# The New International Commentary
## on the
## New Testament

*General Editors*

Ned B. Stonehouse
(1946–1962)

F. F. Bruce
(1962–1990)

Gordon D. Fee
(1990–2012)

Joel B. Green
(2013–      )

# Paul's Letter to the
# PHILIPPIANS

*by*

## GORDON D. FEE

WILLIAM B. EERDMANS PUBLISHING COMPANY
GRAND RAPIDS, MICHIGAN / CAMBRIDGE, U.K.

© 1995 Wm. B. Eerdmans Publishing Co.

Wm. B. Eerdmans Publishing Co.
2140 Oak Industrial Drive N.E., Grand Rapids, Michigan 49505 /
P.O. Box 163, Cambridge CB3 9PU U.K.
www.eerdmans.com

Printed in the United States of America

19  18                    17  16  15  14

**Library of Congress Cataloging-in-Publication Data**

Fee, Gordon D.
Paul's Letter to the Philippians / by Gordon D. Fee.
p.        cm.        — (The New International commentary on the New Testament)
Includes bibliographical references and indexes.
ISBN 978-0-8028-2511-7 (alk. paper)
1. Bible. N. T. Philippians — Commentaries.   I. Title.   II. Series.
BS2705.3.G67   1995
227'.6077 — dc20

95-17640
CIP

*For Sven Soderlund*
*Colleague*
*and*
*Friend*

# CONTENTS

*Editor's Preface*                                          ix
*Author's Preface*                                          xi
*Abbreviations*                                             xv
*Bibliography*                                             xxi


**INTRODUCTION**

   I. PHILIPPIANS AS A LETTER                        1

   II. THE OCCASION OF PHILIPPIANS                  24

   III. THE QUESTION OF AUTHENTICITY —
       SOME NOTES ON 2:6-11                        39

   IV. THEOLOGICAL CONTRIBUTIONS                    46


**ANALYSIS OF PHILIPPIANS (with page references)**     54


**TEXT, EXPOSITION, AND NOTES**

   I. INTRODUCTORY MATTERS (1:1-11)                 59

   II. PAUL'S "AFFAIRS" — REFLECTIONS ON
       IMPRISONMENT (1:12-26)                     106

   III. THE PHILIPPIANS' "AFFAIRS" — EXHORTATION TO
       STEADFASTNESS AND UNITY (1:17–2:18)        155

   IV. WHAT'S NEXT — REGARDING PAUL'S AND THEIR
       "AFFAIRS" (2:19-30)                        258

V.  THEIR "AFFAIRS" — AGAIN (3:1–4:3)                     285
VI.  CONCLUDING MATTERS (4:4-23)                          398


**INDEXES**

    I.  SUBJECTS                                     463
    II.  AUTHORS                                     468
    III.  SCRIPTURE REFERENCES                       476
    IV.  EARLY EXTRABIBLICAL LITERATURE              491
    V.  GREEK WORDS                                  494

# EDITOR'S PREFACE

Although the author of this commentary and editor of this series are the same person, it seemed fitting in this case to have an editor's as well as an author's preface. The reasons for this are three:

First, this is the first volume to appear in the NICNT under my editorship. It is also the second volume to appear under the new format and book design. Hopefully, this new design will make the series much more user friendly; it came about in fact as a response to the many complaints about the two larger volumes in this series (Morris on John and Fee on 1 Corinthians), that they will not lie open on the desk as one is trying to use them. Thus, I herewith offer my gratitude to the Eerdmans Publishing Company for undertaking the new design; in time all the former volumes will be brought into conformity.

Second, although coincidental, it has turned out that the second and third editors of the series have written the replacement volumes on Philemon and Philippians, which originally appeared in a single volume by J. J. Müller (1955). In the original series, the commentaries on Colossians (by F. F. Bruce) and Ephesians (by E. K. Simpson) also constituted a single volume. As the second editor of the series, Professor Bruce updated his Colossians commentary and wrote the replacement volumes on Ephesians and Philemon, which were then published together in one volume. That left the unusual situation of a set of commentaries having two works on Philemon. Meanwhile, the sheer volume of literature on Philippians over the past forty years — and the many new directions that Philippians studies have taken — has called for a replacement volume on this letter as well. Since I was scheduled to write a more popular commentary on this letter (in the IVP NT commentary series), the publishers asked if I would be willing to write the Philippians volume for the NICNT as well. With the consent of the editors at InterVarsity Press, I agreed to do so.

Third, it became clear to me early on that the editor needed an editor.

So in fact the true editor of this volume has been my colleague at Regent College, Sven Soderlund, who brought the experience of years of teaching the Captivity Letters to the task, as well as an uncommon devotion to detail and a keen eye for "Feeism's" of all kinds (including impossible sentences and various malaprops) — although I resisted his efforts at times and must be held accountable for those that remain. Thus, even though the final product is my own, and for good or ill I am responsible for the points of view put forward, Sven has saved me from many an embarrassment, for which I am truly grateful. Indeed, I have learned much about the task of editing from his very careful working through my first draft. For his untiring efforts on my behalf — and on behalf of all who may profit from this commentary — I offer my grateful thanks by dedicating the volume to him.

# AUTHOR'S PREFACE

For the rationale as to the form and style of this commentary, one is invited to read carefully the Author's Preface to my volume on 1 Corinthians in this series (pp. ix-xii), which I had the opportunity to spell out in greater detail in a symposium on the writing of commentaries in *Theology* 46 (1990) 387-92.

But I do need here to reiterate some presuppositions and idiosyncrasies for the sake of the reader. First, without apology I have consciously written this commentary to help the parish minister and teacher of Scripture better understand this letter as the Word of God for a contemporary congregation. At the same time I have been very well aware of the scholar and the classroom teacher. Everything about the format and style gives evidence of this twofold audience. For the primary readership I have tried to make the exposition as uncluttered and as readable as possible. Hopefully, even those Bible students without formal training (and who are not turned off by the appearance of so many footnotes!) will find much profit by reading the text and skipping the notes altogether. For that reason, I have reserved almost all technical discussions of textual criticism, grammar, and lexicography, for the footnotes. There also one will find my indebtedness to, and (sometimes vigorous) interaction with, those who have written on Philippians before me. The notes, therefore, are full of many things; and the user is invited to read around as many of these as he or she needs to in order to keep a steady eye on the meaning of Philippians itself.

That leads me, second, to say a further word about my relationship to previous literature. As with the commentary on 1 Corinthians, I assiduously avoided reading anything on a given paragraph — and tried to keep out of mind what I had read previously — until I had written and rewritten my own exposition of the text, along with the various textual, grammatical, and lexical notes. I then went through the literature (basically 25 commentaries covering a broad range of time and perspective, plus all known specialized studies on the passage) *in chronological order* (through early 1994), after which I interacted, rewrote, or made adjustments, as the case may be — and acknowledged indebtedness for points of view I had not noted before. For this reason the references in the notes are also in generally chronological, not alphabetical, order — although that became difficult to sustain at times when there was more than one edition to a commentary. It also meant that, for me, I always saved the best till last. Even though I differ from them at times, sometimes with characteristic vigor, I learned much from the recent commentaries by three friends: Gerald Hawthorne, Moisés Silva, and Peter O'Brien. Of the older commentaries I found those by Meyer, Lightfoot, and Vincent consistently to be the most helpful (for a very useful overview of commentaries on Philippians, see I. H. Marshall, "Which is the Best Commentary? 12. Philippians," *ExpTim* 103 [1991] 39-42).

Third, although the writer of a commentary assumes that its users will never read the Introduction (!), here is an instance when it seems quite important that the user do so — at least Part I on Philippians as a first-century letter, since the entire commentary has been written from the perspective spelled out there. On other introductory matters, I simply forewarn that there is nothing new, and that the traditional provenance (Rome) and dating (ca. 62 CE) are presupposed — with explanation but with little argumentation.

Fourth, since I think there is some usefulness in doing so, the references to Paul's letters are given in their presumed chronological order (1 and 2 Thessalonians, 1 and 2 Corinthians, Galatians, Romans, Philemon, Colossians, Ephesians, Philippians, 1 Timothy, Titus, 2 Timothy); as before I consider the Pastoral Epistles "Pauline" in the sense that they ultimately derive from him in the first half of the seventh decade CE (between 62 and 64).

Finally, in a day like ours, when Greek is no longer required in the majority of seminaries, and when sociological and literary concerns have far outstripped grammatical ones in exegesis, one is a little hesitant to make too many references to "the Greek." Hopefully, this commentary has taken into account, not always in agreement with the secondary literature, what we can learn from the sociology of the first century and from its various literary and rhetorical devices. But let me here enter a plea for grammar, which also counts for something. To be sure, I am on the side of those who find many of my predecessors — and some contemporaries — to engage in finding more "meaning" in grammar and words than surely Paul intended. (I wonder if he thought through his talk anymore than many of us do, especially in the writing of letters.) "Over-exegeting," I call it. On the other hand, neither do I think Paul simply wrote willy-nilly; I am convinced on the contrary that the *way* he says things often gives us clues to *what* he says — and intends. Therefore, in this commentary I have engaged in several very lengthy grammatical discussions in the footnotes, where I have the sense that grammar has received short shrift in our day of greater expertise in matters sociological (see, e.g., nn. 58 and 59 on 2:17; n. 12 on 4:8; and n. 16 on 4:19). I fear that at times I have been a bit ruthless with my colleagues in these notes, to whom I herewith apologize for the "style" but not for the substance.

It remains, then, to acknowledge those to whom I am indebted for making the writing and publishing of this commentary possible (besides my indebtedness to Sven Soderlund noted in the Editor's Preface):

To my wife Maudine, who not only "suffered" with me through the six months during which this commentary was written, but also read most of the sections — with a keen eye for language and general usefulness for the lay reader — who also creatively interacted with me (and Paul) during the long sessions (usually at meals) where she had to endure the overflow of my exegetical work of the day. (I mention her *first* as yet another example in this commentary of breaking with "formal" traditions!)

To Regent College, whose generous sabbatical policy made it possible for me to be relieved of all other responsibilities from January to June, 1994, during which time this work was undertaken.

To my two teaching assistants (stretching over two academic years), Rick Beaton and Michael Thomson. Rick gathered the vocabulary data that made the analyses on pp. 18-20 possible; he also served as my legs and eyes, spending hours chasing rabbits down library paths and through bibliographical briar patches. Michael prepared the list of abbreviations and collected the comprehensive bibliography from the footnotes, as well as prepared the Scripture and Author indexes.

To students in two seminars over the past five years, who listened and interacted with new ideas about this letter, and from whose papers I also often learned much — especially from those who dug in their heels and would not let me find "division" and "opposition" where there was none.

To Zondervan Publishing House for permission to use the NIV, which is very useful as a translation, but sometimes difficult to use as the basis of comment because of its (correctly so) use of the principle of dynamic equivalence.

As in my 1 Corinthians commentary, I have used brackets occasionally to modify the NIV, where its gender-specific language (especially "brothers" and "man") no longer reflects contemporary English usage and thereby misses the generic intent of the Greek.

I save (what for me is) the best till last. The writing of this commentary is unlike anything I have heretofore experienced as a part of the church. In a regular stream of divine appointments, in a variety of church settings over the four and half months in which I wrote the first draft of the commentary, one Sunday after another either the worship (including liturgy) or the sermon was in some very direct way associated with the text of the preceding week. It was as though the Lord was letting me hear the text played back in liturgical and homiletical settings that made me pause yet one more time and "hear" the text in new ways. It is hard to describe these experiences, which had a profound impact on my sabbaths during the sabbatical; and their regularity seemed beyond mere coincidence. All of which made my Mondays take on a regular pattern as well, as I would go back to the prior week's work and think and pray it through yet one more time. Some of these moments have made the footnotes as well (e.g., n. 42 on 2:9-11, easily the most memorable of these moments; but see also n. 22 on 4:4 and n. 35 on 3:20-21). So the final word is Paul's — his doxology in 4:20: "To our God and Father be glory for ever and ever. Amen."

GORDON D. FEE
JULY 1994

# ABBREVIATIONS

| | |
|---|---|
| AB | Anchor Bible |
| *ABD* | *Anchor Bible Dictionary* |
| adj. | adjective |
| adv. | adverb |
| *AF²* | *Apostolic Fathers* (J. B. Lightfoot; 2nd ed. by M. W. Holmes) |
| *AJA* | *American Journal of Archaeology* |
| *AJT* | *American Journal of Theology* |
| AnB | Analecta Biblica |
| *ANQ* | *Andover Newton Quarterly* |
| *ANRW* | *Augstieg und Niedergang der römischen Welt* |
| Aristotle | |
| *Eth.Nic.* | *Ethica Nicomachea* |
| ASNU | Acta seminarii neotestamentici upsaliensis |
| ASV | American Standard Version |
| *ATR* | *Anglican Theological Review* |
| *AusBR* | *Australian Biblical Review* |
| *AUSS* | *Andrews University Seminary Studies* |
| AV | Authorized Version (= KJV) |
| *BA* | *Biblical Archeologist* |
| BAGD | W. Bauer, W. F. Arndt, F. W. Gingrich, and F. W. Danker, *Greek-English Lexicon of the New Testament and Other Early Christian Literature* |
| *BBR* | *Bulletin for Biblical Research* |
| BCE | Before the Common Era |
| BDF | F. Blass, A. Debrunner, and R. W. Funk, *A Greek Grammar of the New Testament and Other Early Christian Literature* |
| BECNT | Baker Exegetical Commentary on the New Testament |
| *Bib* | *Biblica* |

| | |
|---|---|
| *BibLeb* | *Bibel und Leben* |
| BJRL | *Bulletin of the John Rylands University Library of Manchester* |
| *BSac* | *Bibliotheca Sacra* |
| BST | Bible Speaks Today |
| *BT* | *The Bible Translator* |
| *BTB* | *Biblical Theology Bulletin* |
| *BZ* | *Biblische Zeitschrift* |
| BZNW | Beihefte zur *ZNW* |
| c. | century |
| ca. | *circa* (about) |
| CASB | Cambridge Annotated Study Bible |
| *CBQ* | *Catholic Biblical Quarterly* |
| CBSC | Cambridge Bible for Schools and Colleges |
| CE | Common Era |
| cf. | *confer* (compare) |
| chap. | chapter |
| Cicero | |
|    *Amic.* | *De Amicitia* |
|    *Att.* | *Epistulae ad Atticum* |
|    *Fam.* | *Epistulae ad Familiares* |
|    *Fin.* | *De Finibus* |
|    *Inv.* | *De Inventione* |
|    *Rab.Post.* | *Pro Rabirio Postumo* |
|    *Verr.* | *In Verrem* |
| CIL | Corpus Inscriptionum Latinarum 1863-1909 |
| CNT | Commentaire du Nouveau Testament |
| ConNT | Coniectanea neotestamentica |
| *CTJ* | *Calvin Theological Journal* |
| *CTR* | *Crisswell Theological Review* |
| Dio Chrysostom | |
|    *Or.* | *Orationes* |
| disc. | discussion |
| *DPL* | *Dictionary of Paul and His Letters* (ed. G. F. Hawthorne et al.) |
| e.g. | *exempli gratia* (for example) |
| EBC | The Expositor's Bible Commentary (ed. Frank Gabelein) |
| ed. | editor, edited by |
| *EDNT* | *Exegetical Dictionary of the New Testament* |
| Ep.Ar. | Epistle of Aristeas |
| Ep.Diog. | Epistle of Diognetus |
| EPC | Epworth Preacher's Commentaries |
| Epicurus | |
|    *Gn* | *Gnomologium Vaticanum* (Vatican Sayings) |

| | |
|---|---|
| *EQ* | *Evangelical Quarterly* |
| esp. | especially |
| *EstBib* | *Estudios Bíblicos* |
| *ETL* | *Ephemerides theologicae lovanienses* |
| *ETR* | *Etudes théologiques et religieuses* |
| Euripides | |
| *Or.* | *Orestes* |
| *ExpTim* | *The Expository Times* |
| FFNT | Foundations and Facets: New Testament |
| *FNT* | *Filología neotestamentaria* |
| Gk. | Greek |
| GNB | Good News Bible (= Today's English Version) |
| *GOTR* | *Greek Orthodox Theological Review* |
| *GTJ* | *Grace Theological Journal* |
| Herm | Hermas |
| *Man* | *Mandate* |
| *Sim* | *Similitudes* |
| HNT | Handbuch zum Neuen Testament |
| HNTC | Harper's New Testament Commentaries |
| *HorBibTh* | *Horizons in Biblical Theology* |
| HTKNT | Herders Theologische Kommentar zum Neuen Testament |
| *HTR* | *Harvard Theological Review* |
| *IBS* | *Irish Biblical Studies* |
| ICC | International Critical Commentary |
| i.e. | *id est* (that is) |
| *IKZ* | *Internationale kirkliche Zeitschrift* |
| *Int* | *Interpretation* |
| *ITQ* | *Irish Theological Quarterly* |
| JAC | Jahrbuch für Antike und Christentum |
| JB | Jerusalem Bible |
| *JBC* | *The Jerome Biblical Commentary* (ed. R. E. Brown et al.) |
| *JBL* | *Journal of Biblical Literature* |
| *JETS* | *Journal of the Evangelical Theological Society* |
| *JFSR* | *Journal of Feminist Studies in Religion* |
| *JGWR* | *Journal of Gender in World Religions* |
| Jos. | Josephus |
| *Ant.* | *Antiquitates Judaicae* (The Jewish Antiquities) |
| *BJ* | *Bellum Judaicum* (The Jewish War) |
| *JSNT* | *Journal for the Study of the New Testament* |
| JSNTSup | Journal for the Study of the New Testament Supplement Series |
| *JTC* | *Journal for Theology and the Church* |

| | |
|---|---|
| *JTS* | *Journal of Theological Studies* |
| KJV | King James Version (= AV) |
| LCL | Loeb Classical Library (Harvard University) |
| LD | Lectio divina |
| LEC | Library of Early Christianity (ed. W. A. Meeks) |
| lit. | literally |
| *LS* | *Louvain Studies* |
| LSJ | Liddell-Scott-Jones, *Greek-English Lexicon* (Oxford) |
| Lucian | |
|   *Patr. Laud.* | *Patriae laudatio* (My Native Land) |
| LXX | Septuagint |
| MajT | Majority Text (= Byzantine texttype) |
| MeyerK | H. A. W. Meyer, *Kritisch-exegetischer Kommentar über das Neue Testament* |
| MHT | J. H. Moulton, W. F. Howard, and N. Turner, *Grammar of New Testament Greek* (4 vols.) |
| M-M | J. H. Moulton and G. Milligan, *The Vocabulary of the Greek New Testament* |
| MNTC | Moffatt New Testament Commentary |
| Moffatt | James Moffatt, *The New Testament: A New Translation* |
| MS(S) | manuscript(s) |
| n. (nn.) | note(s) |
| NA$^{26}$ | E. Nestle, K. Aland, *Novum Testamentum Graece* (26th ed.) |
| NAB | New American Bible |
| NAC | New American Commentary |
| NASB | New American Standard Version |
| NCB | New Century Bible |
| NCBC | New Century Bible Commentary |
| NEB | New English Bible |
| *Neot* | *Neotestamentica* |
| *New Docs* | *New Documents Illustrating Early Christianity* (Macquarie University 1981-) |
| NIBC | New International Bible Commentary |
| NICNT | New International Commentary on the New Testament |
| *NIDNTT* | *The New International Dictionary of New Testament Theology* |
| NIGTC | New International Greek Testament Commentary |
| NIV | New International Version |
| NJB | New Jerusalem Bible |
| *NKZ* | *Neue kirchliche Zeitschrift* |
| *NovT* | *Novum Testamentum* |
| NovTSup | Novum Testamentum, Supplements |
| NRSV | New Revised Standard Version |

| | |
|---|---|
| NT | New Testament |
| NTC | New Testament Commentary |
| NTD | Das Neue Testament Deutsch |
| *NTS* | *New Testament Studies* |
| NTTS | New Testament Tools and Studies |
| OL | Old Latin |
| OT | Old Testament |
| p. (pp.) | page(s) |
| Philo | |
|   *Virt.* | *De Virtutibus* (On the Virtues) |
|   *Congr.Qu.Er.* | *De Congressu Quaerendae Eruditionis Gratia* (On the Preliminary Studies) |
| Plato | |
|   *Rep.* | *Republic* |
| Plutarch | |
|   *De Amic. Mult.* | *De Amicitiae Multitudinae* (On Having Many Friends) |
|   *De Lib. Educ.* | *De Liberis Educandis* (On the Education of Children) |
|   *De Util.* | *De Capienda ex Inimicis Utilitate* (How to Profit by one's Enemies) |
| PNTC | Penguin New Testament Commentaries |
| *PRS* | *Perspectives in Religious Studies* |
| q.v. | *quod vide* (which see) |
| *RB* | *Revue biblique* |
| REB | Revised English Bible |
| *RelSRev* | *Religious Studies Review* |
| repr. | reprint |
| *ResQ* | *Restoration Quarterly* |
| rev. | revised |
| *RevExp* | *Review and Expositor* |
| *RHPR* | *Revue d'histoire et de philosophie religieuses* |
| *RivB* | *Rivista Biblica* |
| RNT | Regensburger Neues Testament |
| *RSPT* | *Revue des sciences philosophiques et théologiques* |
| *RSR* | *Recherches de science religieuse* |
| RSV | Revised Standard Version |
| *RTR* | *Reformed Theological Review* |
| SBLDS | Society of Biblical Literature Dissertation Series |
| SBLSBS | Society of Biblical Literature Sources for Biblical Study |
| SBT | Studies in Biblical Theology |
| SD | Studies and Documents |
| Seneca | |
|   *Ben.* | *De Beneficiis* |

| | |
|---|---|
| *Ep. Mor.* | *Epistulae Morales* |
| *Vit. Beat.* | *De Vita Beata* |
| *SE* | *Studia Evangelica* |
| Sib. Or. | Sibylline Oracles |
| Sir | Sirach |
| Str-B | H. Strack and P. Billerbeck, *Kommentar zum Neuen Testament* |
| *SJT* | *Scottish Journal of Theology* |
| SJTOP | SJT Occasional Papers |
| SNTSMS | Society for New Testament Studies Monograph Series |
| SO | Symbolae osloenses |
| *SR* | *Studies in Religion/Sciences religieuses* |
| *ST* | *Studia Theologica* |
| TCNT | The Twentieth Century New Testament |
| *TDNT* | *Theological Dictionary of the New Testament* |
| THKNT | Theologischer Handkommentar zum Neuen Testament |
| *ThZ* | *Theologische Literaturzeitung* |
| TNTC | Tyndale New Testament Commentaries |
| *TQ* | *Theologische Quartalschrift* |
| TR | Textus Receptus |
| tr. | translated by |
| *TrinJ* | *Trinity Journal* |
| *TSK* | *Theologische Studien und Kritiken* |
| TU | Texte und Untersuchungen |
| *TWOT* | *Theological Wordbook of the Old Testament* |
| *TynB* | *Tyndale Bulletin* |
| *TZ* | *Theologische Zeitschrift* |
| UBS[3,4] | United Bible Societies Greek New Testament (3rd, 4th ed.) |
| v. (vv.) | verse(s) |
| WBC | Word Biblical Commentary |
| WC | Westminster Commentaries |
| *WTJ* | *Westminster Theological Journal* |
| WUNT | Wissenschaftliche Untersuchungen zum Neuen Testament |
| Xenophon | |
| *Mem.* | *Memorabilia* |
| ZBK | Zürcher Bibelkommentare |
| Z-G | M. Zerwick and M. Grosvenor, *An Analysis of the Greek New Testament* |
| ZKNT | Zahn's Kommentar zum Neuen Testament |
| *ZNW* | *Zeitschrift für neutestamentliche Wissenschaft* |

# BIBLIOGRAPHY

The following bibliography includes works that were consulted, most of which are cited in the commentary. Commentaries are consistently cited by author's last name, with page numbers; all others appear in the commentary by "short title," whose full citation is given here.

## I. Commentaries

Alford, Henry. *The Greek Testament* (repr. Chicago, 1958; original 1845-60).

Barth, Gerhard. *Der Brief an die Philipper* (ZBK; Zürich, 1979).

Barth, Karl. *The Epistle to the Philippians* (tr. J. W. Leitch; Richmond, 1962).

Beare, Frank W. *The Epistle to the Philippians* (HNTC; New York, 1959).

Benoit, P. *Les épîtres de saint Paul aux Philippiens, a Philémon, aux Colossiens, aux Ephésiens* (Paris, ²1956).

Bonnard, P. *L'épître de saint Paul aux Philippiens et l'épître aux Colossiens* (CNT 10: Neuchâtel, 1950).

Bruce, F. F. *Philippians* (NIBC; Peabody, 1989).

Caird, George B. *Paul's Letters from Prison* (NCB; Oxford, 1976).

Calvin, John. *The Epistles of Paul the Apostle to the Galatians, Ephesians, Philippians and Colossians* (tr. T. H. L. Parker; Grand Rapids, 1965).

Collange, Jean-François. *The Epistle of Saint Paul to the Philippians* (tr. A. W. Heathcote; London, 1979).

Craddock, Fred B. *Philippians* (Interpretation; Louisville, 1984).

Dibelius, Martin. *An die Thessalonicher I, II. An die Philipper* (HNT; Tübingen, ²1925).

Eadie, John. *A Commentary on the Greek Text of the Epistle of Paul to the Philippians* (London, 1859).

Ellicott, Charles J. *St. Paul's Epistles to the Philippians, the Colossians, and Philemon* (London, 1965).

Ernst, J. *Die Briefe an die Philipper, an Philemon, an die Kolosser, und an die Epheser* (RNT; Regensburg, 1974).

Ewald, P. *Der Brief des Paulus an die Philipper* (rev. by G. Wohlenberg; ZKNT; Leipzig, [4]1923).

Fitzmyer, Joseph A. "The Letter to the Philippians," in *JBC* (ed. R. E. Brown, J. A. Fitzmyer, and R. E. Murphy; London, 1968) 2.247-53.

Friedrich, G. *Der Brief an die Philipper* (NTD; Göttingen, [10]1965).

Gnilka, Joachim. *Der Philipperbrief* (HTKNT; Freiburg, 1976).

Grayston, Kenneth. *The Letters of Paul to the Philippians and the Thessalonians* (EPC; Cambridge, 1967).

Haupt, E. *Die Gefangenschaftsbriefe* (MeyerK; Göttingen, [7]1902).

Hawthorne, Gerald F. *Philippians* (WBC; Waco, TX, 1983).

Hendriksen, William. *Philippians* (NTC; Grand Rapids, 1962).

Houlden, J. L. *Paul's Letters from Prison* (PNTC; Baltimore, 1970).

Jones, Maurice. *Philippians* (WC; London, 1918).

Kennedy, H. A. A. "The Epistle to the Philippians," in *Expositor's Greek Testament*, Vol. 3 (ed. W. R. Nicoll, 1903 = Grand Rapids, 1976).

Kent, Homer A., Jr. "Philippians," in *EBC* (Grand Rapids, 1978).

Lenski, R. C. H. *The Interpretation of St. Paul's Epistles to the Galatians, to the Ephesians, and to the Philippians* (Minneapolis, 1937).

Lightfoot, J. B. *Saint Paul's Epistle to the Philippians* (London, [6]1881).

Loh, I.-J., and Nida, E. A. *A Translator's Handbook on Paul's Letter to the Philippians* (Stuttgart, 1977).

Lohmeyer, Ernst. *Der Brief an die Philipper, an die Kolosser und an Philemon* (MeyerK; Göttingen, [13]1964).

Martin, Ralph P. *The Epistle of Paul to the Philippians* (TNTC; London, 1959).

———. *Philippians* (NCBC; Grand Rapids, 1980).

Melick, Richard R., Jr. *Philippians, Colossians, Philemon* (NAC; Nashville, 1991).

Meyer, H. A. W. *Critical and Exegetical Handbook to the Epistles to the Philippians and Colossians* (tr. of 4th edition by J. C. Moore and W. P. Dickson; New York, 1875).

Michael, J. Hugh. *The Epistle to the Philippians* (MNTC; London, 1928).

Michaelis, W. *Der Brief des Paulus an die Philipper* (THKNT; Leipzig, 1935).

Motyer, J. A. *The Message of Philippians* (BST; Downers Grove, 1984).

Moule, H. C. G. *The Epistle to the Philippians* (CBSC; Cambridge, 1923).

Müller, Jac. J. *The Epistles of Paul to the Philippians and to Philemon* (NICNT; Grand Rapids, 1955).

Müller, Ulrich B. *Der Brief des Paulus an die Philipper* (THKNT; Leipzig, 1993).

O'Brien, Peter T. *Commentary on Philippians* (NIGTC; Grand Rapids, 1991).

Plummer, Alfred. *A Commentary on St. Paul's Epistle to the Philippians* (London, 1919).

Schenk, W. *Die Philipperbrief des Paulus. Kommentar* (Stuttgart, 1984).

Scott, Ernest F. "The Epistle to the Philippians," in *The Interpreter's Bible* (ed. G. A. Buttrick et al.; New York, 1955).

Silva, Moisés. *Philippians* (BECNT; Grand Rapids, 1992).

Staab, K. *Die Thessalonicherbriefe. Die Gefangenschaftsbriefe* (Regensburg, 51969).

Synge, F. C. *Philippians and Colossians* (London, 1951).

Vincent, M. R. *Critical and Exegetical Commentary on the Epistles to the Philippians and to Philemon* (ICC; Edinburgh, 1897).

## II. Other Works

Abrahamsen, Valerie. "Christianity and the Rock Reliefs at Philippi," *BA* 51 (1988) 46-56.

———. "Women at Philippi: The Pagan and Christian Evidence," *JFSR* 3 (1987) 17-30.

Achtemeier, Paul J. "*Omne Verbum Sonat:* The New Testament and the Oral Development of Late Western Antiquity," *JBL* 109 (1990) 3-27.

Ahern, B. M. "The Fellowship of His Sufferings (Phil 3,10)," *CBQ* 22 (1960) 1-32.

Alexander, Loveday. "Hellenistic Letter-Forms and the Structure of Philippians," *JSNT* 37 (1989) 87-101.

Antin, P. *"Mori Lucrum* et *Antigone 462, 464,"* *RSR* 62 (1974) 259-60.

Arzt, Peter. "The 'Epistolary Introductory Thanksgiving' in the Papyri and in Paul," *NovT* 36 (1994) 28-46.

Bahr, Gordon J. "Paul and Letter Writing in the First Century," *CBQ* 28 (1966) 465-77.

Bakken, Norman K. "The New Humanity: Christ and the Modern Age, A Study Centering in the Christ-Hymn: Philippians 2:6-11," *Int* 22 (1968) 71-82.

Bandstra, Andrew J. " 'Adam' and 'The Servant' in Philippians 2:5ff.," *CTJ* 1 (1966) 213-16.

Banks, Robert. *Paul's Idea of Community. The Early House Churches in Their Historical Setting* (Grand Rapids, 1980).

Barclay, John M. G. "Mirror-reading a Polemical Letter: Galatians as a Test Case," *JSNT* 31 (1987) 73-93.

———. *Obeying the Truth: A Study of Paul's Ethics in Galatians* (Grand Rapids, 1988).

Barclay, William. "Great Themes of the New Testament — I. Philippians ii.1-11," *ExpTim* 70 (1958) 4-7, 40-44.

Barnes, Elizabeth. "Women in Ministry: A Matter of Discipleship," *Faith and Mission* 4 (1987) 63-69.

Bartchy, S. Scott. ΜΑΛΛΟΝ ΧΡΗΣΑΙ: *First-Century Slavery and the Interpretation of 1 Corinthians 7:21* (SBLDS 11; Missoula, 1973).

Barth, Markus. *Ephesians* (AB 34; Garden City, NJ, 1974).

Basevi, Claudio and Juan Chapa. "Philippians 2.6-11: The Rhetorical Function of a Pauline 'Hymn'," in *Rhetoric and the New Testament, Essays from the 1992 Heidelberg Conference* (JSNTSup 90; ed. S. E. Porter and T. H. Olbricht; Sheffield, 1993) 338-56.

Baumbach, G. "Die von Paulus im Philipperbrief bekämpften Irrlehrer," in *Gnosis und Neues Testament* (ed. K. W. Tröger; Berlin, 1973) 293-310.

Baumert, N. "Ist Philipper 4,10 richtig übersetzt?" *BZ* 13 (1969) 256-62.

Baumgarten, J. *Paulus und die Apokalyptik* (Neukirchen-Vluyn, 1975).

Becker, J. "Erwägungen zu Phil. 3,20-21," *TZ* 27 (1971) 16-29.

Beekman, John and John Callow. *Translating the Word of God* (Grand Rapids, 1974).

Bengel, J. A. *New Testament Word Studies,* Vol. 2 (tr. of *Gnomon Novi Testamenti,* 1742; Grand Rapids, 1971).

Bertram, G. "Ἀποκαραδοκία (Phil. 1,20)," *ZNW* (1958) 264-70.

Best, Ernest. "Bishops and Deacons: Philippians 1,1," *SE* 4 (1968) 371-76.

Betz, Hans Dieter. *Galatians* (Hermeneia; Philadelphia, 1979).

—————. *Nachfolge und Nachahmung Jesu Christi im Neuen Testament* (Tübingen, 1967).

Betz, Otto. "Paulus als Pharisäer nach dem Gesetz. Phil. 3,5-6 als Beitrag zur Frage des frühen Pharisäismus," in *Treue zur Thora. Beiträge zur Mitte des christlichjüdischen Gesprächs. Festschrift für Günter Harder zum 75. Geburtstag* (ed. P. von der Osten-Sacken; Berlin, 1977) 54-64.

Binder, H. "Erwägungen zu Phil. 2,6-7b," *ZNW* 78 (1987) 230-43.

Bjerkelund, C. J. *Parakalō. Form, Funktion und Sinn der parakalō-Sätze in den paulinischen Briefe* (Oslo, 1975).

Black, C. C. "Keeping Up with Recent Studies: 16. Rhetorical Criticism and Biblical Interpretation," *ExpTim* 100 (1989) 252-58.

Black, David A. "The Authorship of Philippians 2:6-11: Some Literary-Critical Observations," *CTR* 2 (1988) 269-89.

—————. "Paul and Christian Unity: A Formal Analysis of Philippians 2:1-4," *JETS* 28 (1985) 299-308.

—————. *Paul, Apostle of Weakness. Astheneia and its Cognates in the Pauline Literature* (New York, 1984).

Blevins, J. L. "Introduction to Philippians," *RevExp* 77 (1980) 311-25.

Bloomquist, L. Gregory. *The Function of Suffering in Philippians* (JSNTSup 78; Sheffield, 1993).

Bornhäuser, Karl. *Jesus imperator mundi (Phil. 3,7-21 u. 2,5-12)* (Gütersloh, 1938).

————. "Zum Verständnis von Philipper 2,5-11," *NKZ* 44 (1933) 428-34, 453-62.

Bornkamm, Gunther. "Der Philipperbrief als paulinische Briefsammlung," in *Neotestamentica et Patristica: eine Freundesgabe Herrn Professor Dr. O. Cullmann* (NovTSup 6; Leiden, 1962) 192-202.

————. "Zum Verständnis des Christus-Hymnus, Phil. 2.6-11," in *Studien zu Antike und Urchristentum* (München, 1959) 177-87.

Böttger, Paul C. "Die eschatologische Existenz der Christen, Erwägungen zu Philipper $3_{20}$," *ZNW* 60 (1969) 244-63.

Bousset, Wilhelm. *Kyrios Christos* (tr. J. E. Steely; Nashville, 1970).

Bouttier, M. *En Christ* (Paris, 1962).

Bowen, C. R. "Are Paul's Prison Letters from Ephesus?" *AJT* 24 (1920) 112-35.

Boyer, J. L. "First Class Conditions: What Do They Mean?" *GTJ* 2 (1981) 75-114.

Brant, Jo-Ann A. "The Place of *mimēsis* in Paul's thought," *SR* 22 (1993) 285-301.

Brauch, Manfred T. *Hard Sayings of Paul* (Downers Grove, 1989).

————. "Perspectives on 'God's Righteousness' in Recent German Discussion," in E. P. Sanders, *Paul and Palestinian Judaism* (London, 1977) 523-42.

Brewer, Raymond R. "The Meaning of *Politeuesthe* in Philippians $1_{27}$," *JBL* 73 (1954) 76-83.

Broneer, O. "The Isthmian Victory Crown," *AJA* 66 (1962) 259-63.

Bruce, F. F. "St. Paul in Macedonia. 3. The Philippian Correspondence," *BJRL* 63 (1980-81) 260-84.

Buchanan, C. O. "Epaphroditus' Sickness and the Letter to the Philippians," *EQ* 36 (1964) 157-66.

Bugg, Charles. "Philippians 4:4-13," *RevExp* 88 (1991) 253-57.

Bultmann, Rudolf. *Theology of the New Testament,* 2 vols. (London, 1952 and 1955).

Burdick, Donald W. "οἶδα and γινώσκω in the Pauline Epistles," in *New Dimensions in New Testament Study* (ed. R. N. Longenecker and M. C. Tenney; Grand Rapids, 1974) 344-56.

Burn, J. H. "Philippians ii.12," *ExpTim* 34 (1922-23) 562.

Burton, Ernest de W. *Syntax of the Moods and Tenses in New Testament Greek* (Edinburgh, ³1898).

Campbell, J. Y. "Κοινωνία and its Cognates in the New Testament," in *Three New Testament Studies* (Leiden, 1965) 1-28.

Campenhausen, Hans von. *Ecclesiastical Authority and Spiritual Power: The Church in the First Three Centuries* (tr. J. A. Baker; London, 1969).

Capper, Brian J. "Paul's Dispute with Philippi: Understanding Paul's Argument in Phil 1–2 from his Thanks in 4.10-20," *ThZ* 49 (1993) 193-214.

Carmignac, Jean. "L'importance de la place d'une négation: ΟΥΧ ΑΡΠΑΓ-ΜΟΝ ΗΓΗΣΑΤΟ (Philippiens II.6)," *NTS* 18 (1971-72) 131-66.

Carr, Wesley A. *Angels and Principalities. The Background, Meaning and Development of the Pauline Phrase HAI ARCHAI KAI HAI EXOUSIAI* (SNTSMS 42; Cambridge, 1981).

Carson, D. A., Douglas J. Moo, and Leon Morris. *An Introduction to the New Testament* (Grand Rapids, 1992).

Cavallin, A. "(τὸ) λοιπόν," *Eranos* 39 (1941) 121-44.

Cerfaux, Lucien. "L'hymne au Christ-Serviteur de Dieu (Phil 2,6-11 = Is 52,13–53,12)," in *Recuil Lucien Cerfaux. II. Études d'exégèse et d'histoire religieuse* (Gembloux, 1954) 425-37.

———. *Christ in the Theology of St. Paul* (London, 1959).

Champion, L. G. *Benedictions and Doxologies in the Epistles of Paul* (Oxford, 1934).

Christou, P. "ΙΣΟΨΥΧΟΣ. Ph. 2.20," *JBL* 70 (1951) 293-96.

Clark, Kenneth W. "The Meaning of ἐνεργέω and κατεργέω in the New Testament," *JBL* 54 (1935) 93-101.

Clements, Ronald E. "Is 45:20-25," *Int* 40 (1986) 392-97.

Collart, P. *Philippes, ville de Macédonie depuis ses origines jusqu' à la fin de l'époque romaine* (Paris, 1937).

Combrink, H. J. Bernard. "Response to W. Schenk, *Die Philipperbriefe des Paulus,*" in *Semeia* 48 (1989) 135-46.

Conybeare, W. J. and J. S. Howson. *The Life and Epistles of St. Paul* (London, 1898).

Cook, David. "Stephanus Le Moyne and the Dissection of Philippians," *JTS* 32 (1981) 138-42.

———. "2 Timothy IV.6-8 and the Epistle to the Philippians," *JTS* 33 (1982) 168-71.

Coppens, J. "Phil. 2:7 et Is. 53:12," *ETL* 41 (1965) 147-50.

Cox, Samuel. "Our Heavenly Citizenship. Philippians iii.20," *Expositor* 2/8 (1882) 303-13.

Cullmann, Oscar. *The Christology of the New Testament* (Philadelphia, 1959).

———. "Immortality of the Soul or Resurrection of the Dead?" in *Immortality and Resurrection* (ed. K. Stendahl; New York, 1965).

Culpepper, R. Alan. "Co-Workers in Suffering. Philippians 2:19-30," *RevExp* 77 (1980) 349-58.

Dacquino, P. "Date e provenienza della lettera ai Filippesi," *Rivista Biblica* 6 (1958) 224-34.

Dahl, N. A. "The Messiahship of Jesus in Paul," in *The Crucified Messiah and Other Essays* (Minneapolis, 1974) 37-47.

Dailey, Thomas F. "To Live or Die, Paul's Eschatological Dilemma in Philippians 1:19-26," *Int* 44 (1990) 18-28.

Dalton, William J. "The Integrity of Philippians," *Bib* 60 (1979) 97-102.

Dana, H. E. and Julius R. Mantey. *A Manual Grammar of the Greek New Testament* (New York, 1927).

Dassmann, E. "Hausgemeinde und Bischofsamt," in *Vivarium* (J. Klausner *Festschrift;* Münster, 1984) 82-97.

Davies, W. D. "Paul and the Dead Sea Scrolls: Flesh and Spirit," in *The Scrolls and the New Testament* (ed. K. Stendahl; New York, 1957) 157-82.

Dawe, D. G. "A Fresh Look at the Kenotic Christologies," *SJT* 15 (1962) 337-49.

Dean, H. "Christ's True Glory," *ExpTim* 71 (1960) 189-90.

De Boer, W. P. *The Imitation of Paul* (Kampen, 1962).

Deidun, T. J. *New Covenant Morality in Paul* (AnB 89; Rome, 1981).

Deissmann, Adolf. "Zur ephesinischen Gefangenschaft des Apostels Paulus," in *Anatolian Studies Presented to Sir William Ramsay* (ed. W. H. Buckler and W. M. Calder; Manchester, 1923) 121-27.

————. *Bible Studies* (Edinburgh, 1901).

————. *Light from the Ancient East* (London, [4]1927).

————. *Die neutestamentliche Formel "In Christo Jesu"* (Marburg, 1892).

————. *Paul, A Study in Social and Religious History* (London, [2]1926).

Delling, Gerhard. "Lexikalisches zu τέϰνον," in *Studien zum Neuen Testament und zum hellenistischen Judentum* (ed. F. Hahn, T. Holtz, and N. Walter; Göttingen, 1970) 270-80.

————. "Zum steigernden Gebrauch von Komposita mit ὑπέρ bei Paulus," *NovT* 11 (1969) 127-53.

————. *Worship in the New Testament* (London, 1962).

Denis, A. M. "La fonction apostolique et la liturgie nouvelle in Esprit. Étude thématique des métaphores pauliniennes du culte nouveau," *RSPT* 42 (1958) 401-36, 617-56.

————. "Versé en libation (Phil. 2,17) = Versé son sang? A propos d'une réference de W. Bauer," *RSR* 45 (1957) 567-70.

Denton, D. R. "Ἀποϰαραδοϰία," *ZNW* 73 (1982) 138-40.

de Silva, David A. "No Confidence in the Flesh: The Meaning and Function of Philippians 3:2-21," *TrinJ* 15 (1994) 27-54.

de Vogel, C. J. "Reflexions on Philipp. i 23-24," *NovT* 19 (1977) 262-74.

Dewailly, L.-M. "La part prise à l'Évangile (*Phil* I,5)," *RB* 80 (1973) 247-60.

Dockx, S. "Lieu et date de l'épître aux Philippiens," *RB* 80 (1973) 230-46.

Dodd, C. H. "The Mind of Paul," in *New Testament Studies* (Manchester, 1953).

Dormeyer, Detlev. "The Implicit and Explicit Readers and the Genre of Philippians 3:2–4:3, 8-9: Response to the Commentary of Wolfgang Schenk," in *Semeia* 48 (1989) 147-59.

Doty, W. G. *Letters in Primitive Christianity* (Philadelphia, 1973).

Droge, Arthur J. "*Mori Lucrum:* Paul and Ancient Theories of Suicide," *NovT* 30 (1988) 263-86.

Duncan, G. S. "A New Setting for Paul's Epistle to the Philippians," *ExpTim* 43 (1931-32) 7-11.

————. "Paul's Ministry in Asia — The Last Phase," *NTS* 3 (1956-57) 211-18.

————. *St. Paul's Ephesian Ministry* (London, 1929).

Dunn, J. D. G. *Baptism in the Holy Spirit* (SBT 2/15; London, 1970).

————. *Christology in the Making* (London, 1980).

————. *Jesus, Paul and the Law* (Louisville, 1990).

————. "Once More, ΠΙΣΤΙΣ ΧΡΙΣΤΟΥ," in *Society of Biblical Literature 1991 Seminar Papers* (ed. E. H. Lovering, Jr.; Atlanta, 1991) 730-44.

Du Plessis, P. J. ΤΕΛΕΙΟΣ. *The Idea of Perfection in the New Testament* (Kampen, 1959).

Dupont, J. "The Conversion of Paul, and its Influence on his Understanding of Salvation by Faith," in *Apostolic History and the Gospel. Biblical and Historical Essays presented to F. F. Bruce on his 60th Birthday* (ed. W. W. Gasque and R. P. Martin; Grand Rapids, 1970) 176-94.

————. ΣΥΝ ΧΡΙΣΤΩΙ. *L'union avec le Christ suivant Saint Paul* (Paris, 1952).

Earle, Ralph. *Word Meanings in the New Testament. Volume 5. Philippians-Philemon* (Grand Rapids, 1977).

Eckman, Barbara. "A Quantitative Metrical Analysis of the Philippians Hymn," *NTS* 26 (1979-80) 158-66.

Ehrhardt, A. A. T. "Jesus Christ and Alexander the Great," *JTS* 46 (1945) 45-51.

Eichholz, G. "Bewahren und Bewähren des Evangeliums: de Leitfaden von Phil 1–2," in *Tradition und Interpretation* (München, 1965) 138-60.

Ellis, E. Earle. "Paul and his Co-Workers," in *Prophecy and Hermeneutic in Early Christianity. New Testament Essays* (Grand Rapids, 1978) 3-22.

————. "Paul and his Opponents," in *Christianity, Judaism and Other Greco-Roman Cults. Studies for Morton Smith at Sixty* (ed. J. Neusner, Part I, New Testament; Leiden, 1975) 268-98.

Eltester, F. W. ΕΙΚΩΝ *im Neuen Testament* (Berlin, 1958).

Euler, K. *Die Verkündigung von leidenden Gottesknecht aus Jes 53 in der griechischen bibel* (Stuttgart, 1934).

Evans, O. E. "New Wine in Old Wine Skins: XIII. The Saints," *ExpTim* 86 (1975) 196-200.

Exler, F. X. J. *The Form of the Ancient Greek Letter of the Epistolary Papyri (3rd c. B.C.-3rd c. A.D.)* (Chicago, 1923).

Ezell, D. "The Sufficiency of Christ. Philippians 4," *RevExp* 77 (1980) 373-81.

Fairweather, E. R. "The 'Kenotic' Christology," in Beare, 159-74.

Fee, Gordon D. "Christology and Pneumatology in Romans 8:9-11 — and Elsewhere: Some Reflections on Paul as a Trinitarian," in *Jesus of Nazareth: Lord and Christ, Essays on the Historical Jesus and New Testament Christology* (I. H. Marshall *Festschrift*; ed. J. B. Green and M. Turner; Grand Rapids, 1994) 312-31.

———. *The First Epistle to the Corinthians* (NICNT; Grand Rapids, 1987).

———. "Freedom and the Life of Obedience (Galatians 5:1–6:18)," *RevExp* 91 (1994) 201-17.

———. *God's Empowering Presence, The Holy Spirit in the Letters of Paul* (Peabody, MA, 1994).

———. "On the Text and Meaning of John 20,30-31," in *The Four Gospels 1992, Festschrift Frans Neirynck* (ed. F. Van Segbroeck et al.; Leuven, 1992) III.2193-2205.

———. "Philippians 2:5-11: Hymn or Exalted Pauline Prose?" *BBR* 2 (1992) 29-46.

———. "Pneuma and Eschatology in 2 Thessalonians 2.1-2: A Proposal about 'Testing the Prophets' and the Purpose of 2 Thessalonians," in *To Tell the Mystery: Essays on New Testament Eschatology in Honor of Robert H. Gundry* (ed. T. Schmidt and M. Silva; Sheffield, 1994) 196-215.

———. "Some Reflections on Pauline Spirituality," in *Alive to God, Studies in Spirituality presented to James Houston* (ed. J. I. Packer and Loren Wilkinson; Downers Grove, 1992) 96-107.

———. *1 and 2 Timothy, Titus* (NIBC; Peabody, 1989).

———. "Toward a Theology of 1 Corinthians," *Society of Biblical Literature 1989 Seminar Papers* (ed. David J. Lull; Atlanta, 1989) 265-81.

———. "The Use of Greek Patristic Citations in New Testament Textual Criticism: The State of the Question," in E. J. Epp and G. D. Fee, *Studies in the Theory and Method of New Testament Textual Criticism* (SD 45; Grand Rapids, 1993) 344-59.

Feinberg, Paul D. "The Kenosis and Christology: An Exegetical-Theological Analysis of Phil 2:6-11," *TrinJ* 1 (1980) 21-46.

Ferguson, Everett. *Backgrounds of Early Christianity* (Grand Rapids, ²1993).

———. "Spiritual Sacrifice in Early Christianity and its Environment," in *ANRW* (Berlin/New York, 1980) Band II, vol. 23.2, 1151-89.

Feuillet, A. "L'hymne christologique de l'épître aux Philippiens," *RB* 72 (1965) 352-80, 481-507.

———. "Mort du Christ et Mort du chrétien d'après les épîtres pauliniennes," *RB* 66 (1959) 481-513.

Filson, Floyd V. *'Yesterday': A Study of Hebrews in the Light of Chapter 13* (SBT 2/4; London, 1967).

Finlayson, S. K. "Lights, Stars and Beacons," *ExpTim* 77 (1965-66) 181.

Finley, Mitchel B. "The Spirit of *Kenosis*," *Bible Today* 69 (1973) 1389-94.

Fiore, Benjamin. *The Function of Personal Example in the Socratic and Pastoral Epistles* (AnB 105; Rome, 1986).

Fitzmyer, Joseph A. "The Aramaic Background of Philippians 2:6-11," *CBQ* 50 (1988) 470-83.

———. "The Consecutive Meaning of ΕΦ' Ω in Romans 5.12," *NTS* 39 (1993) 321-39.

———. "The Gospel in the Theology of Paul," in *To Advance the Gospel* (New York, 1981) 149-71.

———. "'To Know Him and the Power of His Resurrection' (Phil 3.10)," in *Mélanges Bibliques en hommage au R. P. Béda Rigaux* (ed. A. Descamps and A. de Halleux; Gembloux, 1970) 411-25.

Flanagan, Neal. "A Note on Philippians 3:20-21," *CBQ* 18 (1956) 8-9.

Fleury, J. "Une société de fait dan l'Église apostolique (Phil. 4:10 à 20)," *Mélanges Philippi Meylan 2: Histoire du Droit* (Lausanne, 1963) 41-59.

Forbes, C. "Comparison, Self-Praise and Irony: Paul's Boasting and the Conventions of Hellenistic Rhetoric," *NTS* 32 (1986) 1-30.

Forestell, J. T. "Christian Perfection and Gnosis in Philippians 3,7-16," *CBQ* 18 (1956) 123-36.

Fortna, Robert T. "Philippians: Paul's Most Egocentric Letter," in *The Conversation Continues, Studies in Paul and John in Honor of J. Louis Martyn* (ed. R. T. Fortna and B. R. Gaventa; Nashville, 1990) 220-34.

Fowl, Stephen D. *The Story of Christ in the Ethics of Paul, An Analysis of the Function of the Hymnic Material in the Pauline Corpus* (JSNTSup 36; Sheffield, 1990).

Fridrichsen, A. "EN ΔE, zu Phil. 3.13," *ConNT* 9 (1944) 31-32.

———. "'Ισοψυχος = ebenbürtig, solidarisch," *SO* 18 (1938) 42-49.

———. "Συμψυχος," *Philologische Wochenschrift* 58 (1938) 910-12.

Friedrich, G. "Lohmeyers These über 'Das paulinische Briefpräskript' kritisch beleuchtet," *ZNW* 46 (1955) 272-74.

Funk, Robert W. "The Apostolic *Parousia*: Form and Significance," in *Christian History and Interpretation. Studies Presented to John Knox* (ed. W. R. Farmer, C. F. D. Moule, and R. R. Niebuhr; Cambridge, 1967) 249-68.

———. *Language, Hermeneutic and Word of God* (New York, 1966).

Furness, J. M. "The Authorship of Philippians ii.6-11," *ExpTim* 70 (1958-59) 240-43.

————. "Behind the Philippian Hymn," *ExpTim* 79 (1967-68) 178-82.

————. "ἁρπαγμός . . . ἑαυτὸν ἐκένωσε," *ExpTim* 69 (1957-58) 93-94.

Furnish, Victor Paul. *II Corinthians* (AB 32A; Garden City, NY, 1984).

————. "The Place and Purpose of Philippians III," *NTS* 10 (1963-64) 80-88.

————. *Theology and Ethics in Paul* (Nashville, 1968).

Gärtner, B. "The Pauline and Johannine Idea of 'to know God' against the Hellenistic Background," *NTS* 14 (1967-68) 209-31.

Gamber, K. "Der Christus-Hymnus im Philipperbrief in liturgie-geschichtlicher Sicht," *Bib* 51 (1970) 369-76.

Gamble, Harry. *The Textual History of the Letter to the Romans* (SD 42; Grand Rapids, 1977).

Garland, David E. "The Composition and Unity of Philippians. Some Neglected Literary Factors," *NovT* 27 (1985) 141-73.

————. "Philippians 1:1-26: The Defense and Confirmation of the Gospel," *RevExp* 77 (1980) 327-36.

Genths, P. "Der Begriff des καύχημα bei Paulus," *NKZ* 38 (1927) 501-21.

George, A. Raymond. *Communion with God in the New Testament* (London, 1953).

Georgi, Dieter. "Der vorpaulinische Hymnus Phil ii,6-11," in *Zeit und Geschichte Dankesgabe an Rudolf Bultmann zum 80. Geburtstag* (ed. E. Dinkler; Tübingen, 1964) 263-93.

————. *The Opponents of Paul in Second Corinthians* (Philadelphia, 1986).

Gibbs, John G. *Creation and Redemption. A Study in Pauline Theology* (Leiden, 1971).

————. "The Relation between Creation and Redemption according to Phil. II$_{5-11}$," *NovT* 12 (1970) 170-83.

Giblin, Charles H. *In Hope of God's Glory: Pauline Theological Perspectives* (New York, 1970).

Giesen, H. " 'Furcht und Zittern' — vor Gott? Zu Philipper 2.12," *Theologie der Gegenwart* 31 (1988) 86-94.

Gifford, E. H. *The Incarnation: A Study of Philippians II:5-11* (New York, 1911).

Gillman, Florence M. "Early Christian Women at Philippi," *JGWR* 1 (1990) 59-79.

Glasson, T. F. "Two Notes on the Philippians Hymn (ii.6-11)," *NTS* 21 (1974-75) 133-39.

Gloer, W. Hulitt. "Homologies and Hymns in the New Testament: Form, Content and Criteria for Identification," *PRS* 11 (1984) 115-32.

Glombitza, O. "Der Dank des Apostels. Zum Verständnis von Philipper iv 10-20," *NovT* 7 (1964-65) 135-41.

————. "Mit Furcht und Zittern. Zum Verständnis von Philip. II 12," *NovT* 3 (1959) 100-106.

Gnilka, Joachim. "Die antipaulinische Mission in Philippi," *BZ* 9 (1965) 258-76.

Giglioli, A. "Mihi enim vivere Christus est. Congettura al testo di Phil. 1,21," *RivB* 16 (1968) 305-15.

Goguel, M. "ΚΑΤΑ ΔΙΚΑΙΟΣΥΝΗΝ ΤΗΝ ΕΝ ΝΟΜΩΙ ΓΕΝΟΜΕΝΟΣ ΑΜΕΜΠΤΟΣ (Phil., 3,6): Remarques sur un Aspect de la Conversion de Paul," *JBL* 53 (1934) 257-67.

Grayston, Kenneth. "The Opponents in Philippians 3," *ExpTim* 97 (1986) 170-72.

Grelot, P. "Deux expressions difficiles de Philippiens 2,6-7," *Bib* 53 (1972) 495-507.

———. "Deux notes critiques sur Philippiens 2,6-11," *Bib* 54 (1973) 169-86.

———. "La valeur de οὐκ . . . ἀλλα . . . dans Philippiens 2,6-7," *Bib* 54 (1973) 25-42.

Griffiths, D. R. "ἁρπαγμός and ἑαυτὸν ἐκένωσεν in Philippians ii.6, 7," *ExpTim* 69 (1957-58) 237-39.

Gundry, Robert H. "Grace, Works, and Staying Saved," *Bib* 66 (1985) 1-38.

———. *SŌMA in Biblical Theology with Emphasis on Pauline Anthropology* (SNTSMS 29; Cambridge, 1976).

Gundry Volf, Judy M. *Paul and Perseverance* (WUNT 2/37; Tübingen, 1990).

Gunther, J. J. *Paul: Messenger and Exile* (Valley Forge, PA, 1972).

———. *St. Paul's Opponents and Their Background. A Study of Apocalyptic and Jewish Sectarian Teachings* (NovTSup 35; Leiden, 1973).

Guthrie, Donald. *New Testament Introduction* (Downers Grove, IL, [4]1990).

Güttgemanns, E. *Der leidende Apostel und sein Herr* (Göttingen, 1966).

Haacker, K. "War Paulus Hillelit?" *Das Institutum Iudaicum der Universität Tübingen* (1971-72) 106-20.

Hagner, Donald A. "Paul and Judaism — The Jewish Matrix of Early Christianity: Issues in the Current Debate," *BBR* 3 (1993) 111-30.

Hájek, M. "Comments on Philippians 4:3 — Who was *'Gnésios Syzygos'?"* *Communio Viatorum* 7 (1964) 261-62.

Hall, D. R. "Fellow-Workers with the Gospel," *ExpTim* 85 (1974) 119-20.

Hamilton, Neill Q. *The Holy Spirit and Eschatology in Paul* (SJTOP 6; Edinburgh, 1957).

Hammerich, L. L. "An Ancient Misunderstanding (Phil. 2:6 'robbery')," *ExpTim* 78 (1967) 193-94.

Hanhart, Karl. *The Intermediate State in the New Testament* (Franeker, 1966).

Hanson, Anthony T. "Paul and Pre-existence," in *The Image of the Invisible God* (London, 1982) 59-76.

———. *The Paradox of the Cross in the Thought of St Paul* (JSNTSup 17; Sheffield, 1987).

Harris, J. Rendel. "Epaphroditus, Scribe and Courier," *Expositor* 8 (1898) 101-10.

Harris, Murray J. "Paul's View of Death in 2 Corinthians 5:1-10," in *New Dimensions in New Testament Study* (ed. R. N. Longenecker and M. C. Tenney; Grand Rapids, 1974) 317-28.

————. *Raised Immortal. Resurrection and Immortality in the New Testament* (Grand Rapids, 1983).

Hartman, D. "Social Relationships and Letter Writing in the Early Roman Empire: The Use of Petitions/Requests in Paul and the Papyri," unpub. Ph.D. dissertation, Macquarie University, 1990.

Harvey, John. "A New Look at the Christ Hymn in Philippians $2^{6-11}$," *ExpTim* 76 (1964-65) 337-39.

Hawthorn, T. "Philippians i.12-19. With special reference to vv. 15.16.17," *ExpTim* 62 (1950-51) 316-17.

Hawthorne, Gerald F. "The Interpretation and Translation of Philippians $1^{28b}$," *ExpTim* 95 (1983) 80-81.

————. *Word Biblical Themes: Philippians* (Waco, 1987).

Hays, Richard B. *Echoes of Scripture in the Letters of Paul* (New Haven, 1989).

————. *The Faith of Jesus Christ. An Investigation of the Narrative Substructure of Galatians 3:1–4:11* (SBLDS 56; Chico, CA, 1983).

————. "ΠΙΣΤΙΣ and Pauline Christology: What Is at Stake?" in *Society of Biblical Literature 1991 Seminar Papers* (ed. E. H. Lovering, Jr.; Atlanta, 1991) 714-29.

Hemer, Colin J. *The Book of Acts in the Setting of Hellenistic History* (WUNT 2/49; Tübingen, 1989 = Winona Lake, 1990).

Hengel, M. "'Christos' in Paul," in *Between Jesus and Paul* (London/Philadelphia, 1983) 65-77.

————. "Hymns and Christology," in *Between Jesus and Paul* (London/Philadelphia, 1983) 78-96.

————. *Crucifixion* (London, 1977).

————. *Judaism and Hellenism. Studies in their Encounter in Palestine during the Early Hellenistic Period* (Philadelphia, 1974).

Heriban, Josef. *Retto* φρονεῖν *e* κένωσις. *Studio esegetico su Fil 2,1-5, 6-11* (Rome, 1983).

Héring, Jean. "Kyrios Anthropos," *RHPR* 16 (1936) 196-209.

Hill, David. *Greek Words and Hebrew Meanings* (SNTSMS 5; Cambridge, 1967).

Hock, Ronald F. *The Social Context of Paul's Ministry* (Philadelphia, 1980).

Hoffmann, P. *Die Toten in Christus* (Münster, $^2$1969).

Hofius, O. *Der Christushymnus Philipper 2,6-11* (WUNT 17; Tübingen, 1976).

Holladay, C. R. "Paul's Opponents in Philippians 3," *ResQ* 12 (1969) 77-90.

Holmberg, Bengt. *Paul and Power. The Structure of Authority in the Primitive Church as Reflected in the Pauline Epistles* (Philadelphia, 1978).

Hooke, S. H. *Alpha and Omega: A Study in the Pattern of Revelation* (London, 1961).

Hooker, Morna D. "Interchange in Christ," *JTS* 22 (1971) 349-61.

———. "Philippians 2:6-11," in *Jesus und Paulus. Festschrift für Werner Georg Kümmel zum 70. Geburtstag* (ed. E. E. Ellis and E. Grässer; Göttingen, ²1978) 151-64.

———. "ΠΙΣΤΙΣ ΧΡΙΣΤΟΥ," *NTS* 35 (1989) 321-42.

Hoover, Roy W. "The HARPAGMOS Enigma: A Philosophical Solution," *HTR* 64 (1971) 95-119.

Howard, George. "The 'Faith of Christ,'" *ExpTim* 85 (1973-74) 212-14.

———. "On the 'Faith of Christ,'" *HTR* 60 (1967) 459-65.

———. "Phil 2:6-11 and the Human Christ," *CBQ* 40 (1978) 368-87.

Hudson, D. F. "A Further Note on Philippians ii:6-11," *ExpTim* 77 (1965-66) 29.

Hultgren, Arland J. "Paul's Pre-Christian Persecutions of the Church: Their Purpose, Locale and Nature," *JBL* 95 (1976) 97-111.

———. "The *Pistis Christou* Formulation in Paul," *NovT* 22 (1980) 248-63.

Hunt, A. S. and C. C. Edgar, eds. *Select Papyri I* (LCL; Cambridge, MA, 1932).

Hunzinger, C. H. "Zur Struktur der Christus-hymnen in Phil 2 und 1. Petr 3," in *Der Ruf Jesus und die Antwort der Gemeinde* (Jeremias *Festschrift;* ed. E. Lohse, C. Burchard, and B. Schaller; Göttingen, 1970) 142-56.

Hurst, L. D. "Re-enter the Pre-existent Christ in Philippians 2:5-11?" *NTS* 32 (1986) 449-57.

Hurtado, L. W. "Jesus as Lordly Example in Philippians 2:5-11," in *From Jesus to Paul: Studies in Honour of Francis Wright Beare* (ed. P. Richardson and J. C. Hurd; Waterloo, 1984) 113-26.

Jaeger, W. W. "Eine stilgeschichtliche Studie zum Philipperbrief," *Hermes* 50 (1915) 537-53.

Jeremias, Joachim. "Paulus als Hillelit," in *Neotestamentica et Semitica: Studies in Honour of M. Black* (ed. E. E. Ellis and M. Wilcox; Edinburgh, 1969) 88-94.

———. "Zu Phil. ii 7: ΕΑΥΤΟΝ ΕΚΕΝΩΣΕΝ," *NovT* 6 (1963) 182-88.

———. "Zur Gedankenführung in den paulinischen Briefen," in *Studia Paulina in Honorem J. de Zwaan* (ed. J. N. Sevenster and W. C. van Unnik; Haarlem, 1953) 146-54.

Jervell, J. *Imago Dei. Gen 1,26f. im Spätjudentum, in der Gnosis und in den paulinischen Briefen* (Göttingen, 1960).

Jewett, Robert. "Conflicting Movements in the Early Church as Reflected in Philippians," *NovT* 12 (1970) 362-90.

———. "The Epistolary Thanksgiving and the Integrity of Philippians," *NovT* 12 (1970) 40-53.

———. "The Form and Function of the Homiletic Benediction," *ATR* 51 (1969) 18-43.

————. *Paul's Anthropological Terms. A Study of Their Use in Conflict Settings* (Leiden, 1971).

Johnson, L. "The Pauline Letters from Caesarea," *ExpTim* 68 (1957-58) 24-26.

Johnson, Luke T. *The Writings of the New Testament: An Interpretation* (Philadelphia, 1986).

Jonge, H. J. de. "Eine Konjektur Joseph Scaligers zu Philipper II 30," *NovT* 17 (1975) 297-302.

Joüon, P. "Notes philologiques sur quelques versets de l'épître aux Philippiens," *RSR* 28 (1938) 89-93, 223-33, 299-310.

Judge, Edwin A. "Paul's Boasting in Relation to Contemporary Professional Practice," *AusBR* 16 (1968) 37-50.

Käsemann, Ernst. "A Critical Analysis of Philippians 2:5-11," *JTC* 5 (1968) 45-88.

————. "Philipper 2,12-18," in *Exegetische Versuche und Besinnungen* (Göttingen, 1960) 1.293-98.

Kee, Howard Clark, ed. *Cambridge Annotated Study Bible* (Cambridge, 1993).

————. "The Linguistic Background of 'Shame' in the New Testament," in *On Language, Culture and Religion: In Honor of Eugene A. Nida* (ed. M. Black and W. A. Smalley; The Hague/Paris, 1974) 133-47.

Kennedy, George. *New Testament Interpretation Through Rhetorical Criticism* (Chapel Hill, NC, 1984).

Kennedy, H. A. A. "The Financial Colouring of Philippians 4:15-18," *ExpTim* 12 (1900-1901) 43-44.

Kidd, Reggie. *Wealth and Beneficence in the Pastoral Epistles* (SBLDS 122; Atlanta, 1990).

Kilpatrick, George D. "ΒΛΕΠΕΤΕ, Philippians 3:2," *In Memorium Paul Kahle* (ed. M. Black and G. Fohrer; Berlin, 1968) 146-48.

Kim, Chan-Hie. *Form and Structure of the Familiar Greek Letter of Recommendation* (SBLDS 4; Missoula, 1972).

Kim, Seyoon. *The Origin of Paul's Gospel* (Tübingen, 1981).

Klein, Günter. "Antipaulinismus in Philippi: Eine Problemskizze," in *Jesu Rede von Gott und ihre Nachgeschichte im frühen Christentum: Beiträge zur Verkündigung Jesu und zum Kerygma der Kirche: Festschrift für Willi Marxsen zum 70. Geburtstag* (ed. D.-A. Koch et al.; Guterslöh, 1989) 297-313.

Klijn, A. F. J. "Paul's Opponents in Philippians III," *NovT* 7 (1965) 278-84.

Koch, G. "Neue Religiosität ausserhalb der Kirche: Bedrohung oder Chance für den Glauben?" *Theologie der Gegenwart* 31 (1988) 67-75.

Koester, Helmut. "The Purpose of the Polemic of a Pauline Fragment (Philippians III)," *NTS* 8 (1961-62) 317-32.

Koperski, V. "The Early History of the Dissection of Philippians," *JTS* 44 (1993) 599-603.

————. "The Meaning of *Pistis Christou* in Philippians 3:9," *LS* 18 (1993) 198-216.

Koskenniemi, Heikki. *Studien zur Idee und Phraeseologie des griechischen Briefes bis 400 n. Chr.* (Helsinki, 1956).

Kraftchick, S. J. "A Necessary Detour: Paul's Metaphorical Understanding of the Philippian Hymn," *HorBibTh* 15 (1993) 1-37.

Kramer, W. *Christ, Lord, Son of God* (SBT 50; London, 1966).

Kreitzer, L. J. *Jesus and God in Paul's Eschatology* (JNSTSup 19; Sheffield, 1987).

Krinetzki, L. "Der Einfluss von Is 52,13–53,12 Par auf Phil 2,6-11," *TQ* 139 (1959) 157-93, 291-336.

Kühl, E. "Über Philipper 2,12.13," *TSK* 71 (1898) 557-81.

Kümmel, Werner G. *Introduction to the New Testament* (London, ²1975).

Kurz, William S. "Kenotic Imitation of Paul and of Christ in Philippians 2 and 3," in *Discipleship in the New Testament* (ed. F. F. Segovia; Philadelphia, 1985) 103-26.

Larsson, E. *Christus als Vorbild. Eine Untersuchung zu den paulinischen Tauf- und Eikontexten* (Uppsala, 1962).

Lee, G. M. "Philippians I,22-23," *NovT* 12 (1970) 361.

Leivestad, R. " 'The Meekness and Gentleness of Christ': II Cor. X.1," *NTS* 12 (1965-66) 156-64.

Lemaire, A. *Les ministères aux origines de l'église* (LD 68; Paris, 1971).

Levick, B. M. *Roman Colonies in Southern Asia Minor* (Oxford, 1967).

Levie, J. "Le Chrétien Citoyen du Ciel (Phil 3,20)," in *Studiorum Paulinorum Congressus Internationalis Catholicus* (Rome, 1963) 2.81-88.

Lightfoot, J. B. *The Apostolic Fathers* (2nd rev. ed. by M. W. Holmes; Grand Rapids, 1989).

Lincoln, Andrew T. *Paradise Now and Not Yet: Studies in the Role of the Heavenly Dimension in Paul's Thought with Special Reference to His Eschatology* (SNTSMS 43; Cambridge, 1981).

Linton, O. *Zur Situation des Philipperbriefes* (ASNU 4; Uppsala, 1936)

Lohmeyer, Ernst. "Probleme paulinischer Theologie. I. Briefliche Grussüber-schriften," *ZNW* 26 (1927) 158-73.

————. *Kyrios Jesus. Eine Untersuchung zu Phil. 2,5-11* (Heidelberg, 1928).

Lohse, Eduard. "Die Entstehung des Bischofsamtes in der frühen Christen-heit," *ZNW* 71 (1980) 58-73.

Longenecker, Richard N. *Galatians* (WBC 41; Dallas, 1990).

Loofs, F. "Das altfirchliche Zeugnis gegen die herrschende Auffassung der Kenosisstelle (Phil. 2.5 bis 11)," *TSK* 100 (1927-28) 1-102.

López Fernández, E. "En torno a Fil 3,12," *EstBib* 34 (1975) 121-23.

Losie, Lynn Allan. "A Note on the Interpretation of Phil 2⁵," *ExpTim* 90 (1978) 52-53.

Lüdemann, Gerd. *Opposition to Paul in Jewish Christianity* (Minneapolis, 1989).

Lütgert, W. *Die Vollkommenen im Philipperbrief und die Enthusiasten in Thessalonich* (Gütersloh, 1909).

Lyons, George. *Pauline Autobiography: Toward a New Understanding* (SBLDS 73; Atlanta, 1985).

Mackay, B. S. "Further Thoughts on Philippians," *NTS* 7 (1960-61) 161-70.

Malherbe, Abraham J. *Ancient Epistolary Theorists* (SBLSBS 19; Atlanta, 1988).

———. "The Beasts at Ephesus," *JBL* 87 (1968) 71-80.

———. *The Cynic Epistles* (Missoula, 1977).

———. *Moral Exhortation: A Greco-Roman Sourcebook* (LEC, Philadelphia, 1986)

Malinowski, F. X. "The Brave Women of Philippi," *BTB* 15 (1985) 60-64.

Manson, T. W. "The Date of the Epistle to the Philippians," *Studies in the Gospels and Epistles* (ed. M. Black; Manchester, 1962) 149-67.

———. "St. Paul in Ephesus: The Date of the Epistle to the Philippians," *BJRL* 23 (1939) 182-200.

Marshall, I. Howard. "The Christ-Hymn in Philippians 2:5-11," *TynB* 19 (1968) 104-27.

———. "Incarnational Christology in the New Testament," in *Christ the Lord. Studies in Christology presented to Donald Guthrie* (ed. H. H. Rowdon; Leicester, 1982) 1-16.

———. "What is the Best Commentary? 12. Philippians," *ExpTim* 103 (1991) 39-42.

Marshall, John W. "Paul's Ethical Appeal in Philippians," in *Rhetoric and the New Testament: Essays from the 1992 Heidelberg Conference* (JSNTSup 90; ed. S. E. Porter and T. H. Olbricht; Sheffield, 1993) 357-74.

Marshall, Peter. *Enmity in Corinth: Social Conventions in Paul's Relations with the Corinthians* (WUNT 2/23; Tübingen, 1987).

Martin, Ralph P. "Μορφή in Philippians ii.6," *ExpTim* 70 (1959) 183-84.

———. *An Early Christian Confession. Philippians 2:5-11 in Recent Interpretation* (London, 1960).

———. *Carmen Christi. Philippians 2:5-11 in Recent Interpretation and in the Setting of Early Christian Worship* (Cambridge, 1967; Grand Rapids, ²1983).

———. "The Form-Analysis of Philippians 2,5-11," *SE* 2 (= TU 87 [1964]) 611-20.

———. "Some Reflections on New Testament Hymns," in *Christ the Lord. Studies in Christology presented to Donald Guthrie* (ed. H. H. Rowdon; Leicester, 1982) 37-49.

Mayer, Bernhard. "Paulus als Vermittler zwischen Epaphroditus und der Gemeinde von Philippi, Bemerkungen zu Phil 2,25-30," *BZ* 31 (1987) 176-88.

McDermott, M. "The Biblical Doctrine of KOINΩNIA," *BZ* 19 (1975) 64-77, 219-33.

McMichael, W. F. "Be Ye Followers Together of Me: Συμμιμηταί μου γίνεσθε — Phil. III.17," *ExpTim* 5 (1893-94) 287.

Mearns, Chris. "The Identity of Paul's Opponents at Philippi," *NTS* 33 (1987) 194-204.

Meecham, H. G. "The Meaning of (τὸ) λοιπόν in the New Testament," *ExpTim* 48 (1936-37) 331-32.

Meeks, Wayne A. *The First Urban Christians, The Social World of the Apostle Paul* (New Haven, 1983).

Mengel, B. *Studien zum Philipperbrief. Untersuchungen zum situativen Kontext unter besonderer Berücksichtigung der Frage nach der Ganzheitlichkeit oder Einheitlichkeit eines paulinischen Briefes* (WUNT 2/8; Tübingen, 1982).

Metzger, Bruce M. *A Textual Commentary on the Greek New Testament* (London/New York, 1971).

Michael, J. Hugh. "The First and Second Epistles to the Philippians," *ExpTim* 34 (1922-23) 106-9.

———. " 'Work Out Your Own Salvation'," *Expositor,* 9/12 (1924) 439-50.

Michaelis, W. von. "Teilungshypothesen bei Paulusbriefen," *TZ* 14 (1958) 321-26.

Michel, O. "Zur Exegese von Phil. 2,5-11," in *Theologie als Glaubenswägnis. Festschrift für K. Heim zum 80. Geburtstag* (Hamburg, 1954) 77-95.

Miller, Ernest C. "Πολιτεύεσθε in Philippians 1.27: Some Philological and Thematic Observations," *JSNT* 15 (1982) 86-96.

Minear, Paul S. "Singing and Suffering in Philippi," in *The Conversation Continues: Studies in Paul and John in Honor of J. Louis Martyn* (ed. R. T. Fortna and B. R. Gaventa; Nashville, 1990) 202-19.

Moehring, H. R. "Some remarks on σάρξ in Philippians 3,3ff.," *SE* 4 (= TU 102 [1968]) 432-36.

Moffatt, James. *An Introduction to the Literature of the New Testament* (New York, 1911).

———. *Love in the New Testament* (New York, 1930).

———. "Philippians II 26 and 2 Tim IV 13," *JTS* 18 (1917) 311-12.

———. "The History of Joy; a Brief Exposition of Phil. 4:4-7 (R.V.)," *ExpTim* 9 (1897-98) 334-36.

Montague, G. T. *Growth in Christ. A Study of Saint Paul's Theology of Progress* (Fribourg, Switzerland, 1961).

Moo, Douglas J. *Romans* (Chicago, 1991)

Morrice, W. G. *Joy in the New Testament* (Exeter, 1984).

Morris, L. "ΚΑΙ ΑΠΑΞ ΚΑΙ ΔΙΣ," *NovT* 1 (1956) 205-8.

Moule, C. F. D. "Further Reflexions on Philippians 2:5-11," in *Apostolic History and the Gospel. Biblical and Historical Essays Presented to F. F. Bruce on his 60th Birthday* (ed. W. W. Gasque and R. P. Martin; Grand Rapids, 1970) 264-76.

————. *An Idiom Book of New Testament Greek* (Cambridge, [2]1963).

————. "The Influence of Circumstances on the Use of Eschatological Terms," *JTS* 15 (1964) 1-15.

————. "The Manhood of Jesus in the NT," *Christ Faith and History* (ed. S. W. Sykes and J. P. Clayton; Cambridge, 1972) 95-110.

————. *The Origin of Christology* (Cambridge, 1977).

————. "St Paul and Dualism: The Pauline Conception of the Resurrection," *NTS* 12 (1966) 106-23.

Müller, Ulrich B. "Der Christushymnus Phil $2_{6-11}$," *ZNW* 79 (1988) 17-44.

————. *Prophetie und Predigt im Neuen Testament* (Gütersloh, 1975).

Müller-Bardorff, J. "Zur Frage der literarischen Einheit des Philipperbriefes," *Wissenschaftliche Zeitschrift der Universität Jena* 7 (1957-58) 591-604.

Mullins, T. Y. "Benedictions as a NT Form," *AUSS* 15 (1977) 59-64.

————. "Disclosure. A Literary Form in the New Testament," *NovT* 7 (1964) 44-50.

————. "Visit Talk in New Testament Letters," *CBQ* 35 (1973) 350-58.

Murphy-O'Connor, Jerome. "Christological Anthropology in Phil. II,6-11," *RB* 83 (1976) 25-50.

Nagata, T. *Philippians 2:5-11. A Case Study in the Contextual Shaping of Early Christology* (Ann Arbor, MI, 1981).

Neary, Michael. "The Cosmic Emphasis of Paul," *ITQ* 48 (1981) 1-26.

Neugebauer, F. *In Christus. Eine Untersuchung zum Paulinischen Glaubens-verständnis* (Göttingen, 1961).

Nygren, Anders. *Agape and Eros* (London, 1939).

O'Brien, P. T. "The Church as a Heavenly and Eschatological Entity," in *The Church in the Bible and the World* (ed. D. A. Carson; Exeter, 1987) 88-119.

————. "The Fellowship Theme in Philippians," *RTR* 37 (1978) 9-18.

————. "The Importance of the Gospel in Philippians," in *God Who is Rich in Mercy. Essays presented to D. B. Knox* (ed. P. T. O'Brien and D. G. Peterson; Grand Rapids, 1986) 213-33.

————. "Thanksgiving and the Gospel in Paul," *NTS* 21 (1974-75) 144-55.

————. "Thanksgiving within the Structure of Pauline Theology," in *Pauline Studies in Honour of Professor F. F. Bruce* (ed. D. A. Hagner and M. J. Harris; Grand Rapids, 1980) 50-66.

————. *Introductory Thanksgivings in the Letters of Paul* (NovTSup 49; Leiden, 1977).

Ogara, F. " 'Dominus propre est' (Phil 4,4-7)," *VD* 17 (1937) 353-59.

O'Neill, J. C. "Hoover on *Harpagmos* Reviewed, with a Modest Proposal Concerning Philippians 2:6," *HTR* 81 (1988) 445-49.

Omanson, R. L. "A Note on the Translation of Philippians 1:3-5," *BT* 29 (1978) 244-45.

————. "A Note on the Translation of Philippians 1:12," *BT* 29 (1978) 446-48.

Palmer, D. W. " 'To Die is Gain' (Philippians i 21)," *NovT* 17 (1975) 203-18.

Panikulam, G. *Koinonia in the New Testament. A Dynamic Expression of Christian life* (Rome, 1979).

Patitsas, Christos. "*Kenosis* according to Saint Paul," *GOTR* 27 (1982) 67-82.

Pedersen, Sigfred. " 'Mit Furcht und Zittern' (Phil. 2,12-13)," *ST* 32 (1978) 1-31.

Perkin, Vincent. "Some Comments on the Pauline Prescripts," *IBS* 8 (1986) 92-99.

Perkins, Pheme. "Philippians: Theology for the Heavenly Politeuma," in *Pauline Theology, Vol. 1* (ed. J. M. Bassler; Minneapolis, 1991) 89-104.

Pesch, R. "Zur Theologie des Todes," *BibLeb* 10 (1969) 9-16.

Pesch, Rudolf. *Paulus und seine Lieblingsgemeinde: Paulus — neu gesehen: Drei Briefe an die Heiligen von Philippi* (Freiburg, 1985).

Peterlin, Davorin. "Paul's Letter to the Philippians in Light of Disunity in the Church," unpub. Ph.D. dissertation (Aberdeen, 1992).

Peterman, Gerald W. "Giving and Receiving in Paul's Epistles: Greco-Roman Social Conventions in Philippians and in Other Pauline Writings," unpub. Ph.D. dissertation (University of London, 1992).

———. " 'Thankless Thanks': The Epistolary Social Convention in Philippians 4:10-20," *TynB* 42 (1991) 261-70.

Pfitzner, V. C. *Paul and the Agon Motif* (NovTSup 16; Leiden, 1967).

Picard, C. "Les Dieux de la Colonie de Philippes vers le I<sup>er</sup> siècle de notre ère, d'après les ex voto rupestres," *RHR* 86 (1922) 117-201.

Pobee, John S. *Persecution and Martyrdom in the Theology of Paul* (JSNTSup 6; Sheffield, 1985).

Polhill, John B. "Twin Obstacles in the Christian Path. Philippians 3," *RevExp* 77 (1980) 359-73.

Pollard, T. E. "The Integrity of Philippians," *NTS* 13 (1966-67) 57-66.

Porter, L. "The Word Ἐπίσκοπος in Pre-Christian Usage," *ATR* 21 (1939) 103-12.

Porter, Stanley E. "Word Order and Clause Structure in New Testament Greek. An Unexplored Area of Greek Linguistics Using Philippians as a Test Case," *FNT* 6 (1993) 177-206.

Powell, W. "Ἁρπαγμός . . . ἑαυτὸν ἐκένωσε," *ExpTim* 71 (1959) 88

Pretorius, E. A. C. "A Key to the Literature on Philippians," *Neot* 23 (1989) 125-53.

Price, J. D. "A Computer-aided Textual Commentary on the Book of Philippians," *GTJ* 8 (1987) 253-90.

Proudfoot, C. Merrill. "Imitation or Realistic Participation? A Study of Paul's Concept of 'Suffering with Christ'," *Int* 17 (1963) 140-60.

Rahtjen, B. D. "The Three Letters of Paul to the Philippians," *NTS* 6 (1959-60) 167-73.

Ramsay, William M. "On the Greek Form of the Name Philippians," *JTS* 1 (1900) 115-16.

————. *The Bearing of Recent Discovery on the Trustworthiness of the New Testament* (Grand Rapids, 1953).

————. *St. Paul the Traveller and the Roman Citizen* (New York, 1898).

Räisänen, H. "Paul's Conversion and the Development of his View of the Law," *NTS* 33 (1987) 404-19.

————. *Paul and the Law* (Tübingen, 1983).

Rapske, Brian. *The Book of Acts and Paul in Roman Custody* (Grand Rapids, 1994).

Reed, Jeffrey T. "The Infinitive with Two Substantival Accusatives, An Ambiguous Construction?" *NovT* 33 (1991) 1-27.

Reeves, Rodney R. "To be or not to be? That is not the Question: Paul's Choice in Philippians 1:22," *PRS* 19 (1992) 274-89.

Reicke, Bo. "Caesarea, Rome and the Captivity Epistles," in *Apostolic History and the Gospel. Biblical and Historical Essays Presented to F. F. Bruce on his 60th Birthday* (ed. W. W. Gasque and R. P. Martin; Grand Rapids, 1970) 277-86.

————. "Unité chrétienne et diaconie, Phil. ii 1-11," *Neotestamentica et Patristica. Eine Freundesgabe O. Cullmann* (ed. W. C. van Unnik; Leiden, 1962) 203-12.

Renan, Ernst. *Paul* (New York, 1869).

Reumann, John. "Contributions of the Philippian Community to Paul and to Earliest Christianity," *NTS* 39 (1993) 438-57.

————. "Philippians 3.20-21 — a Hymnic Fragment?" *NTS* 30 (1984) 593-609.

Ridderbos, H. *Paul. An Outline of His Theology* (Grand Rapids, 1975).

Rienecker, Fritz and Cleon Rogers. *Linguistic Key to the Greek New Testament* (Grand Rapids, 1976).

Rissi, Mathias. "Der Christushymnus in Phil 2,6-11," in *ANRW* (Berlin/New York, 1987) Band II, vol. 25.4, 3314-26.

Robbins, Charles J. "Rhetorical Structure of Philippians 2:6-11," *CBQ* 42 (1980) 73-82.

Roberts, Richard. "Old Texts in Modern Translation, Philippians i.27 (Goodspeed)," *ExpTim* 49 (1937-38) 325-28.

Robertson, A. T. *A Grammar of the Greek New Testament in the Light of Historical Research* (Nashville, [4]1923).

Robinson, D. W. B. "ἁρπαγμός: The Deliverance of Jesus Refused?' *ExpTim* 80 (1968-69) 253-54.

————. " 'Faith of Jesus Christ' — A NT Debate," *RTR* 29 (1970) 71-81.

————. " 'We are the Circumcision,' " *AusBR* 15 (1967) 28-35.

Robinson, H. Wheeler. *The Cross in the Old Testament* (London, 1957).

Robinson, J. A. T. *The Body: A Study in Pauline Theology* (SBT 1/5; London, 1952).

Robinson, William C., Jr. "Christology and Christian Life: Paul's Use of the Incarnation Motif," *ANQ* 12 (1971) 108-17.

Rolland, P. "La structure littéraire et l'unité de l'Épître aux Philippiens," *RSR* 64 (1990) 213-16.

Ross, J. "ΑΡΠΑΓΜΟΣ (Phil. ii.6)," *JTS* 10 (1909) 573-74.

Ross, J. M. "Some Unnoticed Points in the Text of the New Testament," *NovT* 25 (1983) 59-72.

Rousseau, François. "Une disposition des versets de Philippiens 2,5-11," *SR* 17 (1988) 191-98.

Russell, Ronald. "Pauline Letter Structure in Philippians," *JETS* 25 (1982) 295-306.

Saller, Richard P. *Personal Patronage under the Early Empire* (Cambridge, 1982).

Sampley, Paul. *Pauline Partnership in Christ: Christian Community and Commitment in Light of Roman Law* (Philadelphia, 1980).

Sanday, William and Arthur C. Headlam. *The Epistle to the Romans* (ICC; Edinburgh, 13 1911).

Sanders, E. P. *Paul and Palestinian Judaism* (Philadelphia, 1977).

―――. *Paul, The Law and the Jewish People* (Philadelphia, 1985).

Sanders, J. A. "Dissenting Deities and Philippians 2 1-11," *JBL* 88 (1969) 279-90.

Sanders, J. T. "The Transition from Opening Epistolary Thanksgiving to Body in the Letters of the Pauline Corpus," *JBL* 81 (1962) 348-63.

―――. *The New Testament Christological Hymns* (Cambridge, 1971).

Sass, G. "Zur Bedeutung von δοῦλος bei Paulus," *ZNW* 40 (1941) 24-32.

Satake, A. "Apostolat und Gnade bei Paulus," *NTS* 15 (1968-69) 96-107.

Schenk, W. "Der Philipperbrief in der neuen Forschung (1945-1985)," in *ANRW* (Berlin/New York, 1987) Band II, vol. 25.4, 3280-3313.

Schep, J. A. *The Nature of the Resurrection Body* (Grand Rapids, 1964).

Schmidt, R. "Über Philipper 2,12 und 13," *TSK* 80 (1907) 344-63.

Schmithals, W. *Paul and the Gnostics* (Nashville, 1972) 65-122.

Schmitz, O. "Zum Verständnis von Phil 2,21," in *Neutestamentliche Studien für G. Heinrici* (Leipzig, 1914) 155-69.

Schnider, Franz and Werner Stenger. *Studien zum neutestamentlichen Briefformular* (NTTS 11; Leiden, 1987).

Schöllgen, G. "Hausgemeinden, *oikos*-Ekklesiologie, und monarchischer Episcopat," *JAC* 31 (1988) 74-90.

Schoon-Janssen, Johannes. *Umstrittene "Apologien" in den Paulusbriefen: Studien zur rhetorischen Situation des 1. Thessalonicherbriefes, des Galaterbriefes und des Philipperbriefes* (GTA 45; Göttingen, 1991).

Schrage, W. *Die konkreten Einzelgebote in der paulinischen Paränese* (Gütersloh, 1961).

Schreiner, T. R. "Is Perfect Obedience to the Law Possible? A Re-Examination of Galatians 3:10," *JETS* 27 (1984) 151-60.

———. "Paul and Perfect Obedience to the Law: An Evaluation of the View of E. P. Sanders," *WTJ* 47 (1985) 245-78.

Schubert, Paul. *Form and Function of the Pauline Thanksgivings* (Berlin, 1939).

Schulz, A. *Nachfolgen und Nachahmen. Studien über das Verhältnis der neutestamentlichen Jüngerschaft zur urchristlichen Vorbildethik* (München, 1962).

Schütz, John H. *Paul and the Anatomy of Apostolic Authority* (SNTSMS 26; Cambridge, 1975).

Schweitzer, Albert. *The Mysticism of Paul the Apostle* (London, 1931).

Schweizer, Eduard. "Dying and Rising with Christ," *NTS* 14 (1967-68) 1-14.

———. *Church Order and the New Testament* (SBT 1/32; London, 1961).

———. *Erniedrigung und Erhöhung bei Jesus und seinen Nachfolgern* (Zürich, 1955, ²1962).

Seesemann, H. *Der Begriff* KOINΩNIA *im Neuen Testament* (Giessen, 1933).

Sevenster, J. N. *Paul and Seneca* (Leiden, 1961).

Sherwin-White, A. N. "The Early Persecutions and Roman Law Again," *JTS* 3 (1952) 199-213.

———. *Roman Society and Roman Law in the New Testament* (Oxford, 1963).

Siber, P. *Mit Christus leben. Eine Studie zur paulinischen Auferstehungshoffnung* (Zürich, 1971).

Silva, Moisés. "The Place of Historical Reconstruction in New Testament Criticism," in *Hermeneutics, Authority, and Canon* (ed. D. A. Carson and J. W. Woodbridge; Grand Rapids, 1986) 109-33.

Snyman, A. H. "Persuasion in Philippians 4.1-20," in *Rhetoric and the New Testament: Essays from the 1992 Heidelberg Conference* (JSNTSup 90; ed. S. E. Porter and T. H. Olbricht; Sheffield, 1993) 325-37.

Soards, M. L. "The Righteousness of God in the Writings of the Apostle Paul," *BTB* 15 (1985) 104-9.

Soderlund, Sven. "Focus on Philippians: A Review Article," *Crux* 20 (1984) 27-32.

Spicq, C. "Note sur ΜΟΡΦΗ dans les papyrus et quelques inscriptions," *RB* 80 (1973) 37-45.

———. *Agape in the New Testament* (St. Louis and London, 1965).

———. "*Epipothein*, Désirer ou chérir?" *RB* 64 (1957) 184-95.

———. *Notes de Lexicographie néo-testamentaire,* 2 vols. (Göttingen, 1978).

Spörlein, B. *Die Leugnung der Auferstehung* (Regensburg, 1971).

Stagg, Frank. "The Mind in Christ Jesus: Philippians 1:27–2:18," *RevExp* 77 (1980) 337-47.

Stalder, Kurt. "Episkopos," *IKZ* 61 (1971) 200-232.

Stambaugh, John E. and David L. Balch. *The New Testament in Its Social Environment* (LEC; Philadelphia, 1986).

Stanley, David M. " 'Carmenque Christo Quasi Deo Dicere . . . ,' " *CBQ* 20 (1958) 173-91.

————. *Boasting in the Lord* (New York, 1973).

————. *Christ's Resurrection in Pauline Soteriology* (Rome, 1961).

Steenburg, Dave. "The Case Against the Synonymity of *MORPHE* and *EIKON*," *JSNT* 34 (1988) 77-86.

Stein, Robert H. *Difficult Passages in the Epistles* (Grand Rapids, 1988).

Stewart, James S. "Philippians iv.6, 7 (Moffatt)," *ExpTim* 49 (1937-38) 269-71.

Stowers, Stanley K. "Friends and Enemies in the Politics of Heaven: Reading Theology in Philippians," in *Pauline Theology, Vol. 1* (ed. J. M. Bassler; Minneapolis, 1991) 105-21.

————. *Letter Writing in Greco-Roman Antiquity* (LEC 5; Philadelphia, 1986).

Strecker, Georg. "Freiheit und Agape. Exegese und Predigt über Phil 2,5-11," in *Neues Testament und christliche Existenz. Festschrift für Herbert Braun* (ed. H. D. Betz and L. Schottroff; Tübingen, 1973) 523-38.

————. "Redaktion und Tradition im Christushymnus Phil $2_{6-11}$," *ZNW* 55 (1964) 63-78.

Strimple, Robert B. "Philippians 2:5-11 in Recent Studies: Some Exegetical Conclusions," *WTJ* 41 (1979) 247-68.

Suggs, M. Jack. "Concerning the Date of Paul's Macedonian Ministry," *NovT* 4 (1960-61) 60-68.

————. "Koinonia in the New Testament," *Mid-Stream* 23 (1984) 351-62.

Sullivan, K. "Epignosis in the Epistles of Paul," in *Studiorum Paulinorum Congressus Internationalis Catholicus* (Rome, 1963) 2.405-16.

Swift, Robert C. "The Theme and Structure of Philippians," *BSac* 141 (1984) 234-54.

Talbert, Charles H. "The Problem of Pre-existence in Philippians 2:6-11," *JBL* 86 (1967) 141-53.

Tannehill, Robert C. *Dying and Rising with Christ. A Study in Pauline Theology* (Berlin, 1967).

Tarn, W. W. *Hellenistic Civilisation* (Cleveland, 1952).

Tellbe, B. Mikael. "*Christ and Caesar:* The Letter to the Philippians in the Setting of the Roman Imperial Cult," unpub. Th.M. thesis (Vancouver, 1993).

————. "The Sociological Factors behind Philippians 3:1-11 and the Conflict at Philippi," *JSNT* 55 (1994) 97-121.

Thekkekara, M. "A Neglected Idiom in an Overstudied Passage (Phil 2:6-8)," *LS* 17 (1992) 306-14.

Thomas, Thomas A. "The Kenosis Question," *EQ* 42 (1970) 142-51.

Thomas, W. Derek. "The Place of Women in the Church at Philippi," *ExpTim* 83 (1971-72) 117-20.

Thornton, L. S. *Christ and the Church* (Westminster, 1956).

————. *The Dominion of Christ* (Westminster, 1952).

Thräde, Klaus. *Grundzüge griechisch-römischer Brieftopic* (Munich, 1970).

Thrall, Margaret E. *Greek Particles in the New Testament. Linguistic and Exegetical Studies* (Leiden, 1962).

Torjesen, Karen Jo. *When Women Were Priests* (San Francisco, 1993).

Towner, Philip H. *The Goal of Our Instruction: The Structure of Theology and Ethics in the Pastoral Epistles* (JSNTSup 34; Sheffield, 1989).

Trudinger, Paul. "ἁρπαγμός and the Christological Significance of the Ascension," *ExpTim* 79 (1968) 279.

———. "Making Sense of the Ascension, The Cross as Glorification," *St. Mark's Review* 133 (1988) 11-13.

Turner, G. A. "Paul's Central Concern: Exegesis of Phil. 3,10-15," *Asbury Seminarian* 29 (1975) 9-14.

Turner, N. *Grammatical Insights into the New Testament* (Edinburgh, 1965).

Tyson, Joseph B. "Paul's Opponents at Philippi," *PRS* 3 (1976) 82-95.

Urquhart, W. S. "Glorifying Christ: A Meditation (Phil. 1,20f.)," *ExpTim* 34 (1922-23) 548-50.

van Unnik, W. C. "The Christian's Freedom of Speech in the New Testament," *BJRL* 44 (1962) 466-88.

Vokes, F. E. "ἁπαργμος in Phil. 2:5-11," *SE* 2 (= TU 87 [1964]) 670-75.

Vos, G. *The Pauline Eschatology* (Grand Rapids, 1961).

Wagner, G. "Le scandale de la croix expliqué par le chant du Serviteur d'Isaïe 53. Réflections sur Philippiens 2/6-11," *ETR* 61 (1986) 177-87.

———. *Pauline Baptism and the Pagan Mysteries* (Edinburgh, 1967).

Wallace, D. H. "A Note on morphē," *TZ* 22 (1966) 19-25.

Walter, Nikolaus. "Christusglaube und heidnische Religiosität in paulinischen Gemeinden," *NTS* 25 (1978-79) 422-42.

Wanamaker, C. A. "Philippians 2.6-11: Son of God or Adamic Christology?" *NTS* 33 (1987) 179-93.

Warren, J. "Work Out Your own Salvation," *EQ* 16 (1944) 125-37.

Warren, W. "On ἑαυτὸν ἐκένωσεν," *JTS* 12 (1911) 461-63.

Watson, D. F. "A Rhetorical Analysis of Philippians and Its Implications for the Unity Question," *NovT* 30 (1988) 57-88.

Watson, F. *Paul, Judaism and the Gentiles* (Cambridge, 1986).

Webster, J. B. "The Imitation of Christ," *TynB* 37 (1986) 95-120.

Wedderburn, A. J. M. "Some Observations on Paul's Use of the Phrases 'in Christ' and 'with Christ,'" *JSNT* 25 (1985) 83-97.

Wegenast, K. *Das Verständnis der Tradition bei Paulus und in den Deuteropaulinen* (Neukirchen-Vluyn, 1962).

Westermann, W. L. *The Slave Systems of Greek and Roman Antiquity* (Philadelphia, [3]1964);

White, John L. "Ancient Greek Letters," in *Greco-Roman Literature and the New Testament: Selected Forms and Genres* (ed. D. E. Aune; SBLSBS 21; Atlanta, 1988) 85-105.

———. *The Form and Function of the Body of the Greek Letter* (SBLDS 2; Missoula, MT, 1972).

———. *Light from Ancient Letters* (FFNT; Philadelphia, 1986).

White, L. Michael. "Morality between Two Worlds: A Paradigm of Friendship in Philippians," in *Greeks, Romans and Christians: Essays in Honor of Abraham J. Malherbe* (ed. D. L. Balch, E. Ferguson, and W. A. Meeks; Minneapolis, 1990) 201-15.

Wibbing, Siegfried. *Die Tugend- und Lasterkataloge im Neuen Testament und ihre Traditionsgeschichte unter besonderer Berücksichtigung der Qumrantexte* (BZNW 25; Berlin, 1959).

Wick, Peter, *Der Philipperbrief: Der formale Aufbau des Briefe als Schlüssel zum Verständnis seines Inhalts* (BWANT 7.15; Stuttgart, 1994).

Wiedemann, Thomas. *Greek and Roman Slavery* (New York, 1981).

Wiederkehr, D. *Die Theologie der Berufung in den Paulusbriefen* (Freiburg, Schweiz, 1963).

Wikgren, Allen P. "The Problem in Acts 16:12," in *New Testament Textual Criticism: Its Significance for Exegesis: Essays in Honour of Bruce M. Metzger* (ed. E. J. Epp and G. D. Fee; Oxford University, 1981)

Wilder, Amos N. *Early Christian Rhetoric: The Language of the Gospel* (Cambridge, MA, 1971).

Wiles, G. P. *Paul's Intercessory Prayers. The Significance of the Intercessory Prayer Passages in the Letters of St Paul* (SNTSMS 24; Cambridge, 1974).

Williams, Sam K. "Again Pistis Christou," *CBQ* 49 (1987) 431-47.

———. "The 'Righteousness of God' in Romans," *JBL* 99 (1980) 241-90.

Wilson, S. G. *The Gentiles and the Gentile Mission in Luke-Acts* (SNTSMS 23; Cambridge, 1973).

Wishmeyer, O. "Das Adjective ΑΓΑΠΗΤΟΣ in den paulinischen Briefen. Eine Traditionsgeschichtliche Miszelle," *NTS* 32 (1986) 476-80.

Witherington, Ben III. *Friendship and Finances in Philippi: The Letter of Paul to the Philippians* (Valley Forge, PA, 1994).

Wong, T. Y.-C. "The Problem of Pre-existence in Philippians 2,6-11," *ETL* 62 (1986) 167-82.

Wright, N. T. "Adam in Pauline Christology," in *Society of Biblical Literature 1983 Seminar Papers* (ed. K. H. Richards; Chico, 1982) 359-89.

———. "ἁρπαγμός and the Meaning of Philippians 2:5-11," *JTS* 37 (1986) 321-52.

———. "The Paul of History and the Apostle of Faith," *TynB* 29 (1978) 61-88.

Zerwick, Max. *Biblical Greek* (Rome, 1963).

——— and Mary Grosvenor. *An Analysis of the Greek New Testament* (Rome, 1974).

Ziesler, John A. *The Meaning of Righteousness in Paul. A Linguistic and Theological Enquiry* (SNTSMS 20; Cambridge, 1972).

# INTRODUCTION

This commentary is written from the perspective that Philippians was one letter, written by the Apostle Paul from Rome in the early 60s, to his longtime friends and compatriots in the gospel who lived in Philippi, an outpost of Rome in the interior plain of eastern Macedonia. The aim of this Introduction is to "introduce" both the *letter* as I see it and this *commentary* on the letter. Although the various critical questions that belong to such an introduction will be touched on, one will need to go to the more traditional NT Introductions for fuller treatment of many of these issues.[1] Here is what I perceive the letter to be about, which the commentary that follows will spell out in greater detail.

## I. PHILIPPIANS AS A LETTER

It is common to "introduce" the Pauline letters by "reconstructing" the historical situation to which they were written. While that kind of reconstruction is extremely important for our understanding of Philippians (see section II below), here is a case where the question of "genre" must precede the questions of "history."[2] Thus we will first look at the letter as a piece of first-century "literature."

---

1. For a broad range of views on these matters, see the NT Introductions by Kümmel, 320-35; Guthrie, 541-63; Carson-Moo-Morris, 317-29. For an Introduction of a different kind, toward which I have personal proclivities, see L. T. Johnson, *Writings,* 338-49. Reading the chapters on Philippians in these volumes will give one a good sense of the issues as well as of different approaches.

2. I had already settled on this some months before I read Stowers, "Friends," who argues essentially the same thing. I have learned much from this article, to which I am indebted for some of the insights presented here. Where I differ from Stowers is at the point of history. Although he brings the letter to bear on the situation in Philippi, he is much more interested

## A. Philippians and Ancient Letter Writing

In contrast to many of Paul's other letters, especially the more polemical and/or apologetic letters such as Galatians and 1 and 2 Corinthians, Philippians reflects all the characteristics of a "letter of friendship," combined with those of a "letter of moral exhortation." Several matters point in this direction.

1. *Philippians as a Letter of Friendship.*[3] Letter-writing, which was something of an "art" in pre-typewriter, pre-computer Western culture, was likewise taken with great seriousness by the ancient Greeks and Romans.[4] Formal schooling would have included instruction in letter-writing.[5] Two of the manuals for such instruction are extant, those by Pseudo-Demetrius and Pseudo-Libanius[6] — although they were probably intended for professional scribes rather than for school children. That by Pseudo-Demetrius lists and offers illustrations of twenty-one different types of letters. The first of these, the "friendly type," was well known to all, and according to Cicero was the reason for the "invention of letter-writing."[7] In many ways this is the most "artless" of the letters, since what are now known as "family letters" very often belong to it.[8] Nonetheless, certain characteristics are discernible, and most of these fit very well with one dimension of Paul's letter to the Philippians.

First the theory, as illustrated by Pseudo-Demetrius' example "letter":

---

in the question of "genre" per se, so that one gets the feeling that the letter itself is "generic" in the sense that because it is a "hortatory letter of friendship," it could have been written to any of Paul's churches and come out pretty much the same way. Whereas I am equally convinced that it is a letter of friendship, I think it can only be understood as case specific, written to a very concrete situation in Philippi in the early 60s.

3. See also L. T. Johnson, *Writings,* 338-49; L. M. White, "Morality"; Stowers, "Friends."

4. On this matter, see esp. Malherbe, *Theorists,* 1-11, plus his many examples; S. Stowers, *Letter Writing,* 27-40; J. L. White, *Light,* 189-220; cf. n. 14.

5. See Malherbe, *Theorists,* 6-7; Stowers, *Letter Writing,* 32-35; White, *Light,* 189-90.

6. "Epistolary Types," by Pseudo-Demetrius (falsely attributed to Demetrius of Pharlerum, 4th c. BCE), cannot be dated with precision (from 2nd c. BCE to 2nd c. CE); for text and translation see Malherbe, *Theorists,* 30-41. "Epistolary Styles," by Pseudo-Libanius, dates from the 4th to 6th c. CE; for text and translation, see *ibid.,* 66-81. This work has expanded the list from 21 to 41. Interestingly, his first "type" is the "hortatory" letter; he lists the "friendly letter" as no. 7.

7. See n. 15 below.

8. It should be noted here, as Stowers points out (*Letter Writing,* 71), that the so-called "family letter," which abounds among the papyri, was not recognized as a distinct type by the ancient theorists. But that is because, as the illustration by Pseudo-Demetrius makes clear, the content of the so-called family letter belonged to the category of "friendly letter"; cf. Pseudo-Libanius, "the friendly style is that in which we exhibit simply friendship only."

Even though I have been separated from you for a long time, I suffer this in body only. For I can never forget you or the impeccable way we were raised together from childhood up. Knowing that I myself am genuinely concerned about your affairs,[9] and that I have worked unstintingly for what is most advantageous to you, I have assumed that you, too, have the same opinion of me, and will refuse me nothing. You will do well,[10] therefore, to give close attention to the members of my household lest they need anything, to assist them in whatever they might need, and to write about whatever you should choose.

Although this illustration leans heavily toward the "reciprocation" of friendship (see next section), three features of this theoretical example are noteworthy for Philippians: (1) the note at the beginning that friendly letters are related to "absence" between friends (cf. Phil 1:27; 2:12); (2) that such letters are concerned with "the affairs" of both the sender and recipient (cf. Phil 1:12; 1:27; 2:19, 23); and (3) that the recipient "does well" in looking after the needs of the sender (cf. Phil 4:14).

More significantly, Loveday Alexander has recently subjected a series of "family letters" to an empirical "formal" analysis, and has shown, persuasively to my thinking, that a certain pattern emerges in these letters that is also in evidence in Philippians.[11] She isolates seven items, including the salutation and concluding greetings (I have put the corresponding parts of Philippians in brackets):[12]

1. The address and greeting [1:1-2]
2. Prayer for the recipients [1:3-11]
3. Reassurance about the sender (= "my affairs") [1:12-26]
4. Request for reassurance about the recipients (= "your affairs") [1:27–2:18; 3:1–4:3]
5. Information about movements of intermediaries [2:19-30]
6. Exchange of greetings with third parties [4:21-22]
7. Closing wish for health [4:23]

9. Gk. τὰ πρός σε; see n. 17 on 1:12.

10. Gk. καλῶς οὖν ποιήσεις; cf. on 4:14, but in the past tense.

11. See "Letter-Forms." One needs to be properly cautious here, as to whether the "form" or the reality came first; i.e., whether a preexistent form determined how the letter was written, or the "form" is our discovery based on empirical data (cf. Alexander, 88-89). Surely in this case it is the latter.

12. I should note here that I read Dr. Alexander's article after I had written the commentary, with the present outline already in hand. Her analysis has given clear evidence that this general pattern had already existed in some of the "family letters" from among the papyri.

It will also be recognized that 3:1–4:9 and 4:10-20 do not easily fit the scheme. While

There is also evidence for leaving a "thanksgiving" until the end[13] — although in Philippians this is more likely a matter of rhetoric than of letter form (see on 4:10-20). The point to make is that at the "formal" level much of Philippians is explicable as a letter of friendship, of the "friendly, familial type."[14]

On the other hand, Cicero considers "friendly letters" such as those noted in the papyri as not worthy of correspondence between true friends, since most of the former deal with mundane matters, while letters between friends should engage in conversation about weightier issues.[15] Thus what we have in Philippians is a letter that has the *formal* character — and the "logic" — of a "friendly" or "family" letter; whereas in terms of *content* it carries on conversation at a much deeper level of friendship.

But "friendship" itself, of the kind Cicero was talking about, was another matter that the Greeks and Romans took with a kind of seriousness most moderns can scarcely appreciate. Since there are several indications within our letter that Paul understood his relationship with the Philippians to be a modified expression of "friendship," a brief overview of this phenomenon is also necessary in order for us to understand Paul's letter to them.

2. *Friendship in the Greco-Roman World.*[16] As with most ancient societies friendship played a primary role in basic societal relationships in the Greco-Roman world, including politics and business. So important was this matter that it became a regular topic of philosophical discussions. Aristotle devoted a considerable section of his *Nichomachean Ethics* to a discussion of friendship, while Cicero and Plutarch have entire treatises on the topic, and

---

some see this as evidence for dismembering our present letter into three (see below, pp. 21-23), I have argued in the commentary, on the basis of content and the striking parallels between chaps. 2 and 3, that there are better solutions as to how these sections fit in. See the discussion below (pp. 37-39).

13. Cf. Alexander, "Letter-Forms," 97-98.

14. Stowers ("Friends," 107) points out that this has long been recognized by classicists dealing with ancient letter writing (e.g., Koskenniemi, *Studien,* 115-27; Thräde, *Grundzüge*).

15. Cicero, *Fam.* 2.4.1: "Letter writing was invented just in order that we might *inform those at a distance* if there were anything which it was important for them or for ourselves that they should know. A letter of this kind you will of course not expect from me; for as regards *your own affairs* you have your correspondents and messengers at home, while as regards *mine* there is absolutely no news to tell you" (LCL, 25.101; cited also in Malherbe, *Theorists,* 21; emphases mine, to show the ties with Pseudo-Demetrius noted above). Cicero then goes on to indicate that he intends to write on "something more serious."

16. For discussions in the secondary literature, see Saller, *Personal Patronage,* 7-39; P. Marshall, *Enmity,* 1-34; Stowers, "Friends," 107-14. Among the primary sources, see Aristotle, *Eth. Nic.,* Book 8; Cicero, *Amicitia;* Seneca, *Ep. Mor.* 11; Plutarch, *De Amic. Mult.*

Seneca addresses the issue in several of his "moral letters." According to Aristotle (and others who followed his lead), there were three kinds of "friendship" between "equals": (1) true friendship between virtuous people, whose relationship is based on goodwill and loyalty (including trust); (2) friendship based on pleasure, that is, on the enjoyment of the same thing, so that people enjoy the society of those who are "agreeable to us"; (3) friendship based on need, a purely utilitarian arrangement, which Aristotle disdains, as do most of his successors. Somewhat condescendingly, Aristotle also admitted the word *friendship* for relationships between "unequals" — parents and children, (generally) an older person and a younger, husband and wife, and ruler and the persons ruled.

The philosophical discussions of friendship deal primarily with the first kind, where a certain "core of ideals" emerge that were thought to be applicable to all genuine friendships.[17] These included "virtue," especially fidelity or loyalty; affection, in the form of mutual goodwill toward the other for his or her own sake; and especially the basic matter of mutual "giving and receiving (= social reciprocity) benefits" (= of goods and services, although reciprocity sometimes took the form of gratitude only).[18] The matter of "benefits" called for some of the lengthiest discussions, because friendship could not be understood apart from "benefits," but these could also be abused so as to undermine mutuality and trust. Because it entailed reciprocity whatever else, friendship also included a sense of "obligation" and expressions of "gratitude" (further goodwill). Moreover, and in ways very difficult for moderns to appreciate, friendship of this more or less "contractual" kind was also "agonistic" (competitive) in the sense that it was often discussed in the context of "enemies."[19] That is, to have friends automatically meant to have enemies, so that "constant attention to friends meant constant watchfulness of enemies."[20]

One will easily see that many of these "ideals" are characteristic of

---

17. Cf. Saller, *Personal Patronage,* 12; see his discussion on pp. 12-22; cf. P. Marshall, *Enmity,* 21-24.

18. On the matter of "benefits" and its larger significance for society in general, see G. Peterman, "Giving," 63-104.

19. See esp. chap. 2 in P. Marshall, *Enmity,* 35-69, and Stowers, "Friends," 113-14. I am indebted to these scholars for these insights.

20. Stowers, "Friends," 113, referring to Plutarch (*De Util.* 87B); cf. Plutarch in *De Amic. Mult.* 96A-B (LCL, 2.63): "Enmities follow close upon friendships, and are interwoven with them, inasmuch as it is impossible for a friend not to share his friend's wrongs or disrepute or disfavor." Cf. the threat to Pilate recorded in John 19:12, "If you let this man go you are no friend of Caesar's," implying that since Jesus as a rival "king" was therefore Caesar's enemy, Pilate must act in accordance with "friendship" or he automatically becomes Caesar's enemy.

Paul's relationship to the Philippian believers in this letter. The letter in its entirety is predicated on his and their mutual goodwill; this is the "bottom line," which is so secure that Paul has no hesitation in addressing, even exhorting, them as he does. Theirs has been a "participation/partnership" in the gospel from the very beginning, a partnership that involved the Philippians themselves in evangelism and in furthering the gospel through their "benefactions" to Paul. That same "partnership" now also includes mutual suffering for the gospel (1:29-30; 2:17). Friendship is further demonstrated by the oft-noted expressions of deep affection (e.g., 1:7, "I have you in my heart"; 1:8, "I long for you with the affection of Christ Jesus"; 4:1, "my beloved brothers and sisters, whom I long for, my joy and my crown, beloved"). Even more so, friendship is demonstrated in their mutuality and reciprocity, exhibited in a variety of ways: his earnestness to see them again for their own "progress" in the faith, since they have just recently "benefited" him in a material way; his praying for them (1:4) and their praying for him (1:19); but especially by their recent gift, Paul's acknowledgment of which (4:10-20) is full of language indicating reciprocity in friendship. The sometimes "agonistic" character of friendship, which meant to have friends in the context of also having "enemies," probably lies behind much of the language of "opposition" that marks the letter throughout (1:15-17, 28; 2:21; 3:2, 17-19). And friendship surely lies behind his concern that within their own community they "have the same mindset" (2:2-5; 4:2-3), for his and their friendship will be on rocky ground if theirs with one another is not sustained.

These expressions of friendship are further heightened by the fact that in this letter Paul studiously avoids any indication of a "patron-client" (or "patron-protégé") relationship,[21] which emerges so frequently in his other letters (either in the form of "apostleship" or in the imagery of "father" with children). Thus he begins by identifying himself and Timothy as "slaves" of Christ Jesus (1:1), who himself had become slave for all by dying on a cross (2:7-8). And though the major parts of the letter are exhortative, there is no appeal to Paul's authority as the basis of his exhortation; rather he appeals to their mutuality in Christ (2:1) and to his own example, as he himself follows Christ's example (3:4-14; so also 1:12-26 and 4:14).

In sum. Many of the aspects of letters of friendship are clearly evident in

---

21. On this matter see Saller, *Personal Patronage,* 8-39; see also the discussion of 4:15-16. In his relationship with other churches, this whole matter caused no end of personal tension for Paul, having to do with (1) his role as apostle and thus his authority over his churches, which (2) gave him the right to material support, but which (3) he rejected everywhere but in Philippi; in so doing (4) he inevitably experienced hunger, thirst, being poorly clad, sleepless, etc., a path (5) he appears to have chosen so as to model Christ as "servant of all." In the final analysis, the gospel prevails over everything else, but one cannot miss the moments of tension in his letters because of that choice.

Philippians, not only in some of the "formal" matters, but even more so at key points along the way in the body of the letter. These include the "agonistic" nature of friendship in the Greco-Roman world, which is the probable key to one of the more perplexing issues in Philippians, that of "opponents."

3. *The Question of "Opponents."* There is nearly universal agreement that the Philippians are being harassed by "opponents" of some kind (some would say "kind*s*"); there is likewise nearly universal *dis*agreement as to the "who," "how many," and "where" of these "opponents." Indeed, the secondary literature on this issue[22] is second only to the huge output on 2:6-11 (see p. 192).[23] But when, by one count, the hypotheses number at least eighteen, it is safe to say that the data in Philippians on which these hypotheses are constructed are less certain than are the assertions about "opponents" which appear in the literature.

The primary reason for the differences is the one never spoken to — methodology:[24] how does one go about detecting the presence of opponents, and having done that, how should one assess the nature of their "teaching"? There are basically two ways of proceeding: first, to examine carefully all

22. See Gunther, *Opponents,* 2.

23. For bibliography see O'Brien, 26-27, whose overview of the discussion is also helpful for those who wish to pursue this question further.

24. The basic method is called "mirror-reading," in which statements made by Paul are "mirror read" as reflecting the statements and/or positions of the "opponents." A very useful attempt to bring some order into the current chaos on this matter may be found in J. M. G. Barclay, "Mirror-reading," whose cautions and criteria were worked out in the context of a "polemical" letter (Galatians); they are all the more noteworthy here since Philippians is *not* a polemical letter, although that is often assumed and sometimes asserted. Barclay isolates four "cautions" (= the primary errors in methodology) and offers seven positive criteria.

The cautions (dangers): (1) *Undue selectivity* (= the need to determine which of Paul's statements are most revealing [as to the Philippian situation]); (2) *Over-interpretation* (the inclination to read into every statement by Paul some counter-statement as to the "teaching" of opponents); (3) *Mishandling of polemics* (the tendency to read the *intention* of opponents strictly from the heated, polemical descriptions by Paul); (4) *Reading too much into very little* (the tendency to latch onto a word or phrase, that occurs only once or twice, and reconstruct the whole problem in light of that). On this matter see further n. 60 on 3:3.

The criteria: (1) *Type of utterance* (e.g., assertion, denial, command, prohibition, all of which function differently); (2) *Tone* (the kinds of urgency or lack thereof in the various types of utterance); (3) *Frequency* (an occasional remark does not seem to carry the same weight as those items to which Paul returns again and again); (4) *Clarity* (we can mirror-read with confidence only those statements that are reasonably clear); (5) *Unfamiliarity* (with due cautions imposed, we may consider the presence of unfamiliar themes in a letter a reflection of the unique situation to which it is addressed); (6) *Consistency* (unless there is strong evidence to the contrary, one should *assume* one type of opponent or argument); and (7) *Historical plausibility.*

7

direct statements about "opponents," with an eye toward those that might be *in Philippi;* second, assuming that opponents have been discovered at step one, to "mirror read" other statements so as to determine what they were "teaching." Most of the difficulties, and almost all of the differences of opinion, lie with either a confusion of these two steps or with giving precedence to the second step, but without a controlled methodology.[25]

In the case of Philippians, two matters make this exercise tenuous: (1) As will be noted momentarily, the direct statements are themselves so ambiguous, indeed contradictory, that agreement as to identification is nearly impossible to come by. Moreover, (2) nothing in the letter itself implies anything remotely bordering on "capitulation" on the part of the Philippians.[26] The closest thing to it might be the application of Paul's personal story in 3:15-16 (q.v.); but in comparison with Galatians or 2 Corinthians 10–13, this is mild stuff indeed, and fits better the reality of friendship in any case.

Here, then, are the data, the "direct statements":

1. In 1:15-17, Paul speaks of some who "preach Christ out of rivalry/selfish ambition and envy," supposing thereby to "stir up trouble" for Paul "in my chains." These people can be excluded from consideration of opposition *in Philippi,* since v. 14 makes it certain that we are dealing with people in the same city where Paul is imprisoned (Rome, in our view).[27]

2. In 1:27-28 Paul urges the Philippians not to "be frightened in any way by those who oppose you." This is the one place in the letter where the language of "opposition" actually occurs. In this case the context implies: (a) that these opponents are not believers (they are destined for destruction), and (b) they are harassing the Philippians, and thus the cause of their "suffering for Christ's sake" (vv. 29-30).

3. In 2:21 Paul sets Timothy in contrast to "all the others," who, in the language of 2:4, "look out for their own interests, not those of Jesus Christ." While it is less clear here to whom Paul refers — I have argued that this is a second swipe at the people mentioned in 1:15-17 — it is clear they are not in Philippi, so at least they do not constitute "opponents" in that city.

25. The primary methodological errors in the case of Philippians are two: first the unwarranted assumption that Philippians can be "mirror read" as though it were a *polemical letter;* second, little methodological care is given as to which, or what kind of, statements are "fair game" in order to determine the nature of the opposition. The literature is full of examples of abusing cautions 2 and 4 noted above (preceding n.).

26. The point is that whenever Paul begins to take on "opponents" in his letters, one is no longer dealing with more or less calm and rational conversation, but with something much more polemical, which varies from letter to letter, *depending on the degree to which the community is capitulating.*

27. Although I suggest in the commentary that Paul's primary reason for mentioning them is probably paradigmatic.

Our difficulties, therefore, have to do with identifying the people referred to in the final two statements:

4. In 3:2-3 Paul warns: "Beware of the dogs; beware of the evil workers; beware of the 'mutilation' [of flesh]." "For," he goes on, in contrast to them "*we* are the circumcision who worship/serve by the Spirit of God and boast in Christ Jesus, and place no confidence in flesh." Both this description and the first part of his personal narrative that follows (vv. 4-9) indicate that Paul is once again referring to some Judaizers, people who try to bring Gentile believers in Christ under Jewish identity symbols, especially circumcision.[28] But (a) unless they are to be recognized in 3:18-19 (a moot point indeed), there is not another direct mention of them nor allusion to them, and (b) there is no suggestion in the text that they are actually present in Philippi. This text is a *warning* against them, pure and simple; those who consider them *present in Philippi* either assume that or read it into the text.

5. Finally, in 3:18-19 Paul contrasts some who walk differently from him. Paul himself, desiring to be conformed to Christ's death and with eyes firmly focused on his sure future, strains every nerve so as to reach the goal and attain the prize (3:10-14). These others, whom he has mentioned to the Philippians many times before and now mentions with tears, "live as enemies of the cross of Christ, whose end is destruction, whose god is their belly, whose glory is in their shame, and whose minds are set on earthly things." Apart from their being enemies of the cross, not a word in this description faintly resembles what Paul says elsewhere about those who promote the circumcision of Gentile believers. Who these people are over whom Paul weeps cannot be known for certain, but again, even less so in this case, there is not a hint that they are actually present in Philippi as opponents of Paul and his gospel there.

What that leaves us with, then, is:

(1) one certain mention of opposition of a sort against Paul in Rome (1:15-17), and perhaps a second (2:21), but Paul can rejoice over their preaching Christ because even if they are doing so to increase Paul's affliction, they are failing in that while succeeding in the former;

(2) one certain mention of opposition in Philippi (1:27-28), opponents who are *outside the church* and, in the context of vv. 29-30, almost certainly to be understood as the source of the Philippians' present suffering; plus

(3) one fairly certain warning against Judaizers, whose presence in Philippi is neither expressed nor necessarily to be assumed; and

28. On other options (Jewish proselytizers; "Gnostic missionaries"), see n. 38 on 3:2.

9

(4) one thoroughly ambiguous mention of people over whom Paul weeps because by their current way of "walking" they have opted out of life in Christ and have chosen to become his enemies.

Since neither of these latter two can be placed in Philippi with certainty, and since nothing further is said explicitly about their teaching, to "mirror read" other data in this letter as having to do with "opponents" in Philippi is a tenuous procedure at best.

On the other hand, by recognizing Philippians as a "letter of friendship," and noting the frequently "agonistic" nature of friendship in the Greco-Roman world, one can recognize all of these passages as fitting into that context. As we will note momentarily, for Paul "friendship" has to do primarily with his and the Philippians' "partnership/participation" together in the advance of the gospel, both in Philippi and elsewhere. But as we will also note (p. 33), the reason for the exhortations in this letter are related primarily to his concern over some "posturing" within the community which, if left unchecked, will surely impede the cause of the gospel. The warnings are most likely related to these latter concerns.

Thus Paul's mention of "opponents" is not to be understood as anxiety on his part lest his Philippian friends capitulate to false teaching. In this regard Philippians stands in bold relief over against Galatians and 2 Corinthians 10–13. Rather, in exhorting them to stand firm in the one Spirit for the gospel in the face of opposition and suffering (1:27–2:18), and thus not to lose sight of their sure eschatological future (3:10-21), he appeals to their long-term friendship (see esp. 2:1) and places that in a context over against "enemies." Paul has warned them about such people many times before (3:1, 18), people who turn out not to be so much his and their "enemies" as they are "enemies" of Christ himself (3:18).

The reality of friendship, and the formal characteristics of letters of friendship, therefore, account for much in this letter — both Paul's affectionate language toward the Philippians and the strong language, sometimes full of pathos, about others who are "enemies" of the gospel. But friendship is only part of the story, the rest of which is found in another type of letter from the hellenistic world, the letter of exhortation.

4. *Philippians as a Letter of Moral Exhortation.* Another area in which first-century sociology differs considerably from ours is in the matter of ethics and morality. Deeply influenced as we are by the Law, the Prophets, the Gospels, and the Epistles, we find it difficult to dissociate "religion" from ethics. But such was not the case in the first century CE, where ethical instruction did not belong to Greco-Roman religion, but to philosophy.[29] Moreover,

29. On this matter see esp. Malherbe, *Moral Exhortation,* 11-15.

moral instruction often took place in the context of friendship — of the second kind, where a "superior" instructed an "inferior," often by means of letters. Although these letters lacked "form" as such, they had two "fundamental elements" that characterized them: (1) the writer was the recipient's friend or moral superior;[30] and (2) they aimed at "persuasion" or "dissuasion."[31] Because the persuasion or dissuasion was toward or away from certain "models" of behavior, the author frequently appealed to examples, including sometimes his own. Pseudo-Libanius's brief "example" of such a letter thus reads: "Always be an emulator, dear friend, of virtuous men. For it is better to be well spoken of when imitating good men than to be reproached by all men while following evil men."[32]

Philippians is also easily recognizable in this description. Indeed, the larger part of the letter is taken up with two considerable hortatory sections (1:27–2:18 and 3:1–4:3), in which the appeal is made on the basis of mutuality and friendship (2:1; cf. the "let *us*" in 3:15) and the aim is to "persuade" toward one kind of behavior and to "dissuade" from another. This becomes even more evident in Paul's appeal throughout the letter to exemplary paradigms.

5. *The Use of Exemplary Paradigms.* Significantly, the heart of the two sections of "moral exhortation" is taken up with the best-known materials in the letter, the Christ story in 2:6-11 and Paul's personal story in 3:4-14. In both cases he explicitly says that the narratives have been given to serve as "models" for the Philippians' own "way of thinking" and of behavior appropriate to such a "mindset." What is being "modeled" in each case is a "mindset" that is in keeping with the gospel: in the case of Christ he is the paradigm for the injunction of 2:3, "do nothing out of selfish ambition or vain conceit, but in humility consider others better than yourselves." In the case of Paul, they are urged to follow his example, which has "knowing Christ" as its singular focus, both in the present by living a "cruciform" lifestyle in keeping with that of Christ while at the same time straining to obtain the prize, the final and complete knowing of Christ at the end.

Given these explicitly paradigmatic narratives, one is probably justified in reading the rest of the personal matters in the same way. Thus, even though the opening narrative about "Paul's affairs" in 1:12-26 fits with a letter of

30. These words are Stowers's (*Letter Writing,* 96).
31. In Stowers's words, "the writer recommends habits of behavior and actions that conform to a certain model of character and attempts to turn the recipient away from contrasting negative models of character" (*Letter Writing,* 96). See esp. the descriptions by Pseudo-Demetrius (of his "advisory type"), "we exhort (someone to) something or dissuade (him) from something" (Malherbe, *Theorists,* 37), and by Pseudo-Libanius (of his "paraenetic style"), "Paraenesis is divided into two parts, encouragement and dissuasion" (*ibid.,* 69).
32. Cited in Malherbe, *Theorists,* 75.

friendship, there is every reason to believe that it is also intended to be paradigmatic.[33] So also with the two important interlude narratives as to "what's next" between him and them, namely the coming of Timothy shortly (2:19-24) and of Epaphroditus now (2:25-30, as bearer of this letter). Both men are well known to the Philippians, yet are "commended" to them precisely because both exemplify the gospel: Timothy is set in contrast to "non-friends" (= "enemies") who look out for their own interests (over against the exhortation of 2:3-4); moreover, he is well known to them as one who "will take a genuine interest in your affairs" (v. 20), which is the same as "looking out for the interests of Christ" (v. 21; cf. 2:4). And Epaphroditus is one who in the Philippians' service to Paul "risked his own life for the work of Christ" (v. 30). They are to "honor people like him."

6. *Philippians as a Christian "Hortatory Letter of Friendship."* In light of the foregoing, Philippians is rightly called "a hortatory letter of friendship."[34] The marks of the "letter of friendship" are everywhere.[35] It is clearly intended to make up for their mutual absence, functioning as Paul's way of being present while absent (see on 1:27; 2:12).[36] Thus he informs them about "his affairs," speaks into "their affairs," and offers information about the movements of intermediaries. Evidence of mutual affection abounds; and the reciprocity of friendship is especially evident at the beginning and the end, and thus is probably to be seen in the other parts as well.[37] At the same time, in the two sections in which he speaks into "their affairs" the letter functions as "moral exhortation," which is tied very specifically to exemplary paradigms.

The twofold character of the letter is especially evident in the proemium, the introductory thanksgiving and prayer report (1:3-8, 9-11), which anticipate

---

33. Especially since (a) he narrates his own present response to suffering at the hands of the Empire, which corresponds to their situation, and (b) the "centre of gravity" (Martin; see n. 3 on 1:12-26) for the whole narrative is v. 18, with its "in this I rejoice; what is more, I will further rejoice," which becomes a primary imperative throughout (cf. esp. 2:18).

34. See L. M. White, "Morality," 206 ("Philippians . . . is primarily a friendly hortatory letter"), and Stowers, "Friends," 107 ("a hortatory letter of friendship").

35. But as Johnson (*Writings,* 341) points out, "In calling Philippians a letter of friendship, I do not suggest that it precisely follows a letter form for the friendly letter. . . . I mean, rather, that Paul uses the rhetoric of friendship to evoke appropriate responses in his readers."

36. Cf. Seneca, *Ep. Mor.* 75.1, "I prefer that my letters should be just what my conversation would be if you and I were sitting in one another's company or taking walks together" (LCL, 2.137; cf. Cicero's letter cited in n. 15); Seneca plays this in reverse in *Ep. Mor.* 40.1, "I never receive a letter from you without being in your company forthwith" (LCL, 1.263).

37. As Peterman, "Giving," 105-38, has argued (although his argument on 1:3, following O'Brien, lacks persuasion).

12

so much in the body of the letter. The thanksgiving is full of the matters of friendship: acknowledgment on Paul's part of the Philippians' partnership/participation in the gospel (v. 5), especially now in the context of Paul's present imprisonment (v. 7); his thanksgiving and joy before God for them (vv. 3-4); his deep affection for them (vv. 7-8); his recognition that God has been at work in them and will complete that work at the day of Christ (v. 6). Likewise the prayer report, while predicated on the friendship expressed in the thanksgiving, anticipates the major concerns of the hortatory sections: that their love, which already marks their corporate life, will abound all the more (v. 9); and that their behavior be blameless in every way as they bear the fruit of righteousness (vv. 10-11). And both the thanksgiving and prayer report emphasize their sure future (vv. 6 and 10), anticipating both this motif as such and the exhortation to "stand fast" (1:27; 4:1) that frames the two hortatory sections.

But "hortatory letter of friendship" is only part of the story, and in many ways the least significant part at that. For in Paul's hands everything turns into gospel, including both the formal and material aspects of such a letter. Most significantly, friendship in particular is radically transformed from a two-way to a three-way bond — between him, the Philippians, and Christ. And obviously it is Christ who is the center and focus of everything. Paul's and their friendship is predicated on their mutual "participation/partnership" *in the gospel*. This involves them in most of the conventions of Greco-Roman friendship, including especially social reciprocity, but it does so in light of Christ and the gospel. This three way bond, which is the glue that holds the letter together from beginning to end, may best be illustrated with the following graphic:

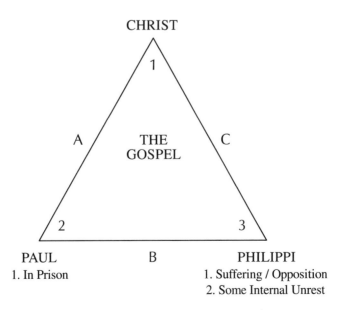

Paul's overarching concern is with the gospel, a word that occurs more often in this letter than in any of the others.[38] His specific concern for the Philippians in this regard is with their ongoing relationship with Christ (Line C); all of the hortatory sections and much else has the strengthening of this relationship as their primary aim. Because of his and their long-time relationship in the gospel (Line B), evidenced again most recently by their gift to him (both of material substance and of the coming of Epaphroditus), Paul writes a letter of friendship that assumes the secure nature of that relationship. The reason for these exhortations is Point 3, their present historical situation, which occasions the letter (see below, pp. 29-34). The paradigm for these appeals is threefold (Christ himself, Point 1; Paul's own imprisonment, Point 2; and Paul's relationship with Christ, Line A). Everything in the letter can be explained in light of one of these items.

The present commentary is thus written from the perspective that in terms of "form," Philippians is a "hortatory letter of friendship," with the conviction that this gives insight into a large number of its special features. But above all Philippians is an especially Pauline, and therefore intensely Christian, expression of that letter form, so that in his hands form does not come first, Christ and the gospel do, first and always. Thus the letter reflects known first-century conventions; but the conventions themselves are mere scaffolding for Paul. He is altogether concerned for his friends in Philippi and their ongoing relationship to Christ.

## B. Other Literary Matters

Not all, to be sure, have viewed the letter in this way; therefore, some further literary matters need to be noted. Some of these are in support of the foregoing analysis; some are by way of contrast with other ways in which the letter has been read. Here also is the place to say a few words about the transmission of the letter in the history of the church.

1. *The Questions of Rhetoric and Orality.* Since the appearance of H. D. Betz's commentary on Galatians (1979), in which he analyzed that letter in the light of the theoretical discussions of Greco-Roman rhetoric, and G. Kennedy's *New Testament Interpretation Through Rhetorical Criticism* (1984), the analysis of the NT letters as documents patterned on ancient rhetoric[39]

---

38. See n. 47 on 1:5, and Part IV below (pp. 47-48); cf. O'Brien, "Importance."

39. For a useful overview see C. C. Black, "Rhetorical Criticism." From Aristotle's analysis, there are three basic forms of rhetoric: *deliberative,* which aims to persuade or dissuade (or both); *epideictic,* whose basic purpose was to praise or blame someone; *forensic,* which occurs in situations of controversy, very often therefore apologetic. One can well understand, given what we have noted above about "letters of moral exhortation,"

has burgeoned apace,[40] so that every letter in the Pauline corpus has now been analyzed through these lenses. Philippians, the one letter that on the surface would seem to resist such an assessment, has been analyzed rhetorically twice,[41] neither of which, despite several helpful insights, carries much conviction as to the overall scheme of our letter.[42] The reason for this is simple:

---

why the hortatory sections of Philippians might have led to seeing the letter as a whole as "deliberative rhetoric." It should be further noted that the rhetorical theorists are speaking primarily of orations and secondarily of tracts or treatises. Rhetoric becomes applicable to letters only when they function as a substitute oration, or more commonly as a tract. The "form" of rhetorical address has at least four parts (although there are sometime others, including "digression," "exhortation," or "epilogue"):

1. An *exordium* (not necessary in deliberative rhetoric), which attempts both to "win over" the audience and to prepare them in advance for what is coming. (It is not difficult to see that Paul's thanksgivings often function in these ways, but it is doubtful that he deliberately intended them to be *exordia* as such.)
2. A *narratio,* which in effect gives the "history" of the matter (past, present, and future), so as to put the audience "on board" with regard to the argument that is to follow.
3. The *argumentatio,* which is the main aim of the oration, in which the attempt to persuade by argument takes place, the part which also, understandably, has the greatest amount of "formal" flexibility.
4. The *peroratio,* which aims both to summarize and to offer, sometimes by exhortation, final arguments to persuade the audience.

40. Indeed, it has now become something of a fad, which nonetheless when the dust is cleared will have contributed considerably to our knowledge of the NT letters and especially to how their "argumentation" works. But it is doubtful that this way of looking at the letters is as much an end-all answer to our quest for understanding as some of its stronger advocates would have us believe. Cf. especially the cautious words of D. E. Aune's review (*RelSRev* 7 [1981] 323-28) of Betz's commentary on Galatians: "Perhaps one of the chief perils of the enterprise is the tacit assumption that all ancient literary compositions worthy of the name were consciously or unconsciously patterned after generic models which, when recognized, can provide the necessary keys for unlocking some of the enigmatic features of such texts. Literary variation, however, was one of the hallmarks of the Greco-Roman period" (323).

41. See Watson, "Rhetorical Analysis," and Bloomquist, *Function,* esp. pp. 84-96, 119-38; see also the three articles that appeared in 1992 Heidelberg symposium volume (Snyman, "Persuasion"; Basevi and Chapa, "Philippians 2.6-11"; J. W. Marshall, "Ethical Appeal").

42. Not surprisingly, the two analyses are about as far apart from each other as one could imagine it to be possible. While both see the letter as "deliberative" rhetoric, they see the "parts" quite differently. Watson labels 1:3-26 as "exordium," while Bloomquist (more convincingly) limits it to 1:3-11; Watson views 1:27-30 as "narratio," while Bloomquist narrows it to 1:12-14; the latter sees 1:15-18a as "partitio" (= "where he agrees with his opponents but controversy remains"); Watson thus views 2:1–3:21 as "argumentatio" ("probatio" is his term), divided into four parts (first development 2:1-11, second development 2:12-18, digression 2:19-30, third development 3:1-21), which Bloomquist

both analyses have seized on the hortatory dimension of the letter as "the rhetorical situation" which Paul is addressing, while failing to recognize the more significant dimension of friendship.[43]

This is not to deny the presence of rhetorical features within the letter. Rhetorical analyses may prove helpful in showing how the hortatory parts of the letter work, that is, in demonstrating how Paul aims to persuade. But more important are several other rhetorical devices that seem intended to catch the attention of, and thus to carry conviction with, the hearer of the letter. Many of these (assonance, asyndeton, chiasmus, repetition, word plays) are pointed out throughout the course of the commentary.[44]

What is most important about these rhetorical features is related to another reality, seldom noted in discussing Paul's letters,[45] namely that the first century CE was primarily an oral (and thus aural) culture — which would have been especially true for the majority to whom this letter was addressed. All of Paul's letters, and Philippians in particular, were first of all oral — *dictated* to be *read aloud* in the community.[46] Much of Paul's rhetoric comes into play precisely at this point. His use of assonance and word plays, for example, are "designed"[47]

---

sees as 1:18b-4:7, divided into five parts ("confirmatio," 1:18b-26; "exhortatio," 1:27–2:18; "exempla," 2:19-30; "reprehensio," 3:1-16; second "exhortatio," 3:17–4:7); Watson then sees 4:1-20 as the "peroratio," which Bloomquist sees as 4:8-20. A careful reading of these two pieces side by side does not lead to one's finding one more convincing than the other, but to the conviction that both represent a basically wrong approach to the analysis of Philippians. Nothing exhibits this more than the rather cavalier way the concept of "narratio" is treated by both. At no point in Philippians does Paul use narrative to give a "history" of their relationship or of the matters with which this letter deals; and to turn the first imperative (1:27-30) into "narratio," as Watson does, is to superimpose a rhetorical template onto this letter that simply does not fit.

43. In this regard Bloomquist's study tends to fare much better, in that he attempts to take the epistolary features of Philippians with equal seriousness. Unfortunately, his epistolary analysis is limited to the basic elements of "form" (salutation, body, closing greetings), without evidence of concern for epistolary types. The result is that his rhetorical analysis wins the day altogether, which is again unfortunate in that he regularly lets his (very questionable) analysis of rhetorical form dictate meaning.

44. See, e.g., n. 8 on 1:21; n. 3 on 3:7-11; n. 5 on 4:8-9.

45. Although in this regard, see Wilder, *Rhetoric;* G. Kennedy, *New Testament;* and Achtemeier, *"Omne Verbum."*

46. Perhaps we should add, "and not pored over by exegetes and theologians so as to milk every word and sentence for all it's worth." In fact, even when read privately, all the evidence we have is that people read aloud, by articulating as they read. "Silent reading" appears to have come in at a much later time. See the discussion by Achtemeier, *"Omne Verbum."*

47. I use this word in a nontechnical sense, since one cannot know how much Paul thought through such matters and how much of it was simply inherent to his being part of a predominantly oral culture.

to be memorable, precisely because oral cultures had a very high level of retention. In literary cultures we are bombarded by so many words in print that very few, if any, are kept in memory in a precise way.

Most significantly for our present purposes, these features, rhetoric and orality, best explain an aspect of the letter that has been greatly puzzling for moderns — why Paul left his "thanksgiving" for the gift to the very end. For most of us such delay borders on rudeness, if not impropriety, and for scholars it has been the source of considerable speculation. But rhetoric and orality best account for it (see the introduction to 4:10-20); these are intentionally the last words left ringing in their ears as the letter concludes, words of gratitude, theology, and doxology that simply soar.[48] Which in turn explains the extreme brevity (for Paul) of the final greetings (vv. 21-22) as well.

2. *The Use of the Old Testament.* Those who consider Philippians 3 to be a three-way conversation between Paul, the Philippians, and some opponents, tend also to read Philippians as "polemical" at this point. But another striking feature of Philippians, Paul's unusual (for him) use of the OT, suggests otherwise, and again fits squarely within a "hortatory letter of friendship."

In this regard, two things stand out. First, whenever Paul is carrying on an "argument" with his churches, and especially so when some form of "Judaizing" persuasion is afoot (as in 2 Corinthians, Galatians, and Romans), he invariably *argues* from the OT, as a way of supporting his understanding of the gospel. Sometimes it is enough simply to say, "it is written"; at other times he feels compelled to explicate the meaning of what stands written in light of the event of Christ and the Spirit. All such form of argumentation is noticeably missing from Philippians, and nowhere more so than in chapter 3, where in warning against such a Judaizing perspective Paul instead offers himself as an example of one who had been there but had given it all up for Christ.

In this letter, second, Paul's use of the OT is of an altogether different kind, one which occurs throughout his letters but is used exclusively here. It is what social scientists call "intertextuality," which by definition means "the *conscious* embedding of fragments from an earlier text into a later one."[49] Such "intertextuality" assumes (a) that the readers/hearers will know the former text intimately, both its language and very often its setting, and (b) that they will hear those echoes used in a new, or newly applied, way in the present setting. Thus, while one might expect the Philippians to hear Paul's (conscious or unconscious)

---

48. Cf. Achtemeier (*"Omne Verbum,"* 26), who notes regarding Philippians that the "changes of topics" in the letter are "clearly signaled" for the *hearer:* "a doxological form in 1:11; 4:9, 19; words expressing closure in 3:1 . . . and 4:1 . . . , with the whole letter concluding with a doxology. Each of those closures would have alerted the listener that one topic had ended and another was about to begin."

49. For this matter in Pauline studies see R. B. Hays, *Echoes.*

use of OT language in many places (1:11; 3:1; 4:5), intertextuality seems especially to occur at several key points in the letter (1:19; 2:10-11; 2:14-16; 2:17[4:18], q.v.). This kind of appeal, especially in 2:14-16 where he presupposes the Philippians' place in the story of Israel, is not the stuff of polemics but of mutuality, thus of friendship. He never "argues" from the OT on the basis that "it is written," because *he assumes that he and they are on common ground* with regard to their *understanding* of the gospel. His concern here is with some practical implications of that common understanding.

We should further point out that such a use of the OT presupposes (a) that as in all the Pauline churches these early Gentile believers were thoroughly acquainted with their Bibles,[50] (b) that they would recognize this application of the OT texts to Paul's and their situation, and (c) that they would do so because of the basically oral nature of the culture, in which the constant hearing of the same "stories" would reinforce them deeply into their memories. To put it bluntly, we may rightly assume that these early Gentile believers knew the OT infinitely better than most Christians do today.

3. *The Matter of Vocabulary.* Because Philippians is a comparatively short letter,[51] one should probably not make too much of its distinctive vocabulary. Nevertheless, an analysis of the words Paul uses in this letter offers further corroboration of our seeing Philippians as a Christian hortatory letter of friendship. Four kinds of vocabulary interest us: *hapax legomena* (words that occur only here in the NT), Pauline *hapaxes* (words that occur only here in the Pauline corpus), the "special vocabulary" of Philippians (words that occur in this letter more frequently than in others), and Paul's use of his distinctively Christian vocabulary in this letter.

There are 1633 words in Philippians,[52] with a vocabulary of 438 words, of which 42 are New Testament *hapax legomena*[53] and 34 are Pauline

---

50. In their case, the only Bible they had, the OT, whose "story" they knew well because they understood themselves as being in continuity with that story. In this regard see esp. 1 Cor 10:1-11, where Paul actually says to a predominantly Gentile church about the OT people of God that "all *our* ancestors were under the cloud and passed through the sea." This phenomenon renders irrelevant the frequent suggestion that because Philippi was without a Jewish contingent, therefore Paul argues from a more Greco-Roman perspective (see, e.g., L. M. White, "Morality," 205-6; and others he cites there; cf. Reumann, "Contributions," 444 [n. 30]).

51. By Pauline standards, that is; it is much longer by far than the ordinary papyrus letter, but matches favorably with some of the letters of Cicero and Seneca.

52. Including all of the recurrences of the definite article, prepositions, and particles. This count is based on the NA[26] text and includes the words they put in brackets as doubtful. The exact number, of course, is ultimately irrelevant; this count simply gives one an idea of length.

53. ἁγνῶς (1:17); αἴσθησις (1:9); ἀκαιρέομαι (4:10); ἄλυπος (2:28); ἀναθάλλω (4:10); ἀπουσία (2:12); ἁρπαγμός (2:6); αὐτάρκης (4:11); γνησίως (2:20); ἐξανάστασις

*hapaxes.*[54] Our interest in these figures is not in their number,[55] but in their nature — in two ways. First, several of the *hapax legomena* belong to the historical context of Philippi's being a Roman colony; thus the singular mention of the "Praetorian Guard" (1:13), of "Caesar's household" (4:22), and especially the metaphorical play on "citizenship" in 1:27 and 3:20 all reflect Paul's conscious awareness of the "Roman" provenance of both his and their situations.

Second, and especially noteworthy, is the high concentration of "friendship" language in this letter, much of which is found in these *hapaxes.* Thus the singular mention of his "absence" (2:12), of his calling them his "longed for ones" (4:1), the concern for their "safety" (3:1), his desire that they "cheer" him (2:19), the specialized language of reciprocity ("giving and receiving" and "accounts") in 4:15, the high concentration of *"syn"* compounds (= they together with him) including "participating together with him in his affliction" in 4:14, all belong to this category. So also does the high concentration of "my affairs/your affairs" language (1:12, 27; 2:19, 20, 23),

---

(3:11); ἐπεκτείνομαι (3:13); ἐπιπόθητοι (4:1); ἑτέρως (3:15); εὔφημα (4:8); εὐψυχῶ (2:19); ἰσόψυχον (2:20); κατατομή (3:2); καταχθόνιος (2:10); κενοδοξία (2:3); λῆμψις (4:15); μεγάλως (4:10); μυέω (4:12); ὀκταήμερος (3:5); παραβολεύομαι (2:30); παραμύθιον (2:1); παραπλήσιος (2:2); πολίτευμα (3:20); προσφιλής (4:8); πτύρω (1:28); σκοπός (3:14); σκύβαλα (3:8); σύζυγος (4:3); συμμιμητής (3:17); συμμορφίζω (3:10); σύμψυχος (2:2); συναθλέω (1:27); ὑπερυψόω (2:9), plus five names: Ἐπαφρόδιτος (2:25); Εὐοδία (4:2); Κλήμεντος (4:3); Συντύχη (4:3); Φιλιππήσιοι (4:15).

54. ἀδημονέω (2:26); αἴτημα (4:6); ἀναλύω (1:23); ἀποβαίνω (1:19); ἀρετή (4:8); ἀσφαλής (3:1); ἀφίδω (2:23); βεβαίωσις (1:7); βίβλος (4:3); γογγυσμός (2:14); διαστρέφω (2:15); δόσις (4:15); εἰλικρινής (1:10); ἔντιμος (2:29); ἐξαυτῆς (2:23); ἐπιλανθάνομαι (3:13); ζημία (2:7, 8); ἴσα (2:6); καίπερ (3:4); Καίσαρος (4:22); κύων (3:2); μορφή (2:6, 7); οἴομαι (1:17); πολιτεύομαι (2:27); πραιτώριον (1:13); σκολιός (2:15); συγκοινωνέω (4:14); συλλαμβάνω (4:3); ταπείνωσις (3:21); ὑστέρησις (4:11); φαρισαῖος (3:5); φωστήρ (2:15); χορτάζω (4:12).

55. Which are deceptively high in this letter. One must be especially careful in the use of these statistics, since they include, *inter alia,* proper names, compounds, and cognates (i.e., other words that belong to the same semantic field). In analyzing vocabulary it is of very little value, e.g., to separate χαίρω ("I rejoice"), συγχαίρω ("I rejoice with"), and χάρα ("joy"), since they clearly belong together. When one eliminates the dubious hapaxes (proper names, some compounds, those that result from citation of the LXX, and cognates [e.g., adjectives where the noun occurs elsewhere with precisely the same meaning]), the numbers reduce to 30 and 20 respectively. If one is interested in statistics, these are the only ones that count! It may be of interest also to note that when hapaxes concentrate, they do so in three kinds of material: where the subject matter is unique to this letter and calls for the language (e.g., the "friendship" materials in 4:14-15), where a metaphor calls for the language (e.g., 3:12-14), or where Paul is apparently deliberately using the language of "hellenism" in a Christianized way (4:8, 11-12). It should be noted that the concentration is much greater here than 2:6-11, where an alleged high concentration of hapaxes has been used to condemn it as non-Pauline.

which occurs elsewhere only in Col 4:8 and Eph 6:21-22. Even the naming of names in 4:3 is an indication of friendship, as we point out in the discussion of that passage. Likewise the special language used to describe their mutual friend Timothy in 2:20-21 (of "like-soul" with me, who is "genuinely" concerned about you) and even more so of Epaphroditus, one of their own whose presence has made up in part for this "lack" of them (2:30), who "risked his life" for the sake of the gospel and should be "honored" in return.

Similarly the *special* vocabulary of Philippians also points to friendship, including exhortation, and away from polemics and argumentation. The word "chains," describing his own situation, occurs in 4 of its 8 Pauline appearances here. So too with the vocative "brothers and sisters," whose 7 occurrences is proportionately higher than elsewhere (except in the other "friendship" letter in the corpus, 1 Thessalonians); similarly the vocative "beloved" appears 3 of its 8 occurrences here. Not only so, but the basis of that friendship, Christ and the gospel, are mentioned proportionately more times in this letter than anywhere else in the corpus.[56] Paul's concerns for the Philippians are also reflected in the "special vocabulary," especially, for example, the use of "consider" (of them, Christ, and himself) and "have a mindset," plus the unusually high incidence of the adjective "all."[57]

But what is most noticeable in this letter is the general paucity of Paul's more specialized theological vocabulary and the infrequency of the explanatory "for,"[58] which is always a dead giveaway that Paul is involved in heavy argumentation. Thus, there is not a single occurrence of one of the verbs for "salvation" in the letter.[59] Such words as "believe," "faith," and "grace" appear but rarely. Even though there is a considerable concern about the Philippians' focus on their sure future, the theological language of "hope" does not occur. If this were the only Pauline letter to have survived, it would be well-nigh impossible to reconstruct his theology adequately; nor would we have any sense at all that Paul's apostleship counted for something! In the one specific moment of theological concentration in the letter, 3:3-14, it comes by way of personal example that they are to emulate rather than by argumentation as such. It is not that the letter is not theological; it is quite impossible for Paul to say anything without presupposing or explicating his theology. But the letter lacks theological *argumentation* as such (with the possible exception of 3:9). Thus the singular most frequent word group in the letter is "joy," which comes as often by way of imperative — and thus full of theological

---

56. See n. 47 on 1:5.

57. On these matters see respectively n. 76 on 2:4; n. 79 on 1:7; and n. 41 on 1:1.

58. It occurs only 13 times in Philippians; cf. the 105 in 1 Corinthians, 77 in 2 Corinthians, 36 in Galatians, and 144 in Romans.

59. The closest thing to it is "and be found in him" in 3:9.

import — as of experience. And the concern here is with Christian experience, how to live in the face of suffering, not with correct "doctrine," as it were.

4. *The Question of Integrity.* As with several others of the Pauline letters, many scholars find Philippians impossible to understand in its present form and have thus dismembered the letter into three (sometimes two) letters.[60] In this case, it is argued that all three of the letters are from Paul, that all were written to Philippi within a relatively short span of time, and that a generally unthinking redactor put them together to create our Philippians. The reasons for this view are basically three: (1) In 3:1 Paul says *to loipon* (= "finally" or "as for the rest"), as though he were about to conclude the letter, which does not happen, so that the "finally" is picked up again in 4:8. Similarly the command to "rejoice in the Lord" in 3:1 is "started again" in 4:4. (2) The suddenly strong attack of some (apparent) Judaizers in 3:2 does not seem easily to fit with the apparently "concluding" words of 3:1, "Finally, rejoice in the Lord." Chapter 3 is therefore seen to be a "fragment" of a different letter from chapters 1–2. (3) Since some papyrus letters begin with the language "I rejoiced greatly" (usually over receipt of a letter), and since it is regarded unthinkable that Paul should wait until the very end to thank them for their gift, it is argued that 4:10-20, which begins "I rejoiced greatly," should also be seen as a separate note of thanks. Thus three letters are hypothesized: Letter A (4:10-20), written first as a quick note of thanks immediately upon receipt of their gift; Letter B (3:1b-to some point in chap. 4), an "interpolated fragment" from a basically polemical letter, whose date and provenance cannot be determined; Letter C (1:1–3:1a, perhaps some part of 4:1-9, and 4:21-23), the letter sent back with Epaphroditus on his return home.

These points are responded to in some detail in the commentary itself. Here we need simply to note the considerable weaknesses of this point of view, which finally creates more problems than it solves.

(1) Despite the mask of some allegedly "objective criteria," the reason for this dismemberment of our letter is primarily subjective — and boils down to a single issue: The "argument" of Philippians is not as tidy as we could wish it to be; and since we would not produce a letter like this, then in all likelihood neither did Paul.

(2) That few can agree on the extent of letter B in itself indicates how problematic this point of view is. The reasons for this lack of agreement are the very ones that have led to the theory in the first place: one still does not know what to do with the repeated *to loipon* in 4:8 and "rejoice in the Lord" in 4:4. What is never explained is how this repetition, which is alleged to make little sense if Paul did it, can somehow now be "logically" explained if it is the product of someone else.

---

60. For a considerable list of those who take this view (up through 1983) see Garland ("Composition," 141 n. 3).

(3) The real difficulties with this view are historical, and go in two directions. First, there are no known analogies for this kind of "scissors-and-pasting" together of someone's letters.[61] The only analogies offered turn out to be examples of circular reasoning. Similar "reconstructions" of other Pauline letters are brought forward as "proof"; but when the "proof" itself needs proving, one's methodology becomes suspect. The one letter from antiquity that has the best possibility to serve as a historical analogy is our 2 Corinthians (1–9 and 10–13),[62] but in this case we are dealing merely with attaching two letters together in their assumed chronological order,[63] not with an intricate, unchronological, and — to most people's view — whimsical weaving together of three letters.

Second, this latter item is what makes this view basically unhistorical, for the common assumption is that someone with these three letters in hand, "pasted" or "tied" them together in this way. But in this case that is a historical impossibility. The only way someone could have created our Philippians out of parts of three different letters would have been to have *copied* the whole in this fashion. If one has difficulty with Paul's having created the apparently unmanageable "seams" in our letter, how is it easier to imagine a scribe-turned-redactor to have done so?[64] Why did he leave the "Finally, rejoice in the Lord" at 3:1? Or why did he not eliminate them in 4:4 and 8? And why 3:2-21 at *this* point in the compilation of letters? On the contrary, we have in fact abundant evidence that scribes, when they were not making mindless and therefore easily detectable errors, copied their manuscripts so as to make them *easier to read and understand*. But to push what is "unmanageable" from our point of view back one remove from Paul, so as to make him a "tidier writer" than we should necessarily believe he was, is to create a historical difficulty of another kind; thus it "solves" nothing.

(4) The ultimate reason for rejecting this hypothesis[65] is that the various parts of our current letter hold together so well as one piece. We begin by noting that the Pauline thanksgivings regularly anticipate many, if not most,

61. It is a cause for some wonder that some scholars have not only convinced themselves that this letter is at best a patchwork quilt — without design — but that they can assert as much, as though this were as common as writing letters itself, which it is not.

62. Some have followed P. N. Harrison in dividing Polycarp's letter to the Philippians into two as well (1-12, 13-14), but his criterion was too subjective to convince the majority (see the second edition of Lightfoot's *Apostolic Fathers,* edited by M. W. Holmes, 120-21).

63. At least that is how many understand 2 Corinthians (for good internal reasons, esp. the future coming of Titus and "the brother" in 8:18, which are spoken of in the past tense in 12:18).

64. Cf. Kümmel, 334, "incomprehensible."

65. And it is and ever will be only that — a hypothesis. We do have the letter in its present form, and this is what all should be under some kind of obligation to make sense of.

of the items in the letter itself. In this case both the language and content of 1:3-11 anticipate matters from all three of the alleged letters. Thus the language of "partnership" in the gospel in vv. 4-5 anticipates 4:10-20; the language of "loving one another still more" anticipates the exhortation of 1:27–2:18, and the mention of their sharing in his "bonds" for the defense of the gospel leads directly to 1:12-18; the language of "longing for them" in 1:7 anticipates the vocative of 4:1, while the "fruit of righteousness" of v. 11 and the eschatological urgency of vv. 6 and 10 point directly to 3:4-14. Did the "redactor" rewrite the obviously Pauline thanksgiving in order to make this work?

In the same vein the two major hortatory sections of the letter, despite addressing different specific issues, are held together by (a) several linguistic phenomena (especially the use of "have the same mindset") as well as (b) by the two paradigmatic narratives — Christ's and Paul's — whose main thrust is to urge a cruciform way of looking at and living out their present existence in the midst of opposition and suffering.[66] Was the alleged redactor himself responsible for this insight, and if he *was* this clever, why then did he bungle the "stitching" job so badly? And is this "bungler" also responsible for the most ingenious rhetorical stroke of all, of putting the "first letter" last, so that its powerful theological rhetoric at the end (4:18-20) are basically the last words in the letter?

The answer to these rhetorical questions, of course, is the obvious one: The person who both "bungled" the seams and arranged things so ingeniously is the apostle himself. It remains only to show that the present arrangement in fact "works" perfectly well when viewed as a "hortatory letter of friendship," which we will attempt to do at the end of the next major section (part II).

5. *The Question of Text.* Although unrelated to the foregoing questions, this seems to be the proper place to say a few words about the Greek text of the letter, which has to do with how Paul's words in this letter were transmitted to us. Basically two matters need to be noted. First, as with all the letters of Paul, we have no textual evidence for any of them before they were brought together as a corpus. Thus when dealing with the textual evidence for Philippians, we are basically dealing with the evidence for the transmission of the corpus as a whole, which, as best we can tell, was brought together sometime in the late first/early second century. This means that errors that made their way into the text before that can only be detected by "conjectural emendation." There seems to be no good reason to resort to such emendation at any point in our letter, since one can usually make sense of the text that has come down to us — despite an occasional (apparently) grammatical *faux pas.*

Second, I have included rather full textual notes throughout the commen-

---

66. Cf. Kurz, "Kenotic Imitation," who has argued particularly in this vein, but who leaves the question of redaction somewhat open.

tary. I note here the four differences from the text in the NA[26] (the basic Greek text behind the NIV), none of which is critical to the sense of the passage:

1:6   "Jesus Christ" for "Christ Jesus"
1:23  remove the brackets around the "for"
2:4   read the plural in each occurrence of "each"
3:7   omit "but"

The NA[26], however, is to be preferred at the one place where the NIV differs from it (in omitting "of God" in 1:14).

Finally, the secure nature of the text of this letter is further demonstrated by the following short list of the translationally significant textual differences between the NA[26] and the *Textus Receptus* (which lies behind the KJV):

| | |
|---|---|
| 1:6 | noted above |
| 1:16-17 | transposition of the two sentences (see n. 1 on 1:15-18) |
| 1:17 (KJV 16) | "raise up" instead of "add" |
| 1:28 | "your" instead of "to you" |
| 2:5 | "have this mindset" instead of "let this mind" |
| 2:9 | "*the* name" instead of "*a* name" |
| 2:30 | "not risking his life" instead of "not regarding his life" |
| 3:21 | omit "that it may be" |
| 4:13 | "through him who strengthens me" instead of "through Christ" |
| 4:23 | "with your spirits" instead of "with you all" |

In this letter, therefore, it is safe to conclude that the text we have is basically that which came from the apostle, and that early scribes apparently had less reason to alter it than in many other parts of the New Testament.

## II. THE OCCASION OF PHILIPPIANS

Given that Philippians is a (very Christian) "hortatory letter of friendship," the question remains, why *this* letter, to *this* people, as *this* time? Thus we turn to the historical situation to which the apostle was writing — an exercise beset with its share of pitfalls, since it also requires a degree of "mirror reading" (see n. 24). Even though we know much about ancient Philippi, some things about its character in the (presumably) seventh decade of the first century CE are more speculative; and the actual situation in the church in Philippi must be picked up from one end of a two-way conversation. In each of the following sections, therefore, we begin with what seems more certain before offering some "best guesses" as to the interpretation of the available data.

## A. The City and Its People[67]

Philippi was located at the far eastern end of a large fertile plain (Datos) in central Macedonia; it sat astraddle the Egnatian Way, nestled on the edge of the plain at the initial ascent up a considerable acropolis, 16 kilometers inland and across a low range of coastal mountains from the seaport of Neapolis (modern Kaválla). Originally founded as Krenides by some Greek colonists from the island of Thasos (ca. 360 BCE), it was taken over and renamed after himself by Philip of Macedon (father of Alexander the Great) in 356. Its reason for existence and for Philip's taking it over are related to its strategic location:[68] it sat as sentinel to the large agricultural plain of Datos; it was well-protected by its acropolis; and, most importantly to Philip, it was nearby to Mount Pangaion on the northern side of the plain, which at that period was rich in mineral deposits, including gold.

Philippi (and all Macedonia) came under control of the Romans in 168, who abolished the ancient Macedonian dynasty and eventually created a Roman province, divided into four parts. According to Luke, Philippi was "the leading city of that district of Macedonia" (Acts 16:11).[69]

Our interest in the history of the city stems particularly from 42 BCE, in which year two major battles were fought nearby in the plain — between Cassius and Brutus (the assassins of Julius Caesar) and the victors, Octavian (later the emperor Augustus) and Mark Antony. Following these victories Octavian honored Philippi by "refounding" it as a Roman military colony,[70] thus endowing its populace with Roman citizenship. Always astute politically, Octavian populated the town and its surrounding agricultural area with discharged veterans from the war. This both alleviated a population problem in

---

67. For a useful overview of the city and its history see the entry in *ABD*, 5.313-17 (by H. L. Hendrix; see p. 317 for further bibliography).

68. As with all cities and towns in antiquity, the final resolution of placement was a combination of the need for protection, proximity to something of significance (e.g., agriculture), and water. Philippi was well supplied with the latter by a small, still flowing, stream where Paul first met Lydia and the other women who were to form the core of this community.

69. On the vexed textual question regarding this designation see especially Wikgren, "Problem."

70. He renamed it (in honor of his daughter) *Colonia Augusta Julia Philippensis*.

Rome and ensured allegiance to the Empire (through its emperor) at this strategic spot along the major highway across Macedonia and northern Greece which connected Rome with Asia Minor and other points east. In an even more astute move Octavian did the same once again after he defeated Antony in the battle of nearby Actium in 30 BCE, this time with veterans from Antony's army, thus creating loyalty from those who had once fought with him and more recently against him. Although these events happened some ninety-plus years before the writing of our letter, they have a considerable effect on several key matters in Philippians.

By the time Paul came to the city in 49 CE (Acts 16:11-15), Philippi was the urban political center of the eastern end of the plain. Its population was both Roman and Greek; and although Latin was the official language, Greek was the predominant language of commerce and everyday life — all the more so in a city located in Greece.

Of the four people from the early Christian community whose names we know, three bear Greek names (Lydia, Euodia, Syntyche) and the other Roman (Clement). We know very little otherwise about the socio-economic makeup of the congregation itself. Lydia, a merchant from Thyatira, bears the name of her home province. That she had a household large enough to include Paul and his companions suggests she owned a villa; at least some of the women who were gathered with her at the river for worship, perhaps including Euodia and Syntyche, were very likely members of her household. The jailer, on the other hand, who also had a household, probably belonged to the artisan class; whereas the young girl from whom Paul had cast the divining spirit belonged to the slave class that often made up a large part of early Christian congregations (as members of Christian households or, as in her case, on their own). What this suggests is that the socio-economic range is similar to what one finds in churches in other urban centers. Finally, the fact that three of the people whose names are known to us are women is probably not accidental, since there is good evidence that in Greek Macedonia women had long had a much more significant role in public life than in most other areas in Greco-Roman antiquity.[71]

## B. The Situation of the Church

The specific historical context of the church to which Paul wrote our letter stems from a combination of three factors: its own history, its location in Philippi, and its long-term relationship with Paul in terms of Greco-Roman friendship.

71. In this regard see especially the citation from Tarn in n. 31 on 4:2, and the further bibliography noted there.

1. *Their History.* The history of the founding of this church sometime during 49 CE, recorded in Acts 16:11-40, is well known. Although this report and chronology have been called into question from time to time,[72] there are no good historical reasons for doubting the picture that Luke presents.[73] According to his report its nucleus was formed by a group of "God-fearing" women, who, because of the lack of a Jewish synagogue in the city, met by the river on the Sabbath for "prayer." Given the prominent place of women in Macedonian life in general, it is not surprising that the core group of first converts were women, nor that the location of its first house church was in the home of a woman merchant. That Paul and his entourage also accepted patronage from Lydia, including becoming temporary members of her household, also plays a considerable role in some of the matters in our letter (see on 4:14-17).[74]

We cannot be sure from any of our sources how long Paul and his companions (Silas, Timothy, and Luke[75]) stayed in Philippi. But whatever its length, it was long enough to establish a close friendship between the apostle and this community of believers, undoubtedly aided by Luke's staying on in Philippi after Paul, Silas, and Timothy had departed for Thessalonica (see on 4:3). The evidence for the kind of nearly "contractual" friendship outlined above (pp. 4-6) is to be found in particular in Paul's statement in 4:15 that "no other church entered into partnership with me in the matter of 'giving and receiving' except for you alone." Social reciprocity is the primary "stuff" of Greco-Roman friendship.

---

72. See, e.g., Suggs, "Concerning," who on the basis of the grammar of 4:15-16 suggested a ministry in Macedonia as early as 40 CE.

73. It seems especially to be corroborated by two statements from Paul's letters, evidence of a kind that we are often lacking elsewhere. In 1 Thess 2:2 he reports, "We had previously suffered and been insulted in Philippi, as you know," and in our present letter (4:15) he testifies, *"At the beginning of the gospel,* when I set out *from Macedonia,* not one church shared with me in the matter of giving and receiving, except you only; for even when I was in Thessalonica, you sent me aid again and again when I was in need." Since this squares so perfectly with Acts, there is every reason to accept Acts as reliable history. Cf. the important discussion in Rapske, *Acts,* 115-34.

74. Cf. Torjesen, *When Priests,* 53-109, who has correctly assessed the sociological significance of Lydia's role as head of her household and patron of Paul and for her probable role as primary leader of the church that met in her house.

75. This assumes Luke to be the identity of the "we" in the "we-sections" in Acts, which begin in 16:10-16. One cannot prove, of course, either that Luke wrote Acts or that he was the person who wrote its "we" sections, but despite the modern consensus against this identification, there are good *historical* reasons to think so — far better from my perspective than the "evidence" against it, which has much too much subjectivity (= theological presuppositions) in it for my liking. For further discussion on this matter see on 4:3 below.

The eventual departure of Paul, Silas, and Timothy was the direct result of the affair of casting out the divining spirit from a young slave girl, which was followed by imprisonment (in which Paul and Silas sang joyful songs of praise during the night), an earthquake, the conversion of the jailer, and the anxiety of the town officials when they realized they had both beaten and imprisoned an uncondemned Roman citizen.

Paul's relationship with this community thereafter is sketchy. On the basis of statements in 1 and 2 Corinthians he apparently paid at least two visits to Philippi not recorded in Acts. In 1 Cor 16:5, his intent had been to go through Macedonia — from Corinth on to Jerusalem. But according to 2 Cor 1:16, those plans had changed and he showed up (apparently unexpectedly) in Corinth, with a new itinerary (Corinth-Macedonia-Corinth). But everything erupted in Corinth, so Paul (apparently) went on to Macedonia, and then decided to write to Corinth instead of returning. Later (2 Cor 2:13/7:5) he came again into Macedonia, where he met Titus, and dispatched him and two other brothers (Luke? 8:18 "the brother who is praised by all the churches for his service in the gospel"), along with our 2 Corinthians, which he wrote from there. According to Acts, because of a plot against him, he paid yet another visit to the city (20:3) on his way to Jerusalem with the collection.[76]

Paul's deep affection for this congregation, evident throughout this letter, is also evidenced in his extravagant testimony about them in 2 Cor 8:1-5:

> And now, brothers and sisters, we want you to know about the grace that God has given the Macedonian churches. Out of the most severe trial, their overflowing joy and their extreme poverty welled up in rich generosity. For I testify that they gave as much as they were able, and even beyond their ability. Entirely on their own, they urgently pleaded with us for the privilege of sharing in this service to the saints. And they did not do as we expected, but they gave themselves first to the Lord and then to us in keeping with God's will.

Significant for our purposes is not only the affection on display here — further evidence of friendship — but the equation of "joy" + "poverty" = "generosity." These, too, have bearing on our letter.

---

76. 1 Tim 1:3, which I take to be Pauline and reliable history (see Fee, *1 Timothy,* 7-10), mentions a further visit, apparently the one anticipated in our letter (1:26; 2:24), while the combined evidence of Tit 3:12 and 2 Tim 4:13 suggest yet another visit before his final arrest and death in Rome. Since Nicopolis is west of Philippi and he was apparently arrested in Troas, which is east (and south), he would most likely have gone back through Macedonia on his way from Nicopolis to Troas. But this is more conjectural, since it assumes that the plans of Tit 3:12 were followed through.

The *occasion* of our letter is to be found both in the elements of friendship (the return of Epaphroditus; Paul's reporting on his "affairs"; his acknowledgment of their gift) and in its "hortatory" sections, assuming that the latter are as case-specific to the situation in Philippi as are the former. There is general agreement that at least two matters coalesce in some way as the driving force behind the exhortations: (1) suffering because of current opposition in Philippi, and (2) internal unrest of some sort.[77] Both of these appear together in the initial imperative (1:27-28): "that you *stand firm* in the *one Spirit, striving together as one person* for the faith of the gospel, without being frightened in any way by *those who oppose you*," which is followed by a clause explaining their suffering (vv. 29-30) and by an appeal to have the same "mindset" (2:1-2). Significantly, Paul uses these same verbs ("stand firm," "have the same mindset") in the appeals that conclude the second hortatory section (4:1-3). Thus these two concerns "frame" the two hortatory sections in the letter, and do so with identical language.[78] But the precise nature of these two matters, how they interrelate, and how much the matter of "opposition" noted earlier comes into play, are less certain.

2. *Opposition and Suffering.* That the Philippian congregation is undergoing suffering as the result of opposition in Philippi is explicitly stated in 1:27-30 and metaphorically so in 2:17. Once this is recognized, it is then easy also to recognize this reality as underlying a variety of other moments in the letter — although to go so far as Lohmeyer and to see the entire epistle as having to do with *martyrdom* takes this theme far beyond the realities of the text itself.[79] We begin with the two basic texts.

In the initial — and probably primary — imperative in the letter (1:27-30), Paul urges the Philippian believers to "stand fast" in the one Spirit, as they "contend together" for the gospel, and thus "not be intimidated in any way by those who oppose you." That this opposition has led to suffering is clear from the final clause (vv. 29-30), which offers *theological reasons* for it. Paul reminds them that their suffering "on behalf of Christ" has been

---

77. It is of some interest that two dissertations that came to hand while I was in the process of writing this commentary take up one and the other of these two matters, in each case seeing the one as the primary cause over against the other. See Bloomquist *(Function)*, who sees their suffering as the key to the whole, and Peterlin ("Paul's Letter"), who sees "disunity" in the church as what drives the letter.

78. It is also noteworthy that the two intermediate narratives about Timothy and Epaphroditus (2:19-24, 25-30), while functioning as "letters of commendation," also seem to present these two brothers as models regarding these two matters: Timothy of the "mindset" that stands over against selfish ambition, the root cause of the unrest (see on 2:3-4); and Epaphroditus of one who had risked his life to the point of death for the sake of Christ.

79. Although this view has been adopted by Blevins, "Introduction," 318-20.

"graciously given" to them, and that it is precisely of a kind with Paul's ("you are going through *the same* struggle"). He then returns to this motif in a metaphorical way at the end of the first hortatory section (2:17-18), where he pictures his suffering as the "drink offering" poured out in conjunction with their "sacrificial offering and priestly service," resulting from their faith.

While suffering is not the dominant motif in Philippians, it constitutes the church's primary historical context *in Philippi* and thus underlies much of the letter. Two items are noteworthy. First, this context helps to explain Paul's emphasis on his imprisonment and suffering in the thanksgiving (vv. 3-8) and in the narrative about his affairs (vv. 12-26). Part of his reason for thanksgiving is for their "joint-partnership" with him "in my chains, for both the defense and confirmation of the gospel," which he terms "this grace" (v. 7). Both parts of the narrative about "my affairs" that immediately follows (vv. 12-18a, 18b-26) seem intended to illustrate "how I am responding," first, to his suffering at the hands of the Empire, and second, to the selfish ambition/rivalry of other believers who are trying to cause him grief in the midst of it. Thus the narrative, which functions as a typical (expanded) expression of friendship, also functions as an exemplary paradigm (= this is how you, too, should respond in your own suffering at the hands of "Rome" in Philippi).

Second, opposition and suffering probably lie behind a further — seldom noted — major motif in the letter: Paul's repeated emphasis on the believer's sure future with its eschatological triumph. This motif begins in the thanksgiving and prayer report (vv. 6 and 10); it dominates the second part of his report on "my affairs" (1:21-24); it serves as the glorious climax (vv. 9-11) to the Christ story in 2:6-11; it is the penultimate word in the appeal that follows (v. 16); it holds the dominant place in his own story in 3:4-14, as the climax of both the story itself (vv. 12-14) and of the appeal that follows (vv. 20-21; 4:1), which is explicitly paradigmatic at this very point; it serves as the singular affirmation (4:5) to the concluding imperatives (4:4-9); and it is integral to the final words of theology and doxology in the letter (4:19-20).

The tie of this eschatological motif to opposition and suffering is especially to be seen in Paul's personal story and its application in 3:4–4:1. Here Paul yearns to know Christ, both the power of his resurrection and *participation in his sufferings* (vv. 10-11), the former being necessary for the latter and the latter explained further as "being *conformed to Christ's death*" (cf. 2:6-8). In the appeal that immediately follows the Philippians are urged to "imitate" Paul's "mindset" (vv. 15, 17), who, while "being conformed to Christ's death," vigorously pursues the ultimate eschatological prize of "knowing Christ" finally and completely (vv. 13-14), which is explicated at the end in terms of receiving a "glorified body" like Christ's (vv. 20-21).

The *source* and *reason for* this suffering are less clear. The clue lies with the first explicit mention of it in 1:29-30. They are suffering, Paul says, because they are involved in "the *same* struggle as *I am now* in." If we take this seriously — and literally — then the reason for the preceding "reflections on imprisonment" (1:12-26) also takes shape. Paul's suffering is both "for the defense of the gospel" and at the hands of the Empire. The Philippian believers are opposed by a "crooked and depraved generation" (2:15), who are "destined for destruction" (1:28). These passages can only refer to the pagan populace of Philippi, who happen also to be citizens of Rome. Thus they are the *source* of the suffering.[80]

That the opposition, and thus their suffering, is a direct result of the Roman character of their city is further indicated by the twin play on the Philippian believers' "dual citizenship" in 1:27 and 3:20. Although themselves Roman citizens, they also constitute a "colony of heaven" in this colony of Rome in Macedonia. Since their true "citizenship" is in heaven (3:20), they are to "live their heavenly citizenship in Philippi in a manner worthy of Christ" (1:27). The pro-Empire character of Philippi also explains another phenomenon in the letter: the unusually high incidence of references to Christ, especially the emphasis on Christ's having obtained sole privilege to the title *Kyrios* ("Lord"; 2:9-11) — at whose name every knee shall someday bow — and the unique appellation of Christ as *Sōtēr* ("Savior"; 3:20), all the more noteworthy in light of the Romans' utter disdain for crucifixion (see on 2:8).

With this we come to the most probable *cause* of the suffering.[81] Philippi owed its existence as a Roman colony to the special grace of the first Roman emperor, thus ensuring that the city would always have special devotion for the emperor. By the time of our letter, the primary titles for the emperor were *Kyrios* and *Sōtēr* ("lord and savior"). Not only so, but the cult of the emperor, where the emperor was honored in a way approaching deification, had found its most fertile soil in the Eastern provinces. In a city like Philippi this would have meant that every public event (the assembly, public performances in the theater, etc.) and much else within its boundaries would have taken place in the context of giving honor to the emperor, with the acknowledgment that (in this case) Nero was "lord and savior." Which is precisely the place where believers in Christ could no longer join in as "citizens of Rome in Philippi." Their allegiance was to another *Kyrios,* Jesus Christ, before whom every knee would someday bow and every tongue confess, including the citizens of Philippi who are causing their suffering, as well as the emperor himself. The Philippian believers in Christ were thus "citizens" of a greater "dominion" and their allegiance was to another *Sōtēr,* whose coming from heaven they awaited with eager expectation. If this were not enough to make

---

80. So also D. W. B. Robinson, "Circumcision," 28.

81. For a more detailed expression of the view outlined here, see M. Tellbe, "Christ and Caesar."

31

the citizens of Philippi begin a methodical persecution of these (now) expatriates living among them, the fact that the Christian's "lord and savior" had taken the form of a "slave" in his becoming human, and in that humanity died on a cross (2:6-8), would have been the final straw. But to this one, Paul says, whom the Philippian pagans scorn, God has given the name above all names, the name of the Lord *(kyrios)* God himself.

Although one cannot be sure of all the details of this picture, there is good reason to believe that it reflects the heart of things regarding the historical context of our letter. As will be pointed out throughout the commentary, such a reconstruction, based on the data and emphases of the letter itself, explains much. It is in this light that the Philippians would hear Paul's triumphant note about the whole Praetorian Guard — the emperor's own select troops — coming to know about the gospel through Paul's imprisonment. So also with the final word of the letter (before the concluding grace-benediction), "all the saints (in Rome) greet you, especially those who belong to *Caesar's household*" — who themselves join you in saying "Jesus is Lord." The gospel, with its proclamation of a heavenly Lord who had become the incarnate Savior, had penetrated the household of the (merely earthly) Roman "lord and savior," who stands ultimately behind "the same struggle" both Paul and the Philippians are currently experiencing. And this, just a couple of short years before the "struggle" breaks out with vengeance in Rome itself, with Nero's pogrom against believers in Christ.

3. *Internal Unrest.* While opposition and suffering at the hands of the Roman citizens of Philippi serves as the "historical context," thus the crucible of the letter, Paul's ultimate concern in its hortatory sections is over some internal "posturing" going on. The Philippians are in a life-and-death struggle for the gospel in Philippi, and if their present unrest goes uncorrected, it could bid fair to blunt, if not destroy, their witness to Christ in their city. There can be little question that this issue lies behind the major moments in the letter. It is the first item mentioned in the opening imperative (1:27), to which he returns in 2:1-4 after the momentary focus on their suffering. It explicitly lies behind both the Christ story in 2:6-11 and its application in 2:12-16. It seems also to lie behind the description of Timothy in 2:20-22 and parts of Paul's story in 3:4-14, as well as the concluding imperative in 4:2-3, where Euodia and Syntyche are singled out by means of the identical imperative as in 2:2.

But the exact nature of the problem, and how far-reaching it is, is much more speculative; and here the pronouncements of scholarship regularly go beyond the actual data themselves. The language "strife" and "division," which occur together in 1 Cor 1:11 but are noticeably missing in Philippians, are nonetheless the stock-in-trade of the secondary literature. But the use of such terms for the Philippian situation not only outstrips the evidence, it noticeably contradicts the dimension of friendship and the expressions of affection that permeate the letter. Even the naming of Euodia and Syntyche is evidence that the problem, though real, has not yet assumed significant proportions, since one of the signs of "enmity" in antiquity was to let the "enemy" remain nameless — as Paul does in all his earlier letters. But these women are named because they are his friends, not enemies (see on 4:2).

On the basis of *what* Paul says and *how* he speaks to this matter, three things seem fairly certain. First, what lies behind the unrest is some form of "selfish ambition" — or "posturing," as I prefer to call it. When appealing to the community to have the "same mindset" so as to complete Paul's joy (2:2), he singles out "selfish ambition/rivalry" and "empty glory" as the attitudes that must be rejected (v. 3). In their place he calls for "humility," which evidences itself by each one "looking out for the interests of the others" (v. 4). It is scarcely accidental (a) that "selfish ambition/rivalry" is used of the attitudes prompting those in Rome who are trying to make life miserable for Paul in his imprisonment (1:17), or (b) that "looking out for the concerns" of the Philippians, over against those who care only for their own interests, is the way Paul describes Timothy to the Philippians, who know Timothy well (2:20-21). The Christ narrative thus speaks directly to this matter, since as God he "emptied himself" (over against doing anything on the basis of selfish ambition) and as man he "humbled himself" (over against doing anything on the basis of vain glory).

But, second, these attitudes have not yet led to "division" or "strife,"[82] the language Paul uses in 1 Cor 1:10-12, which there he goes on to describe in clear terms of "disunity." The closest thing to such language in our letter is "grumbling and murmuring" (2:14, "complaining and arguing," NIV). Such language is a far cry from "division." But if unchecked, it is the stuff that leads to division, which is precisely why Paul feels compelled to speak to it, and to send Timothy to look into it (2:19-20), before he himself comes (2:23-24).

Third, this is probably the place where the warning against "enemies" in chapter 3 fits in. While there is no evidence for the actual presence of outsiders who are "stirring up the pot" in Philippi, the unrest in the church has very likely taken the form of one or some of them being open to listen to foreign matter. What might lie behind their readiness to do so is most likely related to the issue of suffering. The apparent security of "being Jewish" (the matrix out of which some of them originated as God-fearers) while also being in Christ may have begun to look better to them now, since Judaism was a "legitimate religion" in the Empire, exempted from persecution. But people who think so are "enemies," Paul reminds the Philippians with the stern warning of 3:2-3. He himself had been there, and there is no future to the

---

82. See on 2:3 (and n. 70).

past. The future lies strictly with Christ; hence Paul's weeping over others, who have become enemies of the cross of Christ by setting their minds strictly on earthly things (3:18-19).

While one may not have certainty about these "best guesses," they reflect an attempt to tie the various items of the letter together as a whole. In any case, the situation in Philippi is serious, but not disastrous. And since these people are his friends, having recently renewed the evidence of their friendship by a gift to minister to the apostle's needs in prison, and since his imprisonment forbids his current presence with them, he does what friends always did in such situations, he wrote a "hortatory letter of friendship" to serve as his "presence" in his "absence" (2:12).

## C. The Situation of Paul

At the time of his writing Philippians Paul is clearly in detainment, which he describes no less than four times as "being in chains" (1:7, 13, 14, 17). The questions of "where" and "when" have been assumed throughout the Introduction (and the commentary) to refer to his Roman imprisonment in the early 60s CE (between 60 and 62); but since many reject this tradition (in favor of either Caesarea or Ephesus), a few words are needed regarding this matter.[83]

The internal evidence of the letter specifically favors the tradition, especially the mention in 1:13 (q.v.) that "it has become evident to the *whole* Praetorian Guard that I am in chains because of Christ," and the final greeting in 4:22 from "the saints especially of Caesar's household." Against many who protest to the contrary, the natural reading of these texts implies a Roman provenance to the letter, in both cases.[84]

First, the mention of the *whole* praetorium is such that it seems intended to elicit delight and wonder from the Philippians. Although the word *prae-*

83. Since this is much-covered ground, and since there are no significant reasons for rejecting the tradition, I do not here intend to "reinvent the wheel," but simply to give my reasons for staying with the (in this case very solid) tradition and briefly noting why the other options have little in their favor — from my point of view. For the arguments pro and con, one should read on all sides of the issue to see how different scholars handle the same evidence (e.g., for Rome: see Guthrie, O'Brien, Reicke ["Caesarea," 282-86]; for Caesarea: Hawthorne; for Ephesus: Duncan, Kümmel, Carson-Moo-Morris).

84. It is of some interest that this evidence is often turned on its head by proponents of other views (cf. n. 13 on 4:22). So, e.g., Kümmel (*Introduction,* 328): "Since there are no unambiguous arguments for the writing of Phil in Rome, and some evidence against it. . . ." But that should be stated precisely in reverse: "While there is some evidence in favor of a Roman imprisonment, there is no evidence against it."

*torium* can refer to a "governor's palace" in the provinces (as in Mark 15:16 and Acts 23:35), the word more naturally refers the Praetorian Guard, the emperor's own elite troops stationed in Rome (see on 1:13).[85] Those who favor an Ephesian imprisonment can only hypothesize the presence of the guard in Ephesus, since (a) there is no evidence to support it[86] and (b) there was no *praetorium* in Ephesus.[87] Likewise, although the word could refer to the governor's palace in Caesarea, there would be little cause for wonder to mention that the "whole praetorium" in Caesarea had come to learn that his imprisonment was for Christ. Paul's sentence implies that this "became evident" to a large number of people over a period of time and through his direct

85. Bruce (11) points out that Paul's use of this loanword "suggests that it bears its technical sense."

86. It has been common to find the presence of the guard there on the basis of an inscription in the vicinity of Ephesus (cf. CIL, iii. 6085, 7135, 7136). But this inscription refers not to the presence of the guard in that city, but to a former member of the guard who is now on police duty on a road outside of Ephesus. On this matter see Bruce, 12, who describes the inscription as "irrelevant" (see further, "St. Paul in Macedonia," 263 n. 3). Despite the large number of scholars who embrace an Ephesian provenance (first suggested by Deissmann, it owes its present popularity to Duncan's *Ephesian Ministry*), I find myself in full sympathy with Bruce, who bluntly asserts, "Ephesus . . . may be ruled out" ("St. Paul in Macedonia," 263); indeed, there is not a single piece of *historical evidence* in favor of this view, yet it has recently been noted that "Ephesus has been adopted by an increasing number of scholars and now rivals or even surpasses Rome as the imprisonment site favored by most" (Fitzgerald, *ABD*, 5.322). The reasons for espousing an Ephesian provenance are often closely related to the issue of integrity (see pp. 21-23 above), and the need for a shorter distance for the sending of three brief letters within a short time frame. But this is an example of one unlikely hypothesis building on another. Most damaging to this hypothesis, besides the lack of a *praetorium* (= "governor's palace") there (see next n.) or praetorian guard stationed there, is the nature and duration of Paul's present imprisonment. Those who favor an Ephesian provenance hypothesize an imprisonment there as though it were as natural as eating (on the basis of 2 Cor 11:23, "in prisons often"! and then reading between the lines in 1 Cor 15:31-32 and 2 Cor 1:8-11). But besides being an altogether unlikely interpretation of these two texts (being rescued from a deadly peril sounds very little like an imprisonment), and even if one were to allow that Paul might have been imprisoned at some point during his stay there, the imprisonment described in Philippians seems historically impossible in Ephesus (esp. in light of the evidence from Acts 19–20 and 1 Corinthians, which was written from Ephesus): of considerable duration; under *imperial custody* for preaching the gospel; whose outcome could result in death. The evidence of Acts 23–24, written by an eyewitness, stands in strong opposition to such an imprisonment having happened to a Roman citizen in the first half of the sixth decade (between 52-55) in Ephesus.

87. Since Ephesus was in a senatorial, not imperial, province; and there is no known evidence that refers to a senatorial governor's palace as a *praetorium*. One must finally therefore resort to the unlikely hypothesis that Paul either did not know what he was talking about, or that he used language loosely — neither of which makes much sense in this case, since what Paul says is hardly "in passing."

involvement, whereas in Caesarea[88] the number of people involved would be relatively small; and in any case, his arrival on horseback under the protective care of seventy cavalry, followed by a very quick hearing, would have been a major "event" in the *praetorium* in Caesarea and scarcely what Paul is referring to in 1:13.

Likewise, second, regarding the mention in 4:22 of "members of Caesar's household." There can be little question that Nero had members of his "household" scattered all over the Empire looking out for his interests in the provinces. But nowhere outside of Rome is there a known concentration of them of such size that some of its "members" are noteworthy for having become believers in Christ, nor is there any evidence for the use of this terminology outside of Rome. Indeed, in contrast to the mention of the Praetorian Guard, "household" *(oikia)* is *not* a technical term, and Paul uses it on several occasions, always to refer to "the house and its occupants." Therefore, if *oikia* in 4:22 does not refer to Caesar's household in Rome, it would mean that Paul in this case had abandoned his normal usage. One would seem to need hard evidence and particularly compelling reasons for making such an argument and hence for rejecting the Roman provenance of this letter.

But compelling reasons for rejecting the tradition are precisely what is lacking. Only two have a degree of substance, but neither carries conviction. First, it is argued that in writing to Rome Paul expected to start a mission in the West, not to return East (Rom. 15:23-24), whereas in our letter Paul expects to be released and to return to Philippi (1:26; 2:24). Second, the distance between Rome and Philippi (ca. 800 miles [1300 kms]) is argued to be too great for the "five trips" to and fro that this letter is alleged to presuppose.[89]

With regard to the first matter, there is every imaginable difference between what Paul hoped to do when speaking as a free man some three or four years before our letter and what he now plans to do at the end of a long and trying imprisonment — especially so with some storm clouds hovering over his churches in the East.[90] Likewise, the second matter is hardly an issue at all, since it presupposes more "trips" between Paul and Philippi than are

88. Which Bruce rightly describes as "a political backwater" ("St. Paul in Macedonia," 264). He adds, "certainly everybody in Herod's *praetorium* would know that [Paul] was there and why he was there, but would there be anything very remarkable about that?" For arguments in favor of a Caesarean origin of our letter see Lohmeyer, Hawthorne, and Gunther (*Paul,* 98-107).

89. On this matter, and its refutation, see the comments on 2:26, and especially nn. 28, 29, 31.

90. That Paul should be held to his "word" regarding planned itineraries is shaky business at best, given the row this very matter created in Corinth (see 2 Cor 1:15-20). In any case, it hardly "creates a real difficulty for the theory of a Roman origin for Phil," as Kümmel suggests (*Introduction,* 326).

warranted and assumes the historically unlikely scenario that Epaphroditus was traveling alone.[91] Philippi, after all, sat astride the Egnatian Way, which put people in Rome from Macedonia and vice versa in a relatively short time by ancient standards. The alleged distance factor, therefore, is more imaginary than real.[92] Thus, even though these arguments could be seen as supporting the Ephesian hypothesis, they do not in fact call into question the Roman hypothesis. I do not hereby assert that the tradition must be correct, but that in fact the data favor it, and that there is no good reason to reject it. Hence the commentary proceeds from this perspective.

As to the time frame of this imprisonment, the traditional suggestion of between 60 and 62 fits most of the data best. Although some of this evidence is capable of another interpretation, the internal evidence of Philippians would put the writing of this letter toward the latter end of the imprisonment,[93] rather than early on, thus closer to 62 than to 60.

## D. How Philippians "Works"

On the basis of the foregoing discussion, we may assume Philippians to have been occasioned by the following: (1) Paul's imprisonment, to which the Philippians have responded with a gift by way of Epaphroditus, thus renewing their commitment to "friendship" with Paul in the matter of "giving and receiving." (2) That Ephaphroditus has apparently told him about the situation back home, which involved opposition and suffering at the hands of their pagan neighbors and some internal unrest, especially between two of the women who were probably leaders of some kind.

Paul's response takes the basic "form" of a letter of friendship, which in this case weaves in his exhortations regarding their present situation at the

91. The point is that if Epaphroditus took ill along the way, as is implied by the grammar of 2:30, one of his companions could easily have broken off and taken this news back to Philippi, which cuts out at least two of the alleged trips back and forth. On the unlikelihood of his traveling alone, see n. 30 on 2:26.

92. Indeed, it would seem to exist only because one is committed to other reasons for rejecting the tradition. It presupposes far more than is warranted and dissipates completely if one takes seriously — as the internal evidence of the letter would lead one to — that Philippians was written toward the end of the imprisonment (which Luke put at two years).

93. This is based partly on the "sense" one gets that the detention has been long and trying. For it both to have resulted in the *whole* Praetorian Guard being apprised of it as for Christ and to have evoked the various responses to it noted in 1:15-17 implies a certain amount of time. So, too, with the events surrounding the coming of Epaphroditus noted above. But a later rather than earlier date is based mostly on the fact that Luke mentions a two-year incarceration, and Paul in this letter is anticipating his release, which he apparently expects to happen reasonably soon (2:19, 24).

chronologically appropriate places, saving his acknowledgment of their gift until the end, so that it will not get lost in the midst of the exhortations.

Thus, following the proemium (1:1-11) in which he anticipates both dimensions of the letter (friendship and exhortation), the letter is structured around the typical language of friendship, "my affairs" and "your affairs." But at the same time it follows a basically chronological scheme. Thus:

1. The letter begins at the point of Epaphroditus's arrival, which had a twofold purpose: (a) to present their gift to Paul (reflecting their concern for him); and (b) to inform him about the situation back home (which becomes the focus of Paul's concern). For Paul, these two matters merge at one point: the *progress of the gospel.*

2. Paul is currently "absent" from them, which calls forth the first two sections of the letter. First he reports about *his* "affairs" (1:12-26), that from his perspective (beyond what Epaphroditus would tell them) his imprisonment is *advancing the gospel;* at the same time he joyfully (and wistfully) contemplates the outcome — that it will go in his favor (meaning "life") but against his desire (to "depart" and be with Christ).

3. But Paul's real concern is with *their* "affairs," which in their present condition are unlikely to advance the gospel. Although he expects to come soon for the sake of "their progress," in the meantime a letter will take his place; thus 1:27–2:18 addresses their current situation, in which he points to Christ as the paradigm of the selflessness and humility necessary to make unity work.

4. At 2:19 two kinds of chronology are at work: (a) from the perspective of *his writing the letter* (with both Timothy and Epaphroditus present); (b) from the perspective of the Philippians, *as the letter is being read.* Thus he writes a letter to accompany the return of Epaphroditus, which comes next in terms of actual chronology, but second (after vv. 19-24) in terms of his concerns for writing.

5. Thus very soon he hopes to send Timothy, whose task is twofold: (a) to inform the Philippians about the (expected) outcome of the trial; but (b) to return to inform Paul as to whether the letter had done any good. Thus Timothy is to *return* to Paul, before Paul himself sets out, which event will transpire (apparently) shortly thereafter (2:19-24).[94]

---

94. On the question as to whether Paul expected release or martyrdom, the texts are clearcut: he expected to be released and never once contemplated that it might go the other way. See the commentary on 1:23-24, 25-26; 2:17, 19-24 (esp. v. 24). On this matter, which drives much of his "Egocentric Letter," Fortna is psychologizing, not working with the data from the text, when he speaks of, "[Paul's] imprisonment and the possibility, seeming to him at times the certainty, of execution ([1:]7)." Paul may indeed prefer that his trial go against him (as 1:22-23 indicate), but there is nothing in the letter that implies that he thinks indeed it will.

6. In the meantime he has sent Epaphroditus back home with this letter (2:25-30).
7. The next hortatory section (3:1–4:3) is written from the perspective of Epaphroditus's return and his reading this letter in their midst (which takes the place of Paul's presence). Framed by the imperative to rejoice in the Lord (3:1; 4:4), it warns them — for their safety — of matters he has often brought to their attention before, and uses that warning to refocus their attention on their sure eschatological future.
7. At 4:4 he begins the final set of imperatives (vv. 4-9) with which he regularly concludes his letters.
8. But he breaks that off just before the final greetings (4:21-23) to acknowledge their gift to him, so that the final words they hear will be those of gratitude, reciprocity from God himself, and doxology (4:10-20).

The Analysis of the letter that appears on pp. 54-55, and the commentary that follows, proceed along the above lines.

As to the specific *purpose* of the letter, the way forward might be to ask a hypothetical question: Would Paul have written this letter if Epaphroditus were not returning home, having now recovered from his illness? One is tempted to say No, since Paul intends to come himself in the near future; and much of what he says here could have waited until then. But that is also why we must finally answer Yes; because he intends to send Timothy on ahead in any case. Had he not sent a letter by Epaphroditus, he would surely have done so with Timothy. All of which suggests that in the end, the real purpose of the letter lies with the phrase "your progress in the faith" (1:25), which for Paul ultimately has to do with the progress of the gospel, both in their lives and in their city. In the final analysis "their affairs" is the real reason for the letter. That is why Epaphroditus carries a letter with him now, why Timothy will follow on shortly, and why Paul will return East rather than go West once he is released.


# III. THE QUESTION OF AUTHENTICITY — SOME NOTES ON 2:6-11

By anyone's reckoning, 2:6-11 constitutes the single most significant block of material in Philippians. So much is this so, that the secondary literature on this passage, which has mushroomed incrementally over the past forty years, exceeds that on all the rest of the letter combined. The result has been that most contemporary commentaries have been compelled to offer an excursus of some kind simply to deal with the critical issues that have been raised on this passage. Three matters are at issue: (1) the "form" of the passage, which was first argued by Lohmeyer in 1928 to be a hymn and has now become the unquestioned assumption of nearly all who write on the passage; if a hymn, then the question of its strophic arrangement becomes the first matter of discussion; (2) the question of background and authorship, since it is common to assume that the "hymn" is both pre-Pauline and therefore non-Pauline; and (3) understanding its place in its present context. The latter question has been dealt with at some length in the commentary itself. But since the first question has led to the second, and since "authenticity" is one of the traditional matters taken up in the "Introduction" to a commentary, a few words about these two matters need to noted here — especially so, since I have taken a view that runs counter to much of the secondary literature.[95]

## A. The Question of Form

The nearly universal judgment of scholarship is that in Phil 2:6-11 we are dealing with an early hymn about Christ.[96] The reasons for this judgment are basically four: (1) The "who" *(hos)* with which v. 6 begins is paralleled in other passages in the NT also understood to be christological hymns (Col 1:15, 18; 1 Tim 3:16); (2) the exalted language and rhythmic quality of the whole; (3) the conviction that the whole can be displayed to show structured parallelism, of a kind with other pieces of Semitic poetry; (4) the language and structure seem to give these verses an internal coherence that separates them from the discourse of the epistle itself at this point.[97] For the sake of this discussion, I give here the most commonly accepted structural arrangement (that of NA[26], in literal English) with numbered lines:

> 6 a  Who in the form of God being
>   b  Not grasping considered
>   c    to be equal with God,
> 7 a  But himself emptied
>   b    the form of a slave taking,

---

95. Much of the substance of this excursus appeared in *BBR* 2 (1992) 29-46, under the title "Philippians 2:5-11: Hymn or Exalted Pauline Prose?" For a more thorough (and more objective) discussion of these matters, see O'Brien, 186-202, although his discussion is equally carried on in the framework of conviction — in his case that it is in fact a hymn.

96. Thus the title of Martin's monograph (*Carmen Christi* = "hymn of Christ").

97. On the matter of criteria for distinguishing hymns and confessional materials in the NT, see esp. Gloer, "Homologies"; cf. Martin, *DPL,* 420-21. Although this passage reflects several of Gloer's criteria, the fact that vv. 9-11 fit them all so poorly should give everyone reason to pause.

> c In the likeness of human beings becoming;
> d     And in appearance being found as a human being
> 8 a He humbled himself
>   b Becoming obedient unto death,
>   c    but death of a cross
> 9 a Therefore also God him highly exalted
>   b And bestowed on him the name
>   c    that is above every name,
> 10 a So that at the name of Jesus
>    b Every knee should bow
>    c    of those in the heavens and on earth and under the earth
> 11 a And every tongue confess that
>    b The Lord [is] Jesus Christ
>    c    to the glory of God the Father.

Despite the nearly universal acceptance of this point of view, there are good reasons to pause.

First, if originally a hymn, it has no correspondence of any kind with Greek hymnody or poetry; therefore, it would have to be Semitic in origin. But the alleged Semitic parallelism of this piece is unlike any *known* example of Hebrew psalmody. The word "hymn" properly refers to a *song* in praise of deity; in its present form — and even in its several reconstructed forms — this passage lacks the rhythm and parallelism that one might expect of material that is to be sung.[98] And in any case, it fits very poorly with the clearly hymnic material in the Psalter — or with Luke 1:46-55, 68-79, or 1 Timothy 3:16b, to name but a few certain NT examples of hymns.

Second, exalted — even poetic — *prose* does not necessarily mean that one is dealing with a hymn. The same objections that I have raised as to the hymnic character of 1 Corinthians 13 must also be raised here.[99] Paul is capable of especially exalted prose whenever he thinks on the work of Christ.

Third, the *hos* in this case is *not* precisely like its alleged parallels in Col 1:15 (18b) and 1 Tim 3:16. In the former case, even though its antecedent is the "Son" of v. 13, the resultant connection of the "hymn" with its antecedent is not at all smooth.[100] In the latter case, the connection of the *hos* with the rest of the sentence is ungrammatical, thus suggesting that it

98. On this matter see n. 4 on 2:5-11.

99. See G. D. Fee, *First Corinthians,* 626.

100. Indeed, there is nothing else quite like this in Paul, where, in vv. 14-15, one has the order ἐν ᾧ/ὅς ("in whom"/"who"), rather than the expected ὅς/ἐν ᾧ. The subsequent ὅτι in v. 16b, which looks like a *berakoth* formula from the Psalter, plus the second ὅς in 18b, also makes one think that we are here dealing with a hymn fragment of some kind.

belonged to an original hymn (and should be translated with a "soft" antecedent, "he who"). But in the present case the "who" belongs to a perfectly normal Pauline sentence in which it immediately follows its antecedent, Christ Jesus.

Fourth, as pointed out in the commentary, these sentences, exalted and rhythmic as they are, follow one another in perfectly orderly prose — all quite in Pauline style. They begin (a) with a relative clause, in which two ideas are set off with a typically Pauline "not/but" contrast, followed (b) by another clause begun with "and," all of which (c) is followed by a final sentence begun with an inferential "therefore also," concluding with a result clause in two parts, with a final noun (*hoti*, "that") clause. Not only is this as typically Pauline "argumentation" as one can find anywhere in his letters, but also there are scores of places in Paul where there are more balanced structures than this, but where, because of the subject matter, no one suspects Paul of citing poetry or writing hymnody.[101] His own rhetorical style is replete with examples of balanced structures, parallelism, chiasmus, etc.

Fifth, many of the alleged lines are especially irregular if they are intended to function as lines of Semitic poetry. For example, in the commonly accepted structural arrangement given above, there are no verbs at all in six of the "lines":[102]

| | |
|---|---|
| 6c | to be equal with God |
| 8d | but death of a cross |
| 9c | the name above all names |
| 10a | in order that at the name of Jesus |
| 10c | of those in the heavens and on earth and under the earth |
| 11c | unto the glory of God the Father |

Without discounting for a moment the "rhythmic" and "poetic" nature of some parts of this passage, such alleged "lines" as these are simply not the stuff of poetry as such; nor are they natural to the text as "lines" at all, but are simply the creation of the scholars who have here found a "hymn."

Not all scholars, of course, adopt this scheme; indeed there are at least five other basic proposals, with modifications in several of them.[103] It is of little moment here to outline these various schemes. The very fact that there

101. E.g., several passages in 1 Corinthians come immediately to mind: 1:22-25; 1:26-28; 6:12-13; 7:2-4 (!); 9:19-22, etc.
102. There is also no verb expressed in line 11b, "The Lord Jesus Christ," but this is a nominal sentence in which a form of "to be" is presupposed. It is not surprising that four of these verbless "lines" are in vv. 9-11, which has nothing at all of the quality of poetry to it.
103. On this matter see the discussion in Fee, "Philippians 2:5-11," 32-34.

is so little agreement on this *crucial* matter calls the whole procedure into question. If one were to respond that there is agreement at least on the *fact* that it is a hymn, the rebuttal still remains: if so, then one should expect that its parts would be plainly visible to all. Such is certainly the case with Col 1:15-18 and 1 Tim 3:16; but here, and this seems decisive, *all the arrangements are flawed in some way or another.* Either one must (1) excise lines, (2) dismiss the obvious inner logic of the whole, or (3) create lines that are either without parallelism or verbless.

It should be noted finally that any excision of words or lines, so as to reproduce the "original" hymn, is an exercise in exegetical futility. It implies, and this is sometimes vigorously defended,[104] that the first concern of exegesis is the meaning of the "hymn" on its own, apart from its present context. But such a view is indefensible, since (1) our only access to the "hymn" is in its present form and present position, and (2) we must begin any legitimate exegesis by assuming that all the present words are included because they contribute in some way to Paul's own concerns. To assume otherwise is a form of exegetical nihilism, in which on nondemonstrable prior grounds, one determines that an author incorporated foreign material for no ostensible reason. And that leads directly to the question of "authenticity."

## B. The Question of Background/Authorship

The questions of background and authorship are closely related, in that once the passage was isolated as a "hymn," then certain features were "discovered" to be "un-Pauline" (with alleged Pauline features "missing"), which in turn led many to argue that the whole was both pre-Pauline and therefore non-Pauline.[105] Once that was established, then it was necessary to find its original "life setting." It should not surprise us, given the assumptions of the methodology, that scholars found what they were looking for. Nor should it surprise one that, as with form, every imaginable background has been argued for:

   a. Heterodox Judaism (Lohmeyer)
   b. Iranian myth of the Heavenly Redeemer (Beare)
   c. Hellenistic, pre-Christian Gnosticism (Käsemann)
   d. Jewish Gnosticism (J. A. Sanders)
   e. OT Servant passages (Coppens, Moule, Strimple)

---

104. E.g. by Käsemann, Martin, and Murphy-O'Connor.
105. By "un-Pauline" I mean "that which is uncharacteristic of Paul"; "non-Pauline" means that it is judged as quite foreign to Paul.

f. Genesis account of Adam (Murphy-O'Connor, Dunn)
g. Hellenistic Jewish Wisdom speculation (Georgi)

The very diversity of these proposals suggests something of the futility (dare one say irrelevance?) of this exercise. After all, one comes to these positions by *guessing* at what are alleged to be "Pauline adaptations and interpolations," which means that one is fairly free to create as one wills.

All of this becomes thoroughly questionable, when one argues[106] that since Paul did *not* compose it, then one may not use other Pauline words — or even the present context! — to interpret it. That is, not only *can* it be isolated from its context, it is argued, but since Paul did not write it, it *must* be so isolated and must be understood on its own, without reference either to Paul or to its present Pauline context. That is an exegetical tour de force of almost unparalleled boldness.

The primary objection to these views is that they show very little sensitivity either to Paul or to the nature of composition in antiquity. On the one hand, Paul is quite capable of citing,[107] when that suits him. And in such cases we have something that is not speculative to guide us, namely his abundant use of the OT, where sometimes he adapts, sometimes he cites rather closely, and sometimes he takes over its words in an intertextual way. But in all cases, the citation is both clearly identifiable and capable of making at least fairly good sense in its context. That is, Paul chooses to cite because he wants to support or elaborate a point. On the other hand, there are all kinds of evidence that in other cases ancient authors — and probably Paul as well — also took over other material rather wholesale and adapted it to fit their own compositions (the Gospels being a clear case in point). In these latter cases, even when they may have carried over some of the language from their source(s), their authors clearly intend for the present material not to be identifiable as to its source precisely because for them it is now their own material. So in the present case. Here Paul dictates, and the amanuensis transcribes word by word (or syllable by syllable), without any sense that a source needs to be noted. Indeed, in the original letter what we call vv. 5 and 6 would have been "run on," without breaks for words or sentences and without signals indicating the presence of new material.

In this kind of process, one can only speak of "writing in" or "composition"; the language "interpolation" or "insertion" is altogether misleading as to the actual historical process. What Paul dictates he takes ownership

<hr/>

106. As does Murphy-O'Connor, "Christological Anthropology."
107. By "citing" I refer to that kind of quotation from the OT or elsewhere, where some kind of introductory formula is used, or as in the case of 1 Cor 10:26, a γάρ is used with a quote that the apostle can assume will be well known to his readers.

of, even if it had prior existence elsewhere. To argue that what he thus dictates, in thoroughly Pauline sentences, does not reflect his own theology is to argue for exegetical anarchy.[108]

That leads, then, to some final observations about "authenticity." First, by definition "authenticity" or "inauthenticity" means that a written document, or parts thereof, was either written by the person to whom it is attributed, or it was not. With regard to *whole* documents, this is a simple matter. Peter either did or did not write 2 Peter; Didymus the Blind either did or did not write *De Trinitate,* which has been attributed to him and transmitted among his writings. When it comes to *parts* of a document that is otherwise believed to be authentic, then it is a matter of "interpolation" *by a later hand.* Though now transmitted as part of the document in hand, because the material is "inauthentic" it is not necessary to comment on this material as by the author — although one should at least try to discover how such "foreign matter" came to be in the text. The most obvious place where this phenomenon occurs is in the area of textual criticism, and includes such major interpolations as John 7:53–8:12 and 1 Cor 14:34-35,[109] as well as hundreds of lesser ones for each NT document. But in the discussion of this passage, "authenticity" has taken on a new meaning: that Paul has himself "interpolated" a piece of traditional, pre-Pauline, and therefore non-Pauline, material — of which he was not the original "author" — into his letter at 2:6, either as a piece of whole cloth or as "redacted" by him to some degree or another;[110] and therefore, even though he "wrote" it, he did not "author" it and it is thus "inauthentic" and may not be used to reconstruct *Pauline* theology. This is a strange use of language indeed, since by this new definition most of the Gospel of Matthew must be judged "inauthentic"; after all, none of his Markan or "Q" materials was originally "authored" by him.

But that would seem to push the concept of "inauthenticity" beyond recognizable limits. Whether the passage had pre-Pauline existence is a moot point, which cannot be proved one way or the other. But that Paul "interpolated" the material into his letter in such a way that it is not to be understood as his own borders on fantasy; it would be as though he did not intend the

---

108. Cf. the critique by Strimple, "Philippians 2:5-11," 250-51. Others, especially Käsemann ("Critical Analysis") and Martin *(Carmen),* seem to make the same exegetical error, though a little more subtly. In their case the meaning of the "hymn" is discovered first of all in isolation from its present context, then *that* meaning is contended for as the one *Paul himself intends* in context. There is an obvious circularity to this kind of reasoning; thus it does not surprise one that almost all who go this route have the common denominator of opposition to the so-called ethical interpretation of the passage.

109. See the excursus on this matter in *Presence,* 272-81.

110. For this new understanding of authenticity, put in this very forthright way, see Fitzgerald, *ABD,* 5.319-20.

doxology in Rom 11:33-36 to reflect his own point of view because it is so obviously full of "traditional" (including OT) material.

Finally, it needs to be stressed (1) that Paul is the *author* in terms of its inclusion, including *all* the present words of 2:6-11, and (2) that although Paul often quotes, this passage does *not* come by way of quotation. The alleged "hymn" is a *grammatical piece* inextricably connected to the present context. Whereas one might legitimately look separately at a piece of quoted material, speculate as to its original meaning, and then wonder whether an author has correctly understood that original meaning, neither the grammar, the content, nor the context allow such a procedure here. As Morna Hooker put it: "For even if the material is non-Pauline, we may expect Paul himself to have interpreted it and used it in a Pauline manner."[111] Indeed, of this whole enterprise Hooker says (correctly):

> If the passage is pre-Pauline, then we have no guide lines to help us in understanding its meaning. Commentators may speculate about the background — but we know very little about pre-Pauline Christianity, and nothing at all about the context in which the passage originated. It may therefore be more profitable to look first at the function of these verses in the present context and to enquire about possible parallels within Paul's own writings.[112]

"Of course!" one wants to respond to such an eminently reasonable proposal; otherwise why did Paul dictate it in this context as something that in v. 12 he will argue from?[113] In any case, this material appears in the present commentary as part of Paul's letter to the Philippians, with all the grammatical, lexical, and contextual questions that are raised in the process.

# IV. THEOLOGICAL CONTRIBUTIONS

For a "hortatory letter of friendship" Philippians reveals an extraordinary amount of Pauline theology, and not just in the one passage (2:6-11) that has long held interest in this regard. My concern here is not to write a "theology of Philippians," but to highlight both the implicit and explicit theological

---

111. See her "Philippians 2:6-11," 152.

112. Ibid.

113. Most of those who write on this passage simply fail to come to terms with the ὥστε that begins v. 12. Not only is this a thoroughly Pauline form of argumentation, but it is so in such a way that what precedes forms the theological basis for the concluding paraenesis. See the discussion in the commentary.

concerns that are the driving force behind the letter. It is, however, significant to note — in keeping with the nature of this particular letter — that theology for Paul is not philosophical or academic in nature, but is confessional (cf. 1:18-24; 3:3-14) and doxological (4:19-20). Theology in Philippians first of all takes the form of story; to isolate the theology from the story, as if the story were irrelevant to the theology, would be in effect to eliminate one of the primary *theological* contributions of the letter!

## A. The Gospel

We noted above (p. 14) and will have occasion to note throughout the commentary that the ultimate urgency of this letter is *the gospel,* which in this letter takes the form of "the advance of the gospel": Paul's and the Philippians' relationship is described in terms of "participation/partnership in the gospel" (1:5; 4:15); Paul himself is in prison "for the defense and confirmation of the gospel" (1:7, 16), an imprisonment that has in fact brought about "the advance of the gospel" (1:12); Paul's concern for the Philippians is for their own "advance/progress in the faith (= the gospel)" (1:25); and his major concern in this regard is that they get their corporate act together for the sake of the gospel in Philippi (1:27; 2:16). The gospel, therefore, has to do first of all with evangelism, "preaching Christ" (1:18) so that others will hear it for the good news that it is.

On the other hand, in contrast to other letters, there is very little that is said in Philippians as to the *content* of the gospel — which should surprise us none, since this is not a polemical letter but a letter of friendship, and on this matter he and they have long been in accord. What we do learn from its various incidental theological affirmations (e.g., 2:6-11; 3:3, 9, 13-14, 20-21; 4:19) is that the central core of his understanding of the gospel is consistently the same.[114] The absolute heart of the Pauline theological enterprise is the Triune God effecting "salvation in Christ," and thus creating a people for his name, whose present existence is thoroughly eschatological; predicated on the death and resurrection of Christ and the gift of the eschatological Spirit, God's people are both "already" and "not yet" as they live the life of the future in the present, awaiting God's final wrapup, the final consummation of "salvation in Christ." Every significant theological moment in the letter reflects this central core in some way or another, sometimes with emphases unique to the "contingencies" of Philippians, but at all times expressed in "coherence" with what Paul says elsewhere in his letters.

114. On this matter see Fee, "Toward a Theology," and *Presence,* 2-5, 11-13, 799-801.

## B. The Trinity as the Theological Key

Although Christ always plays the central role in the Pauline theological enterprise — after all, it is not for naught that "salvation *in Christ*" lies at the heart of things — in fact one does not long do theology in Paul without taking seriously that the living God, indeed the Trinity,[115] is the heart and soul of everything for him. God, now known in a Triune way through the coming of Christ and the Spirit, is the fundamental presupposition of Paul's existence and worldview. Thus "salvation in Christ" is initiated by God the Father, it is effected in our human history by Christ Jesus the Son,[116] it is appropriated as an experienced reality through the gift of the eschatological Spirit. We will look at the central role of Christ momentarily; here we need to note the consistent way this understanding about the Father and the Spirit carry through in this letter.

As always in Paul, God the Father stands as the primary reality at the beginning and end of all things, and especially of "salvation in Christ." Salvation is God's thing; it is his story whatever else.[117] God both initiated it (1:6; cf. 3:9, 14) and will bring it to completion (1:6); God is the one who makes it work in the present (2:13); and all that God has done through Christ and the Spirit has "the praise and glory of God" as its ultimate goal (1:11; 2:9-11; 4:18, 20). Hence, God's people have been "called" by him to obtain the final eschatological prize (3:14); their salvation and righteousness come "from God" (1:28; 3:9); they are "God's children" (2:15), whose every need will be supplied in keeping with his riches in glory as they are in Christ Jesus (4:19; cf. 4:6-7). God is the "God of peace" who is present among his children (4:9), so that his peace may "rule" in both their individual and corporate lives (4:7). Presuppositional to all of this is God's character. Full of mercy (2:27) and grace (1:2), he lavishes grace on his people in keeping with the immensity of his own riches inherent in his glory (4:19); moreover, it is a "good work" that God is effecting in his people (1:6), which he does for the sake of his own good pleasure (2:13). Paul's basic theology is thus derived from his biblical roots; as with the Psalmist he knows that "God is good," whose "steadfast love endures forever" (Ps 136:1).

Although the Spirit does not play an explicitly major role in this letter,

---

115. Some NT scholars will not be congenial toward this alleged anachronism. For a defense of this usage — even though Paul does not engage in Trinitarian speculation — see Fee, *Presence,* 827-45; cf. "Christology and Pneumatology."

116. Although "Son of God" language is noticeably missing from this letter, it is presupposed in three instances where God is called "Father" (1:2; 2:11; 4:20), since in each instance this appellation comes in a context where God is mentioned in close proximity with Christ.

117. As is the judgment that comes on those who reject his salvation (1:28).

he is mentioned at four key points, all in keeping with his role in "salvation in Christ" as that is spelled out elsewhere. Thus the experienced reality of the "Spirit of God" is the first reality brought forward in 3:3 as evidence not only that "we, who boast in Christ Jesus" are the true circumcision, but also that the true "worship/service" of God is not to be found in religious observance but through life in the Spirit. Thus the Spirit will be the key to Paul's magnifying Christ (and thus vindicating Paul and his gospel) at his upcoming trial (1:19); and the Spirit (who is presupposed as the way "God is at work in them" in 2:13) is the key to the Philippians' standing firm as a united people on behalf of the gospel (1:27; 2:1). Again, there is nothing unique here; this is the recurring explicit and implicit theology of the apostle.

## C. The Central Role of Christ

On anybody's reading, Christ plays the absolutely central role in Paul's life and thought, and nowhere is that more evident than in Philippians. For Paul Christ is his "life," so that death is "gain" (1:21) because it means the ultimate realization of life, namely "being with Christ" (1:24). Thus the ultimate gain of life — now and forever — is the "surpassing worth of knowing Christ Jesus *my* Lord," because of whom everything else is considered "foul-smelling street garbage" fit only for dogs (3:8). Knowing Christ — intimately, fully, and finally — this is the prize, the ultimate goal of the upward calling of God that has taken place in Christ Jesus (3:13-14). Everything else that matters in life, therefore, is "in Christ" or "through Christ" in some way or another.

It is therefore of more than mere passing interest that there is scarcely an explicit word about Christ's central role in "*salvation* in Christ" in the entire letter. On the other hand, given the nature of this letter, neither should that be surprising. In fact such a soteriological role is assumed everywhere, especially with the some twenty-one occurrences of the phrase "in Christ" and its equivalents. The vast majority of these presuppose both the *prior work* of Christ and Christ as the *sphere* of present existence, which his saving work has made possible.

The saving work itself is implied throughout: Christ is the content of the gospel that is proclaimed (1:15-18; cf. 1:27, "the gospel *about Christ*"); his death by crucifixion as "for us" is the presupposition both of our suffering "for him" (1:29) and of Christ as paradigm for life in our present "already/not yet" existence (2:8; cf. 3:10, 18); present righteousness is by "faith in Christ," which means that one is "found *in him*," not having one's own righteousness but that which is from God. Thus we "boast/glory" in Christ Jesus (3:3), precisely because he has effected God's salvation in our behalf (1:11; 3:12). Christ is therefore the ground of present confidence (2:24), hope (2:19), and joy (3:1; 4:4).

But most of this theology is expressed in presuppositional ways; it is seldom explicit and never argued for as such. That presupposition, however, is the key to the primary role Christ plays in this letter: as the one who in his saving death fully revealed God's character and is thus the ultimate paradigm of life in the present. And here is where the particularly "high Christology" of this letter comes into focus, a Christology that is presupposed in a number of off-handed ways[118] and is made explicit in the marvelous Christ narrative in 2:6-11. If paradigm of "selflessness" and "humility" is the *reason* for that narrative, what makes it *work* is its Christology: that the one who in coming as a human being "took the form of a slave" and "humbled himself unto death on a cross" is none other than the one who is "in the 'form' of God" and thus "equal with God" in every way. Although this explicitly expresses pre-existence,[119] that is less Paul's concern than is the demonstration of what true "equality with God" looks like, since the clear implication of vv. 7-8 is that in the "humiliation" of his humanity Christ did not cease to be "equal with God." The full vindication of Christ's death as expressing ultimate "God-likeness" is found in vv. 9-11, where God bestows on Christ the divine "Name," the name of the "Lord God" himself.

This is what makes Paul's personal narrative in 3:4-14 work as well. The goal of everything is to "know Christ," which means through the power of his resurrection to "participate in his sufferings" and thus to be "conformed to his death" (3:10-11). Thus Christ's death by crucifixion — that most hated and execrable of deaths from the Roman point of view — is not only the place of God's redemption but the place of the full revelation of his "likeness." Only the very high Christology expressed in 2:6 could make this work. Hence, the absolutely central role Christ plays in the Pauline theological enterprise, not to mention the experience and understanding of God in everyday life.

## D. The Eschatological Framework

The fundamental framework for all of Paul's theologizing, especially for "salvation in Christ," is his eschatological understanding of present existence — as both "already" and "not yet." With the resurrection of Christ and the gift of the promised Holy Spirit, God has already set the future inexorably in motion; thus salvation is "already." But the consummation of salvation awaits the (now second) coming of Christ — "the Day of Christ," Paul calls it (1:6, 10; 2:16); thus salvation has "not yet" been fully realized. The fact that the

118. In this regard see the comments on 1:2 and 2:11; cf. n. 25 on 1:1; n. 65 on 1:6 and n. 38 on 4:5.
119. Cf. n. 41 on 2:6-7.

future has already begun with the coming of God himself (through Christ and the Spirit) means two crucial things for Paul: that the consummation is absolutely guaranteed, and that present existence is therefore altogether determined by this reality. That is, one's life in the present is not conditioned or determined by present exigencies, but by the singular reality that God's people belong to the future that has already come present. Marked by Christ's death and resurrection and identified as God's people by the gift of the Spirit, they live the life of the future in the present, determined by its values and perspective, no matter what their present circumstances.

This essential framework finds expression both explicitly and implicitly throughout Philippians. It begins in the thanksgiving ("God has *begun* a good work . . . which he will *bring to completion* at the day of Christ Jesus," 1:6), is essential to the prayer report (1:10), underlies the Christ narrative in chap. 2 (esp. vv. 9-11; cf. v. 16), and is the essential matter in Paul's own narrative in chap. 3 (esp. vv. 10-14, 20-21). Already is our "citizenship in heaven," from whence we await the (not yet) coming of our Savior, Jesus the Lord. Indeed, only in Philippians does Paul insert the (perhaps purposefully ambiguous) indicative, "The Lord is near," in his concluding exhortations (4:4-9).

At this point what is theologically at stake in Philippians is the twin reality of the Philippians' present suffering and of the (apparent) diminution of their clear vision of the sure future that awaits. On the one hand, it is the guaranteed future — the "power of Christ's resurrection" (3:10) — that makes it possible, not to mention necessary, to live in a cruciform way in the present (3:10-14), because in any case these present "bodies of humiliation" shall be transformed into the likeness of Christ's present "body of glory" (3:21). It is this kind of eschatological existence — the guaranteed future determining all of life in the present — that is Paul's "secret" to knowing how both "to abound and to be abased." Neither determines life in the present; only Christ does, whose death and resurrection have already marked us as citizens of heaven. That is why Paul can say so strongly, "To live is Christ; to die is gain." Either way, Paul wins. So present suffering does not dictate present existence; suffering on behalf of Christ has been graciously given to those who follow him (1:29), whose present lives are in process of "being conformed into the likeness of his death" (3:11).

On the other hand, in ways he seldom does elsewhere, there is regular emphasis in this letter on "standing fast" and in so doing by giving full effort to the pursuit of the heavenly prize, the final, full knowing of Christ (3:12-14). While the future is sure, guaranteed by Christ's resurrection and the gift of the eschatological Spirit, one's stance and focus in the present is on that sure future. Like the runner in the games, Paul sets himself before them as a model of one who is singularly given to crossing the goal and obtaining the prize;

and he weeps over those who have given up on the future, whose "minds are set on earthly things" (3:18-19). To lose sight of the future is to lose sight of Christ himself, and thereby to become an enemy of the cross.


## E. The Christian Life

In Philippians all of the preceding theological undercurrents and foci find expression for a single purpose: that the Philippians as a community of believers in Philippi will live the "righteousness" of the gospel in the present as they await its consummation. They are a "colony of heaven" (see on 3:20), living the life of heaven in their lives together as the people of God in Philippi. What Paul is concerned about is their "Christ-likeness," which in this letter is clearly spelled out as "God-likeness" (= "godliness").

At issue is love within a community (1:9; 2:2) where some "posturing" is taking place — "selfish ambition/rivalry" and "vain glory" (2:3) — leading to some internal "grumbling and murmuring" (2:14). And love is grounded in God's own character, "humbleness of mind," which is defined in terms of "putting the needs of others before one's own," and is exemplified by the One who as "equal with God" poured himself out into our humanity and in that humanity humbled himself to the ultimate obedience of death on a cross. This is the "fruit of righteousness" for which Paul prays for them (1:11) and the "knowing of Christ" for which he longs (3:8-11), thereby offering himself as one to imitate by the way they "walk" (3:15-17).

Here, then, is also the key to life in the present as cruciform — not just individually, but corporately. We not only believe in Christ but are graciously privileged to "suffer for his sake" (1:29). For only as our lives are thus cruciform (3:11) do we begin to "know Christ." The people of God not only model such "God-likeness" in their life together, but in their standing firm in the one Spirit for the sake of the world (1:27; 2:15). Thus Christ is the beginning and end of everything for the believer: salvation means to "be found in him," not having one's own righteousness, but that which comes from God through faith in Christ; but Christ is also the paradigm for what "salvation" looks like when it has been effected in the life of his followers — it looks like him.

All of which leads to the best known of the theological motifs in this letter — joy in the midst of suffering. But joy is not the primary motif; rather it is a leitmotif. Joy is how believers who know Christ and whose futures are guaranteed by Christ respond in the context of present difficulties, not because they like to suffer, but because their joy is "in the Lord." But joy is not a feeling, it is an activity. In keeping with the Psalmists, Paul urges them to "rejoice in the Lord," which can only mean to vocalize their joy in song and word. Above everything else, joy is the distinctive mark of the believer in Christ Jesus; and in this letter it comes most often as an imperative. Believers are to "rejoice in the Lord *always*" (4:4), because joy has not to do with one's circumstances but with one's relationship with *the Lord;* and they are to do so both on their own, as it were, and together with others (2:18). Whatever else, life in Christ is a life of joy. To miss this reality is to miss Philippians altogether; and to miss Philippians at this point is to miss out on an essential quality of Christian life.

In sum: Our letter invites us into the advance of the gospel, the good news about Christ and the Spirit. It points us to Christ, both for now and forever. Christ *is* the gospel; Christ is Savior and Lord; thus Christ is our life; Christ is our way of life; Christ is our future; Christ is our joy; "to live is Christ; to die is gain"; and all to the glory of our God and Father. Amen.

# ANALYSIS OF PHILIPPIANS

I. INTRODUCTORY MATTERS (1:1-11)                                    59
   A. SALUTATION (1:1-2)                             60
   B. THANKSGIVING AND PRAYER (1:3-11)               72
      1. Prayer as Thanksgiving — for Partnership in the
         Gospel (1:3-8)                              74
      2. Prayer as Petition — for Increased Love and
         "Fruitfulness" (1:9-11)                     95

II. PAUL'S "AFFAIRS" — REFLECTIONS ON
    IMPRISONMENT (1:12-26)                        106
   A. THE PRESENT — FOR THE ADVANCE OF THE
     GOSPEL (1:12-18a)                           108
      1. The Gospel Advances inside and outside Prison
         (1:12-14)                                   109
      2. The Gospel Advances outside Prison — despite
         Ill-will (1:15-18a)                         117
   B. THE FUTURE — FOR THE GLORY OF CHRIST
     AND THE GOOD OF THE PHILIPPIANS (1:18b-26)  126
      1. Paul's Ambition — that Christ be Glorified (1:18b-20)  127
      2. The Desired Outcome — to be with Christ (1:21-24)  139
      3. The Expected Outcome — Reunion in Philippi (1:25-26)  151

III. THE PHILIPPIANS' "AFFAIRS" — EXHORTATION
     TO STEADFASTNESS AND UNITY (1:27–2:18)       155
   A. THE APPEAL — TO STEADFASTNESS AND UNITY
     IN THE FACE OF OPPOSITION (1:27-30)         158
   B. THE APPEAL RENEWED — UNITY THROUGH
     HUMILITY (2:1-4)                            174
   C. THE EXAMPLE OF CHRIST (2:5-11)                191

1. As God He Emptied Himself (2:5-7)     197
2. As Man He Humbled Himself (2:8)     214
3. God Has Exalted Him as Lord of All (2:9-11)     218
D. APPLICATION AND FINAL APPEAL (2:12-18)     229
    1. General Application — An Appeal to Obedience
       (2:12-13)     230
    2. Specific Application — For the World's and Paul's
       Sake (2:14-18)     240

IV. WHAT'S NEXT — REGARDING PAUL'S AND
    THEIR "AFFAIRS" (2:19-30)     258
    A. TIMOTHY AND PAUL TO COME LATER (2:19-24)     262
    B. EPAPHRODITUS TO COME NOW (2:25-30)     271

V. THEIR "AFFAIRS" — AGAIN (3:1–4:3)     285
    A. THE APPEAL — AGAINST CIRCUMCISION (3:1-4a)     287
    B. THE EXAMPLE OF PAUL (3:4b-14)     303
    1. There Is No Future to the Past (3:4b-6)     305
    2. The Future Lies with the Present — Knowing Christ
       (3:7-11)     311
    3. The Future Is Also Future — Attaining Resurrection
       (3:12-14)     337
    C. APPLICATION AND FINAL APPEAL (3:15–4:3)     351
    1. Application — Having a "Mature" Mindset (3:15-16)     352
    2. Appeal and Indictment (3:17-19)     362
    3. Basis of the Appeal — Heaven Now and to Come
       (3:20-21)     375
    4. Final Appeals — To Steadfastness and Unity (4:1-3)     385

VI. CONCLUDING MATTERS (4:4-23)     398
    A. CONCLUDING EXHORTATIONS (4:4-9)     400
    1. A Call to Christian Piety — and Peace (4:4-7)     402
    2. A Call to Wisdom — and the Imitation of Paul (4:8-9)     413
    B. ACKNOWLEDGING THEIR GIFT: FRIENDSHIP
       AND THE GOSPEL (4:10-20)     421
    1. Their Gift and Paul's "Need" (4:10-13)     426
    2. Their Gift as Partnership in the Gospel (4:14-17)     436
    3. Their Gift as a Fragrant Offering (4:18-20)     449
    C. CLOSING GREETINGS (4:21-23)     456

# Paul's Letter to the Philippians

# I. INTRODUCTORY MATTERS (1:1-11)

Almost all letters from the Greco-Roman period[1] begin with a threefold salutation: The Writer, to the Addressee, Greetings.[2] Very often the next item in the letter would be a wish (sometimes a prayer) for the health or well-being of the addressee. Paul's letters, which generally follow this standard form, usually include a thanksgiving;[3] in some of these, as here, he also includes a prayer-report.[4] But in contrast to most of the ancient letters, which tend to be stereotyped, Paul tends to elaborate these formal items; and in so doing, everything Paul's hands touch come under the influence of the gospel, and thereby become distinctively Christian.

In contrast to most extant letters from the Greco-Roman world, Paul's "introductory matters"[5] are quite long, made so usually because they are full of items that foreshadow the concerns of the letter itself.[6] In this regard the proemium of Philippians is typical. All sorts of motifs and concerns within the letter surface initially here: the central focus on Christ and the gospel, the language of servanthood and "fellowship," the relational basis of this "fellowship," Paul's "chains" (thus the motif of "suffering"), the future orientation of present life in Christ, and the need for love and fruitful living in the present. There is in fact very little that is distinctive to this letter that is not anticipated in some way in the three sections of these introductory matters.

---

1. For helpful studies of letter writing in the Greco-Roman period, see J. L. White, *Light,* whose analysis is based on the Greek papyri, and Stowers, *Letter Writing,* who throws the net more widely. Either (or both) of these is essential reading for the serious exegesis of one of the NT letters. Along with the useful collection of such letters in Stowers and White, see also Hunt and Edgar, *Select Papyri I,* for further examples from the Greek papyri.

2. All the true "letters" in the NT follow this pattern (including the letter from James in Acts 15:23-29), except for 3 John, which lacks the standard greeting. For a collection of examples from the papyri, see Exler, *Form,* 23-68; for a further collection and detailed study, see Schnider and Stenger, *Studien.*

3. Noticeably absent in Galatians, 1 Timothy, and Titus.

4. Cf., e.g., 2 Thess 1:11-12; Col 1:9-11.

5. The word *proemium* is the technical one to cover all of these matters, both the "prescript," which refers to the salutation proper, and the thanksgiving-prayer report.

6. Although sometimes noted by earlier commentators, awareness of the significance of this phenomenon for Paul's letters took root with Paul Schubert's *Form and Function of the Pauline Thanksgivings* (1939).

## A. SALUTATION (1:1-2)

> 1*Paul and Timothy, servants of Christ Jesus,*[7]
> *To all the saints in Christ Jesus at Philippi, together with*[8] *the overseers*[a] *and deacons:*
> 2*Grace and peace to you from God our Father and the Lord Jesus Christ.*

[a]Traditionally *bishops*

Although the Philippians themselves would not have been privy to our broader knowledge of Paul as a letter-writer, the most convenient way for us to enter into the significance of this salutation is by comparison with the other letters in the corpus. In such a comparison, several matters stand out: its comparative brevity, the fixed nature of the greeting proper (v. 2), and the inclusion of "overseers and deacons." Some other items need to be noted as well, as we take up the various elements in turn.

**1** *(A) The Writer(s).* Even though the practice is extremely rare among the extant Greco-Roman letters, Paul frequently includes his present companions with himself in his salutations.[9] This is especially so regarding Timothy. One is not quite sure what to make of the phenomenon (of co-authorship). In the case of 1 and 2 Thessalonians, which are written mostly in the first person plural, a genuine co-authorship seems to be involved, and when Paul wishes to distinguish himself from the others, he does so as in 1 Thess 2:18, "I, Paul, once and again." Second Corinthians likewise appears most often in the first person plural, although frequently also in the first singular; however, the subject matter makes it certain that in this case the letter is primarily from Paul himself, and very little from Paul *and* Timothy. When we come to the three Captivity Letters in which this phenomenon appears (Philemon, Colossi-

---

7. The later MajT has the word order, "Jesus Christ," against all the early evidence of all kinds.

8. Several MSS, including K 33 1739 1881, read σὺν ἐπισκόποις as one word, συνεπισκόποις, thus turning "overseers" and "deacons" into indirect objects. The resultant text, "to all the saints in Christ Jesus at Philippi, to the fellow-bishops and deacons, grace and peace," is a patently secondary reading, reflecting the ecclesiology of a later time. Cf. Metzger, *Textual Commentary,* 611.

9. He does so in seven letters in the corpus: 1 and 2 Thessalonians (Timothy and Silas), 1 Corinthians (Sosthenes), 2 Corinthians (Timothy), Philemon (Timothy), Colossians (Timothy), and here (Timothy). There are no known *examples* outside the Pauline corpus. The only known *reference* to co-authorship is in Cicero, *Att.* 11.15.1: "For my part I have gathered from your letters — both that which you wrote in conjunction with others and the one you wrote in your own name . . ." (LCL 2.363). See the discussion in Bahr, "Letter Writing," 476-77.

ans, Philippians), the apparent claim of co-authorship gives way to the reality that Paul is the sole author.

Very likely, therefore, the appearance of Timothy in the six letters that also bear his name is to be understood in two ways. First, it is probable that Timothy served as Paul's secretary, as the actual writer of the letter at Paul's dictation.[10] Evidence for Paul's use of a secretary appears in 2 Thess 3:17, where he signs off the letter with his own hand, after someone else had penned the rest.[11] One cannot be sure, of course, that Timothy was the secretary in that case, or in the case of Philippians, but it is reasonable to think so. Second, in most cases Timothy is well known to the recipients,[12] hence the ease with which he is included as the "co-author," especially in a letter of friendship.[13] Thus, even though Timothy was not involved in the actual composition of the letter,[14] he is involved by being present (probably) as secretary, and thus present to offer reminders and/or corrections as the need may arise. Since he is so well known to the Philippians,[15] and since he is soon himself to come to Philippi (2:19-22), the letter is to be understood in this lesser sense as coming from both of them — Paul as author, with Timothy's concurrence.

But this salutation is unique in another way, which is best seen in contrast to four of the other letters in which Timothy's name also appears. In 1 and 2 Thessalonians, written primarily in the first person plural, the names of the senders appear simply, with no elaboration: Paul and Silvanus and Timothy. In Colossians and Philemon, however, Paul begins as always with

10. So also Jones, Müller, Bruce. Most commentaries think otherwise, often following Meyer (11), who asserts on the basis of Rom 16:22 that "the amanuensis *as such* is not included in the superscription" (emphasis his). More likely the difference between Tertius (who is clearly the amanuensis of Romans but not mentioned in the salutation) and Timothy and Sosthenes (1 Corinthians) is that the latter were Paul's co-workers, and were also known to the recipients.

11. Cf. 1 Cor 16:21 and Gal 6:11, the latter in a letter that lacks any internal information as to who the secretary might be. This is probably an indication that Paul wrote that letter at a time when Timothy was not with him — although it also may be that Timothy was not personally known in the churches of Galatia.

12. This is especially true in the case of 1 and 2 Thessalonians, 2 Corinthians, and Philippians; it is more problematic for Colossians and Philemon.

13. On Philippians as a letter of friendship, see the Introduction, pp. 2-7.

14. After all, in v. 3 Paul assumes the role as the only writer, a stance that carries throughout the letter. Furthermore, in 2:19 he speaks of Timothy in the third person while referring to himself still in the first singular. By way of contrast cf. the reference to Timothy in 1 Thess 3:2.

15. This is made evident by how Paul speaks of him to them in 2:19-23; it is further corroborated by Acts 16:1, 13, where he was present at the founding of the church; cf. 17:14, where he is also present at the founding of the church in Thessalonica. According to Acts 19:22 and 20:3-4, Timothy visited Philippi twice more during Paul's so-called Third Missionary Journey.

his own name, followed by a word of self-identification (apostle/prisoner),[16] which in turn is followed by "and Timothy our brother." In Philippians alone does Paul include Timothy in the self-identification. Thus, "Paul *and Timothy,* slaves of Christ Jesus." The reasons for the inclusion of Timothy in this case are not hard to find, being related to two other matters.

First, after 1 and 2 Thessalonians, only here and in Philemon is there no assertion of Paul's apostleship. This of course explains why on other occasions Timothy's name is separated from Paul's in his self-identification; Timothy is not an apostle.[17] But he is a fellow "slave." The reason for Paul's not identifying himself as an apostle is more speculative; most likely it is related to the nature of both the present letter and Paul's relationship with this community. A letter primarily of friendship and exhortation,[18] not of persuasion, does not need a reminder of Paul's apostleship; indeed, the summons to obedience in this letter is predicated altogether on the secure nature of their mutual friendship.[19]

Second, the identification itself, " 'slaves' [*douloi*][20] of Christ Jesus," anticipates a significant motif of the letter. While "servant," found in most English translations,[21] is an acceptable rendering, it also causes the English reader to lose something of its force. For the (basically Gentile) readers of

---

16. "Paul, apostle of Christ Jesus by the will of God" (Col 1:1); "Paul, prisoner of Christ Jesus" (Phlm 1).

17. Cf. 1 Cor 1:1, where the same distinction occurs between Paul as an apostle and Sosthenes as a "brother," and Phlm 1, where Paul likewise distinguishes himself from Timothy ("Paul, prisoner of Christ Jesus, and Timothy our brother") because Timothy was not in fact a prisoner; only Paul was. This evidence should occasion some caution as to how much weight one puts on Paul's having joined Timothy's name with his in this case (as, e.g., Hawthorne, 3-4). Of the various terms of self-identification used by Paul in his salutations, this one (i.e., "slave of Christ Jesus") in particular can include others on equal grounds, without the need to distinguish himself from his writing companion(s).

18. See the Introduction, pp. 2-7, 10-14.

19. In this regard see esp. the comments below on 1:7-8, 25-26, 27; 2:1-2, 12, 17-18; 4:1, 10, 14-16; cf. the Introduction, pp. 13-14.

20. Altogether this word group appears 59 times in the Pauline corpus: δοῦλος, "slave" (30x); σύνδουλος, "fellow-slave" (2x); δουλεύω, "to perform the duties of a slave, to serve" (17x); δουλεία, "slavery" (4x); δουλόω, "to enslave" (6x). On the meaning of this word in Paul see, *inter alia,* K. H. Rengstorf, *TDNT* 2.261-80; H.-G. Link and R. Tuente, *NIDNTT,* 3.589-98; A. Weiser, *EDNT,* 1.349-52; Sass, "Bedeutung."

21. Cf. KJV, AV, RSV, NRSV, NIV, GNB, NEB, NAB, JB. Weymouth and the NASB have "bondservants"; Confraternity has "bondsmen." The latter are attempts to find a middle way between the rather totally negative connotations of "slave," conditioned as it is by slavery in American history, and the less than servitude connotations in the word "servant." The latter, to be distinguished from a slave, was designated by the word διάκονος, which appears in the next phrase where it is translated "deacons." But because the word "slave" often carries the connotation of "servility," which δοῦλος never does in Paul (so also Vincent, 2), it fares little better than "servant" as an adequate translation into English. Cf. Michael, 2-3.

this letter, this word would have only meant "slave." Indeed, *douloi* were so common in Greco-Roman society that no one would have thought it to refer other than to those owned by, and subservient to, the master of a household.[22] To be sure, the institution of slavery in antiquity[23] was a far cry from the racial slavery that blighted American society — and the English society that made it possible by the slave trade. Even so, the slave in the Roman Empire was not a free person, but "belonged to" another. Thus, whatever else, the word carries connotations of humility and servitude.

Gentile converts to Christianity, however, were no longer members only of Greco-Roman culture. They had entered the "society"[24] of a people whose roots were in Judaism and whose story had its origins in the Old Testament, a story that the Philippians by now would have known well in its Greek form — the Septuagint (LXX). And here the Greek word *doulos,* used for true "slaves" of course, was also used to designate "servants of God," where it carried the sense of distance from and dependence upon God, but at the same time became a kind of honorific title for those in special service to God.[25]

It is this double connotation that is probably at work in Paul's designating himself and Timothy by this word. They are Christ's slaves, bound to him as slaves to their master, but whose "slavery" is expressed in loving service on behalf of Christ for the Philippians — and others. It is noteworthy that Paul does not often use it as a title.[26] Much more often he uses this language to designate any and all of those who "serve" God as "free bondslaves," that is, as those who are free in Christ Jesus, but who have used that

22. Cf. Bruce, 26, who dismisses altogether the possibility of a second connotation (as suggested below).

23. Their slavery, which originated with captives from war, became primarily a socioeconomic phenomenon. For overviews of Greco-Roman slavery, see S. S. Bartchy, *ABD,* 6.65-73, and E. Ferguson, *Backgrounds,* 56-59; see their bibliographies for more detailed studies.

24. On the sociological question of the early churches as a religious "society" in the Greco-Roman world, see esp. W. A. Meeks, *Urban,* 74-80; J. E. Stambaugh and D. L. Balch, *Social Environment,* 124-26, 140-41; and Ferguson, *Backgrounds,* 131-36.

25. See, e.g., Moses (2 Kgs 18:12; Ps 104:26); Josh 24:29 ("Joshua, the servant of the Lord, died"); Jon 1:9 ("I am the servant of the Lord" [δοῦλος κυρίου]); Neh 1:6 (where Nehemiah in prayer calls himself "your servant"); Ezek 34:23 (referring to David as "the Lord's servant"); Ezek 38:17 ("my servants the prophets"; cf., Jer 25:4; Amos 3:7; Dan 9:6, 10). That Paul should substitute "Christ Jesus" for "the Lord [= Yahweh]" is another of those subtle, but significant, moments in Paul where his "high Christology" emerges as presupposition, not argumentation (cf. Sanday-Headlam, *Romans,* 3).

26. Only here and in Rom 1:1, where it appears as his first self-designation, before he also reminds them that he has been "called" to be an "apostle" of the gospel. But cf. Gal 1:10 ("Christ's slave"), and Col 1:7 and 4:7, where Epaphras and Tychicus are each called a συνδοῦλος, "fellow slaves/servants in the Lord."

freedom to "perform the duties of a slave"[27] in the service of God and of his people. Of special significance in our letter is Paul's use of this word in 2:7 to designate Christ in the humiliation of his incarnation. As God's ultimate suffering servant he humbled himself to death on a cross — on the Philippians' behalf — which serves as the proper ground for the humility to which Paul calls them in 2:4. They are to "have this mindset that is also that of Christ Jesus" (2:5), a concern probably anticipated by this self-designation.[28]

Paul and Timothy are thus to be thought of as "slaves/servants *of Christ Jesus.*" Here is the absolutely predominant motif in this letter. Everything is in, of, by, and for Christ Jesus. Christ Jesus is the basis of their common existence; he is the focus and content of the gospel in which Paul, Timothy, and the Philippians are partners; and he is the Lord, to whom every knee shall bow, including those in Philippi who are currently bowing to "Lord Caesar," the emperor Nero. As "slaves of Christ Jesus," Paul and Timothy are thus designated as belonging to him alone; at the same time they are Christ's "servants" on his behalf for the sake of the Philippians,[29] whom he will go on to designate as "in Christ Jesus," and whom he will greet with grace and peace that come from both God the Father and "our Lord Jesus Christ."

*(B) The Addressees.* The letter is addressed "to all the saints in Christ Jesus, who are in Philippi." By this designation Paul repeats three (for him) standard items. First, he calls them "saints,"[30] a common designation for the new covenant people of God, but a translation that has far too many misleading connotations to be useful to the ordinary English reader.[31] This is one of several OT terms used to designate Israel — especially as God's elect — which has been appropriated by the NT writers for the people of God newly constituted by Christ and the Spirit. Its origins can be traced to the covenantal setting of Exod 19:6, where among other things God speaks to Israel as "my people . . . a holy nation" — a people consecrated and subject to Yahweh and his service. The language is picked up regularly in Leviticus, still as an

---

27. For this translation of the verb in Gal 5:13, see Fee, *Presence,* 425 n. 201.

28. Cf. Collange, 26; Hawthorne, 4.

29. In this regard, see esp. 2:16-18 (of Paul toward the Philippians); 2:22 (of Timothy); 2:25-26 (of Epaphroditus).

30. Gk. οἱ ἅγιοι, which occurs in 6 of the 9 letters addressed to churches (1 and 2 Corinthians, Romans, Colossians, Ephesians, Philippians). It also occurs in 4:22 to designate God's people in Rome who return greetings (cf. 2 Cor 13:12).

31. Most often it carries an "elitist" sense, co-opted by the later church to designate its "special" people, as, e.g., "Saint Paul." This is about as far removed from biblical usage as one can get. The word also carries a more popular sense, referring to anyone who is well known for godliness or good deeds, as in "my uncle Alton was a real saint." This is a bit closer to the biblical sense, which presupposes such "sanctity" as being common to all who belong to Christ.

adjective;[32] but in the Psalter and elsewhere it becomes a substantive to refer to God's people as such.[33] The preferable translation here and elsewhere in the NT is "God's holy people," which keeps both dimensions of the term intact — believers in Christ as constituting *God's people,* who are by that very fact also called to be his *holy people,*[34] set apart by the Holy Spirit[35] for God's purposes and distinguished as those who manifest his character in the world.[36] Concern that they be God's holy people in Philippi will be picked up throughout the letter (1:10, 11; 2:14-15; 3:17-19; 4:8).

Second, their becoming "God's holy people" is the direct result of their relationship to Christ Jesus; they are "the saints *in Christ Jesus.*"[37] Much has been written on this latter phrase, including the suggestion that there is a kind of "Christ-mysticism" in Pauline usage,[38] but most of that is to push a common phrase much too far.[39] The Philippian believers are "in Christ Jesus" precisely because they are first of all "by Christ Jesus." That is, Christ Jesus is both responsible for their becoming the people of God, and as the crucified and risen One, he constitutes the present sphere of their new existence. They live as those who belong to Christ Jesus, as those whose lives are forever identified with Christ. We have already noted the emphasis on this theme throughout the letter, which becomes predominant both in Paul's reflections on his own life (1:20-23; 3:7-11) and in his affirmations of and exhortations to the Philippians (1:27; 2:1, 5-11; 3:3; 4:7).

32. In the repeated, "you shall be holy, for I the LORD your God am holy."
33. Cf. Ps 16:3 (LXX 15:3), "As for the saints who are in the land"; 34:9 (LXX 33:9), "Fear the Lord, you his saints"; 74:3 (LXX 73:3), "All this destruction the enemy has wrought among your saints." See esp. Dan 7:8, 18, 21, 22. See the helpful discussion by Evans, "New Wine."
34. Thus trying to keep intact both the "ontological" (= people) and "ethical" (= holy) dimension of this term.
35. Although Paul does not make that point here, there can be little question of this connection in his own thinking; see, e.g., the discussions of 1 Thess 4:8; 1 Cor 6:11; and esp. Rom 15:16 in Fee, *Presence,* 50-53, 127-32, 626-27. Cf. Kennedy, 416, on the present text.
36. Lightfoot, 81-82, notes that it was probably the "moral idea" in this word, almost entirely wanting in the word for "sacred" (ἱερός), that led the LXX translators to choose ἅγιος to render the Hebrew word for "holiness."
37. On the possible significance of the word order ("Christ Jesus" instead of "Jesus Christ"), see Kennedy, 415, who sees the order as "strik[ing] the keynote of Paul's attitude toward his Master."
38. An idea first made popular by A. Deissmann in *Formel.* For English readers a succinct overview of his position can be found in *Paul,* 123-35. The idea was carried forward vigorously by W. Bousset in *Kyrios Christos* and esp. by A. Schweitzer, *Mysticism.*
39. Cf. Collange (37): "The long history of interpretation of the Pauline *'en Christo'* is familiar enough, and it is sufficient for the present to say that the *'en'* ('in') has temporal and historical, not spatial, force here."

Third, they are "God's holy people *in Philippi.*"[40] Again, while one can scarcely make much of it here, this becomes another important motif in this letter. In the present instance it is merely descriptive; but in 4:15 he calls them "Philippians" by name, something he rarely does in his letters. In light of the word play on their Roman "citizenship" in 1:27 and 3:20, this is not an insignificant matter. In this bit of Rome located in the province of Macedonia, with its unique history and therefore special devotion to the emperor — as a divine *Kyrios* ("Lord") — the *Philippian believers* in Christ Jesus, by their allegiance to another Lord, are thereby "God's holy people," his elect, in that city.

Beyond these standard expressions, there are two other items in the address that call for special attention. First, the letter is addressed to "*all* the saints . . . in Philippi." As Lightfoot (p. 83) pointed out many years ago, the "studied repetition of the word 'all' in this epistle, when the Philippian Church is mentioned" makes it nearly "impossible not to connect this recurrence of the word with the strong and repeated exhortations to unity which the epistle contains."[41] Thus, this motif appears at the very beginning of the letter, and is frequently repeated throughout the proemium.[42]

Second, and the most striking feature of the salutation, is the addition of the phrase, "with the overseers and deacons."[43] Surprisingly, this is the

---

40. On the geography, history, and sociology of the first century city, see the Introduction, pp. 25-26, and the bibliography cited there.

41. See 1:2, 7 (2x), 8, 25; 2:17; 4:21. For this emphasis see esp. D. Peterlin's dissertation ("Paul's Letter," 29-31), although as with many theses the influence of the element of "disunity" in the letter is overdone, partly because of methodological weaknesses related to "mirror-reading" (see the Introduction, p. 7 n. 24). The only other letters where this word appears in the salutation are Romans (1:4), a letter addressed to a situation where Jew-Gentile relations are at stake, and 2 Corinthians (1:1) in a prepositional phrase that expands the greeting to include "all who are in Achaia."

42. Although one should also observe that in this, its first occurrence, there is no reason to think it emphatic. The emphasis comes in its "studied repetition."

43. For the considerable bibliography on these two words, see the excursus in the commentaries by Lightfoot, 95-99, 181-269; Vincent, 36-51; Gnilka, 32-41; Collange, 37-41; as well as the significant studies on church order in the early church (E. Schweizer, *Church Order;* von Campenhausen, *Ecclesiastical Authority*); cf. Best, "Bishops." Schenk (78-82) has argued against the authenticity of the phrase; but his arguments are circular and ultimately based on subjectivity (a distrust of the titles in such an early letter). The basic objection is that it requires hypothesizing a kind of scribal activity for which there is no analogy (the fact that these words are secure in the entire textual tradition of Philippians and that they were never transported from here to other letters indicates how unlikely it is that a scribe would have created such a phrase here "out of thin air"). Cf. Peterlin's counter-arguments to each of Schenk's points ("Paul's Letter," 27-28). It is equally unlikely that the καί is epexegetic, thus forming a hendiadys (= "overseers who serve"), as Collange (39-40) and Hawthorne (9-10), following Lemaire (*Les ministères,* 96-103), who picked up the suggestion from Chrysostom.

first designation of its kind in Paul's letters;[44] even more surprisingly, after being thus singled out in the address, they are not hereafter spoken to.[45] As with the salutation itself, the letter is always and only addressed to the whole community. Three matters call for further comment.

(1) Even though these titles occur only here and in the Pastoral Epistles in the Pauline corpus, one should not construe this to suggest either that the other Pauline churches did not have such leaders or that this is a later development in his churches. Leaders are singled out for "honor" in the earliest of the letters (1 Thess 5:12-13); it is not conceivable that the other churches did not have them. That there is little or no evidence for a *hierarchy* in the Pauline churches does not mean that *leadership* did not exist; it undoubtedly did, and there is no good reason to think that the titles given here, and found again in 1 Timothy and Titus, did not exist from the beginning.

(2) Exactly as one finds in the earliest (1 Thessalonians) and later (1 Timothy) letters, both references are plural. No evidence exists for a single leader as the "head" of the local assembly in the Pauline churches.[46] The most probable reason for this relates to the role Paul himself played in his churches. Although he was not regularly present with them, they were his churches and owed their existence and obedience to him (cf. 2:12!).

(3) The language used for this addition, "together with/along with,"[47] is the sure giveaway as to the role of leadership in the Pauline churches. The community as a whole is addressed, and in most cases therefore the "overseers and deacons" are simply reckoned as being within the community. When they are singled out, as here, the leaders are not "over" the church, but are addressed "alongside of" the church,[48] as a *distinguishable* part of the whole, but as *part of the whole,* not above or outside it.

44. Because of the predominant view that the Pastoral Epistles are "deutero-Pauline," most would say the "only" such designation in Paul's letters. On the probable authenticity of these letters, see Fee, *1 Timothy,* 23-26; in any case, they are far more Pauline than otherwise. That is, even if "deutero-Pauline," they are in that sense very clearly Pauline, and thus are filled with Pauline themes and concerns. For similar judgments in recent studies, see Towner, *Goal;* Fowl, *Story;* and Kidd, *Wealth.*

On the improbable suggestion made by some (e.g., Houlden, 49; allowed as possible by Hawthorne and O'Brien) that these terms are likely parallel to the "helpers, administrators" of 1 Cor 12:28, see Fee, *First Corinthians,* 621-22; this is to read back into Paul the concerns of a later time and has no basis in either Paul's use of words or his concerns.

45. Another observation that is seldom made in the commentaries. On Schenk's suggestion that these words are a later interpolation see n. 43 above.

46. Although it seems very likely on sociological grounds that the head of the household, the *paterfamilias,* functioned in a similar role of leadership in the house church that met in his or her household as he or she did in the household itself.

47. Gk. σύν, which carries the connotation of "accompaniment, association."

48. Cf. Motyer, 40-41.

But who were these people, and what was their function?

*Overseers.*[49] The origin of the word *episkopos* as a title for one form of leadership in the NT church is shrouded in mystery, and therefore an object of scholarly debate; but there can be little question that in Pauline usage, as with all his designations of church leaders, it first of all denotes a "function," rather than an "office."[50] The first clue to understanding lies with the verb from which it is derived, whose primary meaning is to "visit" in the sense of "looking after" or "caring for" someone.[51] Thus in the speech in Acts 20:28 Paul is reported to urge the Ephesian elders to "give heed to . . . the flock, *among whom* [not 'over whom'] the Holy Spirit has placed you as *episkopoi,* so as to shepherd God's church."[52] While one need not doubt the titular implications of this usage, the accent is on function. And in 1 Timothy 3 and Titus 1, although the concern is with character qualifications, even there they are described as those who "care for God's church" (1 Tim 3:5). The nature of this designation, together with the fact that it occurs in first position,[53] makes it reasonably certain that those who bore this title held the primary

---

49. Gk. ἐπίσκοποι, found here and in 1 Tim 3:2 and Tit 1:7 in Paul; cf. Luke's version of Paul's "speech" in Acts 20:28. Because of the inherent interest both in the term itself and in early church leadership in general, there is a considerable literature on this term. Among many other items, one should note H. W. Beyer, *TDNT,* 2.606-22; L. Coenen, *NIDNTT,* 1.188-92 (further bibliography, 200-201); Lohse, "Entstehung"; J. Rohde, *EDNT,* 2.35-36; Porter, "ἐπίσκοπος"; Stalder, "Episkopos," plus the items noted above (n. 43). For an earlier view, still worth reading, see the excursus in Lightfoot, 181-269.

50. So esp. in the LXX, where it is altogether a "functional" term. See, e.g., Num 4:16 (ἐπίσκοπος; Eleazar, who was "in charge of" the oil); Num 31:14 (those in charge of the army are called "the ἐπίσκοποι of the forces"); Jdgs 9:28 (Zebul, Abimelech's "deputy" [v. 28], is the ἐπίσκοπος of the city). In some more recent literature a septuagintal background has been called into question, finding it instead in Greek usage for governmental supervisors or officials in societies; see Reumann, "Contributions," 449-50 (following E. Dassmann, "Hausgemeinde," and G. Schöllgen, "Hausgemeinden"). This may well be so, especially since it would have been a convenient term to adopt; but the emphasis is all the more on function rather than on title as such.

51. In Greek literature the noun and verb are frequently used to refer to a "god," whose primary function would be to "care for" people. This usage occurs of Christ in 1 Pet 2:25; cf. 1 Clem 59:3 (of God).

52. Lightfoot, 95-99, followed by many others, argued that πρεσβύτεροι ("elders") and ἐπίσκοποι ("overseers") are interchangeable terms. While that is true to a degree — they are almost certainly not coterminous — more likely, on the basis of the evidence in the Pastoral Epistles, "elder" is the broader term that included all people in leadership, including "deacons" (see Fee, *1 Timothy,* 78).

53. Both here and in 1 Timothy. This is further confirmed by the fact that by the second c. it had become the primary title for local, apparently area-wide, leaders. The translation "bishop" derives from this latter usage and should never be used, since it has altogether misleading implications for this plural, which refers to local leaders of some sort.

leadership roles in the local church. They were probably responsible for "caring for the people" in most senses of that term, including administration, hospitality, and pastoral care.

*Deacons.* This is the more difficult term, because Paul uses it in so many different ways. The word itself *(diakonos)* means "servant," and this is its most common usage in Paul. He uses it of Christ (Rom 15:8), of government officials (Rom 13:4), of himself (1 Cor 3:5; 2 Cor 3:6), and of his co-workers (1 Thess 3:2; Col 1:7). In each of these cases, as with "overseer," it is primarily a "functional" term, designating someone who serves others. But in Rom 16:1 Paul uses *diakonos* to refer to Phoebe in a way that seems very close to a title as well, which is certainly the case here — and in 1 Tim 3:8. From our distance it is nearly impossible to know either what their function was or how they are to be distinguished from the "overseers," although it is almost certain that they are. If the functional sense of these terms is also the clue to their titular use, then the "overseers" are probably those who give general oversight to the congregation, while the "deacons" are distinguished by their actual deeds of service.[54]

The ultimate, but finally unanswerable, question is "Why?" Why in this letter are the "overseers and deacons" singled out in the salutation? A recent suggestion relates it to the grumbling and murmuring of 2:14, since in the OT text alluded to in v. 15 these complaints were directed against God through Moses. Thus the leaders are included in the salutation so as to remind the community of their place in Christ.[55] While this is possible, it seems more likely to be related to 4:2-3, where Euodia and Syntyche, who are most likely to be reckoned among these leaders, apparently are not in full accord with each other. Thus, both the "all" with which the address begins and the addition of "with the overseers and deacons" at the end anticipate the problem of friction that has arisen within this community,[56] perhaps within the leadership itself.

54. All of this acutely raises the question of translation, so as not to mislead. Do we use "titles" (such as "deacon" has become in English) or "functional" equivalents, such as "helpers" (as GNB)? The latter would seem preferable, although it is also bland, considering the "servant" implications of the word.

55. See Silva, 144; for other (earlier) suggestions see Meyer, 13, who opts for a much earlier tradition that they had been responsible for seeing that the gift had been collected and transmitted to Paul (cf. *inter alia,* Barth, Beare, Benoit, Martin), which seems to focus on a lesser concern in the letter, and fails to explain why they are not further mentioned in 4:10-20.

56. So also Michael, 6; Collange, 41; Hawthorne, 10; Garland, "Philippians 1:1-26" (although Michael sees the friction as between the congregation and its leaders ["the members wanting in due respect to the officials"], concerning which, one should note, there is not the slightest hint in this letter).

**2** *(C) The Greeting.* The greeting itself has by now become so standard in Paul that the form found in Philippians is precisely that found first in 1 Corinthians and repeated in 2 Corinthians, Romans, Philemon, and Ephesians.[57] Here is a marvelous example of Paul's "turning into gospel" everything he sets his hand to. The traditional greeting in the Hellenistic world was *chairein* — the infinitive of the verb "to rejoice," but in salutations meaning simply "Greetings!" (see Acts 15:23; Jas 1:1). In Paul's hands this now becomes *charis* ("grace"), to which he adds the traditional Jewish greeting *shalom* ("peace,"[58] in the sense of "wholeness" or "well-being").[59] Thus instead of the familiar "greetings," Paul salutes his brothers and sisters in Christ with "grace to you — and peace."[60]

It is worth noting that this is the invariable order of Paul's words, not "grace and peace to you" as in most translations. Very likely there is significance to this order: the grace of God and Christ is what is given to God's people; peace is what results from such a gift. Hence, "grace to you — and peace." In a profound sense this greeting therefore nicely represents Paul's larger theological perspective. The sum total of God's activity toward his human creatures is found in the word "grace"; God has given himself to his people bountifully and mercifully in Christ.[61] Nothing is deserved, nothing can be achieved. The sum total of those benefits as they are experienced by

57. The whole phrase "from God our Father and the Lord Jesus Christ" is missing in 1 Thessalonians; the "our" is missing in 2 Thessalonians and Galatians; "and the Lord Jesus Christ" from Colossians; while "mercy" is added in 1 and 2 Timothy (but not Titus) and the "our" is transferred from God to Christ in the Pastoral Epistles (in Titus "Savior" is substituted for "Lord").

58. Gk. εἰρήνη; on this word see V. Hasler, *EDNT*, 1.394-97; and H. Beck, C. Brown, *NIDNTT*, 2.780-82. It is just possible that, since this Hebrew word had connotations of "well-being" inherent to it, Paul is here using this Jewish greeting as an equivalent of the "health wish" found in many of the papyrus letters (so Russell, "Structure," 298); but one should perhaps also remember that the English "hello" derived from "health to you"! Whether the greeting "shalom" carried with it a wish for health by the time of Paul seems moot, though possible.

59. At the same time, he may also be modifying a Jewish blessing formula (ἔλεος καὶ εἰρήνη, "mercy and peace"), found, e.g., in 2 Bar 78:2 and echoed (in reverse order) in Gal 6:16. This cannot be demonstrated, of course, since Paul could very easily have made his theological point by adopting the blessing without modification. More likely the blessing formula lies in the background, but the modification is the result of his being a man of two worlds, as suggested here.

60. It should perhaps be noted that one cannot be sure that Paul himself is responsible for this "transformation into gospel" of traditional formulas. But his is the earliest evidence for it, and it is quite in keeping with what he does elsewhere; see, e.g., on 4:8 and 4:11-13.

61. Thus the letter also signs off with "the grace of our Lord Jesus Christ be with your spirits."

the recipients of God's grace is "peace,"[62] God's eschatological *shalom,* both now and to come.[63] The latter flows out of the former, and both together flow from "God our Father" and were made effective in our human history through our "Lord Jesus Christ."

The collocation of the Father and Son in such texts as these must not be overlooked.[64] In Pauline theology, whose central concern is "salvation in Christ," God the Father is understood to initiate such salvation,[65] and his glory is its ultimate *raison d'être.* [66] Indeed, God the Father is the subject of nearly all the Pauline "saving" verbs, whose saving action was effected in our human history through Christ the Son.[67] But texts such as this one, where Father and Son are simply joined by the conjunction "and" as equally the source of "grace and peace," and many others as well, make it clear that in Paul's mind the Son is truly God and works in cooperation with the Father and the Spirit for the redemption of the people of God.

Although one hesitates to make too much of a Pauline prescript, the contemporary church fits into this salutation at several key points. Those in roles of primary leadership too easily slip into a self-understanding which pays lip service to their being "slaves of Christ Jesus" but prefers the more honorable sense of this term found in the OT, than in the paradigm either of Christ (in 2:6-8) or of Paul (2:17). Not only so, but the emphasis on *all* of God's *holy* people, *together* with the leaders, could also use some frequent "dusting off" so as to minimize the frequent distance between clergy and people that otherwise exists in the church. *All* of us are "in Christ Jesus"; and all are in Christ Jesus in whatever "Philippi" God has placed us, since contemporary Western culture is no more a friend to grace than theirs was to these early believers. And, finally, as with them, the key to life in Christ in our Philippi lies first of all in our common experience of grace and peace from God our Father provided by Christ our Lord.

---

62. In Paul "peace" can refer in turn to (1) peace with God (= cessation of hostilities), (2) peace within the believing community, (3) inner peace in place of turmoil, and (4) rest or order within a context of worship. Other commentaries express more confidence than I could muster that one can isolate any of these nuances in the Pauline salutations. In the context of greetings to a community it at least includes (1) and (2), and perhaps (3).

63. On the probable eschatological dimension of this word in Paul, see C. H. Giblin, *Hope,* 96.

64. On the (rightly rejected) possibility that Paul means "from God our Father as well as the Father of our Lord Jesus Christ," see Hawthorne, 12.

65. In Philippians see esp. 1:6, 27; 2:9, 13; 3:9.

66. In Philippians see 1:11; 2:11; 4:20.

67. In Philippians see 1:11; 2:8; 3:9-11, 12, 20-21.

## B. THANKSGIVING AND PRAYER (1:3-11)

In all of Paul's letters to churches, except Galatians, either a thanksgiving report or a benediction[1] immediately follows the salutation. But unlike what he does with his salutations, where he modifies and thereby Christianizes a standard formula, Paul's thanksgivings[2] represent a uniquely Christianized *transformation* of, thus substitution for, the common "health wish" that appears as the next item in many ancient letters.[3] These "health wishes," found in the NT only in 3 John 2, are the ancient equivalent of our "I trust this letter finds you well." They tended to take three different forms: a simple wish,[4] a prayer,[5] or a thanksgiving,[6] the latter being the less common. Thanksgivings of the Pauline type — to God, and for people — simply do not occur.[7] But right at the place where the ancients stereotypically wish the health of another, Paul does a radically Christian thing — thank God *for* his friends in Christ,

1. As in 2 Corinthians and Ephesians — although Ephesians contains both a benediction (1:3-14) and thanksgiving (1:15-23). In contrast to the thanksgiving report, in which Paul essentially creates something new in the place of a very stereotyped formula (see the discussion), the benedictions are adaptations of a Jewish liturgical formula (see, e.g., Furnish, *II Corinthians,* 116-17).

2. The Pauline thanksgivings have been subjected to careful investigation twice: Schubert, *Form and Function;* O'Brien, *Thanksgivings.*

3. It is common to refer to Paul's thanksgivings as a Christianized form of ancient thanksgivings as such, but scholarship needs to be more cautious in its use of "formulaic" language. A "thanksgiving" as such rarely occurs either in the literary or papyrus letters; and when they do occur they are simply a variation of the true "formula" — a wish for the recipient's health (see nn. 4 and 5 below). On this matter, see Arzt, "Epistolary Introductory Thanksgiving," who has demonstrated beyond reasonable doubt that such a *formula* in ancient letters is a myth of scholarship, not the reality of the letters themselves.

4. This is the most common form, which occurs over and again in a very stereotyped way, either, "If you are well, it would be wonderful (εἰ ἔρρωσαι, ἔχοι ἂν καλῶς)" or as part of the greeting itself ("greetings and good health"). Cf. the letters collected and commented on in J. L. White, *Light;* a quick thumbing through the collection in Hunt and Edgar (*Select Papyri,* LCL 1.268-395) could also be a good introductory excercise in "form-criticism"!

5. See, e.g., letter 109 in White (*Light,* 173), "Before anything else I pray that you are well; I myself am also well. I make obeisance on your behalf daily before the lord Sarapis"); cf. letters 103A, 103B, 104B, 105, 110, 111; and the variation in letter 64 ("May you always be well, just as I pray").

6. Cf. letter 26 in White (*Light,* 52), "I offer up thanks to all the gods (τοῖς θεοῖς πᾶσιν χάριν ἔχομεν) if you yourself are well."

7. The only thing that remotely represents a thanksgiving can be found, e.g., in letter 103 (White, 159), where Apion, in writing to his father, thanks the lord Sarapis for having been rescued at sea (but that is a different thing from thanking the gods *for* someone). The thanksgiving in letter 115 (p. 182) is in fact a letter of thanksgiving.

both for what God has and is doing in their lives and (in this case) for their partnership with him in the gospel.

Ordinarily, and in Philippians in particular, the content of the thanksgiving anticipates the letter itself.[8] Since thanksgiving is expressed in the context of prayer, Paul sometimes, as here, follows with a further prayer-report,[9] specifying how he prays for them. This, too, anticipates many of the concerns of the letter.

The result is a twofold prayer-report: prayer as thanksgiving — for their partnership in the gospel, in every kind of way; and prayer as petition — for continued fruitfulness in living out the gospel in Philippi. Both reports, which focus on their past and present in Christ, also underscore their certain future: as affirmation of God's work in them (v. 6) and as petition for the same (vv. 10-11).

Since thanksgiving is also part of the reason for the letter, one is not surprised to find the whole replete with expressions of friendship, and especially of the three-way bond — between himself, the Philippians, and Christ and the gospel — that informs every part of the letter.[10] Indeed, in this case several difficulties of interpretation are probably the result of the strong feelings of affection involved — in both directions: the Philippians' for Paul, often expressed in their devotion to the gospel; and his for them, especially as they are the result of, and now co-laborers in, the proclamation of that same gospel. Thus the whole passage abounds with joy and affection, focusing primarily on their role of "partnership in the gospel" — the very stuff of friendship.

Although the prayer report looks as though it might be more formal, a kind of "prayer in general" full of Christian generalities, it too is best understood as case-specific. Paul is concerned throughout the letter with their present behavior, as properly reflecting the effective work of the gospel. Here he reports on his prayer for them in this regard. Thus the thanksgiving and prayer together give expression to Paul's deep affection for them and anticipate his reasons for writing.

8. Cf. Jewett, "Epistolary Thanksgiving," who, however, considerably overstates this reality ("The entire letter as it now stands is the product of the author's intention set forth in the epistolary thanksgiving," 53). Bloomquist (*Function,* 121-23, 145-47) considers this section to be the *exordium* of a piece of "persuasive" rhetoric (see nn. 39 and 42 in the Introduction), but his presentation itself is not persuasive. Unfortunately he lets his prior commitment to "form" dictate his understanding of "meaning" (only by such a predetermination would one note that there are no imperatives in a Pauline thanksgiving [p. 121]!).

9. Cf. 1 Thess 1:2-3 ("We thank God for you . . . as we mention you in our prayers"); Rom 1:8, 9; Phlm 4; Col 1:3; Eph 1:16; 2 Tim 1:3. For prayer reports see 2 Thess 1:11-12; Col 1:9-14; Phlm 6; Eph 1:17-21 (cf. 3:14-19, which I take to be a renewal of the prayer report begun in chap. 1).

10. See the Introduction, pp. 13-14.

## 1. Prayer as Thanksgiving — for Partnership in the Gospel (1:3-8)

3*I thank my God*[11] *every time I remember you.* 4*In all my prayers for all of you, I always pray*[12] *with joy* 5*because of your partnership in the gospel from the first day until now,* 6*being confident of this, that he who began a good work in you will carry it on to completion until the day of Christ Jesus.*[13] 7*It*[14] *is right for me to feel this way about all of you, since I have you in my heart; for whether I am in chains or defending*[15] *and confirming the gospel, all of you share in God's grace with me.*[16] 8*God can testify how I long for all of you with the affection of Christ Jesus.*

In 1 Thess 5:16-18, in a series of staccato imperatives that belong together as a package, Paul urged the Thessalonians to "rejoice continually, pray unceas-

11. The Western tradition (D* F G b Ambst Cass^pt) reads ἐγὼ μὲν εὐχαριστῶ τῷ κυρίῳ ἡμῶν ("I, for my part, thank our Lord"). Although favored by Kennedy (418), Michael (9, following Zahn), and Barth (13), this is a secondary reading on all counts. (1) It is the habit of this tradition to offer idiosyncratic readings; and such a reading, supported only by Western MSS, is highly suspect under any circumstances. (2) The addition of ἐγὼ μέν can easily be accounted for on the twofold basis of the inclusion of Timothy (καὶ Τιμόθεος) in the salutation and the first person singular verb (εὐχαριστῶ) with which the thanksgiving begins. (3) Although it is true that the "more difficult reading" is usually to be preferred, this is a case where the reading is simply too difficult; Paul never elsewhere offers thanks "to our Lord" (cf. Collange, 43).

12. In order to clarify the difficult compounding of phrases and participles in this sentence, some MSS (F G Ψ 2495 pc) have inserted a καί between μετὰ χαρᾶς and τὴν δέησιν ποιούμενος. The resultant text is probably to be understood as supporting the punctuation of the NA^26 (followed by the NIV), thus making an independent clause of the insertion, "also making my prayer with joy."

13. A considerable number of significant MSS have the reverse word order, "Jesus Christ" (א A F G K P 33 81 104 365 614 1175 1739 1881 2464 pc). The text is read by P^46 B D Ψ Maj lat. This is a tough call. The external evidence is rather evenly divided; and one can make a good case on internal grounds for either: the order "Christ Jesus" predominates in this letter, and in the thanksgiving in particular. Did Paul use this predominant form, which scribes then changed either accidentally or to conform to another usage with which they were familiar? Or, as seems more likely to me, did Paul himself here write the less usual "Jesus Christ," which scribes then conformed to the usage in v. 1 and v. 8?

14. The NIV, following NA^26 (but not UBS^3), has vv. 7-8 as a separate paragraph. Although this represents a common position, these verses are better understood as a continuation of the sentence that began in v. 3 (see the discussion below).

15. A few MSS omit the ἐν which here precedes τῇ ἀπολογίᾳ, thus making a three-member prepositional phrase ("in my bonds and defense and confirmation of the gospel"). This is patently secondary. Paul's prepositions suggest a two-sided reality: "in my chains" and "in the defense and confirmation of the gospel."

16. See n. 86 below for comment on the NIV's handling of this complex set of clauses.

ingly, and give thanks in all circumstances," for these constitute one dimension of God's will for his people. Paul is as good as his word. Not only does this combination appear elsewhere in 1 Thessalonians (3:9-10), but now in a Roman prison, with possible trouble brewing on the Philippian horizon, Paul again gives evidence that prayer, thanksgiving, and joy go together in a kind of indissoluble union.

In modern translations the thanksgiving is often broken into two parts, sometimes into two paragraphs (vv. 3-6, 7-8; cf. NIV). In fact, however, this is a single (especially difficult and convoluted) sentence in Paul's Greek.[17] The difficulties are basically three: (1) how to make sense of the compounding of clauses and phrases in vv. 3-5; (2) to determine how vv. 6-8 fit in as part of the thanksgiving; and (3) to determine the direction of the "remembrance" in v. 3 (whether Paul's toward them or theirs toward him).[18] A word about each of these will give perspective to the whole passage.

1. The difficulties of the first three verses can best be shown by a very literal, "interlinear" kind of presentation of the Greek-English equivalents, in which each word or phrase is marked off by a diagonal:

> I thank my God / at *(epi)* every remembrance (of you/your) / always / in every prayer of mine / for all of you / with joy / the prayer making / for *(epi)* your fellowship / in the gospel / from the first day / until now . . .

The problem, besides determining the direction of the remembrance, is to resolve the function of the modifiers in relationship to each other and to the main verb ("I give thanks"). Although one cannot have final certainty, both Pauline usage elsewhere and the particular concerns of this letter suggest that the best approach is to consider this material as consisting of two parts, each controlled by the two verbs ("give thanks" and "making my prayers"), each of which is immediately modified by an *epi* ("at/for/on the basis of") prepositional phrase.[19] The result is two clauses that look something like this:

> I thank my God
>     in all my remembrance (of you)

17. Despite breaking it into two paragraphs (n. 14), the NIV has otherwise done a good piece of work in bringing some degree of order to the sentence.

18. Some scholars would add the similar apparent ambiguity in v. 7 regarding who is whose heart. But as noted there (n. 83), that has been satisfactorily resolved on grounds of grammar (usage).

19. Similarly, Kennedy, Michael, Lohmeyer, Hawthorne, Silva, Melick, thus taking v. 5 to be primarily expressing the reason for his joy in prayer and thanksgiving. Others (e.g., Lightfoot, Gnilka, Martin, O'Brien, Omanson ["Note"]; cf. RSV) take v. 4 as parenthetical, understanding v. 5 therefore as further dependent of the main verb ("I thank my God for you [. . .] for you participation . . .").

always in every prayer of mine for all of you
(I make) my prayer with joy
    for your participation in the gospel
    from the first day until now[20]

The two clauses, it should be noted further, thus express two primary matter of friendship: his affection for them and their partnership in the gospel.[21]

2. This last matter (friendship) also helps to explain the mild digression in vv. 6 and 7. Remembrance of their past and present participation in the gospel through thick and thin encourages Paul to express confidence that God will continue his larger work in them to the very end.[22] That in turn causes him to offer the *reasons* both for his confidence (v. 6) and for his gratitude and joy (vv. 3-5), with a clause that begins, "just as it is right for me to think this about you all." The reasons are two, corresponding precisely to those expressed in vv. 3-5. So deep is his affection that he concludes in v. 8 by calling on God himself to bear witness to it. At the same time, the content of v. 7 also especially anticipates some items that are to follow (his bonds and the defense of the gospel in 1:12-26, and his longing for them, especially in light of some mild differences among them, spoken to in 1:27–2:18 and 4:1-3). The petition report (vv. 9-11) flows readily out of these final matters in v. 7. The net result is a kind of (conceptual) chiastic arrangement:

    A      I thank God at all my remembrance of you (personally)
      B     I pray with joy because of your fellowship in the gospel
        C    I am convinced God will keep this going until the end
      B′    I have every right to this confidence because I have you in
              my heart and because of your fellowship in the gospel
    A′    God is my witness as to my deep longing for you all

3. This analysis further suggests that since the phrase in question in v. 3 (whose remembrance of whom) lies within a context of his expressing

---

20. Since the second clause is grammatically dependent on the former, however, the whole should be thought of as on a continuum: thanksgiving and joyful prayer happen together, which include his grateful remembrance of them and his joy in that remembrance occasioned by their long-time association in the cause of the gospel. Cf. Silva, who (rightly) notes that "the ambiguities, touching no matter of substance, probably did not even occur to Paul" (44), and "how easy it is for Paul to shift or readjust his thought in the middle of a sentence" (48). His further caution against interpreters making far too much out of very little is wisely taken.

21. See the Introduction, pp. 12-14.

22. See especially the strong future orientation of so much in the letter (cf. the Introduction, p. 30).

affection for them, this matter is best settled, as with the NIV, as flowing from him toward them — although this will need the more careful investigation given below.

Thus thanksgiving and petition blend in Paul, resulting in a combined thanksgiving/prayer-report: offered to God with joy because of their long-term, and now recently expressed, partnership in the gospel, and based on his confidence in God's work among them and full of deep affection for them.

**3** Paul begins with his standard formula of thanksgiving, "I thank my God."[23] Thanksgiving and prayer in Paul are always directed toward God. The "my," which occurs in each of his thanksgivings where the verb is singular,[24] denotes personal relationship. The expression has its roots in the OT, especially the Psalter, where "the God of our fathers" is addressed over and again as "the Lord, *my* God." On the one hand, of course, "my God" refers to the only God there is, who is therefore God over all; on the other hand, this God had arrested Paul and made him his own (cf. 3:12). Hence on the basis of divine election, God is "my God" in a very personal way, the One in whom Paul puts his trust and the One whom alone he serves.[25]

What follows this standard formula has most of the elements found in Paul's other thanksgivings; but they are now expressed just differently enough to produce some ambiguity for us. Ordinarily the next element is the adverb "always,"[26] followed by "for you."[27] Three things happen here that generate our difficulties: (1) these two elements are in reverse order; (2) the usual preposition *peri* ("concerning/for") is replaced by *epi* ("on/at"), which can mean either "on the basis of = because of" or "on the occasion of"; and (3) instead of simply thanking God "for you," he thanks God "*epi* every remembrance of you," which theoretically could mean either "at all my remembrance *of you*" or "because of *your* every remembrance."[28]

---

23. The formula appears in 1 Thess 1:2; 1 Cor 1:4; Rom 1:8; Col 1:3; Phlm 4. In 2 Thess 1:3 and 2:13 there is the slight alteration to "we are bound to give thanks to God."

24. That is, in 1 Cor 1:4; Rom 1:8; Phlm 4; and here — which also explains the variant reading in 1 Cor 14:18. Whenever the verb is plural, "we thank," the possessive is missing. The phrase "my God" also occurs in 4:19 and 2 Cor 12:21.

25. Cf. Acts 27:23 ("whose I am and whom I serve"). The contrast between this expression of personal relationship and the more general expressions of piety in the contemporary Greco-Roman letters is especially striking. See the illustrations in nn. 5 and 6 above.

26. Gk. πάντοτε, which is missing in Rom 1:8 (but is picked up in the resumption of the thanksgiving in v. 10).

27. Gk. περὶ [πάντων] ὑμῶν. The "all" occurs in 1 Thess 1:2 and Rom 1:8.

28. The alleged ambiguity lies with the genitive ὑμῶν, which technically could be either "objective" or "subjective." But as noted below, there is no known instance of the combination of this noun with a personal pronoun in the genitive where it is not an objective genitive.

77

These differences are just enough to cause some scholars to think that Paul intends the latter, "because of your every remembrance [of me],"[29] occasioned by their recent gift sent with Epaphroditus (2:25, 30; 4:10, 18). What favors this view primarily — singularly, some would say — is the appearance of *epi,* which in a similar situation in 1 Cor 1:4 most likely means "on the basis of."[30] Since this same preposition recurs in v. 5 below, where it clearly means "because of," it is argued that in contrast to his other thanksgivings, Paul begins by immediately thanking God for their "renewed concern" for him (cf. 4:10). This view, it is argued further, also eliminates an otherwise awkward "accumulation of temporal phrases in direct succession,"[31] as well as explains why there is no mention of the gift until 4:10.[32]

Despite the apparent cogency of these arguments, however, the traditional view has the better of it by far. The most significant consideration is linguistic: In Greek, verbs and nouns denoting "memory" take the genitive as their object; thus the normal reading of the combination "remembrance[33] of you" would be as an "objective" genitive. Indeed, in the other occurrences

29. This view was adopted, *inter alia,* by T. Zahn, A. Harnack, Ewald, Kennedy, Schubert (*Form and Function,* 74), Martin, O'Brien, Jewett ("Epistolary Thanksgiving," 53), Garland ("Defense," 329-30), Reumann ("Contributions," 441); Peterman ("Giving," 108-14); Houlden is open to it. O'Brien (58-61; cf. *Thanksgivings,* 41-46) presents the most significant case for this view. The only English translation known to me which adopts it is Moffatt ("I thank my God for all your remembrance of me"), which, however, is argued against by Michael in the Moffatt NT Commentary. The traditional view is adopted, *inter alia,* by Meyer, Lightfoot, Plummer, Robertson, Müller, Barth, Beare, Hendriksen, Lohmeyer, Gnilka, Collange, Bruce, Hawthorne, Silva, Melick (in some cases [Plummer, Beare, Lohmeyer, Melick] without discussion). N. Turner (*Insights,* 91) suggests that Paul is intentionally ambiguous, which is unlikely. When authors *are* ambiguous (from our point of view, as here), they usually do not intend to be; their intent, after all, is perfectly clear to themselves (which is why authors have editors!).

30. See, e.g., Martin, 64, who makes this comparison the primary reason, not noting how many — and more significant — *dis*similarities with the other thanksgivings such an interpretation imposes on the present text. See further n. 37 below.

31. O'Brien, *Thanksgivings,* 45.

32. Cf. esp. Martin; but that is not quite so, since their gift seems to be a first point of reference in v. 5 (q.v.), not to mention its being alluded to in 2:25 and 30.

33. Gk. μνεία, which occurs only in Paul in the NT (1 Thess 1:2; 3:6; Rom 1:9; Phlm 4; Eph 1:16; 2 Tim 1:3), thus six times in his thanksgivings. In the other instances in Paul's thanksgivings, it means something very close to "mention," i.e., to "remember" by "mentioning." It can perhaps mean that here as well (BAGD, Hawthorne), although in the other cases it means "mention" in conjunction with the participle ποιούμενος (= "making mention"). But the word is used in 1 Thess 3:6, as here without the participle, in the sense of "to remember," where Paul unambiguously says, "*you* always have good remembrance *of us.*" One should also note this usage in hellenistic letters; e.g., Apion (Antoninus Maximus) to his sister Sabina (2nd c. CE): "making mention of you (μνείαν σου ποιούμενος) before the gods here" (White, *Light,* 160).

of this noun *(mneia)* with a genitive in biblical Greek, the genitive is almost always the object of the remembering or mentioning,[34] and invariably so in all known Greek when the genitive, as here, is a personal pronoun.[35] Besides, to think otherwise in this case is simply against all analogy, since in his other thanksgivings Paul regularly[36] thanks God in some way *for* the recipients of his letter, and the "remembrance" motif in his thanksgivings invariably refers to his memory of them.[37]

Finally, even if the phrase truly were ambiguous, in light of his deep feelings for them elaborated in vv. 7-8, it simply makes more sense of the flow of Paul's thought to see this unusually expressed phrase to be the equivalent of his usual "for you," in this case as a slight elaboration of it. Thus, on the occasion of "all[38] of his remembrance of them," triggered most recently

---

34. In the LXX, Job 14:13; Ps 110(111):4; Wis 5:14; Zech 13:2; Isa 23:16; Jer 38(31):20; Bar 4:27; 5:5; Ezek 21:32(37); 25:10. In the NT, Rom 1:9; Eph 1:16 (v.l.); 1 Thess 1:2 (v.l.); 3:6; Phlm 4. The passage in Bar 5:5, τῇ τοῦ θεοῦ μνείᾳ, is the only subjective genitive, made so in this case by the "enclosed genitive" and the repeated definite article. That is scarcely analogous to the usage here.

35. In light of the linguistic data, one should also note the role of orality in a matter like this. Both in Paul's dictation and in their hearing, his remembering them is the only possible sense. There would be no "marker" in the text that would cause them to go back and "rehear" it in a reversed way.

36. Philemon is the lone exception.

37. There are further supporting reasons for the standard interpretation: (1) In two cases where Paul remembers his converts while in prayer, he also, as here, uses the preposition ἐπί in conjunction with "making remembrance," where it can only mean "*on the occasion of* my prayers." It does not help to argue, as some do, that when this preposition accompanies the verb "to give thanks," it tends to mean "on the basis of," because it may just as easily mean, as it almost certainly does here, "I give thanks *on the occasion of* my every remembrance of you." (2) This view in fact creates a most unusual Pauline thanksgiving, namely that "*always,* in *my every prayer* for *you all,*" what I thank God for is your gift to me! While remotely possible conceptually, such a view is contrary to all analogy. (3) Most significant is a point of grammar seldom noted. If "you" were the "subject" of the verbal idea in "remembrance," that leaves the phrase *without an object at all.* Whereas that might seem remotely possible, it founders in this case precisely because the otherwise unexpressed object must be carried over *from the preceding phrase,* where Paul is the *subject.* To put this another way, since by any reading of the text, a reference to Paul must be carried over from the opening clause, the natural implication is that the *subject* is unexpressed in the ensuing phrase precisely because it would be understood to be *the same as the subject of the sentence.* The alleged ambiguity, therefore, exists only because the normal reading of the sentence is circumvented.

38. Gk. πάσῃ τῇ μνείᾳ, which technically means "all the" (with the implication that he remembers them "all the time"), rather than "every time." But there is good reason to doubt whether this differentiation can be unswervingly sustained during the *koine* period. Paul is very likely intending his "all the" to be all embracing; but in reality the remembrance of them happened from time to time, especially in prayer. Cf. Silva, 49.

by their gift, to be sure, he thanks God *for* his beloved Philippian sisters and brothers in Christ. The *basis* of the thanksgiving will be given in the second *epi* phrase (in v. 5) — their past and present partnership in the gospel. Paul, after all, rarely thanks God for "things"; his thanksgivings are for people, for those special "gifts" whom God has brought into his life, who, despite whatever frustration or grief they may also cause him, are invariably a source of great joy and thanksgiving. Here, I would offer, is a beginning point for understanding the nature of Pauline spirituality.[39]

**4** It is also Paul's habit not only to note that he thanks God *for* his friends, but also (a) that he does so *regularly* ("always") and (b) that such thanksgiving is a regular part of his *praying* for them. Having reminded the Philippians of his thanksgiving for them at all times, he now turns to these other matters.[40] But in so doing he compounds phrases in a way that makes the rest of this opening clause (through v. 5) particularly awkward.

First, he reminds them that he "always" gives thanks for them when praying for them. This does not mean that he offers unceasing thanksgiving, but that he does so continually — over and again. On every occasion when he remembers them in prayer he always does so first with thanksgiving.

Second, his thanksgiving takes place in the context of "*all my prayers*[41] for all of you." That is, on every occasion that he petitions God on their behalf, he does so with thanksgiving. It is difficult to get around the significance of this collocation for our understanding Paul as a person of the Spirit.[42] Not only is he a man of prayer, but a man whose prayer is as filled with thanksgiving as with petition, and whose thanksgiving is for God's people, for whom Paul himself feels deep and passionate longing.

Third, his prayer and thanksgiving are for "all of you." We have already noted (in v. 1) the possible significance of this emphasis in Philippians,

---

39. Cf. Fee, "Pauline Spirituality." The point is that gratitude expressed by way of thanksgiving is the beginning point, the proper stance of humility before God for his grace; in recognizing his congregations both as belonging to God, not to himself, and as God's "gifts" to him, he is thus set free to thank God for them — for all of them.

40. Because of the ἐπί in v. 5, many see this material (v. 4) as parenthetical, but that seems to miss what Paul is up to. See the introductory discussion of this paragraph (and n. 19).

41. Gk. ἐν πάσῃ δεήσει (lit. "in every prayer," which the NIV makes plural, "all my prayers"). This is one of only two occurrences of δέησις in the Pauline thanksgivings (cf. 2 Tim 1:3). Ordinarily he uses the close synonym προσευχή, which is the more general word for prayer (of all kinds). In biblical Greek δέησις is almost always directed toward God and carries the narrower sense of supplication or intercession. It occurs again in 4:6 in combination with προσευχή and "thanksgiving."

42. On this matter, see Fee, "Pauline Spirituality." Granted the Spirit is not mentioned, but prayer for Paul is especially an activity of the Spirit in the believer's life (see Fee, *Presence,* 866-68).

where some posturing is apparently under way that has all the possibility of leading to real division among them. Thus, in this letter, Paul's "all of you" includes *both* Euodia and Syntyche, not to mention everyone else.

Fourth, the combination of "every prayer of mine" and "for all of you" triggers yet another reminder, that when he does offer up prayer for them, now meaning "petition," he does so with joy. Whatever else the Philippians meant to Paul, they were for him a cause of great joy. This little phrase, however, also creates the awkward repetitions in this clause.[43] The word order ("with joy the prayer making") gives this phrase special emphasis; indeed this is the first of 16 occurrences of this word group ("joy") in the letter. While this may not be as dominant a motif in the letter as some contend, it is a recurring motif, and can scarcely be missed. The very awkwardness of the phrase in this case forces it upon the Philippians' — and our — attention.

Joy, it should be noted, which occurs only here in the Pauline thanksgivings, lies at the heart of the Christian experience of the gospel; it is the fruit of the Spirit in any truly Christian life, serving as primary evidence of the Spirit's presence (Gal 5:22; Rom 14:17). Precisely because this is so, joy transcends present circumstances; it is based altogether on the Spirit, God's way of being present with his people under the new covenant. Hence joy prevails for Paul even in prison; he will urge that it prevail for the Philippians as well in their present suffering in the face of opposition.

Here, then, is the paradigm of Pauline spirituality: thanksgiving and prayer, filled with joy, on behalf of *all* of God's people in Philippi. See further on 4:4-7.

**5** But Paul's thanksgiving is not finished. Verses 3-4 focused on the Philippian believers themselves. Having just mentioned that his petitions on their behalf — for *all* of them — are filled with joy, he now offers a brief word as to the basis of[44] his joy, which also serves as further reason for his thanksgiving.[45] The reason is expressed in terms of their *koinōnia* in the spread of[46] the gospel and focuses on the long, enduring nature of their participation/partnership.

---

43. That is, Paul has already mentioned his standard "thanksgiving for you always in every prayer of mine." By adding the phrase "with joy," he feels compelled to note that the joy comes in the context of "his every prayer." Thus he repeats, "the prayer making," all of which means, "thanking God for you always in every prayer of mine for all of you, making that prayer with joy."

44. Gk. ἐπί, which is not quite causal in the strictest sense, i.e., that their participation in the gospel causes his joy, but in the sense that it serves as a basis for such joy and thanksgiving.

45. Cf. Collange, 44, and Silva, 44-45, who also see v. 5 as offering the reason for his joy and thanksgiving together.

46. Gk. εἰς, here with the sense of "unto," i.e., "with the furtherance of the gospel in view." Cf. ASV ("in furtherance of the gospel"), GNB ("in the work of the gospel");

It does not take much reading of Paul's letters to recognize that the gospel is the singular passion of his life; that passion is the glue that in particular holds this letter together.[47] By "the gospel," especially in Philippians, Paul refers primarily neither to a body of teaching nor to proclamation. Above all, the gospel has to do with Christ, both his person and his work. To preach Christ (vv. 15-16) is to preach the gospel, which is all about Christ; to preach the gospel is to proclaim God's good news of salvation that he has effected in Christ. As elsewhere, "Christ" and "the gospel" are at times nearly interchangeable. Living "worthy of the gospel of Christ" in 1:27, therefore, means to live worthy of Christ as he has been made known and proclaimed in the gospel which has him as its focus and content. Thus Paul's joy in prayer is prompted by their "partnership *for (the furtherance of) the gospel.*"

The rest of the thanksgiving is an elaboration of Paul's and their mutual relationship with Christ in the gospel — Paul's as a prisoner in the defense and vindication of the gospel, theirs as partners with him in the spread of the gospel, expressed both in their gift and in their living out the truth of the gospel in Philippi. But the present focus is on the Philippians' *long-time association* with Paul *in the gospel,* thus "your participation/partnership[48] toward the advance of the gospel from the first day until now."[49] Determining the precise sense of *koinōnia* in this clause, however, is not as easy as recognizing its role in the argument. Although this word is usually translated into English as "fellowship," its primary referent is to *participating in* something, rather than to sharing something in common with others.[50] At the least,

---

NAB ("helped promote the gospel"). On the significance of this preposition with the noun κοινωνία, see n. 50 below.

47. The noun εὐαγγέλιον, which occurs 9 times in this letter, is thus mentioned far more frequently (in terms of occurrences per hundred words) in Philippians than in any of the other letters in the corpus (there are also 9 occurrences in Romans, plus two occurrences of the verb; but Romans is four times longer than Philippians).

48. Gk. κοινωνία; the word group appears six times in this letter (1:7; 2:1; 3:10; 4:14, 15).

49. This clear shift in focus, not to mention the word order itself, is what makes altogether unlikely the possibility suggested by Silva (45, but correctly not adopted) that this phrase refers to v. 3.

50. At least this seems to be true for the most part, and especially when it is accompanied by a genitive as in v. 7, 2:1, and 3:10. Cf. J. Hainz (*EDNT,* 2.304): "The neutral rendering, 'participant,' 'participate,' 'participation,' is overwhelmingly preferred [to its religious character in Pauline usage]." But in the two other cases in Paul where this word is followed by the preposition εἰς (2 Cor 9:13; Rom 15:26), it refers to the collection for the poor in Jerusalem, and means something close to "participation" in the sense of "contributing unto them." For bibliography, see Fee, *First Corinthians,* 466 n. 18. Hawthorne, 19, argues that the use of εἰς here supports the view that their gift to Paul is primarily in mind. While I do not doubt, esp. in light of the verb in 4:15, that this passage

therefore, its basic sense is "*participation* in the spread of the gospel."[51] But since that "participation" is expressly linked in v. 7 to Paul's own work in the gospel, very likely in this clause it carries the further connotation of their "participation" in "*partnership* with Paul" in the advance of the gospel.[52]

But what specifically does Paul have in mind by this reference to their "participation/partnership in the gospel"? In light of 4:15-16, especially the language "at the beginning of the gospel . . . you *participated* in the matter of giving and receiving," this phrase at least refers to their sharing with him of their material means as he is imprisoned for the sake of the gospel.[53] This is corroborated further by the collocation of these two words (*koinōnia* and gospel) in 2 Cor 9:15 with specific reference to the Corinthian — and Macedonian — participation in the offering for the poor saints in Jerusalem.[54]

On the other hand, the much broader concern for their relationship to the gospel that permeates this letter makes it difficult to believe that Paul was referring exclusively to their partnership with him by means of their gift.[55] Although Paul is truly grateful for this very tangible participation in his

---

*includes* their gift, Paul's language does not suggest that their gift to him is the first, or even primary, referent. The εἰς functions quite differently here than it does in 2 Cor 9:13 and Rom 15:26, where it points to the people who benefit from the "participation" in the fund for the the poor. Here it is telic pure and simple; the advance of the gospel — not a gift to Paul — is the goal of their "participation."

51. One should note at this point, what will become clear as the letter unfolds, that inherent to Paul's understanding of "the gospel" is the notion of evangelism (see the Introduction, p. 47; cf. vv. 12, 27). Hence it is difficult not to see evangelism as inherent in this phrase as well.

52. Indeed, the compound <u>συγ</u>κοινωνούς in v. 7, repeated in its verb form in 4:14, is the clue to its present focus (cf. n. 87). The σύν implies their joint participation in the same reality; Paul and the Philippians have not only together experienced the benefits of the gospel, but have mutually shared in its proclamation and in (present) suffering for its sake.

53. On the much larger issue of how Paul supported himself, see the discussion below on 4:15-16.

54. Cf. in this regard the use of κοινωνία to refer to the collection itself in Rom 15:26.

55. But see Plummer, 9; Robertson, 61; Martin, 65; Silva, 46-47, who tend to limit it to this concern (see Meyer, 17, for earlier scholars who took this position). Likewise difficult to sustain are those interpretations that see the usage as general here, without specific reference to their gift (e.g., Seesemann, Lohmeyer, Gnilka, Panikulam). On Sampley's view that κοινωνία is here a Greek equivalent for a "consensual *societas*" (legal partnership for a common purpose), see n. 4 on 4:14-17. Besides lacking hard linguistic evidence for this equation (cf. the critique in Peterman, "Giving," 230-31), Sampley seems to have it quite backward in suggesting that Paul's preaching of the gospel beyond Macedonia is "as the representative of the Macedonians." To the contrary, Paul says in 1:7 and 4:14 that the Philippians are participants *with him* in the gospel. They are involved in *his* ministry, not he in theirs.

defense of the gospel in Rome, his greater concern in this letter is *with the gospel in Philippi.* This is the "partnership" in the gospel that concerns him. Indeed, in what follows (1:12-26) he refers to his present situation in a semi-paradigmatic way,[56] himself rejoicing over the further proclamation of the gospel *in Rome* (1:15-18), which joy he wants them to bring to completion by getting their act together in Philippi (2:2). He further urges their prayer for the Spirit in his behalf so that Christ alone will be magnified when he stands trial there (1:20); but all of this so that he might urge them both to proclaim and to live in keeping with the gospel *in Philippi.* Thus he urges them to "live out their [heavenly] citizenship [in Philippi] in a way that is *worthy of the gospel*" and thus to "contest as one person [in Philippi] for the 'faith *of the gospel*' " (1:27). Similarly in 2:15-16 he wants them to be blameless in their conduct as they "hold fast the *word of life*" in the "crooked and depraved generation" in which they are thus to "shine like stars in the world." So also the prayer report that follows this thanksgiving is expressed in terms of their being "filled with the fruit of righteousness that comes through Jesus Christ" (v. 11).

In light of all of this, the best understanding of "your *koinōnia* in the gospel" is that which takes the word first of all in its "neutral" sense to refer to their participation in spreading the gospel itself, in every possible way, which in particular includes their recent partnership in the gospel by sending him a gift while he is imprisoned for the defense of the gospel.

This understanding of *koinōnia* seems further substantiated by the phrase, "from the first day until now," which refers neither to the patronage he received while living and preaching Christ in Philippi (cf. Acts 16:15) nor to their early participation in material support when he first left Philippi (referred to below in 4:15-16)[57] — although it very likely includes the latter. The gospel itself is Paul's first concern here, not his material support; hence he is most likely referring to their participation in the advance of the gospel that stems from the time of their conversion. In light of v. 6, this might even include their "participation" by themselves having responded to the gospel and thus becoming Christ's people in Philippi.[58] But it would especially include their involvement in sharing the gospel with others.[59] This, then, is the most probable sense of their "participation/partnership in the gospel *from*

---

56. On this matter see the Introduction, pp. 11-12; cf. the introduction to 1:12-26 and comments throughout that passage.

57. So Lightfoot, 83; Hawthorne, 20.

58. Cf. Peterman ("Giving," 118): "This active participation (working to propagate the gospel message) presupposes static participation (receiving the gospel message)."

59. Indeed, in 4:2-3 he refers back to his time in Philippi, when Euodia, Syntyche, Clement, and the rest "contended by my side *in the gospel.*"

*the first day.*" Every word spoken and every deed done in behalf of the gospel from the moment of their conversion(s) to the present, including their gift to Paul, are thus "your partnership in the furtherance of the gospel *from the first day until now.*" That this is Paul's primary intent seems corroborated by the otherwise curious participial clause that follows (v. 6).

**6** This next clause is so familiar that its place in the immediate, as well as the larger, context of Philippians is easily overlooked, especially since it is not at once clear as to how it functions in the present sentence. Some scholars, to be sure, have gone the other direction, placing it in context in a very narrow sense — the "good work" referring specifically to the Philippians' material support of Paul that God will continue to perform through them.[60] The clause is best understood, however, in terms of their relationship to Christ and the gospel in the broader sense argued for in v. 5. Its language and grammar also support such a view. First, then, some words about *what* is said, followed by some observations about context.

The clause begins with another participle, "having been persuaded" (= being confident), whose link to what precedes is more conceptual than grammatical. The clue to its place in the sentence lies in the final words of v. 5, "from the first day until now."[61] "Not only so," Paul now adds in a somewhat digressive way, "but I am likewise persuaded that the good work God began in you, in terms of your long-term partnership in the gospel in every possible way, he will bring to glorious consummation at the end, when Christ returns."

But despite this grammatical connection to what *precedes,* Paul's emphasis rests on what he is *about to say*: "being confident," he thus digresses momentarily, "of *this very thing.*"[62] His confidence is that their lifelong

---

60. E.g., Hawthorne, 29 (Plummer, 11, and Martin, 65, who take the narrower view of v. 5, abandon it here).

61. Grammatically, it could be dependent either on the main verb, "I give thanks," or on the preceding participle, "making my prayer." Although a case can be made for either of these, most likely it is dependent on the preceding participle in a rather loose way. Thus Paul is neither offering yet another reason for thanksgiving (as, e.g., O'Brien) or offering an additional reflection on what happens to him when he prays and thanks God for them (as, e.g., Vincent), but while keeping his sentence going by means of a participle, he is actually offering further — theological — reflection on the immediately preceding phrase "from the first day till now." Cf. Meyer, 18, who sees the confidence as "accompanying" the thanksgiving.

62. Gk. αὐτὸ τοῦτο (lit., "this same thing"), an emphatic combination stressing "this very thing" that has been or is about to be mentioned. In this case, the ὅτι that follows makes it clear that it points forward. Cf. 2 Cor 2:3; 7:11; Col 4:8; Eph 6:22, all of which point forward with similar constructions. *Contra* Meyer, 18-19, who, on the analogy of Gal 3:10, argues that it means "for this very reason" and refers to their participation in the gospel in v. 5.

participation in the gospel, "from the beginning until now," will continue until the day of Christ. But this confidence has very little to do with them and everything to do with God, who both "began" a good work in them and will "bring it to completion[63] at[64] the day of Christ." Thus, having reminded them of *his* own joy over their good past and present, he turns now to assure them of *their* own certain future.

The "day of Christ Jesus" is the eschatological goal of present life in Christ. Paul, and perhaps the early church before him, took up the term "day of the Lord" from the OT to refer to the Parousia, the (now second) coming of Christ.[65] Paul thus uses the term in his earliest letters,[66] and frequently thereafter.[67] While at times the term may emphasize the aspect of judgment inherent in its OT usage, much more often the emphasis in Paul is on the eschatological consummation that has Christ's coming — and therefore his final exaltation and glorification, including those who are his — as its central focus. This is the "not yet" of salvation that Christ has "already" secured and the Spirit appropriated in the life of the believer. Thus the focus, as everywhere in Paul, is on Christ; whatever else the final wrap-up entails, it is *Christ's* day above all.

Although it is not certain to what precisely Paul is pointing with the language "good work," it is unlikely that he is referring exclusively to their grace of giving,[68] since one would then have expected him to say "good work

63. Gk. ἐναρξάμενος . . . ἐπιτελέσει. For this way of talking about the present and future of salvation in Christ, as evidenced by the life of the Spirit, see Gal 3:3. The same confidence about the future, predicated on the work of Christ in the present, can also be found in the thanksgiving in 1 Cor 1:4-9, but with different vocabulary.

64. Gk. ἄχρι, which normally does not mean "at" (Paul always uses temporal ἐν for this nuance; e.g., 1 Cor 1:8), but "until." The usage here is dictated first of all by its appearance in the preceding clause; hence: "from the first day *until now*," which in turn is related to the "good work that God is also doing in your lives (lit., among you) and will continue to do *until the day* of Christ's coming." The obvious implication of the two verbs ("began" and "will bring to completion") is that the latter will be fully realized "*at* the day of Christ," although it is obviously understood that there is an ongoing process *until* the day of his coming." Cf. the unique use of εἰς ἡμέραν Χριστοῦ in 1:10 and 2:16, which probably = "*for* the day of Christ," thus reflecting the same "already but not yet" sense that this phrase does.

65. The "Lord" in the OT phrase now understood as referring to Christ — another subtle but significant expression of a very high Christology (cf. the final comment on v. 2). See the Introduction, pp. 49-50.

66. See esp. 1 Thess 5:2 (4); 2 Thess 2:2 (cf. 1:10).

67. See 1 Cor 1:8; 5:5; 2 Cor 1:14; and 1:10 and 2:16 in our letter. So also the shortened form "the day" in 1 Cor 3:13; Rom 2:16; 13:12; and "that day" in 2 Thess 1:10; 2 Tim 1:12, 18; 4:8 (cf. "day of wrath," Rom 2:5; "day of redemption," Eph 4:30).

68. See n. 55 above.

*through* you."[69] The accent instead is on what God is doing *in* (or "among") them, not what he is doing *through* them. Most likely, therefore, the term points to their "salvation in Christ,"[70] and in this case is yet another way of speaking about their "participating in the gospel" — not so much about their sharing it, but about their experiencing it and living it out in Philippi.[71] Thus with this theological affirmation in the thanksgiving, that God has begun and will complete his "good work" of salvation among them, Paul anticipates the appeal in 2:12-13: that they "work out their salvation," meaning to live out in Christian community the salvation that Christ has effected, precisely because "God is at work in you, both to will and do what pleases him."[72]

That Paul in this instance should call their salvation a "good work" is hardly accidental, since this is language he uses elsewhere to refer to the ethical dimension of salvation in Christ.[73] For him there is no salvation that does not include a transformed life; hence this present emphasis. By this language Paul is pointing ahead to the content of the prayer report that follows (vv. 9-11), and thus to the larger concern of the letter that they "live out their heavenly citizenship in Philippi in a manner that is worthy of the gospel" (1:27).

But why this particular way of rounding off the thanksgiving, with its note of joyful prayer based on their long-time partnership with Paul in the gospel? Since such eschatological moments occur elsewhere in Pauline thanksgivings,[74] this may well be either another reflection of the same, or perhaps another typical theological "spin-off": having mentioned "from the

69. Not only so, but one would expect him also to say "*this* good work," not the indefinite "good work" or "a good work." Moreover, the theological and eschatological emphases seem to have more than mere material support in purview. Hawthorne, 21, suggests that the ἐν here could be instrumental, and (wrongly) offers Gal 3:3 as support (the latter *is* instrumental, but does *not* have the ἐν); the context calls for a locative sense to the ἐν here.

70. So most commentaries, though not always with this language. For "salvation in Christ" as the central theme of Pauline theology, see Fee, *Presence,* 11-13. Paul's language here assumes a connection between this passage and 2:12-13.

71. Similarly, Kennedy, 419; Michael, 13; Hendriksen, 54-55; Caird, 107; O'Brien, 64.

72. As with that text, therefore, *contra* Silva and Melick, the focus is first of all on the church as the people of God in Philippi, rather than on all of them as individuals — although of course God's work "in them" is carried out first of all at the individual level. Cf. on 2:4 and 13.

73. See 2 Thess 2:17; 2 Cor 9:8 (where it also includes the grace of giving!); Rom 2:7; 13:3; Col 1:10; Tit 1:16; 3:1; 2 Tim 2:21; 3:17. Cf. also those places where he speaks of "working [or doing/pursuing] what is good": 1 Thess 5:15; Gal 6:10; Rom 2:10; 12:9; 16:19. Many (Gnilka, Martin, Collange, O'Brien) have suggested an allusion here to Gen 2:2, but that seems irrelevant at best and far-fetched at worst (see the response in Silva, 51-52).

74. See, e.g., 1 Thess 1:3; 1 Cor 1:7-8; Col 1:12 (in the prayer report).

first day till now," he simply cannot help himself but also to point out their certain eschatological future. One can hardly disallow such an option in Paul! Nonetheless, while the final phrase in v. 5 undoubtedly *triggered* this clause, its form — especially the language of "persuasion" and the emphasis on God's "bringing to conclusion" what he has begun in/among them — suggests that its primary *raison d'être* has to do with a larger issue brewing in the Philippian community. We may not have full certainty as to the reasons for it, but several moments in this letter suggest that some of them had begun to lose the basic eschatological orientation that marks all truly Christian life.[75] This is especially in evidence in: (1) the way Paul concludes his personal testimony in 3:4-14 (12-14), as forgetting the past and pressing toward the eschatological prize, (2) the appeal that follows for them to do the same (3:15-17), (3) the sad note about those who have not persevered (3:18-19), and (4) the final eschatological notes in the exalted passages in 2:9-11 and 3:20-21 and Paul's own "desire to depart and be with Christ" (1:23). All told, these later affirmations and appeals serve as the most likely clues to our understanding the present affirmation, which also explains its slightly digressive nature in the present sentence.

Believers in Christ are people of the future, a sure future that has already begun in the present. They are "citizens of heaven" (3:20), who live the life of heaven, the life of the future, in the present in whatever circumstances they find themselves. To lose this future orientation, and especially to lose the sense of "straining toward what is ahead, toward the goal to win the prize for which God has called us heavenward" (3:13-14), is to lose too much. Thus, triggered by their present gift, which also reminds Paul of their long association in the gospel, Paul digresses momentarily to remind them that even in the midst of present difficulties, God has in Christ both guaranteed their future and blessed their present situation in Philippi.

**7** But Paul is still not finished with his thanksgiving, at least not with the (now convoluted) *sentence* that began as a thanksgiving. The NIV and most English translations notwithstanding, Paul's sentence begins with the comparative conjunction *kathōs* ("just as"),[76] suggesting that what he is about

---

75. Jewett ("Conflicting Movements," 375, following Lütgert) seems to turn this dimension of the passage on its head by associating it with the language "fear and trembling" in 2:12, and thus to suggest that the Philippians were rejecting such "fear and trembling" having to do with the coming day of judgment. Thus Paul's concern is once again to put the proper "fear" of future judgment before them. That seems quite foreign to this motif in Philippians.

76. *Contra* BAGD, who suggest that καθώς has a "causal" sense when used as a conjunction at the *beginning* of a sentence and include this reference. But καθώς does not in fact begin a sentence here; it concludes the one that began in v. 3. The whole of vv. 3-6 are to be understood as the οὕτως, for which v. 7 will now serve as the proper

to say is to be compared to what has been said. The subsequent phrase, "this way,"[77] therefore, probably refers to the whole of the sentence to this point, especially the content of vv. 3-5, but now by way of his confidence about their future expressed in v. 6. What he is about to do, then, is to *justify* his joyful thanksgiving, both the feelings expressed in vv. 3-4 and the basis for them given in v. 5. "It is, after all," Paul goes on, after the momentary eschatological digression in v. 6, "quite right[78] for me to feel this way about all of you," which he then elaborates in the rest of the sentence, and attests by oath in v. 8. There are certain realities — three are singled out — about their mutual relationship that call for such an attitude: his own deep affection for them (cf. vv. 3-4); their past partnership with him in the gospel (cf. v. 5); and the extension of that partnership to his imprisonment — and the defense of the gospel (v. 7, anticipating vv. 12-26).

The verb which the NIV translates "feel" is particularly noteworthy in the present letter.[79] It refers neither to "thinking" in general, nor "reasoning" as such, nor is it used for a specific act of thought; rather, it has to do with having or developing a certain "mindset," including attitudes and dispositions.[80] This, then, is the proper verb to introduce the clause that follows and its companion in v. 8, a passage full of friendship motifs toward which this verb points; it also anticipates the kind of "mind" he will urge on them later in the letter. Thus, the NIV's "feel this way about all of you,"[81] in the

---

comparison. Thus, "so I give thanks in this way, just as it is fitting for me to feel this way about you." Analogy for the present usage is to be found in 1 Thess 1:5 and 1 Cor 1:6, in the thanksgivings of those letters (on this question, see Fee, *First Corinthians,* 40). The other passages cited by BAGD are likewise suspect on this matter.

77. Gk. τοῦτο, the first of several (somewhat ambiguous) appearances of this demonstrative in this letter. See the discussion on 2:5.

78. Gk. δίκαιον, the ordinary adjective for "righteous, just, upright" (cf. 4:8), which in this usage has the sense of something "obligatory" in view of what is "right" in a given situation; cf. BAGD.

79. Gk. φρονεῖν; BAGD offer "think of, be intent on, be careful about, set one's mind on, be disposed," as its basic range of meaning. Although not especially frequent in Paul's earlier letters, it occurs no less than 10 times in Philippians, and usually at critical moments. It is the key verb in the appeals to harmony in 2:2 (twice) and 4:2, in the appeal to Christ's example in 2:5, in the appeal to keep alive their keen sense of future orientation in 3:15 (twice), as well as in the sad description of those who are doing otherwise in 3:19. It also occurs twice in 4:10 with reference to their renewed concern for Paul.

80. It is of interest that the verb occurs 7 times in the paraenetic section of Romans (chs. 12-15), which begins with emphasis on the "renewing of the *mind,*" and otherwise only 6 times in the rest of the corpus. The clue to its special nuance in Philippians is to be found in its cognate noun (φρόνημα), which occurs three times in Rom 8:6-7 with the sense of "mindset."

81. On this kind of language as common to the "letter of friendship" in Greco-Roman antiquity, see Stowers, *Letter Writing,* 58-60.

sense of having you in mind — or being well disposed toward you — is good colloquial English for this idea.

In giving the reason for his having them in mind in this way, Paul once more emphasizes their mutual relationship, one side of the three-way bond around which this letter finds focus. Thus he returns to the point of v. 5 (their "participation/partnership in the gospel"), but now presses it in terms both of their ministry toward him (v. 7b) and his deep affection for them (v. 8). In place of the NIV's "since I have you in my heart," some have suggested that he intends rather, "because you hold me in your heart" (NRSV),[82] referring to their partnership with him in the gospel to which he will speak in the immediately following clause. But besides the fact that the language of feeling and affection throughout has been about his toward them, two matters of usage indicate that the NIV has it right. (1) Two recent studies on word order with Greek infinitives in the NT make it certain that in this kind of clause (the infinitive before two accusatives) the author normally intends the first to be the subject and the second the object.[83] (2) The explanatory "for" with which the next sentence begins makes almost no sense as referring to the final matters in v. 7, but offers a perfectly understandable explanation of v. 7a.[84] Thus Paul says: "It is quite right for me to have you in mind in this way [referring to vv. 3-6], because I have you in my heart, since you are so well-disposed toward me; . . . *for* God is my witness how deeply I long for all of you with the compassion of Christ."

For the second time in the thanksgiving[85] he emphasizes that his feelings toward them are "for all of you." His own affection, as with that of Christ (v. 8) — and of a parent with squabbling children — refuses to take sides. "All of you," Paul again emphasizes, are "in my heart." In biblical understanding the "heart" refers to the deepest center of human consciousness, the seat of both the will and decision-making, as well as of the emotions. Although rare with this connotation in secular Greek, it has come into the NT from the Hebrew OT by way of the Septuagint. This is what will be further explained in the final oath in v. 8, that Paul has this deep longing for them in the "entrails" (= heart, therefore "compassion/affection") of Christ.

---

82. Cf. NEB, Hawthorne. The problem lies with the Greek infinitive, which as in English takes both its subject and object in the accusative (English, objective) case (e.g., "I thought her to be him").

83. J. T. Reed, "Infinitive" (disc. of our text on p. 10); S. E. Porter, "Word Order" (see p. 197). So most interpreters (Meyer, Lightfoot, Vincent, Michael, Hendriksen, Lohmeyer, Collange, Martin, Bruce, Silva, O'Brien, Melick); for others (e.g. Plummer, Beare) it is so clearcut that they do not even discuss the alternative.

84. So also Meyer, Lightfoot ("[the 'for'] requires it"), Vincent, Hendriksen.

85. See v. 3; cf. v. 1. See the next paragraph and v. 8 as well.

The basic reason[86] for such affection is that "you *all* [that's three (see n. 85)] are participants together[87] with me in the grace[88] [of Christ, cf. v. 2]." Here is one of those remarkable moments in Paul, too easily passed over. The definite article with "grace" indicates that he is referring either to a prior mentioned "grace" or to a well-known "grace." Many[89] take the "well-known" grace to refer to God's saving grace; others[90] to Paul's apostolic ministry. But in light of v. 29, where the verb of this noun occurs in conjunction with their mutual suffering for Christ,[91] Paul very likely is referring to the "grace" of being "partners together in the defense and vindication of the gospel" even in the midst of present "chains."[92]

But *how* they are, or have been, "partners in this grace" is now uppermost in Paul's mind; hence the clause begins on the twin notes[93] of

---

86. At this point the NIV (probably correctly) renders as an explanatory clause ("for whether I am . . .") what in Paul's Greek is a much more complex set of clauses. Woodenly transferred into English, his sentence reads: ". . . me in the heart you both in my chains and in the defense and confirmation of the gospel fellow participants of me of the grace all of you being." Two matters are at issue grammatically: (a) whether "both in my chains etc." belongs to the preceding clause ("I have you in my heart both in my chains and in the defense and confirmation of the gospel" [so Meyer, but surely incorrectly; the word order in this case is emphatic — in both of these ways they are participants together with him]); (b) the relationship, and thus nuance, of this participial clause to its preceding clause. The explanatory clause of the NIV is probably right; the problem is that in so rendering it, they eliminate the explanatory γάρ by which v. 8 is explicitly tied to v. 7, by means of which, in turn, Paul goes on to explain how it is that he has them in his heart.

87. Gk. συγκοινωνούς; cf. 4:14, where the cognate participle occurs (cf. n. 52 above). The compounding of κοινωνός with σύν is probably the sure giveaway that the word κοινωνία on its own does not mean to fellowship in the sense of "share something together" or "be partners in something" (as Sampley, *Partnership,* 60-61), but to "participate in" something. The compound means precisely what many have considered the basic word to mean, "to share together in," hence to be "participants *together*" in the grace of God.

88. Gk. συγκοινωνούς μου τῆς χάριτος. The μου is ambiguous. Grammar disallows that it means "with me," since that would require a dative. Thus it is possessive, most likely going with the "fellow-partners," hence "my fellow-partners." This is the ordinary word order in Greek. Cf. the discussion in O'Brien, 70. On the so-called vernacular possessive, where the possessive pronoun precedes its noun — in Paul almost always emphatic — see on 2:2 ("my joy").

89. E.g., Vincent, Müller (partly), Martin, Motyer, O'Brien.

90. E.g., Bonnard, Collange, Bruce, Hawthorne, Silva, Melick; this in light of Paul's frequent reference to his ministry as "the grace given to me" (e.g., 1 Cor 3:10; Gal 2:9).

91. Lit. "You have been 'graced' (ὑμῖν ἐχαρίσθη) on account of Christ not only to believe in him but also to suffer for his sake."

92. So also Müller, 43; Loh-Nida, 14; Martin, 66; Hawthorne, 23.

93. The Greek is quite clear that Paul here intends to speak of their "partnership

"both in my chains and in the defending and confirming of the gospel." Again, the three-way bond. The gospel, as always, is the primary matter; both he and they have had a part in the defense and confirmation of the gospel. But the Philippians are also "partners together with him" in his present circumstances of imprisonment. But to what specifically do the two phrases ("in my chains," "in defending and confirming of the gospel") refer? One thing noted twice, or two different things?

There can be little question that the first phrase, "in my chains," refers to Paul's present imprisonment. Here is the first mention of the "suffering" motif, which surfaces throughout this letter, and probably carries more significance than many interpreters are ready to allow.[94] Although "chains" could possibly be a metonymy for imprisonment as such, most likely Paul was literally chained to his guards.[95] The way this similar idea is expressed in 2 Tim 2:9 makes it difficult to imagine anything other than literal chains in that case. Probably the same is true here, since in Roman prisons "imprisonment without chains was a concession to high status."[96] In any case, the repetition of the phrase, "my chains," in vv. 13, 14, and 17 indicates that he is smarting under the imprisonment, in part perhaps because he is not free to roam about.

But how do the Philippians "share in God's grace with me" in this matter? Does this refer merely to their gift[97] to him while he is presently in chains? Or does it possibly allude to what he will affirm in v. 30, that some of them are undergoing "the *same* struggle" in a nearly identical way in Philippi? One cannot be sure. Very likely the recent gift is more immediately in view; but one cannot rule out the latter, especially in light of his referring to his present imprisonment for the gospel in terms of "grace," which he will repeat as an aphorism in v. 29.[98]

---

with him in the gospel" in two aspects: ἐν τοῖς δεσμοῖς μου and ἐν τῇ ἀπολογίᾳ καὶ βεβαιώσει τοῦ εὐαγγελίου (cf. n. 15). This is made certain by the τε . . . καί and the repeated "in" following the καί. Meyer, 21, suggests (plausibly) the two phrases refer to Paul's *position* and his *employment* in this position.

94. See the discussion of the theme in the Introduction, pp. 29-32. The primary reason for downplaying it is in reaction to Lohmeyer's "martyrological" understanding of the whole letter (see, e.g., O'Brien, 70). For a historical overview of the handling of the motif in Philippians, see Bloomquist (*Function,* 18-70), although his own approach, based on a questionable use of ancient rhetoric, is less than satisfactory.

95. On the matter of chaining prisoners see Rapske, *Acts,* 25-28.

96. Rapske, *Acts,* 28.

97. It is not, of course, that any gift is "mere." The question throughout this thanksgiving, however, is whether, even though it has undoubtedly been triggered by their gift, his gratitude is limited only to their recent gift, or whether it has a much broader horizon.

98. So Plummer, 12.

So also with "the defense and confirmation of the gospel." Since the first part of this phrase occurs again in v. 16, referring specifically to the reason for Paul's imprisonment,[99] the present phrase may simply be another way of referring to his own imprisonment in which they have had a share by sending him a gift. But in light of what is said in the rest of the letter, especially 1:27-28, very likely Paul's vision has again enlarged somewhat, to refer to their situation in Philippi as well as to his in Rome. Just as he is imprisoned for the defense of the gospel — and thus for its vindication as well — so, too, they will be urged both to live in a way that is worthy of the gospel and to contend for it side by side in the face of similar (Roman) opposition in Philippi. In this way they exhibit their real participation with him in the cause of the gospel.

In sum: the language and the context suggest that Paul minimally has in mind their most recent "sharing with him in the gospel," by means of a material gift while he is in prison. That, after all, is the immediate cause of his thanksgiving. Nonetheless, in light of how the rest of the letter unfolds, he seems here also to be embracing them for their long-term association with him in the gospel — by their helping him to share the gospel in other settings, to be sure, but also by their own activity in Philippi, especially in the face of similar hostility to his. The hostility, after all, comes from the empire itself, of which they are both citizens, both of whom are now in trouble because they hold allegiance to a citizenship in which Lord Christ holds sway even — especially — over Lord Caesar.

**8**   The mild oath with which the thanksgiving report finally concludes provides the key to much about this letter. The "for" with which it begins is explanatory — of how "I have you in my heart" (v. 7). Both the oath itself and its content reveal the depth of feeling out of which the letter is written. The affection that one senses throughout the thanksgiving now spills out as open and unfeigned feelings toward them. Epaphroditus is about to return home, and Paul's thoughts turn toward Philippi — in remembrance of their long-term close relationship in Christ, expressed most recently by their gift. At the same time he is experiencing a measure of distress, because all is not right with them, and he can only sit in prison and pray. Pray he will do momentarily, but now, having just noted their own love for him in Christ, he returns to the affirmation in v. 7 that he has them in his heart.

---

99. Cf. Deissmann (*Bible Studies,* 108-9), who has demonstrated that these two words together carry a technical sense of "defense" and "vindication" (cf. Moffatt, "as I defend and vindicate the gospel"). This suggests, therefore, that although the gospel is "confirmed" in various ways, especially as it has reached into the Praetorian Guard — the emperor's elite troops — as well as the emperor's own household, Paul's present concern is with its *vindication,* even (or, especially) by his imprisonment and subsequent trial (cf. Hawthorne, 23-24). See further on vv. 19-20.

This is one of several such oaths in Paul's letters,[100] where he wishes to emphasize a point that usually has to do with his own thinking or feelings. God must serve as witness, of course, because this is a matter of the heart, and only God can know his heart in this way. In effect, he says to them, "God himself knows how[101] I feel about you."

The content of the oath has to do with how much he "longs for" them. This is not the only community to which he expresses such "longings."[102] Since in the other instances his "longing" refers to his intense desire to be reunited with them, one may minimally assume the same to be true here, especially in light of 1:24-25 and 2:24. He longs for them, he says, not to be present merely by this letter, but also to be there among them in person. But in this case the language goes beyond the mere yearning to be reunited.[103] In 4:1, in a passage of equally deep feeling expressed by a piling up of vocatives of affection, he uses this same word and calls them his "beloved and 'longed-for' brothers and sisters," which in that case does not imply "longing to see." Thus, his "longing" for them in the present instance is probably not simply to be with them again, true as that may be, but suggests an especially deep yearning *for* (= concern about) his friends themselves, that they remain true to the gospel to which they have been so faithfully committed over these many years.

That this is the sense of Paul's present yearning is suggested first by the repeated (now for the fourth time) "for you all." Whatever in fact was going on among them, reported to him by Epaphroditus, he wants them to know how strongly he feels toward them — toward *all* of them. This understanding of his "longing for" them is also supported by the final phrase, "with the affection[104] of Christ Jesus," in which the three-way bond between him and them and Christ is once more brought into focus. His own relationship

100. He calls on God as his witness also in 1 Thess 2:5, 10; 2 Cor 1:23, and Rom 1:9. In other cases he asserts, "I am telling the truth, I am not lying" (Rom 9:1; 1 Tim 2:7; cf. 2 Cor 11:31; Gal 1:20). Such an oath probably derives from the OT practice of calling on God as witness between two parties (so Str-B, Collange, O'Brien); see, e.g., Josh 22:27; 1 Sam 12:5; 20:23; Jer 42:5.

101. Gk. ὡς; Hawthorne, 24-25, and O'Brien, 71, make a bit too much of the conjunction as equivalent to ὅτι (= "that") here. But it must be pointed out that Paul does not use ὅτι. Most likely he means something like our cumbersome, "how that."

102. Gk. ἐπιποθέω; cf. 1 Thess 3:6; Rom 1:11; 2 Tim 1:4. In our letter the same verb is also used of Epaphroditus's "longing" for "the folks back home" (2:26). Here it refers especially to his deep feelings for them.

103. *Contra* Hawthorne, 25.

104. Gk. ἐν σπλάγχνοις (= the entrails), referring to the "inner parts" of one's being — probably because of the physical, deeply visceral, internal "feelings" that one sometimes experiences in the emotion of deep affection for another. Meyer, 24, takes the ἐν as locative (= "by virtue of the dwelling and working of Christ in me").

to them, on such vivid display in this expression of deep affection for them, nonetheless serves as the *second* predicate on which the letter itself rests. The first predicate, the primary one, is their own relationship to Christ, which is the ultimate urgency of the letter. Thus, Paul concludes the thanksgiving by reminding them, first of all, of his own deep longings for them, but also, secondly, that those longings are "with the affection of Christ Jesus" himself, referring almost certainly to "the love Christ has for you, which is also at work in me for you."

That Paul is not an academic, but a passionate lover of Christ Jesus, is made plain by the deep and uninhibited expressions of affection that permeate this thanksgiving, since academics tend to be embarrassed by such displays! But there is much here to be learned by those in the church who have pastoral care of any kind, including that of parents for their children. The emotion, after all, in Paul's case is simply the outflow of his theology and the spirituality that issues from such theology. The theology has to do with the gospel, which has God as its source and sustainer. Whatever else, those whom we love in Christ first of all belong to God. God has begun the "good work" in them that he has committed himself to concluding with eschatological glory. That "good work" is the result of "the affection of Christ Jesus," through whom God has brought about this "good news" on behalf of his people.

The net result in terms of pastoral care is thanksgiving and joy for the people themselves, for "all of them," even those whose antics so often seem to bring more grief than pleasure. They belong to God; it is ours to be grateful for what God has done, is doing, and will continue to do in their lives. And all of this works much better if the care giver also shares in "the affection of Christ Jesus," by having a good measure of the same affection, predicated on being participants together in the gospel.

## 2. Prayer as Petition — for Increased Love and "Fruitfulness" (1:9-11)

> 9*And this is my prayer: that your love may abound*[1] *more and more in knowledge and depth of insight,* 10*so that you may be able to discern what is best and may be pure and blameless until the day of Christ,*

---

1. A few not insignificant MSS (B D Ψ 81 2464 2495) read the aorist περισσεύσῃ for Paul's (almost certainly) original present (περισσεύῃ). Since the aorist is the "normal" tense in the subjunctive, the change from the present to the aorist is frequent in the copying tradition (for this matter in the Gospel of John, see Fee, "John 20,30-31"). Whether tense is "meaningful" here is moot; the present subjunctive was probably used because it goes more naturally with "more and more." Thus, "that your love will keep on growing more and more" (GNB).

95

11*filled with the fruit[2] of righteousness that comes through Jesus Christ — to the glory and praise of God.[3]*

In articulating his reasons for joy and thanksgiving in vv. 7-8, despite their digressive appearance, Paul has not lost sight of what he is about. His thanksgiving for the Philippians takes place in the context of prayer, as he emphatically reminded them in v. 4. Now he proceeds to give content to his prayer, indicating some specifics regarding the "good work" begun in them which he repeatedly prays that God will bring to completion on the day of Christ.

As with the thanksgiving, the prayer report is also a single (less convoluted, but nonetheless complex) sentence, whose overall concern, as well as the meaning of most of its details, lies close at hand. The connections between the various parts are easily traced:

> Paul prays (1) for their love to abound yet more and more;
>> that (2) this be accompanied by full knowledge and moral insight,
>>> so that (3) they might approve those things that really matter,
>>>> so that (4) they might be unsullied and blameless when Christ returns,
>>>>> as (5) they are now full of the fruit of righteousness,
>>>>>> fruit that is (6) effected by Christ Jesus
>>>>>>> and (7) for the glory and praise of God.

Items 1, 2, 3, and 5 thus give the *what* of his prayer for them; item 4 gives the *why,* while item 6 offers the *means* to the (ultimate) *end* expressed in item 7. The *what* begins on a familiar note, that their love grow still more and more. It ends on a similar note, that they bear the fruit of *righteousness.*

2. Perhaps influenced by the LXX of Prov 3:9 and 13:2, the later manuscript tradition (Ψ Maj sy) changed Paul's singular καρπὸν . . . τόν to the plural καρπῶν . . . τῶν.

3. In one of the more puzzling sets of variation in this letter (not to mention the NT), the phrase found in the majority of witnesses, εἰς δόξαν καὶ ἔπαινον θεοῦ ("unto the glory and praise of God"), is read three other ways: D* εἰς δόξαν καὶ ἔπαινον Χριστοῦ ("unto the glory and praise of Christ"); F G Ambst εἰς δόξαν καὶ ἔπαινον ἐμοί ("unto my glory and praise"); P[46] εἰς δόξαν θεοῦ καὶ ἔπαινον ἐμοί ("for the glory of God and my praise"). The evidence of P[46] suggests that the variation had a more troubled history than one might guess; nonetheless the corruption is most likely due to the unusual usage — for Paul — of the word ἔπαινος as directed toward God rather than people. The text of D is a simple change toward the repeated mention of Christ in this passage; the texts of F G and P[46] represent independent errors that lean toward the more standard usage of ἔπαινος — although the text of F G is preferred by Ross ("Unnoticed Points," 70); Hawthorne (14) is ambivalent. Metzger (*Textual Commentary,* 611) adopts the standard reading on the basis of the external evidence.

The middle item (3), though a bit puzzling, is likewise concerned with be-havior — that their knowledge (of God) and moral insight (into God's will) also increase so that they may test and approve what really counts. The whole, therefore, is singularly concerned with their behavior, with the ethical life of the believer in Christ.[4]

As with the thanksgiving, and despite first appearances, the prayer is not "in general," but rather is full of items that anticipate the content of the letter. That their love overflow toward one another is the basic urgency of the exhortation in 1:27–2:18, explicitly expressed in 2:2; that they might be full of the fruit of *righteousness* is the ultimate reason for Paul's personal testimony in 3:4-14;[5] that they might be found so on the day of Christ, a note already struck in v. 6, is a concern that surfaces throughout;[6] that their knowledge of God and moral insight into his will might increase finds further expression in the exhortation in 4:8-9 and (probably) in the practical appli-cation in 2:3-4; and that they might thereby be in position better to determine what really counts anticipates the long warning in 3:1-21. That all of this is through Christ Jesus and for God's glory is the dominant theological predi-cate of the letter.

The upshot is a prayer report in which Paul prays in part for the continuation of the very things for which he has just given thanks. Which should surprise us none, since both reports reflect the same basic theological framework — present existence in Christ as both "already" and "not yet." This is where the *what* and the *why* join: Paul's prayer for them is that they might live the life of the future in the present, so that they might thereby be blameless at its consummation on the day of Christ. The concern is with present life in Christ; the orientation is toward its consummation — that they live for Christ now, and do so in light of his coming Day.

**9** At the beginning of his thanksgiving (v. 4), Paul told the Philippians that he prayed for them on a regular basis, and that he made those prayers

---

4. Thus the prayer comes very close to being a compendium of Pauline ethics, whose *purpose* is God's glory, whose *pattern* is Christ, whose *principle* is love, and whose empowering is the Holy Spirit (see Fee, *Presence,* 879). Missing here is the empowering dimension of the Spirit (Christ as "pattern" is the point of 2:5-11), although it may well be implied by the language of "fruit" (of righteousness) with its apparent anticipation of 3:2-11, a passage that begins by asserting that "we are the true circumcision who 'serve' by the Spirit of God."

5. However see Silva, 62, who sees the anticipation in the prayer as emphasizing "progressive sanctification" vis-à-vis some form of perfectionism (3:12-14). While one can easily recognize an emphasis on "progression," Paul's concern seems less related to the possibility that some think they have already arrived than to their need to "overflow all the more" in behavior that already characterizes them.

6. See on v. 6 above, p. 88.

with joy. Now, flowing directly[7] out of his own longing for them "with the affection of Christ Jesus" (v. 8), he tells them *what* that prayer consists of.

First, he prays (item 1) that[8] "your love may abound more and more." Many years earlier, where an existing love also needed some further prodding, Paul prayed similarly for the Thessalonians that their "love [might] increase and overflow" (1 Thess 3:12).[9] In that case he specified the direction of the love for which he prayed: "for each other and for everyone else." The linguistic and contextual similarities between these two prayers suggest a similar direction to the love for which he now prays — that their love *for one another* abound all the more, a concern that is expressly picked up in 2:2 ("that you have the same love [for one another]").[10]

"Love" is such a common word to us that it is easy to miss Paul's concern. As used by Paul, and following the lead of the Septuagint,[11] "love" first of all points to the character of God, and to God's actions toward his

---

7. The present sentence begins with a καί ("and"). Since parataxis (sentences beginning with "and") are relatively rare in Paul, one can usually show good reason for such when it happens. In this case it suggests the closest possible tie of the prayer to what has preceded, flowing directly out of v. 8, but also thereby picking up the mention of the *fact* of his praying for them in v. 4; cf. Silva (57, 62), who sees it as resumptive of v. 4, and O'Brien (73) for what is argued here. On this kind of parataxis in Paul, see Fee, *Presence*, 45-46, 672 n. 43 (on 1 Thess 1:6; Eph 2:1).

8. Gk. ἵνα. Earlier commentators (e.g., Kennedy) debated as to whether or not this clause expressed purpose. It does not, at least not in any direct sense. This is a common *koine* idiom, where ἵνα, following τοῦτο as in this case, functions like ὅτι, giving the content of the "this" (cf. Hawthorne, 25).

9. Perhaps surprisingly these are the only two instances in a *prayer report* he uses this kind of language (in 2 Thess 3:5 he prays that their hearts might be directed "into God's love," but in that case it refers to God's love for the Thessalonians). This motif, however, appears often in his *thanksgivings*. See 1 Thess 1:3; 2 Thess 1:3; Col 1:4; Phlm 5; Eph 1:15.

10. Otherwise Spicq, *Agape,* 2.277; Lohmeyer, 31; Hawthorne, 25; O'Brien, 74; who suggest that since there is no expressed object, Paul refers to love in its most comprehensive sense, going in every possible direction, that they thus be people of love as God is. The context of the letter, however, suggests a more focused concern.

11. Gk. ἀγάπη *(agape),* a word found only sparsely among Greek writers. It was chosen by the LXX translators to render the Hebrew root אהב, apparently to distinguish it from ἔρος ("desiring love") and φιλία ("natural sympathy" or "mutual affection"). Thus it is used both of God's love for his people (e.g., Deut 7:7) and in the two love commands (for God [Deut 6:5 and passim] and neighbor [Lev 19:18]). This usage, which thus fills an otherwise empty word full of theological grist, is unquestionably the source of its usage among the early Christians, for whom it became the ultimate theological word both to describe God's character and to articulate the essence of Christian behavior. For useful overviews see the articles by G. Schneider, *EDNT,* 1.8-12; and W. Günther and W. G. Link, *NIDNTT,* 2.538-47. Cf. the longer article in *TDNT,* 1.221-54 (by G. Quell and E. Stauffer), as well as the monographs by James Moffatt and A. Nygren.

people based on that character. God's love is demonstrated especially in his "forbearance" and "kindness" (1 Cor 13:4), manifested ultimately in the death of Christ for his enemies (Rom 5:6-8). Thus its primary connotation is not "affection," as in the preceding phrase about Christ (v. 8), but rather "a sober kind of love — love in the sense of placing high value on a person or thing,"[12] which expresses itself in actively seeking the benefit of the one so loved. And this is what Paul now prays will "abound[13] yet more and more" among the Philippian believers. The rest of the prayer, after all, emphasizes "love" not as "affection" but as behavior, behavior that is both "pure" (stemming from right motives) and "blameless" (lacking offense).

On the other hand, both the present tense of the verb[14] and the qualifier "yet more and more"[15] indicate that Paul is not by this prayer "getting on their case," as it were, for something they lacked. Quite the opposite. His concern is that they not let behavior motivated by "selfish ambition or vain conceit" (2:3) undermine the very thing that has long characterized them, to which 2 Cor 8:1-6 bears eloquent testimony. The problem is similar to that occasionally experienced by families, where love is sometimes more easily shown toward those on the outside, who are known very little and with whom one does not have constant association. But actively to love on the inside, those with whom one is in constant relationship and where one's own place in the sun is constantly being threatened, that can be another matter. Thus he prays that the love that has long characterized them will continue "still more and more" toward one and all.

Second (item 2), he prays for a similar increase "in knowledge and depth of insight."[16] The single preposition controlling both nouns suggests a

12. So V. Warnach, "Love," in *Encyclopedia of Biblical Theology* (ed. J. B. Bauer; ³1967) II.518.

13. Gk. περισσεύῃ, a favorite Pauline word (26 of 39 NT occurrences), which reflects his own understanding of the lavish nature of life in Christ, effected by the Spirit. At various times he either urges or acknowledges that believers "overflow" in love (1 Thess 3:12; 4:10), building up the church (1 Cor 14:12), the work of the Lord (1 Cor 15:58; cf. 2 Cor 9:8), thanksgiving (2 Cor 4:15; 9:12; Col 2:7), faith, speech, knowledge, earnestness, and the grace of giving (2 Cor 8:7), and hope (Rom 15:13). And all of this because God's own grace and love have "overflowed" toward us (Rom 5:15; Eph 1:8).

14. See n. 1 above.

15. Gk. ἔτι μᾶλλον καὶ μᾶλλον. The NIV (cf. RSV, NRSV, JB, NAB) leaves out the ἔτι as redundant; but cf. the NASB ("still more and more") and NEB ("ever richer and richer").

16. Gk. ἐν ἐπιγνώσει καὶ πάσῃ αἰσθήσει. It has sometimes been pointed out (e.g., Bonhöffer, *Epiktet;* Gnilka; Hawthorne) that αἴσθησις and the phrase τὰ διαφέροντα that follows are also found in the Greek moral philosophers. So also with the language of 4:8 and 11-12. Whether "dependent" on the philosophers or not, as 4:13 makes abundantly clear (q.v.), this reflects Paul's habit of adapting, and thereby transforming for his own purposes, language well-known to, or used by, his readers. Cf. Hawthorne, 27.

very close relationship between them. The first word *(epignōsis)* is probably the key. Its primary sense is not so much "knowledge about" something, but rather the kind of "full," or "innate," knowing that comes from experience or personal relationship.[17] The second word *(aisthēsis),* which occurs only here in the NT, is more difficult to pin down.[18] In secular Greek it denotes moral understanding based on experience, hence something close to "moral insight." This is the sense which the translators of the LXX picked up, for whom it becomes a near synonym for "wisdom" *(sophia)* or "insight/understanding" *(sunesis).* Very likely, therefore, this phrase is something of an abbreviated equivalent of the similar phrase in the (roughly contemporary) prayer in Col 1:9 ("that by means of all of the Spirit's wisdom [*sophia*] and insight [*sunesis*][19] you might be filled with the knowledge [*epignōsis*] of God's will").

Thus, even though the phrase grammatically modifies "that your love may abound more and more," and may indicate the "manner" in which he hopes that love will abound, more likely the grammatical link is with the verb ("I pray") alone, so that conceptually Paul has moved in a new direction with the prayer. This seems to be verified by the clause that follows, which again grammatically should modify the whole of the preceding clause, but in fact seems to be related singularly to the prepositional phrase ("in knowledge and depth of insight"). If this be the case, then Paul is now praying a second thing, that along with an ever-increasing love they may also experience an ever-increasing knowledge (of God and his will) and moral insight. An increased knowledge of God is what is needed in order for them to "walk worthy of the gospel" and in the one Spirit to contend for that gospel as one person (1:27).

**10** The opening clause of the prayer, for ever-increasing love accompanied by ever-increasing knowledge and moral insight, is followed by two

---

17. In this regard see esp. 1 Cor 13:12, where the cognate verb occurs. Ἐπιγνῶσις is the kind of "knowledge" of us that God has, and that we will eventually experience when "we see him as he is." The usage in Rom 3:20 is likewise instructive, that "through the Law comes the ἐπιγνῶσις of sin." That is, with the coming of the Law people who were otherwise already sinners came to "know" sin for what it really is. Cf. Phlm 6, where Paul prays that Philemon's active sharing of his faith will be "with the ἐπιγνῶσις [full understanding, NIV] of every good thing that is ours in Christ Jesus." See the fuller discussion in O'Brien, 75-76, who notes Paul's dependence on the OT for this concept, and thus points out: "In the OT, as well as in the writings of Paul, knowledge was not a fixed *quantum* but rather something that developed in the life of people as they were obedient." Cf. K. Sullivan, "Epignosis."

18. Cf. the discussion by Delling, *TDNT,* 1.187-88.

19. For the understanding of the clause reflected in this translation see Fee, *Presence,* 640-43.

purpose clauses. The first (item 3) expresses immediate purpose — why they need ever-increasing "knowledge and (moral) insight." The second (item 4) expresses the ultimate purpose of the whole prayer — why they need ever-increasing love and ever-increasing knowledge and insight in order to determine what really counts.

The reason for an overflow of "knowledge and (moral) insight" is so that they will "be able to discern[20] what is best," that is, so that the faculty for making proper assessments about what is absolutely essential[21] regarding life in Christ will increase as well. For truly Christian life, some things matter, and others do not. In light of the term "fruit of *righteousness*" in v. 11 and the contrast between "*righteousness* in terms of Law-keeping" and that which is through faith in Christ in 3:1-11, it is possible that this anticipates the warning and personal testimony of that passage. Especially so, (a) since Paul begins that passage by reminding them that he is once again returning to that oft-repeated subject for their "safety," and (b) in light of what he says elsewhere about circumcision. *Neither* circumcision nor uncircumcision counts for a thing, Paul says; one is no better off with one, or worse off with the other (1 Cor 7:19; Gal 5:6; 6:15). "What counts," he goes on, "is keeping the commandments of God[!]" (1 Cor 7:19), which in Gal 5:6 is interpreted as "faith that manifests itself *through love.*" Whether this part of the present prayer intentionally anticipates 3:1-11 or not, this is the kind of "insight" he prays for them to have, so that they will be able to continue to "discern what counts."[22]

---

20. Gk. δοκιμάζειν, which always carries the connotation of "proving" — thus "approving" — something by putting it to the test. In this sense only does it mean to "discern."

21. Gk. τὰ διαφέροντα; cf. Rom 2:18 ("approve of what is superior," NIV). Its proper opposite is *adiaphora,* "non-essentials." Some earlier commentators (Kennedy, 431-32; Vincent, 13 [with a list of others before him]) suggested that the meaning should be to "test things that differ," i.e., what is good and bad. But that does not seem to be the concern in this context and disregards Paul's usage in Rom 2:18. It is not possible, of course, for such "discerning" or "approving" of "what counts" to be without a degree of comparison. But the emphasis here is not on the comparative process, but on their being able to discern that which God has already marked off as essential or "superlative" regarding life in Christ.

22. Other matters may be anticipated here as well. Some items in this letter are less clear to us than others, especially how some (apparently) disparate elements might be related: the nature of the "posturing" that is going on, so that Euodia and Syntyche have to be urged to "have the same mind" (4:2-3); why the sudden (repeated) warning against circumcision in 3:2; who the people are who have left off striving for the heavenly prize because their minds are on earthly things (3:18-19); and why Paul's final exhortation in 4:8-9, still in the context of urging harmony among themselves, urges them in the language of the highest ideals of Hellenism to "think on whatever is true, honorable, upright, pure, lovely, and admirable," and in this matter to imitate what they have seen and heard in Paul

But if the reason for the penultimate purpose clause is not fully clear, there is no ambiguity as to the *ultimate* purpose for the preceding concerns — that they might be "pure and blameless until[23] the day of Christ."[24] This reflects the urgency already voiced in the thanksgiving that they be found "complete" at the coming of Christ.[25] The only surprise is the *language* Paul uses to express concern for their being "blameless." The word translated "pure"[26] appears twice in 2 Corinthians to describe Paul's apostleship as absolutely sincere, without the "mixed motives" he ascribes to his opponents (2:17). In 1 Cor 5:7, in a corresponding ethical context, it bears the sense of a pure lump of dough, "unmixed" with leaven. In the present context it most likely refers to purity (sincerity) of motive, in terms of relationships within the community.[27] Likewise, *aproskopos*[28] is not Paul's regular word for the idea of "blameless." Ordinarily, as in 2:15 and 3:6, he uses a form of *amemptos,*[29] a word denoting behavior that is without observable fault. But *aproskopos* has to do with being "blameless" in the sense of "not offending" or not causing someone else to stumble.

Thus this choice of words that speak to Paul's desire for the Philippians

---

himself. Although certainty may forever allude us here, very likely there is a close connection between "thinking on merely earthly things" and thus abandoning one's keen sense of striving for the heavenly prize and the posturing by some in the community that is more closely aligned with "selfish ambition and vain conceit" (2:3) than it is with the pure gospel of our Lord Jesus Christ. Perhaps the present concern over "full knowledge and moral insight so as to approve what really counts" may be related to some of this as well.

23. Gk. εἰς ἡμέραν (cf. 2:16). These are the only two instances of εἰς with this term in the Pauline corpus. It simply cannot mean "on" (as the NIV translates in 2:16), for which Paul invariably uses the temporal ἐν (cf. 1 Cor 1:8; 5:5; 2 Cor 1:14; Rom 2:5, 16). Since he has already used ἄχρι in v. 6 to express this reality in terms of "until," and since in Eph 4:30 he uses εἰς with "the day of redemption," which in that case is almost certainly telic (= "*for* the day of redemption"; see Fee, *Presence,* 716-17), that is most likely the sense here (*contra* BAGD). Thus he prays that they might be pure and blameless "for the day of Christ," that is, with the day of Christ in view as their ultimate goal.

24. One might note again the similarity with the prayer in 1 Thess 3:12-13, where an increase and overflow of love is linked to being "blameless . . . when our Lord Jesus comes."

25. On the phrase "day of Christ" and the future orientation that marks so much of this letter see the comments above on v. 6.

26. Gk. εἰλικρινεῖς, the only occurrence of the adjective in Paul (elsewhere in the NT, only in 2 Pet 3:1); but cf. Paul's use of the cognate noun, which bears exactly the same sense (1 Cor 5:8; 2 Cor 1:12; 2:17). See the discussion by H. Goldstein, *EDNT,* 1.391.

27. Otherwise Kennedy, 422, who thinks it refers to their "openness toward God," while the next word picks up the horizontal dimension.

28. Used elsewhere in Paul only in 1 Cor 10:32, where it clearly carries its primary denotation of "giving no offense."

29. Cf. the disc. below on 2:15 and 3:6.

when they stand before God at the end also seems to reflect the present situation in Philippi. The behavior of some appears to have the latent possibility of "mixed motives," or at least is a potential source of "offense." Paul prays that they may stand blameless on the day of Christ, not having offended others through equivocal behavior.

**11** Not one to leave such a prayer hanging on what may sound like a negative note, Paul immediately qualifies: by "pure and blameless until the day of Christ" he means for them to arrive at that day as those "filled[30] with the fruit of righteousness" (item 5). At first blush, the metaphor seems strained; ordinarily one "bears" fruit. But the perspective is now from that of the preceding clause. What Paul wants is for them to stand on *that* day *"full* of the fruit of righteousness." But to do so they must *now* be *living out* such righteousness. Here again, as in v. 6, the "already but not yet" of life in Christ is played out before their eyes.

But to what does "the fruit of righteousness" refer? Here is one of the standard "classroom examples" of the ambiguities of the Greek genitive. Does Paul intend, "filled with the fruit that *comes from* the righteousness that Christ has provided," thus emphasizing the kind of fruitfulness that has God's gift of right-standing with himself as its *source?* Or does he intend, "filled with the fruit *consisting of* the righteousness that marks one who belongs to Christ," thus emphasizing the kind of righteousness that, coming through Christ, has a new kind of *content?* Although this is not an easy choice, and one's *theological* proclivities are with the former,[31] both the OT background of the language and the grammar of the sentence favor the latter.[32]

First, Paul's use of "religious language" like this has been altogether conditioned by his lifelong reading of the OT. The phrase itself comes from the LXX (Amos 6:12; Prov 3:9; 11:30), where it refers to the righteous *behavior* of the righteous person.[33] Similarly, in Ps 15:2 (LXX 14:2), those

---

30. Gk. πεπληρωμένοι, a perfect passive participle that modifies "that you might be." This is an excellent example of the nuance of the Greek perfect, which is not easily carried over into English. It reflects the present state of something that happened in the past; in this clause, which is from the perspective of the future day of Christ, the "past" is the present.

31. Preferred, *inter alia,* by Beare, Hendriksen, Caird, Collange, Ziesler *(Righteousness),* O'Brien — although it should be noted that both views end up at the same point: that Paul's concern is with their "righteous" behavior.

32. Although it also needs to be noted that in Paul one cannot have the latter without the former, so in that sense the gift of a right relationship with God is also included in "the fruit of righteousness that comes through Jesus Christ," even though the concern here is with ensuing behavior.

33. Cf. Jas 3:18 ("the fruit of righteousness is sown in peace for those who make peace"), which both the NIV and NRSV tranlate as "a harvest of righteousness," where again the emphasis is on righteous behavior.

who will be allowed to live on God's holy hill (= dwell in his presence) are they whose "walk is *blameless* and who *do righteousness.*"

Second, on the matter of grammar: The "that" which in the NIV precedes "through Jesus Christ" reflects (correctly) Paul's use of the Greek definite article which here functions like a relative pronoun. This article is without ambiguity; it modifies "fruit," not "righteousness." Paul's emphasis, therefore, is on "the *fruit, consisting of* righteousness," which comes to them through their relationship to Christ. Had the article modified "righteousness," then Paul would have unambiguously meant that righteousness itself, as a gift of right standing with God, came through Christ. But Paul's present emphasis is on Christian behavior, not on how one becomes related to God so as to produce such behavior. After all, it must be noted finally, the whole participial phrase of v. 11a modifies the final clause in v. 10, having to do with their being blameless and without offense at the coming of Christ.

But what does this righteousness look like for which Paul prays? Two observations from our letter give us the clues. (1) The word "righteousness" is probably anticipatory of its usage in 3:6 and 9, where in contrast to "blameless righteousness in keeping with the Law" (including especially circumcision), Paul says that *we* — he and they together — are the true circumcision, who "serve by the Spirit" (v. 3). The "fruit consisting of true righteousness" has not to do with circumcision, or with any other measurable, religious expression of law-keeping; rather it has to do with boasting in Christ and "serving" by the Spirit, and thus being formed into God's own character, evidenced by the way one lives. When one is "filled with the fruit" of this kind of righteousness, then one's life is characterized by the fruit of the Spirit (Gal 5:22-23), which means in part, and now back to our prayer, to "have one's love overflow" (v. 9).

(2) In our letter the way that love expresses itself (2:2), as righteousness of the kind that "really counts," is by adopting a "cruciform" lifestyle, like that of Christ (2:6-11) and his apostle (3:10-11). Thus it means to go the way of the cross, self-emptying so as to become servant of all in place of "selfish ambition," and in that servanthood, humbling oneself to the point of dying for another in place of "vain conceit" (2:3-8). This is what it means for Paul to "know Christ." All other righteousness, especially "religious righteousness," is refuse in comparison (3:8).

Such righteousness as this, it must be emphasized, comes only "through Jesus Christ" (item 6); it is quite unrelated to being religious, which for Paul is but another form of "boasting in the flesh" (3:4). And in this sense, both dimensions of "righteousness," both of which "come through Jesus Christ," join together: the gift of Christ's righteousness means a life of righteousness, without either of which there is no righteousness at all from Paul's point of view.

Furthermore, such righteousness as this is alone "to the glory and praise of God"[34] (item 7). Here is the ultimate goal of all things. In v. 6 Paul reminded the Philippians that "the good work" begun in them was God's doing, as also will be its completion. Now he prays for them — that the fruit of righteousness that comes through Christ Jesus might increase among them more and more, precisely so that God will receive glory through the work that he is doing in their lives.[35] Everything is to that end. Love that reflects God's own love is the only righteousness that "counts," the only righteousness that is to God's glory and to his praise.

It has often been noted that the Lord's Prayer in Matthew serves as a paradigm for prayer in the kingdom ("pray, then, *like this*"), while Luke's version justifies our praying those very words as well ("when you pray, *say*"). So with this prayer. On the one hand, case specific though it is, the very things for which Paul prays seem to be ever relevant for those who are care givers in the church — be it pastors, leaders, parents, or what have you. Most people entrusted to our spiritual nurture, as with all of us, need "love to overflow," not to mention our need to have knowledge of God and insight into his will also overflow so that they (we) may give themselves only to what really counts as believers in Christ. Who of them — of us — does not need to be filled with the kind of righteousness that characterizes God and that Christ has modeled? Thus, "when you pray [for your children or grandchildren or students or parishioners or study group] say. . . ."

On the other hand, there is paradigm here as well. Here is one who has a keen sense of priorities in Christ, and who is concerned when those in his care grow slack in some areas. That this prayer anticipates so much of the letter itself tells us much about Paul in prayer. Before talking to them about some matters that need an "increase," he talks to God about them — and tells them so. We could learn much here.

---

34. On the significant textual variation involved in this phrase, see n. 3 above.

35. Many scholars have pointed out that these words are similar to those that regularly conclude the prayers of Jewish piety (e.g., Ps 21:13; 35:28; Sir 39:10; 1QSb 4:25). Such comparisons only indicate how deeply Paul's piety is rooted in his Jewish heritage. O'Brien (82) goes on to argue that these final words are intended to be a doxology that brings the entire thanksgiving to its conclusion. If so, it is not a formal doxology of the kind with which he concludes the letter in 4:20 (q.v.). More likely, this is simply the conclusion of Paul's prayer, whose ultimate concern is that the Philippians live to the glory and praise of God.

# II. PAUL'S "AFFAIRS" — REFLECTIONS ON IMPRISONMENT (1:12-26)

What follows the thanksgiving and prayer-report is a commonplace in letters of friendship:[1] the writer informs the recipient(s) about his or her own situation — often with the very words Paul uses here.[2] This material is usually brief, and sometimes comprises the whole of a (very brief) letter. In this case, however, it is quite long (vv. 12-26), and as with so much else in Paul's letters, is thoroughly transformed by the gospel. What begins, typically for such material, as a word to relieve the Philippians of anxiety (v. 12) thus evolves into a word about the current spread of the gospel (vv. 13-18a), followed in turn (vv. 18b-26) by a reflection on his desires and expectations regarding his forthcoming tribunal — again focusing altogether on Christ.[3]

Common as a word like this is for Greco-Roman letters, however, this passage is striking for its uniqueness in the Pauline corpus.[4] There is simply

---

1. On Philippians as a letter of friendship, see the Introduction, pp. 2-7. On the possibility that Paul is also reflecting some features of ancient rhetoric, see Bloomquist (*Function,* 119-57), whose analysis disregards Paul's own structural signals (see n. 17 below) and the fact that all of 1:12-26 is a first person singular narrative, while 1:27–2:18 is second person plural and functions as exhortation; cf. the critique in the Introduction, pp. 14-16.

2. Paul begins, γινώσκειν δὲ ὑμᾶς βούλομαι, ἀδελφοί, ὅτι. Among the letters collected by Hunt and Edgar *(Select Papyri),* see, e.g., pp. 303, 317, 327, 329, 342. Thus, a certain Apollinarius writes to his mother (2nd c. CE):

"Apollinarius to Taesis, his mother and lady, many greetings. Before all I pray for your health. I myself am well and make supplication for you before the gods of this place.

*I wish you to know, mother, that* [γινώσκειν σε θέλω, μήτηρ, ὅτι] I arrived in Rome in good health on the 25th of the month Pachon and was posted to Misenum, etc." (p. 303)

Or this one from an Isis to her mother (3rd c. CE):

"Isis to Thermouthion her mother very many greetings. I make supplication for you every day before the lord Sarapis and his fellow gods.

*I wish you to know that* [γινώσκειν σε θέλω ὅτι] I have arrived in Alexandria safe and sound in four days. etc." (p. 341)

For an earlier study of this phenomenon as a "form" see T. Y. Mullins, "Disclosure," who calls it a "disclosure formula"; cf. also J. L. White, *Form.*

3. These two sections are divided by Paul's use of the present and future of χαίρω in v. 18 (καὶ ἐν τούτῳ χαίρω. Ἀλλὰ καὶ χαρήσομαι; "and in this I rejoice. But I shall also rejoice . . ."), which Martin, 70, calls "the centre of gravity" for this section. The failure to note this clear rhetorical device and to observe the shift from reflection on the present to anticipation of the future marks Bloomquist's handling of this section as altogether suspect (see n. 1 above). See the discussion on v. 18b below.

4. Most noticeable is the large number of first person pronouns and verbs that

nothing else quite like it, where he reflects at such length on "his affairs." Granted, as will be pointed out, that the section also functions in a semi-paradigmatic way — and is thus in part for the Philippians' sakes as well — nonetheless, Paul begins by responding at once to their interest in him, which had been evidenced by their recent gift.

A number of significant linguistic ties link this section to what has preceded and to what follows. Thus Paul begins (v. 12) by picking up a major motif in the thanksgiving, the advance of the gospel (vv. 5, 7). Similarly, his being in "chains" (vv. 13, 14, 17) and his being so "for the defense of the gospel" (v. 16) repeats the language of v. 7, while the motivation of "love" in v. 16 echoes his prayer for them in v. 9. Going the other direction, "good will" (v. 15), "love" (v. 16), and "selfish ambition" (v. 17) are echoed again at significant points in the ensuing exhortation (2:13, 2, and 3 respectively). The section itself is framed by the word "advance, progress." In v. 12 Paul speaks of the "advance of *the gospel*"; in v. 25 his concern is for *their* "progress."[5]

Very likely, therefore, more is going on here than at first meets the eye, especially in light of 1:27–2:18. There Paul urges the Philippians to stand firm for the gospel in the midst of their own present difficulties, both external and internal. In v. 30, regarding these difficulties, he writes: "you are going through the *same* struggle you saw I had, and now hear that *I still have*." Since he and they are currently both experiencing opposition from the same source (Rome), and since he also is experiencing less-than-loving attitudes from some within the Christian community in Rome, this passage, besides offering a reflection on his imprisonment, is probably also intended as a paradigm: how the believers in Philippi should respond to such difficulties.[6]

In any case, one can scarcely miss the focus of Paul's concern, here and always: Christ and the gospel. His present imprisonment has ultimately been to the advantage of the gospel, which is cause for joy (vv. 12-18); his singular longing regarding his trial is that Christ will be magnified, whether through life or death (vv. 19-20); if it were to result in death (execution), that

---

occur in these verses (23 in all). In v. 24 a shift begins toward the second person plural, which just as noticeably dominates 1:27–2:18. Galatians, to be sure, begins with a considerable narrative regarding Paul's calling and commission as an apostle, but that is *apologia* (*pace* G. Lyons, *Pauline Autobiography,* 75-176). Nowhere else is there anything like this — reflection on his own present and future circumstances.

5. Noted also by Garland, "Defense," 331; Peterman, "Giving," 124; et al. (usually after the fact at v. 25).

6. Silva, 66, sees the reason as more directly related to their gift ("supporting Paul . . . they have a 'right' to find out about his affairs"). But the suggestion made here not only fits well with the whole of the letter (esp. the recurring "imitation" motif), it also gives a satisfactory reason for vv. 15-17.

means he finally reaches the goal of his life — Christ himself — and if choice were his, he would go this route (vv. 20-23); but most likely the outcome will be life (freedom), which will cause their own "boasting" to "abound in Christ Jesus" (vv. 24-26).

## A. THE PRESENT — FOR THE ADVANCE OF THE GOSPEL (1:12-18a)

Common to letters of friendship, Paul first offers information about his present circumstances, mention of which serves as a kind of structural signal for the first half of the letter.[7] Thus when he turns to exhortation in v. 27, Paul begins with a desire to hear (more) about their affairs. In 2:19-24 he brings these two themes together in terms of "what's next" regarding his and their relationship.

Most remarkable about this opening reflection (vv. 12-18a) is how little it says about Paul personally — in spite of the frequency of first person singular verbs and pronouns. Two things account for this. First, the Philippians already know about his imprisonment, evidenced by their recent gift. Thus his present focus is not so much on himself — he probably expects Epaphroditus to fill them in on personal matters[8] — as it is on *how he views* what has happened to him, very likely with an eye toward them. Since he has just thanked God for their partnership with him in the gospel, it is natural for him to contemplate his imprisonment in these terms. Second, Paul's personal life is so completely taken up with his calling that to reflect on how his imprisonment has furthered the gospel *is* to reflect on his life!

The present reflection falls out into two closely related parts (vv. 12-14, 15-18a). Paul begins by turning their attention immediately to "the progress of the gospel." His confinement has furthered the gospel in two ways: his captors and guards have been made aware of Christ (v. 13); and believers in Rome are more actively proclaiming Christ (v. 14).

Although this second matter is a cause for joy, it has not been without some personal wounds, which leads to the second part: a sub-paragraph flowing out of v. 14, in which he reflects on the twofold motivation — envy and goodwill — behind this renewed activity (v. 15). Verses 16-17 reiterate these in reverse order, in terms of love and selfish ambition directed toward him. But v. 18, where he expresses his response to this activity, is the obvious concern of the whole passage: Christ is being proclaimed, and in that Paul

---

7. See n. 17 below; cf. the Introduction, p. 3.

8. For evidence of this expectation from the bearer of his letters, see esp. Col 4:7-8; cf. Eph. 6:21-22.

rejoices. Whatever else, although suffering, Paul is scarcely languishing in prison.

## 1. The Gospel Advances inside and outside Prison (1:12-14)

12*Now I want you to know, brothers [and sisters],*[9] *that what has happened to me has really served to advance the gospel.* 13*As a result, it has become clear throughout the whole palace guard*[a] *and to everyone else that I am in chains for Christ.* 14*Because of my chains, most of the brothers {and sisters} in the Lord have been encouraged to speak the word of God*[10] *more courageously and fearlessly.*

[a]Or *whole palace*

This first paragraph is a single sentence in Greek, composed of an informational clause (v. 12), plus a compound result clause (vv. 13, 14), indicating the two ways the gospel has been advanced — within prison and without. Thus Paul informs his Philippian friends, probably contrary to their expectations, that his imprisonment has fallen out to do the very thing they should have desired — to further the gospel. Given how this section concludes with emphasis on the *Philippians'* "advance" (vv. 25-26), very likely even these opening words are in part for their sake: here is how one for whom Christ and the gospel are uppermost responds to adversity.

**12**  The transition from the proemium to the body of the letter is marked in three ways: by the *de* ("now"), which in this case is a "transitional particle, pure and simple";[11] by the vocative, "brothers and sisters," which

---

9. That the vocative ἀδελφοί means "brothers *and sisters*" in the Pauline letters is made plain from Phil 4:1 and 2, where Paul uses this vocative and then specifically addresses two women.

10. Although the genitive modifier τοῦ θεοῦ ("of God") is found in most of the early and best MSS (א A B [D*] P Ψ 33 81 104 326 365 629 1175 1241* 2464 lat sy^p.h** co Clement; F G read χυρίου; it is missing in P46 1739 MajT r Marcion), it is highly suspect as an addition by a later hand (so Lohmeyer, Gnilka, Houlden, Hawthorne, Metzger [*Textual Commentary*]). Two matters make one think so: (1) Although Paul at times refers to the message of the gospel with the absolute "the word" (1 Thess 1:6; Gal 6:6; Col 4:3; 2 Tim 4:3), more often he adds a genitive qualifier (either "of God," "of the Lord," "of Christ," "of truth"). In light of Pauline usage elsewhere, the scribal tradition would more likely have added such words than they would have omitted them. That is especially true in this case where the absolute use of "the word" seems to cry out for a genitive qualifier. (2) Although the reading of F G could easily be a corruption of τοῦ θεοῦ, the more likely explanation for the two variations is that we have here two different ways of "emending" Paul's own text.

11. This is the language of BAGD, 2.

is often used by Paul in transitional sentences;[12] and by the formula "I want you to know that . . . ," which occurs only here in the Pauline corpus,[13] but is often found as the first matter in letters of friendship.[14]

The language "brothers and sisters" is one of the more significant Pauline images for the church. Although not unique to Christians,[15] this usage was taken up by them to express their understanding of relationships within the believing community: They are "brothers and sisters" because first they are God's "sons" through *the* Son, whose Spirit cries out from within them in the language of the Son *("Abba")* as the sure evidence of "adoption" (Gal 4:4-6);[16] their ultimate end is conformity to the likeness of the Son, the Firstborn among many *brothers [and sisters]* (Rom 8:29). Thus in this letter, besides the vocatives which refer to the Philippians, Paul uses this appellation to denote fellow believers in Rome (1:14) and to his present companions (4:21). Whatever else, believers in Christ Jesus are God's children, hence "brothers and sisters" in Christ.

What Paul wants the Philippians to know is that "what has happened to me[17] has really served to advance the gospel." The thrice-repeated phrase "my chains" (vv. 13, 14, 17; cf. v. 7) attests that he is referring to his imprisonment. They are to understand that its effect has been quite the reverse of what they might have expected. It has "really[18] served," he explains,

12. See 3:1, 17; 4:1, 8; cf. the more personal ἀγαπητοί μου ("my beloved friends") in 2:12 and 4:1. Thus these vocatives usually appear at the beginning of a new section, but sometimes elsewhere, as in 3:13, to emphasize a point, or as in 1 Cor 15:58, to bring an argument to conclusion.

13. A somewhat similar formula does occur twice at the beginning of new sections of an argument (1 Cor 11:3; Col 2:1: θέλω δὲ ὑμᾶς εἰδέναι); cf. "I do not want you to be 'not knowing' " in 1 Thess 4:13; 1 Cor 10:1; Rom 1:13; 11:25.

14. See n. 2 above. What is striking in this formula is that it appears so often with the same words and in the same word order. It should be noted that the formula also occurs in other forms of client-patron relationships, where the "client" begins the letter by informing the "patron" of present circumstances. See the example in Kennedy, 422.

15. On this matter, see BAGD; cf. M-M, 8-9; J. Beutler, *EDNT,* 1.29.

16. For the significance of this passage to Pauline theology, see Fee, *Presence,* 398-412.

17. Although "what has happened to me" (cf. NRSV) catches the sense of Paul's language, it also tends to obscure the structural tie of this verse with v. 27 (τὰ κατ᾽ ἐμέ = "my circumstances/affairs"; τὰ περὶ ὑμῶν = "your circumstances/affairs"). On this as the sense of τὰ κατ᾽ ἐμέ, see BAGD, κατά II,6. Cf. esp. the usage in Col 4:7 (τὰ κατ᾽ ἐμὲ πάντα γνωρίσει ὑμῖν Τύχικος, "Tychicus will make known to you all about my affairs"); cf. the parallel in Eph 6:21, where τὰ κατ᾽ ἐμέ, in a slightly rearranged sentence, has become τὰ περὶ ἡμῶν! On the use of this formula in letters of friendship, see the Introduction, p. 3. Collange's suggestion (53) that the phrase here refers to a specific recent event, viz., Paul's revealing of his Roman citizenship so as to be set free, is not only purely speculative, but fails to recognize these parallels and this usage in letters of friendship.

18. This is good colloquial English for Paul's μᾶλλον ("rather"). Some (e.g.,

"to[19] advance[20] the gospel." Here is Paul's obvious concern. He wants them not to be anxious about him, because his circumstances, rather than being a "hindrance" *(proskopē)*[21] to the gospel, as they might well believe, have in fact led to its "advance" *(prokopē)*. "To advance the gospel" has been his lifelong passion; he has thus ordered his life so that nothing will hinder, and everything advance, the message about Christ.[22]

For Paul, of course, this is the language of evangelism.[23] In a world of religious pluralism, where evangelism has become something of a dirty word, one must not thereby recreate Paul in one's own image, which downplays this dimension of his life in Christ.[24] Evangelism was his "meat and potatoes" (or "rice," in the case of Asian Christians), since he believed not only that the gospel is God's "message of truth" (Gal 2:5, 14), but that it thereby contains the only good news for a fallen, broken world.

Paul will eventually reflect on his own feelings as to his imprisonment (vv. 20-23), but his first concern is to make sure that his friends in Philippi

---

Kennedy, 423; Collange, 9, 51-52) have suggested that this word implies that a change in Paul's circumstances had occurred. But as Omanson ("Philippians 1.12") has correctly pointed out, here μᾶλλον announces that the reverse of what they might have expected has come true; cf. Lightfoot, 87; Vincent, 16; Plummer, 19; Collange, 53; O'Brien, 90. There is no need, therefore, to postulate that Paul is trying to counteract rumors that are floating about (as Hawthorne, 34). More recently B. J. Capper ("Dispute," 208-9) has suggested that the μᾶλλον indicates a "rift" between Paul and the Philippians. But this represents "mirror-reading" of a most unfortunate kind (see the Introduction, pp. 7-8; cf. the critique of this view in n. 4 on 4:14-17).

19. Gk. εἰς; for this kind of telic use of this preposition see v. 5 (cf. vv. 15, 19, 25).

20. Gk. προκοπή; for this usage in Greek philosophy, see Stählin, *TDNT,* 6.704-7, where it refers to the "progress" toward wisdom (cf. Sir 51:17). Paul here reflects its nontechnical sense found frequently in the papyri, where it refers simply to making progress, in a good sense (see M-M, 542; cf. *New Docs* 2,95; 4,36). For an illustration of the present usage, where something impersonal "advances," or "makes progress," see Jos. *Ant.* 4.59: a sedition "progresses from bad to worse." Closer to Paul's sense is 2 Macc 8:8, referring to the beginnings of the campaign of Judas Maccabeus against the Syrians: "When Philip saw that the man [Judas] was making progress [εἰς προκοπήν] little by little."

21. This is the word Paul uses in 2 Cor 6:3; in 1 Cor 9:12 he uses the cognate ἐγκοπή.

22. As noted in the introduction to this section, this word occurs again in v. 25, regarding the Philippians, as to why Paul expects to be released from prison: It would be for their own "progress and joy regarding the faith." Thus the word functions as a kind of *inclusio* for the section.

23. See the discussion on v. 5; for the concerns articulated here, see 1 Cor 9:3-18, esp. vv. 12, 16, 18, which in vv. 19-23 is stated explicitly, "that I might win some."

24. Indeed, those who rather thoroughly dislike Paul for this passion understand him far better than others, especially among scholars, who profess love for the apostle, but are embarrassed by his fashioning his whole life around this singular concern — to know Christ and to make him known.

have a clear understanding as to how it has affected the gospel. To his delight, and perhaps their surprise, it has advanced it. The next clause (vv. 13-14) spells out how so.

**13** The "so that" (NIV, "as a result") with which this clause begins offers the twofold evidence for the assertion of v. 12. First Paul reveals the effect of his confinement on *unbelievers* — "in[25] the whole Praetorium and to everyone else." What all have come to know is that (literally) "my chains[26] have become manifest[27] in Christ[28]." Although awkward in its expression, Paul's overall intent seems plain enough: it has become clear to all who have had any association with him that his imprisonment has to do with his Christian faith, with his "gospel." This at least means that they have come to know that it is a religious matter; but for Paul it surely means as well that he has tried to evangelize "the palace guard" itself.

The awkwardness of the clause results from the phrase "in Christ." The difficulty in this case lies first with the word order and second with its nuance.[29] That it follows "manifest" emphasizes minimally that the various pagans who have contact with him have become well aware that his imprisonment is neither for crime nor for politics, but with his being "in Christ" (= a follower of Christ). The whole clause therefore probably means first of

---

25. Gk. ἐν, which as in Rom 1:19 is locative, expressing not what is clear *to* them (as NEB, NJB), although that is certainly implied, but the *extent* to which it has been manifested, namely, throughout the entire Praetorian Guard (but all 9,000 of them? and in any case, how could he know its actual extent?). This is conventional hyperbole, where "the whole" stresses the considerable breadth to which this has become known. On the other hand, even as hyperbole, this phrase tends to cut the ground from under hypotheses of either an Ephesian or Caesarean provenance for this letter, since (1) the guard cannot be demonstrated ever to have existed in Ephesus and (2) Herod's *praetorium* in Caesarea was scarcely of a size to call for this emphasis. See the Introduction, pp. 34-36.

26. On this expression see the discussion on v. 7.

27. Gk. φανερούς, which means "plain for all to see"; in Paul cf. Rom 1:19; Gal 5:19.

28. Gk. ἐν Χριστῷ; see also 2:1 (cf. ἐν Χριστῷ Ἰησοῦ in 1:26; 2:5; 3:3, 14; 4:17, 19, 21; and ἐν κυρίῳ in 1:14; 2:19, 24, 29; 3:1; 4:1, 2, 4, 10). On this phrase in Paul, which has had a long history of interpretation, see the discussion by M. A. Seifrid in *DPL,* 433-36, and the bibliography there.

29. Some (e.g., Plummer) have taken it adverbially ("in the power of Christ"); cf. F. Neugebauer *(In Christus),* who likewise takes it adverbially, but as referring to Christ's saving activity, by which Paul's life is forever determined. While this phrase may ultimately point in that direction, it is doubtful whether it can be so overloaded in the present clause. Others (e.g., Ellicott, Michael), who recognize that it goes with φανερούς, suggest that it does not stress the *cause* of his imprisonment being revealed but the *spirit* in which he endured it. This seems overly subtle. The best solution is to see the sentence as somewhat elliptical here; thus, "so that my chains have been manifest [as being] in Christ."

all what the NIV suggests: "that I am in chains *for* Christ." That is, his imprisonment has to do with his Christian faith.[30] But since he does not use the preposition *hyper* ("on behalf of"), but *en* ("in"), and because of the close relationship of this phrase to "my chains," very likely he is saying something more, something about his understanding of the *nature* of discipleship, that it means to "participate in Christ's sufferings" (3:10). Thus, he probably means something like, "it has become clear that I am in chains because I am a man *in Christ,* and that my chains are in part a manifestation of my discipleship as one who is thereby participating in the sufferings of Christ himself."[31] As Paul says in this letter and everywhere else, his life finds its meaning "in Christ" (1:21), even as he himself is "in Christ" and thus lives "for Christ" in the sense of making him known to others.

The term translated "palace guard" *(praetorium)* is one of the cruxes of this letter and impinges on the question of Paul's location at the time of writing.[32] At issue is whether he is referring to a place or to a group of soldiers, and where it was/they were located. The word originated to denote "the general's tent" or "the headquarters within a camp," evolving over time to refer to a governor's palace.[33] But by the first Christian century it was frequently used also to denote the Praetorian Guard, the emperor's own elite troops, stationed in Rome.[34] If Paul is in Rome, as is most likely, then he is referring to this guard, since there was no Praetorium (= "governor's palace") there. Although they would have guarded Paul around the clock, they would also have given him access to visitors, to the writing of letters, and to other routine matters. Since they would rotate on a basically four-hour shift, Paul would have had access to several — or many — of them, from whom eventually "the whole[35] guard" would have known the reason for his bonds.

30. So most interpreters; cf. Beare's paraphrase: "it has come to be recognized by the whole Praetorian Guard . . . that if I am in fetters, it is because of my activities as a Christian."

31. So also Bruce, 41; Silva, 68; O'Brien, 92.

32. Cf. the Introduction, pp. 34-36.

33. As in Mark 15:16 and Acts 23:35, where the palace is called "the Praetorium." Hence the marginal note in the NIV, which indicates the possibility that Paul is referring to the palace itself, not to the guard. The usage in Acts 23:35 is the source of the theory that this letter was penned in Caesarea. But against this is (a) that Paul is clearly referring to a *body of people,* and (b) that there is no *lexical* evidence that this word was ever used to denote the *people* associated with a governor's residence (cf. Reicke, "Caesarea," 283).

34. See esp. Lightfoot, 99-104, whose arguments on this matter have never been overturned. A further view, however, was offered by W. Ramsay (borrowing [incorrectly, it appears] from Mommsen), to the effect that it refers to "persons connected with the imperial court." But no hard evidence for this view was ever forthcoming.

35. Gk. ὅλῳ τῷ πραιτωρίῳ; on its size and the difficulty this phrase creates for other than a Roman imprisonment, see n. 25.

That Paul was "in chains for Christ" also became known "to everyone else."[36] This refers to another group of people outside the Praetorian Guard, most likely to others who had dealings with imperial affairs.[37] Thus anyone in Rome who had occasion to know about Paul's confinement had also come to learn that it had to do with his being the propagator of the nascent Christian religion.

One should not miss Paul's obvious delight in this mild "triumph" regarding his arrest, the same kind one senses at the end of the letter when he sends greetings from "all the saints, especially those who belong to Caesar's household" (4:22). While this might be interpreted as a kind of "one-upmanship," Paul's concern would be to encourage the Philippians in their own current suffering, resulting in part from their lack of loyalty to the emperor. To the world — and especially to the citizens of a Roman colony — Caesar may be "lord"; but to Paul and to the believers in Philippi, only Jesus is Lord (2:11), and his lordship over Caesar is already making itself felt through the penetration of the gospel into the heart of Roman political life.[38]

**14** From the effects of his imprisonment on his captors and others, Paul turns to its effects on the Christian community in Rome.[39] Again he emphasizes "my chains." His "chains," which have resulted in Christ's becoming known among his captors, have also served as the immediate cause of newfound boldness among the "brothers and sisters" in Rome. What is remarkable is how Paul reflects on this matter. Though he would surely prefer freedom himself to evangelize, he recognizes that God has used his curtailment to prod others. The rejoicing that ensues (v. 18) must be taken seriously. Here is one for whom the gospel is bigger than his personal role in making it known.[40]

But the sentence has some inherent ambiguities; therefore, a more

---

36. Gk. καὶ τοῖς λοιποῖς πᾶσιν, lit. "all the rest"; cf. 2 Cor 13:2. Some earlier interpreters (Chrysostom, Calvin) suggest "in all other places" (KJV; cf. Moffatt). But that is against all analogy, and in this case is nearly impossible. Paul may not always be tidy, but neither would he be so obscure when such an idea could be stated easily and unambiguously.

37. Cf. Bruce ("St. Paul in Macedonia," 265), who suggests, "those who were in any way concerned with the arrangements for the eventual hearing of his case."

38. Cf. Houlden, 58: "In getting himself put in prison, in Rome above all, he has acted the Trojan horse, entering into the very heart of the Gentile world to which Christ had despatched him as an apostle."

39. This clause is joined to v. 13 with a καί ("and"), and thus concludes the sentence that began in v. 12. The "nuts and bolts" of his sentence thus runs: "What has happened to me has served to advance the gospel, so that (1) the whole Praetorian Guard and all the rest know that my imprisonment is for Christ, and (2) the brothers and sisters here have been emboldened to speak the message fearlessly."

40. My own experience is that not all are so generous, including the writer of this commentary. Does this man always sing in prison?

wooden rendering will make the following comments easier to follow: "and [so that] the majority of brothers and sisters, having become confident[41] in the Lord by my chains, have been so much the more[42] emboldened fearlessly to speak the word."

"Most of the brothers and sisters" refers to the Christian community[43] in the location of his imprisonment — Rome in our view. That Paul is not referring to believers in other churches[44] seems certain, since as loyal partners of his in the advance of the gospel, the Philippians would have been among the first of his churches to have been so spurred on, yet he feels the need to inform them about this recent development. Thus, it is not "brothers and sister" in Corinth, Thessalonica, and elsewhere, but in Rome, who have been emboldened by his imprisonment. Moreover, "most" in this case probably means simply that the church as a whole has been largely affected in this way by his imprisonment.[45]

That he refers to them *all* as "brothers and sisters" needs especially to be kept in mind when we come to the next sentence (v. 15). For even though he smarts from knowing that some are trying to inflict further pain on him, he clearly intends them to be included among the "brothers and sisters" of this sentence.[46]

Moreover, despite the NIV,[47] Paul does not refer to them as "brothers

41. Gk. πεποιθότας; the NIV's "have been encouraged" is foreign to any known nuance of this verb, which means to "persuade," and in the perfect, as here, takes on the nuance of "being convinced or confident" (cf. Paul's "persuasion/confidence" about the Philippians' sure future in v. 6, and of his release from prison in v. 25).

42. Gk. περισσοτέρως, an adverb whose cognate verb (περρισεύω, "to abound or overflow") appears in v. 9. The translation is that suggested by BAGD.

43. Michael, 37, observes (correctly) that Paul is speaking of all believers, not just about those in leadership (ministers, e.g.); cf. O'Brien, 94, *contra* Silva, 69, who is more cautious. E. E. Ellis proposes that "brothers" at times becomes a quasi-technical term for Paul's "co-workers," or at least for "leaders in ministry" (see *Prophecy*, 6-15). But in view of Paul's usage elsewhere, and especially in view of his use of the vocative to address the entire community of believers to whom he writes (e.g., Phil 1:12; 3:1, 13, 17; 4:1), one seems hard pressed to make that work here.

44. But see Martin, 72, who leans this way. Schmithals's view (*Paul*, 75) that Paul is referring to the situation in Philippi has nothing in the text to commend it and everything against it (cf. Bruce, 45: an "extraordinary argument").

45. See also Bruce, 42. As with the case of the "whole Praetorian Guard" (see n. 25), Paul has not counted noses so as to know that well over half of the individuals in the churches are now evangelizing. This is more popular language to refer to the way the whole of the Roman church has been affected by his being imprisoned there.

46. Although see n. 5 on 1:15-18a for interpreters who in an earlier time challenged this.

47. And a few others (KJV, NASB, Alford, Kennedy, Lohmeyer, Beare, Houlden, Bruce; cf. Moule, *Idiom Book,* 108).

and sisters *in the Lord.*" Such a redundancy quite misses Pauline usage, not to mention the emphases of this sentence.[48] First, Paul regularly uses the phrase "in the Lord" to qualify the verb "being confident."[49] Second, all the other modifiers in this clause also stand in the emphatic first position. He thus intends, "have become *confident in the Lord.*" Its emphatic position reveals Paul's perspective: their present "persuasion/confidence" does not stem ultimately from his imprisonment but from the prior work of the Lord in their lives. The phrase "in the Lord," therefore, refers to the *ground* of their confidence, while the following phrase, "by my chains," is *instrumental* (= the means God has used).[50] Thus his "chains" have served to make them all the more "confident *in the Lord*" so as to proclaim Christ more boldly.

The actual response of the Roman church to Paul's imprisonment is described with two emphatic adverbs, "so much the more" and "fearlessly," which respectively modify the two final verb forms in the sentence. First, they have taken on an extraordinary boldness[51] to witness for Christ as the result of their newfound confidence in the Lord brought on by Paul's imprisonment. This probably reflects the historical situation in Rome in the early 60s, when Nero's madness was peaking and the church there had begun to fall under suspicion, as Nero's pogrom against them just a couple of years later bears witness. The present situation in Rome for the followers of Christ had perhaps (understandably) led them to a more quiescent form of evangelism than was usual for early Christians. For good reason, then, Paul joyfully explains to the Philippian believers that the net effect of his own imprisonment has been to give their Roman brothers and sisters extraordinary courage to proclaim Christ, at the heart of the empire itself, where storm clouds are brewing.

Second, their boldness has led them "fearlessly to speak forth the word." This absolute use of "the word"[52] occurs frequently in Paul to describe the gospel, the message about Christ.[53] That it does so here is confirmed by

---

48. One wonders how one escapes the conclusion that to qualify "brothers and sisters" in this way implies another option, brothers and sisters who are *not* in the Lord. The appeal frequently made to Col 1:2 is not relevant, since in that case the whole phrase modifies, and thereby more narrowly defines, "those who are in Colosse" to whom he writes; they are the "holy and faithful brothers and sisters in Christ," which unpacked means, "those in Colosse who are in Christ, and who are thereby both brothers and sisters [with all other believers in Christ] and likewise with them God's holy and faithful children."

49. Thus, in 2:24 he is "confident in the Lord" (NIV) that he will see them soon; cf. Gal 5:10; Rom 14:14.

50. So also Vincent, 17; O'Brien, 95.

51. Cf. NEB, "with extraordinary courage."

52. On this usage and the textual question involved see n. 10 above.

53. See 1 Thess 1:6; Gal 6:6; Col 4:3; 2 Tim 4:2. Elsewhere, depending on whether the emphasis is on its source or its content, he refers either to "the word of God" (= the message that comes from God; see 1 Thess 2:13; 1 Cor 14:36; 2 Cor 2:17; 4:2; Col 1:25;

vv. 15-16, where "speaking forth the word" becomes "preaching Christ." A part of the reason for Paul's present joy, therefore, is that his arrest has somehow helped stem fear among the believers in Rome; they are not only proclaiming Christ all the more, but are doing so "fearlessly."

Thus the furtherance of the gospel is everything for Paul. That his imprisonment, curtailment though it means for him, has been a means used by God to further the gospel is a source of genuine joy (v. 18). But before that, he offers an aside, since his joy is tempered by another reality: emboldened by Paul's imprisonment though they are, the motive of some is less out of love for the gospel than it is out of a desire to rub salt in his wound.

## 2. The Gospel Advances outside Prison — despite Ill-will (1:15-18a)

15*It is true that some preach Christ out of envy and rivalry, but others out of good will.* 16*The latter[1] do so in love, knowing that I am put here for the defense of the gospel.* 17*The former preach Christ[2] out of selfish ambition, not sincerely, supposing that they can stir up[3] trouble for me while I am in chains.* 18*But what does it matter? The important thing is that in every way, whether from false motives or true, Christ is preached. And[4] because of this I rejoice.*

---

2 Tim 2:9; Titus 2:5) or "the word of the Lord/Christ" (= the message about Christ; 1 Thess 1:8; 2 Thess 3:1; Col 3:16). Note also his use of "the word of truth" (= the message containing the truth from God) in 2 Cor 6:7; Col 1:5; Eph 1:13; 2 Tim 2:18.

1. Against all the early evidence (P[46] ℵ A B D* F G P 33 81 365 1175 1739 1881 latt co), the later MajT (including Ψ sy[h]) has transposed vv. 16-17, so that the two follow-up sentences to v. 15 follow the same order as they appear there. There is nothing inherently better, or "more difficult," about one reading or the other — although the secondary text climaxes both sentences on the positive note of good will and love, while the original text appears as a form of chiasmus (see p. 118 below). This is one of the few major transpositions of this kind in the textual transmission of the Pauline corpus.

2. There is textual variation between τὸν Χριστόν ("*the* Christ" [P[46] ℵ A D Maj]) and simply Χριστόν ("Christ" [B F G Ψ 1739 1881 pc]). The omission is probably secondary; in any case, the articular usage in v. 15 (where Christ is the object, as here) and the nonarticular usage in v. 18 (where Christ is the subject) indicate that the presence or absence of the article carries no significance.

3. In place of the original ἐγείρειν ("raise up, lift up, erect, stir up" [one of the verbs for resurrection in the NT]), read by the earliest and best evidence (ℵ A B D* F G P 33 1739 1881 pc latt co), the later MajT reads ἐπιφέρειν ("bring upon, inflict"). This is secondary by the very fact that had such an appropriate verb as ἐπιφέρειν been in the text originally, one cannot imagine the circumstances whereby it would have been changed (so early and so often) to a verb like ἐγείρειν, which would scarcely be the first to come to a copyist's mind under any circumstances.

4. The earliest witness to the Pauline corpus, P[46], supported by some MSS of the Bohairic version, insert an ἀλλά ("but") before the καί, with which this clause begins. This

Most of us know this material so well that we tend to overlook how surprising it is. The preceding sentence gave no inkling whatever of these tensions;[5] it simply explained to his friends that his imprisonment has continued the progress of the gospel, both inside and outside the context of his "chains." And they surely know him well enough to appreciate what sheer joy that would be for Paul. But now we discover that this progress has not been without its personal drawbacks. Some who have been emboldened by his imprisonment have become more aggressive in their evangelism precisely because they hope to add to Paul's "affliction" (v. 17). The surprise comes in his large-heartedness about this — not that he could be large-hearted, but that he could be so toward people of a kind whom he elsewhere seems to inveigh so strongly against.[6]

The paragraph is in two parts: in vv. 15-17 Paul describes, in terms of their motivation, two kinds of evangelism taking place in Rome in response to his imprisonment; in v. 18a he offers his response to all this, namely "joy over the advance of the gospel." The description itself is set forth in a nearly perfect chiasmus:[7]

A    Some preach Christ because of envy and rivalry (v. 15)
  B    Others because of good will (v. 15)
  B′    The latter do so out of love because they know my imprisonment is in behalf of the gospel (v. 16)
A′    The former proclaim Christ out of selfish ambition, not sincerely, supposing they are causing affliction in my bonds (v. 17)

---

is secondary on all counts, and probably is a simple error of sight, where the scribe's eye picked up the beginning of the next sentence (v. 18c) when copying this one.

5. Indeed, some earlier interpreters (e.g., Ellicott, Meyer, Kennedy, Vincent) argue that people who preach out of "envy and strife" could not possibly be included by Paul among "most of the brothers and sisters" in v. 14. But that is an altogether unnatural reading of the Greek. It would take an extraordinary display of contextual evidence to the contrary for the combination τοὺς πλείονας ("the majority"), followed by τινὲς μέν . . . τινὲς δέ ("some . . . others"), not to mean: "Most . . . , some of whom . . . , others of whom" (cf. Michael, 37). For the latter to be "set over against the πλείονας," as Vincent asserts, would seem to require a differentiating word like ἄλλος μέν. Moreover, one is thus put in the awkward situation of detaching the second group (τινὲς δέ) from v. 14 as well. This view has nothing to commend it, and clearly arose to defend Paul from including as "brothers and sisters" those whom he also accuses of preaching from a motive of jealousy.

6. The operative word here is "seems to." The common — almost certainly misguided — assumption is that these people are of a kind with his "opponents" in Galatians, 2 Cor 10–13 (and Phil 3:2); see on vv. 16-17.

7. On the textual question see n. 1 above.

The emphasis in this sentence lies with the A-A' clauses, that is, with those who are trying to inflict suffering.[8] But even though it smarts personally, Paul will have none of it — the supposed affliction, that is. Rather (v. 18), he rejoices because Christ is proclaimed; for him, "to live is Christ" (v. 21), hence his ability to rejoice. Our dilemma is how to square Paul's attitude toward these people with what he says elsewhere about those who oppose him and his gospel.

**15** Paul thus follows the encouraging word of v. 14 with this unexpected note: "It is true that[9] some preach Christ[10] out of envy and rivalry." Here we face our first difficulty, since these two words[11] occur together elsewhere in the vice lists of Gal 5:20-21 and Rom 1:29,[12] where Paul describes the behavior of those "who will not inherit the kingdom of God." In 1 Tim 6:4, they appear together again to describe the false teachers, who were probably elders, and therefore former friends:[13] their "morbid craving" for controversy stems from "envy and strife." In our text these words express the underlying reason for the newfound boldness of some, which, of course, can only have been directed at Paul personally.[14] Jealousy is one of the basest expressions of human fallenness. Out of envy toward Paul, perhaps with a

---

8. So also Silva, 72.

9. Which rather nicely captures Paul's τινὲς μὲν καί; the καί in this case is ascensive (= some, on the one hand, *indeed* . . .).

10. Gk. τὸν Χριστὸν κηρύσσουσιν. Again, this is the language of evangelism (see above on v. 5 [n. 51] and v. 12). On the textual question regarding the definite article (and its apparent lack of significance) see n. 2.

11. Gk. φθόνος ("envy, jealousy"); ἔρις ("strife, discord, contention"). The "rivalry" of the NIV nicely captures this sense, as long as it is understood to be carried out contentiously.

12. By "together" I do not mean next to each other, but in the same list. In Galatians they appear in reverse order as the 7th and 13th items on that list; in Romans in the second grouping, "full of envy, murder, strife."

13. For this view of things, see Fee, *1 Timothy,* on 1 Tim 6:3-5. That the desertions took place among some of the leadership is what makes 2 Tim 1:15 so poignant: "All in Asia have deserted me."

14. Otherwise, Schütz (*Paul,* 162), who makes the surprising assertion that "they . . . are directed toward the entire community, or at least are not directed toward Paul as an individual." This appears to be based on a prior analysis of the words in Galatians, where the community is in view; but to think so here seems to disregard the chiastic structure of these verses and thus of the relationship of vv. 16-17 to v. 15 (those who preach out of "envy" [v. 15] are the same who do so in order to afflict Paul [v. 17]). Jewett ("Conflicting Movements," 364-65; following O. Linton, "Situation") mirror reads the passage to reflect a division in the (he thinks Ephesian) community over Paul's imprisonment, i.e., whether his imprisonment for a private "crime" is jeopardizing "his role as an advocate of the gospel." But that is to find far more than is in the text, or even hinted at.

kind of unsavory delight that enjoys kicking an opponent who is down, they now view Paul's imprisonment (evidence of God's judgment?) as their chance to preach Christ "correctly."

On the other hand, there are the others, those whose pure motive is "goodwill."[15] They see that Paul can no longer be involved in preaching Christ publicly, so they have stepped in to pick up the slack. Among these we should probably number those whom Paul greets in Rom 16:3-16, many of whom he there applauds for their "hard work in the Lord."

**16-17** These two sentences elaborate on v. 15 as to how each group relates to Paul's "chains." Taking them in reverse order, he begins with his friends, those whose motivation[16] is "love," in this context referring to love *for Paul.* Along with the apostle, they understand[17] Paul's imprisonment to be appointed by God: "I am put here[18] for the defense of the gospel," words that echo v. 7 and anticipate the (apparent) tribunal referred to in vv. 19-20. While those around him are free to "advance the gospel" by preaching Christ, his present role also includes "the defense of the gospel." Thus, these friends among the Roman house churches see their role as filling the gap — with regard to evangelism — for a wounded comrade in arms, as it were, who has been divinely appointed to defend the gospel at the highest level of the empire. It takes the love of Christ, it should be noted further, for one to see another's circumstances through such a prism.

In any case, this surely reflects the heart of Paul's understanding of his ordeal. From the *Roman* point of view, Paul is on trial over a matter of *religio licita* — or perhaps of *maiestas.*[19] From *his* point of view, the gospel itself is on trial, and his imprisonment is a divinely appointed "defense of the gospel" at the highest echelons. And that is exactly where the others have got it wrong. Their "proclaiming[20] Christ" is predicated on "selfish

15. Gk. εὐδοκίαν; cf. 2:13. Here it can only mean "good will toward Paul" (so most commentaries).

16. The preposition ἐξ in both cases offers the "grounds," hence the motivation, for the respective reasons for preaching Christ.

17. Indeed, there is very likely a deliberate contrast between those who *know* (εἰδότες) in v. 17 and those who *suppose* (οἰόμενοι) in v. 16. The one group "know" the apostle and the others do not; so also Collange, 57; O'Brien, 101.

18. Gk. κεῖμαι ("lie, recline"), but which in figurative uses can mean, as it almost certainly does here, "appointed, or destined for" something; cf. 1 Thess 3:3; Luke 2:34. See BAGD 2.a.

19. That is, whether or not Christianity, no longer clearly attached to Judaism in its Greco-Roman settings, should receive the same status as its parent religion (as a *religio licita,* "approved religion"); or perhaps the whole issue of whether those who claim "Jesus is Lord" can also recognize Caesar as "lord." If not, it would amount to treason *(maiestas).*

20. Gk. καταγγέλλουσιν, used 6x by Paul for "proclaiming Christ" (here, v. 18; 1 Cor 2:1; 9:14; 11:26; Col 1:28), as a synonym for κηρύσσω (used in v. 15).

ambition,"[21] aiming at gain for themselves in a personal battle against Paul; they are therefore preaching Christ, but not "from pure motives." They *suppose,* incorrectly, that they will "raise up affliction in my bonds." Thus they think in terms of Paul, his imprisonment, and his affliction; he thinks in terms of the gospel, for whose defense he has been appointed. Hence, although they are probably something of an annoyance, they cannot really get at Paul; even their "impurity," Paul recognizes, still advances the gospel![22]

But who are these people, or at least, *what kind of* people are they? Do they relate in any way to the other alleged "opponents" in this letter, especially people mentioned in 1:28-30; 2:21; 3:2; and 3:18-19?[23] And how do we reconcile Paul's attitude here with what we find elsewhere? Since nothing in the text directly helps us with these questions, we are left to our own devices — and the suggestions have been many.[24] On two matters we can be relatively certain. First, as noted above (on v. 14), they are surely members of the Christian community in the city where Paul is imprisoned.[25] Second, and related to the first, they cannot, therefore, be related — in any direct sense, at least — to the other alleged "opponents" who surface in this letter. These people are in Rome (as are those in 2:21); those in 1:27-28 are in Philippi; others are merely warned against (3:2) or wept over (3:18), but are not located geographically.

Of the various answers to the questions of "Who?" or "What kind of?" the best guess is that which takes seriously that this letter comes from Rome, and that Paul has therefore reached his desired goal expressed in a letter to this church some five or more years earlier (Rom 1:13; 15:23) — although under considerably different conditions than he had hoped for! In that letter he addressed some of the internal struggles, most likely related to the existence of several house churches,[26] which he knew existed even then in the church in

---

21. Gk. ἐξ ἐριθείας; a very difficult word to pin down with any precision. Most likely it is a derivative from ἔριθος, a word denoting "hired laborer," from which it derived a secondary, pejorative sense of "mercenary." BAGD consider its meaning in the NT a "matter of conjecture." The choice seems to be between "rivalry" and "selfish ambition," which in this context come out very nearly at the same place. See further on 2:3 below.

22. In the debate over "integrity" and "opponents" (see the Introduction, pp. 21-23, 7-10), it is common to refer to Paul's treatment of these people as "mild" in comparison with what he says of the "dogs" in 3:2 (e.g., Rahtjen, "Three Letters," 170, who overstates this matter with considerable rhetoric). But this is a half-truth, perpetuated for the sake of a theory. Despite his rejoicing over the fact that the gospel is still being advanced, the *language* Paul uses to describe their motivation is that of *indictment,* not amelioration!

23. On this whole question, see the Introduction, pp. 7-10.

24. For a helpful overview, see O'Brien, 102-5, which will not be repeated here.

25. *Pace* Schmithals's assertion to the contrary (*Paul,* 74 n. 45).

26. See Rom 16:3-15; cf. Bruce, "St. Paul in Macedonia," 266.

Rome. At issue was Jew and Gentile acceptance of one another in the same body of Christ. His letter to them in effect tried to do two things: to get Jewish Christians to see how Christ brought an end to Torah as a means of relating to God; and to get the Gentiles to moderate their behavior toward the Jewish believers on matters that did not count. Hence most of the letter is written from the perspective of the apostle to the Gentiles, trying to persuade that Christ and the Spirit have brought an end to the significance of Jewish identity markers; yet the paraenetic sections, especially 14:1–15:13, are written from the perspective of the Gentiles with regard to their acceptance of Jews.[27]

One can make a great deal of sense of this present material, if on arriving in Rome he found that his letter had not been totally successful. The Jewish Christian element, glad for concessions about food, are less convinced that food (and circumcision) have nothing to do with the kingdom of God (Rom 14:17). Since this is not Paul's church (as one he founded), they owe him nothing, as it were. His presence in Rome under house arrest has given them new energy for evangelism, in part at least over against Paul's understanding of the gospel.[28] Nonetheless, Paul recognizes that they are indeed preaching Christ, but out of jealousy and partisanship. While this obviously disappoints him, it still causes rejoicing because the gospel is being preached.

This would also explain the more difficult — and tenuous — question as to how he can rejoice in their preaching when he so roundly scores "opponents" in other contexts. All of Paul's strong language against "opponents," it should be noted, including 3:2 in this letter, is directed toward those who invade his Gentile churches and insist on their conforming to basic Jewish identity markers (circumcision, food laws, observance of days). But not all who might oppose Paul on the matter of Gentiles' not keeping Torah should be thought of as "Judaizers" in this sense (of invading Paul's churches to make "converts"); nor should one think that just because some who strongly disagree with him have not invaded his churches with their point of view that they thereby would consider themselves as his friends. Such people, especially in a city where Paul is well known but not by face, could easily be stirred up by Paul's present imprisonment to preach Christ — from their point of view, of course — out of envy and selfish ambition over against Paul.

Toward such people[29] Paul could easily take a more moderate stance.

27. For a brief overview of this perspective on Romans, see chap. 7 in Fee, *Presence*.

28. Some have suggested options not involving Jew/Gentile distinctions at all (e.g., Kennedy, 424; Vincent, 19); see the discussion of other options in O'Brien (n. 24).

29. I am not herewith contending that this is *in fact* who the preachers in v. 17 are, but am trying to offer a reasonable explanation as to how Paul can so violently oppose "Judaizers" but treat others more kindly who might hold a *theological* point of view similar to the Judaizers. A position similar to that suggested here is also taken by Silva, 73.

To use the vernacular, it is the difference between genuine evangelism and "sheep stealing." Gal 2:6-10 makes clear that Paul recognizes, and accepts, differences of opinion within the larger circle of Christian faith. The agreement hammered out there finally took the form of "spheres of influence." Not for a moment, therefore, would Paul reject circumcision for boys born into Jewish Christian homes. He was, after all, "to the Jew as a Jew." What he finds intolerable are those who enter his turf (the Gentile mission) and insist on Gentile submission to Jewish ways.[30] Thus, from his perspective what is currently taking place in Rome is not the same as what "the mutilators of the flesh" (3:2) have been about in Galatia and elsewhere. The latter are "sheep stealers," pure and simple; they are not trying to make converts to Christ, but to make "Jews" out of Gentiles who are already believers in Christ. Those to whom Paul is here referring are involved in *evangelism,* as the language of the present passage verifies.[31] If that means they see themselves as being in the right over against Paul, that matters little to him, because he really believes, in ways sometimes difficult for us to comprehend, that "neither circumcision nor uncircumcision counts for anything, but only the new creation" (Gal 6:15). In any case, whether this is the correct reconstruction or not, these sentences together make it clear that Paul can distance himself personally from the pain some would inflict on him and that, despite their motivation, he can rejoice because the gospel is advancing — evangelism is taking place in Rome as the direct result of his incarceration.

A final contextual word. Very likely the reason for Paul's including these words here is for the most part related to the situation in Philippi, where they too are undergoing some internal unrest. Thus, as Paul now writes to Philippi, he does so *in light of the local situation in Rome.*[32] In 1:27 he exhorts them to "contend for the gospel in one Spirit as one person"; in 2:3 he urges that they "do nothing from selfish ambition"; in 2:13 he reminds them that God is at work in you "both to will and to act according to his 'goodwill' "; and in 2:21 he remembers again that some "look out for their own interests, not those of Jesus Christ." It seems reasonable to suppose that some strife on

---

30. This is clearly so, e.g., in the case of Galatians (see 5:7-12; 6:11-13); it is very likely so in 2 Corinthians as well (cf. 2:17–3:18 and 11:1-23, esp. v. 22). In our letter see esp. 3:2-9.

31. This distinction is what is missed by those interpreters who think Paul is here referring to "Judaizers" as such, i.e., those who are compelling Gentiles to be circumcised (e.g., Meyer, Lightfoot). There is no hint here that these "preachers of Christ" are trying to make Jewish Christians out of Gentile Christians; indeed Paul's language suggests the opposite, that they are trying to make Christians out of those are not.

32. A point also made by Beare, 60; Melick, 68 (as one reason among several). Barth, Dibelius, Schmithals, Gnilka, *et al.* see the paragraph as basically an "excursus," a viewpoint that fails to see its interconnectedness with the whole letter.

the local scene has heightened his concern for the situation in Philippi. Thus with vv. 15-17 Paul anticipates the exhortations of 1:27–2:16 and 4:2-3.

**18** Here is the evidence that vv. 15-17 in some ways have been something of an aside for (probably) paradigmatic reasons. Paul began this paragraph by explaining that the net fallout of his imprisonment has been to advance the gospel. That, and that alone, is the cause of his joy:[33] "Christ is preached. And because of this I rejoice." His joy is not over his imprisonment as such; that kind of morbid "thanking God for all things" lies outside Paul's own theological perspective. No, the pain is there, and some are indeed preaching Christ "from false motives."[34] Paul's joy lies with his perspective — his ability to see every pirouette both for its own beauty and for its place in the whole dance. He had long desired to come to Rome, so that he might share with the Roman believers his understanding of the gospel and proclaim Christ to those who do not know him (Rom 1:11-14; cf. 15:23). Now he is there, although in circumstances not of his own choosing. But even so, neither are these circumstances a cause for complaint, but for joy, because God in his own wisdom is carrying out his purposes, even through Paul's imprisonment.

But to get to this expression of joy, which could easily have followed v. 14, he instead goes by way of vv. 15-17. Without doubt the newly emboldened, fearless preaching of the gospel by his friends was cause for joy under any circumstances. What he wants the Philippians to hear is that the preaching which intended as one of its side affects to afflict him is also a cause for joy. Thus, "but[35] what does it matter?" What counts[36] "is that in every way" — and now he inserts by way of vv. 15-17, "whether from false motive or true" — "Christ is proclaimed." Once again, Paul's focus is on evangelism — on Christ as God's good news for all, and therefore to be proclaimed to all. That people are hearing the good news about Christ is also good news for Paul, hence he concludes, "and in this I rejoice."

In 2:17-18 Paul will encourage the Philippians to rejoice with him,

---

33. On the theme of "joy" in this letter see the Introduction, pp. 52-53; see also on 1:4; 2:2, 18; and (esp.) 4:4.

34. Gk. προφάσει, having to do with one's ostensible reason, or pretext, for doing something, but not based on truth or reality. Cf. 1 Thess 2:5, where it appears in close connection with hypocrisy.

35. Gk. γάρ ("for"), which never means "but," under any stretch of the polyvalence of words. Paul says simply, τί γάρ ("For what?"). His more usual expression in such moments is τί οὖν ("What, then?" cf. Rom 3:9; 6:15; 1 Cor 14:15, 26). The γάρ here is to be understood as tying what is said directly to v. 17 in a sort of "explanatory" way: "For (even in light of those mentioned in v. 17) what does it matter?"

36. Gk. πλήν, an adverb used as an adversative conjunction. Here it stands in contrast to the "for what?" "In any case," he adds, meaning something very close to the NIV's "the important thing is"; cf. on 4:14.

even if it means that his present circumstances are a form of "libation," a sacrifice poured out to God on their behalf. Here he anticipates that exhortation by offering himself as a pattern for them to follow.[37]

It would be easy to dismiss this passage (vv. 12-18a) either as anecdotal narrative or as Paul's simply putting the best possible face on a bad situation. But that would be to miss too much. Paul can write things like this because, first, his theology is in good order. He has learned by the grace of God to see everything from the divine perspective. This is not wishfulness, but deep conviction — that God had worked out his own divine intentions through the death and resurrection of Christ, and that by his Spirit he is carrying them out in the world through the church, and therefore through both himself and others. It is not that Paul is too heavenly minded to be in touch with reality, or that he sees things through rosy-tinted glasses. Rather, he sees everything in light of the bigger picture; and in that bigger picture, fully emblazoned on our screen at Calvary, there is nothing that does not fit, even if it means suffering and death on the way to resurrection. Such theology dominates this letter in every part; we should not be surprised that it surfaces at the outset, even in this brief narrative.

Second, and related to the first, Paul is a man of a single passion: Christ and the gospel. Everything is to be seen and done in light of Christ. For him both life and death mean Christ. His is the passion of the single-minded person who has been "apprehended by Christ," as he will tell the Philippians in 3:12-14.

Third, Paul's passion for Christ led him to an understanding of discipleship in which the disciple took up a cross to follow his Lord. Discipleship, therefore, meant "to participate in the sufferings of Christ" (3:10-11), to be ready to be poured out as a drink offering in ministry for the sake of others (2:17). His imprisonment belongs to those trials for which "we were destined" (1 Thess 3:3), and thus come as no surprise.

Interestingly, these three theological realities are what also make for Paul's largeness of heart. True, he lacks the kind of "largeness" for which religious pluralists contend. Is that because such pluralists have not been apprehended by Christ and the gospel, as God's thing — his only thing — on behalf of our fallen world? Unfortunately, such pluralism often has very little tolerance for the Pauls of this world. Tolerance seems easier to one's left than to one's right! But in Paul's case it is his theological convictions that lead both to his theological narrowness, on the one hand, and to his large-heartedness within those convictions, on the other — precisely because he recognizes the gospel for what it is: God's thing, not his own. And that, it should be

---

37. Even though that is not said here, it is said twice later on (3:17; 4:9). Here is surely one of the things they are to "practice" which they have "heard and seen in him." All the more so, in light of the close connection between his "rejoicing" over the gospel in the midst of his pain, which he reaffirms in 2:17 and then explicitly urges them to emulate in 2:18.

added, also stands quite over against many others who think of themselves as in Paul's train, but whose passion for the gospel seems all too often a passion for their own "correct" view of things.

At stake for the Philippians — and for us, I would venture — is the admonition finally made explicit in 4:9: to put into practice for ourselves what we *hear* and *see* in Paul, as well as what we have learned and have received by way of his teaching.

## B. THE FUTURE — FOR THE GLORY OF CHRIST AND THE GOOD OF THE PHILIPPIANS (1:18b-26)

Having apprised the Philippians of the present effect of his imprisonment (vv. 12-18a) — which is cause for joy in that the gospel has been advanced — Paul now turns toward the future, to reflect on the expected outcome of his (apparently) soon coming trial. The future is also cause for joy, partly because he expects vindication — for himself and the gospel (vv. 19-20) — and partly because he expects to be released and to find his way back to Philippi again (vv. 24-26). Thus the paragraph is framed by "joy" — Paul's joy as he anticipates Christ's being "magnified" at his trial, and their joy when his expected return to Philippi is realized.

The section is in three parts, each flowing naturally out of the other and held together by the common thread of reflection on "what's next" regarding his imprisonment. (1) Vv. 19-20 offer the reason for his continuing to rejoice. He expects through their prayers and the supply of the Spirit that he will be "saved/vindicated," thus fulfilling his hope that Christ be "magnified," whether through "life" or "death" (= whether he gains his release or is given the death penalty). (2) The mention of "whether by life or by death" leads him in vv. 21-24 to ponder those options (knowing that he has no real choice in the matter). The focus is on Christ; the orientation is eschatological. Paul's clear preference is death, since that means to gain the eschatological prize — Christ himself (cf. 3:12-14). Nonetheless, he has little doubt that it will be "life," since that is what is best for them. Thus "death" would be to his advantage, but "life" to theirs, so life is what he expects it to be. (3) Vv. 25-26 then offer the end result of his being given "life" — their own "advance" (cf. v. 12) in the faith and the joy they will experience when they see him again.

In contrast to what has preceded, this reflection is far more personal.[1] Even though Paul expects to be released (vv. 24-26; 2:24), his mentioning the possibility of life or death (v. 20) sets him to musing over these alternatives

---

1. E.g., in comparison with the preceding paragraph, there are considerably more first person verbs (9 to 3) and personal pronouns (8 to 4).

(vv. 21-24). Here is the closest thing to soliloquy that one finds in the extant letters. Yet even here the focus is still on Christ and the gospel. By a fresh supply of the Spirit *of Jesus Christ* he expects his "hope" to be fulfilled, that *Christ will be magnified* whether Paul lives or dies; for to live means *Christ* and to die means to gain *Christ.* If he had a choice, therefore, he would choose death, because that would mean to be *with Christ;* but since he has no choice, "life" is the expected outcome, leading to his return to Philippi and their overflow of joy *in Christ Jesus.*

Most likely all of this is for the Philippians' sakes as well, thus it is not true soliloquy. For reasons not known to us (present suffering and/or internal bickering?), some of them apparently have lost their firm grip on future certainties.[2] Hence even this personal musing functions as paradigm.[3] The future — the full realization of Christ — is a glorious prospect, Paul reassures them, even if it were to mean in his case to arrive there prematurely at the hands of others!

Again, one can hardly miss the three-way bond — between him, them, and Christ — that informs every part of the letter.[4] The present emphasis is on Paul's relationship with Christ (to live is Christ; hence his desire is to be with Christ); it concludes on the note of his relationship with them (they will glory in Christ *in him* when he comes to be *with them*), which has their relationship with Christ as its ultimate concern (their progress and joy in the faith).

All told this is one of the apostle's finer moments, a passage to which God's people have turned over and again to find strength and encouragement in times of difficulty. We all are the richer for it.

### 1. Paul's Ambition — That Christ be Glorified (1:18b-20)

*Yes, and I will continue to rejoice,* 19*for*[5] *I know that through your prayers and the help given by the Spirit of Jesus Christ, what has*

---

2. See the discussion of vv. 6 and 10 above, pp. 87-88, 102.

3. Especially so in light of 3:15-17, where exhortation to "imitation" immediately follows vv. 12-14, which emphasizes completing the race so as to obtain the prize. See also on v. 17 above, pp. 123-24, where a similar suggestion was made regarding the place of 1:15-17 in the letter.

4. See the Introduction, pp. 13-14; cf. on 1:3-8 above (p. 73).

5. P[46] B 1175 1739 1881 Ambrosiaster read δέ. Although one is reluctant to go against this combination of witnesses, most likely the δέ is secondary here. If it were original, the preceding ἀλλά would seem to lose its genuinely contrastive force, and the clause ἀλλὰ καὶ χαρήσομαι would then belong to v. 18 (as many hold [see n. 6 below]): "Christ is preached and in this I rejoice, indeed I shall rejoice. But I know. . . ." The γάρ, which is by all counts the more difficult (otherwise, Kennedy, 426), and therefore original, reading, means that Paul has begun a new clause, giving reasons for his avowal of future joy: ". . . and in this I rejoice. And not only so, but I shall also rejoice, *for* I know that . . ." (cf. Hawthorne, 39; O'Brien, 107).

*happened to me will turn out for my deliverance.*[a] 20*I eagerly expect and hope that I will in no way be ashamed, but will have sufficient courage so that now as always Christ will be exalted in my body, whether by life or by death.*

[a]Or *salvation*

That this clause begins a new section is verified by the deliberate shift from present to future rejoicing and by the explanatory "for" which ties vv. 19-20 to 18b (see n. 5).[6] As his present joy is expressed in the face of conflict (some believers in Rome against him), so with his future joy, which will find expression in the face of external opposition — a point that seems directed in part at least toward the situation in Philippi.

This opening paragraph, however, is an extremely complex sentence, whose difficulties (for us) stem in part from the word *sōtēria*[7] (whether it means "deliverance [from prison]"[8] or "salvation" in some other sense) and in part from its flow of thought, including some unclear relationships of the various parts to one another. It complexities can best be seen by a more literal rendering of Paul's Greek, set out according to the grammatical relationships of its various parts:[9]

> What is more, I *will* rejoice,
>> for
> I know that:
>> (a) this for me will turn out    unto *sōtēria*
>>> (a[1])  through your prayers
>>>> and
>>>> the supply of the Spirit
>>>>> of Jesus Christ

6. Otherwise, KJV, ASV, NASB, Meyer, Kennedy, Michael, Kent. A few (e.g., Vincent, 21-22; Jones, 16; Lohmeyer, 49; Beare, 60; Silva, 75) begin the new paragraph with v. 18. On this matter see n. 3 on 1:12-26.

7. Gk. σωτηρία, which in Paul always refers, directly or indirectly, to "eschatological salvation," never "deliverance" (see on 1:28 and 2:12 below). For this latter idea Paul uses the verb ῥύομαι, as in 2 Thess 3:2; 2 Cor 1:10 (3x); Rom 15:31; 2 Tim 4:17-18.

8. As in the NIV; cf. RSV, NRSV, NASB, NEB, GNB. See Hawthorne, 39-44, for the most recent advocacy of this view, which, despite the translations, is a decidedly minority view among commentaries.

9. It will be noted that this display, and the interpretation that follows, differs from that given in the NIV, which has taken considerable liberties with the text in this instance. Since the sentence is so dense, and its flow of thought not easy to follow under the best of circumstances, one may wish to return to this overview after working through the more detailed discussion that follows.

    (a²)  according to my earnest expectation
               and
               hope
   (b) <u>that</u>
      (b¹)       in no way
                 will I be brought to shame,
                 <u>but</u>
      (b²)       with all openness/boldness
                   as always,
                   even now,
               Christ will be magnified
                   in my body
                 whether  through life
                 or        through death

Most of the sentence gives the content of what Paul "knows," namely (a) "that this for me will turn out unto *sōtēria*." The two prepositional modifiers (a¹, a²) and the final clause (b), which spells out the content of Paul's "earnest expectation and hope,"[10] imply that God is the presumed subject of everything.[11] Thus, "God will turn this [Paul's present circumstances] unto 'salvation' " for him; God will do so (a¹) "through the Philippians' prayers and the (subsequent) supply of the Spirit of Jesus Christ," and (a²) "in keeping with Paul's own earnest expectation and hope." His "hope" is then explicated in terms of God's not allowing Paul to be brought to shame (b¹), but to the contrary that "in my 'body,' by life or by death (= acquittal or execution) God will magnify Christ" (b²).

    The second prepositional phrase (a²) functions as the fulcrum: that Paul's present circumstances will turn out for salvation is "in keeping with his fervent expectation and hope," which is defined in terms of Christ's being magnified through Paul's trial, however it turns out. This means, further, that Paul's "salvation" in clause (a) is to be understood in part in light of the content of clause (b). But herein lies the difficulty: this final clause, which is

---

10. Otherwise Hawthorne, 39-43 (and Hofmann, according to Meyer), who understands this ὅτι as a second object clause with the verb "I know" ("I know that . . . , that . . ."). Besides putting considerable strain on this second ὅτι-clause (the absence of a preceding καί is esp. difficult), this seems to miss the point of the sentence as a whole.

11. This is especially so if the suggestion made below is correct, that the Philippians' "salvation" in v. 28 is to be understood as in parallel to Paul's in this sentence. Theirs is explicitly stated to be "from God." The present sentence, therefore, is best understood as expressed in the divine passive, in which the passives ("will turn out," "I will not be brought to shame," "Christ will be magnified") can be reformulated in the active with "God" as the subject.

clearly the aim of the whole,[12] enjoys a measure of tension with the opening clause,[13] which in turn leads to the question of how we are to understand "salvation" in that clause.

**18b-19** Without breaking stride Paul begins this new section by picking up where he has just concluded, moving from his present joy ("because of this I rejoice") to his prospect of still greater joy ("what is more,[14] I will continue to rejoice"). The explanatory "for" indicates that vv. 19-20 are intended to *explain* why he "will continue to rejoice."

The place to begin our way through Paul's "explanation" is with a phenomenon literary critics call "intertextuality,"[15] the *conscious* embedding of fragments of an earlier text into a later one. Since Paul's spiritual life and theology are thoroughly imbued with OT realities, we should not be surprised that he not only quotes the OT[16] but also at times borrows or "echoes" the *language and setting* of a specific OT passage (or motif) and refits it into his own setting.[17] In this sentence he echoes the situation of the "poor man" in the OT, especially Job and the Psalmists, who in their distress look to God for "vindication," which will function as "salvation" for them. Paul's first clause is in fact a verbatim borrowing from Job 13:16 (LXX);[18] and the second

---

12. Both the structure of the whole and the typical "not/but" clause by which it concludes indicate that the final "but" clause expresses the concern of the sentence.

13. This "tension" exists between what in v. 19 appears to be a positive expectation about the future, which at the end of v. 20 seems to be expressed with a measure of doubt (or at least of open-endedness). This tension exists especially for those who take the point of view about the main clause found in the NIV, which "resolves" the tension by a disjuncture between vv. 19 and 20 that is grammatically unjustifiable (by divorcing the prepositional phrase from the clause it modifies and thus starting a new *sentence* with the preposition!) and conceptually misleading (as though Paul expected "deliverance," v. 19, but hoped in any case that Christ might be magnified, v. 20). Hawthorne's resolution fares little better (see n. 10). While it is true that almost everyone would read v. 19 as referring to deliverance were it not for the ὅτι-clause, it is that clause which in fact tells us *not* to read v. 19 in this way.

14. For this translation of the ἀλλά, see M. Thrall, *Greek Particles,* 14; cf. BAGD, who note this usage as "ascensive," to be explained elliptically (= and not only this [v. 18a] but also . . .).

15. On this question see esp. R. B. Hays, *Echoes,* who uses this text in his first chapter (pp. 21-24) as an illustration of such intertextuality, where Paul "echoes" the earlier text with its literary milieu, and thus seems to have transferred some of that setting to his own situation, but does so with some obvious contrasts between himself and — in this case — Job. This view, without the refinement of a later time, was first proposed by Michael, 46-48; cf. Gnilka, 65-66; Collange, 59; O'Brien, 108-9.

16. As in most cases, usually to support an argument.

17. For further illustrations in Paul, see Fee, *Presence,* 489-93 (on Rom 2:29) and 712-17 (on Eph 4:30).

18. This was often overlooked by earlier interpreters, because in this case we

clause, with its collocation of "shame" and "magnifying," picks up the language of the "poor man" in such Psalms as 34:3-6 and 35:24-28.[19] Thus, even though this is now Paul's own sentence, and must be understood within its present context, it is best understood as intentionally echoing the analogous circumstances of Job.

Job 13 contains one of the more poignant of Job's speeches, where he abjures the perspective of his "comforters," who insist that his present situation is the result of "hidden sin." Job knows better and pleads his cause with God, in whom he hopes and before whom he would plead his innocence. Indeed, the very hope of appearing before God in this way will be his "salvation" because the godless shall not come before God (v. 16). And "salvation" for Job means "I know that I will be vindicated" (v. 18).[20] So with Paul, but in quite different circumstances.[21]

The "this," which belongs to the Job citation, now means (probably), "this whole affair (= my present circumstances)."[22] Thus, "my present circumstances will issue in my *sōtēria*." Also in light of the Job citation, *sōtēria* probably refers first to Paul's final eschatological "salvation," when he appears among the redeemed at the heavenly tribunal.[23] But the final clause indicates that it also, especially, entails "vindication," God's "vindication" of him and his gospel by "magnifying Christ — now as always — through

---

have no introductory formula (e.g., "Scripture says"). But the language is so precise, and the "settings" so similar, it is nearly impossible for Paul's language to be mere coincidence.

19. Noted also by Gnilka, 67-68, and O'Brien, 114. This second instance, of course, is an "echo" of a slightly different kind, where in a less case-specific way than with the Job "citation" Paul echoes a repeated OT motif. See on v. 20.

20. In Paul's sentence, therefore, the word σωτηρία carries in part its ordinary sense of "salvation before God," but in this case, as in the LXX, in the special sense of the final vindication of the passion of Paul's life, the gospel of Christ and therefore of Christ himself. See the discussion.

21. But the circumstances are surely analogous. Job's cry for vindication/salvation stems from his suffering, which is made the more so by his "comforters"; his only recourse is to cry to God for vindication. Similarly, some would intensify Paul's present suffering by their preaching Christ out of envy. That they fail in their effort to distress Paul does not make his appeal to God's vindication/salvation any less a reflection of Job. Cf. Garland, "Defense," 333.

22. Cf. Kennedy, 426. Many (Lightfoot, Vincent, Plummer, Jones, Hawthorne, O'Brien, Melick) see it as pointing backward (to all of vv. 12-18b), but this would seem to require the plural ταῦτα (which Meyer, 42, skirts by making it refer to the ἐν τούτῳ of v. 18 [= Christ's being proclaimed in every way], which makes little sense of the present sentence). The NIV takes considerable liberty in translating τοῦτο "what has happened to me," which not only seems to require ταῦτα, but also adds a "to me" that is not justifiable under any circumstances.

23. So Gnilka, Collange, Bruce, Silva, O'Brien, Melick.

Paul" before the Roman tribunal,[24] whichever way it turns out. Such "salvation/vindication" is his "earnest expectation and hope." The result is a sentence which reads (paraphrased): "This whole affair will turn out to my ultimate salvation and present vindication, when, through your prayers and the supply of the Spirit of Christ my earnest expectation and hope are realized at my trial and not only am I not brought to shame but in a very open (or bold) way Christ is magnified in every way — whether I am given 'life' or sentenced to death."[25]

The initial modifier indicates *how* Paul expects God to bring all of this about: "through your prayers[26] and the supply of the Spirit of Jesus Christ." The grammar[27] assumes the closest kind of relationship between their prayer and the supply of the Spirit. Through their prayers, and with that, God's special provision of the Spirit, his most eager expectation and hope about Christ's being magnified through him will be realized. But as the NIV reveals, not all interpreters think so. At issue are (1) the meaning of the word "supply,"[28]

24. So also Hendriksen.

25. It should be further noted that the reflective soliloquy that follows offers further evidence that Paul's concern is not with "getting out of prison," but exactly as in vv. 12-18: that whether released or not, Christ will be glorified, and for Paul that could happen through his death as well as by his life. Besides, he will go on, "as for myself personally, if I could choose, *death* would be preferable because that would mean finally to have 'gained Christ,' but in reality I have no choice, and *life* will be better for you, because that will mean growth and joy for you." That is hardly the reflection of one whose "ardent hope" is to be delivered from prison.

26. Even though δεήσεως is singular, this is the proper understanding of what is almost certainly a "distributive singular." See the discussion, *inter alia,* on Gal 6:18 in Fee, *Presence,* 469. The word order τῆς ὑμῶν δεήσεως is striking. The ὑμῶν has probably been brought forward for clarity and emphasis (on *their* role in his experiencing a fresh supply of the Spirit); cf. Meyer, 43; O'Brien, 111 (see also the discussion of the "vernacular possessive" ["my joy"] on 2:2).

27. The two nouns ("prayers" and "supply") serve as compound objects of one preposition with one definite article. Cf. Zerwick, *Biblical Greek,* 59: "The use of but one article before a number of nouns indicates that they are conceived as forming a certain unity. . . . In Php 1,19 . . . the use of . . . one article shows that in the writer's mind the prayers of the faithful and the ἐπιχορηγία τοῦ πνεύματος Ἰησοῦ Χριστοῦ were intimately connected." Otherwise Meyer, 43, and Vincent, 24; but Paul's way of *distinguishing* between the two is by bringing the ὑμῶν forward (see preceding n.).

28. Gk. ἐπιχορηγία, whose cognate verb appears in Eph 4:16 ("with which it is supplied," RSV), where M. Barth, *Ephesians,* 448, has convincingly shown that the normal meaning ("supply") is both lexically and contextually to be preferred (cf. Col 2:19; 2 Cor 9:10). There is some debate in the literature as to whether the compound form (ἐπιχορηγία) implies *generous* supply. Lightfoot, Michael, Beare, and Motyer are so inclined; Vincent thinks not. Most do not mention the possibility. This is more difficult to determine, since both the noun and its cognate verb appear infrequently in the extant literature. In any case, if it does not imply "generous," all known uses do suggest "full" or "adequate" supply.

translated "help"[29] by the NIV (and others), and (2) whether "Spirit" is the object or subject of "supply" (= supply or supplier). These are related issues, since "help" is an invented meaning which apparently evolved because scholarship was generally convinced that the Spirit was the subject of "supply," not its object.[30]

The noun derives from its cognate verb, which invariably means "to supply, furnish, or provide for." Its non-compounded form originated as a term for supplying choristers and dancers for festive occasions. But even as it moved beyond that original specific sense, it always kept the nuance of supplying or providing someone with something. Thus the verb, and the verbal idea of this noun, is clearly transitive, requiring or expecting an object in terms of what is supplied.[31] That Paul here intends the Spirit as the "supply" is confirmed by the almost identical usage of the cognate verb in Gal 3:5, where it can only mean "God supplies you with the Spirit." There he appeals to believers who had already "received" the Spirit (v. 2) that God's continuing "supply" of the Spirit, including miracles, is further certain evidence that "works of Law" do not count. Likewise here he is not thinking of the Spirit's "help" but of the gift of the Spirit himself, whom God continually provides.[32] The oft-debated question as to whether the genitive is "objective" or "subjective" is therefore nearly irrelevant. Since the noun does not mean "help," but "supply," and an object is implied by the word itself, the Spirit in this case can only be the object[33] — to be supplied so as

29. See e.g. NIV, RSV, GNB, JB, NAB, Phillips, Hawthorne.

30. One can trace the evolution of this meaning through Bauer and the commentators (see esp. Müller, 58 n. 2, and Hendriksen, 74 n. 50; both of whom move from "supply" to "help" without offering lexical evidence). Convinced that the Spirit is the subject of the verbal idea in this noun, and having difficulty offering an object to the translation, "through the Spirit's supply," the evolution was an easy one. Since the verb is used in the papyri in marriage contracts, where husbands promise to "provide for" their wives, the English word "support" in this financial sense came to be used (indeed, this is the only meaning offered in BAGD). The next step, from "support" to "help" or "aid," seemed only natural — but in English (and German [Bauer]), one might add! There is simply no evidence for such a meaning in the Greek materials.

31. It needs to be pointed out that the English word "help," which almost never carries such a nuance, has to do with coming to someone's aid. One would not deny that when the rich provide for the poor, or a husband contracts to provide for his wife (two of the specific uses in the literature; see 1 Clem 38:2 and the papyri cited by M-M, 251), in that sense the recipients are being helped. But the nuance of this word is *not* with the idea of helping, but with the "provision" or "supply" itself.

32. Moffatt's translation has thus captured the sense: "and as I am provided with the Spirit of Jesus Christ."

33. One needs to emphasize this point, over against the decided majority of commentators who argue for a subjective genitive. The evidence in this case seems overwhelming, especially since the word is such a rare one, yet Paul himself uses it in precisely this way in

to magnify Christ — not the one who as "subject" will help Paul as he faces trial.[34]

This understanding is further supported by the unusual designation, "the Spirit *of Jesus Christ.*"[35] This qualifier, yet another genitive construction, again could be construed as subjective (i.e., the Spirit sent by Christ[36]). But the close tie of this phrase to the prayer of the Philippians suggests otherwise. Prayer for Paul would be directed toward God the Father, in this case to supply Paul with the Spirit of his Son.[37] This is how Christ lives in him — by his Spirit (Rom 8:9-10).[38] The reason for this unusual qualifier lies in the context. Paul's concern throughout the "explanation" is on Christ and the gospel. In anticipation of the final clause expressing the nature of his "salvation/vindication," Paul knows that Christ will be glorified in his life or death only as he is filled with the Spirit of Christ himself.[39] That is, it is Christ resident in

---

the only other instance where "supply" and "Spirit" stand in juxtaposition. Those who argue for a subjective genitive tend to dismiss this one piece of solid Pauline evidence much too casually (e.g., Eadie). An objective (or, similarly but less likely, appositional) genitive is also adopted (or allowed as probable), inter alia, by Moule, 23; Michael, 49; Lohmeyer, 52; Bruce, 53; Motyer, 85; Silva, 79 (cf. Zerwick, *Biblical Greek,* 59; Wiles, *Prayers,* 280). Lightfoot, followed by Michael, argued for both meanings (gift and giver).

34. Although in the final analysis that idea cannot be lingering very far behind. What we must not do, however, is to let our own theological proclivities invent meanings for Paul that would have been foreign to him. Paul had none of our hang-ups over whether a Spirit person can "receive the Spirit." Cf. the objection voiced by Meyer, 43, which seems to lie unexpressed behind that of others: "as genitive of object . . . the expression would be inappropriate, since Paul already *has* the Spirit" (emphasis his). Some have also argued for an analogy with the Johannine Paraclete, as the one who comes alongside to aid the believer. But here is a clear case where John can be of very little help in understanding Paul. If Paul's language does not work well for us, it did for Paul. He could not imagine the Spirit in static terms. Hence he can refer to believers' being "given" the Spirit (1 Thess 4:8), or being "supplied" with the Spirit (Gal 3:5; here), or of fanning the Spirit into flame (2 Tim 3:6). For Paul the resident Spirit is ever being given or "supplied" anew in the believer's or community's life. So here. Paul knows his own need of the Spirit in a fresh way if Christ is to be magnified in him personally in the soon-to-be-unfolding events of his present imprisonment. Cf. the discussion in Fee, *Presence,* 52-53, 864.

35. In fact, this exact phrase is found only here in Paul. On two other occasions he refers to the Spirit as "of Christ" (Gal 4:6; Rom 8:9), but in neither instance with the full name.

36. So Eadie, 45; Michael, 49; Kent, 117; Collange, 60; O'Brien, 111.

37. Very much as in Gal 4:6, where God is said to have sent forth "the Spirit of his Son."

38. It needs further to be pointed out that when Paul reflects on the Spirit as helper he invariably speaks in terms of the Spirit *of God.*

39. Cf. Meyer 43. This seems much more likely than the more theological explanation offered, e.g., by Eadie, that the genitive is of origin or source; thus the Spirit is bestowed by the exalted Lord; cf. Michael 49.

him by the Spirit[40] who will be the cause of Paul's — and therefore the gospel's — not being brought to shame and of Christ's being magnified through him.[41]

Thus this phrase, "the supply of the Spirit of Jesus Christ," is not incidental. Here is the key to Christ's being glorified in every way: by Paul's being "supplied" the Spirit of Jesus Christ himself, who will live powerfully through Paul as he stands trial. At the same time, from such a phrase and its close relationship with the prayer of the believing community, one learns a great deal about Paul's own spiritual life and his understanding of the role of the Spirit in that life. He simply does not think of Christian life as lived in isolation from others. *He* may be the one in prison and headed for trial; but the Philippians — and others — are inextricably bound together with him through the Spirit. Therefore, he assumes that their praying, and with that God's gracious supply of the Spirit of his Son, will be the means God uses yet once more to bring glory to himself through Paul and Paul's defense of the gospel (vv. 7, 16).

**20**   The second phrase modifying the Job citation indicates that all of this (Paul's *knowing* that his present circumstances will issue in his salvation/vindication through their prayers and the supply of the Spirit) is quite in keeping with "my earnest expectation[42] and hope." These two words presume a near unity of ideas, so that "hope" does not mean "wishfulness," but something like "hope-filled expectation."[43] As in most cases in the NT, therefore, "hope" is full of content, in the sense that it reflects the highest degree of certainty about the future.

That content is delineated in the final "that" clause,"[44] in the form of a "not/but" contrast (typical of Pauline argumentation) between his experiencing

---

40. Cf. Barth, 34, "the *Spirit* . . . is the Lord in Person."

41. Hamilton (*Holy Spirit,* 12, 35) offers the improbable suggestion, without argument or lexical support, that Paul sees the Spirit as God's "equipment . . . against losing his relationship with Christ in the face of death" (12).

42. Gk. ἀποκαραδοκίαν; cf. Rom 8:19 ("the eagerly awaiting creation"), its only other use in the NT. A great deal more ink has been spilt over this word than seems warranted by the context. Both the Romans passage and the present context rule out the nuance of "anxiety" suggested as possible by G. Bertram, "Ἀποκαραδοκία," and followed by Gnilka, 67, and Collange, 60. See the refutation by D. R. Denton, "Ἀποκαραδοκία"; cf. H. Balz, *EDNT,* 1.132-33. On this matter Bloomquist (*Function,* 153-54), despite the general failure of his rhetorical analysis, is quite right that the whole passage breathes confidence, not anxiety.

43. So Hawthorne, 41; cf. O'Brien, 113.

44. Which functions grammatically as the object of the verbal idea in the noun "hope." Cf. the similar usage in 2 Cor 10:15, where the infinitive μεγαλυνθῆναι (the same verb that appears figuratively in our clause, "may be magnified [= glorified]") functions as the object of the noun "hope" ("we have hope . . . that our sphere of activity among you will be magnified [= enlarged]").

"shame" and Christ's being "magnified."[45] The "not" side is simply put: "that in nothing[46] will I be brought to shame." The verb "to be brought to shame" could possibly mean something close to "being ashamed" (= feeling shame over something, thus having to do with one's inner feelings[47]); however, in biblical Greek (by way of the OT) it normally carries the sense of disgrace that one will experience from failing to trust God, or contrariwise, that the humble who do trust will *not* experience, despite present appearances to the contrary.[48] Paul's present usage appears to be another case of intertextuality,[49] in this case picking up a motif from the Psalms, where the same words ("shame" and "be exalted") often stand in collocation (e.g., Ps 34:3-5 [LXX 33:4-6]; 35:26-27 [LXX 34:26-27]).[50]

In Paul's present circumstances, and especially in light of the words of Job just cited, the reason for this contrast, especially for the "not" side of it, is perfectly understandable. As vv. 12-18 have made clear, *Paul* is experiencing no shame or disgrace from being in prison; his concern is that there will be no reason for disgrace as far as *the gospel* is concerned when he finally stands before the Roman tribunal. Shame, of course, is *not* what he expects, given their prayers and the supply of the Spirit of Christ.

What Paul *does* expect, the "but" side of the contrast, is that his trust in Christ will issue in Christ's being "magnified/glorified."[51] *How* Paul expects this to happen is spelled out by the several modifiers.

First, he hopes that Christ will be "magnified" with[52] "all[53] openness"

---

45. Not as some have it (e.g., Vincent, Plummer, Craddock), between "shame" and "boldness," on the basis of 1 Jn 2:28. This misses Pauline usage by too much, as if the contrast had to do with "fear" and "courage."

46. Gk. ἐν οὐδενί, which in this clause means something close to "in no respect, in no possible way."

47. So Moffatt: "that I may never feel ashamed"; cf. Beare, 62. This sounds altogether too Western. It is also unlikely that the GNB's "I shall never fail in my duty," defended by Loh-Nida (30) as a "dynamic equivalent," is even remotely possible.

48. Cf. the entry by J. Oswalt in *TWOT,* 1.97-98.

49. Esp. so in light of Paul's use of the unusual verb μεγαλύνω (ordinarily = "make large," thus "magnify"), which is used throughout the Psalter with the nuance it carries here of "exalt, glorify, praise, extol." In its only other appearance in Paul (2 Cor 10:15; see n. 44), it carries its ordinary sense.

50. Note esp. Ps 34:3-5, which begins, "O magnify (μεγαλύνατε) the Lord with me," which after speaking of seeking the Lord and being delivered (ἐρρύσατο in this case, see n. 7), he continues, "Look to him and be radiant, so your faces shall never by ashamed (καταισχυνθῆ)" (NRSV). In Psalm 35 those who "magnify" themselves will be brought to "shame"; whereas those who seek the Psalmist's "vindication" will say, "Let the Lord be 'magnified.' " Cf. Gnilka, 67; O'Brien, 114.

51. For the meaning of this verb see nn. 44, 49, 50.

52. Gk. ἐν; see Wedderburn, "Observations," 85, who classifies the preposition as "modal" in this case, i.e., reflecting accompanying circumstance or manner.

53. Gk. πάσῃ (= in every kind of), standing in stark contrast to ἐν οὐδενί (n. 46);

(or "boldness").[54] This is one of the more difficult words in the Pauline letters. Its basic meaning is "outspokenness" or "plainness of speech" that "conceals nothing and passes over nothing" (BAGD); but it soon crossed over to mean "openness to the public," hence "publicly," and eventually took on the nuance of "bold speech," hence "confidence/boldness," of the kind that only the privileged would have before those in authority. Here it probably has to do with "openness" bordering on "bold speech"; thus, in a very open and public way Christ will be magnified through Paul's bold defense of the gospel,[55] however the trial turns out.

Second, he wants this to happen (literally) "as always also now." This phrase signifies, first, that since his conversion, Paul has thought of his own life singularly as in praise of Christ ("as always"), a theme that emerges over and again in the corpus.[56] Indeed, Paul's rejoicing in vv. 12-18 over the advance of the gospel resulting from his imprisonment offers a prime example of what Paul here intends. But, second, the "also now" signifies that Paul, well aware of his present situation, is looking forward to its resolution. This is the phrase that justifies our speaking of his "apparently soon coming" trial.

Third, this hoped-for glorification of Christ will take place "in my body," by which Paul intends his "physical presence," not his "whole person" as a kind of periphrasis for "in me," which is a doubtful meaning for this word in any case.[57] That he intends the former is clarified in vv. 22 and 24, where he refers to present existence as "in the flesh." Ordinarily Paul uses "in me" when he emphasizes that God will be glorified in him in some way.[58] His reason for using "body" in this case has to do the context; he is writing

---

cf. Vincent, 26 ("every way in which boldness can manifest itself"). This contrast also rules out the alleged contrast between "shame" and "boldness" noted above (n. 45).

54. Gk. παρρησία; see the discussions in *NIDNTT*, 2.724-37 (H.-C. Hahn) and *EDNT*, 3.45-47 (H. Balz).

55. It is doubtful that this phrase can properly bear the sense of the NIV ("sufficient courage"; cf. GNB, "full of courage"). The nuance has to do with "forthrightness; frankness of speech," not with courage, as that word is traditionally understood (= over against cringing or fear).

56. See, e.g., 1 Cor 4:4-5; 2 Cor 4:10; Rom 8:28-30.

57. Cf., e.g., GNB, "with my whole being." Despite O'Brien (115) to the contrary, there is no known *linguistic* justification for this translation. The idea that "body" in Paul functions as an anthropological term, very much like ψυχή ("soul"), was propounded especially by R. Bultmann (*NT Theology*, 1.194-95); J. A. T. Robinson *(Body);* and E. Schweizer, *TDNT*, 7.1065-66. Even though this became a byword in NT studies, it does not hold up well under close exegetical scrutiny. See esp. the refutation in R. H. Gundry, *SŌMA;* cf. the exegesis of key texts, such as 1 Cor 6:13-14 (Fee, *First Corinthians*, 254-56) and Rom 12:1 (Fee, *Presence*, 589 n. 372).

58. See v. 26 below; cf. Gal 1:16, 24; 1 Tim 1:16.

about what will happen to him "physically," that is, whether his trial will result in (physical) life or (bodily) death.[59]

That this is Paul's intent is made certain, fourth, by the final phrase, "whether through[60] life or through death." Here, and throughout the elaboration that follows, "life" refers to deliverance, to his being granted a reprieve regarding "life in the flesh." "Death," of course, refers to possible execution. Paul's singular passion — and this is what he surely wants his beloved Philippians to hear — is that even though he expects a favorable outcome,[61] he wants Christ to be glorified as he stands trial, and beyond, even if it were to result in death. That would only hasten Paul's eschatological "salvation/vindication" before the heavenly tribunal. But for now, his singular "hope" is that Christ — and thus the gospel — will be "vindicated" through his life or death.

Thus concludes one of the more complex sentences in the Pauline corpus (see the overview at the beginning). But when all the parts are put back in place, Paul's concern is singular — and is precisely in keeping with what has preceded in vv. 12-18b — the advance of the gospel. Just as Paul looked back over his incarceration to this moment, and could rejoice at its being a catalyst for the progress of the gospel in Rome, so now he looks forward and again rejoices, eagerly anticipating that his trial will further glorify Christ. Although he expects release, as vv. 24-25 will make clear, here he has little interest in release and full interest in the vindication of the gospel at his trial. For that he needs their continued prayer so that he will have a fresh supply of the Spirit of Christ when the trial comes. All the other parts of the sentence are supporting matter for this singular concern.

Because of its complexity, one can also easily overlook the *theological* thrust of the whole, namely Paul's unshakable confidence in the living God, who through Christ has brought eternal salvation and through the Spirit will once again glorify his Son through his apostle. That Paul will turn to momentary soliloquy over the prospect of life and death does not indicate doubt or anxiety on his part;[62] quite the opposite. The whole passage breathes confidence that God will fulfill Paul's "eager expectation and hope." Indeed, the trinitarian substructure of the whole exudes with that confidence. The soliloquy, therefore, has another reason for existence: to encourage the Philippians regarding the certainty of their own future, as long as for them, too, "to live is Christ."

The heart of everything, of course, is Paul's utter devotion to Christ,

---

59. So *inter alia,* Vincent, 25; Silva, 80.

60. Gk. διά, normally, as here, indicating secondary agency. The Spirit is to be understood as the primary agent; but it will happen "through" Paul, whether he is released or condemned.

61. All the available evidence indicates that he expects to be released. In this letter, 1:24-26; 2:24; cf. Phlm 22.

62. As suggested by Bertram and others (cf. Houlden, 61); see n. 42 above.

and his desire that Christ alone be "magnified" in his life, however present circumstances turn out. Here surely is a word for all seasons, if we also are to be effective bearers of the gospel in our day.

## 2. The Desired Outcome — to be with Christ (1:21-24)

> 21*For to me to live is Christ and to die is gain.* 22*If I am to go on living in the body, this will mean fruitful labor for me. Yet what shall I choose? I do not know!* 23*I am torn between the two: I desire to depart and be with Christ, which*[1] *is better by far;* 24*but it is more necessary for you that I remain in*[2] *the body.*

With the well-known words of v. 21 Paul's "reflection on imprisonment" takes a considerable turn. Up to this point, his primary concern has been with the "advance of the gospel" (through his detention) and "Christ's being glorified" (through his trial). Now he turns to purely personal reflection,[3] but reflection of a different kind from what one might have expected following vv. 19-20.[4] Although the apostle assumes he will go free, the final words of v. 20 raised the possibility of execution. What he sets out to explain,[5] therefore,

---

1. Besides some minor variants in this verse (P[46] et al. omit μᾶλλον), the evidence is divided as to the presence or absence of γὰρ ("for"), which is found in an impressive array of early and significant witnesses (P[46] ℵ[1] A B C 6 33 81 104 326 365 1175 1241[s] 1739 1881 pc vg[mss] Augustine; NA[26] with brackets). Despite the brackets in NA[26], the external evidence for its inclusion is especially good; and here is a place where one can well understand its omission by scribes, since it thereby offers a text in keeping with the translation in the NIV. Most likely with this phrase Paul is explaining his preference for death: "*for* this is better by far." But see Lightfoot, 93-94, who observes, "a reading which comes to the relief of a disjointed syntax must be regarded with suspicion."

2. This reflects the ἐν found in P[46] B D F G Maj (in brackets in NA[26]); it is lacking in ℵ A C P Ψ 6 33 81 1739 2495 al Clement. Although something of a toss-up in terms of supporting witnesses, one can make a stronger case for a secondary "addition" on the basis of the ἐν σαρκί in v. 22 than for an "omission" (on the basis of the article?). However, some interpreters who adopt the reading without ἐν make too much of the difference between this usage and that in v. 22, which in this case is probably a matter of usage pure and simple (the verb ἐπιμενεῖν regularly takes the dative, thus not calling for an ἐν).

3. Note the emphatic ἐμοί with which the sentence begins (= "as far as I personally am concerned").

4. That is, following the unmistakable ring of confident expectation about Christ's being glorified, one might have expected this particular theme to be elaborated in some way. According to Meyer (47) Weiss interpreted v. 21 this way, as justifying his joy (v. 18), a view that Jones (20) also allows.

5. Note the explanatory γάρ with which v. 21 begins, which is all too easily overlooked in our gnomic citation of this sentence. Michael (53) finds the "for" unclear and thus tries to justify Moffatt's translating it out.

is his desire for Christ to be glorified even if the verdict were to go against him.[6] Picking up on the final words of v. 20 ("whether through life or through death"), he avows that since Christ is the singular passion of his life, he wins in either case, whether released or executed![7]

He then begins a personal reflection on these two alternatives, whose point seems easy enough. If he had a real choice between the two, he would choose execution, for clear christological and eschatological reasons. But the way this is said — both form (a very complex set of clauses with particularly strong language) and content (especially his longing to "depart and be with Christ") — have resulted in some considerably different understandings of the whole, especially as to (a) how one reconciles the language of choice and desire for death in vv. 22-23 with the plainly expressed expectation of release in vv. 24b-26, and (b) how we are to understand what it means to "be with Christ" at death.

**21** This sentence, striking for its laconic style and focused content, would have been even more striking to its original *hearers,* because of its alliteration and assonance[8] which are impossible to put into English. In transliteration, the two lines go:

| | | | | |
|---|---|---|---|---|
| *to zēn* | *Christos* | | to live | Christ |
| *to apothanein*[9] | *kerdos* | = | to die | gain |

6. Thus Kennedy (428) rightly points out that this verse is the direct result of Paul's having said, "or through death"; cf. Lohmeyer, Barth, Silva.

7. This is surely Paul's point, not some lesser concern about his deep emotion or about his desire to be released from present suffering (as, e.g., Palmer, " 'To Die'," followed by Garland, "Defense," 334, and Hawthorne, 45-46). A longing for release from hardship is a note that cannot be found elsewhere in Paul's letters, nor in this one; indeed, it is altogether foreign to the context and to the theme of joy that pervades the whole. Palmer's case is based on an impressive array of texts from hellenistic writers who talk of death as "gain," because present life is "full of toil" and wearisome, and they want release from it. But there is no hint of "human toil" in this passage, nor in all of Philippians, in which Paul's eschatological framework and future orientation determine everything. See the Introduction, pp. 50-52. This is not to remove the "human factor" from Paul, but it is to argue that evidence from "parallels," when there is no internal evidence for Paul's use of such, must not dictate over the clear evidence from both the immediate context and the letter as a whole. Such a view hardly squares with Paul's "glorying in suffering" (Rom 5:3), or with his desire to "know Christ" by participation in his sufferings (Phil 3:10), or with the totally christological focus of this passage. So also Beare, 62; O'Brien, 123.

8. Those of us in a predominantly *reading* culture sometimes forget that for most early believers these words were primarily experienced by hearing them read, not by reading (see the Introduction, p. 16). The assonance between κέρδος and Χριστός could hardly have been missed. Four consonants correspond (ch/k, r, t/d, s), with only one vowel/consonant transposition (ri/er) and an additional sigma in the first syllable.

9. On the folly of making too much of this aorist (vis-à-vis the present ζῆν), as

This is rhetoric at its best; its potency, however, lies not in form alone, but in its singularly focused affirmations. If Paul is released, as he expects (vv. 24-26; 2:24), that means he will continue ("now as always") to be a man "in Christ,"[10] participating in Christ's sufferings (3:10) and serving him in the gospel. Indeed, here is a kind of maxim that, had Paul not done so, we could easily have penned for him, to epitomize his entire life since Damascus. Such singular focus does not make him otherworldly; rather, it gives heart and meaning to everything he is and does as a citizen of two worlds, his heavenly citizenship determining his earthly.[11] As he puts it in 3:12-14, having been "apprehended by Christ Jesus," Christ thus became the singular pursuit of his life. "Christ" — crucified, exalted Lord, present by the Spirit, coming king; "Christ," the one who as God "emptied himself" and as man "humbled himself" — to death on the cross — whom God has now given the name above all names (2:6-11); "Christ," the one for whom Paul has gladly "suffered the loss of all things" in order to "gain" him and "know" him, both his resurrection power and participation in his sufferings (3:7-11); "Christ," the name that sums up for Paul the whole range of his new relationship to God: personal devotion, commitment, service, the gospel, ministry, communion, inspiration, everything.

Likewise, if Paul is executed, that means the goal of "living" has thus been reached: he will finally have "gained" Christ (as v. 23 verifies).[12] The

---

some do (e.g., Lightfoot, Martin, Hawthorne), see Silva, 82-83. Here is a clear example of "much ado about nothing," since these are the natural "tenses" with these two verbs in Greek. Living has continuity; death happens at a point in time. There is simply no further "meaning" to this ordinary usage.

10. Cf. Gal 2:20, "I live, yet not I, but Christ lives in me; and the life that I now live in the flesh I live by faith in the Son of God." But Barth, 37 (cf. Haupt; Schmitz, "Verständnis"; Dibelius; Hanhart, *Intermediate State;* Hoffmann, *Toten*), goes too far in making Gal 2:20 the primary commentary on the present passage, and thus to see the infinitive "to live" to denote "life" in its more comprehensive sense as "(spiritual) life in Christ." Despite its theological attractiveness, this view has very little to commend it contextually. See the larger discussion and refutation in O'Brien, 119-22. The place to find "definition" for this first line is not in Galatians, but in Philippians itself (as Hendriksen, 76, also notes). A. J. Droge (n. 37), on the other hand, in order to make his interpretation of vv. 22-23 work (that Paul is contemplating suicide), suggests that the meaning of this clause ("for me to live is Christ") is problematic, "while there is no doubt about the interpretation of its counterpart [to die is gain]" (280), an interpretation which in itself seems especially problematic.

11. I put it this way because this is the metaphor he will use with the Philippians (1:27; 3:20); both he and they are citizens of the empire, but both are now in a bit of trouble because they acclaim a higher citizenship.

12. But see Barth, who because of his view of the first line (see n. 10 above) contests that v. 23 serves as "commentary" for this line. Others (e.g., Lohmeyer, Collange, Martin, Loh-Nida; O'Brien is open to it) suggest on the basis of vv. 19-20 and the use of καρπός in

*reason* for this unusual way of putting it — the word *kerdos* ordinarily denotes "profit" — lies in the assonance;[13] the *sense* lies in Paul's understanding death to be the ultimate "gaining" of his lifelong passion. This expresses neither a death wish nor dissatisfaction with life nor desire to be "done with troubles and trials";[14] it is the forthright assessment of one whose future in terms of "life in the flesh" is somewhat uncertain, but whose ultimate future is both certain and to be desired. Death, after all, because it is "ours" in Christ Jesus has thereby lost its sting.[15] It should go without saying that such a statement has meaning only for one to whom the first clause is a vibrant, living reality. Otherwise death is loss, or "gain" only in the sense of escape.

Paul picks up this language again in 3:8, referring to his already having "gained" Christ, which he immediately qualifies with the passive, "that is, and be found in him." Such unusual terminology can scarcely be accidental. Since that whole passage (vv. 4-14) is intended to be paradigmatic for the Philippians — that even though he has "gained" Christ, he still presses on to gain "the prize," and the "mature" in Christ must "imitate" him on this matter — it is very likely that that exhortation is anticipated here, especially since this whole passage (from v. 12) is overlaid with paradigmatic implications (see on vv. 15-18 above).

**22** This sentence is a clear follow-up to v. 21. Picking up on the first clause, Paul assesses what its outcome will mean for him "in the flesh,"[16]

v. 22, plus the use of this word for evangelism in 1 Cor 9:19-22, that Paul here sees his death as "gain" for the gospel. But that seems too obscure to have merit. How would the Philippians have known this usage from 1 Corinthians, one wonders; and this sentence begins with an emphatic "for me," meaning "for me personally," not "for the sake of the gospel."

13. This is contested by Palmer (" 'To Die' ") and those who follow him (see n. 7), who sees it as borrowed language, indicating death as a welcome relief from human drudgery. One need not doubt that Paul knew of this kind of language in the world around him; but both the assonance and the usage in 3:8, where he returns to this language to speak of "gaining Christ" in the "already" (cf. Motyer, 87), not to mention the radically different sense Paul gives it, are reasons enough to doubt that these parallels have any significance for understanding Paul. Even less viable is the suggestion made by earlier interpreters that Paul is here reflecting a position over against the foolish in Wis 3:1-3, since there are no linguistic parallels of any kind, and in any case there is considerable doubt whether Paul knew or used the Wisdom of Solomon. On this question see further, Fee, *Presence,* 911-13.

14. And certainly not with a view toward martyrdom, as Lohmeyer suggests.

15. See Fee, *First Corinthians,* on 3:21-23 and 15:55, for this perspective in Paul.

16. Gk. ἐν σαρκί, a very flexible Pauline word whose meaning here falls somewhere on a spectrum between "body" and "humanity in its creatureliness," both meanings going back to the OT. Some have suggested that Paul adds the phrase following v. 21 to indicate that "life" in v. 21 is not limited to life in the physical body and that death therefore does not bring "life" to an end. Perhaps, but in any case, it refers here to "bodily, physical" existence with no pejorative overtones.

namely, "fruitful labor."[17] If he did have a choice in the matter, he goes on, his initial response is ambivalence: between "fruitful labor," on the one hand, and what is far better, "being with Christ," on the other. This, at least, is the perspective of the NIV, which most likely has it right; but behind this translation is another complex set of clauses. To see the difficulty, here is Paul's sentence in "literal" English:

> but *(de)*
> if "to live"[18] in the flesh,
>> this for me fruit of labor,
> and what I might choose,
>> I do not know/reveal.[19]

Besides the fact that the first two clauses are verbless (continuing the style from v. 21), at issue are: (1) the nuance of the *de* (untranslated in the NIV) in relationship to v. 21; and (2) which clause functions as the "then" clause (apodosis) to the "if" clause (protasis) with which it begins. Does he mean (a):

> If [it is] "to live" in the flesh,
>> *then* this for me [means] fruitful labor;
> and what I shall choose, I cannot tell[20]

or (b):

> If "to live" in the flesh this [means] fruitful labor for me,
>> *then* what I shall choose, I cannot tell[21]

The first of these issues is more easily handled. Despite some translations and commentaries to the contrary,[22] the *de* most likely signals a progres-

---

17. Gk. καρπὸς ἔργου; the NIV has properly captured the sense of the genitive, which Beekman-Callow (*Translating,* 264) describe in terms of "result-reason," where the one event (fruit) is the result of the other (labor). For a similar use of the metaphor "fruit," see 1 Cor 3:6-8; Rom 1:13. Some have suggested that the phrase means to "reap the fruit of past labor"; but everything in the context, and esp. vv. 24-25, speaks against it.

18. Gk. τὸ ζῆν, which is clearly anaphoric, i.e., picking up the exact phrasing of the previous sentence and elaborating on it.

19. See n. 28 below for the meaning of this verb.

20. Cf. NIV, NRSV, REB (*contra* NEB), NAB, Moffatt; cf. Kennedy, Michael, Hendriksen, O'Brien.

21. Cf. GNB, NJB; this view was held by most early interpreters (e.g., Chrysostom, Calvin); it is also held by Lightfoot (hesitantly), Meyer (vigorously), Vincent, Jones, Bonnard, Gnilka, Collange, Loh-Nida, Bruce, Silva, Melick.

22. E.g., NEB, NASB, NJB; cf. most interpreters, who opt for the second position.

sion of thought, not a contrast to the final clause of v. 21.[23] Thus: "*now* if 'to live' in the flesh is what transpires. . . ."

The second matter is more complex.[24] Option (b), which offers a reasonably good sense of the whole, also eliminates the need to supply two verbs in the first set of clauses. Even so, the NIV more likely moves in the right direction.[25] One may easily surmise as to what happened. A follow-up to v. 21 could have gone in one of two directions: either Paul could contemplate what the two alternatives would mean for him; or he could contemplate the two alternatives themselves, as to which he might prefer. What he seems to have done is both. That is, he begins with the first, what the alternatives would mean to him personally.[26] But he gets only as far as the first, "If [it is] 'to live' in the flesh, this for me [means] fruitful labor." At which point he shifts gears. Both v. 21b ("to die is gain") and the reflection in v. 23 (that death is preferable) indicate that what is in tension is not a choice between "life" and "death" per se — as if he really had such a choice — but between the ultimate "gaining" *of Christ* and present "fruitful labor" *for Christ*. Thus, the mention of "fruitful labor" as the outcome of "living in the flesh" triggers a shift in reflection, namely, to the two alternatives themselves.

This view also makes sense of the "I do not know" by which Paul responds (honestly) to his hypothetical question,[27] and of vv. 23-24, which in turn, but in reverse order, take up these two alternatives. The verb translated

---

23. That is, in contrast to the second line of v. 21. Thus the NJB: "but then death would be a positive gain. On the other hand again, if to be alive in the body gives me an opportunity for fruitful work. . . ." Against this is the striking repetition of the infinitive τὸ ζῆν, which certainly looks as though Paul were about to pick up on both ends of v. 21.

24. Other options have been suggested: Lightfoot, 92-93, makes it more interrogative, "But what if my living in the flesh will bear fruit, then. . . ." Vincent and Hawthorne offer a slight moderation of option (b): "If 'to live' in the flesh, if this means fruitful labor." Michael, 56, elides the offending lines; but that is a counsel of despair.

25. For two reasons: (1) the τοῦτο in the second clause is emphatic, and thus seems more likely to point to the option itself (= to live in the flesh, this . . .), while at the same time serving as a form of "then"; in the other option the pronoun is not only unnecessary, but cumbersome in the highest degree (Meyer's and Vincent's appeal that it is emphatic regarding "to live in the flesh" is hardly helpful, since there is no analogy for such a thing in Paul); (2) the καί that begins the next clause does not function well as a "then," and has no analogies in the Pauline corpus (some have suggested 2 Cor 2:2, but as Lightfoot points out, the analogy does not hold). Melick, 85 n. 97, recognizes these difficulties but still opts for it as having "fewer difficulties." This seems strange, since the only difficulty with the first option is discomfort over *two* elliptical sentences, whereas in any case everyone must assume *one*.

26. Hence the "for me" in the second clause.

27. On this matter see n. 38 below.

"I do not know"[28] is one of Paul's regular verbs for "disclosure." Given Pauline usage elsewhere, the English idiom "I can't tell"[29] (meaning, "in light of the alternatives, I don't know what to say") is probably closer to Paul's intent. His point, of course, is that if he really *had* a choice, the alternatives would put him into a genuine quandary, since *from a given perspective either is to be preferred.*[30]

**23-24**   Nevertheless, if choice were to be had, Paul now goes on, he would certainly opt for execution, since that would mean the realization of his lifelong passion; but, he returns in v. 24, since choice cannot be had, remaining "in the flesh" for their sakes is more likely the divine choice.[31]

For anyone who knows Paul well, this follow-on to the ambivalence expressed in v. 22 should come as no surprise. Whatever else, Paul was both a Christocentric and a thoroughly eschatological man, whose life and theology were altogether framed by his "already but not yet" understanding of what God had done through Christ and the Spirit. Thus, even though he throws himself with abandon into life in the present, the entire orientation of his life is toward the (absolutely certain) future. Indeed, it is this orientation that explains his singularly focused life in the present ("for me to live is Christ").[32] What we learn in this sentence is what we could have

---

28. Gk. γνωρίζω, which he regularly uses in the formula, "I make known to you" (1 Cor 12:3; 15:1; 2 Cor 8:1; Gal 1:11; cf. Col 4:7, 9; Eph 6:21 [of Tychicus]). Elsewhere he uses it of divine disclosure (Rom 9:22, 23; 16:26; Col 1:27; Eph 1:9; 3:3, 5, 10). This is the only place where it borders on the sense of "I do not know," preferred by Lightfoot. Most interpreters opt for its regular meaning here ("I do not make known [to you]"; so Kennedy, Vincent, Jones, Hendriksen; cf. REB; M-M; Z-G, 594); but the difficulty with this view is its contradictory nature, since in vv. 23-24 he *does* make it known to them. Some of these suggest "I cannot tell" in a less colloquial sense, of his *not being able to* reveal it (esp. Lohmeyer, O'Brien). But that presses language too much, not to mention misses the context. As v. 23 makes clear, Paul has nothing to hide as far as his own preference is concerned.

29. Suggested, *inter alia,* by Kennedy, Z-G (594; cf. REB).

30. Cf. T. E. Dailey, "To Live," 19: "Each of these very real possibilities has a value of its own."

31. The net result is a piece of (not pure) chiasmus:

A    If "life" in the flesh it is to be, then that means "fruitful labor,"
  B    which would put me in a real quandary, if I had to choose between the two.
  B′   If I could choose, it would be "death," hands down,
A′   but since there is no choice (but God's), it means "fruitful labor" among you.

This is not true chiasm, since line B does not actually mention "death." But if our analysis is correct, then Paul's preference for "death" vis-à-vis the obvious advantages of "life" is what creates the quandary. Hence item B picks up "death" in this extended sense.

32. Cf. Dailey, "To Live or Die," who likewise recognizes the combination of these realities as the key to our understanding Paul's "dilemma."

easily guessed: Had he a real choice, that would be hands down in favor of death, precisely because execution would mean "to depart and be with[33] Christ." From his eschatological vantage point (of "already/not yet") this would be "better by far."[34] In light of 3:12-21 this is clearly the vantage point he desires for the Philippians as well — not death, of course, but the happy prospect of "being with Christ."

At the same time, however, also with the Philippians in view, he acknowledges that to "remain in the flesh" is the more necessary for their sakes. Thus the final clause (23b-24) is set forth in nearly perfectly balanced constructions, representing his (theoretical) dilemma:[35]

> (having the desire)     to depart and be
>                            with Christ
>                            [which is] better by far
>                                 but
>                to remain
>                            in the flesh
>                            [is] more necessary for you

Paul thus does two things, as far as this "reflection" is concerned: first, with yearning he points the Philippians toward his (and therefore their) triumphant certainty — being with Christ finally and forever; second, he begins the transition from "my affairs" to "your affairs" (v. 27), with his expected return to Philippi (vv. 25-26) serving as the hinge.

He begins by responding directly to the ambivalence expressed in v. 22.

---

33. A considerable literature has sprung up on Paul's use of σύν with "Christ," stemming in part from J. Dupont's "ΣΥΝ ΧΡΙΣΤΩΙ," and in part from W. Grundmann, *TDNT*, 7.766-97. It is thus suggested by many that this is a "unique phrase, coined by Paul," which, although it has some flexibility in usage, here means "in fellowship with Christ" as over against merely being "together with" Christ (see the discussions in Collange, 66-67; Hawthorne, 49-50; O'Brien, 133-37). But one wonders, even if Paul intended this subtlety, how the Philippians could have so understood it. Why should they think that σύν with Χριστῷ has a more profound sense than with ἐμοί in 2:22 or 4:21, or with ἐπισκόποις in 1:1? This is surely to find a "theology of prepositions" where none exists. For a similar usage in Paul, see 1 Thess 4:17 and 5:11. These all mean "in association with," not "in fellowship with," as in Rom 6:1-11, where a considerably different concern is being expressed, and where this latter nuance of σύν is not subtle but is inherent to the argument.

34. Gk. πολλῷ μᾶλλον κρεῖσσον, a remarkable compounding of superlatives. There can be little question where Paul's sympathies lie.

35. Hawthorne (48) argues for the two infinitives (ἀναλῦσαι/ἐπιμένειν) both to be objects of Paul's desire, by way of one εἰς. But that puts too much pressure on the clearly contrastive δέ of v. 24, which in this view must function as a καί.

"I am torn[36] between the two," he tells them. Despite the strong verb, this is purely hypothetical[37] — and theological and paradigmatic.[38] After all, he is

36. Gk. συνέχομαι, which in the active originally meant "held together, sustained," but moved toward a variety of cognate meanings ("press hard, crowd, hold in custody") and in unfavorable circumstances toward "attack, distress, torment." For this verse BAGD offer *"I am hard pressed* (to choose) *between the two."* The NIV has given it a nice idiomatic flavor.

37. Cf. Lightfoot, 92, "if I consulted my own longings." *Contra* A. J. Droge, *"Mori Lucrum,"* who argues that to take v. 22 seriously we must allow that Paul was contemplating suicide. But that seems methodologically in reverse, since the rest of the passage, and the letter as a whole, hardly allow such a view. This fails to take seriously Paul's understanding of apostleship — and of discipleship in general — in which one's longing to know Christ includes "participation in his sufferings," because of one's equal certainty of the resurrection. Paul has spent his whole Christian life living in happy tension between the "already" and "not yet." Nothing in this letter suggests that he is now ready to bail out of the "already" so as to hasten the "not yet."

38. Not all see it this way, of course. Besides idiosyncratic views put forward by, *inter alia,* Collange (n. 17 on v. 12), Palmer (n. 7), Droge (n. 37), Reeves (n. 39), the predominant view, based on Paul's language suggesting difficulty in "choosing" between life and death, plus this especially strong verb, is that Paul is here expressing "a genuine dilemma" (the language is Martin's [77], but the sentiment occurs throughout the literature; cf. Dailey ["To Live," 19], "personal turmoil and emotion"), as though Paul were faced with a real choice and that in this dilemma he prefers death but yields instead to the divine necessity of obligation. This interpretation, however, becomes especially problematic when one comes to vv. 24-26, where Paul expresses unquestioned confidence that he will be released — which is expressed even more forthrightly in 2:24 ("I am confident *in the Lord* that I will come soon").

Various ploys have been entertained to get around what is now *our* dilemma over this kind of alleged contradiction. See esp. in this regard O'Brien, 138-39, who suggests that Paul's "confidence" in vv. 25-26 has not to do with his release as such, but "that his presence will be a blessing to the Philippians in the future *if* he is to be released." That seems far less confident than Paul himself is. (It is of some interest that 2:24 is not mentioned in O'Brien's entire discussion of this passage.) To read this as a *Pauline* dilemma misses both the immediate context and that of the letter as a whole. Methodologically, one should begin with what is unmistakable, that Paul clearly *expects* to be released (as in 2:24, which makes no allowance for "if"). That means that we need to take the present "reflection," including its very strong language, as the "soliloquy" that it really is, which arose not because Paul has such strong emotions over whether or not to live or die, but because in v. 20 he had opened the possibility that he could in fact be executed. In light of that possibility, he reflects on his own future in terms of "whether through life or through death." Although apparently reflecting on "life" or "death" in the abstract, in reality he is pondering what it would mean for him to be either released or executed.

The only real question, then, is why this emotion, when in fact he faces no real dilemma at all? The answer to which, I suggest, lies with the Christocentric focus and eschatological framework that governs all of Paul's life and thinking — and with the paradigmatic value of this perspective for the situation in which the Philippians find themselves. That is, since Christ is everything for him (his Christocentric focus), the possibility of his soon

not talking about life or death in the abstract, but about being set free ("life") or executed ("death"),[39] and he has no choice whatever in this matter. His "choice," therefore, is a matter of yearning, pure and simple; and here is where he is "hard pressed" — between finally "obtaining the prize" (3:14) and continuing on in "fruitful labor" for Christ and his kingdom.[40]

His preference is clear: "having the desire[41] to depart and be with Christ." But what Paul understands by this is not so clear, and is therefore a clause around which considerable, but ultimately unresolvable, theological ferment has boiled.[42] What Paul says is plain enough: Death means to "depart"[43] and "be with Christ."[44] At issue is the question of consciousness,[45]

---

gaining the eschatological prize of "knowing Christ" fully and finally (see on 3:12-14) — by means of Roman execution — causes him to "yearn" for the realization of the prize. But eschatological yearning should not be interpreted as an "existential dilemma," since he has none. What gives the language its force is his desire to rekindle eschatological longings in his Philippian brothers and sisters (as 3:15-21 makes clear).

39. A matter that is correctly seen by R. R. Reeves, "To Be," but who still insists on a genuine choice as confronting Paul, which he resolves in terms of Paul's refusing to use the Philippian gift as a means of buying his way out of prison — to their chagrin, which is what he is trying now to explain to them. As intriguing as this option is, in order to make it work Reeves must offer up too many moments of questionable exegesis (e.g., "to be with Christ" = to be with him in Philippi on his release).

40. Cf. Lincoln (*Paradise,* 103-6) for a helpful discussion of this passage, who correctly sees the resolution to lie in the tension that exists inherently in Paul's "already but not yet" eschatological framework.

41. Gk. τὴν ἐπιθυμίαν, a word that in Paul is primarily pejorative, having to do with "desiring something forbidden" (BAGD). The usage here is similar to that in 1 Thess 2:17; cf. Gal 5:17, where the Spirit has "desires" that stand in utter opposition to those (evil desires) of the "flesh." To make it pejorative here (as Bonnard and Collange do) is to allow predominant usage (exceptions belie Collange's "always") dictate over context, which is methodologically suspect (so Bruce, 54).

42. The bibliography here is large. For an earlier, and very useful, discussion, see G. Vos, *Eschatology,* 136-50; see also L. S. Thornton, *Christ and the Church,* 137-40; O. Cullmann, *Immortality,* 48-57; C. F. D. Moule, "Influence"; *idem,* "St Paul and Dualism"; K. Hanhart, *Intermediate State;* R. H. Gundry, *SŌMA,* 147-56; C. J. De Vogel, "Reflexions"; Lincoln, *Paradise,* 103-6.

43. Gk. ἀναλῦσαι, used literally for "breaking camp" or of a ship's "loosing from its moorings"; but found in several Greek authors as a metaphor for death (cf. 2 Tim 4:8, where the cognate noun occurs). De Vogel ("Reflexions," 264) rightly points out that both the metaphor in itself and Paul's language in 2 Cor 5:1 demonstrate that what Paul desires is "to leave the body and be with Christ."

44. This is said equally clearly in 2 Cor 5:8: "to be 'absent from the body' is to be 'present with the Lord,'" a passage which also implies a period in which one is with the Lord in "body-less" existence.

45. Most would say the issue is over "the intermediate state," but this very language assumes a perspective "from below" that is determined by our inability to think

for which in Paul we have no *direct* evidence one way or the other. On the one hand, he uses the metaphor "sleep" for Christians who have died;[46] on the other hand, the implication of a passage like this is that he expects to be consciously "with Christ" — since both the language "depart" (= leave the body) and "remain in the body" and the strong feelings expressed in these sentences make very little sense otherwise.[47] Not only so, but he belonged to a theological-spiritual milieu wherein his Lord could speak of God as "the God of the living, not of the dead," referring to Abraham, Isaac, and Jacob (Mark 12:18-27 and //'s), and wherein Moses and Elijah appear with Jesus at the Transfiguration. It seems most likely, therefore, that Paul expected to be "with the Lord" in full consciousness.

That such a view exists in some tension with belief in a future bodily resurrection[48] is probably to be resolved in terms of the inherent tension between the "spatial and temporal elements"[49] in Paul's eschatology. His present existence "in Christ" makes it unthinkable that he would ever — even at death — be in a "place" where he was not "with Christ." Hence death means "heaven now." At the same time, a person's death did not usher him or her into "timeless" existence. Hence the bodily resurrection still awaits one "at the end." Ultimately this matter lies in the area of mystery. At issue is the interplay between "time" and "eternity" involved in the implied period of "time" between death and resurrection. From our human perspective, earthbound and therefore time bound as it is, we cannot imagine "timeless" existence; whereas from the perspective of eternity/infinity these may very well be collapsed into a single "moment," as it were.

In any case, Paul understood death as a means into the Lord's immediate presence, which for him and countless thousands after him has been a comforting and encouraging prospect. Very likely he also expected such "gain" to include consciousness, and for most believers, that too has been a matter of encouragement — although in this case such a conclusion goes beyond the certain evidence we possess from Paul himself.

Paul expected all of this, of course, at the time of his death, which in

---

of existence apart from the category of "time." See the ensuing discussion. For a helpful overview of the issues involved in this discussion (intermediate state), including the question not addressed here at all, as to whether Paul's thinking on these matters went through stages of development, see L. J. Kreitzer, "Intermediate State," *DPL*, 438-41.

46. Cf. 1 Thess 4:14, 16; 1 Cor 15:51, 52.

47. Cf. De Vogel, "Reflexions."

48. But this is a tension of our making, not of Paul's, as 3:20-21 in this letter verifies. These two ideas rest easily side by side in Paul because "being with Christ" at death is not the final goal; resurrection is. But the former is nonetheless "gain" to Paul, precisely because Christ is the beginning and end of all for Paul.

49. The language is that of Lincoln (*Paradise*, 106).

this hypothetical sentence he could wish were sooner than later. But in fact he expects the opposite, "to remain[50] in the flesh," precisely because that is "more necessary"[51] for "your sakes." With these words we meet for the first time what he actually anticipates regarding these matters. He would *prefer* "death," since that would be to *his* advantage ("better by far"); he *fully expects* "life," since that would be to *their* advantage. How so, is what he takes up in the concluding sentence (vv. 25-26).

Although the larger section in which this passage lies (vv. 18b-26) begins and ends on the note of "joy" and of "Christ's being glorified," the key to everything, both to this letter and to Paul's life as a whole, is to be found in this paragraph, even though it is a bit of an "aside." Paul's saying "for me to live is Christ and to die is gain" puts everything into focus for us, as far as our understanding the apostle is concerned. First, he is a man of one passion: Christ and him alone. As noted above, this title, which has become Paul's favorite appellation of his Lord, covers the whole waterfront as far as his new relationship with and understanding of God is concerned. It seems clear that this is what he also desires for the Philippians — and for us as well. Both our "progress" and that of the gospel is contingent upon such a maxim (to live is Christ; to die is gain) characterizing our individual and corporate lives.

Their problem — and ours — is the strong tendency to speak thus, but in effect to live otherwise. One wonders what the people of God might truly be like in our "post-modern" world if we were once again people of this singular passion. Too often for us it is, "for me to live is Christ — plus work, leisure, accumulating wealth, relationships," etc. And if the truth were known, all too often the "plus factor" has become our primary passion: "For me to live is my work," etc. Both our "progress" and "joy" regarding the gospel are altogether contingent on whether or not Christ is our primary, singular passion. This is surely an infinitely greater option than the self-gratification which dominates the culture within which this commentary has been written.

Second, "to die is gain" expresses, in relationship to Christ, the thoroughgoing eschatological orientation of Paul's existence. Here, too, the contemporary church has tended to lose too much.[52] In a world that has lost

---

50. Gk. ἐπιμενεῖν; cf. μενῶ and παραμενῶ in v. 25. This verb conveys the sense of "staying on."

51. Gk. ἀναγκαιότερον. As suggested above (v. 22) this is neither Paul's "choice" nor "necessity" laid on him by his being set free; rather, it reflects the similar usage in 1 Cor 9:16, where his ministry is not by "free choice" under any circumstances, but has been laid on him by "*divine* necessity." Thus he is not yielding up his "dilemma" to God's choice, as it were, but indicating that God's choice means his "dilemma" was purely hypothetical after all, no matter how much he may have wished it be real.

52. On this matter, see Fee, *Presence,* 803-6, 896-903.

its way, believers in Christ Jesus have the singular word of hope. We expect eventually "to depart and be with Christ." For Paul this was a yearning, for us it is too often an addendum. The point to make, of course, is that such an orientation gives us both focus and perspective in a world gone mad.

## 3. The Expected Outcome — Reunion in Philippi (1:25-26)

25Convinced of this, I know that I will remain, and I will continue[1] with all of you for your progress and joy in the faith, 26so that through my being with you again your joy in Christ Jesus will overflow on account of me.

This sentence serves as the transition from "my affairs" (v. 12) to "your affairs" (v. 27). As with vv. 18b-20, the bulk of the sentence expresses what Paul "knows,"[2] here based on his "persuasion" that the alternative expressed in v. 24 will materialize. The sentence takes the form of two clauses. In verse 25 Paul picks up his conviction from v. 24 and offers the first, more immediate reason[3] for his release: it is for the Philippians' "progress and joy in the faith." In v. 26 he offers the ultimate reason: that his release and coming (parousia) to them will cause their "boasting" in Christ Jesus to overflow.[4] Although this sentence deals with his remaining alive for their sakes and is thus "quietly transitional,"[5] its content fully anticipates the two major sections of exhortation that follow (1:27–2:18 and 3:1–4:3), both of which have to do with their present "progress" and concomitant "joy" with regard to their "faith."[6]

1. The MajT, with no early support, reads συμπαραμενῶ, which puts the emphasis on remaining *with* the Philippians. Meyer, 10, adopts the reading for the sake of an idiosyncratic understanding of the clause (see n. 11 below).

2. Indeed, although probably not intentional and lacking the complexity, this sentence has several formal similarities to the sentence with which the section began (vv. 18b-20). Besides the fact that the larger part of both sentences is the object of οἶδα, the content of what Paul "knows" in both cases is in two clauses, the first modified by (only one in this instance) a compound prepositional phrase, and the latter modified by three phrases.

3. This is a clear telic use of εἰς. For this combination of εἰς followed by a ἵνα clause, see 1 Cor 5:5 (and the discussion in Fee, *First Corinthians*). In this construction the only true purpose clause is the final one (the ἵνα clause); the prepositional phrase with εἰς expresses prior purpose or result, hence in this case the penultimate reason, which gives way to the ultimate reason of "boasting in Christ Jesus."

4. The section thus ends similarly to how it began (in v. 12) and how the prayer-report concluded (in v. 11): on the note of "progress" — theirs in this case — and of "glorying" — in "Christ Jesus" in this case (rather than "God").

5. I do not now know to whom I am indebted for this expressive phrase.

6. E.g., 1:27–2:18 is concerned especially with their "progress" regarding the gospel in the face of opposition in Philippi and in light of some internal unrest; it concludes by noting

**25** Both the "and" and the word order ("and this convinced of"),[7] with which Paul begins, reveal the close connection between this sentence and "what is more necessary for them" in v. 24, namely his release from imprisonment. That the preceding "soliloquy" is just that, expressing his personal longing but unrelated to his actual expectation, is demonstrated by the strength of the verb "convinced," which expresses a persuasion that has evolved into conviction.[8] This passage (and 2:24) makes it certain that the preceding has little to do with some "deep struggle" within Paul and every-thing to do with Paul's eschatological outlook — and yearning — which he undoubtedly wants the Philippians to share.

His conviction is that "I will remain and will continue with all of you."[9] The paired, compound verbs (*menō/paramenō;* "will remain" and "will continue") is a play on words[10] which expresses, first, his conviction that he will "remain" in the sense of "remain alive" (v. 22), and second, his conviction that he will "remain" in the sense of "staying with you" (v. 24).[11] The surprise comes from the qualifier, that "I will continue with *all* of you." This otherwise unnecessary mention of "all"[12] most likely points to the friction that is currently at work among them;[13] that it occurs just before he takes up this issue seems scarcely accidental.

---

that even though their "faith" is currently undergoing stress because of suffering (2:17), they should nonetheless rejoice (v. 18). The next major section (3:1–4:3) is then framed by the imperative to "rejoice in the Lord," as it takes up the issue of their remaining steadfast in their faith in Christ, by maintaining their focus on the future (hence their "progress" in the faith).

7. Gk. καὶ τοῦτο πεποιθώς. The NIV typically translates out the "and," which is fine for reading, but misses the close connection to vv. 23-24. On the verb see on v. 14 (cf. v. 6) above (n. 41).

8. Which is exactly how he expresses it again in 2:24 (πέποιθα ἐν κυρίῳ).

9. As to whether it happened or not depends in part on how one interprets the Pastoral Epistles. In any case, it is probably too skeptical to argue from our hindsight that we know better than Paul would have and thus to deny that he was in fact released, when 2:24 implies that he has every good reason to believe that he will — and there is no evidence that he was not!

10. Gk. μενῶ καὶ παραμενῶ (cf. ἐπιμένω, v. 24), which could otherwise be synonyms (the second expressing a slight intensification), but here must be nuanced toward "remaining alive" and "abiding with you," especially because of the way the second is qualified. Lightfoot suggests "bide and abide," but that is now too archaic to be helpful. Some (Lohmeyer, Bonnard, Martin) take the (altogether unlikely) view that the second verb emphasizes that Paul expects to remain until the Parousia.

11. Meyer, 54, who is not often given to such idiosyncrasies, adopts the reading συμπαραμενῶ (see n. 1) and understands Paul to be saying, "I shall with you be preserved in temporal life."

12. See on vv. 1, 4, and 7 above, esp. the comments on "all the saints" in v. 1.

13. So also Lohmeyer, 67; Hendriksen, 79, suggests the improbable view that Paul intends more than the church in Philippi.

Paul concludes this first clause with the reason why this alternative is "more necessary *for you*," namely, "for your progress and joy in the/your faith."[14] The "your," which modifies both "progress" and "joy," stands in the emphatic first position, thus putting the accent first of all on the Philippians themselves. It is for their sakes that he expects to be released, which he now elaborates to mean specifically for their "progress" and their "joy." These two words together summarize his concerns for them in this letter: the first refers to the quality or character of their life in Christ, and especially to their "advancing," moving forward, in such; the second denotes the quality of their experience of it. And both of these are "with regard to[15] the faith," which may refer to their own faith in Christ, as in 2:17, but in this context more likely refers to the gospel itself.[16]

This long reflection began (v. 12) on the note of the "progress of the gospel," referring to evangelism; it ends on a similar note, only the concern now is more personal — with the Philippians' own "progress" regarding the faith. In this letter that will include their "contending as one person *for the faith of the gospel*" (v. 27) — in the face of opposition and doing so "in one Spirit." Such "progress regarding the faith" will manifest itself as their love for one another increases (1:10; 2:2), as in humility they consider the needs of others ahead of their own (2:3-4), as they "do all things without grumbling and complaining" (2:14), and as they keep focused on the eschatological prize (3:14-21). This is what it means for them to "continue to work out your salvation with fear and trembling" (2:12).

14. Gk. εἰς τὴν ὑμῶν προκοπὴν καὶ χαρὰν τῆς πίστεως. For this very compressed phrase Pauline usage is decisive: the single preposition and article control both nouns and hold them together as a single thought unit, while the "your" that precedes and the genitive "of the faith" that follows are to be understood as qualifying both nouns. On this usage, see v. 19 above (although the ὑμῶν functions differently there; see nn. 26 and 27); cf. 2 Thess 2:17 ("every good work and word"). So most interpreters; otherwise Kennedy, 429.

15. The nuance of the genitive τῆς πίστεως is more difficult to assess. Since it almost certainly refers to both nouns (see preceding n.), most likely it is a "genitive of reference" (Dana-Mantey, *Manual Grammar*, 78; cf. Beekman-Callow, *Translating*, 259, "A is done with regard to B"); thus, "progress and joy, both with regard to the faith, that is, the gospel." On the other hand, if it refers to their faith, as it well might, then it is a more pure genitive (= "your faith's progress and joy").

16. This is also a difficult call. In light of 2:17 and 3:9, one is tempted here to see a reference to "their faith = trust in Christ" (as, e.g., Vincent, Moffatt, Michael, Müller), which in any case may not lurk very far behind if the primary reference is to the gospel. What primarily favors "faith = the gospel" (cf. Hawthorne, O'Brien) is v. 27, where Paul picks up this phrase and specifies it as "the faith of the gospel." Some argue that the definite article (vis-à-vis the personal pronoun, as in 2:17, where he does refer to their faith) also favors this view. But that seems not totally relevant in this case. Since Paul has already used the personal pronoun with "progress" and "joy," it is unlikely that he would repeat it with "faith," since the definite article would serve that purpose.

153

The concomitant of such "progress" is "joy," which they will experience as they "progress regarding the faith." This is now the fourth mention of joy in the letter; the former three (vv. 4, 18 [2x]) had to do with Paul's joy, first in the context of his thanksgiving and prayer for them, and second in the context of two expressions of opposition (by fellow believers [vv. 15-17] and by Rome [vv. 19-20]). His concern here is with the joy that is theirs in the gospel itself, although they will undoubtedly also experience joy in seeing Paul again.[17]

**26** If the first reason Paul is convinced that he will "continue with all" of them focuses on the Philippians themselves — their own progress and joy regarding the gospel — the ultimate reason for all of this (his release and their progress) is expressed in terms of how it affects Christ.[18]

Here in particular the three-way bond that holds the letter together is in full evidence. Thus (literally): "*your* grounds for glorying[19] will overflow[20] in *Christ Jesus* in *me*." Although a bit strained in its expression, the sense of this clause is straightforward enough. The occasion of Paul's coming to them again (thus "in me") will cause their "glorying/boasting" to overflow, and all of this takes place "in Christ Jesus." This is how Christ's being glorified "through life" (v. 20) is to find fulfillment.

The Greek word *kauchēma* ("grounds for boasting/glorying"; NIV, "joy") is especially difficult to render into English. Although it can lean toward "joy," there is no reason to think it here means other than what it ordinarily means in Paul, to "boast" or "glory" in someone. But "boast" is full of pejorative connotations in English — which it can also carry in Paul when one's boasting is wrongly placed. Paul's usage comes directly out of the LXX, especially from Jer 9:23-24, where the truly wise person "boasts" not in "wisdom, might, or wealth," but "in the Lord." "Boast," therefore, does not mean to "brag about" or to "be conceited"; rather, it has to do first

---

17. For the significance of this theme regarding the Philippians themselves, see the discussion on 2:18, 28; 3:1; and 4:4.

18. This is now the sixteenth occurrence of the word "Christ" in the letter to this point, not including "in the Lord" in v. 14. If for Paul, "to live is Christ," so, too, for his beloved friends in Philippi — or he will consider himself to have "run and labored in vain" (2:16).

19. Gk. τὸ καύχημα ὑμῶν; cf. 2:16 (εἰς καύχημα ἐμοί) and 3:3 (καυχώμενοι ἐν Χριστῷ ᾽Ιησοῦ). This is a Pauline word in the NT (55 of 59 occurrences). See the entry in *EDNT,* 2.276-79 (J. Zmijewski) and *NIDNTT,* 1.227-29 (H. C. Hahn); cf. R. Bultmann, *TDNT,* 3.645-54. In contrast to καύχησις, which denotes the act of glorying, καύχημα denotes the "grounds" for such. Most interpreters have rightly rejected the possibility that the "our" is objective, thus referring to Paul's grounds for boasting in them. Everything in the grammar and context of this sentence is against this view.

20. Gk. περισσεύῃ. For this word see on 1:9; cf. 4:12, 18 and the adverb in 1:14.

with putting one's full "trust or confidence in" something or someone and thus, second, in "glorying" in that something or someone. Hence a false "boast" (in the flesh; 3:3-6) lies at the heart of Paul's understanding of sin, whereas its opposite, "boasting/glorying in the Lord," is the ultimate evidence of genuine conversion. In cases such as this one, where the boast is "in someone," the "boast" is still "in Christ." What he has done in and for Paul serves both as the ground for their "glorying in Christ" and the sphere in which such boasting overflows.[21] Thus this part of the clause accents the relationship he and they have with Christ.

But such an overflow of glorying will be the direct result of the other bond, between him and them, that permeates the letter. In this case that finds expression in Paul's *parousia* (= coming, or presence) with them yet once more. Thus this sentence (vv. 25-26) looks beyond the present moment to the time of their joyful reunion; but there is also an "in the meantime" that concerns Paul very much, which what he now turns to address in v. 27 (through to 2:18).

## III. THE PHILIPPIANS' "AFFAIRS" — EXHORTATION TO STEADFASTNESS AND UNITY (1:27–2:18)

In vv. 25-26 Paul concluded his "reflections on imprisonment" (vv. 12-26) with a perceptible shift of focus from himself to his relationship with the Philippians — in terms of an anticipated reunion. He follows that transitional passage by throwing the spotlight now entirely on them and their present circumstances (1:27–2:18). Two matters in the opening sentence (vv. 27-30) drive the whole — (1) concern for the Philippians' steadfastness and unity, (2) in the face of opposition and suffering.[1]

This section is thus as obviously about "their affairs" as 1:12-26 was

21. The fine distinction between Christ as the "object" or "sphere" of their boasting in this case is brought about by the awkwardness of the syntax, where "in Christ" immediately follows "overflow." No doubt that it "overflows in Christ"; but that makes sense precisely because he is first of all the grounds for any and all such boasting.

1. There has been some debate as to which of these two (unity or suffering) is the main concern of the sentence/paragraph. Unfortunately, such debate tends to divide what Paul clearly holds together. In terms of *primary* focus, both the structure of the sentence and the ensuing appeal verify that it has do with "unity." Cf. Martin, 80-81. But that is thoroughly bound up with his concern for the gospel in Philippi, and therefore with their standing firm in the face of opposition, even if it means further suffering. To entitle the whole, "Die Gemeinde im Martyrium" (Lohmeyer), is surely a mistaken emphasis.

about his.[2] In fact, a degree of formal similarity exists between the two sections. Each begins on the same note: "my affairs/your affairs."[3] First person pronouns and verbs dominated 1:12-26;[4] second plural pronouns and verbs now dominate.[5] "His affairs" concluded in a transitional way by focusing on them (vv. 24-26); this section concludes by focusing on Paul (2:16-18), also in a transitional way. And both sections conclude on the note of "joy" (theirs in 1:25; his in 2:17; and his and theirs together in 2:17-18). Finally, just as the heart of the previous section focused on Christ (vv. 21-23), so also with the heart of this section (2:5-11).

But there are three significant differences. First, the previous section was primarily narrative; this one is primarily imperative.[6] If 1:12-26 is the stuff of a letter of friendship, this is the stuff of a letter of exhortation.[7] Second, references to himself appear more frequently throughout this section than references to the Philippians did in 1:12-26, understandably so, since the appeal is based in part on their secure relationship. Third, the focus on Christ stands out in a unique way, in one of the most exalted passages in the NT, again understandably so. That is, if the focus on Christ in 1:21-23 was paradigmatic by implication, this one is explicitly so, as vv. 5 and 12-13 make plain; thus the "story" of Christ serves as paradigm for the "mindset" necessary for unity among them with regard to the gospel, both as they themselves "advance" in the faith (1:25) and as they hold fast the word of life for the sake of others (2:16).

One further formal note. Excluding 2:17-18, which serves as transition to the next section of the letter (vv. 19-30), the several parts of the argument fall out[8] into a nearly perfect chiasm:

2. Thus the lack of a section break here in the NIV with a major break at 2:1 — signaled by the new section title — is especially unfortunate (cf. GNB, Phillips). There is nothing in favor of a major break at 2:1, and everything in favor of one here, including not only the shift from talking about himself to exhorting them noted here, but also such clues as his "being absent/present" with which it begins (v. 27) that is picked up again in 2:12, plus the chiastic structure noted below. The REB has nicely captured the sense by its title, "Unity and witness," which it (correctly) puts here.

3. See n. 17 on 1:12.

4. See n. 4 on 1:12-26 and n. 1 on 1:18b-26.

5. There are 9 second person plural pronouns (plus 2 reflexives), 1 vocative ("my beloved ones," 2:12), 14 second plural verbs (plus 8 participles modifying these verbs).

6. Of the 14 verbs, 10 are imperatives, while 4 others are implied imperatives (στήκετε, 1:27; φρονῆτε, 2:2; γενήσθε, φαίνεσθε, 2:15), as are 5 of the participles.

7. On these matters, see the Introduction, pp. 2-7, 10-14.

8. I put it this way, because I am less certain than others that this kind of "chiasm" is a part of Paul's upfront consciousness. Rather, I think this is simply the way his mind works, as an argument unfolds. The key matter in pointing it out is to show that the whole argument is unmistakably a single piece.

156

A      Appeal to steadfastness and unity in the face of opposition
         (1:27-30)

    B      The appeal to unity, based on Paul's and their common life
           in Christ (2:1-4)

       C     The appeal to Christ's example (2:5-11)

    B′     Application of the appeal, again based on their mutual
           relationship (2:12-13)

A′     Further application: unity in the face of opposition (for the
         sake of witness) (2:14-16)

These formal observations together tell the story. The stage is set by the appeal in vv. 27-30: the need for unity in the face of opposition — with its concomitant suffering — for the sake of the gospel. The Philippians are apparently being sorely tested, which now explains some of the emphases in the foregoing section.[9] But they do not have their act fully together, which also explains some further emphases in the foregoing[10] — and the following. At issue for Paul, however, is not simply their own lives in Christ, but the cause of the gospel in Philippi (where Nero is acclaimed as *kyrios,* "lord"). Thus the reason for the further appeals in 2:1-18, all of which proceed from this initial "table-setting" paragraph.

The next paragraph (2:1-4), predicated on his and their long-term relationship in Christ and the Spirit, is a straightforward appeal to unity, set over against self-centered attitudes ("selfish ambition" and "vain conceit") that destroy the community. That appeal is reinforced by the example of Christ (5-11), who as God and man displayed the opposites of "selfish ambition" and "vain conceit" by, first, "pouring himself out" in taking the form of a servant and, second, humbling himself to the point of death for the sake of others. But the Suffering One is now the Exalted One (future orientation again); not only so, he alone reigns as *Kyrios,* and at his name every knee shall bow and tongue confess (including "lord" Nero!). After applying all of this to their own situation (12-13; God himself at work among them for his

---

9. For example, Paul's joy-filled response to his detainment, since it has served to "advance the gospel," even though some fellow believers — out of "selfish ambition" and "envy" — are doing so hoping to stir up θλῖψις ("tribulation, suffering") for him; so also with the joy-filled anticipation of his forthcoming trial, where he expects Christ to be magnified whether through his release or execution; so too with his explanation that "death is gain," since it means the fulfillment of his yearning to depart and be with Christ; not to mention that the source of their "same struggle" (v. 30) is probably the same, perceived disloyalty to the empire.

10. Especially his readiness to rejoice even when fellow believers through their own selfish ambition try (unsuccessfully) to make his life miserable while in prison; see above on vv. 15-17.

own good purposes), Paul makes a final appeal to harmony (14-16), because believers alone "shine as (God's) stars in the world" — in Philippi ("a crooked and depraved generation") — even as they "hold fast/forth the word of life." For the sake of all this, Paul concludes (vv. 17-18), he is quite prepared himself to suffer still more, being "poured out as a sacrificial libation" in conjunction with the "sacrificial offering" of their own faith(fulness).

With this section we come to the heart of matters, the primary reason for having written this letter — why he takes the occasion of Epaphroditus' return to *write* to them, rather than waiting until he himself returns. And here in particular the three-way bond that holds the letter together stands out.[11] The problem is not schism, but posturing and bickering — selfish ambition, empty conceit, complaining, arguing. At stake is the gospel in Philippi — Christ himself, if you will. Thus Christ and the gospel are Paul's ultimate concern, now as always (point 1 in the diagram); the penultimate concern is with the Philippians' relationship with Christ (line C), and thus for the Philippians themselves (point 3), whose united front for Christ is breaking down under outside pressure ("those who oppose you," v. 28). Thus Paul appeals, on the one hand, to the example of both Christ (vv. 5-11; point 1) and himself (v. 17; point 2), and on the other hand, to his and their long-term and secure relationship in Christ and the Spirit (vv. 1-2; cf. 1:27; 2:12, 16-18; line B).

## A. THE APPEAL — TO STEADFASTNESS AND UNITY IN THE FACE OF OPPOSITION (1:27-30)

> 27*Whatever happens, conduct yourselves in a manner worthy of the gospel of Christ. Then, whether I come and see you or only hear*[12] *about you*[13] *in my absence, I will know that you stand firm in one spirit, contending as one [person]*[14] *for the faith of the gospel* 28*without*

---

11. See esp. the diagrammatic presentation of these matters in the Introduction, p. 13.

12. The manuscript tradition varies between the present (ἀκούω) and aorist (ἀκούσω) subjunctive. The present (read by P[46] ℵ* B D* P 629 1241[s] 2464 pc) is to be preferred on all counts: the aorist is the "normal" tense and would be the one toward which scribes would normally change, whereas it is nearly impossible to account, even by sheer accident, for a change in the other direction. It is doubtful whether the present is "meaningful," unless it reflects the possibility of Paul's hearing more than once.

13. Gk. τὰ περὶ ὑμῶν; while one may perhaps leave out the τά for the sake of dynamic equivalence, to render this "about you" is neither "dynamic" nor "equivalent." On the use of this kind of phrase in letters of friendship (in his case, τὰ πρός σε), see the "example letter" of Pseudo-Demetrius in the Introduction, p. 3. See further n. 17 on 1:12.

14. NIV, "man"; Gk. μιᾷ ψυχῇ, lit. "as one soul." Under no circumstances does the idiom mean "man." See the discussion below.

*being frightened in any way by those who oppose you. This is a sign to them that[15] they will be destroyed, but that you[16] will be saved — and that by God. 29For it has been granted to you[17] on behalf of Christ not only to believe on him, but also to suffer for him, 30since you are going through the same struggle you saw I had, and now hear that I[18] still have.*

Paul now turns to "your affairs," and does so by way of imperative. The whole is a single, nearly impossible, sentence in Greek, which probably assumes this form because Paul tries to include all of the urgencies of the letter (at least as far as their situation is concerned) in this opening word. Indeed, the weakness of some interpretations has been the failure to recognize the initial imperative as the key to the whole, and that everything else in the sentence functions as a modifier in some way. Here especially a structural display will help both to identify its various parts and to follow the train of thought ("stream of consciousness"?).[19]

> Only
> (1) worthy of the gospel of Christ,
>        live out your "citizenship"
>                    so that
> (2)                whether coming and seeing you
>                    or being absent,
>                    I hear about "your affairs,"
>                    that

15. The later manuscript tradition conforms Paul's Greek to a more classical idiom by (1) inserting a μέν, while (2) the majority of these also shift the word order (from ἐστὶν αὐτοῖς to αὐτοῖς ἐστίν — correctly so, in light of the addition), and (3) by changing Paul's ὑμῶν to ὑμῖν, so that the whole is now nicely balanced: "which to them, on the one hand," "to you, on the other hand"). This helps to make sense of a difficult clause, but it is scarcely original.

16. For the textual variation ὑμῶν/ὑμῖν, see the preceding n.

17. Typically — and understandably — a few MSS (A 1241ˢ) replace this "you" (ὑμῖν) with an "us" (ἡμῖν). Although this is a logical place for such an interchange, the focus of the argument to here is on the Philippians, not on the Philippians *and Paul.* That will come in the next clause (v. 30), where Paul appeals to his example of suffering as being the "same" as theirs.

18. Paul's sentence reads (literally): "what you saw *in me,* and even now hear *in me.*" The awkwardness (apparently) of this final ἐν ἐμοί caused it to be omitted in P[46] and 81.

19. Lying behind this overview are a number of exegetical decisions on some difficult questions that receive further explanation in the exposition that follows. Lohmeyer's attempt (72-73; cf. Michaelis) to find strophic patterns to all this must be judged a failure.

(a) you stand firm
in the one Spirit,
(b) as one person
contending together for the faith of the gospel
(3) not being frightened in any way
by those who oppose you
[ which
(4) is for them an "omen"
(a) of destruction
but
(b) of your salvation,
(c) and *this* from God ]
because
(5) it has been granted to you,
on behalf of Christ,
(a) not only to believe on him,
but also to suffer for him
(b) having the same struggle,
which
you saw in me
and now
you hear in me

Thus, Paul's concerns:

(1) The *exhortation:* that they live as worthy citizens of the gospel of Christ;
(2) The *reasons:* that in his current absence, he may hear about "their affairs":
    (a) that they stand firm in the one Spirit
    (b) contending side by side as one person for the faith of the gospel
(3) The *circumstances* that called this forth: intimidation by their adversaries
(4) Which leads to an *aside:*
    (a) Their doing 2 and 3 will become an "omen" of the opponents' destruction;
    (b) but evidence of the Philippians' salvation,
    (c) which has God as its source;
(5) A concluding *theological explanation* of their suffering (implicit in item 3):
    (a) It is a "grace" given to those who believe
    (b) It is consonant with Paul's own struggles (past and present).

160

This paragraph thus holds the keys to much in this letter, especially regarding Paul's concerns about things on their end, which have undoubtedly been reported to him by Epaphroditus. Although he does not explicitly say so (but cf. 4:2-3), 2:2-3 and 14 imply there are some internal tensions among them; at the same time there are some external pressures being applied, which bid fair to make their situation as God's people in Philippi tenuous. Paul's ultimate concern for them is directly related to his concern for the gospel in Philippi. His obvious hope, as 2:1-2 makes plain, is that his and their long-term friendship and participation together in the gospel will pull them through this twofold crisis.

**27** With the adverb "only"[20] Paul moves directly from "your [future] progress and joy in the faith" to the present scene in Philippi, which has all the potential for "regress" rather than "progress." Thus: "*Only* — in light of what I have just said about my coming, but *in the meantime* before I get there — let this be what I hear *you* to be about," namely, "living out your citizenship — the heavenly one of course — in a manner worthy of the gospel of Christ." This imperative controls the argument from here to 2:18.

The rendering of the imperative as "conduct yourselves"[21] is unfortunate[22] — and unnecessary.[23] When Paul intends the general idea of conduct he uses the common Jewish metaphor of "walking."[24] Along with the noun *politeuma* in 3:20 (q.v.), Paul is here making a play on their "dual citizenship" — of the empire by virtue of their being Philippians; of heaven by virtue of their faith in Christ and incorporation into the believing community. On the one hand, the city boasted of its privileged status as a Roman colony, made so by Octavian (later the emperor Augustus) after his decisive victory on the plains of Philippi; hence its people thereby had Roman citizenship conferred

---

20. Gk. μόνον, the neuter accusative of μόνος used as an adverb; cf. Gal 5:13, the other comparable use in Paul. "Lifted like a warning finger" (Barth, 45).

21. Gk. πολιτεύεσθε, a common verb in Greco-Roman authors, which in the active denotes to "live in the *polis* [city state] as a free citizen," but which in the middle (as here) meant "to take an active part in the affairs of the *polis*," hence to "be a citizen" (almost always literally, either of the Greek city state or of the empire). The metaphorical use is rare, since there would be little place for it in the Greco-Roman world.

22. But cf. NASB, RSV, NRSV, GNB, NEB, JB, NAB (cf. Bruce); the metaphor is kept intact by Berkeley, Rotherham, and Goodspeed (cf. O'Brien). Despite Lenski, et al., R. Roberts ("Philippians i.27," 325) had it right: "It is inconceivable that the idea of citizenship should be absent from his mind as he dictated the word πολιτεύεσθε."

23. That is, one can capture the sense of the metaphor in English without such bland language as "conduct yourselves." Cf. O'Brien (144): "as citizens of heaven live . . . worthy of the gospel."

24. As in Phil 3:17, 18, and in 15 other instances in the corpus (see on Gal 5:16 in Fee, *Presence,* 429-30). Indeed, on three occasions Paul uses the present combination with περιπατεῖτε ("walk worthy of"; 1 Thess 2:12; Col 1:10; Eph 4:1).

on them, a matter in which they took considerable pride.[25] The verb thus means (literally) to "live as citizens." On the other hand, by joining it with the adverb "worthily," Paul now uses the verb metaphorically, not meaning "live as citizens of Rome"[26] — although that is not irrelevant — but rather "live in the Roman colony of Philippi as worthy citizens of your heavenly homeland." That, after all, is precisely the contrast made in 3:17-20, where "our 'citizenship' is in heaven," in contrast to those whose minds are set on "earthly things."

As Philippi was a colony of Rome in Macedonia, so the church was a "colony of heaven"[27] in Philippi, whose members were to live as its citizens in Philippi. This suggests a missionary outlook on the one hand (they are "contending for the gospel" in Philippi; cf. 2:14-16), but a concern for the "welfare of the state" — the believing community itself — on the other. Thus this is the fitting verb for the setting. It would be full of meaning in light of their privileged status as Roman citizens, now addressing them as to their "civic" responsibilities to the new "polis," the believing community, of which they are a part and whose responsibilities will be spelled out in what follows.[28]

With the modifier, "worthy of the gospel of Christ," Paul defines both the parameters and the nature of the new "polis" of which they are citizens and to which they have obligation. As noted above (vv. 5, 7, 12), the gospel is the crucial matter. He and they have had a long-term participation together in the cause of the gospel (1:5), for the confirmation and defense of which Paul is now in prison (vv. 7, 15), an imprisonment which in its own way has fallen out for the "advance of the gospel" (v. 12). What was anticipated in the prayer (vv. 9-11) is now spelled out by way of imperative. Whatever they do or suffer in Philippi, they must live in a way that is "worthy of the gospel of Christ."[29] The phrase presupposes that the gospel had known ethical content,[30] and that "selfish ambition, vain conceit, grumbling, and disputing,"

25. See further the Introduction, pp. 25-26.

26. This is the view put forward by Brewer ("Meaning"; cf. Scott), but most interpreters take it the way that is suggested here, and for good reason in light of 3:20. Some (Hendriksen, Hawthorne, Silva) would have both, but that is unlikely, since 3:20 certifies that we are involved in a word play and such plays seldom incorporate the literal reality of the meaning being played on. E. C. Miller ("πολιτεύεσθε") wants to find the background in hellenistic Judaism, thus urging the Philippians to live as "the true Israel." But there is nothing in the immediate context nor in the historical context of Philippi that favors this view.

27. The language is from Moffatt's translation of 3:20, which may not be precise in that instance, but nicely captures the sense of Paul's concern here.

28. So also R. Roberts, "Philippians i.27," 327-28; cf. Martin, 82.

29. As in all other instances, the qualifier "of Christ" refers to the content of the gospel, not its source.

30. Cf. J. Schütz (*Paul,* 50): "The gospel establishes the norm of the Philippians' conduct."

for example, are *not* in keeping with their heavenly citizenship, since they do not reflect the ethical character of the gospel. In God's time Paul will return to Philippi for their own "advance" in "the faith" (= the gospel); for now he writes to encourage the same. Thus, if Paul's "affairs" are all about Christ and his being glorified, so he now urges the same on them, that whatever else, for them, too, "to live is Christ."

The *reason* for this exhortation is given next, but in a way that has been complicated by Paul's urgencies. He begins with a purpose clause that appeals to his and their relationship, whose *content* is finally given in the "that" clause that serves as the object of "I hear." To get there he ties two concerns together (his coming [vv. 25-26] and their present situation). But he also writes in light of two (anticipated) realities: (1) that he is about to send Timothy to "learn about your affairs" (2:19), who will obviously come *after* this letter — and perhaps return to Paul[31] before Paul himself comes; and (2) that Paul intends to come soon, when he can (2:24). This accounts for the grammatical awkwardness. He really is expecting to hear about "their affairs" before he comes; hence this is how the clause concludes: "or whether, being absent, I (nonetheless) hear about your affairs," presumably from Timothy. But because of what was said in vv. 25-26, with the word about his own coming, he begins first with "whether I come and see you," which in fact he expects to happen *after* he first "hears" about their situation.[32]

In the meantime he spells out specifically three coinciding matters he hopes to hear about "their affairs": (1) that by standing firm in the one Spirit (2) they are contending together as one person for the faith of the gospel; and (3) that in so doing they are not themselves intimidated in any way by the opposition that is responsible for their present suffering.[33]

While the above seems clearly to be Paul's point, the first of these matters is most often understood otherwise,[34] not to refer to the Holy Spirit,

31. On this question, see n. 26 on 2:19.

32. This so easily accounts for the grammar of this sentence and is so clearly in keeping with vv. 24-25 and 2:24 that one wonders about Michael's comment (64), "To say the least, the words make it clear that he was far from being certain that acquittal would be his lot." They do no such thing. Nor are the various emendations noted by Loh-Nida (38) necessary or helpful.

33. To which he will then append two explanatory words: (1) that when they do as he urges, it will serve as an omen against their opponents, while it evidences God's salvation of them; (2) that in any case their present suffering is part and parcel of discipleship, as they have already seen and now hear in the case of Paul.

34. Put baldly by Melick (89): "It naturally cannot refer to the Holy Spirit"! If "natural" has anything to do with ordinary Pauline usage, then this is a remarkable overstatement indeed. Several have taken the view argued for here (Erasmus, Weiss, Ewald, Moule, Jones, Dibelius, Bonnard, Collange, Gnilka, Martin; C. Brown, *NIDNTT*, 3.702; L. T. Johnson, *Writings*, 342). Attempts to make it refer to the human spirit or community

but to a kind of "common mind" within the community. The primary reason[35] put forward for this view is the close juxtaposition of this phrase with the "one soul" that begins the next clause. Thus (literally): "that you stand firm in *one pneuma, [as] one psyche* contending together[36] for the faith of the gospel." This is understood to be a piece of semitic parallelism (a distich), in which the second "line" is synonymous with, or explanatory of, the first.[37] While that appears to have much going for it, several matters indicate that Paul is instead referring to their standing firm in the Spirit.

First, "in one spirit," which seems to make perfectly good sense to us, in fact has no analogy in Greek literature, especially not in Paul and the NT. Whereas the term "one *psyche*" occurs frequently to describe oneness or unity between two or more people,[38] the word *pneuma* is never so used. Indeed, it is not easy to determine exactly what "in one spirit" means.[39]

---

spirit as that is influenced by the Holy Spirit (as, e.g., by Michael, Barth) will not work, since it does not take the Pauline data seriously enough. On this whole question, see Fee, *Presence,* 743-46.

35. The only other reason offered is that the modifier "one" seems to put the emphasis on the Philippians' own unity, which it does indeed, but in terms of its source, not its expression, which is the point of the second clause.

36. Gk. στήκετε ἐν ἑνὶ πνεύματι, μιᾷ ψυχῇ συναθλοῦντες, which is also chiastic (A B B′ A′).

37. So, e.g., Eadie, 72; Meyer, 61; Kent, 118; Bruce, 57; and esp. Hawthorne, 56-57; followed by Silva, 94; and O'Brien, 150. This is a perfectly valid observation, of course; but it is purely gratuitous to assume that the "parallel" is synonymous in the sense of the second repeating or explaining the first. Some older commentators (e.g., Lightfoot) not only saw the two terms as anthropological, but also were willing to distinguish the two, with "spirit" designating "the principle of the higher life," vis-à-vis the "soul, the seat of the affections, passions, etc." (106). The juxtaposition is undoubtedly for rhetorical effect, but there is no compelling reason why the meaning of the first of these phrases should be *dictated by the second,* while there are several good reasons why it should not. Moreover, in contemporary understanding of Hebrew poetry, the second line is understood, as happens here, to be advancing the idea of the first in some way. Thus Paul urges them to "stand firm in the one Spirit of God," and in so doing to contend together as one people of God. This both keeps the parallel and fits known usage.

It is often argued that the juxtaposition of these two terms makes a synonymous understanding "more natural." But "natural" is in the eye of the (very Western) reader, since such an understanding of πνεῦμα would have been totally *un*natural both to Paul and to the Greco-Roman hearer, as the linguistic evidence makes clear.

38. See esp. Acts 4:32, where the unity of the believers is described in terms of their being ψυχὴ μία. Aristotle explicitly calls μιὰ ψυχή a common "proverbial" expression about friendship (*Eth. Nic.* 1163b6-7; cf. Euripides, *Orest.* 1046).

39. Thus Eadie (72), "pervaded with one genuine spiritual emotion"; Meyer (61), "the perfect *accord* of their minds in conviction, volition, and feeling"; Michael (65), "the disposition of the community"; Lohmeyer (75) "die innere Geschlossenheit" (= "the inner resolution of purpose"; cf. O'Brien [150], "with one common purpose").

Ordinarily, it suggests something attitudinal,[40] that is, a "community spirit"[41] or (worse yet, in terms of Pauline usage) "a common mind."[42] But Paul himself never elsewhere uses *pneuma* in this way.[43] What is altogether missing in Paul is any hint that "spirit" might be an anthropological *metaphor* for a *community disposition.* Although the French have a word for it (*esprit de corps* = "spirit of the body"), the Greeks apparently did not; and it is highly questionable whether Paul is here creating such a usage.

Second, also regarding a matter of known (especially Pauline) usage, whenever Paul uses the verb "stand firm" followed by the preposition "in," the prepositional phrase is invariably locative; that is, it defines the "sphere" in which one is to stand firm.[44] That regular usage works perfectly with "the one Spirit," by whom they have all been incorporated into Christ, whereas "in one spirit" functions not as a locative but as a dative of "manner," indicating *how* they are to stand firm. There is no Pauline analogy for such usage.

Third, in the resumption of the appeal that follows in 2:1-4, these two words are picked up again by Paul and used exactly as we are suggesting he uses them here. Thus in v. 1, he appeals to their common "participation in *the Spirit*" and in v. 2 argues that they be "*soul* brothers and sisters" in this matter. Thus, just as he has (indirectly) asked for their prayers that he might be supplied afresh with the Spirit of Christ as he faces his ordeal (v. 19), so now in the midst of their ordeal he urges them to stand firm in, and thus by, that same Spirit, the one and only Spirit whom they have in common.

Fourth, and most significantly, Paul himself uses this very language ("in one Spirit") in another Prison Epistle (Eph 2:18; cf. 4:4) as well as in 1 Cor 12:13 to describe the Holy Spirit, *precisely in passages where the emphasis is on believers' common experience of the one Spirit as the basis*

---

40. Cf. Vincent, 33, who suggests "disposition" as the proper sense of πνεύματι here.

41. This is the language of Hawthorne, 56.

42. Cf. Kent, 118.

43. That is, he never uses πνεῦμα as an *anthropological* term for the human mind. Indeed, in this letter he uses the verb φρονεῖν when he wants to make this point (2:2; 4:2); in 1 Cor 1:10 he uses the actual words for "mind" and "opinion" in a context of schism; and in 1 Cor 2:10-16 the πνεῦμα is said to know the mind of God or people. Furthermore, when Paul does use πνεῦμα in the sense of an "attitude," he is dependent on the LXX and thus always qualifies it with a genitive modifier, specifying the kind of "spirit" he intends (e.g. "gentleness"; 1 Cor 4:21).

44. Thus in 4:1, when he renews this charge, he urges them to "stand firm in the Lord." So also in 1 Thess 3:8; while in 1 Cor 16:13 it is "stand firm in the faith." This point is recognized by Meyer, who says correctly (61, emphasis his), "it is the common element, *in which* they are to *stand*"; but he then proceeds to explain it as though it were a dative of manner.

*for unity.* No one would imagine in these cases that "in one Spirit" refers to the *esprit de corps* of the community. Paul's point is that their being one in Christ is the direct result of the *one* Spirit's presence in their individual and community life. So too in this case.

That leads, then, to the further contextual observation that such an understanding not only fits Pauline usage, but also fits the present appeal and his theology as reflected elsewhere. The present appeal is for their unity in the face of opposition. That Paul should *twice* urge them to hold firm and contend with unity of purpose makes for a much weaker appeal than that he should urge them first to stand firm in the "one Spirit," and thereby to contend "as one person" against their opposition.[45] It is, after all, an especially Pauline point of view that the Spirit is the key to unity in the church. This is expressly stated in such passages as 1 Cor 12:13 or Eph 4:4, and is the clear implication of many other texts (including 2:1 that follows). That he should qualify the Spirit as "the *one* Spirit" emphasizes the *source* of their unity. Only by standing firm in the *one and only* Spirit can they hope to contend as "one person" for the gospel against their opposition. We should therefore not be surprised that this is the first thing said in the long appeal for unity (1:27–2:18) that begins with this sentence.

The reason they need to "stand firm in the one Spirit" is so that they might "contend together[46] as one person for[47] the faith of the gospel." The non-compounded verb *(athleō)* means "to engage in an athletic contest." The compounded form, which occurs only here and in 4:3 in the NT, is strictly metaphorical, carrying the sense of "engaging side by side" or "helping one another," in this case in the struggle for the gospel in Philippi. That he repeats the verb again in 4:3, when referring specifically to Euodia and Syntyche, who once "contended side by side with (Paul) in spreading the gospel" in Philippi but who are now at odds, indicates that that passage gives the particulars toward which the imperative in 1:27 is directed. Thus, even though we do not come upon reasons for this stress on unity until later (2:1-4; 4:2-3),

---

45. This is such a thoroughly Pauline point of view that one wonders why it should even be imagined that the phrase might mean something like *esprit de corps.*

46. Gk. συναθλοῦντες. My translation "together" is an attempt to reflect the compound σύν, which in this case, given the metaphor, may mean something like "side by side" (so *EDNT,* 3.296, who also take the metaphor to have moved over into the arena of "battle," which very well may have been the case, since for ancients the "struggle" of the athletic contest was very much like that of "battle"). See further on v. 30, where the more common athletic metaphor, ἀγών, appears.

47. A dative of interest; Lightfoot (106; cf. Plummer, 34) understands this dative to go with the σύν in the participle, hence "striving in concert *with* the faith" (whatever that might mean). He says of the more common understanding that it seems "harsh and improbable." But his view fails to take seriously the emphasis on *unity* being stressed here.

the issue is one that the Philippians are privy to; there can be little question that they heard this emphasis in light of their present situation. This also helps to explain the earlier emphasis on "all of you," especially in 1:25.

What Paul has said in 1:25 also explains the unusual expression, "for the faith of the gospel," which is probably an appositional genitive (= "the faith, that is, the gospel"; or "the faith that is contained in the gospel").[48] As always the gospel is the urgency. Thus it turns out that their own "progress and joy in the faith" (mutual love and unity) is directly related to their contending side by side "for the faith of the gospel" in the face of current opposition in Philippi.

**28** The second participial modifier, "without being frightened in any way by those who oppose you," serves as the fulcrum between his appeal for unity in the face of opposition and the ensuing mention of suffering (vv. 29-30), which together serve as the primary "historical context" of the letter.[49] At the same time this modifier furnishes us with some much-needed historical background in order to make sense of the matter of their suffering. There were those in Philippi who "stood in opposition to them."[50] Since the Philippians knew to whom Paul is referring, he does not elaborate; we can only surmise. But in light of several hints within the letter, especially the emphasis on Christ as "lord" and "savior," and of the loyalty of this colony to the cult of the emperor, it seems very likely that the (Roman) citizens of Philippi, who would have honored the emperor at every public gathering, were putting special pressure on the Philippian believers; their allegiance had now been given to another *kyrios,* Jesus, who had himself been executed at the hands of the empire. The present context, in which Paul asserts that they are undergoing "the *same* struggle" he is *now* engaged in — as a prisoner of the empire — gives us good reason to believe so.

But since the Philippians did not need to be informed along these lines

---

48. Barth (47), as one might well expect, takes "of the gospel" to be subjective: "Faith is not mine but God's." Fair enough; but that simply is not Paul's point here. But cf. Hawthorne (57), who also sees it as subjective, but for less theological reasons.

49. See the Introduction, pp. 29-34.

50. On the question of their "identity," see the Introduction, pp. 7-9. That these are the same people warned against in 3:2 (as Hendriksen, Collange, Hawthorne, Silva) has nothing in its favor (except that both passages occur in the same letter) and everything against it: the adversaries here are a present reality, those in 3:2 are warned against as a "safety" measure (3:1); this situation reflects the "same struggle" as Paul is now experiencing, which can be laid at the feet of the Jewish community only in a very circuitous manner; the present struggle is "the same" as the one they saw with their own eyes, and at no known point when Paul was in Macedonia was a Jewish or Jewish Christian struggle in evidence, whereas conflict with the state was present from the beginning. Cf. O'Brien (153) for a similar assessment.

— after all, they knew better even than Paul what he is here referring to —
why mention it at all? The answer lies first in the participle, "not being
*frightened*[51] in any way," and second in the reassuring "aside" which immediately follows. Thus Paul urges that as they contend for the truth of the gospel
against the opposition in Philippi, they not let the opposition *intimidate* them,
formidable as it might appear. Now one can also better understand Paul's
sounding out the clear note that "to die is gain," since death means to "depart
and be with Christ." People who hold firmly to such an eschatological orientation — the "mature," after all, have this "mindset" (3:15) — will not be
intimidated by opponents. They recognize that, in Luther's words, "the body
they may kill; God's truth abideth still; his kingdom is forever." This, then,
is Paul's (circuitous) way of urging them also to "glorify Christ," whether
"through life or through death."

To plant that eschatological certainty firmly in their hearts, he offers
a brief parenthetical moment, which seems to be much more straightforward
than some interpreters have allowed. That the rest of our v. 28 is parenthetical
most are agreed. At issue are two points of grammar: (1) that the clause is
introduced by the (indefinite) relative pronoun, which does not seem to have
an immediate antecedent; and (2) that the second clause is elliptical (something must be supplied to make it work), which has been considered to be
problematic since the two pronouns ("to them" and "your" ["you" NIV])
are in different cases (dative and genitive respectively). But both of these have
readily available explanations in terms of Pauline usage and Greek grammar,
which point toward the understanding reflected in the structural analysis given
above (pp. 159-60).[52]

The "which" ("this," NIV) with which the clause begins is best
understood as referring to the Philippians' following through on the three
matters he has just urged on them.[53] If they do so, Paul says by way of

---

51. Gk. πτυρόμενοι; the verb occurs most often in the passive, bearing the sense
of "being frightened," or "let oneself be intimidated"; or, since it sometimes appears with
regard to "spooking" horses, it may mean something like, "not be thrown into consterna-
tion" (Meyer).

52. Which is also very close to the "dynamic equivalent" offered in the NIV.

53. The justification for this is to be found in Pauline usage. Two observations:
(1) As in most *koine* Greek, the indefinite relative pronoun (ἥτις in this case) usually
occurs in the nominative case. (2) The reason for the feminine singular is a simple matter
of attraction — in this case, as elsewhere in Paul when using this idiom, to the number
and gender of *the predicate noun that follows*. Thus the indefinite is used because it
refers not to any specific word or idea that precedes (*contra* Hawthorne, who sees τῇ
πίστει as its antecedent), but to the whole of the preceding clause; and the feminine
singular is used because the predicate noun ἔνδειξις is feminine singular. This is precisely
the same phenomenon as in the apparently "ungrammatical" οἵτινές ἐστε ὑμεῖς in 1 Cor
3:17, where the plural οἵτινες in this case refers to the (masculine singular) "temple"

encouragement, that will function with regard to the opposition[54] as an "omen[55] of destruction."[56] How so, Paul does not say, but the answer probably lies with the Philippians' embracing the eschatological outlook just given in vv. 21-24. Such people cannot be intimidated by anyone or anything, since they belong to the future with a kind of certainty that people whose lives are basically controlled by Fate could never understand. Such a united front in spreading the gospel in Philippi, by people whose eschatological certainties give them uncommon boldness, will mean that those who oppose them can in no way intimidate them; indeed, such a disposition will serve as an omen with regard to the opponents of their destruction.

By the same token such resolve and unity in the face of opposition will fall out as salvation for the Philippians. Although the grammar is a bit sticky here, most likely Paul intends that their following through on his exhortations, which will serve as an omen regarding their opponents, will at the same time result in their own salvation,[57] where the word "salvation"

---

that has just preceded; but it is masculine plural because it has been attracted to its predicate noun "you."

Hawthorne constructs an elaborate case for reading the text as though it referred to the opponents' attitude toward the Philippian believers (they see your loyalty to the faith as senselessly leading to your destruction, while you see it as leading to salvation). While this may be remotely possible, it is highly improbable, since it is dependent on several contingent — and necessary — improbabilities for it to work (that the distant τῇ πίστει is in fact intended to be a specific antecedent to the indefinite relative; that Paul's ordinary usage noted above is not at work here; that the contrast between ἀπωλείας and σωτηρίας is not Paul's ordinary one [see n. 56 below]; and [most improbably of all] that in an elliptical second line one may assume words from that line to be read back into the first line). The same must be said of Collange's less carefully worked out, but similar, attempt to read it this way.

54. O'Brien (155), probably correctly, sees this as a dative of reference, thus stressing that it will be a reality for them whether they recognize it or not.

55. Gk. ἔνδειξις; in its three other NT occurrences (2 Cor 8:24; Rom 3:25, 26) it clearly means "proof" or "evidence." It means that here as well, of course, but in light of the context, and since an "omen" constituted "proof" for most ancients, this meaning suggested by BAGD probably captures Paul's nuance. In any case, he did not use the ordinary word for "sign" (σημεῖον), which fact is obscured by rendering ἔνδειξις as "sign." The word ἔνδειγμα functions in a similar way in 2 Thess 1:5, although nouns with the -μα suffix tend to refer to a "concrete expression" of the verbal idea in the noun, hence in that case, a "clear indication."

56. Gk. ἀπωλείας, which in Paul carries the theological sense of utter ruin on the part of those who do not believe. Cf. 1 Cor 1:18, where the cognate verbs of these two nouns are likewise set in contrast to one another. This clear, and very Pauline, contrast tends to undercut the view of Hawthorne and Collange (see n. 53), who apply ἀπωλείας to the Philippians.

57. The resolution of the problem of the change of case from the dative (αὐτοῖς) to the genitive (ἡμῶν) is most likely that offered by Kennedy (432): "The emphasis in Paul's mind changes from the persons to their destinies"; cf. Beare, 67. The result is that the genitive is a "vernacular possessive" (see on 2:2), with probable emphasis on "your."

probably carries a sense very close to that in v. 19. Such salvation/vindication will not necessarily be manifest to the opponents, but it will become clear to the believers themselves. To drive this point of assurance home, Paul adds, "and this (i.e., your salvation/vindication)[58] comes from none other than God himself."

As often in Paul, God is both the first and last word. Salvation is at his initiative; it comes "from" him. Thus it is the first word. But in this sentence, in light of their need for reassurance, it is now the last word as well. Everything is from God; the Philippians can rest assured here. Which is also a necessary word in light of the final theological explanation regarding suffering that he is about to offer.

**29** The final clause in this long sentence (which began in v. 27) offers a theological explanation for their suffering.[59] The explanation is in two parts, corresponding to our current verse divisions. In v. 29 Paul puts the Philippians' present suffering in terms of their relationship with Christ; in verse 30 in terms of their relationship with him.

Because of the parenthetical character of v. 28b, what Paul is setting out to explain is not immediately clear.[60] Most likely these words were triggered by the combination of items in v. 28: his mention of the opposition and the strong affirmation of the Philippians' salvation, as from God. Picking up on the latter, Paul proceeds to explain: . . . will serve as evidence of *your* salvation, *because* the God who has given you his salvation has with that gift also "graced" you to be Christ's people in the world, which means that you will suffer for his sake just as he did for yours, and as I do as well. But what ultimately triggers all of this is the mention of the opposition, undoubtedly filtered through Paul's knowledge of his readers' present, very real, situation.

The keys to understanding the passage lie first in the text, and secondly in the larger context of the letter. About the text, two things stand out: Paul's choice of the verb "graciously given," and its striking Christocentric character.

---

58. Not all agree that τοῦτο should be construed with "salvation." Lightfoot (106; cf. Michael, 71; Bruce, 60) considers the τοῦτο to refer to ἔνδειξις; Plummer (35; cf. Jones, 25; Houlden, 67) to "the fearlessness with its meaning"; Vincent (35; cf. Silva, 93; O'Brien, 157) to both parts of the clause, which it very well may, but surely with the emphasis on the latter.

59. Similar to the kind of thing Paul has done elsewhere; cf., e.g., 1 Thess 3:2-3; 2 Cor 4:17-18; Rom 5:3-4; 8:17-18.

60. That is, at first blush the "because" does not seem to go easily with anything that precedes. Here is a case where Paul's understanding of their present context probably has as much bearing on what he says as the actual grammar of his sentence. Although most interpreters are happy to accept the ὅτι clause in this kind of "free floating" way, some (e.g., Kennedy) see it as going back to the mention of opposition at the beginning of the verse.

Thus Paul begins with an emphatic, "because *to you* has been *graciously given.*"[61] Your salvation which comes from God, Paul explains, graciously given you through Christ, also includes another extension of grace, namely to suffer on his behalf. This may also be the clue to "sharing in God's grace with me" mentioned in v. 7. In any case, suffering should not surprise or overwhelm them; it is rather evidence that "God looks upon you with favor."[62]

What is even more striking to the Greek reader, which is not easily captured in English translation, is how thoroughly Christocentric this clause is, an emphasis that is created in part because of an awkward stylistic feature that probably resulted from dictation. Paul (apparently) began to dictate the subject ("to suffer on behalf of Christ") immediately after the verb ("it has been graciously given"). But he got as far as "on behalf of Christ" and interrupted himself with a "not only" phrase, intending to emphasize their suffering for Christ, but within the context of what he has just said about their salvation.[63] Paul's point is easy enough to see. The God who has graciously given them salvation through Christ ("not only to believe in him"), has with that salvation also graciously given them "to suffer on his behalf." But the interruption has created a striking focus on Christ: thus, "to you has been graciously given *on behalf of Christ . . .* to suffer *on his behalf.*"[64]

And herein lies the clue. What Paul is not doing is offering encouragement to believers about suffering in general.[65] That too is our lot, as Paul explains in Rom 8:17-30. But here he is speaking specifically of their living

---

61. Gk. ἐχαρίσθη; the cognate of the noun χάρις ("grace"). In Paul's letters the verb means "to give graciously" (1 Cor 2:12; Gal 3:18; Rom 8:32[!]; Phlm 22), or by extension, "to forgive" (e.g., Col 2:13; Eph 4:32).

62. Lightfoot, 106.

63. The interruption, and therefore the emphasis, is even more startling in Greek. Ordinarily in Paul when an infinitive serves as the grammatical subject of the sentence, it is also accompanied by the Greek definite article (e.g., τὸ ζῆν and τὸ ἀποθανεῖν in v. 21 above), as well as in the two infinitive phrases as the end of this verse. It is also typical of Paul, when such occurs, to "enclose" a prepositional modifier between the article and the infinitive. Thus the two contrasting infinitive phrases at the end of this clause read τὸ εἰς αὐτὸν πιστεύειν and τὸ ὑπὲρ αὐτοῦ πάσχειν (lit., "the in him to believe" and "the in Christ's behalf to suffer"). This is where Paul was heading when he began to dictate the sentence; but in getting as far as τὸ ὑπὲρ Χριστοῦ, the mention of "Christ" triggers a momentary interruption in the form of a "not only/but also" contrast, thus leaving the original (and now ungrammatical) subject to dangle, but in an especially striking manner.

64. Hawthorne's suggestion (61) that ὑπέρ here means "in Christ's stead" is an unnatural reading in this case and is based on an understanding of Col 1:24 that is not at all firm.

65. A point sometimes overlooked in the literature; but see Michael, Fitzmyer. Silva (97-98), while admitting no direct evidence for it, enters a theological plea for an extension in this direction. While sympathetic with his concern, I am not persuaded.

for Christ in a world that is openly hostile to God and resistant to his love lavished on them in Christ. Those who have received this gracious love of God in Christ are also thereby given the grace to "shine out as stars in this wicked and perverse generation" (2:15). This accent on "for Christ's sake" also explains why Paul goes on (in v. 30) to link their present suffering to his, to which he has just spoken. Indeed, in vv. 19-20, he had solicited their prayers for a fresh supply of the Spirit of Christ Jesus so that Christ will be glorified in his forthcoming trial whether through life or *through death.* Now the Philippians, too, are encouraged to "stand fast in the one Spirit" as they contend for the gospel in the face of similar opposition.

This emphasis in turn must also be understood in light of the "story " of Christ to which he will appeal in 2:5-11. They are to live "on behalf of Christ" in the same way Christ himself lived — and died — on behalf of this fallen, broken world. The Christ in whom they have believed for their salvation effected that salvation because as God he poured himself out by taking the form of a servant and as man he humbled himself to the point of death — death for theirs and the world's sake — even death on a cross. That is why Paul can now explain that their salvation includes suffering "on behalf of Christ," since those who oppose them as they proclaim the "faith of the gospel of Christ" are of a kind with those who crucified their Lord in the first place. And for believers, as with their Lord, the path to glorification leads through the suffering of the cross.

**30** Paul now concludes this exhortation-turned-theological-explana-tion by reminding them that he and they are in it together. With these final words, "having[66] the *same* struggle," the reason for both the length and the content of the preceding narrative about "my affairs" (vv. 12-26) now falls into place. Three points are made.

First, their present "struggle"[67] is *of a kind with his,* both that which they have known about in the past and that which he is currently experiencing. The accent falls on "the same," which minimally points to their common suffering on Christ's behalf brought on by those who oppose the gospel. Very likely, as was suggested above (p. 167), "the same" reflects the common source as well, the Roman Empire.

---

66. Although the nominative (ἔχοντες) could conceivably go back to the participle in v. 28 (so Kent, 120), more likely it is an "irregular nominative"; cf. Col 3:16; Eph 3:18; 4:2.

67. Gk. ἀγῶνα, an athletic metaphor already so used by the philosophers to refer to "the heroic struggle which the pious has to go through in this world" (E. Stauffer, *TDNT,* 1.135; cf. G. Dautzenberg, *EDNT,* 1.25-27; and esp. V. C. Pfitzner, *Agon,* 114-29). For Paul, of course, it refers not to the "heroic struggle of the Christian life," an idea altogether foreign to him, but to the "noble contest" (1 Tim 6:12) of the gospel itself as one "contends" for it in a world altogether hostile to it (cf. 1 Thess 2:2; 1 Cor 9:25; Col 1:29; 4:12; 1 Tim 4:10; 6:12; 2 Tim 4:7).

Second, he reminds them that their "struggle" is identical with that which "you saw I had."[68] Paul and his readers, one must sometime be reminded, lived in a real world of flesh and blood people who knew one another. Among the recipients of this letter, after all, are the jailer and his family and (perhaps) the young slave girl whose having been set free from Satan's tyranny had resulted in the first of his sufferings on behalf of Christ that they "had seen." Indeed, not long after that initial stay in Philippi he wrote to another Macedonian congregation and refers to his Philippian experience in terms of "suffering and being shamefully treated" (1 Thess 2:2). Nonetheless, the "struggle" was always with him, and every time he came through Philippi they saw more of the same, which in time took on a variety of forms.

But, third, and now back to vv. 12-26, he reminds them that their present suffering is precisely of a kind with his current Roman imprisonment. Whatever else, they are in this thing together. And it is that reality — and resource — that he will draw on as he now returns to the appeal that they stand firm in the one Spirit, contending side by side for the gospel (2:1-4).

Although our particulars may differ considerably, the theological concerns that emerge in this paragraph are greatly needed in the church today (especially in our current post-Christian, post-modern world), both in the Western church where the "struggle" is immense, but the suffering itself less so, and in churches in the emerging world, where suffering is often more prevalent but where sectarian strife all too often hampers the cause of the gospel.

One of the reasons most of us in the West do not know more about the content of vv. 29-30 is that we have so poorly heeded the threefold exhortation that precedes: (1) to stand firm in the one Spirit (overall our pneumatology is especially weak); (2) to contend for the faith of the gospel as one person (the "faith of the gospel" has been watered down in so many ways, on all sides [not just by "liberalism," but by the blatant materialism that erodes the evangelical church], that it is sometimes not worth contending for; and our sectarianism has more often resulted in in-house furor than in contending for the gospel in the face of pagan opposition); and (3) to do so by not being intimidated in any way by the opposition (who tend to focus on our many weaknesses, so as continually to deflect our contending for the gospel of our crucified Savior per se).

The net result is that the content of Paul's explanation is something

---

68. Paul's Greek is a bit more emphatic: οἷον εἴδετε ἐν ἐμοί = "of a kind that you saw *in me*" (cf. the emphatic "in me" in v. 26). This does not mean simply "which you saw I experienced," but "which you saw taking place in my life and experience among you." Does this emphasis on "of a kind" mean that some of them had now been imprisoned?

contemporary Christians hear reluctantly, either out of guilt that so many of us look so little like this, or out of fear that it might someday really be true for us. The key is to return to Paul's emphasis, "for the sake of Christ." Our tendency is to focus on the suffering; what is needed is a radical paradigm shift toward Christ — and his apostle — as God's ultimate paradigm for us. Through "death on a cross" he not only "saved us," but modeled for us God's way of dealing with the opposition — loving them to death.

What for Paul was exhortation to a concrete historical situation may well still function that way today in various local situations. But might it not also now take the form of prayer as we look at the church and the world in our day?

## B. THE APPEAL RENEWED — UNITY THROUGH HUMILITY (2:1-4)

> 1*If you have any encouragement from being united with Christ, if any comfort from his love, if any fellowship with the Spirit, if any[1] tenderness and compassion, 2then make my joy complete by being like-minded, having the same love, being one in spirit and purpose.[2] 3Do nothing out of selfish ambition or[3] vain conceit, but in humility consider[4] others[5] better*

1. MSS variously try to alleviate Paul's ungrammatical τις by changing it into a neuter (singular or plural). Various explanations have been forthcoming as to the grammatical breakdown, usually in terms of an early error by a copyist (Lightfoot; Kennedy). Very likely the "error" is Paul's own, related to the nature of his rhetoric.

2. For the sake of better English, the NIV has chosen here to obscure some of Paul's repetitiveness in this set of appeals. Lying behind "and purpose" is yet another participial construction, τὸ ἓν φρονοῦντες ("thinking the *one* thing"), which nearly repeats the purpose/result clause, ἵνα τὸ αὐτὸ φρονῆτε ("that you think the *same* thing"), which all of the following participles and words modify. Understandably, several MSS (ℵ* A C I Ψ 33 81 1241ˢ 2464 pc f vg) conform this final phrase to the main clause by substituting αὐτό for ἕν. The latter, which is surely original, is in keeping with Paul's habits elsewhere, where in a series such as this he interchanges "same" and "one" (see esp. 1 Cor 12:8-10).

3. Paul's Greek (as reflected in NA²⁶), though clear, is awkwardly expressed (lit. "nothing according to selfish ambition, nor according to vain glory"). This engendered a considerable amount of tinkering in the transmissional process, so that the MajT ended up substituting an ἤ ("or") for Paul's μηδὲ κατά ("nor according to"), which is the same route taken by the NIV, even though translated from the NA²⁶ text.

4. For Paul's simple participle ἡγούμενοι, a few scribes (P⁴⁶ D* I K 1175 pc) preferred the compound προηγούμενοι, most likely under the influence of the similar exhortation in Rom 12:10, τῇ τιμῇ ἀλλήλους προηγούμενοι ("with honor preferring/more highly esteeming one another").

5. In a rare moment of singular agreement on a patently secondary reading, P⁴⁶ and B insert a τούς before the participle ὑπερέχοντας, thus particularizing ("others who are better") what Paul leaves open-ended so as to include all others.

174

*than yourselves.* 4*Each*[6] *of you should look*[7] *not only to your own interests,
but also*[8] *to the interests of others.*

Both the "therefore" (omitted in the NIV) and the content of this paragraph
— and those that follow — attest that the main issue in the preceding paragraph (1:27-30) is the exhortation with which it began (to live as "citizens"
worthy of the gospel by standing firm in one Spirit against the opposition),
not the theological explanation of suffering[9] with which it concluded.[10] To be
sure, he begins the renewed exhortation by appealing to the encouragement
and comfort that is theirs in Christ, which flows directly out of the context
of suffering in vv. 29-30. But the present urgency is spelled out in the multi-
plication of synonymous phrases in v. 2, which together urge one thing —
"that you have the same 'mindset,' " that is, that they get along together in
their "struggle" for the gospel, especially in the face of the opposition.

At the same time the paragraph points forward in a variety of ways,
both linguistic and conceptual, to the Christ narrative that follows (vv. 5-11).

6. Because of his proclivities toward the distributive, or collective, singular, Paul's
Greek at times creates some uncertainties for scribes. The editors of NA[26] (and UBS[4])
have opted for the singular ἕκαστος here (with P[46] ℵ C D Maj pc; against A B F G Ψ 33
81 104 1175 pc lat), but for the plural at the end (with P[46] ℵ A B D P Ψ 33 81 104 365
1175 1739 1881 2464 pc; against the MajT). This is an especially difficult textual choice,
the second instance also involving punctuation, whether the (apparently original) ἕκαστοι
belongs with the imperative that follows (thus, ἕκαστοι τοῦτο φρονεῖτε, "each of you has
this mindset") or with the present participial construction (almost certainly the latter, since
it so nicely balances the two halves of v. 4). The more difficult plural should probably
prevail as original in both cases, with scribes changing them to the singular in keeping
with ordinary style, and with Paul's own usage elsewhere.

7. Whether intentional or not, but surely in the interest of rescuing Paul's im-
possibly cumbersome sentence and awkward Greek (see the structural display below),
scribes variously changed Paul's participle, σκοποῦντες, into a form of imperative (either
third singular or second plural). The meaning is not affected, as is evidenced by the
imperative in the NIV, where the (clearly original) participle was so translated.

8. The Western tradition (D* F G it Tert), joined by K pc, omits this καί, probably
for the very reason that the NIV translators have added an "only" to the preceding clause,
namely, to make the two clauses more balanced. The καί is put in brackets in NA[26]; but
omission is surely the secondary process here, since the addition of a καί would create the
very difficulty that (in Paul's original) the NIV translators have tried to get around.

9. Thus the theme of suffering, as with its counterpoint "joy," serves as a kind of
"leitmotif" in the letter, not as its primary theme.

10. Some see Paul as here "turning from the menace of a hostile world to deal
with the equally threatening problem of a divided community" (Martin, 85-86; cf. Bonnard,
Gnilka, O'Brien). But that seems to miss by too much the overall connections of the
argument, and especially the connection of this paragraph with the preceding. Granted the
present paragraph focuses altogether on the issue of their unity; but that is already the point
in 1:27, where the issue was deliberately placed within its real life setting in Philippi.

Both paragraphs begin by urging on them the "same mindset";[11] the two sentences in vv. 6-8 (how Christ acted as God [6-7a] and man [7b-8]) respond directly to the vices singled out in v. 3 ("selfish ambition" and "vain conceit"); finally the verb in the second sentence (v. 8, "he humbled himself") picks up on the "humility" that in v. 3 is offered as the opposite of those vices.[12]

As with 1:27-30, this too is a single (even more) complex sentence.[13] As before, the way into — and out of — its complexities is through a visual display of the whole (again following Paul's wording very literally):

```
                    Therefore
(protasis)      [1] ¹If any   encouragement
                                  in Christ
                [2] If any   solace
                                  of love
                [3] If any   sharing
                                  of Spirit
                [4] If any   compassions
                             and
                             mercies
(apodosis)          ²fulfill my joy,
                             so that
(explanation)        you set your minds on the same thing
(elaboration)          having the same love,
                       united in soul setting your minds on the one thing
                              ³nothing according to selfish ambition
                              nothing according to empty conceit
                                 but
                              with humility
                       considering one another
                                      more important than oneself
                              ⁴each not looking out  for one's own concerns
                              but
                              each also                for others' concerns
```

11. Thus, τὸ αὐτὸ φρονῆτε (v. 2, "have the same mindset"); τοῦτο φρονεῖτε (v. 5, "have this mindset").

12. But rather than, as Collange (77), this paragraph is not the "overture" to the "Christ hymn"; the narrative about Christ exists, on the contrary, to reinforce by ultimate example what is urged here (and in 1:27); cf. Black, "Formal Analysis," 305-6.

13. So most interpreters, although Lightfoot (108) et al. take vv. 3-4 to be a separate sentence, offering that an imperative is to be supposed. But the passages Lightfoot cites in support are suspect; there is no sure evidence for a presupposed imperative.

In *form* this is a "conditional" sentence, with a fourfold protasis (the "if" clauses) and elaborated apodosis (the "then" clause). The overall result is a sentence in four parts: a compound protasis (v. 1); the apodosis (2a); a result (or noun) clause explaining how the apodosis will be "fulfilled" (2b); and a series of modifying participles and nouns (2c-4) offering the means to fulfillment in contrast to some negatives ("selfish ambition/empty conceit"), which undoubtedly give content to the problem in Philippi. The "conditional" nuance, however, disappears as the sentence evolves. The "if" clauses turn out not to express supposition, but presupposition,[14] and should therefore be translated something closer to "since there is . . ."; and the apodosis, instead of expressing the "then" side of a supposition, takes the form of an imperative based on the presuppositions.

This, at least, is how the sentence "works,"[15] and for the most part (vv. 2-4) its sense is plain enough — perhaps too plain for most of us. The major difficulty in interpretation lies with v. 1, partly due to the meaning of some of the words and phrases and partly to the nature of the relationships presupposed by these phrases.

**1** By the "therefore"[16] with which this sentence begins, Paul ties what he is about to say to the preceding paragraph. The conjunction is inferential (= "in consequence of what I've just said") and is probably intended to pick up on the whole of vv. 27-30.[17] Thus with this word he first of all signals a resumption of the appeal to unity that began in vv. 27-28a; but he

14. Cf. in this regard, J. L. Boyer, "First Class Conditions," 106; and BDF §371 (and most commentators), *contra* W. Barclay, "Great Themes," 40, who considers the clause to be suppositional.

15. *Contra* those who have set out more literary schemes, beginning with Lohmeyer, whose effort in this case was no more successful than in the preceding sentence (n. 19 on 1:27-30). But Gnilka modified Lohmeyer's attempt, and in this he has been followed by others (Black, "Formal Analysis"; Silva, O'Brien). Black says of this threefold strophic scheme, "there is much to commend [it] . . . and little for which to criticize it" (300); to the contrary, such a reconstruction implies a kind of conscious literary production that fails to take seriously either the oral nature of the text (see n. 22 below) or the actual syntax of the sentence. Black carries this still further, suggesting that it may also have had prior existence. But this is an exercise in scholarship that has very little bearing on the meaning of the text, except as Paul's own sentence and emphases are realigned to fit a particular scheme that would undoubtedly surprise him. Cf. Hawthorne (64): "Whether this strophic pattern can be demonstrated to the satisfaction of everyone is doubtful, but unimportant."

16. Gk. οὖν; the NIV in this case renders the reader no service in omitting this connective.

17. So also Meyer, 69; otherwise Kennedy, Vincent (cf. Motyer), who would take it only with v. 27. The number of commentators who do not so much as notice the conjunction says much about their predisposition toward an interpretation that finds the οὖν an unfriendly intrusion.

does so now in light of the Philippians' suffering, in a struggle they have in common with Paul. "Therefore," he says in light of that — and to return to the matter at hand — "if there be any 'comfort' in Christ, as indeed there is, . . . then complete my joy."

But what Paul does next is not quite that simple. He begins by appealing to their common experience of Christ's comfort, as a direct response to their common experience of suffering for Christ in the preceding clause (1:29-30). But right at that point, before dictating an apodosis, he adds three more "if" clauses, whose studied accumulation is part of the rhetorical effect[18] — but which turns out to be part of our difficulty, since what precisely Paul is appealing to in each case is less than clear. There are basically three options, depending on whether one sees the context as emphasizing (1) Christ and the Spirit's prior work of grace in their midst,[19] (2) the Philippians' common life in Christ that they have experienced together heretofore,[20] or (3) the relationship that they and Paul have together in the bonds of Christ and the fellowship of the Spirit.[21]

But part of our difficulty may also be related to the nature of dictation, in that what is written from dictation sometimes carries with it the rhetorical effects of oral speech.[22] In this kind of rhetoric precision is a lesser concern than is the persuasive effect created by the accumulation of phrases.[23] It is possible, therefore — probable, I would venture — that the emphasis shifts as Paul warms up to his rhetoric, even though each of the phrases undoubtedly has a primary direction to it, and very likely a secondary as well.[24]

Thus, at the beginning the focus is on Christ — and what is theirs by being "in Christ." But as the preceding clause makes clear, and the "therefore" implies, "Christ's comfort" is shared by him and them together. As Paul

18. Cf. Vincent, 53; Hawthorne, 64.

19. So e.g., Vincent, Jones, Beare, Hendriksen, O'Brien. See esp. O'Brien, 167-76, for a thorough and helpful discussion of the options and their ramifications for understanding — although I differ some with his conclusion and his reason for it.

20. So Lightfoot, Meyer, Moule, Silva.

21. So the Greek Fathers, Eadie, Michael, Barth, Hawthorne; cf. NEB, JB.

22. It is easy to forget that even though sent as written documents, Paul's letters began with orality (Paul dictated their contents to an amanuensis) and were received in the same way (read aloud in the community at worship); on this matter see the Introduction, 16-17. Cf. Lightfoot (108), on the τις/τινα interchange in the fourth clause (see n. 1): "τις . . . can only be explained by the eager impetuosity with which the Apostle dictated the letter." This makes as much sense of the *form* of this sentence as does the strophic arrangement argued for by Gnilka, Black, et al. (see n. 15).

23. Cf. Silva (102): "The clauses are deliberately compressed and vague, since the appeal is primarily emotional . . . and impassioned pleading."

24. On this whole question, see the admonition by Barth (51): "Must *everything* be clear to us here, unless we prefer to confess that *everything* here is obscure to us? At all events, one would almost like to say: why tear it all to pieces in explanation?"

moves to the next two clauses, the primary focus again seems to be on the Philippians' experience of God's love and their participation in the Spirit; but again, he and they share these together as well. When he reaches the fourth clause, however, which noticeably lacks a genitive modifier, the direction seems to shift toward their relationship with him, thus leading directly to the imperative, "complete my joy."[25]

A final note about the first three clauses. In light of their linguistic similarities to 2 Cor 13:13(14) and conceptual parallels with Rom 5:1-5, these three clauses very likely also reflect an intentional Trinitarian substructure.[26] If so, as with the benediction in 2 Corinthians, having begun with Christ, Paul proceeds with phrases expressing the primary qualities of the Father and the Spirit as to their relationship to the believing community. This, at least, seems to make good overall sense of the four clauses,[27] to which we now turn individually.

1. "If there is any encouragement (comfort)[28] in Christ." This first clause is best understood as closely tied to vv. 29-30 and thus predicated on the three-way bond noted throughout. As one would expect in this letter, Paul first grounds his appeal in Christ. *What* he says about Christ responds directly to the motif of suffering just mentioned. Just as they are presently suffering on behalf of Christ, in the midst of their struggle there is also "encouragement

---

25. For a generally similar analysis as to how the clauses unfold in process, see Beare, 71-72.

26. Especially so, since in Paul's view love flows *from* God [the Father] through Christ; cf. Rom 5:5-8. On this matter I have changed my mind from the more hesitant noting of this in *Presence,* 750 n. 68. My hesitation as to whether the Philippians would have caught the Trinitarian nuance still holds; but there is no reason for them not to have caught the specific nuances in each phrase as are suggested here. Thus it comes out Trinitarian, in terms of Pauline presuppositions, whether or not they caught the nuance. So also Lohmeyer, Motyer (and some earlier interpreters noted by Meyer, 70, who himself rejects it).

27. But see Meyer, 69 (cf. Vincent, 53; Plummer, 37; Martin, 87), who sees them in balanced pairs, lines 1 and 3 "referring to the *objective* principle of the Christian life," and lines 2 and 4 "the *subjective* principle," or in Plummer's words, "the one [pair] relating to union with Christ and its benefit, and the other to communion with the Spirit and its benefit." Hawthorne (67) sees the first pair as "focusing on the human side of things" (Paul toward them), the "second on the divine" (God toward them). None of these is compelling and in each case depends on one's interpretation of the parts.

28. Gk. παράκλησις, one of the more difficult NT words to pin down with precision, since its semantic field ranges from "exhortation/appeal" to "encouragement" to "comfort/consolation." In Paul the difficulty is heightened by the fact that its cognate verb παρακαλέω is one of the primary verbs used by Paul in his paraenesis (cf. Phil 4:2). For some that usage determines everything (see n. 30); but here the context seems to rule in a different direction. For the view taken here, see also Barclay, "Great Themes," 40; Collange, 77 (cf. the Vulgate, *consolatia*). O'Brien (169-71) favors "comfort" but in the sense of "encouragement" noted below.

in Christ," in the sense of "comfort." As the preceding clause makes clear, and the "therefore" implies, that "comfort in Christ" is shared by him and them together. Thus, while the focus is primarily on what Christ has done — or in this case, will continue to do — for them, the appeal presupposes that he and they share this comfort just as they do the struggle and the suffering.[29]

Very often, however, this clause has been understood otherwise, as stressing either "exhortation or appeal" or "encouragement," but the latter quite apart from vv. 29-30. That is, the Philippians' being "in Christ" is seen as the grounds for the following exhortations (vv. 2-16),[30] or for encouragement per se.[31] While either of these is possible, it seems more likely in context that Paul's usage here reflects that of 2 Cor 1:5 ("just as the 'sufferings'[32] of Christ have overflowed unto us, so *through Christ* our comfort [*paraklēsis*] likewise overflows").[33]

2. "If there is any solace[34] of love." *What* Paul intends by this phrase seems easy enough, namely, that the further basis of his appeal is the "solace afforded by love" (BAGD). Thus he continues the motif of comfort in light of their common struggle. But based on whose love for whom? On this there is no certainty.[35] If our observations on the possible Trinitarian substructure of the passage are correct, then Paul is referring to the experience of *God's love,* lavished on the Philippians — and him — in Christ and "shed abroad in their hearts" by the Spirit (Rom 5:5). Two things make one think so: that

---

29. This, at least, would seem to be the reason for the choice of *this* word in connection with Christ.

30. E.g., BAGD (as their first choice), "Christian exhortation"; cf. Lightfoot, Meyer, Kennedy, Vincent, Plummer, Jones, Hawthorne, Silva. But as Collange rightly points out, this paragraph is noteworthy "as a kind of 'non-exhortation,' . . . ; Paul is taking every precaution to avoid the appearance of giving orders" (77).

31. So Beare, Hendriksen, Gnilka, Hawthorne, Martin, O'Brien, Melick; this is sometimes based on the combination of παράκλησις with παραμυθία in 1 Cor 14:4, where it seems to carry this nuance; cf. the cognate verbs in 1 Thess 2:12.

32. Gk. τὰ παθήματα; cf. πάσχειν in the present argument (1:29).

33. This seems all the more likely in light of the appellation of God in that passage (2 Cor 1:3) as "the Father of all *mercies* (οἰκτιρμῶν)," the word that appears in the fourth line of the present appeal.

34. Gk. παραμύθιον; the feminine form occurs in 1 Cor 14:4, also in conjunction with παράκλησις; the verb occurs with the cognate verb for παράκλησις in 1 Thess 2:12. Thus of the four occurrences of this word group in the NT (all in Paul) it is used in conjunction with παράκλησις in three. Some (Lightfoot, Kennedy, Müller, Hendriksen; cf. Moffatt, Confraternity) argue on the basis of classical usage for the meaning "incentive, persuasion" here; but that goes against normal *koine* (see M-M, 488, and esp. *NewDocs,* 3.79; 4.14 and 166) and Pauline usage, as documented above.

35. E.g., Meyer (70), "the brotherly love of Christians"; Kennedy (432; cf. Michael, 76), "[Paul's] love toward them"; Beare (71; Martin, 86; Loh-Nida, 49; cf. NIV), "Christ's love for them."

this clause falls between the mention of Christ and the Spirit, and with the same language (in the case of the Father and the Spirit), as in 2 Cor 13:13(14);[36] and that "love," in keeping with Paul's OT roots, is most often expressed as from God, whose "love" for his people is the ultimate predicate of everything that God has done on their behalf. It is that "same kind of love" to which he will appeal in the apodosis that follows.

Again, given the context and flow of the argument, there is every good reason to believe Paul also includes himself with them as a recipient of "love's consolation." Thus, the appeal in this context probably means something like, "if our common experience of comfort from God's love has anything going for it at all, then express that same love toward me, by completing my joy by having the same love toward one another."

3. "If there is any sharing[37] in the Spirit."[38] With this phrase Paul returns specifically to the "one Spirit" in whom, and thus by whom, they are to stand united in contending for the gospel in Philippi (1:27). This clause readily follows the first two. It is the Spirit who put them "in Christ"; so also it is by the Spirit that God's love, the ground of their being, has been shed abroad in their hearts (Rom 5:5). As in the benediction in 2 Cor 13:13(14),[39] the "fellowship with the Spirit" most likely refers to the "sharing in the Spirit" (NRSV) that believers have first with God, but by that very fact, secondly, with one another because they live and breathe by the same Spirit.[40]

---

36. Thus in 2 Cor 13:13, Paul has the order, Christ-God-Spirit; of God he says ἡ ἀγάπη τοῦ θεοῦ, of the Spirit ἡ κοινωνία τοῦ ἁγίου πνεύματος. In our passage it is παραμύθιον ἀγάπης and κοινωνία πνεύματος.

37. Gk. κοινωνία; on the meaning of this word see above on 1:5.

38. In light of the common interpretation of 1:27, and absence of the article, some earlier interpreters took πνεύματος here to refer to the human spirit (noted by Meyer, 70; cf. NAB). But Paul's use of language and the present context disallow such a view altogether. On the irrelevance of the article as signifying the Holy Spirit in Paul, see Fee, *Presence,* 15-24.

39. On this question, see Fee, *Presence,* 362-65.

40. There has been some debate as to whether "of the Spirit" is an objective or subjective genitive. That is, are we in fellowship with the Spirit, or does he create the fellowship of the saints (as Barclay, "Great Themes," 40; Collange, Hawthorne, Silva)? Since the phrase appears first in 2 Cor 13:13, where the two prior clauses reflect something both of God's character and of his activity on behalf of his people in light of that character, it would seem most likely that something similar is in view with this phrase. Since the word primarily means "participation in," the view presented here (first, "sharing in the Spirit" himself; second, by that fact "sharing in the same Spirit" with one another) seems to capture the essence both of the "direction" of the Spirit's activity and of the meaning of the word itself. This view goes back at least as far as Meyer (*2 Corinthians,* 514). It received its recent impetus from H. Seesemann, *Begriff;* cf. the commentaries on the 2 Corinthians passage by Windisch, 428; Lietzmann, 162; Bultmann, 251; Barrett, 344; Furnish, 584; Martin, 505; so also Dunn, *Jesus,* 261.

181

By the Spirit, therefore, they are united to Christ, and in Christ to one another — and thus to Paul. Indeed, the Spirit is the empowering agent of all that God is currently doing among them, "both to will and to do of his good pleasure" (2:13). Thus, just as the comfort from being "in Christ" and the solace of experiencing God's love serves as the ground for his appeal to their unity in Christ, so too (especially) with their common "participation in the Spirit."

4. This (apparently) Trinitarian basis of appeal is followed by, "if any compassions and mercies,"[41] which in some ways is the most difficult of all,[42] since it appears tacked on as a final, passionate appeal based on deep feelings, and since there is no genitive qualifier. But that may also be the clue to what Paul intends. In 1:8 he has already based his longing for them on the "compassion of Christ"; and the word "mercies"[43] is expressly said to belong to God in 2 Cor 1:3 and Rom 12:1. Nonetheless, in Col 3:12, probably written at an earlier stage of the present imprisonment, he had urged those believers to put on, among other Christian virtues, "bowels of mercy,"[44] where the context is clearly that of community life. In light of the imperative that comes next, that is very likely the direction of this final appeal, but not simply toward one another; rather, as before, he is appealing to "compassion and pity" that *he and they have toward one another,*[45] which leads directly to the imperative that follows. Paul thus concludes, "if God's compassion and mercy have produced those same qualities in you toward me, as you know I have toward you, then complete my joy by having a single mindset among yourselves."

Thus, from this view, the *appeal* is for their unity and love toward one another (vv. 2-4), *based on* their shared comfort and love that has its origins in God and found historical expression in Christ and the Spirit, and has been shared mutually by them and for one another. With that he turns to the appeal itself.

**2** Just as part of the power of the appeal in the protasis lay in the compounding of "if" clauses, so in the apodosis there is an equally striking compounding of synonymous phrases[46] of such nature that the "wayfaring

---

41. Gk. σπλάγχνα καὶ οἰκτιρμοί; about which Lightfoot notes (108): "by σπλάγχνα is signified the abode of tender feelings, by οἰκτιρμοὶ the manifestation of these in compassionate yearnings and actions." Thus the two words together express "root and fruit" (Motyer, 104). It is unlikely to be a hendiadys (= "compassions, namely, mercies," thus "affectionate tenderness," Moffatt).

42. So Hawthorne, 66.

43. Gk. οἰκτιρμοί; found elsewhere in Paul in 2 Cor 1:2; Rom 12:1; Col 3:12. The plural in both cases ("compassions" and "mercies") is a direct reflection of the LXX, which used both of these words to translate the Hebrew רחם.

44. Gk. σπλάγχνα οἰκτιρμοῦ, which means something like "heart of pity."

45. As, e.g., Loh-Nida, 49-50; Hawthorne, 66; Motyer, 104 (cf. GNB).

46. Kennedy, 433, citing Vaughan, calls it "the tautology of earnestness."

person though a fool" could not possibly miss the point. Three (or four)[47] times he says it:

> that you set your minds on the same thing;
>> having the same love,
>> together in soul having your minds set on the one thing.

But to get there, in a way similar to the grammar of 1:27, he expresses the apodosis in terms of their relationship to him, in this case by way of an imperative, "complete[48] my joy." For the ultimate urgency of the appeal — their unity — this imperative seems unnecessary,[49] since he could easily have gone directly from the fourfold ground of the appeal to its actual content (as he will in 4:2); this, after all, is his concern. But instead, in keeping with the tenor of the whole letter, he interjects this strong personal appeal. While on the surface this may sound self-serving,[50] in reality it speaks volumes about Paul's pastoral heart.[51] His own life and apostleship are deeply bound up with his converts' well-being, and especially with their perseverance so that they

---

47. Many interpreters (e.g., Vincent, Müller, Hawthorne, Silva, O'Brien; Black, "Formal Analysis"; Fee, *Presence;* cf. the punctuation of NA[26]) take the adj. σύμψυχοι to be a separate "line." On this matter I have changed my mind, since to read it separately one must supply a further participle ("being"), which Paul himself does not do. The (much-to-be-preferred) alternative is to take the adj. as modifying the final participle (φρονοῦντες). Within the ἵνα clause this results in a primary clause ("that you set your minds of the same thing"), modified by two participial phrases (so Meyer, Alford, Ellicott, B. Weiss, Vincent, Beare, Hendriksen, Collange, Kent, Loh-Nida; Silva is open to it). The use τό with ἕν in the last phrase supports this view, since it then becomes anaphoric, meaning "the one thing already mentioned above [i.e., the same thing]." Thus the adj. σύμψυχοι begins the phrase by describing *how* ("together in soul") they are to "set their minds on the one thing" mentioned in the primary clause. This works out much more smoothly in Greek, it should be noted, than in my cumbersome English translation:

ἵνα τὸ αὐτὸ φρονῆτε,
τὴν αὐτὴν ἀγάπην ἔχοντες,
σύμψυχοι τὸ ἓν φρονοῦντες.

48. Gk. πληρώσατε, which variously means "to fulfill, to fill full, to complete, to bring something to its goal." Here it probably means to "fill to the full," and thus to "complete" what is already at work.

49. Cf. Meyer, 72.

50. Indeed, it is taken so by Fortna, "Philippians," who by failing to recognize Philippians as a letter of friendship is quite insensitive both to the formal aspects of the letter and to its character. The result is a caricature of Paul that is based more on Western psychologizing than on the text itself.

51. Cf. Motyer, 102; this clause is therefore too easily brushed aside by Hawthorne, who correctly sees that it expresses the secondary concern of the sentence, but then treats it as nearly irrelevant.

themselves will experience God's eschatological joy (cf. vv. 16-18). Such perseverance calls for their standing firm in the one Spirit. Only so will his own joy be filled to the full; and in any case the entire letter presupposes the secure nature of his and their mutual affection and joy. Thus, he appeals, "If these various realities of life in Christ and the Spirit mean anything to you at all — indeed, if we share these together in Christ — and if there is any compassion and mercy as you think of me in this prison, then make my joy[52] full by being of one mind," that is, by responding to the exhortation of 1:27.

As the Philippians were hearing the letter read aloud, they could hardly have missed associating this imperative with the preceding expressions of joy: first in 1:4, where he makes his prayer and thanksgiving for them with joy — "complete that joy," he now urges; and second in 1:18, where his twofold rejoicing served as the "center of gravity" for his "reflections on imprisonment."[53] Both in his present circumstances, trying as they are, and in anticipation of his trial, he has rejoiced and will continue to do so, since the gospel is being furthered and Christ is about to receive even greater glory. Now he urges them to bring that joy to its full completion, by advancing the gospel still more in Philippi (2:14-16). But to do so they must get their act together; the murmuring and bickering must cease, they must come to a common mind about life together in Christ and must show the same by their mutual love for one another (in fulfillment of his prayer for them in 1:9). If they who are already his "joy and crown" (4:1) are to remain so at the coming of Christ, they must give heed to the imperatives of this sentence (and to the similar ones in 4:1-3).

A few further words about the compounding of words and phrases by which they are thus to complete Paul's joy:

a. The initial clause, "that[54] you set your minds on[55] the same thing," has been rightly captured by the NIV, "that you be like-minded." This verb, which he used in 1:7 to refer to *his* disposition toward them, is also used at the end of the letter of *theirs* toward him (4:10 [2x]). In between it dominates the imperatival moments in this letter.[56] As noted before, the word does not

---

52. Gk. μου τὴν χαράν, a rare example of the "vernacular possessive" (language from Abbott's *Johannine Grammar*) in Paul. In this letter see on 1:28 (possibly); 3:20 ("our citizenship"); 4:14 ("my affliction"); cf. also the enclosed genitives in 1:19 and 2:25. Its very rarity indicates that Paul intends the possessive to be emphasized when it occurs. That is surely so here.

53. On this matter see n. 3 on 1:12-26; the language comes from Martin.

54. Gk. ἵνα, probably introducing a result clause here; so also Lightfoot, 108. But perhaps it is an epexegetical noun clause, giving the content of his "fulfilled joy." Either way it comes out at the same place.

55. Gk. φρονῆτε; see on 1:7 above.

56. Occurring twice here, again in v. 5, twice in 3:15, once in 3:19 (of those who are otherwise-minded) and in the final appeal of 4:2; cf. Rom 12:3 and 16 and 15:5.

mean "to think" in the sense of "cogitate"; rather it carries the nuance of "setting one's mind on," thus having a certain disposition toward something (e.g., life, values, people) or a certain way of looking at things, thus "mind-set."[57] What he means by the "same" mindset will be explained in vv. 6-11, where Paul points them to that of Christ (v. 5). The emphasis is thus on the Philippians' unity of purpose and disposition, unity with regard to the gospel and their heavenly citizenship[58] — exactly as in 4:2, where he qualifies it, "have the same mindset *in the Lord*" — *not* on their all having the same opinions about everything.[59]

b. The "same love" that he wants them to have points back to the second clause in the protasis, "if any solace from (God's) love." The phrase "the same" carries some ambiguity, perhaps purposefully so in this case. The context demands that he is first of all urging them to have "the same love for one another" that they already have experienced in God's love for them — and in theirs and his for one another. But at the same time, he wants them to have shared love, each having "the same love" for the other. In 1:9 Paul told them he prays that their love might abound "still more and more." Love, therefore, is not lacking in this community. At issue is the danger of its being eroded by internal friction, by their not "having the same disposition" about what it means to be God's people in Philippi. Thus, they will fill his cup of joy to the full as they return to full and complete love for one another, which by definition means to care for another for her or his own sake. As someone well said: "Love begins when someone else's needs are more important than my own," which is precisely what Paul will urge in the elaboration that follows.

c. But before that he adds yet another participial phrase. With the rare compound adjective, "together in soul,"[60] joined to a near repetition of the first clause,[61] he now joins soul and mind together (feeling and thinking). Not only does he want their minds set on the same thing, but he wants them to do so with

---

57. Cf. the same use of φρονεῖν in Rom 8:5 and thrice-repeated use of the cognate noun φρόνημα in Rom 8:6-7, where "the mind of the flesh or Spirit" is "fixed on" like concerns.

58. So also O'Brien, 179: "the need . . . to be 'gospel-oriented.' "

59. On this language — and its accumulation in this passage — as that of "ideal friendship" in the Greco-Roman world, see Stowers, "Friends," 112; cf. L. T. Johnson, *Writings,* 342. Sampley (*Partnership,* 62-63) sees this language as supporting his view that Paul and the Philippians have entered into a form of "consensual *societas*" (see n. 4 on 4:14), but this has been critiqued and found wanting by Peterman, "Giving," 144-47, 231.

60. Gk. σύμψυχοι, formed from σύν (together with) and ψυχή (soul), picking up and by means of the compound reinforcing the μιᾷ ψυχῇ of v. 27. The word here means something close to "harmonious" or "together as one person," putting emphasis on "unity . . . in feeling as well as in thought and action" (*EDNT,* 3.291, *contra* A. Fridrichsen, *Philologische Wochenschrift* 58 [1938] 910-12, who proffered "wholeheartedly").

61. See n. 47 above.

their whole being. This adjective harks back to "as one soul/person," which modifies "contending side by side for the faith of the gospel" in 1:27,[62] just as the third line in the protasis ("if there is any sharing in the Spirit") harks back to the call in that same verse to "stand firm in the one Spirit."[63] Again, as in 1:27, the accent is on unity within the community of faith.

**3** Paul's sentence now begins to get away from him, as he piles modifiers upon modifiers.[64] But even that has its own rhetorical effect. With a typical "not/but" contrast the phrases and clauses that make up our v. 3 give "shoe leather" to the appeal in v. 2. The contrasts are stark, which the NIV has rightly turned into yet another imperative: "Do nothing out of[65] selfish ambition or vain conceit, but in humility consider others better than yourselves." With these words Paul specifies what he knows — or suspects — is going on among them. The first item, "selfish ambition" or "rivalry,"[66] was used in 1:17 to describe those in the Roman community who are preaching Christ out of envy, supposing thereby to give Paul grief. Significantly, the "selfish ambition" of the envious was explicitly contrasted to those who preach Christ out of "love" (1:16).[67] "Selfish ambition" stands at the heart of human fallenness, where self-interest and self-aggrandizement at the expense of others primarily dictate values and behavior. People with such a "mindset" not only stand over against the apostle, their dear friend, but also over against God, whose Son fully displayed God's character when he took on a servant's role (cf. 2:7).

The second item, "vain conceit" (lit., "empty glory"[68]), denotes that

62. Cf. Collange, 79 ("obviously"), although this is a point often overlooked in the commentaries.

63. So also Barth, 51, 54.

64. Some think not; see n. 12. But Meyer (74) is surely correct here in seeing the modifiers of this verse to go with the preceding participle (φρονοῦντες) and thus to describe what is *excluded* when they all "set their minds on the one thing."

65. Gk. κατά, which the NIV obscures here, treating it as though it were identical to the ἐξ ἐριθείας of 1:17; but κατά indicates the "standard" to which one conforms one's behavior, not its source. Thus, "do nothing in keeping with (= that conforms to) selfish ambition/rivalry."

66. Gk. ἐριθεία; on this word see the discussion on 1:17 above; while "selfish ambition" is probably to be preferred, the use of "ambition" in this translation needs to be understood as implying "over against others."

67. The repetition of these words here in particular supports the suggestion that a part of the reason for the narrative in 1:15-17 was paradigmatic.

68. Gk. κενοδοξία; cf. κενόδοξος in Gal 5:26. The word is a compound of κενός ("empty, vain") and δόξα ("glory, honor"); the compound thus denotes "vanity, conceit, excessive ambition" (BAGD), and is most often used to describe those who without cause think too highly of themselves. Although one would not make more of it than the apostle himself intended, it is of some interest that these two words ("empty" and "glory") appear at the beginning and conclusion of the so-called Christ-hymn (2:6-11): the first (ἐκένωσεν, v. 6) to describe the kind of self-emptying that is the precise opposite of κενοδοξία; and

kind of "empty glory" that only the self-blessed can bestow on themselves. This word occurs throughout the Greco-Roman world to describe those who think too highly of themselves, not those who might appear to have grounds for "glory," but those whose "glory" is altogether baseless. It occurs elsewhere in Paul in Gal 5:26, also in the context of a church where people are "eating and devouring one another."[69] One does not wish to be too harsh on the sisters (Euodia and Syntyche) who are singled out in 4:2 as not getting along — and the two further words in 2:14 ("grumbling and disputing") must also come into the picture — but Paul well understands that if these attitudes are allowed to continue unchecked, the believing community in Philippi is headed for serious trouble, far more serious than is probably currently present.[70]

At the same time these words point forward as the opposites of the "mindset" of Christ: who as God did the antithesis of "selfish ambition" by pouring himself out and becoming a servant, and as man the antithesis of "vain conceit," by humbling himself unto death on a cross.[71]

In further anticipation of vv. 6-11, especially v. 8, Paul here contrasts "selfish ambition and rivalry" with, "in[72] humility consider others better than yourselves." "Humility"[73] is a uniquely Christian virtue,[74] which, as with the

---

the second (δόξα, v. 11) to express the "glory" that accrues to God as the self-emptying One receives his divine vindication and the worship of all creation.

69. It is worth noting that 8 of the 15 "works of the flesh" in that passage (Gal 5:19-21) are sins of discord, one of which is ἐριθεία. On this passage see Fee, *Presence*, 440-43.

70. So Kennedy, 434; both Kennedy and Michael (74) rightly caution about creating a situation in Philippi that looks more like Corinth or Galatia. In Michael's words: "The utter absence of severity of censure in this exhortation shows that the dissensions and disputes at Philippi had not yet reached an acute stage." See the Introduction, 32-33.

71. Barth (50) observes that this passage reflects "the heart of the Pauline *ethic,* . . . where seemingly so little, but in fact everything, is demanded by saying that each is to climb down from the throne on which he sits, and to mind and to seek after the *one* end, which is then also that of the *others.*"

72. The Greek text has the article, without the preposition (τῇ ταπεινοφροσύνῃ). The article points to "the [well-known quality] of humility" (Meyer, O'Brien, et al.) or functions as a possessive "in your humility" (Lightfoot). The dative is most likely "manner," not "means" (as Meyer), although BAGD suggest, "motivating cause."

73. Gk. ταπεινοφροσύνη, a compound word from "lowly" and "mind" (from the verb φρονεῖν in v. 2), hence the KJV "lowliness of mind." Collange (79) points out the probable assonance with φρονεῖν (φρονεῖν/ταπεινοφροσύνη). This compound is not well-attested outside the NT and early Christian writers; it is found elsewhere in Paul as a Christian virtue in Col 2:23; 3:12; Eph 4:2 (the latter also in the context of promoting unity within the community). The usage in Col 3:12 is telling, where it occurs as one of five virtues (including "bowels of mercy"; cf. 2:1) with which God's beloved are to clothe themselves. It occurs in a negative way in Col 2:18 (of false humility).

74. Among other discussions, see Jones, 28; *TDNT,* 9.1-26 (W. Grundmann); *NIDNTT,* 2.259-64 (H.-H. Esser).

message of a crucified Messiah, stands in utter contradiction to the values of the Greco-Roman world, who generally considered humility not a virtue, but a shortcoming.[75] Here Paul's roots are in the OT — and in Christ. In the OT the term indicates "lowliness" in the sense of "creatureliness," and the truly humble show themselves so by resting their case with God rather than trusting their own strength and machinations.

Humility is thus not to be confused with false modesty, or with that kind of abject servility that only repulses, wherein the "humble one" by obsequiousness gains more self-serving attention than he or she could do otherwise. Rather, it has to do with a proper estimation of oneself, the stance of the creature before the Creator, utterly dependent and trusting. Here one is well aware both of one's weaknesses and of one's glory (we are in his image, after all) but makes neither too much nor too little of either. True humility is therefore not self-focused at all, but rather, as further defined by Paul in v. 4, "looks not to one's own concerns but to those of others."

For Paul this perspective comes from Jesus, where "humility" explains both his own self-understanding and his opposition to pharisaism. Not only so, but in Jesus something essential about God's character is revealed. Jesus' invitation to the heavily laden to come and "learn of him" (Matt 11:29) is thus placed in a context where the Son alone knows the Father and so is revealed as "gentle and *humble (tapeinos)* in heart" — to "babes," it should be noted, not to the "wise and learned" (11:25). Thus the main verb in the second sentence in the ensuing narrative about Christ (vv. 7b-8), describing his Incarnation ("he humbled himself, becoming obedient unto death"), comes from the same root.

Thus, over against doing anything on the basis of "selfish ambition" or "vain conceit," the Philippians are to have the same love for one another as God in Christ has for them, which will find its ultimate expression when "in humility" you "consider[76] each other[77] better[78] than yourselves." As with

75. As Esser (*NIDNTT*, 2.260) points out, "the fundamental difference between the Gk. and biblical use of these words [is that] in the Gk. world, with its anthropocentric view of [humankind], lowliness is looked on as shameful, to be avoided and overcome by act and thought. In the NT, with its theocentric view of [humankind], the words are used to describe those events that bring a [person] into a right relationship with God and [one's fellow-humans]." In fairness to many of the Greek authors, however, it should be pointed out that they use the word very often to describe that kind of servility which we note in the next paragraph is *not* a part of the NT understanding.

76. Gk. ἡγούμενοι, a verb that means consciously to focus on something or someone, to give it due consideration. The verb recurs in v. 6, regarding Christ, who did not "consider" equality with God a matter of personal advantage; in 2:25, where Paul "determined" to send Epaphroditus back home; and in 3:7-8 [3x], referring to how Paul "considers" his former advantages now that he has come to know Christ.

77. Gk. ἀλλήλους, its only occurrence in Philippians, but one of Paul's more significant words in his paraenesis (exhortations), esp. when relationships among believers

humility, this does not mean that one should falsely consider others "better." As v. 4 will clarify, we are so to consider others, not in our *estimation* of them[79] — which would only lead to the very vices Paul has just spoken against — but in our *caring* for them, in our putting them and their needs ahead of our own. After all, this is precisely how Christ's humility expressed itself, as Paul narrates in v. 8. Thus, it is not so much that others in the community are to be thought of as "better than I am," but as those whose needs and concerns "surpass" my own. Here, of course, is the sure cure for "selfish ambition and vain conceit," not to mention "grumbling and bickering" (v. 14).

It needs only to be noted, finally, that in Paul's sentence this final participle modifies the main clause in v. 2, "that you have the same mind-set."[80] Here is the road to true unity among believers; as the use of "one another" demonstrates (see n. 77), this passage deals with attitudes within the believing community. If "selfish ambition and vain glory" are sure bets to erode relationships within the church, then the surest safeguard to a healthy church is when "considering each other as more important than oneself" characterizes its people, especially those in positions of leadership.[81]

---

are in purview. *Everything* is done ἀλλήλων. Believers are members of *one another* (Rom 12:5; Eph 4:25), who are to build up *one another* (1 Thess 5:11; Rom 14:19), to care for *one another* (1 Cor 12:25), to love *one another* (1 Thess 3:12; 4:9; 2 Thess 1:3; Rom 13:8), to pursue *one another's* good (1 Thess 5:15), to bear with *one another* in love (Eph 4:2); to bear *one another's* burdens (Gal 6:2); to be kind and compassionate to *one another*, forgiving *one another* (Eph 4:32; cf. Col 3:13), to submit to *one another* (Eph 5:21), to be devoted to *one another* in love (Rom 12:10), to live in harmony with *one another* (Rom 12:16), and (here) to consider *one another* more important than themselves (Phil 2:3; cf. Rom 12:10). To translate this "others" as in the NIV is to make it too general and thus to tone down the community significance of this exhortation.

78. Gk. ὑπερέχοντας; cf. 3:8 and 4:7. The word can mean "better," but in its two further occurrences in this letter, both adjectival, it has to do with "surpassing," going far beyond anything else. In light of v. 4, this seems to be the sense here as well. Cf. NASB ("regard one another as more important than [one]self") and NJB ("everyone should give preference to others").

79. This is a common interpretation (e.g., Jones, 28-29, "a high appreciation of all that is good and estimable in others"; cf. Martin, 90; Hawthorne, 69); a view rightly rejected by Barth (56-57). After all, ours is not to "find the good qualities" in others, but to see them from the common perspective of grace, as those like ourselves who above all need "looking after" by those who are gracious toward us, who "care for" us not on the basis of worthiness, but of need.

80. At least this is the most natural way to understand the grammar. Otherwise Lightfoot (see n. 13), but his divorce of vv. 3-4 grammatically also makes this too paraenetic on its own right and misses the fact that v. 5 is the next sentence after vv. 1-4, a sentence which takes the content of this one a step farther by locating its basis in Christ himself.

81. This assumes that such is the case with Euodia and Syntyche; see on 4:2-3 below.

**4** This final set of clauses, which again for the sake of readability have been made into a separate sentence in the NIV, is in fact a further participial modifier of the participle "considering" in v. 3. Which in turn means that this clause is not another in a series of exhortations; rather, it clarifies the preceding clause.[82] Here is how one considers the others within the believing community to "surpass oneself," by "looking [out][83] not for oneself, but especially for the needs of others." Here is how he elsewhere describes those whose behavior is genuinely Christian; they "do not seek their own good, but that of others."[84] This is the way, Paul says in Gal 6:2, that we "fill to the full the law of Christ,"[85] by "bearing each other's burdens."

The emphasis is on "each" and "others." Here one finds a kind of tension between the individual and the community that occurs throughout Paul. As always in such passages, the accent rests on the community; it is only as a people of God together that God's people fulfill his divine purposes. But in contrast to ancient Israel, where entrance into the community came through birth within the covenant community, in the people of God newly constituted by Christ and the Spirit, people enter one at a time. Therefore, the emphasis in Pauline paraenesis (exhortation) is primarily on the community, but obedience must begin with the individual (see v. 13 below). Thus, "each one" among them must have this care for the "others" among them.[86] This emphasis is probably to remind some within the community who seem to be out of step with some others.

One must also be careful not to push this clause beyond Paul's own intent, which is not concerned with whether one ever "looks out for oneself" — the "also" in the final line assumes that one will do that under any circumstances — but with the basic orientation of one's life, a life touched by the grace of God that has been lavished on us through Christ and made an experienced reality through the Spirit. All such terms as "enlightened self-

---

82. For a similar perspective as to how v. 4 *functions* in this sentence, see Grundmann, *TDNT,* 9.21-22.

83. Gk. σκοποῦντες; cf. 3:17. In Paul the verb ordinarily means to "look to" in the sense of "keeping one's eyes on" someone or something (BAGD); but here is a case where it almost certainly means "to look out for" in the sense of watching out for the needs of others. It is this sense that is picked up and emphasized in the compound ἐπισκοπέω (to care for, oversee), which in its noun form becomes ἐπίσκοπος ("overseer").

84. 1 Cor 10:24; cf. 10:33; 13:5; Rom 15:2. In our letter see esp. on 2:20-21, where this character trait is illustrated positively by Timothy over against some others, who fail at this very point.

85. On "the law of Christ" as denoting living as Christ himself, who "loved me and gave himself for me," see Fee, *Presence,* 463-64.

86. One would not ordinarily make much of this word at all, since it occurs regularly in Pauline paraenesis (e.g., 1 Thess 4:4; 1 Cor 7:17, 20, 24; Rom 15:2 et passim). The emphasis in this case rests on the plural ("all of you each one") and the repetition (it occurs near the beginning and in the emphatic final position).

interest" belong to modern psychology, not to the basic orientation of life in Christ. While this language may serve as a corrective to the kind of obsequiousness noted on v. 3, all of that lies outside Paul's concerns, that the basic orientation of Christian life regarding relationships with others is to be like that which he will describe in the Christ narrative that follows.

Here, then, is Paul's basic response to the (apparently) petty grumbling and bickering going on among some within the believing community in Philippi, a kind of unrest that not only dulls their witness within that city but at the same times erodes their ability to "contend side by side" for the sake of the gospel in the face of strong opposition.

The *basis of the appeal* is twofold: (a) to their relationship with God as that has been manifest even in the face of suffering by Christ's comfort and God's love, as well as from their common participation in the Holy Spirit; and (b) to their longstanding relationship with Paul, who has not only experienced these same graces with them, but whose joy will now be filled to the full as they allow these realities to inform their present life together in Philippi.

The *concern of the appeal* is with their being a united people in Christ by the Spirit. Only so can they hope to "advance" in the faith themselves (1:25) and to advance the cause of the gospel (1:27).

The *content of the appeal* describes, first, those expressions of our human fallenness that altogether militate against unity within the household of faith, "selfish ambition" and "empty glory"; and, second, those virtues necessary for it to happen, "love" and "humility," which find concrete expression as God's people learn to live as Christ, to consider and care for the needs of others as the matter of first priority.

As Barth rightly pointed out, here is a vivid, miniature expression of the heart of Pauline ethics, not simply because its predicate is grace, but because it is grounded in the character of God as that has been revealed in Christ Jesus, which is the point to be taken up next. As with so much else in this letter, here, too, is a word for all seasons. One can only imagine what might happen if we were to rethink — and re-experience — the love and encouragement that is ours through the Trinity, and on that basis also rethink — and thus reorient — our life in Christ in terms of our relationships to one another. If we ourselves were more truly characterized by the content of this appeal, we might become a more effective people in the world.

## C. THE EXAMPLE OF CHRIST (2:5-11)

Without breaking stride, Paul turns from the appeal in v. 2, as elaborated in vv. 3-4, to a second imperative by which he will now define the "mindset" he is urging on them: "This mindset have among yourselves which was also found in Christ Jesus." And with that he launches into a narrative about Christ that is at once one of the most exalted, most beloved, and most discussed and debated passages in the Pauline corpus.[1] Here is one of Paul's finest hours, which serves both to exalt Christ and to prod the Philippians to emulation (the issue of vv. 1-4), while reassuring them of Christ's exalted position — including over Caesar himself.

Since the seminal work of Lohmeyer, the vast majority of interpreters have assumed the present passage to be an early hymn[2] (whether by Paul or otherwise[3]) in honor of Christ. Whether hymn or not, and I have considerable

1. Unfortunately, the latter item — the profusion of discussion and debate — has sometimes tended to obscure rather than to enlighten, and, even worse, to bog down in debate a passage that should cause the reader to soar. It seems tragic that such a marvelous moment should get inundated by so much talk (and I am among the guilty [see "Philippians 2:5-11"], although part of that article, it should be pointed out, was in protest against the proliferation of literature resulting from its alleged hymnic character). Nonetheless, that talk does exist (the bibliography constitutes well over half of the special literature devoted to Philippians, so that nearly 100 pages [of 555] of O'Brien's commentary, for example, are devoted to this passage alone); and a great deal of it, it must be admitted, is extremely helpful. Much of the literature deals with critical issues, esp. form, authorship, and background. I have dealt with some of this in the Introduction, pp. 39-46, although a few of these questions are also taken up in footnotes (for form see nn. 2, 4, 5; for authorship, nn. 3, 6 [cf. n. 12 on v. 8; n. 9 on vv. 9-11]; for background, nn. 45, 86 [cf. n. 11 on v. 8; n. 35 on v. 10]). For a helpful discussion of the relevant questions, see O'Brien, 186-203, 253-71; also 186-88 for bibliography up to 1990.

2. Reflected in the poetic format of the NIV and NA[26] (the REB is noteworthy among recent translations for not having done so; cf. also UBS[4]). Lohmeyer's dissertation *(Kyrios Jesus)* appeared in 1928, the first edition of his commentary the year following. Adumbrations of this view can be found as early as J. Weiss (1897), and begin to be noted in passing (in English) as early as Moffatt *(Introduction,* 1917) and Plummer (1919), so that Michael (1928), on the basis of Moffatt, can say, "It is not impossible that Paul is making use of the words of some early poem or hymn." The first commentaries in English after World War II (Synge [1951]; Scott [1955]; Müller [1955]) are mixed; Scott discusses the possibility, but rejects it; Müller uses the language of "hymn," but in quotation marks. Soon thereafter the quotation marks disappear and "Christ-hymn" is the coinage of the realm (Caird is a lonely exception). The next major commentary in English (Beare, 1959, now influenced by Käsemann [1950]) adopts Lohmeyer in such a thoroughgoing way that he speaks of Pauline authorship as "impossible," and in his ten pages of commentary on the passage (78-88), Paul's name is mentioned but once, only to deny that he could have authored what he wrote. The upshot is that for these ten pages Beare offers no commentary on Philippians at all, but on an unknown author's "hymn" (cf. Collange, who repeatedly refers to "our hymn," and mentions Paul but once; the same tendency is also at work in Martin); on the matter of authorship see next note. This point of view has only occasionally been called into question; see Hooker, "Philippians 2:6-11"; G. Wagner, "Le Scandale"; Fee, "Philippians 2:5-11"; and especially Fowl, *Story,* 31-45.

3. On the matter of authorship, see the Introduction, pp. 45-46. There is a discern-

doubts here,[4] one can scarcely miss the poetic and exalted nature of much of this. But neither, by calling it a hymn, should one miss the narrative character

---

ible — but nothing approaching a groundswell! — swing back to Pauline authorship on the part of some (see, e.g., Furness, "Authorship"; Hooker, "Philippians 2:6-11"; Strimple, "Recent Studies"; Feinberg, "Kenosis"; Wright, "ἁρπαγμός"; Black, "Authorship"; Fowl, *Story;* and the commentaries by Silva and O'Brien). The steps toward the denial of authenticity are easy to discern: first, the passage is understood to be a hymn (preceding n.); if so, then it is probably pre-Pauline; and if so, given some unique words and phrasing, it must also be non-Pauline. All of this is certainly possible, though unprovable; it becomes pernicious when one also argues that the words in their present context must be understood on the basis of their reconstructed "original form," so that Kreitzer (*Jesus,* 115), *inter alia,* can say, "We should not necessarily presuppose that the christology of the hymn is identical to that of Paul." In fact, methodologically we should do precisely that, since this passage is *not* available to us except in its present Pauline expression.

Throughout the exposition that follows I will assume what one may rightly assume about any piece of writing such as this, that the words used are the "choice" of the author of the text we now have. Since Paul dictated these words, and did so in the form of prose sentences (see next n.), we may assume that he *chose* to use these very words, even if they had existed in prior form. After all, we have all kinds of evidence that Paul "cites" texts (the LXX in particular) in such a way as to make them his own! Cf. Hooker ("Philippians 2:6-11," 152): "For even if the material is non-Pauline, we may expect Paul himself to have interpreted it and used it in a Pauline manner"; and D. J. Moo (*Romans,* 49 [on the same issue about Rom 1:3-4]): "Methodologically it is necessary at least to maintain that whatever Paul quotes, he himself affirms." That is so eminently reasonable one wonders how so many can comment on the passage as though not written by Paul (even if not originally "authored" by him). See also n. 6 below.

4. What seems to favor this view are (1) the obvious poetic nature of vv. 6-8, (2) that it begins with ὅς, which is how two other apparent hymns begin (Col 1:15; 1 Tim 3:16); (3) that it seems to be a self-contained piece, not all of which, some have argued, seems to fit the context (esp. vv. 9-11); and (4) some unusual wording, especially for Paul. Against it are: (1) the word ὑμνός in Greek, including the LXX, is used exclusively to describe songs or poems written in praise of a deity (or honored person), which include an ascription of praise and the reasons for it (see esp. Fowl [*Story,* 31-45], whose evidence seems irrefutable on this matter); (2) that no one has yet produced an analogy (either stylistically or linguistically) that even remotely resembles the structures of our passage; and (3) that vv. 9-11 have almost nothing hymnic about them; the combination of διό ("therefore"), followed by a ἵνα clause ("so that"), concluding with a ὅτι clause (serving as the object of "confess"), is not the stuff of hymns but of argumentation. To say, as Collange (95), that vv. 6-8 and 9-11 are "identical in structure" is to stretch the words "identical" and "structure" beyond recognition. Indeed, if this sentence (vv. 9-11) had appeared elsewhere in the corpus, not following the poetry of vv. 6-8, no one would ever have guessed that it was originally part of a hymn!

This is not to deny the poetic nature of much of this; but poetry does not = hymn, which is poetry intended to be sung or read in praise of God, and giving the *reason* for it. More likely the passage reflects something more creedal, as elsewhere in Paul. Cf. Hooker ("Philippians 2:6-11," 157): "It is of course undeniable that there is something poetic about these lines. Whether this makes them a poem — or whether they would be better

of the passage, which begins with Christ's pre-existence, followed by his incarnation, including his death on the cross, and concludes with his (assumed) return to heaven as the exalted Lord of heaven and earth. Indeed, of the many attempts to find the "original" strophic arrangement of the alleged hymn,[5] the most satisfactory by far are those which follow Paul's own sentence structures. Hence for the purposes of seeing how the narrative functions, and thus how Paul's own *dictated sentences*[6] work, the whole is set out in a structural display (again following Paul's Greek very literally[7]):

[5]*This* mindset have
  among yourselves
*which* also
  in Christ Jesus:
[Part I]  [6]who
 I[1]  being in the "form" of God,
    *not* <u>harpagmon</u>[8] did he consider equality with God,
    [7]*but* himself  he emptied,
     taking     the "form" of a slave
     coming to be   in the likeness of human beings;

---

described as a piece of rhythmic prose — is a different matter. In many ways the latter seems more likely"; but in the end she leans slightly toward the former. This whole matter seems to be a case of cross-pollination, whereby the exalted nature of this passage, plus its obvious poetry, is merged with a more contemporary use of the word "hymn" and then read back into the first century. That Paul is capable of something hymnic is attested by Rom 11:33-36, which, like those in Luke 1 and 2, is a fine mixture of OT words and motifs with his own concerns, and which stands in contrast to this passage, precisely because both its poetry and form are those of a hymn in the first-century use of that word.

 5. For a critique of much of this, see Fee, "Philippians 2:5-11," 30-34. That scholars have come up with five basic arrangements, with countless variations within each, does not offer great confidence that we can ever discover the "original" form of the hymn — especially since it is only recoverable from Paul's prose, and the reconstruction is thus subject to the whims of subjectivity (e.g., one scholar's "inclusio" ["taking the form of a slave," with the opening participle] is another scholar's "parallelism" [with the next participle]; both of which are correct, because they have nothing to do with "strophes").

 6. I emphasize these words, because this passage was dictated, just as was the rest of the letter — not "inserted" or "interpolated" (the reigning language of scholarship), as though by some kind of editorial process. Although taken down word by word or phrase by phrase (usually), what Paul dictated were sentences, not strophes or lines of a hymn. The evidence for this lies in the structural display, all of which makes perfectly good sense as Pauline *sentences,* but parts of which do not fit well in the various strophic arrangements, where many "lines" lack a verb and some are nothing more than prepositional phrases (cf. Fee, "Philippians 2:5-11," 32-33). See the Introduction, pp. 40-43.

 7. Except for the participles in vv. 7-8, which I have translated in keeping with the exegesis that follows, since to do otherwise creates nearly impossible English.

8and

I²     being found in appearance as a human being,

       he humbled himself,

          becoming     obedient unto    death,

                            death on a cross.

[Part II]    9Therefore also

      God     him has highly exalted

               and

          has granted him the name

                   that is above every name,

       10so that

              at the name of Jesus

                every knee should bow

                  in heaven

                    and

                  on earth

                    and

                  under the earth

            11and

              every tongue should confess that

                    the Lord is Jesus Christ

                  to the glory of God the Father.

The narrative is thus in two parts, corresponding to our vv. 6-8 and 9-11.[9] The first part is a compound sentence, with two clauses joined by "and" (I¹ and I²),[10] which are identical in form and in turn show how Christ's "mindset" expressed itself first as God and second as "man."[11] Both of these clauses have a *basic* threefold structure: (a) each begins with a participial phrase indicating the "mode"[12] of Christ's existence (as God, as "man"), followed (b) by the main clause indicating what Christ *did* in each of these modes of existence (he poured himself out; he humbled himself); which (c) in turn is modified by a further participle indicating *how* Christ carried out what was

8. Gk. ἁρπαγμόν, one of the extremely difficult words in the passage; for its probable meaning see the discussion below.

9. Cf. C. J. Robbins, "Rhetorical Structure," who presents a similar, basically two-part, analysis based on the principles of classical rhetoric.

10. Some think otherwise; see n. 3 on v. 8.

11. On the issue of translating this word, see n. 1 on v. 8.

12. Finding proper language to express divine realities is difficult at times. By "mode" I do not intend to suggest "modalism"; this is simply an attempt to find a word that will work on both sides of Paul's compound sentence, just as Paul himself did with his choice of μορφή.

said of him in the main verb (by "taking on the 'form' of a slave"; by "becoming obedient unto death"). In both cases this final participle is further modified, in the first clause by another clarifying participle (Christ's taking the form of a slave has to do with his "being made in the likeness of human beings") and in the second by a clarifying word about his death ("the death of the cross"). The first clause (I[1]), it should be noted, also has a significant difference: the main verb is expressed, typically for Paul, with a "not/but" formulation,[13] intended to set Christ's "divine activity" into the starkest possible contrast ("being in the 'form' of God, he did *not* consider equality with God to be taken advantage of, *but* he emptied himself"). These parallels, plus the sheer power of some of the language, are what give the sense of poetry to this first part.

Part II (vv. 9-11) lacks both the poetry and the balanced clauses of Part I. Instead, it takes the form of basic Pauline argumentation. The ultimate consequence of Christ's "mindset," which led to his "humiliation," Paul asserts, is that God has exalted him "to the highest place" (NIV), by bestowing on him the ultimate name of all: God's own appellation of "Lord," which, not incidentally, is also one of the appellations of Caesar (cf. Acts 25:26). In so doing God vindicated Christ's "mindset" evidenced in vv. 6-8.

The context makes it clear that vv. 6-8 function primarily as paradigm.[14] The two clauses stand in bold relief to the "selfish ambition" and "empty glory" of v. 3, the second clause exemplifying the humility that is likewise called for in that passage. The function of Part II has been debated. Most likely its purpose is twofold: first, to express divine affirmation of Christ's way of expressing his "equality with God" in vv. 6-8; and, second,

---

13. This very important feature in Paul's sentence is generally overlooked in the literature; but see M. Thekkekara ("Neglected Idiom"), who correctly notes that the contrast deliberately highlights the lengths to which Christ went in his self-abasement.

14. So the vast majority of interpreters, although it is vigorously denied by E. Käsemann ("Analysis"), followed by Martin (*Carmen,* 84-88); cf. Losie ("Note"). Käsemann's denial is in strong opposition to Lohmeyer and is thus predicated primarily on his theological aversion to anything that smacks of "imitating Christ," as though ethics were based finally on self-effort rather than on grace; for Martin it also includes the "impossibility" of emulating Christ in vv. 9-11. But these objections are based on a fundamental misunderstanding of "imitatio" in Paul, which does not mean "repeat after me," but (in the present context) "have a frame of mind which lives on behalf of others the way Christ did in his becoming incarnate and dying by crucifixion." The point of vv. 9-11, after all, is not "imitatio" in the "follow me" sense, but in the sense of God's vindication of such a life. Hurtado, whose refutation ("Lordly Example") of the Käsemann/Martin view is especially noteworthy, points out (125) that they object to a view that is overly simplistic (dubbed by Martin "naïve ethical idealism"), their caricature of which, one might add, is not the perspective of most who have written on the subject. See the discussion at the end of vv. 9-11; cf. O'Brien, 253-62, and Fowl, *Story,* 77-101.

in keeping with a motif that runs throughout the letter, to affirm the Philippians' certain future, with its divine vindication. It thus also places Christ in bold contrast to "lord Nero," whose "lordship" they have refused to acknowledge in a city where the cult of the emperor undoubtedly played a significant role.

But quite apart from its function in the argument, this narrative has significance all on its own. Here is the closest thing to Christology that one finds in Paul;[15] and here we see again why the "scandal of the cross" was so central to his understanding of everything Christian.[16] For in "pouring himself out" and "humbling himself to death on the cross," Christ Jesus has revealed the character of God himself. Here is the epitome of God-likeness: the pre-existent Christ was not a "grasping, selfish" being, but one whose love for others found its consummate expression in "pouring himself out," in taking on the role of a slave, in humbling himself to the point of death on behalf of those so loved. No wonder Paul cannot abide triumphalism — in any of its forms. It goes against everything that God is and that God is about. To be sure, there is final vindication for the one who goes the way of the cross; but for believers the vindication is eschatological, not present. Discipleship in the present calls for servanthood, self-sacrifice for the sake of others. Hence Paul concludes the narrative with a further call to "obedience" on the part of the Philippians (v. 12), which will take shape as God works out his salvation among them for his own good pleasure (v. 13); but for God to do so, they must stop the bickering (v. 14) and get on with "having the same love" for one another (v. 2) as Christ has portrayed in this unparalleled passage.

## 1. As God He Emptied Himself (2:5-7)

5*Your*[17] *attitude should be*[18] *the same as that of Christ Jesus:*

15. Those who deny that Paul's concern is pardigmatic (see preceding n.) also argue that the point of the "hymn" is soteriology, a position that seems especially difficult to sustain, in comparison with the profusion of semi-creedal soteriological texts in Paul which use actual soteriological language. True, Christ's death on the cross is ultimately soteriological for Paul — and even indirectly so here (i.e., the one whose "mindset" carried him to the cross is also the one whose death effected their salvation) — but when the cross is mentioned in soteriological contexts there is always a "saving verb" and usually some form of the preposition "for us" — both of which are missing here.

16. Cf. esp. 1 Cor 1:17-31.

17. The relationship between this verse and what precedes has been made the clearer in the manuscript tradition by the insertion of either γάρ ("for," P[46] ℵ[2] D F G Maj lat sy[h]) or οὖν (2492 pc). This is a clearly secondary process: (1) the asyndetic text has by far the best support (ℵ* A B C Ψ 33 81 1241 2464 2495 pc); (2) the variations reflect two separate attempts to remove the asyndeton; and (3) one cannot imagine the reasons for omitting the conjunction, if either were original.

18. As another reflection of the difficulty with Paul's Greek in v. 4, the later MajT,

6*Who, being in very nature*[a] *God,*
*did not consider equality with God something to be grasped,*
7*but made himself nothing,*
  *taking the very nature*[b] *of a servant,*
  *being made in human*[19] *likeness.*

[a]Or *in the form of*
[b]Or *the form*

Following the imperative in v. 5, Paul begins the narrative about Christ with his pre-existence,[20] indicating both what his being God did not entail and what it did. The main thrust of the clause is simple enough: Christ's being God was not for him a matter of "selfish ambition," of grasping or seizing; rather it expressed itself in the very opposite. Thus in a single sentence Paul goes from Christ's "being equal with God" to his having taken the role of "a slave," defined in terms of incarnation. All of this to call the Philippians to similar self-sacrifice for the sake of one another (v. 4).

But the ideas are profound, full of theological grist, and the language not at all simple. Historically, the discussion has centered in four difficult wordings: *morphē* (NIV, "in *very nature* God"), *harpagmon* ("something to be grasped"); *ekenōsen* ("he made himself nothing"); and *homoiōmati* ("in human *likeness*"). Some preliminary observations are needed in order to put these matters into perspective. First, it is of some interest that these difficulties are concentrated in the sentence that deals with divine mysteries. That is, on the basis of *what was known* and *came to be believed* about Jesus' earthly life, Paul is trying to say something about *what could not be observed,* yet *came to be believed* about Christ's prior existence as God. Most of *our* difficulties stem from this reality, plus our prevailing desire to penetrate into the divine mysteries themselves. Second, Paul's primary concern is not theological as such, but illustrative,[21] what *Christ Jesus* did (in keeping with his "mindset") in his prior existence as God

---

which there changed the plural ἕκαστοι to ἕκαστος, likewise changed Paul's second plural imperative (φρονεῖτε) to a third singular (φρονείσθω). This is reflected in the well-known rendering of the KJV: "let this mind be in you." Hawthorne argues for this as the original text, but does so for the very reason that the later scribal tradition corrupted the text — to make Paul a tidier writer than he demonstrates himself to be at this point.

19. Paul's Greek reads (literally), "in the likeness of 'men' having become" (Gk. ἐν ὁμοιώματι ἀνθρώπων γενόμενος). P[46] and some Latin witnesses, probably quite independently, changed the plural "men" to "a man," most likely in assimilation to the next clause. But Paul is precise; see n. 94 below.

20. Some have thought otherwise, esp. those who consider the passage to be based on an Adam-Christ analogy, in which Christ is being portrayed as the second Adam in his humanity. See the discussion below on v. 6 (and nn. 41 and 73).

21. A point that is too often missed in the discussions; on this matter cf. Kennedy, 435.

(which of course does indeed say something theological). Therefore, third, while not primarily intended as such, by its very nature the passage is full of theology (especially Christology) that must be dealt with. And fourth, Paul's actual choice of language[22] is further dictated by two factors: (a) the "not/but" contrast, which dominates the whole, and which called for a word (*morphē*, in this case) that could serve equally well *both* expressions of Christ's existence (as God and as a slave);[23] (b) his primary concern in the passage is to illustrate the kind of selflessness and humility referred to in v. 3.

Each of these provisos must be kept in mind as we look more carefully at the details.

**5**   This opening imperative, which functions as a transition from vv. 1-4 to 6-11, demonstrates that the narrative that follows is intentionally paradigmatic. Although the sentence is elliptical,[24] Paul's point seems plain enough. He begins with an emphatic "this," which is best understood as pointing backward,[25] in this case to vv. 2-4. That is followed immediately by the imperative, "this *think*"[26] (*touto phroneite*, "your attitude should be,"

22. On the matter of "Paul's choice of language," see n. 3 above.

23. Cf. Kennedy (435, written in an earlier day but still apropos): "Much trouble would have been saved if interpreters instead of minutely investigating the refinements of Greek metaphysics, on the assumption that they are present here, were to ask themselves, 'What other terms could the Apostle have used to express his conceptions?' " See further n. 47 below.

24. That is, the second clause is without a verb, which must be supplied either from the first clause or from the sense of the context.

25. As is most often the case in Paul; and so most interpreters. In this letter see the usage in 1:7 (τοῦτο φρονεῖν; clearly pointing backward); 1:22 (this one is debated); 1:25 (τοῦτο πεποιθώς); 3:7 (ταῦτα ἥγημαι), 15 (τοῦτο φρονῶμεν), 15 (τοῦτο ὁ θεὸς ὑμῖν ἀποκαλύψει); 4:8 (ταῦτα λογίζεσθε); 4:9 (ταῦτα πράσσετε). Only in 1:19 (q.v.) does this not seem to be the pattern, and there it is at least in part the result of his citing Job. Whenever τοῦτο clearly points forward, it is followed by a noun clause which explains the content of the "this." One could argue for that pattern here, except that in context the τοῦτο does not pick up a new train of thought, but continues one already in process. *Contra* Käsemann, Martin, Loh-Nida, Losie ("Note," 53), et al., who see τοῦτο as pointing forward, especially to the hymn (although Losie argues this case on the basis of the backward pointing examples of this letter). It is of some interest that those who see "in Christ Jesus" as referring not to Christ's own mindset, but to that of the community as they are "in Christ," almost to a person fail to come to terms with this pronoun. Losie is an exception, but the forced nature of his view highlights the difficulty with it.

26. Here is the place where the translation "have this mindset" ("frame of mind," Z-G) breaks down, since it puts the emphasis on the noun implied in the verb, rather than on the action itself. Which has led to no end of trouble in this case, since it has caused generations of readers (and scholars) to assume the relative pronoun that follows has this non-existent noun as its antecedent, whereas the grammar of Paul's sentence is clear — that the antecedent of ὅ ("which") is τοῦτο ("this"). Cf. Losie ("Note"), who correctly notes that τοῦτο is the object of φρονεῖτε (although he otherwise quite misses Paul's syntax).

NIV), which purposely harks back to v. 2 *(phronēte/phronountes)*. Thus the basic imperative sums up the whole of vv. 2-4: "*This* mindset (i.e., that which I have just described) have among yourselves."

In Pauline paraenesis the prepositional phrase "among yourselves"[27] occurs most often to express what must take place in the community,[28] although that must be responded to at the individual level. Just as v. 4 particularizes ("each" is responsible to apply the imperatives in the context of "one another"), so here, each is to have this mindset *in you,* but it must also be evident *among you.* Thus, "within your community learn to develop attitudes of selflessness and humility, considering the needs of one another as top priority."

This basic imperative is then qualified as that "which [was][29] also in Christ Jesus." This clause needs a verb supplied, which has caused far more difficulty for interpreters than seems necessary. The key lies with the relative pronoun and its adverbial modifier, "which also."[30] The antecedent of "which" is "this," and thus points back to the content of vv. 2-4, meaning that the frame of mind set forth in vv. 3-4 is precisely that which one *also* has seen in Christ Jesus; at the same time "also" begins to point forward. The phrase "in Christ Jesus" is thus to be understood as in parallel with "in/among you," which is the natural reading of Paul's sentence.[31] To be sure, some would treat the "also" as "colorless" and argue that "in Christ Jesus" should have an alleged "technical" sense,[32] thus making the whole sentence refer to

27. Gk. ἐν ὑμῖν; in this letter see on 1:6 and 2:13.

28. But see, *inter alia,* Lightfoot, Meyer, Vincent, Müller, Hendriksen, who see it as referring strictly to the "hearts" (Lightfoot) of individual believers. Meyer and Vincent suggest that if it refers to the community, the parallel with Christ breaks down; but that is to take the concept of "parallel" much too rigidly, as do those who also use the same argument to insist that ἐν Χριστῷ Ἰησοῦ must also be corporate (e.g., Silva).

29. As in 1:21 and 22, this clause is without a verb. Ordinarily in such a sentence one supplies the verb from the first clause. But that makes very little sense here (*pace* Hawthorne, who can make this work only by adopting a patently secondary textual corruption; see n. 18 above). Most likely (as Z-G), in light of the narrative that follows, the verb should be past tense. But a present tense ("is") would also work, as would a verb that keeps the second plural of the first clause (e.g., "you find"). Kennedy (434) objects that to supply ἦν is "harsh, for it would presuppose τοῦτο φρονεῖν (not τοῦτο alone) as the antecedent of ὅ." But that, of course, is not true if one takes τοῦτο, as one should grammatically, as the object of the verb and as pointing back to vv. 2-4 (see n. 25).

30. Gk. ὃ καί; "which also" is the ordinary sense of this idiom. For some who think otherwise, see n. 33 below.

31. That is, rather than viewing ἐν Χριστῷ Ἰησοῦ as a "technical" term (see next n.), which in this case is especially questionable, one should see the ἐν as functioning precisely as in 1:30 ("which you saw ἐν ἐμοί and hear ἐν ἐμοί").

32. Much is made of the "technical" (= formulaic) use of this phrase in Paul, as though it meant to be incorporated into "Christ's mystical body." Besides the particularly

the believers in Philippi: "Have this mind among yourselves, which is fitting [for those] in Christ Jesus."[33] While that might (just barely) work grammatically,[34] it works very poorly contextually, where the issue is neither with soteriology[35] nor with the Philippians' "being in Christ Jesus," but with behavior that is in keeping with Jesus',[36] which is what the next clause defines by way of poetic narration.

---

questionable assumption that there is such a "mystical body" in Paul (see esp. the critique by Yorke, *Body*), to assume that it would have carried such a "technical" sense in most of its appearances is quite unwarranted; that the Philippians would have known such a usage could not be demonstrated under any circumstances. See the discussion by Seifrid in *DPL*, 433-36, whose overview of the data should help to put this idea into perspective. Cf. the discussion on 1:13 and the similar judgment on the phrase "with Christ" on 2:23. See also the next note.

33. See Zerwick (*Biblical Greek*, 156), who recognizes the traditional meaning, but suggests that ὃ καὶ might be more stereotypical here, and therefore "otiose" in this clause. This view can be traced back to Deissmann *(In Christus);* it has been adopted, *inter alia,* by Kennedy, Moffatt, Jones, Michael, Dibelius, Beare, Gnilka, Collange, Silva, Käsemann ("Critical Analysis"); Martin *(Carmen);* Losie ("Note"). But this is an unmanageable, noncontextual tautology (= "think what you think in Christ"; cf. Lohmeyer, Hendriksen, Caird, Marshall, Moule, Strimple) and a most unnatural reading of the text, if word order and "hearing" count for anything. For the majority in Philippi the letter was a matter of hearing, not reading; it seems nearly impossible that they could have "heard" the subtleties demanded by this alternative. Paul's text reads τοῦτο φρονεῖτε ἐν ὑμῖν ὃ καὶ ἐν Χριστῷ Ἰησοῦ (lit., *"this* think in you *which also* in Christ Jesus"), which calls either for an "is" (or "was") before or after "in Christ Jesus" or for another form of second plural verb ("you see or find"), either of which would be readily supplied by the mind of the hearer (because they would *automatically* hear the ὃ as picking up the τοῦτο and the καί as *picking up the prepositional phrase*). Surely this is what Paul intended his audience to do. On the other hand, it would require considerable pauses and re-reading for one to hear, first, that "in Christ Jesus" should be understood in a "formulaic" way and thus refer to "us"; which would require, second, that one reread and drop the καί (Losie's ploy ["Note"] to get around this is especially forced) and then, third, supply something like "is proper" (or in the case of Käsemann and Martin, some form of φρονεῖτε) to complete the sentence. This seems much too subtle for a basically oral culture. It is noteworthy in this regard that the REB ("what you find in Christ Jesus") has thus changed the NEB ("arise out of your life in Christ Jesus"). One wonders how anyone but a scholar could have come by the latter. Caird (118-19) tries to dodge the tautology by offering the wholly unsupportable suggestion that we treat ὃ καί as the equivalent of the Latin *id est;* but καί does not = *est* under any circumstances. Silva resorts to an intensive ("which indeed"), but that seems to intensify the tautology instead.

34. For the reasons for "just barely," see nn. 25, 26, and 33. To make the τοῦτο point forward to the ὅ, it should be pointed out, makes the latter the real antecedent of the former rather than the other way about, which is how Paul's sentence reads.

35. As Käsemann et al. would have it.

36. This is precisely in keeping with Rom 15:5-8. In a context of Jews and Gentiles "living in harmony with one another" so that "with one voice they might glorify God,"

**6**  With the relative pronoun "who,"[37] Paul proceeds from the fore-going imperative directly to the narrative about Christ.[38] Again, even though the details are not easy, his overall concern seems plain enough. Beginning with Christ's pre-existence, and by means of a striking "not/but" contrast[39] (in keeping with the similar contrast of vv. 2-4), he portrays *two* ways of thinking, of "setting one's mind," one selfish, the other selfless. Thus he reminds the Philippians that everything Christ did in bringing them salvation was the exact opposite of the "selfish ambition" censured in v. 3.

The sentence begins with a participial phrase, "who being[40] in the 'form' *(morphe)* of God." Despite some recent interpreters, this language expresses *as presupposition* what the rest of the sentence assumes, namely that it was the

---

and in nearly identical language (τὸ αὐτὸ φρονεῖν ἐν ἀλλήλοις κατὰ Χριστὸν Ἰησοῦν), Paul prays that "God would grant you to *have the same mindset* among one another *according to* Christ Jesus." What that means is spelled out in vv. 7-8, where he appeals to Christ's assuming the role of a servant on behalf of them both. Now, a few years later and from Rome, he makes a similar appeal, which is like the former in all of its particulars: the appeal itself, the setting, Christ as paradigm, and the servant nature of the paradigm. Silva (109) sees this text as supporting the alternative position, but to do so he must make Paul's κατά become "a general expression that calls attention to our relationship with Christ." But that seems to stretch the preposition beyond recognition. The Romans are to have this mind among themselves, precisely because it is "in keeping with" what they know about Christ as that is spelled out in vv. 7-8.

37. Gk. ὅς. For the suggestion that this relative signals the beginning of a hymn, see the discussion in Fee, "Philippians 2:5-11," 31 (cf. the Introduction, pp. 41-42).

38. Cf. the similar appeal to Christ's incarnation in 2 Cor 8:9 ("being rich, for your sakes he became poor"), which functions like this one: an imperative (to give generously), followed by an appeal to Christ's self-giving in his incarnation.

39. Paul's point, of course, could have been made without the contrast, but it would not have been as effective. That is, as always in these Pauline contrasts, one can read the sentence strictly in terms of the "but" clause. Thus, "who, being in the form of God, . . . emptied himself by taking on the form of a slave." But the power of the rhetoric lies in the contrast of Christ's emptying himself vis-à-vis "grasping," or "using to one's own advantage" (for this meaning of *harpagmon* see the discussion).

40. Gk. ὑπάρχων; although at times interchangeable with εἶναι, in this case (*pace* BAGD) it very likely carries its primary sense of "to exist (really)." Earlier interpreters (e.g., Lightfoot, Plummer) argued that the word itself implies prior existence; but in the *koine* period the word on its own will hardly bear that weight. See M-M, 650-51.

The relationship of the participle "being" to the verb "did not consider" is debated. Most consider it concessive (so NRSV ["though he was in the form of God"]; cf. NASB, NAB, Lightfoot, Vincent, Michael, Hendriksen, Silva). Hawthorne (85) and Wright ("ἁρπαγμός," 345 n. 87) follow Moule ("Manhood," 97, in Wright's case from personal conversation) in considering it causal (= "precisely because he was in the form of God . . . he recognized what it meant, etc."). More likely Paul's intent is circumstantial, mean-ing, "who, in the circumstance of being in the μορφή of God, as he always was" did not act selfishly (cf. GNB, "he always had the nature of God"; so also Meyer, 79).

Pre-existent One[41] who "emptied himself" at one point in our human history "by taking the 'form' of a slave, being made in the likeness of human beings." Very likely Paul used the participle rather than the finite verb because of Christ's always "being" so.[42] The participle also stands in temporal contrast with the two aorist participles at the end of the sentence. That is, prior to his "having taken the 'form' of a slave" he was already "in the 'form' of God." Moreover, it also stands in contrast in a substantive way with the final participle, "being born/made in the likeness of human beings," which only makes sense if "being in the *morphē* of God" presupposes prior existence as God.[43]

41. The denial that this clause refers to pre-existence has taken two forms. (1) Many earlier interpreters (including Calvin) understood the whole passage, including v. 6, to deal with the divine Christ in his Incarnation. He who was "in the form of God" even in his earthly life did not consider his equality with God something to be seized upon (see the discussion and refutation in Meyer, 77-79). (2) More recently many have argued, either on the basis of a certain structural arrangement (Howard, "Phil 2:6-11") or of "Wisdom christology" (Murphy-O'Connor, "Anthropology") or of an Adam-Christ analogy (Harvey, "New Look"; Bakken, "New Humanity"; Talbert, "Problem"; Dunn, *Christology,* 114-21), that Paul sees Christ here merely in his humanity, who, e.g., as Adam, was in God's "image" (cf. n. 73 below), but vis-à-vis Adam did not try to seize God-likeness. But against these views are: (1) the grammar and language that do exist must be stretched nearly beyond recognition in order to work; (2) the metaphor inherent in ἐκένωσεν ("he emptied himself") seems strikingly inappropriate to refer to one who is already human; (3) that the one described in v. 6 as "being in the form of God," which means further that he was "equal with God," is later said to "be made/born in human likeness" and is then "found in human appearance"; and (4) the structure itself, in which Part I² ("and being found in appearance as a human being") stands in such clear contrast to I¹ ("who being in the 'form' of God"). (On the unlikelihood that one should begin Part I² with the redundancy of making *both* participles that refer to his humanity begin the final sentence ["coming to be in the likeness of human beings and being found in appearance as a human being"] see n. 43 and n. 3 on v. 8). Dunn's exegesis is suspect methodologically, in that it requires a considerable accumulation of merely possible, but highly improbable, meanings, *all of which are necessary to make it work.* Conclusions based on such a procedure are always suspect. Finally, this view divests the narrative of its essential power, which rests in the pointed contrast between the opening participle ("being in the form of God") and the final coda ("death of the cross"). For refutations see Feinberg, "Kenosis"; Hurst, "Re-enter"; Wong, "Problem"; Wanamaker, "Philippians 2.6-11"; and O'Brien, 263-68. For a helpful overview and sane conclusions on this matter, see Hurtado, *DPL,* 743-46.

42. On this usage of the participle in a very similar context, cf. 2 Cor 8:9.

43. Those who deny this (see n. 41 above) by suggesting that the second sentence *begins* with the participle γενόμενος ("coming to be in the likeness of human beings"), not only create a nearly intolerable redundancy (see n. 3 on v. 8), but also never quite come to terms with the oddity of this second "strophe" in comparison with the first: In the so-called first strophe the human Jesus is already on the scene, whereas the second picks up with his "coming to be" as a human. Moreover, why the "hymn" should emphasize his humanity with a further twofold assertion of it, if the first "strophe" already *assumes* it, is never spoken to.

But what about *morphē*?[44] Our difficulties here are twofold:[45] discovering what Paul himself intended by this word, and translating it into English, since we have no precise equivalent.[46] The key to understanding the word lies with Paul's reason for choosing it, which in turn lies with what transpires in the sentence itself. His urgency is to say something about Christ's "mindset," first as God and second as man. But in the transition from Christ's "being God" to his "becoming human," Paul expresses by way of *metaphor* the essential quality of that humanity: he "took on the 'form' of a slave." *Morphē* was precisely the right word for this dual usage, to characterize both the reality (his being God) and the metaphor (his taking on the role of a slave),[47] since it denotes "form" or "shape" not in terms of the external features by which something is recognized,[48] but of those characteristics and qualities that are essential to it. Hence it means *that which truly characterizes a given reality.*[49]

44. The word occurs in only these two instances in the NT. The literature here is immense. The best of the dictionary articles are those in *TDNT* (4.759-62; J. Behm) and *EDNT* (2.442-43; W. Pohlmann), with a useful bibliography in the latter. The best of the earlier discussions in English (before the influence of the papyri) is by Kennedy (435-36; cited by M-M, 417), which supersedes that of Lightfoot (127-33), which is limited to classical usage (and, in spite of its usefulness in that regard, takes up issues probably not Pauline). See also the discussion by Martin (*Carmen,* 99-133; although he accepts its improbable identity with εἰκών and δόξα), and the more recent commentaries (Hawthorne, Silva, O'Brien).

45. Others see another issue here as well, namely the cultural-historical "background" to this word (and to many other of the ideas found throughout the "hymn"). On this issue, see the discussion in O'Brien, 193-98 — except to point out that the view of Käsemann, who influenced many, that it reflects a pre-Christian Gnostic Redeemer myth is itself a piece of scholarly mythology, since there are no hard (or soft, for that matter) data for such a view in the first Christian century.

46. Cf. Vincent (57): "'Form' is an inadequate rendering of μορφή, but our language affords no better word." In the absence of a better alternative, I will stay with "form," but put it in quotes.

47. Had it not been for the second phrase, therefore, Paul most likely would have written something like φύσει θεός ("being God in nature"), or perhaps ἐν φύσει θεοῦ ("in God's nature"). But φύσις would not work in the second instance, where "slave" is metaphorical and needs the second participle to spell out what is intended. Nor would the σχῆμα of the final participial phrase in v. 7 work, since that word emphasizes external features rather than substance or reality. As Meyer (80) notes: "The μορφή θεοῦ presupposes the divine φύσις."

48. See preceding n. on the use of σχῆμα in v. 7.

49. So M-M, 417 (citing Kennedy): "a form which truly and fully expresses the being which underlies it" (cf. Martin; O'Brien). The second occurrence, it should be pointed out, which in part determines the meaning in this first instance, makes it extremely unlikely that μορφή serves as a synonym for εἰκών ("image"), which is used in 2 Cor 4:4 and Col 1:15 to refer to Christ's revelatory and mediatorial functions respectively; and thus it is

What the earliest followers of Christ had come to believe, of course, on the basis of his resurrection and ascension, was that the one whom they had known as truly human had himself known prior existence in the "form" of God — not meaning that he was "like God but really not," but that he was characterized by what was essential to being God. It is this understanding which (correctly) lies behind the NIV's "in very nature God."[50] And it is this singular reality, lying in the emphatic first position as it does, which gives such extraordinary potency to what follows, and therefore to the whole.

That Paul by this first phrase intends "in very nature God" is further confirmed by the clause that immediately follows, which also happens to be one of the more famous cruxes in the letters of Paul. "Being in the 'form' of God," Paul begins. "Not *harpagmon* did Christ consider to be equal with God," he adds next. But first a closer look at *harpagmon* will aid the discussion that follows.[51]

The difficulties are two:[52] its rarity in Greek literature; and where it does appear it denotes "robbery,"[53] a meaning that can hardly obtain here.[54] This means that

---

equally unlikely that this sentence was shaped with an Adam-Christ contrast in view (see n. 73 below). That μορφή is the equivalent of εἰκών is another piece of scholarly opinion that has gained increasing momentum, being repeated over and again as though the linguistic data actually supported it — which it does not. The second occurrence of μορφή (v. 7) also plays havoc with the view, adopted in various forms (by, *inter alia,* Meyer, Jones, Martin, Strimple, Fowl) that μορφή = δόξα ("glory"), a view that would have much going for it had we only the first instance (ἐν μορφῇ θεοῦ); but to apply "glory" to the role of the slave is to press words beyond their ordinary sense (cf. Collange, Hawthorne).

50. Cf. GNB ("he always had the nature of God"); NEB ("the divine nature was his from the first"; but changed back to the ambiguous "form" in the REB); cf. TCNT, Montgomery, Phillips.

51. Because of the significance and difficulty of this word, I have chosen in this case to set it off as a mini word study, which will need to be read in order to understand the whole, but hopefully by doing it this way will also help to make better sense of the overall passage.

52. Again, as with μορφή, the literature is immense. The best of the recent literature is that by N. T. Wright, "ἁρπαγμός," who both summarizes the preceding debate and offers a solution that is especially satisfactory in light of all the issues, and to which I gladly acknowledge indebtedness. Wright basically adopts the view of Hoover ("Harpagmos," see n. 56).

53. The noun is formed from the Greek verb ἁρπάζω, which means to "snatch" or "seize," usually with the connotation of violence or suddenness.

54. Since it makes very little sense at all (despite the KJV, and those who have tried to comment on the basis of this translation). J. C. O'Neill ("Hoover") argues against Hoover (see n. 56) that "robbery," which is "near nonsense," seems "to be the only choice left" (448), whose counsel of despair is then to emend the text. But in so doing O'Neill

scholars have been left to determine its meaning on the basis either (a) of (per-ceived) context, or (b) of the formation of Greek nouns, or (c) of finding parallels which suggest an idiomatic usage. Also involved is the question as to whether "equality with God" was something Christ did not possess but might have desired or something he already possessed but did not treat in a *harpagmon* way.[55]

Although the jury is still out on this question, the probable sense of this word is to be found in one of two refinements — by C. F. D. Moule and R. W. Hoover — of earlier suggestions.[56] The former based his conclusions on the formation of Greek nouns, in which nouns ending in -*mos* do not ordinarily refer to a concrete expression of the verbal idea in the noun but to the verbal idea itself.[57] In this view *harpagmos* is not to be thought of as a "thing" at all ("something" to be treated by the verbal idea in the noun). Rather it is an abstract noun, emphasizing the concept of "grasping" or "seizing." Thus, Christ did not consider "equality with God" to consist of "grasping" or being "selfish"; rather he rejected this popular view of kingly power by "pouring himself out" for the sake of others. In Moule's terms, equality with God means not "grasping" but "giving away" (272). This view has much to commend it,[58] and in any case, surely points in the right direction in terms of the overall sense of the noun in context.[59]

The alternative is to see the word as a synonym of its cognate *harpagma* ("booty" or "prey"), which in idioms similar to Paul's[60] denotes something like,

---

has called into question only *some* of Hoover's data (the evidence from Heliodorus [Hoover, 102-6] is especially noteworthy); by turning Hoover's findings into a "rule," O'Neill eliminates the "rule" by noting the exceptions. But that is not the same thing as eliminating Hoover's understanding of the idiom.

55. The technical language for these distinctions is *res rapta* ("something grasped" = "robbery") or *res rapienda* ("something to be grasped"), both referring to what was not previously possessed, and *res retinenda* ("something to be clung onto"), referring to something already possessed.

56. See Moule ("Reflexions") and Hoover ("Harpagmos"); these two pieces appeared nearly simultaneously (1971 and 1970 respectively). Hoover built especially on the work of W. W. Jaeger ("Studie"), although its line goes back to Lightfoot. Moule gave a more solid philological base to the previous work of J. Ross ("ΑΡΠΑΓΜΟΣ"), F. E. Vokes ("ἁρπαγμός"), and S. H. Hooke *(Alpha);* cf. also J. M. Furness, "ἁρπαγμός"; H. Dean, "Glory." Although some have followed Moule (e.g., Hawthorne), the general swing (adopted also in this commentary) is toward Hoover, while keeping Moule in view (so Martin, Strimple, Feinberg, Wright, Silva, Fowl, O'Brien, Melick); it was taken earlier by Käsemann, "Analysis," 63 ("to use something for one's own benefit").

57. Cf. the discussion in M-M, 78.

58. The common objection that it still requires an object, i.e., "*what* is not being seized or given away?" has been already answered by Moule, that such an "active" view of the noun does not require an object as such.

59. As Wright ("ἁρπαγμός," 345) also points out.

60. That is, when it occurs as part of a double accusative with a verb like "think" (as here) or "do."

"a matter to be seized upon" in the sense of "taking advantage of it." This view has much to commend it and probably points us in the right direction, although it is arguable that the evidence for the interchangeability of *harpagmos* and *harpagma* is not as strong as its proponents suggest.[61] In either case, it should be pointed out, the clause comes out very much at the same point.

Back then to Paul's point with this "not" clause, which is twofold (= two sides of a single concern). First, he is picking up on, and thereby reaffirming, what he said in the initial participial phrase, that Christ before his incarnation was "in very nature God." This reaffirmation is accomplished by means of two complicated points of grammar,[62] which together make it clear that Paul intends the infinitive phrase ("to be equal with God") to *repeat in essence the sense of what preceded* ("being in the 'form' of God"). Thus Paul intends (by way of a structured elaboration):

> Being in the 'form' of God as he was,
> Christ did not consider a matter of seizing upon to his own advantage,
>     this being equal[63] with God we have just noted,
> but he emptied himself."

This, then, is what it means for Christ to be "in the 'form' of God"; it means "to be equal with God," not in the sense that the two phrases are identical, but that both point to the same reality.[64] Together, therefore, they are among

---

61. Cf. the (much overstated) critique by O'Neill, "Hoover." The first objection to both suggestions (Moule's and Hoover's), of course, is the lack of linguistic evidence as such for this word.

62. First, by the *structure* of the clause. In Greek ἁρπαγμὸν . . . τὸ εἶναι ἴσα θεῷ is a double accusative which functions as the object of the verb ἡγήσατο ("consider"). Thus it is a form of indirect discourse; in direct discourse "to be equal with God" would the subject and ἁρπαγμόν the predicate noun of a sentence that would read: "to be equal with God is *harpagmon*," which is *not* Christ's mindset (cf. Käsemann ["Analysis," 62]). But by putting "not *harpagmon*" in the emphatic first position, Paul indicates that the infinitive that follows *refers back* to the initial participial phrase, in a kind of A-B-A structure. Thus, "in his being in the form of God (A), not *harpagmon* did Christ consider (B) his being be equal with God (A')."

Second, by using the definite article with the infinitive, which, as in 1:21-22 — and ordinarily so in any case — is probably anaphoric, pointing to "something previously mentioned or otherwise well known" (this is the language of BDF, §205); cf. Meyer (88), Hawthorne (84), and Wright ("ἁρπαγμός," 344), who also see the article as anaphoric.

63. Gk. ἴσα θεῷ; for this use of ἴσα as a predicate, Lightfoot notes Job 11:12 LXX. Cf. John 5:18, where Jesus is accused, on the basis of his "working on the Sabbath," of making himself ἴσος τῷ θεῷ.

64. So most interpreters (e.g., Meyer, Müller, Beare, Hendriksen, Collange, Loh-

the strongest expressions of Christ's deity in the NT. This means further that "equality with God" is not that which he desired which was not his, but precisely that which was *always* his.[65]

Second, Paul is thereby trying to set up the starkest possible contrast between Christ's "being in the 'form' of God" and the main clause, "he emptied himself."[66] Equality with God, Paul begins, is something that was inherent to Christ in his pre-existence. Nonetheless, God-likeness, contrary to common understanding, did *not* mean for Christ to be a "grasping, seizing" being, as it would for the "gods" and "lords" whom the Philippians had previously known; it was not "something to be seized upon to his own advantage," which would be the normal expectation of lordly power — and the nadir of selfishness. Rather, his "equality with God" found its truest expression when "he emptied himself."[67]

What is thus being urged upon the Philippians is not a new view of Jesus,[68] but a reinforcement, on the basis of Paul's view of the crucifixion, that in the cross God's true character, his outlandish, lavish expression of love, was fully manifested.[69] This is what Paul is calling them to by way of discipleship. The phrase, "not *harpagmon*," after all, corresponds to "not looking out for one's own needs" in v. 4. Here is Paul's way of saying that Christ, as God, did not act so. Thus, as he has just appealed to them to have a singular "mindset" *(phronēte)*, which will express itself in "humility" as they "consider"[70] one another better than themselves, so now he has repeated

Nida, Bruce, Hawthorne, Silva, O'Brien, Melick; Käsemann ["Analysis," 62-63]; Wright ["ἁρπαγμος," 344]). Those who reject what the grammar seems to require do so either because they take a different view of ἁρπαγμός (e.g., Kennedy, Jones, Michael) or because of prior commitments to an Adam-Christ analogy in which Christ is seen as only human (see nn. 41 and 73).

65. Indeed, the fact that "equality with God" was something he always had is what makes the contrast between the opening participle and the main verb (our next point) work at all.

66. Strimple ("Recent Studies," 263) notes (correctly) that the *res rapienda* view of ἁρπαγμόν (see n. 55) creates a disjunction between being in the *form* of God and being *equal* with God "contrary to the natural force of the grammatical construction which so closely binds together these two clauses which precede the real disjunction, which comes with the ἀλλά at the beginning of verse 7."

67. Cf. Wright, "ἁρπαγμός," 344-46.

68. As a Pauline church, what is presented here is the one they would already have known well.

69. Which is why the "coda" to the final participle in v. 8, "even death on a cross," is expressed in such a way — so as to carry ultimate rhetorical effect. Here is the apogee of true "God-likeness," where the divine Christ gives himself away in the utterly execrable "weakness" (humiliation) of crucifixion. For this understanding of the cross, see esp. 1 Cor 1:18-25 in Fee, *First Corinthians,* 67-78.

70. For this verb (ἡγέομαι) see n. 76 on v. 3.

the injunction to have this "mindset" (*phroneite,* v. 5) which they see in Christ Jesus, who did not "consider" (same verb as in v. 4) being equal with God as something to be taken selfish advantage of, something to further his own ends.

We should note finally that many have seen Paul here to be playing on the Adam-Christ theme[71] that appears elsewhere in his letters.[72] Most who hold this view understand Christ to be set in studied contrast with Adam, who, "being in God's image,"[73] considered his "equality with God" as something to be seized. Christ, on the contrary, disdained such "grasping" and did the opposite; as Adam tried to become "like God," Christ, as God, in fact became man. This is an intriguing analogy, but it must be noted that its basis is altogether conceptual, since there is not a single *linguistic* parallel to the Genesis narrative.[74] Whether the Philippians would have so understood it

71. This possible association with Gen 2–3 goes back at least as far as Ernesti (noted, but rejected, by Meyer); it was also noted, and again rejected, by Vincent and Plummer. It has been much more widely accepted in recent years (*inter alia,* by Caird, Houlden, Kent, Silva; Cullmann, *Christology;* Ridderbos, *Paul;* Bandstra, " 'Adam' "; Hooker, "Philippians 2:6-11"; Dunn, *Christology;* Wright, "ἁρπαγμός") — with varying degrees of conviction as to how much the language has been purposely designed to represent this analogy, from Caird's "the context requires it," to Wright's more cautious "typically cryptic reference to Adam" ("ἁρπαγμός," 348; cf. Silva, "network of associations"). It is rejected by Collange, Glasson ("Two Notes"), Strimple ("Recent Studies"), and Feinberg ("Kenosis"). The most useful current overview of this matter is O'Brien, 263-68.

72. In conjunction with the resurrection (1 Cor 15:21-22, 45-49) and with the universality of human sin (Adam) and God's redemption (Christ; Rom 5:12-21).

73. Those who see the analogy as *intentional* on the part of the "author" of the "hymn" argue (1) that μορφή and εἰκών are interchangeable terms, and (2) therefore that the "author" is deliberately "citing" Gen 1:26-27 with this substitution. They see this as further confirmed by the language τὸ εἶναι ἴσα θεῷ ("to be equal with God"), which is understood to pick up Gen 3:5 and 22 ("be like one of us," although there is *not a single linguistic link* between these passages and Phil 2:6-7). That the two words are fully interchangeable in this sense is scholarly mythology based on untenable semantics (cf. esp. the refutations by Wallace, "Note," and Steenburg, "Case Against"), as though, because in certain instances they have a semantic overlap, therefore an author could — or would — use either one or the other at will. For example, there is a semantic overlap with the words "right" and "just" in English, and they might be fully interchangeable in a sentence that says, "What she did was right/just." But one is in grave danger who thinks they are thereby fully interchangeable, even in comparable sentences (as, e.g., "she is just; she is right"). Since Paul is quite ready to speak of Christ as "in the image (εἰκών) of God," and since that is the word used in Genesis, how could it be possible, one wonders, that Paul was *intending* this analogy and have written μορφή? And it will do no good in this case to say that he was "citing" a pre-formed hymn, because as anyone knows who has watched Paul use the OT, he seldom lets the words in an original text dictate how those words will appear in his own sentence.

74. This seems to me to negate this view as *intentional* on Paul's part; cf. Käsemann

without some linguistic clue probably depends on whether Paul himself had used such an analogy at some point in his time with them.[75]

**7**   That leads us then to the most famous, but unnecessary, crux of all, the main clause of the present sentence, "but [in contrast to his considering equality with God as something to seize on to his own advantage] he emptied *(ekenōsen)* himself." This is a crux, however, that has been generated by scholarship, not by Paul or by Pauline ambiguities. The debate has raged over the concept of "emptying himself," i.e., what *kenōsis* means, and emerged either because of a faulty understanding of *harpagmon* or because it has been assumed that the verb requires a genitive qualifier — that he must have "emptied himself" *of something*.[76] But that is precisely *not* in keeping with Pauline usage. Just as *harpagmon* requires no object for him to "seize," but rather points to what is the opposite of God's character, so Christ did not empty himself *of* anything; he simply "emptied *himself*," poured himself out.[77] This is metaphor, pure and simple.[78] The *modifier* is expressed in the modal participle that follows; he "poured himself out *by* having taken on the 'form' of a slave."

Pauline usage elsewhere substantiates this view, where this verb reg-

---

("Analysis," 64): "The text lends no support to it . . . ; and such support must certainly be expected *in the case of such a concrete reference*" (emphasis mine). Vincent, followed by Glasson ("Two Notes"), also points out that nothing in the Genesis account that suggests seeking "*equality* with God" to be the nature of the Fall; rather, it was the quest for absolute knowledge.

75. Many of those who hold this position, it should be noted further, likewise deny that the passage speaks of pre-existence (see n. 41 above).

76. The literature here covers a broad range (commentaries, theologies, articles), which makes it impossible to offer an adequate bibliography. For the earlier (mostly theological, and mostly Reformed) debate, see Müller, 83-85. For more recent treatments, see E. R. Fairweather, " 'Kenotic' Christology"; T. A. Thomas, "Kenosis"; and C. Patitsas, *"Kenosis"* (for a Greek Orthodox view). At issue in this debate for the most part has been whether Paul considers Christ to have emptied himself of divinity itself in some way or of "the glories, the prerogatives of Deity" (Lightfoot, 112), which in more recent times has had to do with his "glory" (as a way of understanding μορφή; see n. 49 above) or of his power (Müller, Hendriksen, Collange).

77. *Pace* Plummer (44), who argues that "a secondary object must be understood" (cf. Hendriksen, Kent). One wonders why so, since this is not true in Paul's other uses of this word. When metaphors start being pressed like this, one may as well ask other irrelevant questions (e.g., into what was he emptied?). The view argued for here ("poured himself out") was first presented (apparently) by W. Warren, "ἐκήνωσεν"; it has been adopted, *inter alia,* by Jones, Michael, Hawthorne, Silva, O'Brien, Melick, Dean ("Glory"); it was anticipated by Vincent, 59.

78. Cf. Martin, *Carmen,* 195; Müller, 80; Silva, 125; O'Brien, 217. But it is a metaphor, one should note, that demands pre-existence (see n. 41); otherwise why use it, when other more appropriate verbs were at hand ("denied himself," "rejected," etc.)? Indeed, if it does not presuppose pre-existence the metaphor itself has been "emptied."

ularly means to become powerless, or to be emptied of significance.[79] Here it stands in direct antithesis to the "*empty* glory" of v. 3, and functions in the same way as the metaphorical "he became poor" in 2 Cor 8:9. Rather than doing anything on the basis of "empty glory," Christ on the contrary "emptied himself," or as the KJV has it (memorably), "he made himself of no reputation,"[80] whose sense the NIV has captured with its "made himself nothing." As Wright put it well, "The real humiliation of the incarnation and the cross is that one who was himself God, and who never during the whole process stopped being God, could embrace such a vocation."[81] Thus, as in the "not" side of this clause (v. 6b), we are still dealing with the character of God, as that has been revealed in the "mindset" and resulting activity of the Son of God. The concern is with divine selflessness: God is not an acquisitive being, grasping and seizing, but self-giving for the sake of others.

That this is Paul's intent is made even more certain by the two explanatory participial phrases that follow.[82] The first explains the *nature* of Christ's emptying himself, the way it expressed itself in our human history: "by taking[83] on the 'form' of a slave." "Form" *(morphē)* here means precisely what it did above, that in his earthly existence he took on the "essential quality" of what it meant to be a slave. We have already looked closely at the word "slave" in Paul's self-designation in 1:1. Here it probably means something close to its corresponding verb in Gal 5:13 (= "perform the duties of a slave").[84] From Paul's perspective this is how divine love manifests itself in its most characteristic and profuse expression.

79. See 1 Cor 1:17 ("lest the cross of Christ κενωθῇ [be made ineffectual]"), and Rom 4:14 ("faith κεκένωται [has been emptied]"). Why not ask, e.g., of what has faith been emptied? (cf. Silva). The two other passages (1 Cor 9:15 and 2 Cor 9:3) refer to one's "boast" being "emptied," which is precisely the meaning the cognate noun regularly has in Paul (e.g., Phil 2:16 [2x]; cf. Gal 2:2). On this point see esp. Hooker ("Philippians 2:6-11," 152), followed by Wright ("ἁρπαγμός," 345-46).

80. *Contra* Michel, 89.

81. "ἁρπαγμός," 346. The further point to make, of course, is that the text does not imply that he *exchanged* one form of existence for another (*pace* Thomas, "Kenosis," 151; et al.); rather, it is precisely he who is in the form of God (always) who "beggared himself" (Beare) by "taking on" the form of a slave; cf. Bruce (70): "He displayed the nature (or form) of God *in* the nature (or form) of a servant."

82. Which are best understood as modal; i.e., they describe the manner, or circumstances, in which he "emptied himself" (so most interpreters).

83. Gk. λαβών; ordinarily the aorist participle indicates antecedent time. But despite Moule (*Idiom Book,* 100), who recognizes only two such uses in the NT (both in Acts), the majority of scholars understand this participle to express coincident time. Cf. Gal 4:6; Eph 1:9.

84. On this meaning of the verb, see Fee, *Presence,* 425. To argue that he must be *enslaved to someone* ("God" [so Meyer, Plummer], or "the powers" [see n. 86]) is to press the metaphor and therefore to miss it.

It is often suggested that there is more to this word, that by using "slave" Paul has some other "background" in mind than simply slavery as such. Two have been proffered.[85] Altogether unlikely is the suggestion that by becoming human Christ accepted "bondage" to the "powers," so that through death he might destroy them.[86] The obvious difficulty with such a view is that nothing in the text suggests as much; indeed, it is held basically by those who read the whole "hymn" as pre-Pauline and with a meaning in its prior existence, due to its background there, which Paul has then imperfectly imported into its present context. A more likely "background" is the Servant of the Lord of Isaiah 42–53, where some interesting linguistic and conceptual links do exist.[87] In the LXX, however, Isaiah's Servant is designated by a quite different Greek word.[88] If, therefore, such ties exist, and they are at least as viable as the "cryptic reference to Adam" in v. 6, they most likely do so as general background; after all, Jesus himself interpreted his death in light of Isaiah 53, and Paul and the early church were quick to see that Christ's "servanthood" was ultimately fulfilled in the "pouring out of his life unto death" (53:12) for the sake of others. It is hard to imagine that early Christians, therefore, would not rather automatically have heard this passage with that background in view, especially since that passage begins (52:13) the way this one ends, with the Servant's exaltation by God.[89]

But in the present context the emphasis does not lie on Jesus' messianism or on his fulfilling the role of the Servant of the Lord. Rather it lies primarily on the servant nature of Christ's incarnation. He entered our history not as *kyrios* ("Lord"), which name he acquires at his vindication (vv. 9-11),

---

85. Actually three. E. Schweizer (*Erniedrigung*, 21-33, 93-102) suggests the righteous sufferer such as one finds in intertestamental Jewish martyrologies, although apart from Martin, he seems not to have persuaded many.

86. See Käsemann ("Analysis," 67-68), followed by Beare, 82; Gnilka, 120; Caird, 121-22; Bornkamm ("Verständnis," 181).

87. Esp. the repeated εἰς θάνατον (53:8, 12) in the context of his being ἐν τῇ ταπεινώσι (v. 8). Note also the conceptual ties of "he emptied himself" and "he poured out his soul unto death" (53:12); and 52:13 ("my servant καὶ ὑψωθήσεται καὶ δοξασθήσεται σφόδρα [shall be exalted and glorified greatly]"). This was first argued for at some length (apparently) by H. W. Robinson (*Cross*, 104, 105 [first appearing in 1926]) and carried forward by L. Cerfaux (*Le Christ*, 288-98) and J. Jeremias ("Zu Phil ii 7"); it has been adopted, *inter alia*, by Jones, Michael (tentatively), Hendriksen; Martin (*Carmen*, 169-96); Gibbs ("Creation," 275-81); Strimple ("Recent Studies," 260-61); Feinberg ("Kenosis," 36-40). See the helpful discussion in O'Brien, 268-71, although he finally rejects it.

88. He is the παῖς θεοῦ; Paul's word is δοῦλος, and he is not called "the slave of the Lord." This linguistic difference is the most frequently given reason for rejecting the idea altogether (e.g., Plummer).

89. Similarly Silva, who also cites Heriban (*Retto*, 160-62) and Wagner ("Le scandale") in support.

but as *doulos* ("slave"), a person without advantages, with no rights or privileges, but in servanthood to all.[90] And all of this, surely, with an eye to vv. 3-4.[91]

The second participial phrase simultaneously clarifies the first by elaboration[92] and concludes the present sentence by paving the way for the next (v. 8; Part I²). Together these phrases give definition to Christ's "impoverishment." The phrase "in the form of a slave" comes first for rhetorical reasons — to sharpen the contrast with "in the form of God" and to set out the true nature of his incarnation. It thus reflects the "quality" of his incarnation. The second phrase indicates its "factual" side. Thus, Christ came "in the form of a slave," that is, by his "coming to be[93] in the likeness of human beings."[94]

The word "likeness"[95] has been the troubling word in this phrase, especially in light of the even more difficult word "appearance" in the first phrase of the next sentence. But again, the difficulty stems more from philosophical theology than from Paul. The word is used primarily because of Paul's belief (in common with the rest of the early church) that in becoming human Christ did not thereby cease to be divine. This word allows for the ambiguity, emphasizing that he is similar to our humanity in some respects and dissimilar in others. The similarity lies with his full humanity; in his incarnation he was "like" in the sense of "the same as." The dissimilarity, which in Rom 8:3 had to do with his being sinless while in the "likeness" of sinful flesh, in this case has to do with his never ceasing to be "equal with God." Thus he came in the "likeness" of human beings, because on the one hand he has fully identified with us, and because on the other hand in becoming human he was not "human" only. He was God living out a truly human life, all of which is safeguarded by this expression. Even so, one should not miss

---

90. Moule ("Reflexions," 268-69) suggests this as the only motif; cf. Houlden, Hawthorne, Bruce.

91. So also Hurtado ("Lordly Example"); cf. O'Brien, 223-24.

92. Cf. Meyer (90, "specifies"); Kennedy (437, "defines"); Vincent (59, "explains"). Those who deny pre-existence (see n. 41) recognize the difficulties this phrase poses for their point of view and adopt the tautological "strophic" arrangement which sees this and the next participle as introducing the next clause (on this matter see n. 3 on v. 8).

93. Gk. γενόμενος; cf. v. 8 where the same participle appears in a similar qualifying phrase. Cf. further the double use of this participle in the semi-creedal Gal 4:4-5, which in that case = "was born." It is so translated here by Moffatt; cf. NRSV, NAB. The NIV and NASB translate "being made," while GNB suggests "appearing."

94. Gk. ἀνθρώπων; the plural is purposeful, implying his identity with the whole human race, which is then particularized in the next phrase ("as a human being [himself]").

95. Gk. ἐν ὁμοιώματι; cf. esp. Rom 8:3 (ἐν ὁμοιώματι σαρκὸς ἁμαρτίας, "in the likeness of sinful flesh"); on this latter usage BAGD comment ("it is safe to assert that [Paul's] use of our word is to bring out both that Jesus in his earthly career was similar to sinful [people] yet not absolutely like them").

that this phrase is also part of the contrast. Christ "made himself of no reputation" in becoming *human* — whether we humans like that or not.

In sum: In Christ Jesus God has thus shown his true nature; this is what it means for Christ to be "equal with God" — to pour himself out for the sake of others and to do so by taking the role of a slave. Hereby he not only reveals the character of God, but from the perspective of the present context also reveals what it means for us to be created in God's image, to bear his likeness and have his "mindset." It means taking the role of the slave for the sake of others, the contours of which are what the next clause will spell out.

### 2. As Man He Humbled Himself (2:8)

> 8*And being found in appearance as a [human being],*[1]
> *he humbled himself*
> *and became obedient to death —*
> *even death on a cross!*

The narrative that began in v. 6 is continued by this sentence,[2] whose close connection — and narrative quality — is highlighted by the paratactic "and."[3]

---

1. Gk. ἄνθρωπος; while it is true that Jesus was in fact male, thus a man, this word does not point to his being male, but to his being human. On the other hand, against all the rules of inclusive language I have mantained "man" in the title of the section for the sake of poetry. Hence the two clauses in Part I: "As God he emptied himself; as Man he humbled himself." Although the use of "man" is generic here, and therefore against the "rules," let the reader understand it to mean "*a* man."

2. In some ways, therefore, one can scarcely justify commenting on this verse as a distinct entity. I have chosen to do so in order to highlight the three parts of the narrative and their significance for the argument. This is also a place (cf. 2 Cor 13:14[13]) where the versification of the English Bible (which has it correctly!) does not match the Greek (which has v. 8 begin with the main clause, "he humbled himself").

3. Gk. καί. Parataxis has to do with joining sentences with an "and" as over against various forms of subordination. It is a regular feature of Hebrew narrative, picked up most noticeably in the NT in the Gospel of Mark. Parataxis is rare in Paul; where it does occur it is usually in narrative of some kind (e.g., 1 Thess 1:6, 9; Gal 1:14, 24; 2:2; Eph 2:1). It should be pointed out that it is also a feature of Hebrew poetry, although occurring with less frequency than in narrative.

Some see the καί as joining the two participial phrases, rather than the two clauses, either as concluding the preceding sentence (Meyer, Loh-Nida, Hawthorne), or beginning the next (Jeremias, J. A. Sanders, Collange, and all who deny pre-existence [see n. 41 on v. 6]), or as an independent strophe (Martin, GNB). For the most part (Meyer excepted) this is the result of forcing strophic arrangements on the text rather than recognizing Paul's sentences. Apart from these prior commitments to strophic patterns, this has nothing in its favor: (a) it destroys the formal similarities of the two sentences; (b) it creates a nearly intolerable redundancy, whose purpose is difficult to fathom; indeed, viewed this way, the phrase

Apart from the "not/but" contrast in v. 6, it is identical in form to the preceding sentence. It begins (1) with a participle emphasizing Christ's present "mode" of being, in this case "as a human being," followed (2) by the main clause ("he humbled himself"), precisely as in v. 6, followed (3) by a participial modifier, again modal, which spells out *how* he did so ("by becoming obedient unto death"), which in turn (4) is brought to rhetorical climax by specifying the kind of death ("the death of a cross").

**8**   The opening phrase ("and being found[4] in appearance as a human being") picks up the flow of the narrative by reiterating the essential matter from the final phrase of the preceding sentence. At the same time, as with the opening participle in v. 6, it serves to specify the "mode of existence" for Christ's action in this clause. "In the form of God" he emptied himself; now "in the appearance of a human being" he humbled himself.

The word "appearance"[5] is yet another of the troubling words in this passage (vv. 6-11). Most likely the usage here is stylistic pure and simple, in which Paul picks up the idea from the preceding phrase ("in human likeness") but says it in a slightly different way. The primary sense of the word has to do not with the essential quality of something, but with its externals, that which makes it recognizable. Thus, having said that Christ came in the "likeness" of human beings (v. 7b), Paul now moves the narrative on to its next point, by saying he "appeared" in a way that was clearly recognizable as human. Together the two phrases accent the reality of his humanity, just as the first two phrases in the preceding sentence accent his deity.[6]

---

interrupts the otherwise smooth flow of the narrative; (c) this kind of identical parallelism (where two synonymous lines say exactly the same thing) would not only be unique for this passage, but cannot in fact be found elsewhere in Paul; (d) it causes the καί to create a strange relationship between these two phrases ("having become in the likeness of human beings and being found in appearance as a human being" as either the *conclusion* of the prior sentence or *beginning* of the next makes very little sense); and (e) it creates unnecessary asyndeton for the middle sentence (v. 8), over against vv. 9-11. Finally, it should be noted that either of these creates an unnatural *reading* (and thus *hearing*) of the text for those who do not have the strophes before them (cf. Silva, 121). It is therefore understandable that the majority of interpreters (and translations) view the καί as beginning the second sentence.

4. Gk. εὑρεθείς (aorist passive), which ordinarily refers to an event antecedent to the main verb (= having been found); in this case the English present passive participle offers the same sense. On a spectrum εὑρίσκω goes from "finding" by purposeful search, to "finding" in the sense of surprise or discovery, to its least purposeful sense, used here, where it means something close to "he was seen to be." Cf. 3:9 (which is probably more in the middle); 2 Cor 5:3; Gal 2:17.

5. Gk. σχήματι; cf. 1 Cor 7:31, the only other occurrence of this word in Paul, where it seems to mean, "this age in its present expression."

6. That is, his "being in the form of God" which means that he "was equal with God."

As a human being "he humbled himself"; that is, in his human existence he chose, in obedience, to "take the lowest place" *(etapeinōsen).* This word deliberately echoes "in lowliness of mind" *(tapeinophrosynē)* in v. 3; at the same time it anticipates by way of contrast his being "exalted to the highest place" in v. 9. On the place of "humility" in the life of Christ and the believer see on v. 3.

The ensuing participle functions in the same modal way as its counterpart(s) in the preceding sentence, narrating *how* his humbling himself found expression, in this case "by becoming obedient unto death." Although Paul does not often speak of Christ's death in terms of "obedience" (cf. Rom 5:19), the language in the present instance is in keeping with the reason for the passage in the first place — to call the Philippians to "obedience" regarding the appeal in vv. 2-4.[7] In any case, such language fully reflects Paul's theological perspective. In keeping with the rest of the early church,[8] he understood Jesus' death not from the perspective of those who "crucified the Lord of glory" (1 Cor 2:8) — who acted on the basis of human "wisdom," in sheer ignorance of God's "mystery" revealed by the Spirit, that God chose to redeem our fallen race through the weakness (and therefore scandal) of the cross — but from the perspective of one who saw his death as an act of "obedience" to the divine will. "Obedience unto[9] death," therefore, points to the degree to which obedience took him, the readiness of him who, as one of us, *chose* the path that led to a death[10] "decreed before the ages for our glory."[11] Which

---

7. Thus in vv. 12-13 he applies this narrative to their situation, by reminding them that they have "always obeyed" — not Paul, of course, but God himself, just as Christ did by his having died for them.

8. Esp. the Gospel of John and Hebrews (see Jn 4:34; 5:30; 6:38-40; 7:17; 10:15, 17; Heb 5:7-10; 10:5-9).

9. Gk. μεχρί; the preposition for "until," which can denote "space," "time," or "degree." Here it clearly denotes "degree." Jesus' obedience took him to the *n*th degree, to death itself. The use of this preposition is what in part gives one pause as to whether this passage was written with Isaiah 53 *consciously* in the background, where the LXX twice reads εἰς θάνατον.

10. *Contra* those who suggest that it points to a *life* of obedience, which maintained obedience to the very end (as, e.g., Plummer [47]: "He became so by a life of absolutely perfect obedience in all things").

11. See 1 Cor 2:7 (NRSV); for this perspective elsewhere in Paul see also Gal 1:4 ("who gave himself for our sins . . . according to the will of our God and Father"); cf. Rom 1:2-4; 16:25-26; Eph 1:3-7, 11. Some have seen "obedience" otherwise: to the "powers" (Käsemann, et al. [see n. 86 on v. 7]; a view, one should note, that could only have arisen among those who comment on the "hymn" as though Paul had nothing to do with it); or to other human beings as well (Hawthorne); or simply to the *fact* that he obeyed (Barth, O'Brien). But the subject of the next clause, "Therefore *God* highly exalted him," seems to point to the view taken here, that his death is in obedience to the divine will.

is quite in keeping with him who, as God, impoverished himself by taking on the role of a slave.

The final phrase, "death of a cross," which concludes Part I of the narrative, fits the alleged "hymn" so poorly that many scholars have seen it as a Pauline "addition." On the contrary, its rhetorical effect, both in its present clause and as concluding the whole, is so forceful that it is hard to imagine it to be a mere "tack on."[12] In its own clause its effect lies in the repetition of "death" back to back: "unto death, death, that is, of a cross." At the same time it combines with "in the 'form' of God" (v. 6) to frame the narrative to this point with the sharpest imaginable contrast: God and the cross.

Here is the very heart of Pauline theology, both of his understanding of God as such and of his understanding of what God has done and is doing in our fallen world. Here is where the one who as "equal with God" has most fully revealed the truth about God: that God is love and that his love expresses itself in self-sacrifice — cruel, humiliating death on a cross[13] — for the sake of those he loves. The divine weakness (death at the hands of his creatures, his enemies) is the divine scandal (the cross was reserved for slaves and insurrectionists). No one in Philippi,[14] we must remind ourselves, used the cross as a symbol for their faith; there were no gold crosses embossed on Bibles or worn as pendants around the neck or lighted on the steeple of the local church. The cross was God's — and thus their — scandal, God's contradiction to human wisdom and power: that the one they worshiped as Lord of all, including Caesar, had been crucified as a state criminal at the hands of one of Caesar's proconsuls;[15] that the Almighty

12. One of the unfortunate by-products of seeing the alleged hymn as pre-Pauline, and then commenting on it as though Paul had nothing to do with it (e.g., Beare), is to view this final, climactic word as a Pauline addition to the "hymn," which breaks up its original strophic arrangement. On this matter Caird has rightly noted (122): "Lohmeyer's attempt to bracket the words *even death on a cross* as an intrusive gloss, is the reductio ad absurdum of his theory, since the words in fact constitute the climax to which the last three verses have been pointing." Similarly, Hengel, *Crucifixion,* 62-63, with regard to these words as providing the climax of vv. 6-8; in his view they are to be understood precisely in connection with his taking the "form" of a slave, since crucifixion was a slave's penalty, as everyone reading the letter well knew.

13. Cf. Cicero (*Verr.* 5.66; LCL 655-57): "To bind a Roman citizen is a crime; to flog him is an abomination; to slay him is almost an act of murder; to crucify him is — what? There is no fitting word that can possibly describe so horrible a deed." Cf. Heb 12:2: "Who endured the cross, scorning its shame."

14. Nor anywhere else in the early church!

15. See esp. the accusation of the religious in Luke 23:2, where they knew that the only way they could get the state to do their dirty work for them was to trump up a political charge — sedition: "We found this man . . . forbidding us to pay taxes to the emperor, and saying that he himself is the Messiah, a king" (NRSV). On the whole

should appear in human dress, and that he should do so in *this* way, as a "Messiah" who died by crucifixion.[16] Likewise, this is the scandal of Pauline ethics: that the God who did it this way "gifts" us to "suffer for his sake" as well (1:29):

This is our God, the Servant-King,
Who calls us now to follow him,
To bring our lives as a daily offering,
Of worship to the Servant-King.[17]

### 3. God Has Exalted Him as Lord of All (2:9-11)

9*Therefore God exalted him to the highest place*
*and gave him the[1] name that is above every name,*
10*that at the name of Jesus every knee should bow,*
*in heaven and on earth and under the earth,*
11*and every tongue confess[2] that Jesus Christ is Lord,*
*to the glory of God the Father.*

The basic paradigmatic concern of this "Christ story" has been expressed in vv. 6-8.[3] But neither the narrative nor Paul's overall concern for the Philippians

---

question of Jesus' death by crucifixion, its Roman background and its theological significance, see M. Hengel, *Crucifixion;* for a brief, but helpful overview see J. B. Green, *DPL,* 197-99.

16. A form of execution, it should be further pointed out, reserved for *non*-citizens of the Empire. Cf. n. 13 above, to which one might add Cicero's further remark (*Rab. Post.* 5.16; LCL 467): "The very word 'cross' should be far removed not only from the person of a Roman citizen, but from his thoughts, his eyes, and his ears."

17. From the hymn by Graham Kendrick, *The Servant King* (1983).

1. The Western and later Byzantine traditions (D F G Ψ Maj; Clement Origen) omit τό, thus reading as the KJV ("*a* name above all names"). Although one could argue for an addition on the grounds of grammar (ὄνομα τό, without a τό preceding ὄνομα is awkward), both the external evidence and Pauline grammar argue for the article as original. The omission resulted either from an error of hearing (the τό immediately follows αὐτῷ) or (more likely) from a lack of understanding of Paul, so that his definite "*the* name" (= the Lord) came to mean something closer to name = reputation.

2. The large number of MSS have changed Paul's original subjunctive (ἐξομολογήσηται) to a future indicative (-γήσεται). This is an understandable change, which makes v. 11 a final sentence on its own. But the second subjunctive (preserved in P[46] ℵ B Ψ 104 323 2495 pm) is to be preferred; it keeps the sentence with its chiastic structure intact (see n. 6) and represents Paul's ordinary style.

3. That is, the Philippians are to pursue the mindset of the one who as God emptied himself and as man humbled himself, even to death on the cross. On this whole question,

in this context is finished. Thus he concludes on this note of exaltation, affirming that Christ's self-emptying and death by crucifixion revealed true equality with God. In so doing, Paul both affirms the rightness of the paradigm to which he has called the Philippians and keeps before their eyes the eschatological vindication that awaits those who are Christ's,[4] a concern that runs throughout the letter and the note on which this whole section (from 1:27) concludes (2:16). For a suffering community whom Paul repeatedly reminds regarding the absolute centrality of Christ in everything — both present and future — here is the necessary concluding word. Believers in Christ, suffering though they may be, are in Christ both "already" and "not yet." Already they know and own him as Lord of all; not yet have they seen all things brought under his subjection. Here, then, is the eschatological reminder of who, and whose, they are: glad followers of him who is King of kings and Lord of lords, before whom at God's eschatological wrapup every knee shall bow to pay him the homage due his name.

Although the passage has the ring of doxology to it, it lacks the poetry that has preceded, which was abetted primarily by the participial constructions.[5] Indeed, everything has changed. In Part I, Christ is the subject of all the verbs and participles; here God is the subject and Christ the object, who is recipient both of the divine "name" and of the worship offered by "every knee" and "every tongue," all to the glory of God.[6] If this is part of a hymn, it has no known parallels, either in Judaism, Hellenism, or in Paul.[7] The

---

see n. 14 on 2:5-11; cf. the discussion in O'Brien, 253-62, and the theological observations at the end of the paragraph (pp. 226-29 below).

4. The first to note this view of vv. 9-11 among English commentaries was Michael; most neglect it altogether, usually because by the time they come to this verse the context is forgotten in the interest of what Paul says about Christ himself. On the basis of his view of v. 5, Barth sees the vindication to come to the Philippians as a result of their being "in Christ." But such a view arose only for theological reasons — to be done with a kind of "imitatio Christi" that seems to imply personal effort and therefore to circumvent grace.

5. Cf. Silva (127) and O'Brien (232), who both recognize that this is a Pauline prose sentence and begin by describing its obvious parts, but who then continue to use the language of hymnody.

6. The whole, therefore, falls out into a kind of chiastic structure:

A       God has exalted him to the highest place
  B       by bestowing on him "the name" above other names
    C       at which name every knee shall bow
    C′       and every tongue confess (the name)
  B′       namely that the Lord is Jesus Christ
A′       all to the glory of God the Father

7. The lack of a Pauline parallel is highlighted when contrasted with Rom 11:33-36,

parallelism that does exist (in vv. 10-11) is the direct result of another piece of "intertextuality" in this letter;[8] indeed, the whole has been formulated to echo the oracle in Isa 45:18-24, where Yahweh (LXX, the "Lord"), Israel's savior, declares his exalted status over all gods and nations.[9]

**9** With an inferential "therefore also"[10] Paul draws the preceding narrative to its proper conclusion. Although he mentions neither the resurrection nor the ascension,[11] these two realities are presupposed by what he does say.[12] Paul's immediate interest lies elsewhere. Nor is what follows to be understood either as a *reward* for Christ's previous action[13] or as an assertion of his *victory* over the powers.[14] Rather it asserts the divine vindication of Christ's emptying himself and humbling himself in obedience by dying on a cross. As God's "yes" to *this* expression of "equality with God," God the Father "exalted him to the highest place and gave him the name that is above every name." Although expressed as a twofold action, most likely Paul intends

---

a doxologic passage, which appears in nicely balanced semitic parallelism. Cf. the "addition" to the prescript in Galatians, where in v. 4 he says of Christ: who gave himself for our sins, *in order that* he might deliver us . . . , *in keeping with* the will of God, to whom (God) be glory forever." As with the present passage, this is the stuff of creed, not hymn, which is expressed in the exalted language of praise but whose "poetry" is incidental, not hymnic.

8. See above on 1:20 and on 2:14-16 below.

9. It is a cause for some wonder that this sentence could be considered by some to be pre-Pauline and thus not by Paul (e.g., Käsemann, Beare, Martin), in light of (a) the Pauline form that it takes, (b) the typically Pauline intertextuality which forms the heart of it (and the use of Isa 45:23 in particular; cf. Rom 14:11), (c) the Pauline language that abounds (the two main verbs; the confession of Jesus as Lord), and (d) the thoroughly Pauline outlook theologically. And all of this is an undisputed Pauline letter!

10. Gk. διὸ καί; the conjunction itself (διό) is always inferential and never slips into modified expressions, such as resumption, which is so characteristic of οὖν. Although it is possible that the καί is correlative, functioning with the καί at the beginning of the next clause to emphasize "both . . . and" with regard to God's activity of exalting and name bestowing, much more likely it is to be understood as intensifying the conjunction, which BAGD suggest "denot[es] that the inference is self-evident." For this usage in Paul, see 2 Cor 1:20; 4:13 (2x); 5:9; Rom 4:22; 15:22.

11. The absence of which some, therefore, consider to reflect non-Pauline authorship. But in fact many of these kinds of creedal statements, most of which in Paul are soteriological, do not mention the Resurrection.

12. G. Howard, "Phil 2:6-11," has taken the human Jesus view, which denies pre-existence in vv. 6-7 (see n. 41 on v. 6), to its logical conclusion, by arguing that this passage also speaks only of the human (albeit risen) Jesus. But this is to pile still further exegetical improbabilities onto a view that is already loaded with them. It is not surprising that he has found no followers.

13. E.g., Meyer, 99; Martin, 100; Houlden, 77; Silva, 127-28.

14. E.g., Lohmeyer, Käsemann, Beare, Caird, Martin.

the two verbs to point to a single reality: that God highly exalted Christ *by*[15] gracing[16] him with "the name." Both parts of the sentence, however, raise issues that need closer examination.

First, in asserting that God has "highly exalted"[17] Christ, Paul uses a compound of the ordinary verb for "exalt" with the preposition *hyper,* whose basic meaning is "above." On the basis of a certain understanding of v. 6 (what Christ did not "seize" was something *not previously his*), some see Paul as stressing that Christ has been rewarded for his humiliation by having been given a *higher* "position" than he had heretofore.[18] Others see an emphasis on his victory *over* the powers, although that concern is foreign to the narrative and must be inferred on the basis of an (almost certainly) incorrect understanding of "in heaven and on earth and under the earth." But the verb "highly exalted" implies neither of these. Paul virtually holds the copyright on *hyper* compounds in the NT, and in the vast majority of cases they magnify or express excess,[19] not position. No one would imagine, for example, a positional interpretation for the similar compound in Rom 8:37 ("we are *more than conquerors* [probably Pauline coinage] through Christ"). Likewise here, God has "highly exalted" Christ, meaning exalted him to the highest possible degree.

But what does Paul intend by "the name that is above every name"? Here the options are basically two,[20] "Jesus" or "Lord." On the one hand, there is much to be said for "the name" to refer to his earthly name "Jesus."[21] That, after all, is what is picked up in the next phrase, "at the name of *Jesus.*"

---

15. Thus reading the καί as epexegetic and the sentence as a hendiadys, where the second verb elaborates or fills out the meaning of the first. On this usage in Paul, see esp. 1 Cor 11:22 ("or do you despise the church of God *by* humiliating the have-nots"). So also Silva, 128-29.

16. Gk. ἐχαρίσατο, the verb formed from the noun χάρις ("grace") and a Pauline favorite; see the discussion on 1:29 above.

17. Gk. ὑπερύψωσεν, found only here in the NT.

18. It might be in a sense that in the chronology of heaven as it intersects with earth Christ has assumed a "new role" as it were (as sympathetic high priest, for example, who knows our suffering from the inside). But it is doubtful that one can mine "positional" significance out of that kind of understanding.

19. See MHT, 2.326; as they point out, the English equivalent is our "over" compounds (e.g., overjoyed, overburden, overdevelop), or as many have put it, the emphasis is on the superlative, not comparative.

20. "Name" sometimes refers to one's character, or reputation, as in the first petition of the Lord's Prayer; but in light of the definite article with "name" that seems untenable here. So also with Lightfoot's "the title of dignity" (cf. Beare). Both of these miss the role of the Isaiah oracle in the passage as a whole. In this case *the* name, meaning "the well-known" name, probably reflects an OT phenomenon where "the name" was a periphrasis for Yahweh.

21. For this view, see Meyer, Alford, Eadie, Vincent, and more recently, Moule ("Reflexions," 270) and Silva.

If so, then Paul does not mean that he has now been given that name, but that in highly exalting him, God has bestowed on the name of Jesus a significance that excels all other names. Moreover, "Jesus" is in fact a *name,* whereas "Lord" could be argued to be a title.[22]

On the other hand, most believe that the bestowing on him of the name "Lord," as the equivalent of Yahweh, is how Jesus has been exalted to the highest place.[23] Indeed, were it not for the phrase "at the name of Jesus" in the next clause, this would be the universal point of view. In favor of it is the second part of the result clause (v. 11), that every tongue will confess that "the *Lord* is Jesus Christ." But what favors it the most is the clear "intertextuality" that is in process here.[24] The twofold result clause that makes up our vv. 10 and 11 is a direct borrowing of language from Isa 45:23, where Yahweh (the Lord) says that "before me (the Lord) every knee shall bow and every tongue will swear (LXX, confess)" that "in the Lord alone are righteousness and strength." This emphasis on Yahweh, "the Lord,"[25] as the one unto whom all shall give obeisance, seems to certify that what Paul has in mind is none other than *the* name, Yahweh itself, but in its Greek form of "the Lord," which has now been "given" to Jesus.[26] On the meaning and significance of this name, see on v. 11.

We should note finally that this declaration of Jesus as "Lord" would probably not be lost on believers in a city whose inhabitants are Roman citizens and who are devotees of "lords many," including "lord Caesar." Paul well

22. So Meyer, 100.

23. So, *inter alia,* Kennedy, Plummer, Michael, Lohmeyer, Barth, Müller, Beare, Hendriksen, Collange, Bruce, Hawthorne, and most specialized studies on the passage.

24. That the intertextuality is certain is verified by Paul's citation of this same passage from the LXX in Rom 14:11, where it appears to reinforce that all people, including believers, will appear before God's "judgment seat." This citation is especially noteworthy as demonstrating intertextuality in the present passage, for two reasons: first, Paul begins the Romans citation with words from Isa 49:18 ("I live, says the Lord"), which indicates that Paul has the larger context of these Isaianic oracles in view; and second, because in both instances he cites a form of the text with ἐξομολογήσεται rather than ὀμεῖται (see n. 28 below), indicating that in the present instance he is not "loosely reworking" or "alluding" to this passage, as Kreitzer (*Jesus,* 115-16), e.g., suggests. This is a primary example of intertextuality, in which Paul purposely picks up the language of an earlier text (in this case, Isa 45:23), bringing with it the basic contextual concerns of that text, and now reapplies it to his own situation. See the discussion on 1:20.

25. An emphasis, it should be pointed out, that runs through the whole of Isa 41–55 (see esp. 42:8, "I am Yahweh God [ἐγώ κύριος ὁ θεός], that is my name"!; cf. 41:17, 21; 42:5, 6, 13, 21; 43:3, 10, 12, *et passim*).

26. We might note further (1) that this interpretation removes the awkwardness of Christ's being "granted" a name he had already borne during the time of his incarnation; and (2) that it fits the Pauline view of things, in that the basic confession of believers is that Jesus is Lord (v. 11).

222

knows to whom he is writing these words, especially since he is now one of the emperor's prisoners and the Philippians are suffering at the hands of Roman citizens as well.

**10** The result[27] of God's exaltation of Jesus is expressed in two coordinate clauses taken directly from the LXX of Isa 45:23,[28] both of which stress that the whole creation shall offer him homage and worship, presumably at his Parousia. Thus the narrative covers the whole gamut: It begins in eternity past with Christ's "*being* in the 'form' of God," then focuses on his incarnation, and finally expresses his exaltation as something already achieved (v. 9), thus presupposing resurrection and ascension; now it concludes by pointing to the eschatological future, when all created beings shall own his lordship.[29]

First, then, "at[30] the name of Jesus[31]," the Lord, "every knee shall bow." The whole created order shall give him obeisance. The "bowing of the knee" is

---

27. Gk. ἵνα, which in classical Greek expresses purpose, and still does for the most part in the NT, including Paul. But there are several instances in Paul where the purpose seems to embrace result more than aim (cf. v. 2 above; see Fee, *Presence,* 434-37, on Gal 5:17); cf. O'Brien, 239. Most interpreters see it strictly as purpose.

28. Thus Paul: πᾶν γόνυ κάμψῃ [ ] καὶ πᾶσα γλῶσσα ἐξομολογήσηται
   Isa 45:23: κάμψει πᾶν γόνυ καὶ ἐξομολογήσεται πᾶσα γλῶσσα.

There is a considerable textual variant in the LXX manuscript tradition, between ἐξομολογήσεται (A Q ℵ[c]) and ομεῖται (B ℵ Lucian Catenae). The latter reading was almost certainly created by Origen in his Hexapla as a "correction" toward the Masoretic text. In any case, Paul is the certain evidence that this reading existed (in Tarsus?) in the first Christian century. That Paul cites it this way in two instances, once (Rom 14:11) precisely (verbally) as in Codex Alexandrinus (but with the transposition πᾶσα γλῶσσα ἐξομολογήσεται), verifies that this is the reading he knows, not one that he created. Furthermore, the transposition, slight as it is textually, indicates that Paul was probably citing from memory, while at the same time it verifies that Alexandrinus is not an adaptation to Paul.

29. This seems so clearly the perspective of the whole, that one is caught by surprise that there has been debate as to the "time" of this event (see Martin, *Carmen,* 266-70). On this matter, Lohmeyer (97) surely had it right, that it speaks of the eschatological future from the perspective of "a present in God." This is nothing other than the "already/not yet" eschatological framework that informs the whole of Pauline theology. See the Introduction, pp. 50-52.

30. Gk. ἐν; some debate exists as to whether this is the object (so most interpreters) or medium (so Kennedy, Plummer) of worship (the language is Michael's, 96). Ordinarily one would think the latter; the context and structure of the sentence indicate the former, in the sense of "in honor of his name," is in view (as GNB, Loh-Nida, O'Brien). However, to use this preposition as a way of suggesting that the worship is not directed *to* Jesus, but through him to the Father (as e.g., Collange), seems to press for a fixed sense to a flexible preposition, while missing the point of the whole passage.

31. Most likely this genitive means "the name (= Lord) which has been bestowed on Jesus," not "the name Jesus itself."

a common idiom for doing homage, sometimes in prayer, but always in recognition of the authority of the god or person to whom one is offering such obeisance.[32] The significance of Paul's using the language of Isaiah in this way lies with his substituting "at the name of Jesus" for the "to me" of Isa 45:23, which refers to Yahweh, the God of Israel. In this stirring oracle (Isa 45:18-24a) Yahweh is declared to be God alone, over all that he has created and thus over all other gods and nations. And he is Israel's savior, whom they can thus fully trust. In vv. 22-24a Yahweh, while offering salvation to all but receiving obeisance in any case, declares that "*to me* every knee shall bow." Paul now asserts that through Christ's resurrection and at his ascension God has transferred this right to obeisance to the Son; he is the Lord to whom every knee shall eventually bow. There is in this language no hint that those who bow are acknowledging his salvation; on the contrary they *will* bow to his sovereignty at the End, even if they are not now yielding to it.

Also in keeping with the Isaianic oracle, but now interrupting the language of the citation itself, Paul declares the full scope of the homage that Christ will one day receive: every knee "of those in the heavenlies and of those on earth and of those under the earth" shall bow to the authority inherent in his name.[33] In keeping with the oracle, especially that "the Lord" is the creator of the heavens and the earth (45:18), Paul is purposely throwing the net of Christ's sovereignty over the whole of created beings.[34] Those "of heaven" refer to all heavenly beings, angels and demons;[35] those of earth refer to all those who are

32. See, e.g., Ps 95:6; Mark 15:19; Luke 5:8; 22:41; Acts 7:60; 9:40; Eph 3:14; cf. the discussions in *NIDNTT,* 2.859-60 (Schönweiss), and *EDNT,* 1.257-58 (Nützel).

33. Some have argued for universalism on the basis of statements like this; but that flies full in the face of 1:28 (cf. 1 Cor 1:18; 2 Cor 4:3; etc.).

34. But it seems unlikely that the three words are neuter and intend to imply "the whole range of creation," including inanimate creation, as Lightfoot (115) argues, followed by Plummer, 49; Carr, *Angels,* 86-89; Silva, 133.

35. So most interpreters. Although this language will surely include "the powers," there seems to be no particular emphasis on them, nor is there any reason to suppose that all three designations refer to "spirit powers" (as, e.g., Dibelius, Käsemann, Beare, Cullmann, Martin [*Carmen,* 257-65], Gnilka, Traub [*TDNT,* 5.541-42], Nützel [*EDNT,* 1.258]). This view, which has been thoroughly refuted by Hofius (*Christushymnus,* 20-40; cf. Carr, *Angels,* 86-89), is the direct result of faulty methodology, which (1) presupposes that the "hymn" is pre-Pauline (and therefore non-Pauline), (2) seeks to root its "background" in Gnostic or hellenistic cosmology, and (3) then reads that alleged "background" into its present Pauline usage. Against it, besides this metholodological weakness, are: (1) that although Paul understands the powers to inhabit the "heavenlies" (Eph 1:20-21; 2:2; 3:10; 6:12), there is no evidence that he understood them also to inhabit earth and Sheol (on the misreading of 1 Cor 2:6-8 in this way, see Fee, *First Corinthians,* 103-4); (2) that Paul's primary background is the OT, and the present language, though not found in the OT, thoroughly represents the cosmology of the OT (see, e.g., J. Guhrt, *NIDNTT,*

living on earth at his Parousia, including those who are currently causing suffering in Philippi; and those "under the earth" probably refer to "the dead," who also shall be raised to acknowledge his lordship over all.

**11**   Second, not only shall every creature bend the knee and offer the obeisance that is due Christ's name, but "every tongue"[36] shall express that homage in the language of the confessing[37] — but currently suffering — church: Jesus Christ is Lord. In its Pauline occurrences this confession always takes the form, "the Lord is Jesus," to which he here adds "Christ." For Paul this confession is the line of demarcation between believer and nonbeliever (Rom 10:9). Such confession, he argues in 1 Cor 12:3, can come only by way of the Spirit; hence the crucial role of the Spirit in conversion. This confession in Rom 10:9 is linked with conviction about the resurrection of Jesus; that same combination is undoubtedly in view here. When at the End all creation beholds the risen Jesus, they will on that basis declare that *Kyrios* is none other than the Jesus who was crucified and whom Christians worship. But the confession will not then be that of conversion, but of final acknowledgment that "God has made this Jesus, whom you crucified, both Lord and Christ" (Acts 2:36).

Despite an occasional demurrer, there can be little question that this confession arose in the early Jewish Christian community,[38] as the Aramaic "Maranatha" in 1 Cor 16:22 bears striking evidence. Thus, in the very earliest Aramaic-speaking communities, the language that belonged to God alone is now being addressed to Christ in corporate invocation. One can scarcely gainsay the christological implications of this confession in the present passage. On the one hand, in the Jewish synagogue the appellation "Lord" had long before been substituted for God's "name" (Yahweh). The early believers had now transferred that "name" (Lord) to the risen Jesus. Thus, Paul says, in raising Jesus from the dead, God has exalted him to the highest place and bestowed on him the name of God — in the Hebrew sense of *the Name,*

---

1.522-23); and (3) most importantly, there is not a hint in the present letter that the Philippians were distressed by the "powers"; their problem is with people, whose opposition is bringing them considerable suffering. Thus, if there is emphasis at all in such a broad throwing of the net (and there probably is), it would seem to be — for the sake of the Philippians — that it includes those who are currently responsible for their suffering.

36. Gk. γλῶσσα. Although this word sometimes refers to languages, and BAGD think so here ("*every language* = every person, regardless of the language he [or she] speaks"), Paul is more likely picking up the sense of the LXX of Isa 45:23, that the "tongue of every person" shall confess — which is also in keeping with the parallel, "knee."

37. The ὅτι is a ὅτι-recitativum (used to introduce a quote), thus indicating, as elsewhere in Paul, that these are the actual words of the confession.

38. On this question see esp. the article on "Lord" in *DPL,* 560-69, by Hurtado; see also his *One God.*

referring to his investiture with God's power and authority.[39] On the other hand, Paul's monotheism is kept intact by the final phrase, "unto the glory of God the Father."[40] Thus very much in keeping with 1 Cor 8:6, where there is only one God (the Father, *from* whom and *for* whom are all things, including ourselves) and only one Lord (Jesus Christ, *through* whom are all things and we through him), so here, this final sentence begins with God's exalting Christ by bestowing on him "the name" and concludes on the same theological note, that all of this is to God the Father's own glory.[41]

In the light of the grandeur of this passage (all of 2:6-11), one can easily forget why it is here. Paul's reasons are twofold: first, as throughout the letter, to focus on Christ himself, and thus, second, in this instance to point to him as the ultimate model of the self-sacrificing love to which he is calling the Philippians.[42] That Paul himself has not forgotten where he is going becomes evident in the application that immediately follows, where the Philippians are called upon to "obey," just as the self-abasing One "obeyed" the will of his Father. But we should note further that both of Paul's concerns transfer fully into the ongoing life of the church and the believer.

---

39. Cf. Kreitzer (*Jesus,* 116), whose language I have here borrowed.

40. Cf. Kreitzer (*Jesus,* 161), cited also by Hurtado, *DPL,* 565. Cf. 1:11, where the fruit of righteousness comes "through Christ Jesus unto the glory and praise of God."

41. That is, this phrase goes with the whole narrative (from v. 6), not just the final clause (so Meyer).

42. Cf. Francis Bland Tucker's hymn, based on this passage (set to Ralph Vaughan Williams's *Sine Nomine*):

[1]All praise to thee, for thou, O King divine,
didst yield the glory that of right was thine,
that in our darkened hearts thy grace might shine:
allelujah!

[2]Thou cam'st to us in lowliness of thought;
by thee the outcast and the poor were sought,
and by thy death was God's salvation wrought:
allelujah!

[3]Let this mind be in us which was in thee
who was a servant that we might be free,
humbling thyself to death on Calvary:
allelujah!

[4]Wherefore, by God's eternal purpose, thou
art high exalted o'er all creatures now,
and given the name to which all knees shall bow:
allelujah!

[5]Let every tongue confess with one accord
in heaven and earth that Jesus Christ is Lord;
and God the Father be by all adored:
allelujah!

As a wonderful experience of divine appointment (and perhaps humor, given my view that the passage is not a hymn), this was one of three hymns and contemporary choruses (including Graham Kendrick's "Servant King" [see n. 17 on v. 8]) sung in worship on the Sunday after I had finished this section of the commentary. The passage obviously sings, even if it was not originally a hymn!

First, whatever else the Christian faith is, and whatever Christian life is all about, it finds its central focus ever and always on Christ. Here we have spelled out before us in living color both the *what* and the *why* of Paul's affirmation, "for me to live is Christ." This narrative puts it into focus: Paul believed that in Jesus Christ the true nature of the living God had been revealed ultimately and finally. God is not a grasping, self-centered being, but is most truly known through the one who, himself in the form of God and thus equal with God, poured himself out in sacrificial love by taking the lowest place, the role of a slave, whose love for his human creatures found its consummate expression in his death on the cross. That this is God's own nature and doing has been attested for all time by Christ Jesus's divine vindication; he has been exalted by God to the highest place by having been given the name of God himself: The Lord is none other than Jesus Christ. This is therefore why for Paul "to live is Christ." Any faith that falls short of this is simply not the Christian faith.

But second, Paul's point is, in the words of the poet, "'Tis the way the Master went, should not the servant tread it still?" That Christ serves for us as a paradigm for Christian life is not, as some fear, a betrayal of Paul's gospel.[43] On the contrary, it reinforces a significant aspect of his gospel, namely that there is no genuine *life in Christ* that is not at the same time, by the power of the Holy Spirit, being regularly transformed into the *likeness of Christ*. A gospel of grace, which omits obedience, is not Pauline in any sense; obedience, after all, is precisely the point made in the application that follows (v. 12). To be sure, the indicative must precede the imperative, or all is lost; but it does not eliminate the imperative, or all is likewise lost.

The behavioral concern of this passage is precisely in keeping with the Pauline paraenesis found everywhere. Paul's gospel has inherent in it that those who are in Christ will also walk worthy of Christ (1:27). Thus, in Pauline ethics, the principle is love, the pattern is Christ, the power is the Spirit, and their ultimate purpose the glory of God — all of which has been provided for in the death and resurrection of Christ. The appeal in the present passage is to a unity in Christ that for Paul was a *sine qua non* of the evidential reality of his gospel at work in his communities. The bases of the appeal, Christ, God's love, and the Spirit, are set forth in v. 1. The Christian graces absolutely necessary for such behavior are selflessness and humility, in which one looks not only to one's own interests but also — especially — to those of others

---

43. See n. 14 on 2:5-11 above. As noted there, the tendency on the part of some is to rail against something of a "straw man," as though to see Christ as paradigm is to think that "all that a Christian has to do is to follow in the Master's footsteps" (Martin, *Carmen*, 289). That is hardly Paul's point, nor that of those who take the passage as Paul intends — as a paradigm to reinforce unity within the community.

(vv. 3-4). Here is where the example of Christ comes in. Those who are Christ's (v. 1) must also have his "mindset" (vv. 5 — 11).

However, to insist that in context the basic thrust of this passage is "Christ as paradigm" of a certain mindset does not mean that there are no other agenda, including paradigmatic ones. Both the length and pattern of the passage suggest that Paul is laying a much broader theological foundation, probably for the whole letter. In the first place, the mention of Christ's death on the cross as paradigm at the same time reminds them of the basis of their faith in the first place. It is that death, after all, that lies at the heart of everything. To put it another way, the appeal to Christ's example in his suffering and death makes its point precisely because it presupposes that they will simultaneously recall the saving significance of that death.

Moreover, there is also an emphasis in this letter on *imitatio* with regard to suffering (1:29-30; 3:10, 21). Those who are privileged to believe in Christ are also privileged to suffer for him; indeed to share in those sufferings is part of knowing him. Hence, this passage, with Christ's humbling himself to the point of death on the cross, will also serve as the theological ground for that concern. That, indeed, seems to make the best sense of the otherwise unusual emphasis in 3:10 that knowing Christ includes the "participation in his sufferings, being conformed[44] to his death." Thus Christ's death once again serves as paradigm.

Finally, the note of eschatological glory in vv. 9-11 is also struck more than once in this letter (1:6; 1:10-11; 1:21-24; 3:11-14; 3:20-21). For this, too, Christ serves both as exalted Lord and as example or forerunner. His vindication, which followed his humiliation, is found in his present and future lordship, to which both the Philippians and (ultimately) their opponents bow. But that vindication also becomes paradigm. Those who now suffer for Christ, and walk worthy of Christ, shall also at his coming be transformed into the likeness of "the body of his (present) glory" (3:21).

Thus the narrative summarizes the centrality of Christ in Pauline theology. His death secured redemption for his people; but at the same time it serves as pattern for their present life in the Spirit, while finally we shall share in the eschatological glory and likeness that are presently his. And all of this "to the glory of God the Father."

In the final analysis, therefore, this passage stands at the heart of Paul's understanding of God. Christ serves as pattern, to be sure; but he does so as the one who most truly expresses God's nature. As God, Christ poured himself out, not seeking his own advantage. As man — and not ceasing to be God — he humbled himself unto death on the cross. That this is what God is like is

---

44. Gk. συμμορφιζόμενος, where Paul is surely intending them to hear the echo of Christ's μορφή from this passage.

228

the underlying Pauline point; and since God is in process of recreating us in his image, this becomes the heart of the present appeal. The Philippians — and we ourselves — are not called upon simply to "imitate God" by what we do, but to have this very mind, the mind of Christ, developed in us, so that we too bear God's image in our attitudes and relationships within the Christian community — and beyond.

## D. APPLICATION AND FINAL APPEAL (2:12-18)

Because of the splendor of the preceding passage, it is easy to forget its aim. But Paul has not forgotten. At issue is the gospel in Philippi: first of all their own "salvation" (v. 12), evidenced by continuing "obedience" — like that of their Savior (v. 8) — but as always, second, with an eye toward evangelism, the effect of the gospel in the world (v. 16). Thus, he returns to his present concern — "obedience" expressed through a common "mindset," for the sake of Christ and the gospel — by applying to their situation what he has just written in 2:6-11.

The application is in three sentences (vv. 12-13, 14-16, 17-18), which together form a single appeal, reflecting a threefold concern: (1) that they return to their common cause, partly (2) for the sake of the gospel in the world, and partly also (3) for Paul's sake, and thus for their mutual eschatological joy. The first two sentences are imperatives, urging first that they show their "obedience" by getting their corporate act together (working out their salvation, is Paul's way of putting it). To which imperative, and lest he be misunderstood, he immediately appends a theological word, a word of ultimate encouragement: God has committed himself to effecting their "obedience" for his own good pleasure. In the second imperative, echoing language from the Pentateuch and Daniel,[1] Paul forbids "complaining and arguing" — for the sake of the "crooked and depraved" Philippi in which they "shine as lights" as they hold fast the message that brings life. That sentence concludes on the note of Paul's own ministry among them — that if they thus obey, it will not have been in vain — which leads to the final sentence (vv. 17-18), where he returns to the themes of his suffering, their faith, and mutual joy.

With these final words the argument begun in 1:27 thus comes full

1. On the basis of the echoes of Deut 32:5 in v. 15, Michael (followed by Beare and Loh-Nida) proposed that Paul in this section is making a "farewell" speech, consciously adapting Moses' farewell speech to Israel. While there can be little question of the intertextuality in vv. 14-16, it is doubtful whether one can read such a "farewell" speech back into vv. 12-13 as Michael does. See n. 16 below, and the discussion on vv. 14-18.

circle.[2] It began on the note of their walking worthy of the gospel whether Paul is present or absent. This concluding appeal begins on that theme (v. 12) and ends on the motif of their rejoicing together in their mutual suffering (vv. 17-18; cf. 1:18). And that leads directly to vv. 19-30, in which he goes on to "what's next" regarding his and their circumstances — that he expects to hear further about "their affairs," now in light of the present letter, after they have first learned further about "his affairs," and both from the same source, Timothy.

## 1. General Application — An Appeal to Obedience (2:12-13)

> 12*Therefore, my dear friends, as you have always obeyed — not only[3] in my presence, but now much more in my absence — continue to work out your salvation with fear and trembling, 13for it is God[4] who works in you to will and to act according to his good purpose.*

On the basis of what he has just said about Christ, Paul returns to the appeal to harmony that has been the primary concern since 1:27. Picking up the word "salvation" from 1:28, he urges that they flesh it out in their life together in Philippi. At least that is where the appeal is ultimately heading, as vv. 14-16 disclose. This first imperative thus serves as the "theme" sentence for the appeal,[5] by reminding them of three realities: (1) Paul's affection for them

---

2. In some ways it helps to put 1:12-26 into perspective as well. Paul began the narrative about "his affairs" by noting his imprisonment to be for the "advance" *and* the "defense" of the gospel (1:12, 16; cf. 1:7); 2:15-16 indicate that this twofold concern regarding the gospel is likewise the point of his appeal in 1:27-30, namely that they "stand firm" and "contend together" for the gospel. But "complaining and arguing" deflect their calling to "brighten the corner where they are," as God's "blameless" children. The appeal of vv. 15-16, we should note further, also supports what was noted on 2:1-4, that their being of "one mind" does not lean in the direction of their all thinking alike, but of their being committed to the common cause of the gospel.

3. Although Paul's sentence comes out nearly at this point, his Greek actually reads "not *as* in my presence only." The ὡς ("as") has been omitted by a few MSS (B 33 1241ˢ pc). The omission is easy to account for, since the conjunction implies that they might be obedient only when he was present, but not when absent.

4. Although it makes no significant difference in meaning, Paul's Greek is a good example of an idiom that gives the lie to the Jehovah's Witnesses treatment of John 1:1. Θεός is without the article here just as there, and for the same reason: "Colwell's rule," that a definite predicate noun which precedes the copulative lacks the definite article with the noun. D and the later MajT add the article, recognizing that Paul is referring to God, not "a god," but in so doing quash a NT idiom.

5. Cf. Calvin, Meyer, Silva, O'Brien, who also use the language "general admonition/exhortation" for these two verses. But "general" should not then give rise to a noncontextual interpretation, as so often happens, as though Paul were now turning to

and their long-term relationship with him; (2) their own long-time "obe-dience" as far as the gospel is concerned; and (3) God's work in them effecting their obedience for his own good pleasure — the same God who exalted Christ, and for whose glory the whole world will pay homage to his Son.

Everything in the sentence echoes something that has gone before: The vocative "my beloved" recalls the tenderness and affection of 1:8; the re-minder of their long-time "obedience" recalls 1:5 ("their partnership in the gospel from the first"), but now comes hard on the heels of Christ's obedience mentioned in v. 8; Paul's "presence or absence" recalls the same kind of interruptive word in 1:27; their common "salvation" that is to be "worked out" among them picks up the language of 1:28; God as the one who is at work in them for this end echoes their salvation as "from God" (1:28); and God's prompting and leading their obedience for his own "good pleasure" is reminiscent of the immediately preceding "to the glory of God." Although Christ is not mentioned directly in this imperative — indeed, in light of vv. 6-11, is there any need? — everything is once again predicated on the three-way bond that holds the letter together: between him, them, and Christ and the gospel (salvation).

**12** This has long been a difficult passage, especially for evangelical Protestants,[6] who, on the one hand, tend to individualize Paul's corporate imperatives (such as this one) and, on the other hand, cannot imagine Paul suggesting that salvation is something the individual must "work out" for oneself — even though it is with God's help. But Paul's concern lies else-where. The "so then"[7] with which this sentence begins indicates that he is

---

address the matter of their individual salvation (as, e.g., in Meyer, Vincent, Hendriksen, et al., whose comments on this passage are altogether soteriological, in terms of the believer's individual salvation).

6. Evidence for this is the fact that this passage has been included in two recent books on "hard sayings" in Paul, published by evangelical publishers; see R. Stein *(Difficult Passages in the Epistles)* and M. Brauch *(Hard Sayings of Paul).* In earlier years this passage served as the fountain for a good bit of vitriol between Protestants and Roman Catholics over "grace" and "works," the result of coming to a passage with a theological agenda in hand, rather than the primary exegetical concern of hearing the passage within its own historical and literary context.

7. Gk. ὥστε, which usually indicates that an inference is to be made from what has just been said. While there is nothing wrong with the NIV's "therefore" as a translation of this word, it misses some of the flavor of Paul's Greek. This conjunction is used by Paul especially in contexts where he is applying an argument to the local situation (another reason to believe that the issue here is case-specific, not simply general paraenesis). Cf. 1 Thess 4:18; 1 Cor 3:21; 4:5; 10:12; 11:33; 14:39; 15:58; Phil 4:18, all of which are followed by imperatives as here (cf. 1 Cor 3:7; 7:38; 11:27; 14:22; 2 Cor 4:12; 5:16, 17; Gal 4:3; Rom 7:4, 12, where it is followed by an indicative, but still functions to introduce an inferred conclusion of an argument).

about to apply the appeal of 1:27–2:5, now by way of vv. 6-11, to the case specific situation of the believing *community* in Philippi. What follows this imperative (in vv. 14-16) makes that certain.

But it takes a while in Paul's sentence for him to get to the imperative,[8] because first he will remind them of his affection for them and of their long history of "obedience." His affection is expressed in the vocative, "my beloved friends."[9] Even though this vocative occurs elsewhere in Paul, its three occurrences in this letter, as in Phlm 16, should be understood in light of the very personal and warm affection that Paul holds for these friends.[10] That is further evidenced by the appeal to his and their long-term relationship, expressed in terms of their "obedience" both when he is present and absent from them.[11]

Hence he begins, "just as[12] you have always obeyed."[13] But to whom has such obedience been given? On the one hand, Paul can urge "obedience" to his own words (2 Thess 3:15), a sense that probably lies close at hand elsewhere as well (e.g., 2 Cor 2:9; 7:15; Phlm 21). On the other hand, the combination in 2 Cor 10:5-6 of "every act of disobedience" as having to do with "obedience to Christ" probably gives us the clue for all of these passages,

8. Indeed, this is a very Germanic sentence, with the verb in last position preceded by a long clause before one gets to it (in Paul's order, "just as always you have obeyed, not as in my presence only but now all the more in my absence, with fear and trembling your own salvation work out"). Because of the distance between the μή and the verb, it is easy to lose sight of the fact that grammatically it goes with the imperative at the end, and not with "obedience." But some have made far too much of this. If Paul's sentence is not tidy, it works in terms of intent. At issue is "obedience" to the gospel, as that is spelled out in their life together (i.e., as their common salvation is worked out in their midst). That concern is interrupted by the reminder that this is how they "obeyed" when he was present and by "how much more" he wants them to obey in his absence. Thus the μή negates the imperative only *indirectly:* In working out their salvation they are *not* to do so as though such obedience were only forthcoming when he was among them.

9. Gk. ἀγαπητοί μου (lit., "my beloved"); in Paul see 1 Cor 10:14 (cf. 1 Thess 2:8; 2 Cor 7:1; 12:19; Rom 12:19, where it occurs without μου, and 1 Cor 15:58 and Phlm 16, where, as in Phil 4:1, it is also joined to "brothers and sisters").

10. See on 1:8 and esp. 4:1, where it occurs twice, framing that appeal in a most striking way ("My dearly loved brothers and sisters . . . beloved friends").

11. All of this, it should be noted, is the "stuff" of friendship. See the Introduction, pp. 2-7.

12. Gk. καθώς, introducing a comparative clause; see on 1:7 above. But in contrast to that sentence, and others like it, the point of comparison will follow in this case. Thus the basic elements of his sentence read: "Just as you have always obeyed . . . so now work out your own salvation." *Contra* Hawthorne (see n. 24 below).

13. Gk. ὑπακούσατε; for Pauline usage, of churches with regard to obedience to Christ and the gospel, see 2 Cor 2:9; 7:15; 10:5, 6; cf. 2 Thess 3:14 and Phlm 21.

including the present one. As his letter to the Romans makes clear,[14] for Paul *faith in* Christ is ultimately expressed as *obedience to* Christ, not in the sense of following the rules, but of coming totally under his lordship, of being devoted completely to him. This is the only "obedience" to his own words that Paul cares anything about.[15] That this is the sense here seems certain, since it follows so closely the twofold reminder of Christ's own obedience that led to the cross and of his present status as Lord of all. Thus Paul starts on this note of reminder, that they have always given evidence of their faith by their obedience to Christ.

But before he goes on to the "so now," the geographical distance factor which keeps popping up in this letter[16] finds expression once more. The repetition of this language from 1:27, plus the fact that this is what is taken up next (2:19-24), indicates a point of obvious concern. He longs to be with them, not only for mutual joy, but also for their "progress" in the faith (1:25); but he is now absent from them, at a time when some mending is needed. Thus, on the basis of his and their close relationship, Paul speaks this way while "absent from them" as his way of appealing to them, as though he were actually present. This in turn best explains the unusual way of putting it here:

14. See esp. his language "the obedience of faith" (Rom 1:5; cf. 15:18), which in that letter means something like "obedience that characterizes true faith." This is made certain by the interchange of "faith" and "obedience" in 1:8 ("your faith is proclaimed all over the world") and 16:19, which becomes "your obedience is known by all." Thus obedience means to respond to God (Rom 15:18) by receiving the gospel (10:16); whereas those who reject God do so by "not obeying the gospel of our Lord Jesus" (2 Thess 1:8).

15. Thus those who stress obedience only to Paul (e.g., Barth, Dibelius, Gnilka, Martin, Loh-Nida) or to God (e.g., Lightfoot, Melick) do not seem to have it quite right. In light of the following qualifier, about their "obedience" (whether Paul is present or absent), it is hard to escape an emphasis on "obedience" with regard to Paul's admonitions; but in light of the larger context (Christ's obedience [v. 8]; his lordship [vv. 9-11]) it is equally hard to escape that "obedience" to Christ and the gospel is the only obedience to his words that Paul could imagine. So most interpreters.

16. See esp. 1:27 above; but cf. 1:8, 24-26; 2:19-24; 4:10. Michael (99, followed by Beare and Houlden), as part of his overall view of this passage as a "farewell speech," sees this language as referring to "life" and "death," i.e., that Paul is here preparing them to carry on after his death (= they now have to work out their own salvation because the apostle will not be around much longer to help them; so also Hendriksen, Collange, Caird, but without Michael's scenario). But there is nothing in favor of such a view (even the use of the Deuteronomy echo in v. 15 is misguided) and everything against it: (1) these words are a deliberate recall of the similar language in 1:27, where there is not hint of "death"; (2) this language belongs especially to matters of friendship (see n. 11), which culturally has nothing to do with "death"; (3) Paul clearly expects to be released from this imprisonment (1:24-26; 2:24); and (4) he immediately follows this passage not with directions about how to carry on after he is gone, but how to carry on *now*, because he is about to send Timothy and he himself will be coming soon — or so he firmly believes (2:19-24).

"not as (though)[17] in my presence only." They have had a long history of obedience to Christ and the gospel, whether Paul was present or absent; now that he cannot be present, and some differences among them have arisen, he urges them to get on with their obedience "all the more so"[18] in his absence,[19] so that it would not appear as if his presence alone prompted them to obey.

That brings him finally to the imperative, what all of this was aiming at in the first place: "Work out[20] your own[21] salvation." This choice of language is predicated on his prior use of "salvation" in 1:28, which, he asserted, is "from God." But "salvation" is not only something they receive; it is something they *do*. A great deal of unnecessary ink has been spilt over this passage, as to whether "salvation" has to do with the individual believer[22]

17. Gk. ὡς, which (*contra* Collange, Hawthorne, O'Brien) functions here as a comparative particle; it could thus mean "just as you do in my presence" (so Meyer). But the combination μὴ ὡς . . . μόνον suggests a degree of doubt on the part of Paul. Collange's view (argued for in more detail by Hawthorne and followed by O'Brien) is that ὡς = "when" in the sense of "in view of" (although how one can make that leap escapes me) and thus speaks to his anticipated παρουσία. But besides a nearly impossible meaning for ὡς, this view founders on the position of μόνον ("only"), which seems to demand that the obedience spoken of had to do with their obedience *only* when he was present, not "in view only of my coming."

18. Gk. ἀλλὰ νῦν πολλῷ μᾶλλον (= but now by how much more); cf. 1:23. Its force is brought out esp. in 2 Cor 3:9 and 11 (if the older covenant had glory, and it did, how much more the new covenant that is accompanied by the life-giving Spirit).

19. Gk. ἐν τῇ ἀπουσίᾳ μου, the cognate noun for the participle that occurs in 1:27; a NT hapax legomenon. Here, of course, it parallels ἐν τῇ παρουσίᾳ μου ("in my presence").

20. Gk. κατεργάζεσθε, a verb with a degree of flexibility. Its basic sense is to "accomplish" something, not in the sense of "fulfillment," but of "carrying out" a matter (cf. Rom 7:18: "to will is present"; but to "carry out" [κατεργάζεσθαι] what is willed is another matter). Under no circumstances can it be stretched to mean "work at," as though salvation were something that needed our work (as in good works) in order for it to be accomplished. On this see esp. Stein (*Difficult Passages,* 42-45).

21. Gk. (τὴν) ἑαυτῶν (σωτηρίαν). Some see Paul here as emphasizing the reflexive, suggesting either that it puts stress on each believer's salvation, or on *their own* salvation, now that Paul does not expect to be around much longer (see nn. 1 and 16 above — although some who hold this view are thinking only of Paul's present absence, not his anticipated death). But these views make too much of very little. While the reflexive at times does stress what belongs especially to the subject of a sentence (cf., e.g., vv. 3-4 above), that is usually made clear by some inherent contrast in the sentence. In other cases it functions very close to a normal possessive, except that by use of the reflexive it slightly intensifies the possessive as being one's own. This latter seems to be what is going on here. For his purposes Paul could easily have said ὑμῶν σωτηρίαν; he chose rather to use the reflexive, which strengthens the idea of its being their "possession." It must be noted (*pace* Kennedy, Müller, Hendriksen, et al.) that Paul has ways of individualizing plural commands, and the use of this reflexive is not one of them.

22. As, e.g., in Kennedy, Müller, Hendriksen, Silva, O'Brien.

or with the corporate life of the community. But that is a false dichotomy. The context makes it clear that this is not a soteriological text per se, dealing with "people getting saved" or "saved people persevering." Rather it is an ethical text, dealing with "how saved people live out their salvation" in the context of the believing community and the world. What Paul is referring to, therefore, is the *present* "outworking" of their *eschatological salvation* within the *believing community* in Philippi.[23] At issue is "obedience," pure and simple, which in this case is defined as their "working or carrying out in their corporate life the salvation that God has graciously given them." That they must comply with this injunction at the individual level is assumed, and that their final eschatological salvation will be realized personally and individually is a truth that does not need stating, because that is not at issue here. In Pauline theology people are saved one by one to be sure (which is the point of discontinuity with election in the OT), but (in continuity with the OT) they are saved so as to become a "people for God's name." The concern in this passage is with their being his people in Philippi, as v. 15 makes certain ("that you may become blameless and pure, God's children without fault in a crooked and depraved generation").

That "working out your salvation" has to do with "obedience" is verified both by the grammar and context. First, the imperative must be taken seriously for what it is, the apodosis (the "so then" clause) of a comparative sentence ("just as . . . so now"),[24] whose protasis ("just as") offers the

---

23. On the other hand, Silva and O'Brien rightly oppose what they call a purely "sociological" understanding of this imperative, so that "salvation" is watered down to mean something like "wholeness" within the community (as Michael, Beare, Martin, Loh-Nida, Hawthorne; Swift, "Theme," 245). One will have a hard time defending that understanding of this word on the basis of Pauline usage (as Hawthorne's resorting to some papyrus uses indicates). In a (correct, but unfortunate in terms of results) reaction to this view, Silva and O'Brien, despite an occasional demurrer, swing the pendulum to the other side, so that it becomes a case of "either/or" (i.e., either individual or community); whereas in Paul "salvation" is always "both/and." As Caird (125) put it, "Salvation in the New Testament is always an intensely personal, but never an individual, matter." On this question see further, Fee, *Presence,* 846-47, 876, where for the sake of stressing the corporate nature of the Pauline imperative I chose finally to discuss his ethics in the chapter on salvation and the people of God, rather than in the chapter on salvation and the individual. Martin's view, it should be noted, seems strikingly contradictory. On the one hand, he follows Käsemann in vigorously contending for a soteriological view of vv. 6-11 (= the "way of salvation" that serves as the basis for the paraenesis, vis-à-vis the passage serving as a paradigm); yet he then turns about and defines "salvation" in this passage as "wholeness."

24. So Silva (135, noted favorably by O'Brien), although not expressed grammatically. *Contra* Hawthorne, 98, who thinks the clause elliptical, requiring an assumed "so continue to obey" as an apodosis. But that is unnecessary, since the present imperative functions precisely in this way. For this usage in Paul cf. 1 Thess 2:4; 3:4; 5:11; 2 Cor 8:6.

primary clue as to what "working out their common salvation means"; it means to continue in their obedience to Christ. This is then picked up in the next clause; what God empowers in/among them is to will and do regarding the obedience spoken to in this first clause. And contextually that means that they stop whatever squabbling is going on and get on with being "God's blameless children" in pagan Philippi. Thus everything about the sentence and its context indicates that Paul with this imperative is not referring to the "salvation" of individual believers, but the salvation that God has wrought in making them a people of God for his name in Philippi, and that at issue is their getting on with it. Even though as before (vv. 4-5) they will have to respond individually, the imperative itself has to do with what takes place in their community life, as they return to their common cause with regard to the gospel.

Finally, they are to work out their salvation in this way "with fear and trembling." This unusual phrase, taken over from the OT,[25] occurs in some odd moments in Paul, so that it is not at all certain what he intends by these words — especially since the OT sense of "dread" seems to be missing altogether. In its first occurrence (1 Cor 2:3), which probably should give direction to our understanding it in other places, its meaning is especially difficult to pin down. But whatever it might mean specifically in that instance, its being closely connected with "weakness" as further exemplifying the "weakness of the cross" indicates that at the very least it reflects human vulnerability. What people see in one who lives "in fear and trembling" is not self-assurance, but defenselessness. But for that very reason it seems quite wrong, as some have done,[26] to suggest that "fear and trembling" is therefore an attitude that believers have toward one another. On the contrary, while the vulnerability of each will be apparent to the others, the OT background of this language calls for an understanding that has to do with existence vis-à-vis God. The context in this case seems to demand such a view.

25. Gk. μετὰ φόβου καὶ τρόμου; cf. 1 Cor 2:3; 2 Cor 7:15; Eph 6:5. In the LXX it is used primarily of the dread that pagans experience at the presence of the living God (e.g., Exod 15:16; Isa 19:16), which then is transferred to their dread of his people because of the wonders God performs for them (Deut 2:25; 11:25); finally it is also used of the sheer terror of circumstances that bode death (Ps 54:6 [English, 55:5]).

26. See esp. Barth, 71-72, who suggests that the phrase is nearly synonymous with "lowliness of mind" in v. 3, and thus sees it as the theological key to the whole imperative; cf. Collange, Martin, Loh-Nida, Gombitza ("Mit Furcht"), who also see it basically as concerned with relations between people. So also Giesen ("Furcht"), although he more correctly emphasizes the believers' attitude in the midst of their hostile environment. Hawthorne, to a degree following Pedersen ("Mit Furcht"), suggests a meaning here akin to "obedience." Given its OT background, however, and Paul's usage elsewhere, the phrase probably has to do with one's proper awe of God.

This phrase, then, first of all reminds the Philippians of the grandeur of the final words in vv. 9-11. If the whole universe of created beings is someday (soon, from their perspective) to pay homage to their Lord, then they themselves need to be getting on with obedience (= working out their salvation) as those who know proper awe in the presence of God. One does not live out the gospel casually or lightly, but as one who knows what it means to stand in awe of the living God.[27] On the other hand, nothing of failure or lack of confidence is implied.[28] The gospel is God's thing, and the God who has saved his people is an awesome God. Thus "working out the salvation" that God has given them should be done with a sense of "holy awe and wonder" before the God with whom they — and we — have to do.

**13** Paul's concern is obviously with the preceding imperative, that the believers in Philippi get on with being God's people in all respects. But he has stated the imperative in such a way as to make possible a betrayal of his theology. So, typically,[29] he immediately places the imperative within the context of God's prior action. "For," he goes on to explain,[30] "God is the one who empowers you in this regard." They are indeed to "work at" it *(katergazesthe);* obedience, after all, takes "willing and doing." But they are able to do so precisely because God himself is "at work" *(energōn)* in and among them. This verb, as elsewhere, does not so much mean that God is "doing it for them," but that God supplies the necessary empowering.[31] Thus, even though their obedience must be within the context of proper "fear and trembling" — and it is difficult to escape the motivational aspect of that phrase[32] — they are herewith reminded that even so, their obedience is ultimately something God effects in/among them. Paul's real point, therefore, is

27. For the unlikelihood of Jewett's view that this phrase refers to their "fear and trembling" before the final judgment of God, see n. 75 on 1:6.

28. As Vincent (65) suggests.

29. In this regard see esp. 1 Cor 5:7, where Paul uses the imperative in such a way that, if left unguarded, it could undermine his theology. So they must indeed "cleanse out the old leaven so as to become a fresh lump of dough," but of course that is what they already are by grace. Cf. Gal 4:9, where he does the same thing with what appears to be an innocent statement of reality, that the Galatians now "know God," meaning, of course, he immediately qualifies, that they are in fact "known by God."

30. That is, the γάρ in this case indicates that he will now explain *how* they are going to be able to carry out the imperative of v. 12. Collange (110) makes the intriguing, but unlikely, suggestion that it emphasizes his absence; thus, "you do not need to wait for my arrival, for it is God in any case who does the work."

31. The verb ἐνεργεῖν appears in Paul's letters 17 of its 20 NT occurrences. That it means something close to "effective empowering" is supported by the interchange in 1 Cor 12:6 and 11 between God the Father and God the Spirit, both of whom are said to "energize all [these] things" among God's people.

32. So Mundle, *NIDNTT,* 1.623.

not to protect himself theologically, but to encourage the Philippians that God is on the side of his people, that he not only has their concern at heart, but actively works in their behalf for the sake of his own good pleasure. The rest of the sentence gives us the "who, where, what, and why" of that empowering.

The *who* is easy. Just as in the preceding paragraph, which concluded by noting that even the worship of Christ as Lord is ultimately "to the glory of God," so here the emphasis is altogether on God. Even though the name "God" functions as the predicate nominative,[33] it appears first in the clause by way of emphasis. Thus, "the one supplying the power for your obedience is none other than the living God."[34]

The *where* is "in/among you."[35] As before (vv. 1:6; 2:5), when using this phrase in a corporate context, he primarily means "among you"; but for that to happen it must begin "in you," that is, in the resolve of each of them to see to it that God's purposes are accomplished in their community.

The *what* is loaded with theology. Not only does God empower their "doing" (*energein,* the infinitive of the verb just used to describe God's own activity), but also the "willing" that lies behind the doing. This is fully in keeping with Paul's understanding of Christian ethics, which has not to do with obedience to a set of rules that regulate conduct, but first of all with a "mind that is transformed" by the Spirit. Such a mind is "conformed" not to this age, but to the character of God, so that behavior is a reflection of God's will, what is good and pleasing and perfect to him (Rom 12:1-2). The "doing of salvation" for Paul therefore lies in the "willing," which means the radical transformation of life by the Spirit. The believer is not one who has been begrudgingly "caught by God," as it were, so that obedience is basically out of fear and trembling over what might happen if one were to do otherwise; rather, being Christ's means to be "converted" in the true sense of that word, to have one's life invaded by God's Holy Spirit, so that not simply new behavior is now effected, but a new desire toward God that prompts such behavior in the first place.[36]

But Christian ethics lies not just in the "willing." In Rom 7:18, in his description of life before and outside of Christ,[37] but looked at from the

---

33. *Contra* Meyer. On this matter see n. 4 above.

34. In keeping with their view of v. 12, many would limit it to "in the souls of believers" (so Meyer, Vincent, Kennedy, Hendriksen, Silva, O'Brien); but the context seems to rule that out.

35. Gk. ἐν ὑμῖν; cf. n. 72 on 1:6 and the discussion on v. 5 above.

36. Cf. Bruce (82): "This is Paul's teaching about the Holy Spirit, even if the Spirit is not explicitly mentioned here." Cf. Fee, *Presence,* 598-603, for the Spirit as key to Rom 12:1-2 in the same way.

37. See esp. 7:5-6; "When we *were controlled* by the flesh . . . ; but *now* we have been set free to serve in the new way of the Spirit." See the NICNT commentary by D. Moo, for this perspective.

perspective of life in the Spirit, Paul described *pre-Christian life* with these same verbs. To "will," he said, was present with me; he recognized the good and spiritual thing that the Law truly is. But without the Spirit, he goes on, "carrying out *(katergazesthai)* the good" does not happen. As a believer, however, Paul will have none of that (i.e., of their not being able to carry out the good that they will); hence he urges the Philippians to "work it out" precisely because God (by his Spirit, is implied) is present with them both to will and to do "the good."[38]

The *why* ("according to his good purpose," NIV) is debated; indeed, the phrase is perfectly ambiguous.[39] The word translated "good purpose" occurred in 1:15, as the motivation for those among Paul's friends who preach Christ out of love and "goodwill" toward Paul. In light of what is about to be urged (v. 14), that meaning could prevail here as well; that is, God is at work in them both to will and to do what promotes goodwill in the community.[40]

More likely, however, given Paul's theology and the emphasis of the present sentence, he intends the definite article to function as a possessive and thus to refer to God's empowering their obedience for his own *eudokia*. In which case this word probably leans toward "good pleasure,"[41] in the sense that God does this for his people precisely because it pleases him so to do. This also means further that the preposition *hyper* bears its regular sense of "for the sake of."[42] This does not mean that God, despite v. 6, is a self-

38. For this understanding of Rom 7:7-25, see Fee, *Presence,* 508-15; the repetition here of these very verbs as something quite within the grasp of God's Spirit-filled people plays the lie to the interpretation that Paul was there describing some kind of (non-existent) tension between the Spirit within him and the flesh, in which the flesh obviously still had the upper hand.

39. Gk. ὑπὲρ τῆς εὐδοκίας. The ambiguity lies with the article τῆς, which can refer either to "the well-known" goodwill that believers ought to have toward one another (in keeping with v. 4), or "his" good will, reflecting the Greek article as referring back to the subject of the sentence ("God"), and thus functioning as a possessive pronoun.

40. As *inter alia* Michael, 104; Collange, 111; Hawthorne, 101.

41. So most interpreters; Lightfoot has "benevolent purpose."

42. For reasons not at all clear, many find this usage difficult, as though God's effecting something "for the sake of his own good pleasure" were awkward or theologically offensive. The result has been a number of unlikely ploys to get around the ordinary sense of the preposition. BAGD suggest the sense of "above and beyond" for this passage. That would work fine for the accusative, but Paul uses the genitive here, and almost certainly means that God acts "on behalf of" someone's "good pleasure," most likely his own. The NIV implies that it equals κατά here, as though God's empowering their willing and doing were "in keeping with" the standard set by "his good purposes." But grammatically that has no analogies. Collange argues that "in behalf of" carries this nuance in any case; but that is especially difficult to see. Finally, BDF §231.2 offer the extremely unlikely expedient that it goes with the next imperative (v. 14). In light of biblical theology in general and Pauline theology in particular, the view presented here fits perfectly well into the argument.

gratifying being after all. Rather, all that God does he does for his pleasure; but since God is wholly good, his doing what pleases him is not capricious, but what is wholly good for those he loves. God's pleasure is pure love, so what he does "for the sake of his good pleasure" is by that very fact also on behalf of those he loves. After all, it delights God to delight his people.

Thus, with v. 13 Paul puts the imperative into theological perspective. What follows is to be understood as flowing directly out of this word; there he will specify how they are to "work out their common salvation" as God works in and among them for his own good pleasure. What pleases God in this instance, of course, is that they cease the in-fighting that is currently going on among some of them.

## 2. Specific Application — Harmony for the World's and Paul's Sake (2:14-18)

> 14*Do everything without complaining or arguing,* 15*so that you may become*[1] *blameless and pure, children of God without fault in a crooked and depraved generation, in which you shine like stars in the universe* 16*as you hold out*[a] *the word of life — in order that I may boast on the day of Christ that I did not run or labor for nothing.* 17*But even if*[2] *I am being poured out like a drink offering on the sacrifice and service coming from your faith, I am glad and rejoice with all of you.* 18*So you too should be glad and rejoice with me.*

[a]Or *hold on to*

With yet another imperative, Paul spells out how in particular they may "obey" (= work out their salvation) while he is currently absent from them. At the same time he concludes this section of the letter (from 1:27) by bringing into focus all of its various motifs — those that are up front as well as those that form the background situation in Philippi.[3] In the opening imperative

---

1. For Paul's γένησθε some early MSS (P[46] A D* F G latt) substituted ἦτε; this has all the earmarks of a "sense" variation (i.e., they understood γένησθε to = "to be," and thus substituted the latter), especially since much of the evidence is related to the OL Version. But in so doing they mess with Paul's use of the language of the LXX, which dominates the sentence.

2. For the εἰ καί of the majority, which is clearly the Pauline original, F G vg have καὶ εἰ, a variant that very likely arose through the OL Version. Despite the grammarians to the contrary, this variant is probably an indication that εἰ καί is not concessive, but intensive, and that the order of F G is concessive. See n. 59 below.

3. Indeed, apart from a specific focus on Christ himself (and that is very close at hand in vv. 6-11), every major motif of the letter is touched on in some way in these two

(1:27) he had appealed to them to comport themselves in a manner worthy of their heavenly citizenship, which should take the form of (1) standing fast in the one Spirit, (2) contending as one person for the gospel, and (3) not being frightened in any way by the opposition. Along the way it became clear that steadfastness in the face of opposition is also needed because things are not altogether in good order among them, which not only affects their own life in Christ, but their effectiveness as God's people in Philippi as well. All of that is brought together in this final appeal, which concludes by bringing his and their relationship back into the picture, with a final word about suffering and joy.

The net result is a sentence whose flow is easy enough to discern but whose concluding logic is less so. The Philippians first of all are urged to "do all things without murmuring and arguing" (v. 14). This is followed by a purpose clause, whose primary focus is on their role in the world: that they be "the blameless children of God" (15a) and thus "shine as stars" in pagan Philippi by "holding firm the word of life" (15b-16a). That much is manageable. But at this point the sentence takes an unexpected — and abrupt — turn, whose ultimate purpose appears to be transition: namely, to return to the narrative about his and their affairs that was broken off at 1:26. But its immediate aim is less easy to discern. In contrast to vv. 11 and 13, which conclude with God's glory and good pleasure, the final goal[4] of the imperative is for Paul's eschatological "boast" in them (16b), evidence that his ministry will not have been in vain (16c). But never one to leave an admonition on what could be perceived as a down note,[5] he concludes by reflecting on an alternative possibility, that his ministry might be viewed as a drink offering poured out in conjunction with their own sacrificial faith (17a), thus bringing the theme of suffering back into the foreground. If indeed this is the case, he concludes, and it is, so much the more cause for him and them to rejoice together (17b-18). Paul is clearly exhorting what he has been praying: that they be pure and blameless for the day of Christ (1:10).

The abrupt way his ministry is brought into the sentence, with its eschatological focus — also a recurring theme in the letter — is perhaps best explained on the basis of its most striking feature: the sudden and profuse influx of echoes from the OT, which is quite unlike anything else in the Pauline

---

sentences: their need for unity; the gospel (here, "the word of life"); evangelism; the opposition in Philippi ("crooked and depraved generation"); his and their relationship; suffering; and joy.

4. The preceding sentences concluded: εἰς δόξαν θεοῦ πατρός ("for the glory of God") and ὑπὲρ τῆς εὐδοκίας ("for his good pleasure"); this one concludes: εἰς καύχημα ἐμοί ("for my boast"). The prepositions in each case are basically telic, expressing goal or aim.

5. See above on 1:11.

corpus. So unique is this that one scarcely knows what to make of it. A maximal view would see it as intentional intertextuality,[6] with distinct language from a series of LXX texts that recall the story of Israel from its origins, through the desert, to its eschatological hope. A minimal view would see it as the outflow of a mind steeped in Scripture and Israel's story as it has been regularly applied to the new people of God.

The data: It begins in v. 14 with Israel's "murmuring" (Exod 16:12 et al.); the Philippians are urged not to do so. The reason for the prohibition is first expressed in the words God spoke to Abraham at the renewal of the covenant in Gen 17:1; as with the father of the covenant, the Philippians are to "become blameless" before God. This concern is then repeated in the language of Deut 32:5, where in the Song of Moses Israel is judged on account of its rebellion as "blameworthy children, a crooked and perverse generation" (LXX); but for the new covenant people of Philippi all of this is now reversed: by heeding the prohibition against "murmuring," they become "God's blameless children," and the opposition in Philippi the "crooked and perverse generation." Finally, in Dan 12:3 Israel's eschatological hope takes the form: "the wise shall *shine as luminaries (phōsteres),*" with the parallel clause in the Hebrew (MT) adding, "and those who lead many to righteousness as the stars" (for which the LXX has, "those who hold strong to my *words*"); from the perspective of Paul's "already/not yet" eschatological framework, the Philippians, as they live out their calling as God' blameless children, already "shine as stars" as they "hold firm the *word* of life." The eschatological context of Daniel in turn accounts for Paul's concluding with a word about the "not yet" side of eschatological realities: the Philippians must persevere (now) in this kind of obedience or Paul will have no "boast" at the end; indeed, he will have "labored in vain" (yet another clause echoing OT language [esp. Isa 65:23, "my chosen ones will *not labor in vain*"]). Finally, in contrast to that, and now with no specific text in view, he images his ministry and suffering, and their faith and suffering, in terms of the levitical sacrifices.

But what to do with this phenomenon? On the one hand, both its uniqueness in the corpus and the sudden profusion of language not found elsewhere in Paul[7] suggest something more intentional than otherwise; moreover, it seems to "work" too well to be mere chance or coincidence. On the other hand, this might be just our discovery, with nothing intentional on Paul's part at all; after all, he is a man steeped in the story of Israel and is quick to see its application to the people of God newly constituted by Christ

---

6. On this matter see on 1:19 and 2:10-11 above.

7. The following terms are found only here in Paul, and some only here in the NT: "God's blameless children"; "crooked and perverse generation"; "shine as stars"; "the word of life."

and the Spirit. Perhaps there is a middle way, that this reflects something sermonic or some former teaching (and is thus intentional in that sense), of a kind that Paul can draw on at will and weave into a single, meaningful sentence that specifies the kind of obedience he is calling them to, while at the same time placing the imperative within a larger biblical framework that assures the Philippians of their place in God's story.

**14** Both the asyndeton (lack of a connecting or nuancing particle) and the language of this imperative indicate that it has the closest possible tie to what has just been said.[8] Following the verb "obey," meaning to "work your salvation out," because God "works" in/among you to will and to "work" for his good pleasure, Paul now urges, "Do all things." The "do" picks up on the verbs, "obeying" and "working"; the "all things" is all inclusive, having to do with everything that makes up their common and corporate life in Philippi, but especially "working out their salvation" by standing firm and contending together for the gospel in the face of opposition.

The first of the two qualifying nouns, "without complaining,"[9] is undoubtedly an intentional echo[10] of the grumbling of Israel in the desert,[11] made certain by (a) that the only other occurrence of the word in Paul is in 1 Cor 10:10 ("and neither grumble as some of them grumbled"), which explicitly recalls Num 14:1-38, (b) that in the next clause Paul unmistakably echoes the language of Deut 32:5, which recalls the recalcitrance of Israel in the desert, and (c) that Paul adds another noun to *clarify* what their "grumbling" consists of. Here, then, is the place for them to start "working out their salvation with fear and trembling": to stop being like the murmuring Israelites.

But since Israel's grumbling was against Moses and God, and since there is no hint in this letter that the Philippians are doing the same (that is, murmuring against Paul or God),[12] Paul adds another clarifying noun, which puts their "grumbling" into the Philippian context: "and without controver-

---

8. Cf. Michael, 104; O'Brien, 289.

9. Gk. χωρὶς γογγυσμῶν; found only here in Paul, but see the cognate verb in 1 Cor 10:10; elsewhere in the NT in John 7:12; Acts 6:1; 1 Pet 4:9. This is the noun and verb used regularly in the LXX to render *telunnah* and *lun* of the Pentateuch, referring to the "murmuring" of the Israelites against God (and Moses).

10. So most interpreters (Lightfoot, Meyer, Beare, Gnilka, Houlden, Caird, Martin, Kent, Loh-Nida, Bruce, Hawthorne, Silva, O'Brien, Melick).

11. See Exod 16:7-12 (6x); 17:3; Num 14:27-29 (3x); 16:41; 17:5 (2x), 10. Some (Gnilka, Caird, Martin) suggest the imagery of the church as a pilgrim people. Perhaps so, given the various echoes of the Philippians' replacing Israel as God's people in the story.

12. It is possible (as, e.g., Meyer, Vincent, Müller, Hendriksen) to read this imperative to mean, "Carry out these imperatives without grumbling about it," which would then direct it toward God. But the context, and especially the purpose clause that follows, supports the interpretation offered here (so Kennedy, Jones, Michael, Barth, Bruce, Hawthorne, Silva, O'Brien, Melick).

sies."[13] Here, most likely, is the tell-tale word, for which "grumbling" offers a biblical frame of reference. Although it ordinarily means something like "disputatious reasoning," that is, reasonings that have ulterior and malicious design, here, as in 1 Tim 2:8, it refers to the disputes or controversies themselves.[14] In light of the final appeal in 4:1-3, this word very likely spells out negatively what Paul urged in 2:2, that they have the same mindset, the same love for one another which they have experienced from God in Christ.

**15-16a** This clause offers the positive *purpose* behind the opening imperative, and there are no surprises in terms of concerns. As in the prayer report (1:9-11) he wants them, first, to be blameless with regard to their observable behavior, so that they might be recognized for what they are, "the children of God," and that they might thus be blameless for the day of Christ. The arena for such behavior is pagan Philippi, now described in the language of Deut 32:5: "a crooked and depraved generation." But being blameless is the penultimate concern. The ultimate concerns are two: first, the gospel in Philippi, almost certainly in the interest of evangelism, as throughout the preceding narrative about "his affairs" (1:12-26); and second, their own successful eschatological conclusion, expressed in terms of their being Paul's "boast" with the day of Christ in view.[15] Each of these parts of the clause needs closer examination.

1. "That you might become blameless and pure" is a compound which in terms of language is unique, but in terms of concept appears in 1:10. Both contexts reflect Paul's "already but not yet" eschatological framework, the former emphasizing the day of Christ itself, this one emphasizing *present* conduct, with the day of Christ clearly in view. The first part, "become blameless," is precisely how God begins the renewal of the covenant with Abraham.[16] The word has primarily to do with observable conduct, which

---

13. Gk. διαλογισμῶν; elsewhere in Paul in 1 Cor 3:20; Rom 1:21; 14:1; 1 Tim 2:8.

14. So Kennedy, Jones, Plummer, Michael, Barth, Martin, Loh-Nida, Bruce, Hawthorne, Silva, O'Brien. Earlier interpreters, without the benefit of the papyrus finds, and reading it in light of other NT passages, understood it in terms of inner doubts or malicious reasonings against God (e.g., Lightfoot ["intellectual rebellion against God"]; Meyer ["without hesitation"!], in keeping with his view of the whole sentence [see n. 12]).

15. Although this final eschatological note is no surprise in this letter, the way it is expressed, as the conclusion to this sentence, is a surprise, so we will note it separately under v. 16b.

16. Except, of course, that it is now plural. The LXX reads: εὐαρέστει ἐναντίον ἐμοῦ καὶ γίνου ἄμεμπτος (Gen 17:1); Paul says: ἵνα γένησθε ἄμεμπτοι. Had this occurred in another context it would most likely be considered coincidental. What makes one think otherwise here is (1) the use of ἄμεμπτος, which is somewhat rare in Pauline paraenesis (only in 1 Thess 3:13, plus the adverb in 1 Thess 2:10; 5:23; he tends to use other words for this idea); (2) the appearance of this unique combination *in this context;* and (3) the otherwise apparent repetition of this idea in the next phrase.

one can "find no fault" with. Since Paul will repeat this idea with another word in the next phrase, where the context is toward people, very likely this first occurrence, as in the Genesis account, is "blameless toward God." "Pure"[17] is directed more toward the heart, not in the sense of "clean" but of "innocent."

2. With "children of God without fault" Paul begins his "echoes" of Deut 32:5 (LXX). The term "children of God,"[18] which is full of familial overtones (God as Father, believers as children, hence brothers and sisters), is especially appropriate for those who are being urged "to obey." The OT text says that Israel "no longer" has the right to this name, to which the LXX adds the adjective "blameworthy" *(mōmeta),* a term that reflects a cultic setting (= full of blemishes). Paul picks up this adjective, negates it *(amōma* = without fault), and adds "in the midst of"[19] before continuing the rest of the "citation."[20] He thus converts the whole phrase into its opposite with regard to the Philippians.[21] They *are* indeed God's children, and as they stop their internal bickering they will thus be "without fault."

3. By his addition of the preposition "in the midst of," Paul also transforms the next words of Deut 32:5 into their opposite. Originally "a crooked and depraved generation" described "blameworthy" Israel. But since God's Philippian children will become "blameless" as they stop their bickering, they must be so in the context of pagan Philippi, who now receive the epithet, "crooked and depraved generation." Although this language is dictated by the LXX text Paul is citing, it is nonetheless a fair reflection of his view of pagan society,[22] a view he has in common with most of the rest of the NT writers.[23] But in the context of 1:27–2:18, for which this passage functions both as a conclusion and as something of an inclusio with 1:27-

17. Gk. ἀκέραιοι; elsewhere in Paul only in Rom 16:19 ("be *innocent* with regard to evil"; cf. Matt 10:16, "innocent as doves").

18. Gk. τέκνα θεοῦ. Although the idea of believers being God's children occurs throughout the Pauline corpus and in a variety of contexts, this precise term occurs elsewhere only in Romans (8:16, 21; 9:8). The latter instance (Rom 9:8) is especially instructive, since there too Paul deliberately transfers this Abrahamic terminology to believers.

19. Gk. μέσον; the neuter singular of this adjective, used as an "improper" preposition, a form that occurs nowhere else in Paul, and was changed to the grammatically more acceptable ἐν μέσῳ by the later MajT.

20. Meyer (115) seems to miss too much in suggesting that Paul first wrote "children of God without fault," which caused him then to recall the Deuteronomy passage, which in turn prompted him to add the next words from Deuteronomy as well. The "reversal of fortunes" that Paul effects with this material is much too intentional for that.

21. Barth (76): "a triumphant parody of that passage."

22. See, e.g., 1 Cor 6:9-10; Rom 1:28-30; Tit 3:3.

23. Cf., e.g., 1 Pet 4:3-5; Rev 22:15.

30,[24] it is hard to escape the implication that the term is a purposely pejorative reference to "those who oppose" you in 1:28.[25] As we noted there Paul is most likely referring to the general pagan populace in Philippi, who took their devotion to Caesar as "lord" seriously and found those who advocated another "Lord" more than just a little nettlesome. In the midst of such "a crooked and depraved generation" the Philippian believers are to conduct themselves in a way that is otherwise (i.e., ethically) without blame.

4. Having reminded the Philippians of the arena in which they are to live out the gospel, he now turns to the final apocalyptic vision of Daniel[26] (12:1-4) to describe their role in pagan Philippi: "among whom *you shine*[27] *as stars*[28] in the world[29]." It is probably the eschatological context of the

24. See the introduction to 1:27–2:18 on p. 167.

25. It is less likely that it refers to the "mutilators of the flesh" in 3:2, as Collange and Silva suggest: first, because those people are not described anywhere as "opponents"; but second, and more importantly, such people as those described in 3:2 can only be itinerants, while Paul's concern is with ongoing life in Philippi.

26. Given the uniqueness of this language in Paul and that it is precisely that of Dan 12:3 (Daniel: καὶ οἱ συνιέντες φανοῦσιν ὡς φωστῆρες τοῦ οὐρανοῦ; Paul: ἐν οἷς φαίνεσθε ὡς φωστῆρες ἐν κόσμῳ), it was for me a cause of some wonder how so many interpreters (e.g., Meyer, Vincent, Kennedy, Jones, Barth, Müller, Collange, Caird, Kent, Martin, Hawthorne, Silva) have missed this expression of intertextuality — all the more so when the next phrase in Paul seems to be a modification of the second line in Daniel as well, not to mention its context in Hebrew of "bringing many to righteousness." That I have always "heard" Daniel here, even as a boy, says something about my own ecclesiastical background, since the Daniel passage was cited so often as an incentive to evangelism. That experience makes me think the same would have been even more true of the Philippians, who lived in a basically oral culture and would have heard Scripture read over and again, and whose minds would not have been constantly bombarded by thousands of other media and literary sources.

27. Gk. φαίνεσθε. Since in its other two Pauline occurrences (2 Cor 13:7; Rom 7:13), this word means "to appear," some (esp. those who have missed the echo of Dan 12:3; e.g., Lightfoot, Meyer, Vincent, Plummer, Martin) have argued for that sense here. Some (Calvin, Beare, Hawthorne) take this to be an imperative, which in context is altogether unlikely (the verb occurs in a relative clause, and there seems to be no analogy for an imperative in such a clause); as O'Brien points out, everything in this ἵνα clause is already dependent on the single imperative, "Do all things."

28. Gk. φωστῆρες, which technically does not mean "star," but any heavenly light-giving body. Given that its stands in synonymous parallel in Dan 12:3 with "the stars (ἄστρα) of heaven," most likely in that context it is the more all-embracing word that includes the sun and moon as well (as in Gen 1:14-19). Without noting its Danielic origins, and in view of buildings erected as navigational "beacons" (an early expression of the lighthouse), S. K. Finlayson ("Lights") offers this as a (dubious) alternative here, while Martin follows Conzelmann (*TDNT,* 9.324) in the equally dubious suggestion that it might mean "light-bearers."

29. Gk. ἐν κόσμῳ; while this word can easily be all-embracing, and thus mean

Daniel passage that makes his own transition to their eschatological future so easy. But before that, he is concerned still with the "already."

5. The modal qualifier,[30] "as you hold out/on to[31] the word of life," brings us face to face with the inherent ambiguity of this final part of the sentence, which in turn reflects one of the repeated ambiguities of the NT: that the people of God are to "shine" in the world "over against" its darkness, while simultaneously they are to illumine that darkness.[32] That is, by their attitudes and behavior they are to be clearly distinguishable from, and in opposition to, the world around them, while they are also to be God's messengers, bringing the word of life to the dying. It is this tension that one also senses here. The language "crooked and depraved generation among whom you shine as stars in the world," on the one hand, looks very much as if Paul meant "over against" the world; the present phrase, on the other hand, implies their evangelistic mission. The verb itself, which does not necessarily imply as much, is probably a further reflection of the passage from Daniel, being chosen as a more appropriate synonym for the LXX phrase "those who hold strong to my words,"[33] which appears in the second clause (the synonymous parallel in 12:3). In which case it most likely carries the sense of "hold firm" the word of life.

But what suggests evangelism as the ultimate intent of their "holding firm" the gospel is (a) the word order ("*the word of life* holding firm," immediately following "in the world"); (b) the unique language for the gospel, "word *of life,*" which occurs only here in Paul, and makes very little sense if does not carry the thrust of bringing life to others; and (c) the context of Dan 12:3, in which the second line in the Hebrew reads: "and those who

---

"the universe," it is difficult to know why the NIV translators thought so here. By deliberately altering "of heaven" to "in the world," Paul seems to be indicating the present sphere of their shining.

30. So most interpreters; O'Brien (297) follows Gnilka (153) in linking the participle with the main clause, ἵνα γενήσθε, but that seems strained, given the intervening clause with a verb in the second plural. Under any circumstances it is an unnatural reading, and one wonders how the hearers could have caught on.

31. Gk. ἐπέχοντες, which occurs only here and in 1 Tim 3:15 in Paul (cf. Luke 14:7; Acts 3:5; 19:22). The word means to "hold firm" or "stay put" (Acts 19:22), but in 1 Tim 3:15 means "to give one's full attention to."

32. "Influence as well as contrast" (Michael).

33. Gk. καὶ οἱ κατισχύοντες τοὺς λόγους μου. The Hebrew has, "and those who lead many to righteousness." It is hard to know where the LXX version came from. The verb κατισχύω means "to prevail" (which takes the genitive) or "be strong, powerful." Thus this line of the LXX probably means, "those who hold strong my words." Since that would be a rare sense for this verb, Paul simply substituted ἐπέχοντες. This seems to make the best sense of the unusual features of this phrase, both the choice of this verb and the unique reference to the gospel as "*the word* of life." This is the new way that "my words" have made their way into the world.

bring many to righteousness (shall shine) as the stars for ever and ever." Thus, it is not some kind of defensive posture that is in view (as in, "hold the gospel fast so that the enemy does not take it away from you"), but evangelism, that they clean up their internal act so that they may thereby "hold firm" the gospel,[34] the message that brings life to those who believe. Their role in Philippi, by the very nature of things, puts them in strong contrast (hence, in opposition) to the paganism of Philippi, while at the same time they offer "life," the life that Christ has provided through his death and resurrection, to those who will take the time to hear.

**16b**     Although the main point of Paul's sentence has been reached with the preceding participial phrase, the sentence itself has not yet come to an end. In light of the eschatological context of Dan 12:3, whose language Paul has just echoed, he concludes the sentence on an eschatological note, one of the many that permeate the letter.[35] But this final phrase is so abrupt, and so out of character with what has preceded, that one is quite startled by it.[36] For rather than speaking directly about their own eschatological triumph, he concludes the purpose clause that began in v. 15 on what appears to be a personal note regarding his own ministry: (literally) "*for* my grounds for boasting/glorying *for* the day of Christ,"[37] language that recalls their boasting in 1:26 and his prayer in 1:10. Most likely the sentence has gotten away from him a bit, and this final phrase is to be understood primarily in response to their "shining as lights in the world as they hold firm the word of life" in Philippi. Both prepositions are thus to be understood as telic[38]: first, the imperative itself — and their heeding it, of course — is "with a view to" Paul's having grounds for eschatological "boasting/glorying,"[39] all of which, second, has "the day of Christ" as its goal.[40] He will reserve his "glorying" for the day when it counts, when they, along with others,

---

34. Which is almost certainly what the genitive λόγον ζωῆς means. As always in Paul, the use of λόγος for the gospel denotes its message (see on 1:14 above).

35. See the discussion of 1:6; cf. on 1:21-23; 2:9-11 above, and 3:9-16, 18-21 below.

36. Hence the reason the NIV has broken it off with a dash. They also (correctly) turn the phrase into a clause, but in so doing abandon Paul's nuance regarding the "day of Christ." See the discussion.

37. Part of the difficulty with this clause has to do with the sense of these two occurrences of εἰς. See the discussion.

38. Loh-Nida suggest "conditional," but there seems to be no lexical or grammatical warrant for such.

39. Gk. εἰς καύχημα ἐμοί; cf. the discussion on 1:26 above. This noun (καύχημα), vis-à-vis καύχησις, refers not to the actual act of boasting but to the grounds for such.

40. Gk. εἰς ἡμέραν Χριστοῦ, precisely as in 1:10 (q.v., esp. n. 23; cf. n. 64 on 1:6), the only two occurrences of this expression of the phrase in the corpus. As noted, it does not (cannot, *pace* O'Brien) mean "on the day of" nor does it = "until"; it means, "with the day of Christ in view."

become his "crown of boasting" (1 Thess 2:19; cf. Phil 4:1). To which Paul then appends a final word that seems even more surprising, "that I have not run in vain, nor labored in vain."

As noted, the most likely reason for all of this is transitional; that is, just as he brought *them* into the picture in 1:25-26 (at the conclusion of "my affairs"), and with some of the same language, he brings this section about "your affairs" to conclusion by bringing *himself* back into the picture. But why in this way? one wonders. The answer to which lies in the combination of (a) Paul's yearning for his friends and (b) the very close connection he sees between who they are (and what they do) and his own life in Christ. He thus yearns for them in part because, as his converts, their steadfast loyalty to Christ also means that his own life has counted for something. The final word, therefore, is not a word of doubt,[41] but an affirmation: by their heeding these words he will have plenty of cause for "boasting" when they stand together before Christ at his Parousia; indeed, they will be primary *evidence* that he had "neither run in vain nor labored in vain."[42]

As noted on 1:26, "boasting" has nothing to do with what Paul has done, but with what Christ has wrought through him (as Rom 15:18 makes clear; cf. 1 Cor 15:10). When used positively, as here, "boasting" points to the ground of one's confidence and trust, Christ himself, in whom one therefore "glories." Thus Paul concludes his imperative with the sheer glory that he and they will experience together in the presence of Christ[43] — they because of his ministry among them that brought them to that glory; he because his "glorying" in them, as he and they are in Christ's presence together, is but another way of expressing his "boast in the Lord" (1 Cor 1:31; 2 Cor 10:17).

The appended clause, "that I have neither run in vain nor labored in vain," is vintage Paul, who here combines into one clause what appear separately elsewhere in all sorts of contexts.[44] The two verbs, taken from the

---

41. That is, he does not here say "lest I have run in vain," as in Gal 2:2; 1 Thess 3:5. The ὅτι most likely introduces an object clause, although it could be causal (as Kennedy et al. would have it). In either case it is here affirmation, not doubt. Cf. the REB: "proof that I did not run my race in vain or labour in vain."

42. Just as was promised in Isa 65:23 to those who dwell in the New Jerusalem: "they will not labor in vain."

43. For reciprocal "boasting" at the Parousia, see 2 Cor 1:14.

44. For the imagery of ministry and Christian life as "running a race" see 3:13-14; cf. 1 Cor 9:24-25; Gal 2:2; 5:7). Since the imagery is drawn from the games, the ἀγων word group applies here as well, although one cannot be sure "racing" itself is intended (see, e.g., Col 1:29; 4:12; 1 Tim 4:10; 6:12). The imagery of "labor" is far more common, serving as one of his primary verbs for ministry (e.g., 1 Thess 5:12; 1 Cor 15:10; 16:16; Gal 4:11 et passim), but also for every kind of "work" that is associated with living in and for Christ (e.g., 1 Thess 1:3; 1 Cor 15:58, etc.). For the two images in the same letter see Gal 2:2 ("run") and 4:11 ("labor"). Cf. Pfitzner, *Agon,* 103-4.

games and from manual labor[45] respectively, are among his favorite images for ministry. On the one hand, life in Christ has the features of a race, with the eschatological prize awaiting those who finish (see 3:14); on the other hand, and more often in Paul, it involves "labor"; one "works hard in the Lord,"[46] just as the tent maker does in the shop.[47] Paul has invested his whole Christian life in seeing that others also obtain the prize for such running, or realize the fruit of such labor. Hence, at issue for him is not his own personal "prize"; for him that prize will consist primarily in having his "beloved" Philippians (and others) there with him (cf. 4:1).[48]

Thus, based on their long-time friendship, this clause serves as a final incentive for them to "obey by working out their salvation while he is absent from them." In this letter it is included especially for those whose vision of their certain future has diminished in some way. The question as to whether it could really be in vain, of course, is much debated. On the basis of what Paul says here (vv. 17-18) and elsewhere, the answer seems to be twofold. On the one hand, such an expression as this only makes sense if such a potential really exists; on the other hand, Paul has such confidence in God regarding his converts that it would be unthinkable to him that the potential would ever be realized. Which leads us to the final sentences in this present argument.

**17** Having brought his relationship with them back into the picture at the end of v. 16, and apparently as a general response[49] to his confidence

45. Lightfoot (118) considers "labor" in this instance to be an extension of the athletic metaphor, indicating the well-known "labor intensive" training that the games required. But Paul's frequent use of this imagery for ministry, with no connection to the games, seems to suggest otherwise.

46. See the frequency of this expression in the closing personal greetings in Romans 16.

47. Note that Paul uses this same verb to describe his "working hard with his own hands," as one of his apostolic hardships (1 Cor 4:12).

48. *Contra* J. Gundry Volf (*Perseverance,* 262-64), who argues that "loss" would refer to lack of "divine commendation for service at the last day."

49. The sentence begins with ἀλλά ("but"), which in this case is probably to be understood as introducing an "independent clause, to indicate that the preceding is to be regarded as a settled matter, thus forming a transition to someth[ing] new" (BAGD). "Independent" is taken to an extreme by Lohmeyer and Barth, who, because the appeal itself ends with v. 16, consider vv. 17-18 to introduce vv. 19-30; but that is difficult to see (as Barth's own use of dashes is a clear indication), especially since inherent in such a strong adversative is some kind of contrast to what has preceded. O'Brien (303) argues for an "ascensive force" here (= "not only labours, but even death"; cf. 1:18), citing BDF §448 (and others) as in support of such a possibility (and unfortunately, he makes this meaning a part of his case for his understanding of the metaphor, p. 305). While this is attractive, it is questionable whether it can work, since this usage is restricted to ἀλλά with καί or γε καί (see the thorough disc. in Thrall, *Greek Particles,* 11-16). At least, I am not aware of any known analogy for this usage of ἀλλά *by itself.*

in their obedience which will mean that he has not labored in vain, Paul
concludes this long appeal regarding "your affairs" by putting that relationship
into its positive perspective. The precise nature of that perspective, however,
is not at all easy to determine, since it takes the form of a conditional sentence,
whose protasis (the "if" clause) is expressed with a striking shift of images
and whose apodosis returns to the theme of joy. Thus, in a sentence which
was undoubtedly perfectly clear to Paul and probably reasonably understandable to the Philippians as they heard it read, the distance of time and circumstances has left us to wonder both what the imagery denotes and how the
sentence fits into the letter.[50]

Using metaphors drawn directly from the sacrificial system of the OT,[51]
Paul says (literally), "but if indeed I am being poured out as a drink offering at
the sacrifice and service of your faith." The imagery itself is much clearer than
its points of application. Pictured is the Levitical priest, whose "service"[52]
included the offering of a sacrificed animal,[53] and often a grain offering accompanied by a "drink offering" of wine poured out in the sanctuary (Num 28:7).
In the present application Paul is pictured as the drink offering and the Philippi-

---

50. The certain evidence for this, pity the poor reader, is the contradictory nature
of so much that is found on the passage in the commentaries, while using many of the
same data and grammars. Perhaps we should confess that we are fishing for answers to a
very difficult metaphor, on which certainty will be hard to come by.

51. Instead of the OT, it is common for scholars to assume the primary background
for these words is pagan religion — as though the Philippians might not be well acquainted
with the biblical data. But two matters speak against this view: (1) Although Paul does not
use cultic terminology often, whenever he does, his OT heritage is primarily in view (see,
e.g., ὀσμὴν εὐωδίας, θυσίαν δεκτήν in 4:18, a combination which can only come from
such passages as Num 15:3-4 [where the first three words occur in the same sentence] and
Lev 19:5 [where the latter two appear]; cf. also 1 Cor 9:13 in light of 10:18, and Rom
15:16, where the mention of the Gentiles demands the OT sacrificial system as background
to the metaphor). Such sacrifices, after all, are offered *to God* (Rom 12:1; Eph 5:2). (2) In
light of the preceding accumulation of echoes from the OT, it is hard to imagine that he
has now abandoned the OT for something pagan. However, as former pagans — for the
most part at least — it need not be denied that the Philippians would also know this
language well on the basis of pagan religion. But that hardly accounts for Pauline usage.

52. Gk. λειτουργία (from which "liturgy" derives), used primarily in the LXX to
refer to the various duties of the Levites, including the actual "service" at the altar. The
word group appears rarely in Paul (3 of 5 times in this letter; see below on 2:25 and 30;
otherwise only in 2 Cor 9:12 and Rom 15:29, of the offering for the poor in Jerusalem),
always metaphorically of Christian "service" of some kind, and not restricted to "ministers." In this sentence it applies in some way to the Philippians.

53. Gk. θυσία, used for sacrifice in general, but in the Pentateuch (LXX) very
often for the cereal offering that accompanied the burnt offering and drink offering. That
would give good reason to think such imagery is in view here, except that in Eph 5:2 and
Rom 12:1 the imagery clearly refers to the sacrificed animal (see next n.).

ans (apparently) as "serving" by offering the sacrifice, which has to do with their faith in some way. But none of this is easy to decipher, in part because of the context and in part because Paul's use of sacrificial imagery is so flexible that usage elsewhere is of little or no help here.[54]

In light of what is assumed to be the Greco-Roman background of this metaphor, plus the similar usage in 2 Tim 4:6, "drink offering" is most often considered to be a metaphor for Paul's death (or martyrdom).[55] Thus it is usually assumed, or explicitly stated, that the imagery is that of "blood" being poured out over the sacrifice.[56] But there is nothing inherent in the imagery to demand this view;[57] and there are significant grammatical and contextual reasons to doubt it here. The grammar has to do with the nature of the conditional sentence, which in this case is a "first class" or "real" condition. That is, it does not express supposition, either more or less probable,[58] nor

54. E.g., he uses θυσία metaphorically three other times: in Eph 5:2 to refer to Christ's offering himself to God; in Rom 12:1 of believers, who are to be "living sacrifices" as over against the "dead animals" sacrificed on ritual altars; and in Phil 4:18 of their gift to him. He uses ὀσμὴ εὐωδίας ("sweet smelling [sacrifice])" to accompany the "sacrifice" in Eph 5:2 and Phil 4:18; but of his own ministry in 2 Cor 2:14-15 (where because of the imagery of the Roman triumph, it may well pick up that imagery). And the use of "cultic service" language (λατρεία [see on 3:3] and λειτουργία [see on 2:30]) is of even broader range, including Rom 15:16, where he sees his ministry (λειτουργός) of bringing the Gentiles to Christ as "performing the duties of a priest," so that the Gentiles, "sanctified by the Holy Spirit," are a "pleasing offering" to God.

55. As though, as some suggest, by his affirming that "death is gain," he is herewith suggesting that he really expects to be martyred.

56. See, e.g., Meyer, Plummer, Michael, Beare, Loh-Nida. This view has been challenged on lexical grounds by A. Denis (followed by Collange and Hawthorne). It ought also to be challenged on theological ones, since in Paul's Jewish heritage libations of blood were considered idolatrous, as Ps 16:4 makes clear.

57. Classical literature offers only a couple of analogous uses of the metaphor. Lightfoot notes that Seneca uses the metaphor of "drink offering" to refer to his impending death, and Meyer offers an undated source from the Greek side. The other known use of the metaphor is later (Ignatius [Rom 2.2]) and is probably based on 2 Tim 4:6 (or this passage interpreted through 2 Tim 4:6). A second c. papyrus noted in BAGD has been shown to be in error (Denis, "Versé").

58. Which are expressed in Class 3 and 4 conditions (to use Burton's classifications [*Moods,* 100-112]); class 3 (more probable) is expressed with a future in the protasis; class 4 (less probable, and rare in the NT) with the optative. But cf. the translations which assume the metaphor to refer to his (near future) death: "am to be poured out" (RSV [corrected in the NRSV], NAB, REB [NEB has, "if my life blood is to crown that sacrifice"], Goodspeed, Z-G); "perhaps my life blood is to be poured out" (GNB, supported by Loh-Nida); "has to be poured out" (NJB, Moffatt); cf. Meyer, "if I even should be poured out"; Kennedy, "Nay, even though I should even be offered." This has been variously justified on grammatical grounds that appear to be questionable. Silva (152), e.g., has argued on the basis of BDF §372.4 that εἰ can be used for ἐάν, citing Matt 5:29 as an

does it likely express concession in this case,[59] as though he were conceding that his imprisonment might lead to death. The *kai* that goes with the "if" is almost certainly intensive, heightening the actuality. Thus Paul intends: "if indeed, as is the case, I am currently being poured out."

Two contextual matters seem decisive. First, as to the larger context of the letter, Paul nowhere suggests (or even hints) that he expects his imprisonment to end in death. Quite the opposite. He might yearn that it did (1:23), but in fact he expects that he will be vindicated (1:19-20), and that out of (divine) necessity he will live (1:24) and return to see them again (1:25-26); indeed, at the end of the very next paragraph (2:24) he affirms that "I am persuaded *in the Lord* that I myself will come soon." These data make the grammatical issue all the more significant, since in light of what he expresses clearly (and not by metaphor), had he here intended to allude to the possibility of martyrdom, one should have expected some kind of suppositional conditional sentence.

---

example, so that "the clue lies in the extremity of the condition" (apparently followed by O'Brien [305], "the present tense after εἰ simply states the supposition graphically," but without grammatical support or analogy). But this seems to be a case of confusion, since the examples in BDF all refer to present general conditions (Burton's Class 5, which ordinarily take ἐάν with the subjunctive, but in such cases as that cited may take εἰ with the indicative). But none of these examples has anything to do with *suppositions,* something that may or may not happen *in the future.* While it is true that "rules" do not always hold, and that in some cases these classes of clauses may become slightly "mixed," I know of no analogy for a conditional sentence like this one to refer to a future supposition. Silva has rightly rejected the suggestion by some that this is a case of a present tense verb functioning like a future, since that happens primarily in eschatological contexts, and is very often accompanied by a temporal adverb (such as in 2 Tim 4:6, to which O'Brien appeals to make his case here, but which seems in fact to work the other way — the adverb in that case is precisely what is missing here). Thus the emphatic denial by Plummer (54), echoed by many others, that "the present tense does not mean that the sacrifice has begun," is pure assertion, for which he and others offer no analogies. It must be noted, finally, that these various grammatical assertions seem to be the product of determining first what the *imagery* is going to mean, and then trying to find a way around the plain sense of Paul's grammar afterward (see next n. as well).

59. Gk. εἰ καί. Although this idiom (including ἐὰν καί) is regularly understood to be concessive, there are some cases in Paul where concession is clearly impossible (as nonsensical), and where the καί must therefore be understood as intensive ("if indeed"). This is especially true in its first occurrence in the corpus (1 Cor 4:7), where Paul cannot possibly mean, "even if you have received it," but "if indeed you have received it [and you have, is the clear implication], why then do you act as though it were not a gift?"; cf. 1 Cor 7:11, 28; 2 Cor 11:15; 2 Tim 2:5. While in most other cases, a concessive idea works well, there is still no reason to discard the intensive, which not only works as well as concession, but in many cases seems to be better (as, e.g., 2 Cor 4:3, where "if indeed our gospel is hidden, as it is in fact" makes better sense than the more traditional "even if this were the case," especially since it is *in fact* the case; for the intensive as making the best sense in context of 1 Cor 7:21, see Fee, *First Corinthians,* 317).

Second, in terms of immediate context, he has just said that he and they are experiencing "the *same* struggle" (1:30); now he images his drink offering as in close association with their "sacrifice." Since it is altogether unlikely that he is speaking of their martyrdom, as most interpreters recognize,[60] then it is equally unlikely, given what he says elsewhere in the letter, that by this metaphor he intends to speak about his.

But if not, then what? One cannot be certain here, but since this paragraph serves with 1:27-30 as an inclusio ("bracket"), the most likely option is that the metaphor refers to the present suffering (in his case, by imprisonment) mentioned in 1:30. Thus he is suggesting that his imprisonment, besides being a "drink offering" to the Lord, is to be understood as his part of their common suffering,[61] the "drink offering" poured out in conjunction with[62] their "sacrifice."

Unfortunately, the Philippian side of the imagery is equally uncertain. Had Paul said only "sacrifice," this would undoubtedly point to them as the sacrifice. But the addition, "and service,"[63] with the qualifier "of your faith," points to them as those who are "ministering,"[64] but doing so in the context

60. It is of interest that Michael, one of the strongest advocates of "impending death" for this metaphor, also argues vigorously that the next part of the imagery refers to the Philippians, and therefore that Paul is urging that "there is correspondence in sacrifice" (he refers to 1:30 as well). His second point is properly taken, which is what makes the reciprocal rejoicing not tautologous; but it is more difficult to see how their mere "struggle" corresponds to Paul's martyrdom. Under no circumstances does 1:30 refer to Paul's "martyrdom."

61. Cf. Hawthorne and Kee (CASB, 187-88), who have also made the connection with present suffering. Earlier suggestions (by Manson, Denis, and Collange) propose apostolic ministry in general (rather than imprisonment) as the "drink offering," but that does not seem to fit the sacrificial image as well.

62. Gk. ἐπί, which is sometimes brought forward as evidence for a pagan background, since with the dative it often means "upon." But the LXX sometimes uses this preposition with the drink offering *in connection with* the sacrifice (Num 15:5; cf. Gen 35:14; Exod 15:29); and since it was not poured out on the sacrifice itself, the preposition probably means "at," in the sense of "at the time of" (cf. BAGD, ἐπί II.2). O'Brien (307) objects to this meaning on the grounds that "it requires θυσία to be understood as 'the act of sacrificing' " (which he rightly points out it almost certainly does not mean). But the use in Num 15:5 overrules the objection.

63. It should be pointed out that the two words have the article in common, thus indicating that they belong together "as forming one event" (Loh-Nida, 74).

64. Most earlier interpreters (see, e.g., Calvin, Meyer, Jones) think that Paul is still the subject of these activities ("whilst I present your faith as a sacrifice and perform priestly service in respect to it," Meyer), a view allegedly supported by Rom 15:16-17. But Paul makes a quite different point there (see Fee, *Presence*, 626-27). The grammar and sense of the present passage suggest otherwise, as does the mutual joy encouraged in the apodosis and follow-up sentence. Indeed, it is difficult to make much sense of this option at all. How is their faith something Paul sacrifices to God?

of sacrifice that comes as the direct result of their "faith."[65] In light of his use of sacrificial imagery again in 4:18 to refer to their gift to him, the present usage may very well refer to their gift as well.[66] But what is less clear in this case is how his imprisonment might be the "drink offering" poured out in conjunction with their sacrificial gift. Thus, it seems most likely, but by no means certain, that both sides of the imagery recall 1:29-30, that God has "graced" them not only to "believe" in Christ, but also to suffer for his sake. Paul's present imprisonment serves as the "drink offering," which accompanies their own suffering in behalf of Christ.

But how, then, does this connect with v. 16? That is, how does this metaphorical reference to their common suffering serve as response to their obedience to these injunctions serving as eschatological evidence that he has not served Christ in vain? The logic seems to be that, rather than his having run in vain, which in fact is unthinkable, his present suffering, which is also on their behalf in the midst of their own suffering, presents the real picture of their relationship. What is missing is an implied middle step, which on this view would go something like this: "I expect you to be my grounds for boasting at the Parousia, evidence that I have not labored in vain. (And presently my labor includes imprisonment, as yours does suffering in Philippi.) But if indeed my present struggle represents a kind of drink offering to go along with your own suffering on behalf of the gospel, then I rejoice over that."

In any case, he says, "if indeed this is the case" (= if my suffering is to be understood in conjunction with yours — and the condition is a real one), then that too is cause for joy. So he rejoices in prayer and thanksgiving as he recalls their faith(fulness) in the gospel (1:4); he rejoices over the advance of the gospel in Rome resulting from his imprisonment, even by those who do so out of "selfish ambition" (1:18a); he will yet rejoice as he and his gospel are vindicated at his forthcoming trial (1:18b); he wants that joy to be brought to its full measure by their "obedience" to the present appeal (2:2); and now he insists on rejoicing in the midst of their mutual suffering for Christ. "I rejoice," all on my own, as it were, he says first; then he adds "and I rejoice with all of you as well."[67]

---

65. This is to take the genitive as "source or origin" (= your faith is what prompts your present sacrificial "ministry"; cf. Michael, Beare, Hendriksen, Caird, Kent, Hawthorne, Silva). Many (e.g., Vincent, Kennedy, Jones, O'Brien) take it as "objective," or "appositional," suggesting that their faith is what is offered up as sacrifice, although it is not easy to see what exactly that means.

66. As many think (e.g., Martin, Hawthorne).

67. There is good evidence that συγχαίρω can mean "I congratulate you." If so, this would remove the apparent redundancy of "I rejoice, and I rejoice along with you," only to have him turn about in the following sentence and urge them to do what seems already implied in this first clause. So Lightfoot, Meyer, Plummer. But Paul uses this verb

**18**   This final sentence is an invitation for them to reciprocate. In the same way, he adds, "you also rejoice (on your own, as it were) and then join with me in rejoicing together." Although for some this has created an awkward redundancy, very likely it is probably an especially significant moment with regard to this theme in the letter. To this point every mention of "joy," except in 1:25, has had to do with Paul himself.[68] With this imperative a subtle, but noticeable, shift toward them takes place.[69] What began in 1:25 as concern for their "progress and *joy* regarding the faith" is now put into the form of an imperative, an imperative that will recur at further points in the rest of the letter;[70] significantly, its first occurrence (1) is totally intertwined with Paul's joy, and (2) is found in the context of rejoicing in the midst of suffering and opposition.

Here, then, is the most likely reason for this otherwise unusual conclusion to the long appeal of 1:27–2:18. Paul has already modeled joy in the face of opposition and suffering (1:18); his concern for them is both with their "progress" and their *joy* regarding the gospel. Now, in anticipation of the renewal of their joy at the coming of Epaphroditus (2:28) and the imperative to "rejoice *in the Lord* (always)" that frames the final exhortation (3:1; 4:4), Paul begins by linking that imperative to his own joy, both in the context of present suffering and in the mutuality of that suffering. Just as they are in this thing together, as far as the gospel (1:5, etc.) and suffering for Christ (1:29-30) are concerned, so too he wants them to share his joy in the advance of the gospel, no matter what the present circumstances. It is perhaps noteworthy, therefore, that this intentional redundancy occurs in this case hard on the heels of an explicit reminder of his and their mutual eschatological certainty (v. 16); likewise the imperatives of 3:1 and 4:4 frame an appeal that has steadfastness regarding their future orientation as an integral part (3:11-15, 19-21).

Thus, the double repetition, even though it appears unnecessarily redundant, makes perfectly good sense both in the context of the whole letter and at this point in the "argument." What Paul is emphasizing in each case is that, first, he and they rejoice on their own accounts for the privilege of serving the gospel, even in the midst of great adversity, and second that they do so mutually, as they have done so much else mutually.

Joy in suffering, it should finally be noted, is not "delight in feeling

---

elsewhere in the sense given here (1 Cor 12:26; 13:6); and the emphasis in the double repetition makes sense as suggested.

68. See 1:4, 18 [2x], 2:4, 17 [2x].

69. Paul's own "rejoicing" occurs only once more in the letter — at 4:10, where he tells them that "I rejoiced greatly" at their renewed practical concern for him, which rounds off this motif the way it began in 1:4.

70. See 3:1 and especially 4:4; cf. the purpose clause in 2:28 (also 29).

badly"; rather it is predicated on the unshakable foundation of the work of Christ, both past and future. Joy has nothing to do with circumstances, but everything to do with one's place in Christ. And this is probably how we are to understand the "missing link" between vv. 16 and 17. Having just expressed their eschatological future in terms of their being his ground for "glorying" (in Christ, is assumed) with an eye toward the coming Day of Christ, he concludes that sentence with a motivational word: that Paul will not have run in vain. But on this matter he has no real doubt, as these final sentences make clear. They are in this thing together; and he does not expect to have labored in vain. On the contrary, his and their life in Christ are too closely bound up together, both in believing and in suffering, for there to be any doubt about the future. Hence the final word is one of joy: let joy abound, he says, since mine already does, even in this Roman confinement. And on this note the "letter of exhortation" concludes momentarily, as he returns to the matters that have to do with the "letter of friendship."

We need to note in conclusion, however, that this final note is not merely an expression of Christian piety, but of genuine concern for the Philippians in their present circumstances. He concluded the section — 1:12-26, about "his affairs" — on the note of their "progress in the faith (the gospel)" and their joy in his coming to them again; now he concludes this section, which has had their "progress" in the gospel as its primary concern, on the same note of joy. From here he returns to some final matters of chronology about their and his affairs, in terms of three "comings" from Rome to Philippi (Epaphroditus's now, Timothy's very soon, and his own as soon as he can), after which he will return to a final word about their situation and the progress of the gospel in Philippi (3:1–4:3). That section is framed by the imperative, "rejoice *in the Lord*" (3:1; 4:4), which suggests that at issue is not simply their joy as such, but that they find their joy *in the Lord,* so that they will not need to look elsewhere.

Because of the extremely complex nature of this paragraph — including its grammar, the unusually high incidence of intertextuality, and the role of the metaphors in v. 17 — one can easily lose sight of the forest for the trees. But there are some significant theological points that need to be noted at the end. First, one must not lose sight of the fact that everything else that is said is brought to bear on the opening imperative: "Do all things without grumblings and disputings." Because so many of us are prone to such behavior, it is easy to dismiss this as a very "mundane" matter; but the very fact that Paul spends so much energy giving biblical and theological support to it suggests otherwise. This is spoken in the context of their — and our — being God's children in a very fallen, twisted world. Our corporate behavior, especially as that is reflected in our attitudes toward one another, goes a long way in determining how effectively we "hold firm the word of life" in such a world. Thus, evangelism is the bottom line, and internal bickering among the people of God is thoroughly counter-productive activity.

Second, Paul's use of the "story" of Israel (in this case, its failure) as his way of including the Philippians as God's people — indeed, as the eschatological continuity of his people — says much about our own place in God's story. Again, the concern is with our behavior — with our "succeeding" where Israel failed. The underlying theology in all of this is God's own character, as that is now reflected in his children who bear his likeness as we live out the life of the future in the present age. Only as we reflect God's own likeness will our evangelism be worth anything at all, both in terms of its aim and of its being successful.

Third, although not as directly related to vv. 14-16 as it is to the whole of the section (from 1:27), the return to the leitmotif of "joy" in the midst of "suffering" must not be missed. Neither "plastic joy" nor "trumped up suffering" will do. Suffering for Paul is ultimately a theological matter; it has to do with our relationship with Christ and our unyielding commitment to the gospel in our present, very pagan world — which is neither a "friend to grace" nor sympathetic to our confession that *only* Jesus is Lord. Suffering for its own sake will not do; and suffering because "we are right, let the rest be damned" has nothing to do with this text nor with the Christian faith. The joy comes from our relationship with Christ and with one another in Christ, as well as from our eschatological certainty; the suffering must be the direct result of trying to bring others in on the joy, or it deflects from Christ's suffering. Only so can we also rejoice in one another's suffering — as evidence that the proper "sacrifices" are being offered up to God.

## IV. WHAT'S NEXT — REGARDING PAUL'S AND THEIR AFFAIRS (2:19-30)

Having informed the Philippians about "his affairs" (as "reflections on imprisonment," 1:12-26) and appealed to them regarding "their affairs" (that they live worthy of the gospel, 1:27–2:18), Paul now proceeds to "what's next." And "what's next" has to do with visits to Philippi[1] (Timothy's [vv.

1. R. W. Funk, *Language,* 264-74 (cf. "Apostolic *Parousia*"; White, *Body*), uses the language "travelogue" and "apostolic *parousia*" for the various passages in Paul's letters similar to this one, suggesting that they have a common "form" and "normally" occur at the end of the "letter body." But as T. Y. Mullins has correctly pointed out ("Visit Talk"), the "formal" aspects do not hold together at all, in that only one feature isolated by Funk occurs in all the passages he analyzes; and "normal" is in the eye of the beholder,

19-23]; his own [24]; and Epaphroditus's [25-30]), which from the point of view of his writing the letter are all future, but from that of their reading it are partly future (vv. 19-24) and partly completed (vv. 25-30).

After the exalted language of the Christ story in 2:6-11 and the striking metaphors in 2:14-18 by which this was applied to the Philippians' situation, it is easy to view this material as mundane — which in a sense it is — and to neglect it as of little import, which it is not. After all, this is the stuff of which real letters are made, even though we are not quite used to that in Paul! On the other hand, neither should we make too much of it, as some have done, and thus give it greater significance than Paul intends. What this section does for us is to put all kinds of things into perspective as to the reasons for the letter.

The material falls into two clear parts. First (vv. 19-24), he hopes to send Timothy as soon as the outcome of his imprisonment has been resolved.[2] Expecting it to go in his favor, he is "persuaded in the Lord" that he himself will come to them "shortly." He expects to hear back from Timothy, however, *before* he comes (v. 19b). Meanwhile, second (vv. 25-30), out of kindness to them, he has sent the now-recovered Epaphroditus on ahead with this letter. Typically for Paul, both paragraphs also serve as "letters of commendation"[3] — for two brothers who scarcely need such.

All of this is rather straightforward.[4] The only real surprise is that he

---

since such "visit talk" occurs in a variety of other places in Paul's letters as well (in Philippians at 1:25-26; cf. 1 Thess 2:17–3:6; 1 Cor 4:16-20; 2 Cor 8:16-24; 1 Tim 3:14-15). As White himself points out (*Body,* 144) regarding 1 Thessalonians, the placement is "due to the peculiar nature of the epistolary situation." In fact, this can be said in every case, including those that are deemed to be "formally" and therefore "normally" at the end of the letter body.

2. While it is true that Paul does not explicitly say this, such an understanding of v. 23 is quite in keeping with what he has said to this point (in 1:19-20, 24-26, 27; 1:12) and especially with the catch phrase τὰ περὶ ἐμέ (*contra* Hawthorne; see on v. 23).

3. It is remarkable that in the various "formal" analyses of the letter (see n. 1 above) scholars have discussed at some length the so-called travelogue or apostolic *parousia* "form," which is "formal" only in a loose sense, while the much greater ties of these paragraphs to the "letter of commendation," included in various letters to identify and commend the carrier of the letter, have been generally neglected. On this matter see C.-H. Kim, *Form,* 119-43. In Paul see esp. 1 Thess 3:2-3 ("commendation" for Timothy *after the fact!*); 1 Cor 16:15-18; 2 Cor 8:16-24 (which is the true "form" of this material, not "travelogue"; *contra* Funk); Rom 16:1-2; Col 4:7-9. As with the "visit talk" (see n. 1), these various passages have some elements in common, but lack "form" in any meaningful sense of that term. The common features that these two paragraphs have with various of these "commendations" will be pointed out along the way.

4. Or so one would think; but a survey of the literature indicates how easily assumptions and assertions intermingle without the slightest hesitation. These move in a

should send Timothy at all, given Epaphroditus' return and that Paul hopes himself to come as soon as possible. Furthermore, why should he "commend" Epaphroditus to them, who is one of their own? And why this order of the two paragraphs, since they are chronologically in reverse? With the answers to these questions lie some keys to the occasion and purpose of our letter.

We take the chronological matter first, since that will put several things into perspective. To this point, the content of the letter has followed a discernible chronological scheme:[5] Epaphroditus's arrival with their gift and news from Philippi, reflected in the thanksgiving and prayer, is the starting point, followed by Paul's reflections on his imprisonment ("my [present] affairs," 1:12-26) and his appeal regarding their present situation, to stand firm in the midst of suffering and be of one mind in doing so (1:27–2:18). In terms of chronology, therefore, the coming of Epaphroditus with this letter should come next; but in terms of the "logic" of the letter the proposed sending of Timothy and the assurance of his own visit come next, followed by the commendation of Epaphroditus.

The "logic" is to be found in the repetition in the first paragraph of the phrase "your affairs" (vv. 19 and 20) from 1:27, and "my affairs" (v. 23), recalling 1:12.[6] In addition Paul also echoes the language — and concern — of "one's own interests" from 2:4, whose opposite now is not "the interests of others," but "the interests of Jesus Christ" (v. 21) which in fact proves to be the theological undergirding of the former — one seeks "the interests of Jesus Christ" when one "looks out for the interests of others," instead of "one's own." Thus, vv. 19-24 logically follow 1:27–2:18 by taking up his concern about "their affairs," and tying that to Timothy's proposed visit. What drives Paul to write this letter is twofold: thanksgiving for the gift (which, of course, could have been sent orally with Epaphroditus) and the situation in Philippi. Although Paul's response to the latter does not suggest serious problems — yet — they are serious enough to warrant this "pre-arrival" letter.

---

variety of directions, and are often contradictory, based either on prior commitments to a point of view (e.g., Michael, who is so sure that Paul is staring death in the face — despite what is clearly said to the contrary in this letter — that he would excise the paragraph on Timothy altogether) or on the difficulties noted in the discussion as to the order and content of these paragraphs which commend to the Philippians two brothers whom they know well. See further nn. 7, 13, 14, 42, 45 on this paragraph and nn. 7, 8, 12, 19, 21, 28, 29, 38, 50 on vv. 25-30.

5. On this matter, see the Introduction, pp. 37-39.

6. Since this seems to be so clearly what is at work (see n. 17 on 1:12; n. 13 on 1:27; and the discussion on 1:27), one is surprised at how seldom these connections are noted in the literature (as far as I can determine, the clear linkage between 1:27 and 2:19 and 23-24 is not mentioned at all).

Which in turn explains this double sending of Epaphroditus and Timothy, and in that chronological order, before he comes himself.[7]

First, he "must" send Epaphroditus now, because he owes that to them out of friendship — between him and them, and between them and Epaphroditus. But it also gives him opportunity to send this letter in advance. Second, Timothy will come a little later, because he also owes that to them out of friendship — his with them (to let them know the outcome, which he could not wait to find out before sending Epaphroditus), and theirs with him (so as to be strengthened and to work on the issues in 1:27–2:18 before he comes; see on v. 19). But the latter concern is also — especially — for the sake of the gospel in Philippi, which is what causes the Timothy material to come immediately after 1:27–2:18 and before the Epaphroditus material.

Paul's chief concern, and the *ultimate* reason for this letter, is the progress of the gospel in Philippi. This is what he reminds them of in the thanksgiving; this is what he wants them to know about his own situation, that it is advancing the gospel in Rome even in the face of opposition; and this is what he wants to learn about them (1:27), that they are walking "worthy of the gospel" in the face of opposition and suffering in Philippi (2:14-16). Timothy's reason for coming, therefore, besides encouragement (v. 20) and informing them about the outcome of "Paul's affairs" (v. 23), is to "cheer Paul" (v. 19) by reporting back about their situation (addressed in 1:27–2:18 and hopefully "cured" by this letter before Timothy arrives), and to do so before Paul himself comes (v. 24).

This, then, is why he will send Timothy soon, to see how they are doing, both in their suffering and in holding firm the gospel in the unity of the Spirit. In this regard, both paragraphs seem to be written so as to present these two brothers as further models: Timothy as one whom they know to live for the sake of Christ, and thus for the concerns of others; Epaphroditus, as one who in his suffering for Christ that brought him near death did not flag in doing the "work of Christ."[8]

---

7. This, at least, seems to make eminently good sense both of the place and purpose of these paragraphs in the letter, *contra* a variety of other reconstructions: (a) that our Philippians is a collage of three letters to Philippi, one of which was concluded by these paragraphs (e.g., Beare, Collange; see the Introduction, pp. 21-23); (b) that they function as a *digressio* in a piece of deliberative rhetoric (Watson; see Introduction, pp. 14-16); (c) that they are "apologetic" in some form or another: for Epaphroditus's "hasty" return (e.g., Michael, Hawthorne; cf. White, *Body,* 145 n. 96: "Homesickness is no excuse for leaving his post"!); for Ephaphroditus's coming when they were expecting Timothy (Silva); for Epaphroditus, who belongs to one of the dissenting factions back home (Mayer). Some of these belong to the mixture of assumption and assertion noted above in n. 4.

8. Several recent interpreters (e.g., Culpepper, "Co-Workers"; Hawthorne; Watson, "Rhetorical Analysis," 71-72; Bloomquist, *Function,* 128-29) see this as a more dominant motif in these paragraphs than the data seem to allow.

It needs only to be pointed out once again how much the triangular concern that drives the whole letter (between him and them and Christ [and the gospel]) is at work here as well.

## A. TIMOTHY AND PAUL TO COME LATER (2:19-24)

> 19*I hope in the Lord Jesus[9] to send Timothy to you soon, that I also may be cheered when I receive news about you.* 20*I have no one else like him, who takes a genuine interest in your welfare.* 21*For [all are looking] out for [their][10] own interests, not those of Jesus Christ.[11]* 22*But you know that Timothy has proved himself, because as a son with his father he has served with me in the work of the gospel.* 23*I hope, therefore, to send him as soon as I see how things go with me.* 24*And I am confident in the Lord that I myself will come[12] soon.*

Given the place of this paragraph in the "logic" of the letter, it remains to show how it works out. Verse 19 sets out the basic datum and its reason — a proposed visit by Timothy, which turns out to be primarily for Paul's sake. He hopes to be "cheered" by (further) news about "your affairs," presumably whether his letter has had any effect. But this needs explanation, so vv. 20-22 offer a twofold justification for the sending of Timothy, which turns out to be only partly justification for doing so *at all,* and mostly justification for sending *Timothy.* Thus v. 20 indicates why *only* Timothy will do, to which Paul appends a surprising word of contrast (v. 21), explaining that all are not like Timothy. He then (v. 22) reminds them of their knowledge of Timothy, which focuses on his "proven worth" and his long-term service alongside Paul in the cause of the gospel.

These three sentences function like a "letter of commendation" — for

---

9. The "Lord Jesus" is the reading of the majority of MSS, both early and late. Some witnesses (C D* F G 630 1739 1881 pc), quite missing the echo of vv. 9-11, substitute the more common "Christ Jesus."

10. NIV, "everyone looks . . . his"; Gk. οἱ πάντες . . . τὰ ἑαυτῶν. Retaining Paul's plurals eliminates the need for the gender specific "his."

11. In keeping with their more usual order in this letter, the majority of MSS (B MajT pc) have transposed Paul's "Jesus Christ" (found in P[46] ℵ A C D F G P Ψ 33 81 326 1739 1881 it pc; K and Cyprian omit "Jesus") to "Christ Jesus." The "more difficult reading" should prevail as original, since scribes will have conformed to the more usual, and therefore more expected, order than vice versa.

12. Typically, a number of MSS (ℵ* A C P 326 629 1241[s] 2464 a f vg sy[p] sa[mss] bo), some apparently independently of the others, added πρὸς ὑμᾶς ("to you") to the ἐλεύσομαι at the end of Paul's sentence. Such an addition is easily explicable, since Paul's sentence has the feel of having been left hanging.

Timothy, of all things, who is *not* coming with this letter, but will be coming later.[13] Although the paragraph, therefore, fits a well-known letter-writing convention, it also offers "justification" for Paul's sending him to find out about their affairs — after Epaphroditus has returned![14] But this explanation gets away from Paul a bit, so in vv. 23-24 he *resumes* the basic datum — the sending of Timothy — but with two additional pieces of information (filling out some earlier information): Timothy is to be sent as soon as Paul has some sense about "his own affairs"; and he himself will come as soon as possible. These pick up items from 1:19-20 and 24-26.

Thus vv. 19 and 23-24 function as a kind of travel narrative. But it is not possible even here for the apostle to speak without expressing concern for the gospel. So along with the basic issue of his and their relationship, and his concern about them, the explanatory "commendation" of Timothy (vv. 20-22) has the gospel as its underlying current, becoming explicit at the end of v. 22. The *content* of vv. 20-22 suggests that, along with himself (in 1:12-26) and Christ (2:5-11), Timothy is also being set forth as something of a paradigm.

**19** Having brought himself back into the picture at the end of the long exhortation, by reflecting on his and their respective suffering (vv. 17-18), Paul returns to where the narrative left off in 1:26.[15] This opening sentence offers the basic datum ("I hope . . . to send Timothy to you soon"), and his reason for it ("that I for my part may be cheered when I learn about 'your affairs' "[16]). Since

13. On the other hand, he has done the same thing for Timothy in 1 Thess 3:2-3, *after* Timothy had been to Thessalonica and had returned. Collange's assumption (116), therefore, that this commendation is evidence of Timothy's "weakness" ("somewhat spineless character") is altogether unwarranted.

14. Some recent interpreters have suggested that Paul instead is offering reasons "why it was necessary . . . for [Timothy] to stay with the apostle" (Silva, 156; cf. O'Brien, 320, "factors . . . that necessitated Timothy's presence with the apostle"). This takes up a suggestion by Michael (117), followed by Hendriksen (134-35), that the apostle will send him only reluctantly because he can "ill afford to part with [him]." But nothing in the text either explicitly or implicitly suggests that lying behind this paragraph is a justification for Paul's not sending Timothy now, nor does this suggestion capture Paul's *explicit* concerns.

15. The sentence is joined to what has preceded with a δέ, which many of the older commentators (Meyer, Vincent) considered to be contrastive to vv. 17-18 (so also O'Brien, among recent commentators). More likely it is a "transitional particle pure and simple" (BAGD), hence (correctly) left untranslated by the NIV. If translated, it means something like, "now," in the sense of moving the letter along to the next item.

16. Gk. τὰ περὶ ὑμῶν, again in v. 20; cf. 1:27. As in 1:27 (n. 13), the NIV has chosen to bypass the significant τά that precedes περὶ ὑμῶν. Although it is arguably legitimate to translate this phrase in v. 20 as "your welfare," the result is that the reader misses altogether the relationship of these two sentences; and in the case of v. 20 it puts the emphasis more on Timothy's being there for their encouragement, than for the sake of the gospel — which seems to underline Paul's concern. "Your affairs" works fine in both sentences, and allows for the broader view that both their suffering and lack of harmony are in purview.

the outcome of his trial is still future, he "hopes"[17] to do this (repeated in v. 23), in contrast to the actual "I thought it necessary to send Epaphroditus" in v. 25. This hope is qualified as "in the Lord Jesus,"[18] a qualifier which is used in similar ways, and with a whole variety of nuances, throughout the letter.[19] As in 1:14, the emphasis is on the *grounds* for his "hope." From the time he was "found in Christ Jesus" (3:9), so that Christ thus became his whole life (1:21), everything Paul thinks, says, or does is based on his relationship with "the Lord Jesus."[20] Thus, even though "hope" may be watered down at times (as in our idiom, "I hope so," when we have very little confidence about something), this qualifier, plus the change in v. 24 to "I am persuaded in the Lord" when referring to his own coming, suggests that "hope" moves much closer to certainty.[21]

The word "soon,"[22] which ordinarily means "quickly," in the sense of "without delay," can hardly mean that here. In light of its usage in v. 24, it can only mean "as soon as possible"; even so this word is probably used to express the urgency Paul feels about the matters just addressed (in 1:27–2:18). Thus, it will be "without delay," once the present delay regarding the outcome of his incarceration is resolved.

The *reason* for sending Timothy is expressed in terms quite the reverse of his ordinary reason for sending one of his co-workers to a church. In most cases, it is for *their* sakes — to straighten something out, or to bring something started to completion.[23] But here it is first of all for his own sake, that "I for

17. For this use of ἐλπίζω regarding expected travel plans, see 1 Cor 16:7; Rom 15:24; Phlm 22; 1 Tim 3:14.
18. On the textual question see n. 9 above. The expression "in the Lord Jesus" is just unusual enough to suggest that Paul is deliberately recalling vv. 9-11, where Jesus has been given the name above every name, the name of the Lord God himself.
19. See 1:13, 14, 26; 2:1, 24, 29; 3:1, 3, 14; 4:1, 4, 7, 10, 19, 21.
20. O'Brien (317) translates "if the Lord Jesus wills"; but since Paul says that clearly when he so intends (1 Cor 4:19; 16:7; cf. 16:12), and since this prepositional phrase occurs with such regularity in this letter (see preceding n.), it seems difficult to justify that sense here.
21. Of the kind usually expressed with the noun (ἐλπίς), and referring to our certain eschatological future, as in 1:20 (q.v.); cf. 1 Thess 1:3; 4:13; 5:8; 2 Thess 2:16; 2 Cor 3:12; Gal 5:5; Rom 8:24; etc.
22. Gk. ταχέως, the adverb of ταχύς ("quick, swift, speedy"); for this use of the adverb in Paul see 1 Cor 4:19 and 2 Tim 4:9, where in each case it means "as quickly as possible," but does not suggest that it will happen immediately.
23. Cf. the sending of Timothy in 1 Thess 3:2-3 ("to establish and encourage you regarding your faith") and 1 Cor 4:17 ("to remind you of my ways in the Lord"), and of Titus in 2 Cor 8:16-24 — although it is clear that in the case of his sending Timothy to Thessalonica it was also to relieve his own anxiety about their welfare in Christ (as 3:5-8 make clear). On the basis of Col 4:8//Eph 6:22, Silva (155-56) suggests that "the purpose normally was that the church in question may be informed with regard to Paul's affairs and thus receive encouragement." As with the formal considerations noted above (n. 1), "normal" is in the eye of the beholder! Many earlier interpreters, despite what is actually

my part[24] might be cheered,"[25] in the sense of being encouraged or refreshed by good news about them. The implied contrast in "I for my part" is probably what he expects will happen to them as they learn from this letter and from Epaphroditus about "his affairs." Likewise, what will "cheer" Paul will be to "learn about your affairs." In light of the same phrase in 1:27, this can scarcely mean "about you" personally and probably not "about your affairs in general," but "about your affairs" addressed in 1:27–2:18. This is verified by the contrast in v. 21, where concern over one's own interests is contrasted with "those of Jesus Christ." This, after all, is the concern that causes the letter to be written at all. It is this sending of Timothy and expectation of hearing back from him[26] before he himself comes that makes the "soon" in Paul's case so problematic (see on v. 24).

**20** With an explanatory "for," Paul proceeds to "commend" Timothy, even though he is not the bearer of the present letter. Significantly, the commendation does not speak first about their own long-term knowledge of him (see on 1:1), but about Paul's having no one like-minded. What he says about Timothy in this first instance sounds so much like his appeal to them in vv. 3-4, one must assume this to be intentional, and for their sakes.

First, then, "I have no one else *of like soul*[27] (or mind)." Although the

---

said, assume that the primary reason for Timothy's going is to "hearten" the Philippians in their time of need (e.g., Calvin, Lightfoot, Meyer); but see next note.

24. Gk. κἀγώ, which in a sentence like this means "I also," or as suggested, "I for my part." As noted in the discussion, this word indicates that he fully expects them to be cheered about news from him; but to elevate that to an equal reason alongside what Paul explicitly says (as so many do) quite misses Paul's point. As Michael (113) pointed out, "the enheartening of his readers is so obviously a purpose of the mission that the Apostle is content to allude to it in this way." But his *primary* reason for sending Timothy — at least in terms of what he wanted the Philippians to hear — is the one stated here: ἵνα κἀγὼ εὐψυχῶ (presuming that Timothy's report to Paul will indeed "cheer" the apostle, because the present letter will have accomplished its purposes).

25. Gk. εὐψυχῶ, only here in the NT; cf. the usage in Josephus (*Ant.* 11.241): "he cheered Esther and encouraged her to hope for the best."

26. What cannot be determined, of course, is *where* or *how* he expected to hear back from Timothy. Most assume that Timothy will "come back to him with news from there" (Bruce, 91); on the basis of his reconstruction of the events in the Pastoral Epistles, Hendriksen (134, followed by Kent) suggests a pre-arranged rendezvous in Ephesus. In any case, here is a place where we have to take the language at face value and not read into it more than we can ever know.

27. Gk. ἰσόψυχον, a NT hapax legomenon, as with εὐψυχῶ just above; cf. the similar hapax σύμψυχος in 2:2. It occurs in the LXX once (Ps 54:14[55:13]), where the NIV renders, "one like myself." Various attempts have been made to give it a more precise nuance (e.g., Christou, "'ΙΣΟΨΥΧΟΝ" [= confidant]; Jewett, *Anthropological Terms,* 349-50, following Fridrichsen, "Ἰσόψυχος" [= equal status in life, hence sharing equal existence with the Philippians in the new aeon]), but these have not met with much success.

referent of "like-souled" is not immediately clear, most likely Paul means that Timothy is "like-minded to me," rather than no one else is like-minded to Timothy.[28] Thus with a slight word play on "being cheered" (lit., "good souled"), Paul emphasizes that the primary reason for *Timothy's* coming is that he can count on him to carry Paul's own deep concerns at heart. Those concerns, repeating from v. 19, are for "your affairs." That is, when he arrives you can count on it, "he will genuinely[29] show concern[30] for your affairs," referring especially to how they are faring with regard to their standing firm in one Spirit in the face of opposition in Philippi (1:27-30). Paul thus begins with the reasons from his perspective why only Timothy will do; he will go on in v. 22 to the reason from their perspective. But before that he takes a broadside at some people, who are not of his or Timothy's mindset.

**21** With another explanatory "for," Paul now contrasts Timothy's concern for *the Philippians'* welfare with the mindset of others, who "seek their own interests, not those of Christ Jesus." That they stand in direct contrast to Timothy, who will be concerned about "your affairs" when he comes, attests that "the interests of Christ Jesus" have to do with love for God being shown by love for neighbor. This is what the letter to this point has been all about, Paul's own "seeking the interests of Christ Jesus," as he appeals to the Philippians to work out — among themselves and in Philippi — the salvation that Christ has brought them.

28. Although many take the latter stance (e.g., Calvin, Lightfoot, Jones, Michael, Dibelius, Lohmeyer, Müller, Hendriksen, Gnilka, Martin, Kent), both the context and the lack of an expressed object indicates that the implied object is the subject of the sentence (cf. Meyer, Vincent, Bonnard, Houlden, Christou, Collange, Loh-Nida [cf. GNB], Bruce, Hawthorne, Silva, O'Brien, Melick). Cf. the similar discussion on 1:3 (n. 37). As Meyer (126) correctly notes, even though the language differs, in content this echoes the similar passage in 1 Cor 16:10.

29. Gk. γνησίως, yet another NT hapax legomenon; however, it is the adverb of γνήσιος which describes the "yokefellow" whom Paul addresses in 4:3 (cf. 2 Cor 8:8; 1 Tim 1:2; Tit 1:4). The word originally referred to a "legitimate" child, and thus in time came to mean "genuine." Collange (followed by Bruce, Hawthorne), on the basis of the father-son imagery in v. 22, argues for its original sense here. He "is a legitimate son, the sole authorised representative of the apostle" (117). While that works well for the adjective in 1 Tim 1:2 and Tit 1:4, one is especially hard pressed to show that the adverb ever carried that sense.

30. Gk. μεριμνήσει; cf. 1 Cor 12:25, where his concern for the "visible" parts to take note of the (essential but) less visible, is that "the parts might show concern for one another." The future in the present passage indicates that it is not "concern about their welfare in general," as the present tense in the NIV implies, but that *when he gets there* he can be expected to show this concern (cf. Meyer). Several recent commentators recognize that this is what Paul intends, but then assert that the present tense is justified so as not to mislead the modern reader (Silva, O'Brien). How so, one wonders? Paul's concern is to speak specifically to the situation in Philippi, which the future tense makes clear but the present does not.

266

But we are poorly prepared for this sentence. Verses 20 (Paul's reasons from his perspective for sending Timothy) and 22 (Paul's reasons from their perspective) make perfectly good sense. But why *this* interruption, and who are these people, especially since Paul's brush sweeps so widely: "All" are like this.

We begin with the "all,"[31] which can only refer to people in Rome, not Philippi,[32] and which should mean something like, "the whole lot of them." But "the whole lot of whom," since he probably does not intend to indict every believer in Rome? The *form* of the contrast, especially the words in v. 20, "I have no one like-minded," sounds as if he intended to contrast Timothy with other co-workers who might be available for such duty.[33] But in fact Paul does not say that (nor is it necessarily implied, as many suggest).[34] Moreover, the *content* of the sentence makes this understanding difficult to believe. Given what we know of Paul elsewhere and the high regard with which he holds those who travel with him, and that in 4:21 he sends greetings from "the brothers who are with me," it does not seem possible that he should here slander them with this kind of barrage. Furthermore, in light of the next verse, it seems altogether unlikely that he would even have considered sending anyone else.

The contrast, therefore, is not between *Timothy and other co-workers* who could make this trip, but between *Timothy's character qualifications and some other people* who came to mind as Paul was dictating. These people are condemned precisely because they lack the two essential qualities noted of Timothy in v. 20: *like-mindedness* with Paul, which expresses itself in *genuine concern for others,* and thus exemplifies the character of the gospel as that was presented in 2:3-4. This seems verified by the content of the contrast; where we might have expected a contrast at the human level, "they seek their own interests not those of others," what we get is a contrast concerning the gospel: their "concerns" are not "those of Jesus Christ." Probably, therefore, this aside looks

31. Gk. οἱ πάντες, a combination which ordinarily would mean "all of them in contrast to a part" (cf. 1 Cor 9:22, "to all of them I became all things").

32. *Contra* Barth and Collange.

33. The position adopted by the vast majority of interpreters. But the difficulty with this view can be seen in the way they try to exonerate some of Paul's co-workers (arguing, e.g., as well may be the case, that Luke and Aristarchus are not currently with Paul).

34. Primarily on the basis of the verb "I have" and the object "no one." But this observation cuts both ways. Had Paul intended "no one *else*" in v. 20, he could easily have added an ἄλλον; to say "I have" does not imply "in my company," but "of all my companions I have no one like-minded in the same way he is" — an understanding that fits Holmberg's observation: "*Timothy* was undoubtedly the co-worker closest to Paul's heart" (*Paul*, 59).

267

in two directions at once. On the one hand, what prompts it are those people already mentioned in 1:15 and 17,[35] who preach Christ, but "not purely/ sincerely," and who therefore are not truly doing so for Christ's sake. On the other hand, as v. 20 has already hinted, Timothy is being set forth as yet another model of one who "thinks like Christ" and is therefore being singled out in light of some in Philippi who are otherwise-minded (2:3-4).

That means, therefore, that the contrast is not with anyone else whom Paul might be able to send but will not because they are too self-serving, but between Timothy's positive qualities in v. 20 and some in Rome — not to mention Philippi — who are otherwise. That this contrast is intended in part for Philippi seems verified by Paul's language, which is the clue to much. Such people, he says, "seek their own interests";[36] Paul has already appealed to the Philippians to do nothing out of self-interest, but rather in humility to regard the needs of others as having precedence to their own (2:3-4).

**22** From his denunciation of the self-seeking, Paul returns to the commendation of Timothy,[37] reminding the Philippians of their own knowledge of him: "His proven character[38] you know." The word "proven character" has been coined from the verb, "to put to the test." In 2 Cor 8:2 it refers to the "test" that the Philippians themselves had gone through; but in Rom 5:5 it denotes the "character" that such testing has produced. The latter is probably in view here. Because of long associations with Timothy, they know his worth, that his character has been put to the test and thus "he has proved himself" (NIV).

But as with almost everything else in this letter, Paul's interest in Timothy's "proven character" is not with his "character" in general, but as that has been demonstrated in the way "he has served with me in the cause of the gospel." As they well know, that relationship is one of "a son[39] with

35. Cf. Jewett ("Conflicting Movements," 365), "Paul severely indicts precisely the same persons."

36. Elsewhere Paul uses this identical language to describe those who are truly Christian ("love [meaning, the one who loves] does not seek its own interests" [1 Cor 13:5; cf. above on v. 4]; 1 Cor 10:24; 13:5), and in particular his own ministry as being "genuine" (1 Cor 10:33; 2 Cor 12:14).

37. The sentence begins with a δέ, probably in this case intending a contrast between Timothy's proven worth, which the Philippians know, and those in v. 21 who seek their own interests.

38. Gk. δοκιμήν, a strictly Pauline word in the NT (2 Cor 2:9; 8:2; 9:13; 13:3; Rom 5:4 [2x]); indeed, as M-M point out, the occurrence in 2 Cor 2:9 is the earliest known use of this word in the Greek world — although Paul probably did not coin it.

39. Gk. τέκνον, which emphasizes the relationship involved, as over against υἱός, where the emphasis is more on the status of "sonship" itself. For this usage applied to the Philippians, see v. 15 above; for Paul's describing Timothy in this term of endearment, see 1 Cor 4:17; 1 Tim 1:2 (cf. Phlm 10 of Onesimus, and Tit 1:4 of Titus). As Caird (129)

his father." But the emphasis in this case is not on their relationship as such, but on Timothy's being "likeminded" with his "father" in the gospel, alongside whom he has served for so many years. The reminder, therefore, is similar to that in 1 Cor 4:17, "like father, like son." You can count on his being among you as a son who looks and acts just like his father. Thus, "he has served[40] with me in the cause of the gospel," which is very much like what he had earlier thanked God for with regard to them (in 1:5). As with the content of the two preceding verses, this too is expressed in terms that recall earlier moments in the letter, and therefore is very likely intended also to serve in a paradigmatic way.

**23** With a resumptive "therefore,"[41] Paul returns to the basic datum of v. 19, that he "hopes to send Timothy." But now, instead of "soon," he qualifies with a clause that indicates why Timothy is coming later, and has not accompanied Epaphroditus. Although the clause is awkwardly expressed in Greek,[42] Paul's point is clear. As soon as he has any inkling[43] as to the outcome of the

points out, the imagery assumes family life in the Greco-Roman world, where the son learns the family trade from his father by working alongside him.

40. Gk. ἐδούλευσεν (lit., "performed the duties of a slave"), which in this case almost certainly intentionally echoes the noun in 1:1 (referring to himself and Timothy) and 2:7 (Christ).

41. Gk. μέν οὖν, a combination which expresses continuation or resumption, rather than inference.

42. It begins, ὡς ἂν, which in a context like this means "whenever." Thus he says, "whenever I find out about my affairs." To which he adds ἐξαυτῆς as the final word, which is a shortened form of ἐξ αὐτῆς τῆς ὥρας (= from which time), thus "at once" or "soon thereafter." The whole, therefore, means what the NIV renders, "as soon as I see how things go with me." Hawthorne (followed by Silva) objects to this understanding, and prefers "as soon as I see about my own affairs," meaning "that Timothy is presently indispensable to him" and that "his stay with him for the moment is much more important than his anticipated mission to Philippi." Paul is thus alleged to want Timothy to take care of some personal matters for him before he makes the trip. But to arrive at this meaning, Hawthorne must "divide and conquer," by trying to show that, rather than their ordinary meaning, words and phrases *can* mean something else — and therefore *do*. But the immediate context, the larger context of the letter, the meaning of ἀφίδω (next n.), and esp. the meaning of τὰ περὶ ἐμέ (Hawthorne tries to make this mean something quite different from the τὰ κατ' ἐμέ of 1:12; but the interchangeability of these two expressions in Col 4:7-8 plays the lie to this) combine to indicate that the traditional understanding is the correct one. In any case, Hawthorne's view requires that this is a bit ironic, that there is a proper concern for one's own affairs after all. But that seems highly unlikely.

43. Gk. ἀφίδω, a compound which literally means "look away from toward"; hence in Heb 12:2 it means exactly that, "to look away from their present struggles to Jesus, the pioneer and perfecter of their faith." But it is used by the LXX translator in Jon 4:5 to describe how Jonah sat in his shelter, to "wait and see" what would happen to the city. This seems to be the sense here, that Paul can send Timothy only after a "wait and see" period, which he obviously does not expect to be long.

trial, he will send Timothy to fill them in further on "my affairs."[44] Thus Timothy's reason for coming is twofold: in the first instance for Paul's sake, to see how the letter has affected them; and second for their sakes, to be encouraged and brought up to speed about the outcome of his imprisonment.

**24** Having indicated the second reason for Timothy's coming, to report on "my affairs," Paul concludes this brief look into the expected future by repeating what he told them in 1:24-26, this time even more emphatically: "I myself will come soon." Here is the certain evidence that the adverb "quickly" does not mean "right away," as it ordinarily does, but "quickly" in the sense of "at once after I see how things go with me."

In 1:24 this persuasion was expressed in terms of "necessity," implying "divine necessity" that had their "progress in the faith" as its ultimate concern. Now he expresses that persuasion in the strongest kind of language: "I am confident in the Lord," exactly as he has expressed it about those in Rome who have been emboldened toward greater evangelism as the result of Paul's imprisonment (1:14). It is hard to make it plainer, given the outcome is still in the future, that he fully expects to be released, and therefore that the talk about "death" in 1:21-23 was a yearning, not an anticipation of the near future.[45] Which in turn also indicates that the metaphor in v. 17 above is unlikely to be a reflection on martyrdom, but a reference to his present suffering.

Although a passage like this carries much less theological grist than what has preceded, what emerges is of considerable moment. Paul's description of Timothy, especially as that stands in contrast to those in Rome who out of rivalry are trying to increase his affliction, lies at the heart of what Paul understands Christian life to be all about. Reflecting the kind of concern he has raised by way of appeal in 2:3-4 (see v. 21), he reminds the Philippians that Timothy's coming to them would reflect his genuine concern about them; Timothy simply is not one to seek his own interests ahead of those of Christ Jesus. As noted on that passage, it is hard to imagine a more certain antidote to any number of struggles that consistently plague the local church, not to

---

44. Yet one more time in this long narrative — from 1:12 — he uses this terminology (τὰ περὶ ἐμέ), which now, in contrast to 1:12 (where he has τὰ κατ' ἐμέ), is expressed exactly as the phrase occurs regarding "their affairs" in vv. 19 and 20 (τὰ περὶ ὑμῶν; on the basic interchangeability of these expressions see n. 42).

45. *Contra* Michael and Caird, both of whom are so convinced (esp. on the basis of the metaphor in 2:17) that Paul is "staring death in the face," that they have considerable difficulty with this sentence (Michael would use it to argue that the paragraph does not belong to the original letter; and despite what Paul says, Caird suggests, "but he cannot have much confidence in his release, or he would not have needed to send Timothy") — further examples of prior assumptions causing one to read between the lines (see n. 4). Cf. Beare (97), who sees Paul's attitude toward death and liberty as changing "almost from moment to moment."

mention larger bodies and denominations, than this one — that God's people all be as Timothy in terms of their putting the interests of others as the matter of first importance. Here again the way of "humility," taking the lower road by way of the cross, is on full display; and here alone, as the gospel impacts the people of God in this way at the core of our beings, can we expect truly to count for the gospel in a world that lives the opposite, not only as a matter of course, but for the most part as its primary value. One must "look out for number one," after all. Agreed, as long as one recognizes the cross to dictate that "number one" is one's neighbor and not oneself.

## B. EPAPHRODITUS TO COME NOW (2:25-30)

*25But I think it necessary to send back to you Epaphroditus, my brother, fellow worker and fellow soldier, who is also your messenger, whom you sent to take care of my needs. 26For he longs[1] for all of you and is distressed because you heard he was ill. 27Indeed he was ill, and almost died. But God had mercy on him, and not on him only but also on me, to spare me sorrow upon sorrow. 28Therefore I am all the more eager to send him, so that when you see him again you may be glad and I may have less anxiety. 29Welcome him in the Lord with great joy, and honor [people][2] like him, 30because he almost died for the work of Christ,[3] risking his life[4] to make up for the help you could not give me.*

1. A number of MSS add the infinitive "to see" (ℵ* A C D I^vid 33 81 104 326 365 1175 2464 2495 pc sy bo). This is a secondary addition on all counts: (a) its omission would be nearly impossible to explain, whereas the addition can be accounted for on the analogy of 1 Thess 3:6; Rom 1:11; 2 Tim 1:4; (b) the text without ἰδεῖν fits the mood of this letter; as with Paul in 1:8, Epaphroditus longs for them, which included "to see" them, but is not limited to such. Cf. Metzger, *Textual Commentary,* 613-14.
2. NIV, "men"; Gk. τοὺς τοιούτους (= "such people").
3. As often happens with Paul's mention of Christ, especially in genitives like this, the name here has a tortured textual history. The alternatives are "Christ" (P^46 B D F G 6 1175 1739 1881 2464 Maj latt sa) and "Lord" (ℵ A P Ψ 33 81 104 365 1241^s pc sy^h bo); C omits it altogether (favored by Lightfoot, Kennedy, Plummer); 1985 and Chrysostom have "God." Not only is "Christ" better attested, but the phrase "work of the Lord" occurs elsewhere in Paul (1 Cor 15:58; 16:10), whereas "the work of Christ" is unique to this passage, hence the "more difficult" — and in this case surely the original — reading. The MajT (and D) add the article before "Christ," but that is not to designate him as *the* Christ," but to conform to standard usage, since the article occurs with "work" (in genitive phrases, standard usage is for both or neither word to have the article). Cf. Metzger, *Textual Commentary,* 614.
4. In place of Paul's uncommon παραβολευσάμενος, the later MajT substituted παραβουλουσάμενος, reflected in the KJV's "not regarding his life."

From his plans to hear about their affairs (now in response to this letter) and to come himself as soon as possible, Paul turns to the more immediate matter at hand — the return of Epaphroditus, who is also the bearer of the letter. Logically, this paragraph should precede the former: Epaphroditus now, Timothy and myself later. But Paul's logic is that of concern, not chronology. Most striking (for us) about the present paragraph is that it takes the form of commendation, the kind of thing that regularly appears in letters from the Greco-Roman period to "introduce" the bearer of the letter to the one(s) addressed.[5] How much one should make of this is a debated question, raised primarily because Epaphroditus is so well known and because, besides explaining Epaphroditus' long absence and recent recovery, Paul also urges them to welcome him with honor.

The paragraph is in two parts (vv. 25-27; 28-30), both of which (a) begin on the same note (Paul's having sent Epaphroditus), (b) mention Epaphroditus as the Philippians' "minister to my needs," and (c) note that Epaphroditus's illness brought him very near to death. What is being explained in both parts are the reasons for sending Epaphroditus *now,* and not waiting for the outcome of Paul's trial. The first part gives the reason from *Epaphroditus's perspective*: his own deep longing for the community back home in light of their knowing about his illness (v. 26). It begins with the fact of Paul's sending him, including a considerable elaboration of his relationship to Paul and his service to Paul on their behalf (v. 25). Having mentioned Epaphroditus's illness, Paul concludes with a note about the severity of the illness and the greatness of God's mercy (v. 27). Verses 28-30 then give the reason for sending him, now from *the Philippians' perspective*: their own joy in seeing him again which will lessen Paul's present sorrow to some degree (v. 28). He then concludes with the actual commendation (v. 29) and the reasons for it (v. 30) — that Epaphroditus risked his life to "fill up the vacancy of your absence" and thus "of your priestly service toward me."

But why such a commendation in this letter? Because of its length and his urging the community to receive him with joy, some have read this as indicative of the tension in the community, and that Epaphroditus was on one side of that tension,[6] while others see it as a semi-veiled "apology" for sending Epaphroditus home "before he had finished his commission" of staying with Paul and ministering to his needs.[7] But that is probably to read far too much

5. In Paul's case see 1 Cor 16:15-18; 2 Cor 8:16-24; Rom 16:1-2; Col 4:7-9; Eph 6:21-22.

6. See, e.g., Mayer ("Paulus"), noted favorably by Silva (160 n. 98) and O'Brien (341).

7. This view can be traced to Michael, 118-19, who asserts (without evidence) that "it was the intention of the Philippians . . . that Epaphroditus should remain with the Apostle so long as he had need of him." This "twofold mission" view has gained popularity

into very little, both in this paragraph and in the whole letter. Nowhere does Paul hint that tension within the community amounts to open "division." Rather, what is lacking is a common purpose, which has led to some posturing, including (apparently) some disputing and unwillingness to serve one another in love. It is possible, therefore, that Paul is here "covering Epaphroditus's tracks" for him, since he was the obvious bearer of this unhappy news to Paul. But since nothing else in the letter suggests tension between the church and Paul, and since the letter pours forth with affection at every point, far more likely this profusion of commendation is part of that affection. Paul has received their gift from Epaphroditus (cf. 4:18); now in sending him back he commends him to them as one of their own, and in honoring Epaphroditus, Paul honors them. Thus rather than read ulterior motives into words of affection, we should take them at face value.[8] Epaphroditus really has been full of concern for the "folks back home"; that he should have risked his life on their behalf is reason enough for Paul to urge them to receive him back with joy. That God has spared him so that he could come back at all is all the more reason for joy.

Many see this paragraph as paradigmatic as well, and given the role of every preceding narrative to this point, that may well be so again. If so, the paradigm here moves toward the "suffering" side of things in this letter. Epaphroditus models one who was ready to "risk his life," thus to suffer for the sake of Christ on behalf of others. What makes one think so in this case

---

in recent years, allegedly supported by such language as ἀναγκαῖον (v. 26, "necessary"), σπουδαιοτέρως (v. 28, suggested to mean "hastily"), and the lack of a qualifier like "again" with "send" (see n. 12). The frequent flip side of this argument is that Epaphroditus himself had failed in his duty (due to "homesickness"). See, *inter alia,* Bonnard, Beare, Gnilka, Kent, Hawthorne, Silva, White (*Body,* 145), who use such language as "malingerer" (Kent), "he apparently failed in his mission" (Hawthorne), or "leaving his post" (White). But despite its many advocates, this view (of a "twofold mission") remains conjecture only, and an unlikely one at that, since it hangs on such thin threads (see esp. on the meaning of σπουδαιοτέρως below). What Paul does say, both here and in 4:14-19, implies otherwise (see nn. 12, 13, and 19). And in any case v. 29 (that they should hold in honor people like Epaphroditus) speaks strongly against the suggestion that he was derelict in his duty to Paul (cf. Gnilka, 163). On the impossibility of Rahtjen's view ("Three Letters," 169) that "Epaphroditus had already returned home and had been received with coolness if not with hostility," see n. 9 below.

8. Which among recent interpreters is an almost novel idea (see preceding n.). So intent are some on finding ulterior motives that they are quite ready to overthrow what Paul does say in favor of reading between the lines — or else make Epaphroditus out to be emotionally unstable (see esp. Martin, "nervous disorder"; Hawthorne, "emotional instability"). All of this fails to take the letter genre ("friendship") seriously. It is as though because so much in Paul's letters is polemical, one must read even friendship through polemical bifocals.

is the unique phrase "unto death" (v. 30), used elsewhere in Paul only in 2:8 to refer to Christ's death on the cross.

On the further issue raised by this paragraph, having to do with the place of Paul's imprisonment and the number of trips to and fro implied by what Paul says here, see the Introduction, pp. 36-37. See further on v. 26 for a suggestion as to how and when the church heard of his illness.

**25** The "but" with which this paragraph begins contrasts what Paul will now say about Epaphroditus with what he has just said about Timothy's and his own coming. His "hoping" and "being confident in the Lord" did not indicate lack of certainty, but the necessary hesitation when speaking of future events of that kind. But now — and from the perspective of their reading the letter — he affirms, "I considered[9] it necessary" to send Epaphroditus back home, probably as soon as he had recovered sufficiently to make the journey. The rest of the paragraph basically explains why it was "necessary"[10] to do so, and in so doing Paul honors Epaphroditus before the community for his having risked his life on their and Paul's behalf.

That the concern is in part to honor Epaphroditus before them becomes clear by the word order of Paul's sentence. Having mentioned him by name,[11] and before the infinitive "to send[12] him to you," Paul offers no less than five

---

9. Gk. ἡγησάμην; see on 2:3 and 6 (cf. 3:7-8). Along with ἔπεμψα in v. 28, this is an epistolary aorist (present tense at the time of writing, but past from the perspective of the recipients), as the NIV has it. But it seems unnecessary in this case to translate it with the present tense, as though Paul's perspective were more significant than that of the Philippians. Rahtjen's view (n. 7) that Epaphroditus had already returned home, so that these are genuine aorists, is defeated altogether on the formal grounds that Paul's appeal in v. 29 to "welcome him with joy" belongs to a letter of commendation that accompanies its carrier (see Rom 16:2).

10. Gk. ἀναγκαῖον, which stands in the emphatic first position in Paul's sentence: ἀναγκαῖον δὲ ἡγησάμην. Some read this word as evidence for an apologetic stance to this paragraph; but that is to read far too much into a single word. It stands clearly in contrast to what he has just said about Timothy; what Paul is about to explain is why Epaphroditus has returned before the outcome of Paul's trial is known. He has just told them how they will learn of that; now he sets out to explain why he has determined (ἡγησάμην) that Epaphroditus should not wait.

11. Gk. Ἐπαφρόδιτος, only here and in 4:18 in the NT. The name means "honored by Aphrodite," thus "comely," and was common among both Greeks and Romans (as "Venustus"). It is clear from the following description that a (potential) devotee of Aphrodite (assuming he was so named by his parents) has learned of real love through Christ. On the name itself, see J. R. Harris ("Epaphroditus"). Whether or not the name Epaphras was a shortened form of this name, there is no likelihood of any kind that this Epaphroditus and the Colossian Epaphras were the same person.

12. Gk. πέμψαι, which in this case is especially far removed from its verb. Michael (following Bengel, and followed by Martin and Hawthorne) makes the strange suggestion that this verb without a qualifier like "again" (or the compound ἀναπέμπω; cf. Phlm 12)

epithets, three describing his relationship to Paul[13] and two to the community, including the fact that he acted on their behalf regarding Paul. First, he is "my brother," the fundamental term of relationship within the believing community;[14] he is to Paul what the rest of them are as well. Second, he is Paul's "co-worker," Paul's most common term for those who have labored with him in the gospel in some way,[15] including Euodia and Syntyche and others in Philippi (4:3). But in this case, third, Paul further defines his role as co-worker with a military metaphor; he is also "my fellow soldier."[16] Military imagery is not common in Paul; very likely it was evoked by the surroundings (the Praetorian Guard, 1:13), or by the fact that Roman Philippi originated as a

---

implies that he "had not been sent on a brief and hurried mission, but rather with the intention that he should remain with the Apostle." But how so, one wonders, since he is going *back* under any view (cf. Buchanan, "Ephaphroditus' Sickness," 159; O'Brien, 333 n. 26). Besides, this kind of argument cuts both ways, since it is just as plausible that Paul uses ἀναπέμπω in Phlm 12 precisely because he was sending Onesimus back after "failure," and thus he should have used that verb here if the "double mission" view were to prevail. That the church had sent Epaphroditus on a "double mission" (see n. 7 above) is pure conjecture; what Paul actually says here and in 4:18 implies a single mission. In any case that is all that Paul explicitly refers to.

13. Some are enamored by what they see as an ascending order to the threefold, "brother, co-worker, fellow-soldier" (e.g., Lightfoot, Plummer, Hendriksen). While that may hold for the first item in contrast to the next two, it is more difficult to see such intent in the final two items. What is of greater significance is that Paul variously designates those whom he is sending with such epithets, usually two, but sometimes three: 1 Thess 3:2 ("brother and co-worker," of Timothy); 1 Cor 4:17 ("beloved child and faithful in the Lord," of Timothy); Rom 16:1 ("sister and servant," of Phoebe); Col 4:7 ("beloved brother, faithful servant, and fellow slave," of Tychicus); the latter is shortened in Eph 6:21 to "beloved brother and faithful servant." This phenomenon (esp. the after-the-fact usage in 1 Thess 3:2) should cause those who read ulterior motives into this passage (that Paul multiplies epithets for apologetic purposes) to have a moment's pause.

14. But cf. E. E. Ellis (*Prophecy*, 13-18), who argues that the usage in contexts like this one (cf. 4:21) implies a semi-technical usage that is yet another term for "co-worker." One need not doubt that it sometimes borders on such; but one loses too much of significance if the "semantic range" of the word is narrowed (as Ellis tends to) to become the equivalent of "co-worker." The very fact that Paul compounds these designations so often (see preceding n.) argues for the opposite, namely that their semantic range does *not* sufficiently overlap for only one of them to be used.

15. Gk. συνεργόν; it is used variously of Timothy (1 Thess 3:2 [τὸν ἀδελφὸν καὶ συνεργόν, as here]; Rom 16:21); Apollos (1 Cor 3:9); Timothy, Silas, and the whole Corinthian church (2 Cor 1:24); Titus (2 Cor 8:23); Priscilla and Aquila (Rom 16:3); Urban (Rom 16:9); Philemon (Phlm 1); Mark, Aristarchus, Demas, and Luke (Phlm 24); Mark, Aristarchus, and Justus (Col 3:10-11).

16. Gk. συστρατιώτης; used elsewhere of Archippus of Colossae (Phlm 2). The military metaphor is used also of Timothy in 2 Tim 2:3 (cf. 1 Tim 1:18).

military colony.[17] With reference to Epaphroditus, the imagery is that of a wounded comrade-in-arms, who is being sent back home for rest. Since Epaphroditus was almost certainly present at the dictation of the letter, these words are spoken as much for his sake as for that of the community; but they are surely for the community's sake as well, to emphasize that their messenger in Paul's behalf is considered by him to be a fellow soldier for the sake the gospel.

Finally, Paul also designates him as "your messenger[18] and minis-trant[19] to my need." Epaphroditus thus served as an "apostle," one sent on behalf of the congregation to perform a given task.[20] That task is then ex-pressed with a metaphor from the sacrificial system: he "performed a priestly duty" on their behalf "for Paul's needs."[21] This is the first certain mention of their gift to Paul, although as noted on 1:5, it was most likely included already in the phrase "participation with me in the gospel." It is moot whether it is also alluded to by the term "your sacrifice and ministry" in 2:17, although the sacerdotal language used there and here (as well as in 4:18) makes a strong case for such. In any case Paul's present point is clear; in a culture where prisoners were not cared for by the state, but whose "necessities" for life (especially food) had to be supplied by friends or relatives, this is no small thing that they have done. They have thus "offered priestly service" (to God, is implied) by their sending Epaphroditus with the gift necessary for him to sustain life in prison. This present word about Epaphroditus anticipates the full acknowledgment in 4:14-20.

**26** The preceding clause concluded with the words "to send to you." Hard on the heels of those words Paul now offers his first explanation — from Epaphroditus' perspective — as to why it was necessary to send him now, and alone, not waiting for the outcome of the trial: "since he has been

---

17. See the Introduction, pp. 25-26.

18. Gk. ἀπόστολος ("apostle"), the clear indication that this is first of all a functional term for Paul (cf. 2 Cor 8:23), before it is titular.

19. Gk. λειτουργός; on this word see on 2:17; cf. the noun λειτουργία in v. 30. In light of 2:17, 4:18, and Rom 15:16 one wonders how Collange could have persuaded himself of a pagan background to the usage here. The "double mission" view also seizes on this word as implying not just bringing the gift but "attendance" on the apostle as well. But the usage in v. 30 and the language of 4:18 imply quite the opposite, that it refers specifically to the "priestly service" of bringing the gift to Paul. Cf. Buchanan ("Epa-phroditus' Sickness," 158-59).

20. For this usage see esp. J.-A. Bühner, *EDNT,* 1.145 (section 5).

21. Gk. τῆς χρείας μου, a word frequently used for "the necessities of life." In this letter see 4:16 and 19 (cf. the discussion on 4:11-12). Again, this language scarcely favors the "double mission" view (see nn. 7 and 19); to the contrary the usage in 4:16 suggests the opposite, and when Paul wants to enlarge its semantic range he does so in 4:19 by adding πᾶσαν ("every").

longing[22] for all of you[23] and has been distressed[24] because you heard he had taken sick."[25] The point of this clause is plain enough, and it is doubtful that there are hidden agenda. As their messenger and "ministrant" to Paul's needs, Epaphroditus was desirous to return home, partly because of his affection ("longing") for them[26] and partly because he was deeply distressed for their sakes over their having heard about his illness but not about its happy resolution.[27] Only those who have not had such experiences, when one has knowledge both of a sickness and its severity and where communication is not readily available, would ever read ulterior motives into this. Furthermore, such a view calls Paul's integrity into question, which borders on arrogance for those so far removed in time and place from the apostle.

This sentence has also been cause for many to doubt the Roman provenance of this letter, supposing that he took ill in Paul's company and that someone had to carry that news to Philippi (one trip) and another had to carry the news of their distress back to wherever Paul is imprisoned (another trip).[28] The implication is that the distance between Philippi and Rome is

22. Gk. ἐπιποθῶν ἦν; on the use of the verb see on 1:8. This is a periphrastic imperfect; whether it can also function as an "epistolary aorist" (as the NIV, "he longs for you") is highly doubtful (see n. 9 above); and in any case, the imperfect implies, not surprisingly, that this has been going on for the past while. The suggestions that this word implies "homesickness" (as Plummer, Martin, Loh-Nida, Hawthorne, White) is psychologizing pure and simple; and in light of 1:8, it is bad psychologizing as well, since Paul's "affection" for the Philippians scarcely implied "homesickness."

23. On this emphasis in the letter see n. 41 on 1:1.

24. Gk. ἀδημονῶν, used of Jesus in the garden in Mark 14:33 and Matt 26:37. As with "longing" (n. 22), it is pure psychologizing to read "spiritual anguish" and "nervous disorder" (as, e.g., Martin, Hawthorne) into this word. Barth (88) also falls prey here: "what a very strange motive for the behaviour of a grown man!"

25. Gk. ἠσθένησεν, which more often than its cognate noun ἀσθενεία is used to mean "be sick," or in the aorist "took sick," although the aorist may refer to the whole experience (= "was sick"; on this usage see Burton, *Moods*, 20).

26. On the textual variation that adds "to see," see n. 1, an addition that seems to miss Paul's point (*contra* Michael, who suggests that either way makes very little difference). Epaphroditus longs for *them,* out of affection and concern for them, precisely because they knew he was ill and did not know of its happy outcome — although a desire to *see* them as well does not lag very far behind.

27. Kennedy, 446, offers the doubtful suggestion that upon hearing of Epaphroditus' illness, the Philippians had written to Paul, to which our letter is now in response.

28. This is frequently asserted to be five; e.g., Collange (119 n. 2): "[1] the Philippians learn of Paul's imprisonment; [2] Epaphroditus is sent; [3] the Philippians hear of their envoy's illness; [4] *he* hears that his friends are worrying about him; [5] Epaphroditus is sent back." This is so full of conjecture that it is hard to believe it is taken as seriously as it is (see, e.g., Martin, 120-21, who in arguing that an alternative view cannot be proved, implies that this view *is* thereby proven). Under any view, nos. 3 and 4 should be combined; why, one wonders, would there be need of a full journey back to Paul and Epaphroditus

much too great for such comings and goings.[29] But that is a quite unnecessary, and unlikely, scenario to read into this sentence. Given that Epaphroditus was probably carrying a considerable sum of money, it is equally unlikely that he was traveling alone.[30] The most promising scenario, therefore, is the one that sees him as having taken ill on the way to Rome, with one of his traveling companions returning to Philippi with that news (which is how Epaphroditus knew they knew), while another (or others) stayed with him as he continued on his way to Rome, even though doing so put his life at great risk (v. 30).[31] This view is favored in particular by the way Paul phrases v. 30 (q.v.), that he had *risked his life in order that* he might fulfill his mission to Paul on behalf of Philippi.

---

for him to know that they were concerned about him? The implication of the text is clear; Epaphroditus knows they are aware of his illness but not its resolution. He would not need someone to tell him that that would cause anxiety at home! Nor would no. 1 require Paul's arrival in Rome before the Philippians could have known about it (although in this case nothing can be demonstrated one way or the other); the point is that five trips to and fro rests on conjecture pure and simple, not on anything that is explicitly said (or implied by what is said). So also Reicke ("Caesarea," 284), who notes that only nos. 2 and 3 are presupposed by what Paul actually says in the letter.

29. Collange is bold: "This paragraph takes for granted a considerable number of communications to-and-fro between Paul and Philippi which points rather to an Ephesian origin of the letter." In fact this paragraph is nearly irrelevant to that matter, since all questions about distance and the number of trips under any view is based on conjecture, not on what is actually said. If I find my reconstruction more plausible than that of Collange, it is because I think the grammar of v. 30 (see p. 283 and n. 50) moves in this direction, and in any case it seems to fit real life much better than his; but neither view can be proved. See the Introduction, pp. 36-37.

30. In this regard see 1 Cor 16:13 ("the men you approve to accompany your gift to Jerusalem"); 2 Cor 8:16-24, where three brothers are responsible for assisting with the Corinthians gift; 2 Cor 11:9 ("the brothers who came from Macedonia supplied what I needed"); and Acts 20:4, where Luke names the entourage finally responsible for carrying the gift from the Gentile churches to the poor in Jerusalem (cf. 24:17 for Luke's knowledge of the reason for the trip to Jerusalem). That neither Paul nor Luke regularly mentions those who accompany the leader of such a group is evidenced everywhere (e.g., in 2 Cor 8:16-24 the two who accompany Titus are not named, while the second one is not mentioned at all in the further reference in 12:18; cf. Acts 21-26, where in 21:29 Luke mentions only "Trophimus the Ephesian" from among those enumerated in 20:4, because he is the catalyst of the uproar). To mention other than the leader(s) of such a group lies beyond the interests of the narrator.

31. This view was suggested as early as Conybeare and Howson (*Life,* 722); it has more recently been advocated by Mackay ("Further Thoughts," 169); Buchanan ("Epaphroditus' Sickness"); Caird, 129; Bruce, 96; Silva, 161. That Paul does not mention further companions is not a serious problem for this view (see preceding n.), esp. in light of Paul's calling Epaphroditus the church's "apostle." He was their official representative and carrier of the gift. That he should not mention others in this case means only that Epaphroditus's return is not an "official mission" from Paul, and that it was he who had taken ill.

**27** With an emphatic "for indeed,"[32] Paul goes on to bear witness, first, to the severe nature of the illness, and second, to the wideness of God's mercy — both to Epaphroditus and to himself. We have no way of knowing the nature of Epaphroditus's illness; what Paul underscores is how serious it really was, enough to bring him to death's door.[33] The repetition of this motif in v. 30 further indicates its true seriousness.

But the other side of reality, which the Philippians would now be experiencing with his arrival, is that "God had mercy on him" — a clause probably read much too casually by those of us who have the benefits of modern medical science. Far fewer people in antiquity recovered from death's door. In saying "God had mercy on him," therefore, Paul probably does not mean simply that in God's good mercy Epaphroditus simply got better, but that God had a direct hand in it.[34] Most likely his recovery was due to what elsewhere Paul calls "gifts of healings" (1 Cor 12:9, 28, 30).

In this case, however, there is no mention of a "gift of healing"; Paul's emphasis rests altogether on the mercy of God evidenced by Epaphroditus's recovery, which in turn does not so much stress generosity toward the undeserving — although that is always true as well — but the *experience* of mercy itself.[35] This is made certain by the final addendum, "not on him only, but also on me, to spare me sorrow upon sorrow," a clause that once again presupposes his close relationship with this community. They know well Paul's affection for them; the concluding plaintive note simply underscores it.

We can only guess what Paul is referring to by the first level of "sorrow" upon which additional sorrow would have been piled;[36] it probably picks up the recurring motif of suffering, of his continually being poured out

32. Gk. καὶ γάρ, only here in Philippians, but a combination that occurs frequently in Paul's letters where he is trying to persuade (e.g., 1 Thess 3:4; 4:10; 1 Cor 11:9; 12:13, 14; 14:8; etc.). The combination, as here, is usually both explanatory (γάρ) and intensive (καί), thus offering further, emphatic explanation of something that has preceded. "The καί implies that the previous ἠσθένησεν understates the case" (Lightfoot, 123).

33. Gk. παραπλήσιον θανάτῳ (= "coming near to death"). The adjective (used adverbially here), which can also mean "near" in the sense of "similar to," occurs only here in the NT, where the original meaning (by derivation = coming alongside) obtains.

34. This, of course, cannot be demonstrated; but neither can it denied as some do (e.g., Plummer, Hendriksen). Nothing is at stake here, but in view of Paul's understanding of life in Christ as altogether predicated on life in the Spirit (see Fee, *Presence*), this seems to be a very natural way of understanding what lies behind this theological account of Epaphroditus's recovery.

35. A verb that in Paul occurs elsewhere (apart from Romans 9–11) chiefly in connection with his call to apostleship (see 1 Cor 7:26; 2 Cor 4:1; 1 Tim 1:13, 16); see Rom 12:8 for its singular usage at the horizontal level (people showing mercy to others).

36. Gk. λύπην ἐπὶ λύπην; cf. Isa 28:10 (θλῖψιν ἐπὶ θλῖψιν).

as a drink offering (v. 17), especially in his present imprisonment.[37] This little phrase should also be regularly kept in mind when in this letter we repeatedly hear Paul speak of rejoicing. Joy does not mean the absence of sorrow, but the capacity to rejoice in the midst of it. His gratitude in the present case is for mercy, that he has not had sorrow of this kind — the loss of a long-time and dear brother in the Lord — added to the sorrow he already knows.

As usual, therefore, Paul can hardly speak without reflecting on everything from its theological perspective. The God he serves is full of mercy, both in healing the sick and in sparing the heavy-laden from further sorrow.

**28** With another "therefore" Paul returns to the opening words of v. 25, but now as a matter of fact, "I sent him." The qualifier "all the more eager"[38] indicates that the "therefore" in this case, in contrast to v. 23, is not resumptive, but inferential. Thus Paul offers the reciprocal side of Epaphroditus' distress over their knowledge of his illness: "that you may see him again and rejoice." In 1:25 Paul suggested that his own coming would be for their progress, and thus for further joy, regarding the faith itself. Here their joy will be that gladsome, spontaneous delight in seeing their brother again, and especially in seeing him alive and well. But did Paul here intend "see him again and rejoice" or "see him and again rejoice," since the placement of "again" is perfectly ambiguous?[39] Pauline *usage* clearly favors the latter, since this adverb almost always precedes the verb it modifies. Paul, therefore, probably intended that in seeing him they would "rejoice again," which is quite in keeping with the repetition of this imperative in the letter. On the other hand, one cannot be sure that this is how the Philippians would have understood it, since it also seems to go so naturally with the participle

---

37. This is the most common view; Beare (98) suggests "sorrow at his critical illness," but he then has difficulty with the ἀλυπότερος in v. 28, a difficulty that is purely of his own making.

38. Gk. σπουδαιοτέρως, the comparative of σπουδαίως, which is found elsewhere in Paul only in 2 Tim 1:17. In keeping with the "apologetic" view of this paragraph (see n. 6), it is common to suggest (in some cases assert) that this probably means "the more hastily" (Beare adds, "somewhat prematurely"); cf. *inter alia* Michael, Collange, Kent, Hawthorne, Silva, O'Brien); but that is a suggestion predicated altogether on a prior view of the paragraph, not on Pauline usage. Nowhere else in Paul does this word group imply "haste" as over against "eagerness, earnestness, diligence." And in 2 Cor 8:17 he uses the comparative adjective precisely as he does the adverb here, in a sending context indicating the high degree of eagerness involved in getting Titus and the two brothers to Corinth.

39. Paul's Greek can easily be put into English: "in order that in seeing him again you may rejoice," which could be punctuated, "in seeing him again, you may rejoice" or "in seeing him, again you may rejoice." Interpreters are generally divided: the former is favored by, *inter alia,* Hendriksen, Collange, Hawthorne, Silva, and the KJV, NIV, NASB, REB, NRSV, NJB; the latter by Lightfoot, Meyer, Vincent, Plummer, Michael, Müller, Beare, Gnilka, Rienecker-Rogers, Loh-Nida, O'Brien, and the GNB and NAB.

"seeing." In any case, Epaphroditus's return is to be a cause for renewing their joy.

Not only so. Just as he added a word of personal relief at the mercy of God in sparing Epaphroditus, so here Paul adds a similar word, "and I for my part may have less sorrow."[40] Thus, their renewed joy, which was undoubtedly a cause for joy for Paul as well, is here expressed in terms of its opposite, and in response to "sorrow upon sorrow" in v. 27. Epaphroditus' return will thus lessen Paul's sorrow at the first level as well. That is, God's mercy on Epaphroditus meant that Paul was not given extra sorrow; his anticipation of their joy in seeing Epaphroditus again, and their concomitant relief from anxiety over him, will also have the effect of lessening Paul's ongoing grief (related to his imprisonment).

**29** With another inferential "therefore" Paul comes at last to the "commendation" proper, expressed in this case by way of a compound imperative.[41] Since Paul has sent him back for the triple reasons given (for Epaphroditus's, theirs, and Paul's sakes), "therefore," he concludes, "welcome him in the Lord with all joy"[42] and "honor such people as he." Here is a troublesome word for some.[43] Why should Paul have to "command" such a thing, if there were not trouble around the edges? But even to ask the question is to make far too much of the imperative, which is a standard feature of such "commendations" in Greco-Roman letters, not to mention in Paul himself.[44] Having given the reasons for their welcoming him back with joy, Paul now concludes by urging them to do so. Thus, not all imperatives in Paul are "correcting" something that has gone wrong.

---

40. Gk. ἀλυπότερος, comparative of ἄλυπος, occurring only here in the NT. The meaning advocated by BAGD ("free from anxiety") and followed by the NIV, NRSV, and NAB seems to be an invented meaning with no lexical basis whatever (the "be less concerned about you" of the NASB is impossible). The adjective is formed from λυπή ("sorrow, grief") and with the alpha-privative means simply to be without sorrow (or perhaps, trouble). But "anxiety" is not even in the purview of this word, at least not according to LSJ.

41. Cf. esp. Rom 16:1-2, "in order that you may welcome (προσδέξησθε, as here) her and assist her as she has need." What is missing in this case is the language of "commendation" itself, but that is because Epaphroditus is one of their own, in contrast to Phoebe's coming to Rome where she is not formerly known (except, probably, by Aquila and Priscilla).

42. Gk. μετὰ πάσης χαρᾶς, which does not imply "every kind of," as Plummer would have it, but "with fullness of joy."

43. So, e.g., Kennedy (447), followed by others (see n. 6): "The πάσης χαρᾶς and ἐντίμους surely point to some alienation on which we have no light." They do no such thing, of course, although it is a possibility.

44. See, e.g., 1 Cor 16:15 (of Stephanas), that the church should "submit" to such and "recognize" (= honor) such; cf. 2 Cor 8:24 (of Titus and his two companions). Cf. the imperative in 1 Thess 5:12-13, which some would read as implying tensions; but again that is to make much too case specific what are more likely general admonitions.

The first imperative, of course, repeats what he said in the preceding clause as to the purpose of his sending Epaphroditus back home. But it does so with the typical (for this letter especially) qualifier "in the Lord." The nuance of this phrase is again not easy to pin down; but most likely it is similar to Paul's "hope in the Lord" (v. 19) and "confidence in the Lord" (v. 24) in the preceding paragraph. Everything that believers do is "in the Lord" in some way or other. Here it probably reflects the fact that their common existence, theirs and Epaphroditus's, is predicated on the fact that together they are "in the Lord," meaning they belong to him.

The second imperative is also typical, that they hold "such people" in honor. Although this plural may indicate, as suggested above, that others are traveling with him and that in this final word they too are included, more likely this simply reflects a standard idiom. When Epaphroditus is held up for "honor"[45] of this kind, at the same time he belongs to the larger category of "such people" who deserve esteem. Thus the two imperatives together indicate the kind of reception Epaphroditus deserves upon his return, the kind of esteem in which they should hold him for what he has done. Such honor is not drawing glory away from God, but is that properly given to one of God's own, who nearly "poured out his life" on behalf of a brother.

**30** With a final causal clause, Paul repeats, but also elaborates, the two basic reasons given above for their esteeming Epaphroditus highly on his return home:[46] first, because "he almost died[47] for the work of Christ," which is then elaborated, "having risked[48] his life to fill up[49] the help you could not give me."

45. Gk. ἔντιμος, found only here in Paul; elsewhere in the NT with this same general sense only in Luke 14:8, where it has to do with rank, however, not personal qualities that elicit such honor. The use in 1 Pet 2:4, 6 is more purely adjectival (= "precious, valuable").

46. It is possible, of course, that this clause modifies both imperatives in v. 29; but in either case it most immediately qualifies the second one — and makes more sense doing so. The present sentence reiterates the reasons not for their joy (v. 29a), but for their holding him in honor (29b).

47. Gk. μέχρι θανάτου; cf. 2:8 (only in these two instances in Paul's letters). Although the nuance here is slightly different from that in 2:8, it is hard to imagine that in a basically aural culture they would not have heard the echo.

48. Gk. παραβολευσάμενος τῇ ψυχῇ, a word that occurs here for the first time in known literature. An inscription noted by Deissmann (*Light,* 88), which uses the participle in precisely this same way, indicates that Paul did not invent the word. It is most likely a term associated with gambling, which is now used metaphorically. Cf. Acts 13:26 (in James' letter), where it is said of Paul and Barnabas, ἀνθρώποις παραδεδωκόσι τὰς ψυχάς, for which BAGD suggest, "men who risked their lives." Note also that when referring to one's "life" in this way, Paul (typically in Greek) uses ψυχή to reflect this sense. It was not Epaphroditus's "soul" that was at risk, but his present life on earth.

49. Gk. ἀναπληρώσῃ; although this verb can mean "fulfill" or "complete," with

For the first of these see on v. 27. What is added here, which we could have guessed at but without certain evidence, is that his coming so close to death was the direct result of engaging in "the work of Christ." Ordinarily this language has to do with evangelism; but here that would seem to be only indirectly so. The grammar of the sentence indicates that it refers to Epaphroditus' bringing their gift to Paul in Rome; and since Paul's imprisonment is directly related to the "work of Christ," any gift brought to him by fellow believers in this way would be seen as participating in the gospel, as 1:5 suggests.

The next qualifier intensifies "he almost died for the work of Christ." What happened, Paul suggests, is that by his completing his mission in the midst of severe illness, Epaphroditus put his own life in jeopardy. At least that is what the grammar implies. The main clause says, "he almost died for the work of Christ," which is now modified by an aorist participle followed by a purpose clause, which goes with the participle, not the main clause. Thus, "he almost died for the sake of Christ, by having risked his life in order to complete . . . your service to me." The clear implication is that there is "a causal connexion between the bringing of the gift and the risking of his life."[50] This is the phrase that gives credence to the view noted above (v. 26), that he most likely took ill en route to Rome, but pressed on anyway to fulfill his commitment to the church and Paul, and thus exposed himself to the very real possibility of death.

The final purpose clause gives the reason for Epaphroditus' so risking his life, while at the same time it offers the believers in Philippi their ultimate reason for holding him in high honor: he was willing to risk his life so that he might "make up for the help you could not give me." But it is doubtful whether Paul intended to sound quite so pejorative. This combination of the verb "make up for" and the noun "lacking"[51] is used in a similar context in 1 Cor 16:17 to refer to "making up for the absence of the rest." That is almost surely the intent here. Thus, the clause begins, "he has made up for your lack"

---

the noun ὑστέρημα it means to "fill up, fill a gap, replace." For this usage in Paul, see esp. 1 Cor 16:17; cf. Gal 6:2.

50. Mackay, "Further Thoughts," 169. Cf. Caird (129), "The obvious interpretation of v. 30 is that he fell ill on the road and nearly killed himself by completing his journey while he was unfit to travel." Although this, too, is a slender thread on which to hang a hypothesis, at least it is the one linguistic-grammatical moment in the paragraph that actually favors one view over against another. The common assumption, and frequently emphatic assertion, that he fell ill while in Rome, is assumption only, without a shred of evidence from the text itself.

51. Gk. ὑστέρημα, which ordinarily means "deficiency" or "lack" of something. But in the present idiom the "lack" Paul experiences is that of his friends. On this usage see the discussion in Fee, *First Corinthians,* 832. For the more common usage see on 4:11 below.

in the sense of "your absence." Paul's absence from Philippi has created a gap in his life, and Epaphroditus has filled that up to a degree. Having made that point, Paul then returns to the sacrificial imagery of v. 25. With a genitive qualifier he indicates that by the "lack" of their not being present, neither could they minister to his needs as they would have liked; but now Epaphroditus has done so in their behalf. As in v. 25 he expresses their gift to him through Epaphroditus in terms of "performing the duties of a priest" in his behalf. Thus, very much in keeping with 4:10 he recognizes that their "lack" with regard to him was not in the willing but in the opportunity. The result is a clause very awkwardly stated, but whose sense goes something like this: "so that he might make up for your absence, and thus 'minister' to my needs as you have not had opportunity to do recently."

Thus Paul concludes this brief narrative of proposed travel plans. The narrative is full of warmth and pathos, victory and trepidation. His affection for the Philippians spills over to them through his expressions of affection for Epaphroditus, their "ministrant" to his human needs. At the same time the passage echoes with notes of gratitude and joy, gratitude to God for his mercy in healing a brother, joy renewed as they see him again. Paul hints at his sorrows, but does not elaborate; instead, the passage is full of affection and honor for one who dared to risk his life "for the work of Christ" in bringing him material aid. His ultimate concern is that the Philippians themselves appreciate Epaphroditus for what he has done in their behalf for Paul's sake. If he also thus serves as one who was willing to suffer for the sake of Christ, that note, while not played loudly, neither is played so softly that it cannot be heard. Thus, here is very personal material, which receives its theological moments because Paul seems incapable of doing anything otherwise.

A passage like this ought to serve as a constant reminder to all of us (scholar, pastor, student of the Bible) that the NT was written in the context of real people in a very real world. Biblical texts are too often the scholar's playground and the believer's rule book, without adequate appreciation for the truly human nature of these texts — texts written by one whose speech was ever informed by his theology, but who expressed that theology at a very personal and practical level. Without being maudlin or saccharine one may rightly note that Paul lived as a believer in a world surrounded by friends, that those friends brought him joy, and that the untimely death of such friends would have been for him immeasurable grief. Hence the sense of deep relief at the experience of God's mercy is worth noting. That Epaphroditus' illness was itself the direct result of his "risking his life" for the sake of the work of Christ is also worth noting, especially in a culture where taking risks is primarily related to "business ventures," rather than to genuinely personal risks related to one's love for Christ and for his people.

## V. THEIR "AFFAIRS" — AGAIN (3:1–4:3)

The letter now takes an especially intriguing turn — so much so that the majority have despaired of finding any "logic" to its present order, and some see the break as so severe as to posit the presence here of a "fragment" from another letter altogether.[1] Some of the difficulties should be obvious to any reader: the sudden denunciation of false teachers in v. 2 after apparently starting to wrap things up ("finally, rejoice in the Lord"), returning to "finally" and "rejoice" at the end (4:8, 4); how the second part of Paul's testimony, about his not having "arrived" but still pressing on toward the eschatological goal (vv. 12-14), is related to the first part, where he contrasts his former life in Judaism with present righteousness based on faith (vv. 4a-9); how those described in vv. 18-19, over whom Paul weeps, are related to those flailed in v. 2 for promoting circumcision.[2] At first blush one wonders whether something new has happened between 3:1a and 1b that has caused a sudden outburst of warning, followed by a series of new appeals.

On the other hand, all of the basic concerns that have preceded are echoed here: first, in Paul's testimony (vv. 4-14), with (a) its thoroughgoing christocentricity, including the language "gain Christ" (v. 8, which recalls 1:21, "for me to live is Christ; to die is gain"), (b) its emphasis on "participation in Christ's sufferings" (vv. 10-11), which recalls 1:29-30 and 2:17, and (c) the eschatological orientation of its conclusion (vv. 11-14, 20-21), which recalls a primary motif from chaps. 1-2 (see on 1:6). Second, in the final application and appeal of 4:1-3, Paul repeats (a) the exhortation from 1:27 to "stand fast in the Lord" (4:1), (b) the appeal in 2:2 that they "have the same mindset in the Lord" (4:2), and (c) the language "contending together for the gospel" from 1:27. Furthermore, the whole continues to be written in the first person singular and second person plural (with occasional moments of first person plural when Paul includes himself and them together). All of these together suggest, first, that despite appearances there is a genuine relationship

---

1. On this question, see the Introduction, pp. 21-23. The present discussion proceeds on the basis that one must make sense of the text as it now stands, as in keeping with a "hortatory letter of friendship" — all the more so since there are so many words and themes that presuppose what has preceded.

2. On the larger question of "opponents" in Philippi, generated in part by these two passages, see the Introduction, pp. 7-10; see also the introduction to vv. 1-4a below and the discussion of vv. 2 and 17-19. Note especially the matter of "mirror reading" (p. 7, esp. n. 24), since *how* one reads this material is determined in large measure by one's presuppositions — whether it is basically polemical and apologetic (thus assuming a "three-way conversation" between Paul, the Philippians, and some alleged opponents) or a hortatory letter of friendship (thus a two-way conversation between Paul and the Philippians in a context that also, typically, includes the recognition of "enemies").

between this material and what has preceded, and, second, that the repeated "finally" and "rejoice in the Lord," rather than indicating an interruption or digression, more likely function as a framing device for the appeal contained in 3:1 to 4:9, while the repetition of "stand fast" and "have the same mindset" in 4:1-2 functions in the same way as an *inclusio* for 1:27–4:3. Finally, it should be noted that all of the material in this section fits the genre of a hortatory letter of friendship.[3]

What this suggests further is that the warning in 3:2 with its follow-up response in vv. 4-9 and the contrast between "those whose minds are set on earthly things" and "us with our heavenly citizenship" (vv. 17-21) are in some way related to the preceding concerns — even if the precise nature of that relationship may forever allude us. This seems the more certain in light of two other phenomena that are crucial to the present passage: first, that Paul twice reminds the Philippians that he is currently writing something he has told them over and again (3:1b and 18), and that the largest single block of material is Paul's personal testimony (3:4-14), which is followed by no less than three different appeals to "imitate me" (3:15, 17; 4:9).

Very likely, therefore, this section continues the "chronological" dimension of the letter, as Paul returns once more to "their affairs" and their "progress and joy in the faith" (1:25). The whole letter is dictated from the perspective of its being read aloud in the assembly. Thus the first appeal regarding "their affairs" (1:27–2:18) was written in light of his current "absence" from them (1:27; 2:12), and reflects what he had learned from Epaphroditus. Now, in light of Epaphroditus's return and with his assumed presence in the congregation in mind,[4] Paul returns to their circumstances: their need to "progress in the faith" (1:25), to have "joy" renewed[5] and to find that joy *"in the Lord,"* and thus not fall prey to the kind of teaching he has repeatedly warned them about in the past[6] — which is perhaps related to the present tensions among them, as well as to the abatement of eschatological focus on the part of some.

They are therefore urged: (1) to recall prior warnings (against those who would entice them to submit to Jewish "boundary markers" and thus be identified with Israel's former covenant while they also identify with Christ), (2) to find their joy in the Lord — alone — including present participation in

---

3. On this matter, see the Introduction, pp. 2-14; cf. Stowers, "Friends," 113-17.

4. Cf. Furnish ("Place," 88): "Here he deals with certain matters he knows Epaphroditus . . . will discuss with the Philippians in person when [he comes]."

5. See on 1:25; 2:18, 28, 29.

6. Cf. Garland ("Composition," 165): "In chap. 3 Paul is not giving the readers new information nor trying to convince them of something about which they disagreed. He writes of things they already know and with which they concur."

his sufferings as they await the final glory, (3) to hold fast to — indeed eagerly look forward to — their sure hope of Christ's coming, of thus obtaining the final prize of their "upward calling in Christ Jesus," and (4) specifically to those who are the source of current unrest, to do all this with a single mindset, living together in joy, peace, and patience.

Paul begins in 3:1-4a with the primary imperative, "rejoice in the Lord," and the oft-repeated warning and contrast between "Judaizers" and believers in Christ. That is followed by his personal story (vv. 4-14),[7] which begins by setting himself forth as living evidence of the failure of righteousness based on Torah observance (4-9), and concludes by emphasizing participation in Christ's sufferings and thus being conformed to his death (10-11) while striving for the final eschatological goal (12-14). This is then applied to the Philippian situation (vv. 15-21): first urging them to imitate him in these matters (15-17), then contrasting himself to others who as enemies of the cross (= a cruciform lifestyle) have also lost their future orientation (18-19), and concluding on the high note of their "already/not yet" existence in Christ — present heavenly "citizenship" as they await the return of Christ and their glorious transformation into his likeness (20-21).

He then wraps up all the preceding exhortations (1:27–2:18; 3:1-21) by applying the preceding warning and appeal directly to the concern over standing firm as one person for the gospel (4:1-3). This in turn leads naturally to further concluding exhortations, first (4-7) in the form of a typical series of "staccato" imperatives, designed with their circumstances in mind; and second (8-9), as a final appeal to give themselves to "higher things" and to follow his example. All of which leads to a final word about his "affairs" in light of their recent gift (vv. 10-20), in which he once more emphasizes their long-standing partnership with him in the gospel, the note on which the letter began (1:3-8).

If the passage itself is not as tidy as some would count tidy, and if some of the details and relationships between the parts remain something of a mystery, the whole is nonetheless explicable as it stands and does not need the radical dismemberment some would apply to it.

## A. THE APPEAL — AGAINST CIRCUMCISION (3:1-4a)

1*Finally, my brothers [and sisters],*[8] *rejoice in the Lord! It is no trouble for me to write the same things to you again, and it is a safeguard for you.*

---

7. Martin (123) and Pfitzner (*Agon,* 139-53) consider this to be "self-defence"; on the unlikelihood of such, see the discussion in n. 1 on 3:4b-6.

8. See n. 9 on 1:12.

> 2*Watch out for those dogs, those [evil doers],*[9] *those mutilators of the flesh.* 3*For it is we who are the circumcision, we who worship by the Spirit of God,*[10] *who glory in Christ Jesus, and who put no confidence in the flesh* — 4*though I myself have reasons for such confidence.*

The difficulty with this paragraph is reflected in the way various English translations offer paragraph breaks in vv. 1-2,[11] which are based on the assumption that Paul here begins to wrap things up (1a), only to shift suddenly and inexplicably to a severe denunciation of some opponents.[12] But there are good reasons to read vv. 1-2 as they stand and as intentionally dictated in precisely this way. First, the adverb translated "finally" is best understood as transitional toward the final matter to be taken up. Thus Paul does not intend *finally,* but "as for the rest [of what needs to be spoken to]." Second, the five sentences that constitute our vv. 1-2 are asyndetic (lacking the standard nuancing particle), which in Paul is usually for effect, indicating the closest kind of relationship between them.[13] Third, one can make sense of this relationship,[14] without resorting to hypothetical sudden shifts in Paul's circumstances.[15]

9. NIV, "men who do evil."

10. The original text reads either οἱ πνεύματι θεοῦ λατρεύοντες ("who serve by the Spirit of God"; ℵ* A B C D² F G 1739 Byz pler) or οἱ πνεύματι θεῷ λατρεύοντες ("who serve God in spirit" [Moffatt]; ℵ² D* P J 365 1175 pc lat sy) or οἱ πνεύματι λατρεύοντες ("who serve by the Spirit"; P⁴⁶). Both the supporting witnesses and transcriptional probability favor the first option (the phrase seems so unnatural and the concept of "serving God" so normal [cf. Rom 1:9], it is difficult to imagine scribes deliberately changing from either of the latter to the former). Cf. Metzger, *Textual Commentary,* 614. Otherwise Kennedy (449; cf. Moffatt; Michael is open to it), who prefers the dative on the mistaken notion that it provides a better parallel with σαρκί ("flesh") at the end of the sentence. See the discussion.

11. The NIV (cf. NAB, RSV, Phillips) apparently understands 1b to refer to the repeated imperative to "rejoice" (Phillips is explicit; not only does he make a major break after v. 1, but he translates 1b, "it doesn't bore me to repeat a piece of advice like this"). But since that view is so unlikely (see discussion on v. 1), others (NRSV, REB, NJB) correctly recognize that 1b introduces what follows, but cannot believe it follows "finally, rejoice in the Lord," so they offer a major break at 1b, including a section title, so as radically to dismember Paul's argument.

12. Kee (CASB, 188) is typical: "In the middle of this verse there is an abrupt change in tone." Cf. *inter alia,* Lightfoot, Meyer, Jones, Barth, Bruce, Hawthorne.

13. A stylistic feature rarely noted in the literature on this passage, O'Brien (147) being a notable exception. For this stylistic feature in Paul, see N. Turner, *MHT,* 4.85; cf. vv. 4b-6 that follow.

14. So also Meyer, Vincent, Kennedy, Caird, Silva, O'Brien — although not all in the same way.

15. This is the traditional understanding; more recently many have suggested the (much less likely) hypothetical stitching together of two or more independent letters by someone at a later time in Philippi. On this matter, see the Introduction, pp. 21-23.

After the transitional adverb, "as for the rest," Paul begins his final appeal by picking up the imperative "rejoice" from 2:18, to which he now adds "in the Lord." Not only is this a major concern in the letter, but this reminder is also the framework in which they are to hear the final warning and appeal. That means the next sentence (v. 1b), not the threefold "watch out for" (v. 2), is the beginning of this appeal. What he is about to write, he begins, is something they have heard from him often before; to repeat it in this letter is not onerous for him, rather, it is precisely for their security. And with that he warns them one more time, with strikingly emotive language, against those who might try to come into their community and urge Gentile believers to submit to circumcision. The reason they must not give heed to such persuasions, he goes on, rests on the fact that "we" who have received the Spirit and boast in Christ are God's Israel, the "true circumcision." It is the difference between "serving" by the Spirit and trusting in "the flesh," which language serves as the springboard for his personal testimony — Exhibit A regarding the validity of vv. 2-3.

Given the frequency with which Paul speaks to this issue in his letters,[16] one must assume that the arguments of the Judaizing faction had a surface attractiveness to many, despite the (literally) painful consequences if Gentiles were to submit. But Paul appeals not to the physical pain, but to historical and theological realities. *Why* the Philippians should need to be warned again against such "rubbish" (v. 8), and whether it is related to teachings espoused by either of the women in 4:2, are matters of conjecture. Among the better guesses is that which sees a relationship between the attractiveness of "becoming Jewish" (a *religio licita*) and the Philippians' present suffering at the hands of fellow Roman citizens, because they were followers of a *Kyrios* who had been executed as a state criminal. Perhaps by embracing the outward expressions of Jewish identity, they could still belong to Christ but ward off some of the opposition.[17]

In any case, and despite the emotive language of v. 2, there is little hint either here or elsewhere in the letter that such people are actually *present*

16. See Galatians, which is given wholly to this issue, where the "agitators" (Paul's language for those commonly called "Judaizers") are present and totally disruptive, and Romans, where the tension apparently exists within the various house churches in Rome; see also 1 Cor 7:18-19; 2 Cor 2:17–4:6 (which argument makes most sense if again the "peddlers" are pressing Gentiles to accept Jewish identity symbols, especially circumcision; cf. 11:4-22); Col 2:11, 16-23; Tit 1:14-16.

17. See in this regard, M. Tellbe, "Sociological Factors." It should be noted here that the question of "why" is seldom raised, as though it would be a very natural thing for Gentile Christians to be so attracted. For a quite different answer, based on several moments of dubious mirror reading, see Jewett, "Conflicting Movements," 386-87.

*in Philippi* at the time of this writing or that a serious threat is at hand.[18] After all, Paul's primary response takes the form of personal narrative, not argumentation as such;[19] and not once does he threaten them with the *consequences* of such action. His main thrust is altogether positive, setting life in Christ in stark contrast to what he had formerly known as a Torah observant Jew.[20] This suggests that the emotive language is more a reflection of Paul's own distaste for such people, after so many years of struggle against them,[21] than it is a direct attack against anyone currently in Philippi.

**1** The word translated "finally" by the NIV[22] marks a transition to the final matters to be taken up in the letter, not its conclusion. Hence "finally" is a purely gratuitous translation, as though Paul were about to begin what he

---

18. Recognized as early as Calvin (267): "For as they had merely made an attempt on the Philippians and had not overcome them, it was not so necessary to enter into a full-scale disputation and refute errors to which they had never lent an ear. Hence he simply warns them to be diligent and attentive in detecting and guarding against imposters" (cf. Meyer, 147; Bruce, 107; Furnish, "Place," 81; Jewett, "Conflicting Movements," 373, 382-83; W. D. Thomas, "Place," 117 n. 1; Perkins, "Philippians," 90-91; de Silva, "No Confidence," 29-33). This question is often not spoken to at all, in most cases because their presence in Philippi is simply assumed, as, e.g., Pfitzner (*Agon,* 142): "his opponents who . . . in Philippi threaten to destroy his work." That Paul has repeatedly warned them about such itinerants assumes not their presence in Philippi, but Paul's expectation that sooner or later they would make their way to Philippi as they have to other Pauline centers.

19. As noted in the Introduction, pp. 6-7, 11-14, the considerably different way that people read texts based on their presuppositions about genre is especially evident here. The difficulty with reading this section as polemical is that apart from v. 2 nothing else takes a polemical mode. That Paul offers his own testimony in response and that he concludes by urging them to follow his example is not the stuff of polemics or self-defense. In fact apart from the invective of v. 2 and the pathos of vv. 18-19 over some enemies of the cross, there is nothing else in the text that signals "opposition" or polemics.

20. Some "mirror read" this testimony as presupposing "an attack on Paul's apostleship" (Pfitzner, *Agon,* 142); but apostleship is not so much as hinted at in this passage, nor is it mentioned elsewhere in the letter — even in the salutation (1:1, q.v.). This is to read into the text what is simply not there.

21. Koester ("Purpose," 320) rightly observes that Paul's intent here is "not to describe the opponents, but to insult them."

22. Gk. τὸ λοιπόν (lit. = "the rest"; the neuter acc. sing. used adverbially), which occurs in 2 Cor 13:11 without the article and in that context clearly means "finally," as it probably does in 4:8 below (but to conclude the series of exhortations, not the letter). Elsewhere in Paul it either = "henceforth, in the future" (1 Cor 7:19; 2 Tim 4:8) or, as in 1 Thess 4:1; 2 Thess 3:1, and here, marks a transition to the final matters to be taken up in the letter; cf. Meyer (139), "it introduces what is *still* to be done by the readers *in addition to* what has been hitherto communicated" (cf. Vincent, Hendriksen, Hawthorne, Silva, O'Brien; Swift, "Theme," 247; Garland, "Composition," 149). All three uses are illustrated in the papyri (for the present usage, see M-M, 380). See the discussion in Thrall, *Greek Particles,* 25-30.

finally gets to in 4:4 and 8 or that this is the actual conclusion of one of three alleged letters. What it means here is exactly what it meant in 1 Thess 4:1 and 2 Thess 3:1, "as for the rest," meaning "as for what remains to be said." As in previous cases, Paul adds the vocative, "my brothers and sisters," which in this letter appears most frequently at transitional points.[23]

However, as Paul moves toward "what remains," he does not begin with the primary subject matter, but with its essential theological — and experiential — framework:[24] "Rejoice in the Lord."[25] This serves as Paul's first antidote to their being taken in by the possible attractiveness of the Judaizing option.[26] The imperative recalls 2:18 (and 1:25), where the Philippians have been encouraged to rejoice with him in the midst of suffering for Christ's sake, a joy he trusts will be renewed at the coming of Epaphroditus (2:28). But now, as in the framing imperative in 4:4, their joy is to be found *"in the Lord."* As with the Psalmists whose language Paul is using,[27] the Lord who saves is both the basis and focus of joy, which in this imperative does not refer to a feeling but an activity. It means to verbalize with praise and singing. The reason for such "rejoicing in the Lord" has to do with knowing him by being found in him (3:8-9). Knowing Christ far surpasses even blameless Torah observance; it is unthinkable that under the pressure of present sufferings they should lose their joy in *belonging to Christ* by yielding to such

23. See n. 12 on 1:12. It should be noted that the vocative occurs in every instance of (τὸ) λοιπόν used as a transitional (or concluding) adverb; cf. 4:8 below and 2 Cor 13:11.

24. Cf. Caird, 130-32, who argues that the whole passage offers "theological justification for rejoicing in the Lord" (132).

25. It needs also to be noted that Goodspeed's translation of this imperative ("goodbye"; cf. NEB, "farewell," corrected by REB) is in fact impossible (*pace* Lightfoot, Beare; Bruce is sympathetic). Nothing is in its favor, and everything against it: (1) it is predicated on the faulty assumption that this imperative concludes 1:1–2:30; (2) the (alleged) resumptive use in 4:4 makes such a view nonsense (how could one imagine Paul to say something as strange as "farewell in the Lord *always,* again I say, farewell"?); even Goodspeed tries, without lexical warrant, to get around this one (*Problems,* 174-75); (3) it makes the imperative χαίρετε mean something radically different from what it means elsewhere in the letter; and (4), conclusively, there is no lexical justification for it; when this verb does appear in the papyri, it never occurs as an imperative at the end of a letter (see the numerous examples in Exler, *Form,* 35-36, 69-77; cf. the critique by L. Alexander, "Structure," 97).

26. O'Brien (349) observes with insight that in most cases in this letter the theme of joy occurs in the context of "adverse circumstances."

27. See Ps 32:11[31:11]; 33:21[32:21]; 35:9[34:9]; 40:16[39:17]; and many others. The LXX translators consistently avoided χαίρω for this idiom (but see Zech 10:7), using either ἀγαλλιάω or εὐφραίνω. Paul, on the other hand, uses the latter words only once (2 Cor 2:2), not counting LXX citations, preferring χαίρω and its cognates. Given the flexible way this idiom is handled in the LXX and given Paul's linguistic preferences, χαίρετε ἐν κυρίῳ is best understood as Paul's own rendering of this OT idiom.

observance. As in 2:19 and 24 above, the phrase "in the Lord" refers to the grounds (or sphere) of their present existence, and thus points to their basic relationship with Christ which should eliminate all attraction to mere religion or religious identity symbols that have no future in them at all.[28]

With that Paul moves toward his second major concern with regard to their present circumstances,[29] introduced by the reminder that he is repeating himself, and is doing so out of concern for them. Both the existence of this introductory sentence and its form indicate the degree of Paul's concern over what follows. He begins with the object, "the same things,"[30] in the emphatic first position, followed by a contrastive "on the one hand (regarding me)" and "on the other hand (regarding you)," with the word "safety"[31] coming in the emphatic final position. Perhaps anxious lest they take adumbrage over this repetition, he also with a masterful stroke shifts the possibility that such repetition could be "burdensome"[32] from them to himself. Such rhetoric is for their benefit, that in their present suffering they not allow Jewish identity markers to become attractive and thus lose their strong grip on future realities already present in Christ and the Spirit.

To be sure, some have seen this sentence as referring to "rejoice in the Lord,"[33] but that seems nearly impossible, since (1) "the same things" is

---

28. In Paul, of course, the resource for such joy is the Holy Spirit, as in 1 Thess 1:6; Gal 5:22; Rom 14:17 (on these texts, see Fee, *Presence*).

29. The first being his concern that they stand fast as one person for the sake of the gospel in the face of opposition in Philippi (1:27–2:18).

30. Gk. τὰ αὐτὰ, followed by γράφειν; the accent clearly falls on "the same things," not on "to write," thus making the debate as to whether Paul had *written* these things before somewhat irrelevant (*pace* Lightfoot, Meyer, Vincent, Collange). As Calvin (268; cf. Gnilka, Silva; Garland, "Composition," 164) recognized early on, and as v. 18 confirms, Paul is referring to the many times he had previously *told* them about such things — although it is possible that he is also referring to what Epaphroditus will have communicated (as suggested by Furnish, "Place," 86; followed by Jewett, "Conflicting Movements," 383 n. 1; and Martin, 124). It is pedantic to think this emphasis must include former communications by letter, and to translate it accordingly has little warrant (e.g., GNB, "I don't mind repeating what I've written before"; one would expect a πάλιν if this were the case) — although neither can one rule out that Paul had written before; it is simply that this phrase offers nothing by way of *support*. See further on n. 34 below.

31. Gk. ἀσφαλές, the only occurrence of this word group in Paul, having to do with "security" rather than "salvation" as such; cf. Heb 6:19 ("a *sure* and steadfast anchor"); Acts 21:34; 22:30; 25:26. Furnish ("Place," 83-86) has argued at some length for the meaning "certain, dependable knowledge," but that seems unlikely; to my knowledge, he has found no supporters.

32. Gk. ὀκνηρόν, the adjective of ὄκνος ("hesitation, shrinking"), which is used in that way in Rom 12:11; but here it refers to something "arousing dislike or displeasure" (Hauck, *TDNT* 5.167), hence "onerous" or "troublesome."

33. See n. 11 above; cf. Alford, Weiss, Dibelius, Lohmeyer, Caird, Bruce,

plural, not singular, which would be the natural expression if he intended to point to the preceding imperative, (2) this view disregards the asyndeton (see n. 13), which is especially unusual if this were Paul's intent, and (3) one can imagine any number of adjectives that might serve as reasons for him to repeat the imperative to rejoice, but "for you security" is not one of them, whereas it fits perfectly with the warning and exhortation that follows.[34] The view suggested here seems confirmed by the repetition of this idea in v. 18 ("about whom I have told you many times before"). Thus, this sentence sets them up for the warning that follows.[35]

**2** What Paul is about to repeat for their "safety" begins with the threefold warning, "look out for,"[36] expressed with powerful rhetoric,[37] full of invective and sarcasm against (apparently) Jewish Christians who promote

---

Hawthorne. Lightfoot (126) clearly recognizes the unlikelihood of this view, but in keeping with his radical disjunction between vv. 1 and 2, neither can it point forward; hence he suggests it refers to the "dissensions" in 1:27–2:18 (cf. Hendriksen).

34. Cf. Mackay ("Further Thoughts," 164): "It is altogether reasonable to suppose that he had repeatedly warned the Philippians against the 'Judaizers', and that he is apologizing in iii.1 for giving this warning again." So most interpreters (e.g., Meyer, Vincent, Kennedy, Jones, Bonnard, Müller, Kent, Loh-Nida, Silva, O'Brien).

35. Rahtjen ("Three Letters," 172) claims that those who hold to the integrity of Philippians have as much difficulty with this sentence as do those who hold to partition theories. But that seems to be an overstatement, since he admittedly cannot make sense of it at all, whereas the proposed interpretation seems to make perfectly good sense as setting up the warning that follows.

36. Gk. βλέπετε; part of the rhetoric lies in the repetition of this warning imperative with its asyndeton: "look out for the dogs; look out for the evil workers; look out for the mutilation." G. D. Kilpatrick ("ΒΛΕΠΕΤΕ," followed by Caird, Hawthorne; Garland, "Composition," 166; Stowers, "Friends," 116) argued for a weakened sense here ("regard, look at, consider") on the grounds that when it serves as a warning it is followed either by a μή πως or an ἀπό; thus it is not admonitory but setting forth the Judaizers (Jews, in the case of Caird and Hawthorne) as "a cautionary example" (Caird). But this makes very little sense of the rhetoric (why the threefold repetition of an *indicative,* one wonders) or the context (esp. vv. 3-4, which follow very strangely if this is not warning); nor is it an altogether accurate syntactical observation about usage. When followed by a μή πως, the warning still lies in the verb, not in what follows; and, as Silva and O'Brien correctly point out, in this case the μή πως seems clearly implied by the context; furthermore, as evidenced by Caird's discussion, this view has considerable difficulty with the γάρ in v. 3.

37. The rhetoric is threefold: the repetition itself; the use of epithets that "turn the tables" on his opponents; and the assonance with which it is expressed:

βλέπετε τοὺς κύνας,
βλέπετε τοὺς κακοὺς ἐργάτας,
βλέπετε τὴν κατατομήν.

To see three different groups here (as some earlier interpreters noted by Meyer, 146) displays insensitivity both to the context and the rhetoric.

circumcision among Gentile believers.[38] It is this sudden outburst of invective, following so closely the imperative to "rejoice in the Lord," that has caused many to read this as an interruption of some kind. But that is an unnecessary inference, as is the common assumption that these people were actually present in Philippi (see n. 18). In fact, this is warning, pure and simple, which does not require their presence in order to carry weight. That Paul does not mention them again[39] would seem to indicate that they are *not* present — although they surely will have tried their wares in Philippi in times past — and that a present threat of "Judaizing" does not seriously exist.[40] The reason for the invective lies with Paul. Such people have been "dogging" him for over a decade,[41] and as the strong language of Gal 5:12 and 2 Cor 11:13-15 makes clear,[42] he has long ago

38. Some have argued for Jews as such (so Lohmeyer, Rahtjen, Klijn, Pollard, Caird, Hawthorne, et al.), but that view carries little persuasion in light of Pauline usage elsewhere, esp. 2 Cor 11:1-23, where Paul's language can only refer to people who are Christians (they preach "another gospel," to be sure, but it is a "gospel" that speaks of Christ). It is hard to imagine the circumstances whereby Gentiles who had come to follow Christ could possibly be attracted to becoming Jewish proselytes, since that is what most of them avoided as God-fearers. Even less likely are suggestions that the "missionaries" are Jewish "gnostics" (Schmithals) or "gnostics" who "claim special Spirit endowment" (Koester, Martin, Loh-Nida, Polhill, Lincoln); on the latter see n. 60 below.

39. At least not in vv. 3-9; it is moot whether he is referring specifically to them in the generalizing word in vv. 18-19, where he speaks of "many" who "walk" differently from himself. "Judaizers" could easily be included in the phrase "enemies of the cross of Christ," but the verb "walk" in Paul always has to do with how one lives, not with theological aberration, and the context indicates that Paul is there referring to people who are no longer "pressing on toward the prize," who have set their minds on "earthly things" vis-á-vis "us whose citizenship is in heaven." On the improbability that they were currently present in Philippi, see n. 18 above.

40. Cf. Mackay (163): "the change in tone . . . must not be exaggerated" (so also O'Brien, 347). All the more so if one takes seriously the role of "enmity" in letters of friendship (see Introduction, pp. 6-7).

41. This is my own play on words; it is altogether doubtful that the epithet in the Greek carried this word play.

42. In one of the most biting bits of sarcasm to be found in his letters, Paul urges in Gal 5:12 that if they must use the knife, they do so by castrating themselves rather than circumcising his Gentile converts; in 2 Cor 11:13-14, he calls them Satan's dupes, masquerading as apostles of Christ. Rahtjen's assertion ("Three Letters," 170) that "the bitterness of the tone of the first two verses is even greater than the anger shown in Galatians," makes one wonder by what criteria we should measure degrees of emotion. In any case, "bitterness" and "anger" would not be the first words to come to my mind when reading the present text, which has no comparable follow-up in the rest of the letter and nothing comparable to the ringing "anathema" of Gal 1:6 and accusation of being "false apostles" who are servants of Satan "masquerading as servants of righteousness" in 2 Cor 11:15. The latter are categorically stronger denunciations than the present passage, which takes the form of insult but not pronouncements of eternal judgment or of calling their character into question.

had it to the bellyful with these "servants of Satan" who think of themselves as "servants of Christ" (2 Cor 11:15, 23).

On the other hand, we miss too much if we think of this language as merely expressing a personal pique. At issue for Paul is Christian existence itself. The concerns are therefore expressed ultimately in experiential and theological language, as the alleged "opponents" fade into the background rather quickly. As with the exhortations in 1:27–2:18, living the gospel in Philippi is what is at stake. This is why he speaks of such *repetition* as not "burdensome" for him, even though being reminded again of the Judaizers' activities appears to be irksome.

Thus, as in Galatians and 2 Corinthians, Paul uses epithets that "turn the tables" on them, as to what they think themselves to be about in contrast to what he thinks. First, "look out for *the dogs.*"[43] This metaphor is full of "bite," since dogs were zoological "low life," scavengers that were generally detested by Greco-Roman society and considered unclean by Jews, who sometimes used "dog" to designate Gentiles.[44] Paul thus reverses the epithet; by trying to make Gentiles "clean" through circumcision, the Judaizers are unclean "dogs."[45]

Second, they are "evil doers."[46] The clue to this usage lies in its

43. As always with such striking metaphors, one can find numerous suggestions in the literature as to what it points to. Some suggest "those who 'dog' his footsteps" (although there is no known use of such a metaphor in Greek literature); others that he regarded these people as "scavengers" on his congregations, a suggestion that seems to have possibilities. More fancifully, some have pointed to 2 Kgs 9:36, where the "dogs" eat *the flesh* of Jezebel, thus pointing toward the final epithet, "the mutilation." For still more fanciful suggestions see Meyer (145), who notes "shamelessness," "snappishness," "envy," "disorderly wandering about," and "a loud howling against Paul"!

44. A culture that spends millions of dollars on dogs as pets can scarcely appreciate the basic contempt that ancient society had for dogs, who were both scavengers (eating whatever street garbage they could find) and vicious (attacking the weak and helpless). They get nearly universally bad press in the Bible and thus are metaphorically applied to humans only pejoratively (see, e.g., 1 Sam 17:43; 24:14; 2 Sam 9:8; 16:9; 2 Kgs 8:13; Matt 7:6; 2 Pet 2:22). For Jewish attitudes toward Gentiles, see R. Aqiba, who named his two dogs Rufus and Rufina, because the Gentiles are like dogs in their manner of life (Tanch 107b; cited in Str-B 1.725).

45. Grayston ("Opponents") thinks otherwise, that the "dogs" are Gentiles, who are "promoting circumcision as an initiatory rite . . . out of semi-magical belief in ritual blood-shedding" (171). But this fails altogether in light of vv. 3-6.

46. Gk. τοὺς κακοὺς ἐργάτας; cf. 2 Cor 11:13, ἐργάται δόλιοι ("deceitful workers"). ἐργάτης occurs in Paul elsewhere only in 1 Tim 5:18 (where he is citing a piece of Jesus tradition) and 2 Tim 2:15 (metaphorically of Timothy). Some understand the present usage as "ironic" over against their alleged "harping on the necessity of 'works' to secure salvation" (Martin [1959], 137; cf. Barth, Caird, Hawthorne, Silva). But that seems altogether unlikely, since it is doubtful that the Judaizers ever saw themselves as promoting

position between "dogs" and "the mutilation." Since both of these terms express reversals, it is arguable that this one does as well. If so, then the irony derives from the Psalter's repeated designation of *the wicked* as "those who *work iniquity*."[47] The reason for changing the noun from "iniquity" to "evil" is for the sake of the assonance noted above (n. 37). Such people, Paul proffers, in trying to make Gentiles submit to Torah do not work "righteousness" at all, but evil, just as those in the Psalter work iniquity because they have rejected God's righteousness, in the sense of showing their relationship to him by walking in his ways.

Third, and changing from the masculine plural to a pejorative description of their activity, Paul warns, "beware the mutilation," an ironic reference to Gentile circumcision.[48] The Greek word for circumcision is peri*tomē* (= to cut around); kata*tomē,* used here, denotes "cutting to pieces," hence "mutilate." This word play,[49] especially the emphatic "for *we* are *the* circumcision" (v. 3), not to mention that Paul begins his testimony with *this* word — ahead of tribe and people — makes it certain that circumcision is the primary issue between Paul and them. Along with the play on "cutting" in Gal 5:12, where he urges them to "castrate" themselves, this is the ultimate derogation of circumcision, the most "cutting" epithet of all. The cognate verb occurs in Lev 21:5 (LXX), which prohibits priests (who "serve" God) from "cutting" their flesh as pagan priests did (cf. 1 Kgs 18:28). The shift from the people ("dogs, evil workers") to the activity ("mutilation") is probably first of all to keep the rhetoric crisp, but in effect it also highlights the activity, which leads directly to the response in v. 3.

This final epithet also serves as evidence that the issue has to do with "righteousness based on Law" (v. 9), which in Paul invariably refers to Torah observance both as a "means to" and "gauge of" righteousness — i.e., being observant is seen as an attempt to secure one's relationship with God, while at the same time Torah serves as the yardstick to measure

---

"works." H. Koester ("Purpose"), on the basis of usage in Matt 9:37-38; 10:10; *Did* 13:2, sees the epithet as a self-designation denoting missionary activity (cf. Georgi, *Opponents,* 40; Lincoln, *Paradise,* 90; O'Brien), which cannot be proven one way or the other. Paul himself never so uses it at any rate.

47. Gk. οἱ ἐργαζόμενοι τὴν ἀνομίαν; see Ps 5:5; 6:8; 13:4; 35:12; 52:4; 58:2, 5; 91:7, 9; 93:4, 16; 118:3; 124:5; 144:4, 9. The noun ἐργάται occurs with this idiom in 1 Macc 3:6 (so also in Symmachus's translation of Ps 93:16). So also Bruce, 104.

48. Rahtjen ("Three Letters," 170) considers this to refer to their own ("the dogs'") circumcision; but that would be against all analogy in Paul, who never derogates circumcision as such, and especially not that of Jews.

49. The technical term for which is paronomasia, a deliberate use of words with similar sounds for rhetorical effect, another form of which is the assonance of the three clauses (see n. 37 above).

performance, and thus that relationship. What is less clear is what these "dogs" expected of Gentile converts. Traditionally, on the basis of centuries of Protestant theology, it has been assumed that they were putting forward Torah observance as a way of getting right with God.[50] But there is serious doubt as to whether that would have been their primary intent; after all, these Gentiles are already believers in Christ, as are all those upon whom the Judaizers urge circumcision. Most likely, therefore, at issue for them is Torah observance as evidence of Gentiles' truly belonging to God's people and therefore of their genuine obedience to Christ.[51] Nonetheless, even though their first interest is in making Jews out of Gentiles, in the sense of securing their place within the Abrahamic covenant, Paul clearly sees through to the ultimate theological consequences for those who would capitulate — that it has the effect of adding a plus factor to grace, and thus of eliminating grace altogether by exchanging it for boasting in "one's flesh." This in turn explains why the following argument and illustration from Paul's personal history takes the form it does.

50. Except for an occasional demurrer, this view has held almost total sway until it was challenged by E. P. Sanders in *Paul and Palestinian Judaism* (1977), who coined the term "covenantal nomism" to describe a view of the Law that thought of law-keeping as an expression of covenantal relationship vis-à-vis obeying the law to gain God's favor. This point of view, which might be called "religious-sociological" (over against the traditional "theological-religious" perspective), has been advanced by many others, esp. Dunn (see essays collected in *Jesus, Paul and the Law*). See the discussion in Fee, *Presence,* 813-16, for the perspective suggested here, which would embrace both the religious-sociological and theological dimensions of this issue. On the one hand, Dunn is quite right in pointing out that the language "works of the Law" in Paul does not include ethics, but invariably denotes the three "identity markers" (circumcision, Sabbath observance, food laws) which distinguished the people of the covenant from the Gentiles among whom they lived. This is undoubtedly the driving concern of the Judaizers themselves, to bring Gentiles within the "blessings" of the Abrahamic covenant, which was predicated on their becoming circumcised. On the other hand, Paul ultimately argues on a more theological plane, moving the issue to the "means to righteousness" itself, i.e., how one is rightly related to God. At stake for him is whether one's identity with God and his people is predicated on "faith" in God's grace as expressed in Christ's death and resurrection, or on the "doing" of "Torah observance." Cf. D. Hagner, "Jewish Matrix."

51. Paul's own position on circumcision is found in the thrice repeated "neither circumcision nor uncircumcision counts for a thing" (1 Cor 7:19; Gal 5:6; 6:15), precisely because it has no significance with God whatsoever. This further suggests, in keeping with his dictum in 1 Cor 9:20, that he has no difficulty if Jewish parents continue to circumcise their boys. Where he comes out fighting is when Torah observance is given significance, so that Gentiles must conform in order to belong fully to the people of God. At that point, Torah observance takes on theological significance, implying that one's relationship with God in itself is predicated on "works of law."

**3** As immediate response to the ironic "mutilation," Paul asserts: "For[52] *we* [in contrast to what they are trying to get Gentiles to do] *are* the circumcision [hence you do not need literal circumcision], who serve by the Spirit of God and 'boast' in Christ Jesus and put no confidence in the flesh." Here is a sentence at once full of rhetorical power and theological grist.[53] The rhetorical power lies partly in the paronomasia (see n. 49 above) and partly in his choice of a verb from the temple cultus[54] to describe what "we" do (see "c" below). The theological grist is to be found in every phrase. This verse, not v. 2, is the principal sentence in the present appeal, whose theology is going to be explicated by means of Paul's own story in vv. 4-14.

a. The emphatic "we" — not they — by which the sentence begins is the first occurrence of this theological phenomenon in the letter. It is Paul's regular habit in the middle of an argument to shift from the second or third person to the inclusive first person plural whenever the point shifts to some soteriological reality that includes him as well as his readers.[55] Thus, rather than "you" Philippians are the true circumcision, it is "we" — you and us, Gentiles and Jews together — who are such. In this case, of course, the shift in person paves the way toward the "I" of vv. 4-14; but the recurrence of this phenomenon in vv. 15-16 and (especially) vv. 20-21 indicates that it is not simply preparatory here.

b. In saying that "we," both Jews and Gentiles together who have put our trust in Christ, "are *the* circumcision," Paul indicates that the primary issue is not the Philippians' salvation, but rather the identification of the people of God under the new covenant.[56] Lying behind this usage is the theology and

52. Gk. γάρ, in this case offering the "cause, or reason" why they should heed the admonition of v. 2. On the difficulties this raises for the softened view of βλέπετε see n. 36

53. That this sentence represents some kind of prior catechetical teaching (so Collange, Martin) is pure speculation; the context is so precise and the content so Pauline that such speculation is as unnecessary as it is unprovable.

54. See n. 59 below.

55. See, among many examples, 1 Thess 1:9-10 ("*you* turned from idols to the living God . . . and await his Son from heaven, Jesus who delivers *us* from the coming wrath"); Gal 4:5 ("in order that he might redeem *those* under Law, in order that *we* might receive adoption"); Rom 8:15 ("*you* received the Spirit of adoption, by whom *we* cry 'Abba, Father' "); cf. 1 Thess 5:9; 1 Cor 1:18, 30; 5:7; 15:3; Rom 5:1-5; 8:3; *et passim.* Some think otherwise regarding the present passage: e.g., H. Koester, "Purpose," who thinks that the emphatic "we" refers to Paul's Spirit-endowed apostleship as over against that of his opponents, but this is related to his unique view of the passage as a whole; D. W. B. Robinson, "Circumcision," who takes the unlikely view (given vv. 15-16 and 20-21) that it refers to himself and other Jews-turned-Christians; others think it refers to Paul and Timothy. See the discussion in O'Brien, 358-59.

56. For the covenantal emphasis of this language, see Motyer, 148.

intertextuality of a passage like Rom 2:28-29,[57] where Paul takes up the promise of Deut 30:6 and turns "Jew" and "Gentile" end for end — in terms of "circumcision of the heart" by the Spirit.[58] Now the reason for the rich imagery in Phil 2:14-16 comes into focus, where by a similar reversal the Philippians are seen as "the blameless children of God." Paul, it needs to be emphasized, knows nothing of a "new" Israel; for him there is only one people of God, who are now newly constituted — quite in keeping with OT promises — on the basis of Christ and the Spirit; and it is by the Spirit in particular that Gentiles have entered into their inheritance of the blessings promised to Abraham (Gal 3:14).

c. Paul first describes the true circumcision as "we who 'minister'[59] by the Spirit of God."[60] The crucial term here is the verb rendered "worship,"

---

57. For a full discussion of this text, see Fee, *Presence,* 489-93; cf. on 2 Cor 3:6 and Rom 7:5-6 as well (pp. 304-7, 503-8).

58. Cf. also Jer 9:23-25, from which Paul derives his understanding of "boasting in the Lord," which in v. 25 of that passage also reflects on merely outward circumcision.

59. Gk. λατρεύοντες (NIV, "worship"), which is very difficult to render into English (see the discussion; cf. H. Balz, *EDNT,* 2.344-45); cf. Rom 1:9 and 2 Tim 1:3 (of Paul's "service" to God) and Rom 1:25 (of idolatrous "service"). Pauline usage is determined by the LXX; the use of the cognate noun in Rom 9:4 and 12:1 tells the story. To Israel belongs, among other things, the λατρεία (= the temple cultus); now believers, in contrast to idolaters (Rom 1:25, those of "senseless minds," v. 20), offer "service" to God that "makes sense" of their present existence in Christ (for this understanding of λογίκην see Fee, *Presence,* 599-602). In order to support his mirror reading of this text as polemical against "Spirit enthusiasts" (next n.), Koester ("Purpose," 320-21) argues against a cultic background here — despite the context — and offers the unlikely translation, "[we are those] who work as missionaries in the Spirit of God."

60. Many (e.g., Koester, Gnilka, Martin, Polhill, Lincoln, O'Brien), picking up on some "parallels" in 2 Cor 11-12, see this phrase as reflecting the position of "the propagandists," who "claim . . . special possession of the Spirit in their activities" (Lincoln, *Paradise,* 90-91). This is then read into a variety of further moments in the passage (the emphasis on suffering, the mention of the resurrection, the alleged "perfectionism," those who have made a "god of their bellies"). This kind of "mirror reading" (see the Introduction, p. 7 n. 24) represents a clear case of falling into "pitfalls" 2 and 4 of Barclay's guidelines ("over-interpretation" and "latching onto particular words and phrases as direct echoes of the opponents' vocabulary and then hanging a whole thesis on those flimsy pegs"). Besides the plain fact that the Spirit is neither mentioned nor alluded to throughout the rest of this passage, this view does not take Paul's own theology seriously enough, especially his presupposition, expressed throughout his letters in a variety of forms, that Christian life is predicated on the saving work of Christ (hence, "boasting in Christ Jesus") and the appropriating work of the Spirit (hence, "who 'serve' by the Spirit of God"). See further, Fee, *Presence* (13, 78, *et passim*). When Paul speaks in a very Pauline way, as he does here, one is especially hard pressed to discover the "theology" of alleged "opponents" in what he says, all the more so when we also lack the kind of direct evidence provided by explicit statements about their point of view.

which rendering in this case can be quite misleading. Paul's usage is determined by the LXX, where it is used almost exclusively to denote the Levitical "service" in the temple cultus. Here it stands in ironical contrast to v. 2. "Mutilation" is what those who "served" in the temple cultus were forbidden to do. Now, in contrast to the "workers of iniquity" who are engaged in such illegitimate "service," Paul says we are the true circumcision, who "serve" by the Spirit, over against serving by the flesh. The verb, therefore, is not the one for "worship" in the sense of what the congregation does together as a gathered people, but represents the "service" of God's people in terms of their devotion to him as evidenced in the way they live before him. Rather than offer such service by "cutting away the flesh," so as to be identified with the people of God under the former covenant, the true circumcision live (= "serve") in Christ by the power of the Spirit. Thus Paul has in view not external rite over against internal "spiritual"[61] service, but two ways of existing — in the "flesh," which he understands as life centered in the creature as over against God, or as the eschatological people of God, evidenced to be so by the Spirit of God, through whom all life in the present is now service and devotion to God.[62]

Thus, "serve" has to do with "righteousness" — the real thing, which reflects God's likeness and character in Christian behavior (e.g., looking out for the interests of others, 2:3-4, as modeled by him who revealed God-likeness in emptying himself by taking on the form of a slave, 2:5-7); and such "service," which is effected in the life of the believer and believing community by God's own indwelling Spirit, is a million miles removed from "service" in the form of Torah observance. In turning Torah into "laws to be observed" God's people thus turned them into merely human regulations, missing their intent as revelation of God's likeness to be lived out among God's people; hence the need for a circumcision of the heart, effected by the Spirit, to replace that of the "flesh."

61. As, e.g., the NEB (corrected in the REB), "we whose worship is spiritual"; cf. Calvin, 269; Lightfoot, 145; Beare, 105; Hawthorne 126-27, a view often tied to John 4:24. But Pauline usage and theology stand totally against it; indeed, such a view misses the genuinely radical nature of life in the Spirit as Paul elsewhere articulates it (see Fee, *Presence, passim*).

62. This suggests further that this dative, as usual in Paul, is probably not locative, as the NRSV makes it ("who worship in the Spirit of God"; cf. NASB, NAB), as though we render proper service to God as we live in the Spirit. While one could scarcely argue against that theologically, Pauline usage seems determinative here. In most instances, arguably in all, this dative (πνεύματι; ἐν πνεύματι) is instrumental (see the full discussion in Fee, *Presence,* 21-24). We offer such service by means of the Spirit, which in this case probably has little to do with "doing" anything, but rather with simply living and walking by the Spirit as over against putting confidence "in the flesh."

Significantly, Paul qualifies "Spirit" by the genitive "of God."[63] This designation occurs often enough that one should perhaps not make too much of it here — this is who the Spirit is, after all. Nonetheless, since Paul does not often use this qualifier in this construction,[64] there is probably more emphasis here than at first meets the eye. Very likely this is a pointed contrast to those who think of themselves as rendering service to the one God both by their own circumcision and by insisting that believing Gentiles offer themselves to God in the same way. True service to God is that which has been engendered by the Spirit *of God,* where through life in the Spirit the believer thus "boasts in Christ," who has brought an end to the time of "the flesh."

d. But if one begins Christian life as an experienced reality of the Spirit, the basis of that life is Christ himself, which in this sentence is expressed in terms recalling Jer 9:23-24:[65] "who boast/glory in Christ Jesus." On the meaning of this word see on 1:26 above. Here again it carries the nuance of "boasting" in the sense of putting one's full trust and confidence in, and thus to "glory" in. Although the presence of the Spirit functions as Paul's primary contrast both to "works of Law" and to "the flesh," in this letter in particular he can scarcely bring himself to speak of Christian existence without mentioning Christ. In the personal word that follows, this is the theme to which he returns in grand style.

God's new covenant people, therefore, do not need to become Torah observant, precisely because they "boast in Christ Jesus"; they have put their trust in him who has effected God's true righteousness for them. Thus, Christ Jesus, by death on the cross, has brought them into relationship with God through sheer grace; and the goal of Torah is realized not in their becoming observant but in their walking by God's Spirit who now indwells them.

e. Finally, and now in contrast both to "*boasting* in Christ Jesus" and to "serving *by the Spirit of God,*" he adds the telling blow: "and who put *no confidence* in the *flesh.*" This clause is full of irony, Paul's way of moving from their specific expression of Torah observance (the circumcision of the flesh) to what he recognizes to be the theological implications of Gentiles' yielding to circumcision. It reflects the similar argument in Gal 3:2-3, where Paul uses "flesh" exactly as here, referring first to the actual "flesh" cut away

63. On the textual question see n. 10.

64. That is, with the dative πνεύματι; Rom 8:9 is the one exception.

65. For the crucial nature of this text in Paul see 1 Cor 1:31 and 2 Cor 10:17. As noted above on 1:26, Paul's use of this word (καυχάομαι) has been largely determined by the Jeremiah passage, which already uses the preposition ἐν with this verb and means to "put one's confidence *in* and thus to glory *in* [the Lord]." This OT usage calls into serious question all other suggestions as to the meaning of "in Christ Jesus" in the present passage (e.g., GNB [Loh-Nida], "rejoice *in our life in union with* Christ Jesus," which sounds far more like Deissmann and Bousset than it does like Paul).

in circumcision,[66] but at the same time as the primary descriptive word of life before and outside of Christ. Thus, as in that passage, "Spirit" and "flesh" stand juxtaposed as eschatological realities that describe existence in the overlap of the ages.[67] One lives either "according to the Spirit" or "according to the flesh." These are mutually incompatible kinds of existence; to be in the one and then to revert to the former is spiritual suicide from Paul's point of view. And this is where the Judaizers have gone astray; they reject "boasting *in the Lord*" for "confidence *in the flesh*."

Thus with this full description of those who belong to the Israel of God as newly constituted by Christ and the Spirit, Paul sets the Philippians in sharp contrast to what the "mutilation" would do for them. As he will go on to argue by way of personal narrative, there is absolutely no future of any kind in reverting to what is now past, which Christ and the Spirit have brought to an end.

We should note finally the implicit Trinitarianism of this sentence. The true circumcision, thus true righteousness (both one's relationship with God and behavior that reflects his character), comes from God (v. 9), by whose indwelling Spirit believers now serve him in "righteousness," who have first of all put their trust in Christ Jesus, who has effected "righteousness" for them. "Righteousness," of course, is not mentioned in this opening theological sentence; but it is implied in the first clause, "we are the circumcision," as is evidenced by vv. 6 and 9. The key to that righteousness is here set forth by means of its primary new covenant components — Christ and the Spirit.

**4a** As a final addendum to the description in v. 3, but also as a lead-in to the personal word that follows, Paul appends: "though[68] I myself have reasons for such confidence" — although he actually says it a little more starkly: "though I myself have confidence even[69] in the flesh." What this means will be clarified in the following sentence (vv. 4b-6). We who serve by the Spirit, Paul says, who "boast" in Christ Jesus, have thus abandoned altogether "putting confidence in the flesh" — which by implication is what the Judaizers are bringing Gentiles to by urging circumcision. But, he now concedes, if they want to play that game, then I win there as well, since I

66. W. D. Davies ("Flesh and Spirit"; cf. GNB, Loh-Nida) would limit it to this usage; but that seems altogether unlikely (cf. Moehring, "Some Remarks").

67. For this emphasis on "flesh" and "Spirit" as primarily eschatological realities, see Fee, *Presence,* 816-22; cf. Silva 170-71.

68. Gk. καίπερ, used with the participle to express concession; found only here in Paul. There seems neither need nor warrant for Hawthorne's taking the clause as the protasis of an elliptical sentence.

69. The Western witnesses (D* E* F G it pc) omit this καί, but in so doing they deflect Paul's emphasis.

excel on their turf, "having [grounds for] confidence even in the flesh."[70] As before, "in the flesh" refers first to the rite of circumcision, but now carries all the theological overtones of trying to have grounds for boasting before God on the basis of human achievement, the ultimate "self-centered" expression of life. And with that he turns to offer, first, the evidence for such a bold statement (vv. 4b-6) and, second, the zero net worth of such "achievement" in light of having come to know Christ and being found in him.

## B. THE EXAMPLE OF PAUL (3:4b-14)

What follows the warning and affirmation of vv. 2-3, though untypical of the Paul we meet in his earlier letters, fits the present letter well: he offers his personal story as a paradigm for them to follow.[1] In the process many of his basic theological convictions find expression in terms of his own experience of them. This unusual form of "argumentation" is predicated altogether on the secure relationship that exists between him and them.[2] It also further indicates that this section is not an interruption or digression, but a purposeful part of the letter, and that v. 1 intentionally introduces it. These are Paul's close friends, who know his gospel well from years of association with him. Such sharing of the gospel would undoubtedly have included warnings against those who might come to them with a "different gospel," insisting on Torah

70. Lightfoot (145) correctly argues that "the proper force of ἔχων πεποίθησιν may not be explained away." After all, Paul speaks here of having indeed that which he will renounce in vv. 7-9. *Contra* such translations as GNB: ("I could, of course, put my trust in such things").

1. Cf. Collange (129): "So the interest of the apostle does not lie primarily in autobiography but in parenesis; . . . he is simply striving to instruct." Martin (123) suggests otherwise, that this is "self-defence," in which Paul "goes to [great] length to defend himself from the implied criticism of his opponents"; cf. Pfitzner (*Agon,* 142). But (a) that takes the concept of "opponents" to lengths not found in the passage itself (cf. nn. 19, 38, and 60 on the preceding paragraph); (b) there is nothing in the language itself that implies "defense" (the ἐγὼ μᾶλλον simply sets Paul in contrast to the Judaizers in v. 2, but not in terms of "self-defense"); and (c) Paul himself urges that what he says here is to serve as a paradigm for the Philippians (vv. 15-17), which does not fit well the theme of "apology." It is the paradigmatic nature of the present narrative that marks it off from all previous autobiographical moments in his letters (e.g., 1 Thess 2:1-12; Gal 1:13–2:14; 2 Cor 11:23–12:12), which are decidedly "apologetic" in function and tone *(contra* G. Lyon, *Pauline Autobiography)* — although even there Paul reminds converts of his example when among them, so as to reinforce some point of paraenesis (as in 2 Thess 3:7-10).

2. Yet another indication of friendship (see the Introduction, pp. 2-7). Indeed, the present appeal functions similarly to that in 2:1-2, where he urges on the basis of their long-time relationship in Christ and the Spirit that they "complete his joy" by being of one mind regarding the gospel.

observance. Since Paul has gone over this ground with them often before, his own example is sufficient here: "I've been there," he reminds them, "and it is a dead end, offering neither life nor fellowship with Christ. Indeed, it has no future at all; whereas 'knowing Christ' means to 'be found'; it means fellowship with him now and being with him forever." Fellowship with Christ now, of course, also means participation in his sufferings, made possible through the power of his resurrection.

The narrative can be easily traced. It begins with his former "advantages" within Judaism, which in his case far outstrip any that could be exhibited by those who might come to them (4-6); but this "gain" turns out to be total "loss," mere "refuse," in comparison with the ultimate "gain," that of being found in Christ, possessing God's righteousness made available through Christ — now and at the end — and thus knowing him (7-9). But the sentence concludes on a surprising note, reminding them that such life in Christ includes present suffering as well as future glory (10-11), which leads to the conclusion of the story, that the future, which has come present in Christ and the Spirit, is also still future and is fully worthy of vigorous pursuit (12-14).[3]

The "why" of all this is more difficult, since both vv. 12-14 and the transitional vv. 10-11 seem so poorly related to vv. 4-9. The first part (vv. 4-9) clearly flows out of, and seems intended to respond to, the warning and affirmation of vv. 2-3. The transitional clause (vv. 10-11), which reiterates the theme of "knowing Christ" from v. 8, moves in an unexpected direction, returning to the theme of present suffering ("being *conformed* to his death") while awaiting future resurrection. Picking up on "the resurrection," the second part (vv. 12-14) focuses on a second recurring theme, steadfast "pressing on" so as to realize the certain future. At issue is how these various parts relate to each other, and to the letter as a whole; especially so since the application that follows, including the appeal to imitate him (vv. 15-4:1), climaxes explicitly on the theme of vv. 12-14 — their "standing fast" (4:1) in light of their guaranteed future, when they will be transformed into (by "being *conformed* to") Christ's present glorified existence (3:21).

Most likely the reason for this narrative is twofold: (1) to reiterate his gospel, which they know well, but now by way of his own personal history and in light of the warning in v. 2 — apparently a theological "diagnostic"; and (2) using that same story to return to twin urgencies that recur throughout:

3. Some would also see a correspondence with the narrative about Christ in 2:6-11 (e.g., Moule, Wright); but Paul himself makes no point of it, and the parallels are inexact, especially since the paradigmatic point of the present narrative seems to differ considerably from the former one, although the linguistic echoes suggest that Christ's story serves as the premise for this one.

(a) that they "hang in there" in the midst of present suffering, indeed that they see their suffering for what it is — God's way of "conforming" them to Christ's death — and (b) that they not lose their grip on their certain future. In view of how the passage concludes (3:17–4:1), the latter two issues seem to be the primary concern, for which the first part of the story serves as the theological ground. This is what it means to "know Christ": it means not to look elsewhere for "advantages" of any kind, but to be found in him, and thus to participate in his sufferings in the present, in the full light of our certain eschatological future in which we will be finally "conformed" to his present glory.

## 1. There Is No Future to the Past (3:4b-6)

> 4bIf others think they have reasons to put confidence in the flesh, I have more: 5circumcised on the eighth day, of the people of Israel, of the tribe of Benjamin, a Hebrew of Hebrews; in regard to the law, a Pharisee; 6as for zeal, persecuting the church; as for legalistic righteousness, faultless.

With this opening paragraph Paul sets forth his former advantages, what was at one time on the "gain" side of the ledger. After an opening sentence that insists on the superior quality of his "status" as a Jew, he illustrates that superiority with a list of seven items, six of which indicate different ways in which he "excelled." Not surprisingly, given vv. 2-3, he begins with circumcision, then moves on to his membership in the ancient people of God, including his tribal origins; he is "a Hebrew of Hebrews," which can be demonstrated in three observable ways, concluding with the declaration, "blameless, according to the righteousness found in the law."

Little is new here.[4] What is surprising — for this list — is the inclusion of "persecuting the church," plus the final assertion of blamelessness as to the Law. From a sociological point of view, what is reiterated here are items that indicate "status." But the final two (and very likely, therefore, his being a Pharisee as well) indicate "achievement"; so the interest is not simply in what was given to him by birth, but in what he himself did so as rightly to be designated "a Hebrew of Hebrews." All of this, he will go on, amounts

---

4. The first item is everywhere presupposed. His belonging to "Israel's race" is specifically mentioned in 2 Cor 11:22; Rom 9:3; 11:1. He mentions his tribe in Rom 11:1, his being a "Hebrew" in 2 Cor 11:22. His pharisaism is implied in Gal 1:13-14; he mentions his "persecuting the church" in Gal 1:13, 23; 1 Cor 15:9, and 1 Tim 1:13. Only his "faultlessness" in observing Torah is not mentioned elsewhere in his letters, although it is no surprise in light of Gal 1:14.

to nothing more than "refuse" in comparison with knowing Christ, which by implication means "no Torah observance." The future, therefore, is not to be found in taking on Jewish identity; in other words, the future does not lie in his religious past.

**4b** This sentence basically reiterates the preceding addendum to v. 3. It is at once ironical and theological. Even if they did not intend it to be so, putting "confidence in the flesh" is what the Judaizers are all about; not only can Paul play that game — as he has just asserted (v. 4a) — but now, he goes on, "I can play it better than they can."[5] My credentials with regard to Jewish identity are impeccable; indeed, in comparison with their grounds for confidence in the flesh, "I have more."[6]

Some have seen the protasis of this sentence as indicating the presence of Judaizers among them.[7] But that is not a necessary inference; more likely, even though Judaizers serve as immediate background, this is Paul's way of giving perspective to any in Philippi who, because of present suffering, might be tempted to lean this way. After all, in several of the following items, the Judaizers could also boast; Paul's concern in offering his personal testimony is to warn the Philippians against them (= "to write the same things again is for your safety," v. 1b).

**5-6** What follows is a catalogue of seven items that illustrate the foregoing assertion:

(1) "Circumcised on the eighth day."[8] Paul leads with this particular item, not with the next two, for obvious contextual reasons. The Judaizers insist on Gentile circumcision, so that in keeping with Gen 17:3-14 Gentile believers in Christ can also identify with God's ancient people in keeping with the Abrahamic covenant. Thus Paul, who through Christ and the Spirit belongs now to *the* circumcision, begins here: as a Jewish boy, born into a Jewish home, I was "circumcised on the eighth day"; that is, "I received circumcision

---

5. For this emphasis on his "superiority" in Judaism see Gal 1:13-14 and 2 Cor 11:21-23.

6. Gk. ἐγὼ μᾶλλον; for this usage of μᾶλλον, see S. R. Llewelyn, *New Docs* 6.69-70, who notes that in an elliptical apodosis like this, it is not merely contrastive ("rather"), but intensive (= "all the more").

7. Cf. Gnilka (189), followed by Martin, who emphasizes the anonymity of a supposed "debater." This same formula, however, occurs at key points in 1 Corinthians (3:18; 8:2; 14:37), where it points not to outsiders but to people within the Corinthian congregation who have taken the stance proposed in the protasis. In light of the rest of Philippians, it is extremely doubtful that outsiders are being addressed here. On the larger question of Judaizers present in Philippi, see the discussion on v. 2 (esp. nn. 18 and 39).

8. Gk. περιτομῇ ὀκταήμερος. The dative is "reference" (= with reference to circumcision).

long before any of you in Philippi had even heard about Christ and the gospel."9

(2) "Of the people10 of Israel."11 Here is the crucial item. What the Judaizers hope to achieve by Gentile circumcision is to bring them into the privileges of *belonging* to God's ancient people, "Israel's race." Paul had been given this privilege by birth.

(3) "Of the tribe of Benjamin." The reason for this one is almost certainly for effect. Gentiles could become members only of Israel; his membership was of a kind whereby he could trace his family origins. He belonged to the tribe of Benjamin, that favored tribe from whom came his namesake Saul, Israel's first king, the tribe blessed by Moses as "the beloved of the Lord . . . whom the Lord loves [and who] rest between his shoulders" (Deut 33:12), in whose territory sat the Holy City itself. They were also notable because they alone joined Judah in loyalty to the Davidic covenant.12 It is not difficult to hear a ring of pride in this little reminder,13 which then calls for the next designation.

(4) "A Hebrew of Hebrews." This is the "swing" term, summing up the preceding three, and setting the stage for the final three. He was in every way a "Hebrew, born of pure Hebrew stock." The appellation "Hebrews" appears to be a term Jews used of themselves, especially in the Diaspora in contrast to Gentiles.14 That the two terms ("Hebrews, Israelites") occur to-

9. Meyer (151) suggests that the mention of "the eighth day" implies that some of the Judaizers were themselves proselytes, hence Paul's superiority. Although possible, this seems doubtful. Paul is aiming at "the righteousness contained in the law." His "I more" — and what he counts as "filthy street garbage" — has to do with his "achievements," not his status as such. After all, in Rom 11:1-2, he argues that his own "status" (an Israelite of the tribe of Benjamin) is the clear evidence that God has not in fact cast off his ancient people.

10. Gk. γένους, here meaning "race."

11. Georgi (*Opponents,* 46-49) has demonstrated that this term featured prominently in the propaganda of hellenistic Judaism to emphasize their special religious heritage. He has been followed by many (Martin, Bruce, Hawthorne, O'Brien).

12. Hendriksen (156-58) rightly calls into question some of the lavish praise of the tribe of Benjamin that is found in many of the commentaries.

13. Evidenced also by the way it is recalled in a more off-handed way in Rom 11:1.

14. As is evidenced by the inscription from the synagogue in Corinth, "Synagogue of the Hebrews." In recent years it has become common to emphasize the linguistic features of this term (see, e.g., C. F. D. Moule, "Once More"; cf. Martin, Bruce, Hawthorne, O'Brien; Gutbrod, *TDNT,* 3.390; Gunther, *Opponents,* 75), thus to suggest that he intended "Hebrew Palestinian parentage"; but this looks like strapping Paul into a Lukan straitjacket. This usage can be found throughout Jewish literature to distinguish themselves from Gentiles, almost certainly in contrast to the more pejorative term "Jew" which the Gentiles used. Besides, Paul's Greek is such that even if he had

gether in 2 Cor 11:22 in reference to Jewish Christian opponents (probably Judaizers) supports the contention that those warned about in v. 2 are Judaizers as well.

(5) "In regard to the Law, a Pharisee." This is in keeping with the data recorded in Acts 23:6-9 and 26:5 and with Paul's own word in Gal 1:14, that he had advanced in Judaism far beyond his contemporaries, being "extremely zealous for the traditions of his ancestors." Again, as the reminiscence in Gal 1:14 makes clear, this was another area of personal pride for him. The reason for mentioning this feature of his history is at least threefold: (a) It defines his relationship to the Law in a very specific way, as belonging to the Jewish sect who had given themselves to its study and codification. (b) The combined evidence of Matt 23:15 and Acts 15:5 suggests that any Jewish Christians who came to Philippi to promote Torah observance on the part of Gentiles would most likely also belong to this sect. (c) It gives the framework for understanding the next two items.

(6) "As for zeal, persecuting the church."[15] Whereas for us this may sound like a strange matter to include as "grounds for confidence in the flesh," for Paul it regularly served to heighten the contrast between his present "enslavement" to Christ and his former zeal against him.[16] He was not just your everyday, run-of-the-mill Pharisee; his zeal for the Law[17] was demonstrated most surely by his untiring dedication to stamping out the nascent Christian movement, probably related to his conviction that God had especially cursed Jesus by having him hanged (Gal 3:13; Deut 21:23). In their own way, his Judaizing opponents are also persecuting the church; but Paul surpasses them even here. Is this also a way of emphasizing for the Philippians' hearing, and in light of his and their present suffering, that he himself once stood on the other side on this issue? If so, there is a bit of irony in this usage as well.

---

learned Aramaic in his home (which he very likely did), Greek is his first language. See further J. Wanke, *EDNT,* 1.369-70.

15. *Contra* O'Brien (376-78), this usage indicates that "church," which primarily referred to the gathered assembly in any given community, could also carry the more universalizing connotation of the people of God in general. Had Paul intended the former, he most likely would have said "churches," as he does elsewhere.

16. In this regard see Gal 1:13-14 (where his zeal in persecuting the church and his zeal for the Law are the only two items mentioned; cf. 1:23, where it is mentioned again) and 1 Tim 1:13; cf. 1 Cor 15:9. Acts faithfully represents this dimension of his zeal for God (9:1-2; 22:4-5; 26:9-11).

17. That "zeal for the Law" is in view is made clear not only from the parallel in Gal 1:14, but from its place in this context between "as to the Law, a Pharisee" and "as to the righteousness found in the Law, faultless." See further the discussion in O'Brien, 375-76.

(7) "As to righteousness in the Law, blameless." This final item brings the catalogue to its climax; everything else is pointing here.[18] But it is also the item that has generated long debates among later readers, since it seems to contradict what Paul says elsewhere about one's ability to keep the Law. The key to the present usage lies at three points — the term "righteousness," the qualifier "in the Law," and the word "faultless"[19] — which together indicate that he is referring to Torah observance understood as observable conduct.

To begin with the final item, the key to "faultless" lies with the cultic overtones of this word (cf. 2:15). Paul has no "blemishes" on his record, as far as Torah observance is concerned,[20] which means that he scrupulously adhered to the pharisaic interpretation of the Law, with its finely honed regulations for sabbath observance, food laws, and ritual cleanliness. His former blamelessness in these matters makes his Christian pronouncements on these items all the more telling.[21]

This means that "righteousness" in this context does not refer to God's character or to the gift of right standing with God, but precisely as he qualifies

---

18. Some (e.g., Gunther, *Opponents*, 130) read into this phrase presumed "opponents" who "were eager to be blameless (v. 6)," viewing vv. 12-15 as reflecting their alleged emphasis on perfectionism. Martin and Pfitzner (cf. Schmithals, *Paul*, 73), on the other hand, mirror read the same evidence as "presuppos[ing] an attack of Paul's claims to apostolicity" (see n. 1). The implausibility of these reconstructions, besides being methodologically questionable mirror reading (see Introduction, p. 7 n. 24), is found in the preceding phrase, "as to zeal [for the law], persecuting the church," which all such reconstructions conveniently ignore. Pfitzner, e.g., lists all the other items in this list, and then says that "*all* these claims, *on which they seek to base their authority,* Paul for his part now considers loss" (emphasis mine). One wonders how "all these claims" can so easily circumvent "persecuting the church"; and if the latter is not part of their "claims" to "authority" (which is understandably not argued for since it borders on nonsense), then how can one be so sure that the surrounding items reflect the "claims" of "opponents"? The point to note, of course, is that Paul himself elsewhere refers to this matter in his past without hint of "opponents."

19. Gk. ἄμεμπτος; see above on 2:15 (and n. 16).

20. Some see Paul's word here as in conflict with the testimony in 1 Tim 1:13-16; but as with Rom 7:7-25, that testimony is expressed in terms of his now Christian backward look at his life before Christ. Here the perspective is within the framework of Judaism. Cf. the witness of the rich young man in the Gospel records, who claims regarding Torah observance that he had "kept these from my youth."

21. It is clear that Paul lacks a "convert's mentality" on these matters, since he never argues that Jewish believers in Christ should abandon such identity markers. He comes out fighting only when they are given theological significance, as they invariably are when imposed on Gentiles. In this regard, see esp. the argument in Rom 14:1–15:13, where all three of these past "achievements" are argued for as acceptable for Jewish believers, but as totally outside the purview of the Kingdom of God.

it, that "righteousness" which is "in the Law." Although "the Law" cannot always be so narrowly defined in Paul, here he is probably referring to matters of "food and drink" and "the observance of days," since, along with circumcision, these are the two items regularly singled out whenever discussion of Torah observance emerges in his letters.[22] Both the narrative that follows (vv. 8-9) and Rom 14:17 make it clear that for Paul true "righteousness" goes infinitely beyond these matters; indeed, the Kingdom of God has nothing at all to do with "food and drink" but with righteousness (!), peace, and joy in the Holy Spirit. What makes the present kind of righteousness so worthless is that it generates "confidence *in the flesh*"; it is "my own righteousness — my own achievement — predicated on Torah observance" (v. 9), which stands in stark contrast to the "righteousness that comes from God predicated on faith." But the present usage also indicates, as argued in 1:11, that the concern for "righteousness" in this passage is not ultimately with "right standing," but with "right living."

Paul's present point, of course, is not his sinlessness, but his being without fault in the kind of righteousness that Judaizers would bring one to, by insisting on Torah observance. But what has that to do with righteousness at all, is his point. He has excelled here, he says, and found it empty and meaningless; hence he insists for the Philippians' benefit that there is "no future in it."

A passage like this one, especially in light of Paul's language of renunciation in vv. 7-8, should perhaps call into question both the confusion of Christian faith with pride in nation and the various brands of "religiousness" and legalism that variously abound. Confusion of being Christian with being a member of a given nation has a long history in the church; it is one of the pernicious bequests of the conversion of Constantine, which plagues not only officially "Christian" states, but perhaps even more insidiously a country like the United States, where the American flag often holds pride of place in Christian sanctuaries and where patriotic holidays are sometimes the more significant days in the American church calendar.

Equally pernicious is the pride of those who have defined godliness in terms of "food and drink and the observance of days," who still maintain distinctions between "clean and unclean," although variously defined. To be able to claim that one does not indulge in such "sins" is a badge of honor in many circles. Likewise for those who define righteousness in terms of "church" — rites, sacraments, forms — rather than in terms of "knowing Christ." Paul has not given up his heritage, nor is he against "form" of various kinds. What for him is "refuse" is to "put confidence in them," as if righteousness had

22. Otherwise Kennedy, who thinks it includes "the ordinary moral precepts of the law as well." But that seems to run counter to Rom 7:7-12.

anything to do with such. And if that seems too strong for some readers, at least that gives one an opportunity to sense the passion fellow Israelites would have felt toward Paul. Our problem in hearing this text lies with our ability to distance ourselves too easily from their passions, which Paul is treading on in this passage with characteristic single-mindedness. None of these things has anything at all to do with "knowing Christ," he will go on to say.

## 2. The Future Lies with the Present — Knowing Christ (3:7-11)

> 7But[1] *whatever was to my profit I now consider loss for the sake of Christ.* 8*What is more, I consider everything a loss compared to the surpassing greatness of knowing Christ Jesus my Lord, for whose sake I have lost all things. I consider them rubbish, that I may gain Christ* 9*and be found in him, not having a righteousness of my own that comes from the law, but that which is through faith in Christ — the righteousness that comes from God and is by faith.* 10*I want to know Christ and the power of his resurrection and the*[2] *fellowship of sharing in his sufferings, becoming like him in his death,* 11*and so, somehow, to attain to the resurrection from the dead.*

With engaging rhetoric,[3] Paul now revises the balance sheet, reversing "gain"

---

1. This ἀλλά is missing in much of the better early evidence (P⁴⁶ P⁶¹ᵛⁱᵈ ℵ* A [F] G 33 81 1241ˢ 1739* pc b d Lucifer Ambrosiaster); it is found in B D Ψ Maj a f vg sy co. This is a tough call, evidenced by the brackets in NA²⁶. Either addition or omission could be accounted for because of homoeoteleuton (both ἀλλά and the ἅτινα that follows begin and end with alpha). On the whole, the text without ἀλλά is more likely original (so Michaelis, Hawthorne; O'Brien is open): (a) the external evidence strongly favors this reading (B has here abandoned its Egyptian companions); (b) it is easily the more difficult reading, since the context cries out for such a contrastive particle, which was frequently supplied in the transmissional process; (c) the combination of ἀλλά and ἀλλὰ μενοῦνγε καί in successive sentences does not occur elsewhere in Paul, which, although an awkwardness that could have led to its omission, more likely was created by scribes who sensed the need of what Barth (96) calls "the great 'But'!" Even so, the scribes have correctly read the context, which implies such a contrast.

2. The τήν found in the majority of witnesses is missing in P⁴⁶ ℵ* A B 1241ˢ 2464 pc (as is the τῶν that precedes "sufferings" in P⁴⁶ ℵ* B). The text without the article is almost certainly original, since it is difficult to conceive of the circumstances in which a scribe would have omitted it (them). This suggests that Paul understands the closest kind of relationship to exist between "the power of his resurrection" and "participation in his sufferings," since both are controlled by a single definite article.

3. Found in this case in a variety of literary devices, which are striking in effect, especially for a document written to be heard. It includes the asyndeton with which it begins; the studied parallelism of v. 7; chiasm (vv. 10-11); and repetitions of various kinds (ἅτινα-ταῦτα-πάντα-τὰ πάντα; κέρδη-κερδήσω; ζημίαν-ζημίαν-ἐζημιώθην; ἥγημαι-

and "loss" in light of his experience of Christ. He begins with a simple sentence of renunciation, echoing earlier language in the letter[4] and setting up the word plays that follow. "What things were *gains* to me," he affirms, "these things I have come to consider *loss* because of *Christ Jesus my Lord.*" The rest of the paragraph is a single sentence, which begins by spelling out the "gain/loss" metaphor in light of "Christ," and concludes by explaining what it means for him to "gain Christ." The best way to see what is going on is by means of a structural display, again "translating" the Greek very literally (and picking up with the end of v. 6):[5]

(a)  6bAs to the **righteousness** in the Law, faultless.

(b)  7What things  were for me  *gain*

   These things  I consider  *loss*(b)

(c)        because of    CHRIST.

      8aWhat is more

   All things  I consider to be  *loss*(b)

            because of the surpassing worth

(d)            of *KNOWING*    CHRIST JESUS my LORD(c)

         8bbecause of WHOM(c)

   All things  I  have  *lost*(b)

         and

         consider refuse

      8cin order that

   I  might  *gain*(b) CHRIST(c)

      9and

   be found   in HIM(c)

      not having   my own **righteousness** (a)

               which is based on [*ek*] Law

      but      that which is

            through faith in CHRIST(c)

         the   **righteousness** (a)

               from [*ek*] God

            based on [*epi*] faith

---

ἡγοῦμαι-ἡγοῦμαι; διά-διά-δι᾽ ὅν; γνώσεως-γνῶναι; δικαιοσύνην-δικαιοσύνην; πίστεως-πίστει; as well as the clauses in v. 9). Typically, Lohmeyer sees the passage as poetic, dividing it into six strophes; but he has found no followers.

   4. The words κέρδη ("gain"), ἡγοῦμαι ("consider"), and "Christ Jesus my Lord" echo earlier moments in the letter. For "gain" see on 1:21; for "consider" see n. 76 on 2:3.

   5. The letters (a), (b), (c), and (d) isolate the several interwoven motifs, which have also been highlighted by capitalization, bold, italics, and capitalized italics. The (e) item ("being conformed") recurs in v. 21. The A B B′ A′ highlights the chiasm in vv. 10-11.

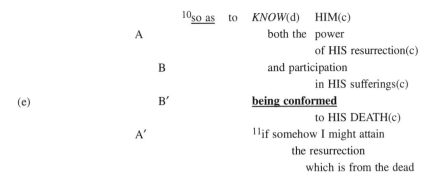

The renunciation in v. 7 sets forth the leading themes of the whole — the "gain-loss" metaphor and its reason, "because of Christ." The elaborating sentence that follows is basically in four parts:

(1) The opening clause (8a) serves as the "theme sentence" for the rest of the sentence-turned-paragraph; it basically repeats v. 7b, with "because of Christ" now taking the form of "knowing Christ Jesus my Lord."

(2) This is repeated again in v. 8b in the form of relative clause, which now *begins* with "because of whom" and then repeats for the final time the motif of "the loss of all [former] things," punctuating with an earthy exclamation point, "refuse." That much goes easily enough, as far as grammar is concerned; but not so with the final two clauses, toward which these opening affirmations are pointed.

(3) The first goal of the "loss because of Christ" theme is expressed in a twin purpose clause, "in order that I might *gain* Christ (8c), that is, be found in him" (9), which is then elaborated by taking up the theme of "righteousness" and "Law" from v. 6b and setting it in contrast to the righteousness that God has provided through Christ; the "when" of this clause is less certain, but most likely looks to the future, while presupposing the present. With that the themes of "righteousness" and "Law" disappear altogether.

(4) The final purpose clause (vv. 10-11), whose grammar is also uncertain, is best understood as modifying vv. 8c-9; it thus concludes the sentence by returning to the theme of "knowing Christ" in v. 8b, putting that into the larger context of the letter by stressing the themes of suffering and future resurrection, set forth in a chiasmus (A B B′ A′).

In getting to the ultimate goal expressed in vv. 10-11, the narrative moves in a kind of circular fashion, anticipating later themes while echoing and repeating present themes. Thus, the themes of "righteousness" and "Law" (a), which on the basis of vv. 2-3 and 4-6 would seem to be the main point, appear only in v. 9, as a kind of "framing" motif around the newly expressed theme of "loss" and "gain" (b) found in vv. 7-8, which is repeated in several forms before Paul lets go of it. Meanwhile, the theme of "*knowing* Christ"

(d) is mentioned in the middle of the "loss/gain" word play (v. 8a), to be picked up again as the main point in the final clause (vv. 10-11). But knowing Christ is a two-sided reality, including both suffering and resurrection. Hence Paul expresses present suffering as "being conformed *(summorphizomenos)* to his death," which word he then picks up at the end (v. 21) to describe what happens to "the bodies of our present humiliation" when they are raised; they will "be conformed *(summorphon)* to the body of his present glory."

But in all of this the central theme is Christ (c), who is the heart of everything from beginning to end: former advantages are now considered "loss" because of "gaining" *Christ;* indeed, they are "street refuse" in comparison with the "surpassing worth of knowing *Christ,"* through whom true righteousness, righteousness from God, has now been made available; and this so that Paul might "know" *Christ* by participating in *Christ's* suffering in the present through the power of *his* resurrection, which includes "being conformed to *Christ's death"* while awaiting "being conformed to his glorified body" at the resurrection (v. 21).

Two further observations. First, this analysis suggests that v. 9, which emphasizes what it means "to be found in him" *positionally,* serves primarily as the *ground* for vv. 10-11: the aim of everything is "to know Christ" *relationally,* both the (present) power of his resurrection (A) and the fellowship of his sufferings (B), "being conformed to his death" (B′) so as to realize the future dimension of the former ("attaining the resurrection from the dead" A′). Since "pressing on to attain" the latter is the theme picked up in the rest of the narrative (vv. 12-14) as well as in the application that follows (vv. 15-21), and since the theme of "righteousness" appears early on only to disappear as the narrative unfolds, it seems highly likely that the latter theme ("righteousness") exists primarily for the sake of theme of "knowing Christ." This is not to downplay either the warning of v. 2 or the contrasts and theological affirmations of vv. 4-6 and 7-9; but it is to suggest that the emphasis in vv. 1-4a is precisely where we suggested them to be — on the Philippians' "continually rejoicing in the Lord" because their common experience (with Paul) of Christ and the Spirit has removed them forever from Torah observance. Indeed, the righteousness they have already received in Christ serves as the theological ground for their "knowing Christ" in the way they are now experiencing, even if it involves suffering.

Second, even though the content differs considerably, both the linguistic echoes and the general "form" of the narrative seem intentionally designed to recall the Christ narrative in 2:6-11.[6] While Christ did not *consider* God-

---

6. This has been frequently noted (e.g., Jones, Bonnard, Silva; Käsemann, "Analysis," 64; Pollard, "Integrity," 62-64; Hooker, "Interchange," 356; Wright, "ἁρπαγμός," 347), with varying degrees of emphasis as to its purposefulness in the letter.

likeness to accrue to his own advantage, but "made himself nothing," so Paul now *considers* his former "gain" as "loss" for the surpassing worth of knowing Christ. As Christ was "found" in "human likeness," Paul is now "found in Christ," knowing whom means to be "conformed" (echoing the *morphē* of a slave, 2:7) to his death (2:8). Finally, as Christ's humiliation was followed by God's "glorious" vindication of him, so present "suffering" for Christ's sake will be followed by "glory" in the form of resurrection. As he has appealed to the Philippians to do, Paul thus exemplifies Christ's "mind-set," embracing suffering and death. This is what it means "to know Christ," to be "found in him" by means of his gift of righteousness; and as he was raised and exalted to the highest place, so Paul and the Philippian believers, because they are now "conformed to Christ" in his death, will also be "conformed" to his glory.

This is one of the truly "surpassing" moments in the Pauline corpus; it would be a tragedy if its splendor were lost in analysis. Finally, therefore, one should go back and read it again and again, until what one learns in the analysis is absorbed in praise and worship over the "surpassing worth of knowing Christ Jesus our Lord." The future does not lie in the past, but in the future, and it is guaranteed precisely because it has already come present through Christ's death, to which we are presently being conformed, and his resurrection, whose power we know now and will realize fully at our resurrection.

**7**  With striking asyndeton,[7] but no less bold contrast, Paul renounces his former advantages, those "gifts" and "achievements" which qualify him above others to have "confidence in the flesh." "Because of[8] Christ," Paul declares, "whatever things[9] were gains for me, these very things I have come

---

7. On the textual question see n. 1. The effective nature of the asyndeton in this case lies in the expectation of a contrastive particle (supplied by the later scribes). Instead Paul gathers up all the preceding advantages in the relative ἅτινα (= "whatever things") and expresses the contrast with the commercial metaphor of (former) "gains" = (present) "loss."

8. Gk. διά, the first of three consecutive uses of this preposition, which with the accusative basically "indicates the reason why some[thing] happens, results, exists" (BAGD). Whereas in some cases a more prospective (final) sense seems probable (see Zerwick, *Biblical Greek,* 36; M. J. Harris, *NIDNTT,* 3.1183-84), there seems to be no compelling reason to think so here (= "for the sake of," NIV, GNB, NASB, RSV, Silva, O'Brien; "because of," NRSV, REB, JB, Hawthorne). Granted the purpose clause in v. 8c ("that [ἵνα] I might gain Christ"), but that comes later in the sentence and does not seem to be Paul's point here. It is not "for the sake of gaining Christ" that he has "revised the balance sheet," but precisely *because of* Christ, who he is and what he has done, that such radical reorientation has taken place. See also nn. 18 and 22 below.

9. Gk. ἅτινα, the indefinite relative pronoun, which here minimally refers specifically to the catalogue in vv. 5-6; the indefinite is used, however, probably to enlarge the purview. Thus, it includes the "what things" of vv. 5-6, but it also includes "whatever [other] things" may be of the same kind.

to consider loss." But this is said with flair. "Whatever things" and its accompanying demonstrative, "these things," occupy the emphatic first position in their respective clauses, while the contrasting "gain" and "loss" occupy the emphatic final position. Thus:

| Whatever things | were for me | | gains, |
| These very things | I consider | because of Christ | loss |

What is being renounced in particular, as v. 9 makes clear, is his "blamelessness as to the righteousness in the law." Still in view is the warning against succumbing to Jewish identity symbols, which now are shown by way of personal example to be quite unrelated to righteousness.

The renunciation is expressed in the language of the marketplace, "gains" ("profit," NIV) and "loss." As v. 8c indicates, the word "gains"[10] harks back to 1:21, where "to die is gain" refers to "gaining Christ" through death.[11] The present usage is a clear play on the metaphor. Paul's former "profits" are now collectively a "loss"[12] because of his ultimate "gain," Christ himself. While he cannot renounce — nor does he wish to[13] — what was given to him by birth (circumcision, being a member of Israel's race, of the tribe of Benjamin, born of true Hebrew stock), he does renounce them as grounds for boasting, along with his achievements that expressed his zeal for the Law. Hence the significance of his use of the verb, "I *have come to consider*[14] them as loss," rather than a simple affirmation, "what things *were* gain *are now* loss," which would have been both imprecise and misleading.

10. Gk. κέρδη. The plural is probably intentional, suggesting that each of the items just enumerated belonged on the "credit" side of the ledger. The verb, which in 1 Cor 9:22 is a "missionary term" (= to "gain" converts; Schlier, *TDNT,* 3.673), occurs in v. 8c as a further expression of the commercial metaphor, which in turn attests that the phrase "to die is gain" in 1:21 almost certainly means "to gain Christ" through death, just as "to live means Christ" in every possible way.

11. It seems also to echo the saying of Jesus recorded in Matt 16:24-26 (// Mark 8:34-36; Luke 9:23-25; so *inter alia,* Kennedy, Michael, Hendriksen, Collange, Silva), where "following Christ" means to "take up one's cross," and thus to "lose" one's life in order to "find" (εὑρέσει) it; for what do people profit who "gain" (κερδήσῃ) the whole world but "lose" (ζημιωθῇ) their souls.

12. Gk. ζημίαν, only here in Paul; but the verb, which occurs in v. 8, and still carries on the commercial metaphor, appears with the more general sense of "utter loss" in 1 Cor 3:15. For a more thorough discussion see Stumpff, *TDNT,* 2.888-92; for illustrations of the commercial use of these two words, see M-M, 273.

13. As Rom 9:1-5 and 11:1-2 make clear.

14. Gk. ἥγημαι (see above on 2:3, 6, 25), here purposefully expressed in the perfect tense (what he came to consider loss when he met Christ still holds true); see also n. 16.

**8a-b** With an emphatic, "not only so, but what is more,"[15] Paul sets out to explain the "how so" of the renunciation of v. 7. He begins with a "thesis sentence," which reiterates v. 7b in grand and expansive language: "I consider[16] all things to be loss" — not just the advantages enumerated in vv. 5-6 — but *all things,* "because of the surpassing greatness of knowing Christ Jesus my Lord." This is a reprise on the theme struck in 1:21, "for to me to live is Christ." What "all things" entails is not immediately apparent; it includes the former "gains" of vv. 5-6, but it implies more (see n. 9). Everything that others might consider to have value in the present age — religious advantages, status, material benefits, honor, comforts[17] — these appear to him as nothing at all, as total "loss," in comparison with Christ.

But in this case, it is not simply "because of Christ" that he considers all things as loss, but "because of[18] the surpassing greatness[19] of knowing[20]

15. Gk. ἀλλὰ μενοῦνγε καί; a combination that occurs nowhere else in Greek literature. Cf. 1:18, where the ascensive ἀλλὰ καί occurs. Thrall (*Greek Particles,* 11-16) argues that the present combination is an ἀλλὰ καί, made more emphatic by the addition of μενοῦνγε. Hence, "not only so, but all the more I consider all things as loss." The καί, which is omitted by P[46vid] ℵ* 6 33 1739 1881 pc lat, is undoubtedly original; it was omitted precisely because of the strangeness of the combination.

16. Gk. ἡγοῦμαι (see n. 14), now in the present tense, expressing that what happened for him at conversion is how he still views things.

17. This listing is based on Paul's own words, both here and in passages like 1 Cor 4:8-13.

18. This is the second διά (see n. 8), for which Lightfoot (148) suggests, "by reason of," which Plummer takes to be equivalent to "in comparison with." But that meaning, adopted as early as Moffatt (cf. Goodspeed, NIV; affirmed as "undoubtedly right" by Michael, 145; cf. Caird), seems to be an invention, pure and simple, since examples are never forthcoming and the grammars and lexicons know nothing of it whatever. But whether, as in v. 7, it is prospective ("for the sake of") or retrospective ("because of") cannot be determined. I think the latter, since the passage seems to be retrospective up to the purpose clause (coming to know Christ serves as the basis, the reason, for his glad loss of all things), which he finally puts into a telic mode (indicating the purpose for which he has done so).

19. Gk. τὸ ὑπερέχον; cf. 4:9 below (also 2:3, in the slightly different sense "to be better"). The verb means "to surpass, excel"; for this substantival use of the neuter participle the NIV follows the suggestion of BAGD ("the surpassing greatness"); but in context it is probably to be understood in light of the prevailing commercial metaphor, hence "surpassing worth" (RSV), "surpassing value" (NRSV; NASB); "overwhelming gain" (Phillips); *contra* "surpassing knowledge" *EDNT,* 3.398 (cf. NAB), on which see the next note.

20. Gk. τῆς γνώσεως, lit., "of the surpassing worth of the knowledge of Christ Jesus my Lord." "Knowledge" here does not denote a quantifiable body of data about someone or something, but the act of "knowing" itself, as v. 10 makes clear. The genitive, therefore, is not appositional (as NAB, Beare, Loh-Nida, Hawthorne, O'Brien) but "objective," or in the language of Beekman and Callow (*Translating,* 257, 260) expressing

Christ Jesus my Lord." This piling up of genitives has as its ultimate goal "knowing Christ Jesus my Lord," which so far surpasses all other things in value that their net worth is zero; they are a total loss. As v. 10 will clarify, "knowing Christ" does not mean to have head knowledge about him, but to "know him" personally (BAGD) and relationally. Paul has thus taken up the Old Testament theme of "knowing God"[21] and applied it to Christ. It means to know him as children and parent know each other, or wives and husbands — knowledge that has to do with personal experience and intimate relationship. It is such knowledge that makes Christ "trust-worthy." The intimacy will be expressed in v. 10 in terms of "participation in his sufferings." In the light of such expansive language, therefore, the object of his "knowing" is not simply "Christ," nor even "Christ Jesus," but "Christ Jesus *my* Lord."

Here is the evidence of intimacy and devotion. Paul regularly refers to Christ with the full title and name, "our Lord, Jesus Christ"; only here does he reverse the order and substitute the first person singular pronoun. The "Christ Jesus," because of whom he gladly considers all else to be loss, is none other than "my Lord." The reason for such devotion and longing is not expressed here, but it rings forth clearly in Gal 2:20, "who loved me and gave himself for me." This is not simply coming to know the deity — it is that, of

the "content" of "surpassing worth." Thus, what has "value exceeding all other values by far" finds expression in "knowing" Christ.

21. Where "knowing God" has first of all to do with revelation; one knows God by observing the "ways of God" and thus his character that lies behind all his ways. God's concern for Israel over and again is that "you may know that I am YHWH" (Exod 10:2 *et passim*). But inherent in such "knowledge of God" was obedience, i.e., loyalty to him through behavior that conformed to his covenant love and faithfulness (righteousness). Hence the promise of the new covenant (Jer 31:34) was that with the law written on their hearts God's people would "know the Lord," since this is what he required more than sacrifices (Hos 6:6) and the failure of which led to judgment (Hos 4:1; where "knowledge of God" is in parallel with "faithfulness and love"). See the helpful overview by E. D. Schmitz, *NIDNTT,* 2.395-96, 399-401.

Since the OT so clearly influences Paul at every turn, and especially since this phrase occurs in the context of "righteousness" based on Torah observance, which he has gladly given up for the surpassing worth of "knowing Christ Jesus my Lord," it is remarkable that some scholars have looked to hellenistic (esp. "Gnostic") sources for the "background" to Paul's usage here (as, e.g., Beare, Bultmann, Schmithals, Koester). Even more tenuous is to mirror read this language as reflecting the position of "opponents" (Schmithals, Koester, Martin, Lincoln; see nn. 38 and 60 on vv. 2-3). Besides being a considerable anachronism in the use of this language, the protest must be registered once again (cf. Fee, *First Corinthians,* 11) that even in Corinth — and especially in this letter, where such terminology is misleading at best — what is essential to Gnosticism (their cosmological mythology; salvation by *gnosis*) is altogether missing. The apparent dualism in the various forms of "opposition" to Paul (in 1 and 2 Corinthians; Colossians; 1 Timothy) can be explained on other grounds.

course — but even more so, it is to know the one whose love for Paul, expressed in the cross and in his arrest on the Damascus road, has transformed the former persecutor of the church into Christ's "love slave," whose lifelong ambition is to "know him" in return, and to love him by loving his people. There is something unfortunate about a cerebral Christianity that "knows" but does not "know" in this way.

One more time, like a composer giving his theme yet another variation, Paul repeats: "because of whom[22] I have lost all things and consider them rubbish." The first element in these two clauses is straight repetition, with the verb "suffer loss" now replacing the noun. But the second element catches us by surprise, expressing as it does the depth of feeling Paul had for those who would "advantage" his Gentile converts with what is so utterly worthless. The word translated "rubbish"[23] is well attested as a vulgarity, referring to excrement (hence "dung" in the KJV); on the other hand, it is also well attested to denote "refuse," especially of the kind that was thrown out for the dogs to forage through.[24] Although it could possibly mean "dung" here,[25] more likely Paul is taking a parting shot at the "dogs" in v. 2,[26] especially since he uses language very much like this in 1 Cor 4:13 to refer to all that is off-scouring and refuse.[27] A translation like "filth" (NJB) perhaps captures both the ambiguity and vulgarity. In either case, it is hard to imagine a more pejorative epithet than this one now hurled at what the Judaizers would promote as advantages. Paul sees them strictly as disadvantages, as total loss, indeed as "foul-smelling street garbage" fit only for "dogs."

**8c-9** Paul expresses the goal of his "revising the balance sheet" with

---

22. This is the third διά (see nn. 8 and 18), and the one that could most easily yield the telic sense of the NIV, "for whose sake" (as most interpreters). The difficulty with that translation in this case is that it is seldom understood as prospective (i.e., "for the purpose of gaining Christ"), but in the sense of doing it with Christ's benefit in view — which meaning the preposition cannot sustain.

23. Gk. σκύβαλα, only here in the NT; in the LXX only in Sir 27:4. Although Lang (*TDNT,* 7.445) dismisses it as popular etymology, its origins are very likely from a combination of "dogs" (κύσι = to dogs) and "cast" (βαλεῖν); cf. M-M, 579. Anyone who has seen — and smelled — this phenomenon in places lacking modern sanitation facilities can well understand the likelihood of such etymology. The alternative etymology is σκώρ, σκάτος ("dung, excrement"; so Lightfoot, et al.), but it is very difficult to account for the -βαλ in this view.

24. Cf. Syb. Or. 7.58, where the combination occurs in an "oracle" against Thessaly ("you will be the mournful refuse of war, O one who falls to dogs," OTP)

25. As M-M (579-80) would have it; cf. Kennedy, Hawthorne, Silva, O'Brien; Lang, *TDNT,* 7.445-47; Hays, *Echoes,* 122 ("crap"). For this usage see Jos. *BJ* 5.571 (lit. of cow dung) and the examples from the papyri in M-M.

26. Cf. Michael, 147; Polhill, "Twin Obstacles," 364.

27. On the meaning of these words, see Fee, *First Corinthians,* 180.

two verbs: "in order that I may gain Christ, that is,[28] be found in him." The first verb completes the metaphor — by turning v. 7 on its head: What *was* gain is now considered loss because of true gain, Christ himself. Paul now implies that the gaining of Christ *requires* the loss of all former things, because to be rich in Christ means to be rich in him alone, not in him plus in other gains. For Paul it is a theological truism that grace and self-confidence are in radical antithesis; grace plus anything cancels out grace. On the other hand, despite Paul's way of putting it, which has been determined by the context, neither is there any sense of calculation, as though he were setting about in a crass way to "gain" eternal life and eventually settled on Christ as the means to that goal. In Paul's case, the "gain" came first, and came in such a way that the rest fell away as utter "refuse" in comparison.[29]

The second verb ("be found"), along with its participial modifier ("not having a righteousness of my own"), elaborates what it means to "gain Christ," contrasting his new experience of "righteousness" with that noted in v. 6, which is now "loss" and "street filth." But how we are to understand this little "meteorite from Romans" is not as easy as describing it.

First, *when* does Paul expect this "gaining" and "being found" to take place? The answer lies with Paul's "already but not yet" eschatological perspective (cf. vv. 10-11 that follow), which determines his existence in Christ and serves as the basic framework for all of this theological thinking.[30] On the one hand, the first point of reference is almost certainly future, looking to the "day of Christ" mentioned in 1:6, 10 and 2:16. Such an understanding fits the future orientation both of the immediate context (vv. 11-14) and of the letter as a whole (see on 1:6).[31] On the other hand, the modifying participial

28. Gk. καί, which is most likely a form of hendiadys, where the second member spells out in greater detail what is meant by the first; cf. on 2:9 (n. 15) and on v. 10 below. So also Hawthorne; cf. Silva, O'Brien.

29. Cf. Houlden (99): "It is not as if consideration of the defects of the Law has prompted Paul to cast about for alternatives." The analogy is with our oldest son the day (when he was six) a neighbor let him ride his bicycle; from that day on the toy trucks were "considered loss" for the "surpassing worth" of knowing how to ride a bicycle. Nothing was calculated; the greater simply replaced the lesser by the sheer force of its "greatness."

30. For this perspective see above on 1:6 and 10-11; cf. Fee, *Presence,* 803-8; cf. Lightfoot, Martin, Bruce, Hawthorne, O'Brien. Others see it as referring to either one or the other: the present only (Vincent, Beare); the future only (Plummer, Michael, Collange, Gnilka, Gundry Volf [*Perseverance,* 258]; cf. Moffatt's "translation": "and be found *at death* in him" [!], defended by Michael).

31. Not to mention (a) that the ordinary sense of a purpose clause is prospective (i.e., one does one thing "in order that" a second thing might result), and (b) that the metaphor "gain" in 1:21, which this clause echoes, clearly points to the future. Indeed, detached from their qualifiers and v. 10 that follows, both of which are very "present" sounding, these two verbs would automatically be understood as eschatological in their orientation.

clause ("having righteousness") is oriented toward the present, as is the final purpose clause (vv. 10-11), which is grammatically dependent on the present clause.

Thus, in keeping with the urgency of this passage, with its concluding emphasis on the "not yet realized" future toward which he — and hopefully they with him — are striving, Paul uses his own story as the paradigm for looking to the future on the basis of the "presence of the future" found in the righteousness that Christ has provided. He expects to "gain Christ and be found[32] in him" on the day of Christ, precisely because this is *already* his experience of Christ.

Second, *where* Paul is now "found" — and expects to be at the end — is "in Christ."[33] He now lives in fellowship with Christ, who is both the source of this new life and the sphere in which it is lived. Having put his trust "in Christ Jesus" (v. 3), Paul is thus "found in Christ," who has given him a righteousness that turns blameless Torah observance into "street garbage."

The participial construction which elaborates this point is a piece of art. It is first expressed in a typical "not/but" contrast, the "not" referring back to Paul's faultless "Torah observant righteousness" in v. 6, the "but" offering the new expression of righteousness, "through faith in Christ Jesus." Together they form a three-part phrase:

> I. a     not having my own righteousness
>    b       that comes from the law,
>     c      but that which is through faith in Christ

which is then repeated in an appositional phrase with the same three parts, the first two "lines" now reflecting the counterpoints to the former phrase:[34]

---

32. Gk. εὑρεθῶ (aorist passive subjunctive, which for some inexplicable reason Collange calls "the future tense of the verb"). On this verb see n. 4 on 2:8. In characteristic fashion Paul with this passive shifts the emphasis from himself to God; i.e., "gaining Christ" is not something Paul hopes to "achieve" by losing everything else; rather, the metaphor of loss and gain, referring to his "before and after" in Judaism and now in Christ, is about to be explained as "from God," the gift of God's gracious love extended to him through Christ. Calvin (274) tries to make the verb active in sense, thus implying that in Christ Paul has "found all things." But the verb simply will not sustain that meaning.

33. On the diverse use of this phrase in Philippians, see above on 1:13, 14; 2:1, 19, 24; 3:1, 3; cf. 3:14; 4:1, 7, 19, and 21 below

34. Schenk (250-51), followed by Silva (185) and O'Brien (394), sets this out as a piece of chiasm, which it obviously is not (although as Plummer, followed by Loh-Nida, pointed out, there is a kind of internal chiasm between the two mentions of "righteousness"; but what value that observation has, which destroys Paul's clause in this way by eliminating the last, ringing, "on the basis of faith," one can only wonder). The rhetoric in this case lies in the repetition (see n. 3 above), not in chiasm. It is of some interest that Silva and

II. a     the righteousness

b     that comes from God,

c     which is based on faith.

That much is easy; some of the parts are less so: especially (a) the nuance of "righteousness";[35] (b) the contrasts "from law/from God"; and (c) the phrase "through faith in Christ."

About "righteousness" Paul makes four affirmations: to gain Christ means (1) to be done with "my own righteousness" which (2) is *ek nomou* (from/predicated on law); this new righteousness (3) is "the from God *(ek theou)* righteousness," which (4) is Paul's "through faith in Christ." The difficulty stems from the first phrase, "not having my own righteousness based on law," which picks up on v. 6, where "righteousness" denotes "upright behavior"; yet in the rest of the present sentence "righteousness" seems to refer to one's relationship with God.[36]

The key lies in the context, especially in vv. 3-4, where in contrast to those who insist on Gentile circumcision Paul asserts that those of the true circumcision "boast in Christ Jesus and put no confidence in the flesh." Thus,

---

O'Brien would approve Schenk's non-existent "chiasm" here, but for theological reasons reject the obvious chiasm of vv. 10-11.

35. Over the past four decades the literature on this term has grown to monumental proportions. The issues, which cannot be resolved here, are several, some interrelated: (a) the relationship of the noun (δικαιοσύνη) to its corresponding adjective (δίκαιος) and verb (δικαιόω), and therefore (b) whether it ever means "justification"; (c) how it is related to the term "righteousness of God," the main theme of Romans, which occurs elsewhere in Paul only in 2 Cor 5:21; and (d) whether it is therefore primarily "relational" or "ethical" (i.e., referring to one's relationship with God or to one's ethical life as a result of that relationship). My own view in sum (and without argumentation): The background of the term lies in the OT, where it has primarily to do with God and his people in their relationship to one another in terms of the covenant; thus "the righteousness of God" refers to his loving faithfulness to his people in terms of the covenant, and their righteousness refers to their reciprocation by keeping the stipulations of the covenant (the law). When Paul uses the noun, therefore, he has in mind God's covenant loyalty to his people, and thus his and their relationship based on the new covenant. Thus it is primarily a term having to do with our relationship with God; but the noun itself does not mean "justification," as though it were primarily a forensic term. It simply refers to our new right relationship with God predicated on the saving work of Christ. Furthermore, in Paul it is unthinkable that that relationship does not also involve right living. Hence the flexibility — and difficulty — in deciding on its precise nuance at several points in Paul's letters. For a discussion of this term in Paul see K. Kertelge, *EDNT,* 1.325-30; cf. Ziesler, *Meaning* (for the Jewish background and its use in the NT), and S. K. Williams, "Righteousness," for a discussion of the debate on "the righteousness of God" in Romans.

36. The earliest commentary in English that seems to recognize this difficulty is Bruce, 120.

despite the way the clause begins, Paul's stress is not primarily on "right living" — that will come next — but on the *predicate* of such living.[37] At issue, one must remember, is the circumcision of Gentile believers. But in this argument Paul has theologically transmuted circumcision from an ethnic-religious identity symbol, whereby in obedience to Torah Gentiles become full members of the covenantal people of God, into a *means to* and an *expression of* "righteousness."[38] However, it is a thoroughly useless expression of righteousness — indeed, "foul-smelling street garbage" — and therefore no means to righteousness at all, because it not only makes an end run around Christ Jesus but puts confidence in the symbol, mere flesh, rather than in the reality. Circumcision — and all other forms of Torah observance — means to "boast" in human achievement; and its "blamelessness" is expressed in ways that count for nothing at all. One is thus neither righteous in the sense of being rightly related to God nor righteous in the sense of living rightly as an expression of that relationship.

Thus Paul's concern for the Philippians. He warns them once more against the Judaizers who would forever try to make them "religious." There is no future in it, he tells them. But his greater concern is with their current behavior, in two directions: (1) that their love for one another will increase (1:9), as they learn in humility to consider the needs of others to be more important than their own (2:3-4) — just as Christ demonstrated by his death on the cross (2:5-8); and (2) that they learn to "rejoice in the Lord" even in the midst of their present suffering (2:17-18; cf. 3:1, 10-11), so that "conformed to Christ in his death" (v. 10b) they might also be "conformed to him" in his resurrection (v. 21).

To make these points he continues his personal story with this description of what it means to be "found in Christ"; it means to have a "righteousness" absolutely antithetical to that promoted by those who belong to the past, who think of relationship with God in terms of Torah observance.[39] Such

---

37. *Contra* Ziesler, *Meaning,* 148-51, who, on the basis of the connection with v. 6, understands "ethical righteousness" to be its only meaning here.

38. Although not put in quite these terms, cf. R. H. Gundry, "Grace"; *contra* E. P. Sanders, *Paul, the Law,* 43-45, 137-41, whose exegesis of this passage is especially forced in order to make it fit his prior assumption, that Paul never thought of "law-keeping" as a means to grace. That may well have been true of Paul before meeting Christ, but the strong language of vv. 2-8 in this passage indicates that as one who had been "apprehended by Christ" (v. 12) he looked back on his former life in Judaism from a radically different theological perspective. After all, there is no escaping the grammar that puts "blameless Torah righteousness" in v. 6 among the ἅτινα of v. 7, which in turn becomes part of the σκύβαλα in v. 8.

39. Cf. Rom 10:3: ἀγνοοῦντες γὰρ τὴν τοῦ θεοῦ δικαιοσύνην καὶ τὴν ἰδίαν ζητοῦντες στῆσαι, τῇ δικαιοσύνῃ τοῦ θεοῦ οὐχ ὑπετάγησαν ("since they did not know

"righteousness" is nothing more than "a righteousness of my own[40] that is *ek nomou* (lit., 'from law')." Even though this phrase stands in *formal* contrast to *ek theou* ("from God"), here it probably expresses not the "source" of the righteousness emphatically described as "of my own," in the sense of its "proceeding from the law," but Torah observance as the basis for it — as in vv. 3-6. Hence the NAB, "based on observance of the law."[41]

In contrast to that, Paul has now experienced righteousness of a radically different kind, a new relationship with God that has come *ek theou* — "from God." This, of course, is what the Judaizers also believe about their righteousness. But Paul sees through such covenantal identity symbols: the Judaizers have trivialized righteousness by making one's relationship with God rest ultimately on observance, on the performance of religious trivia; the latter have nothing at all to do with a "right" relationship with the "righteous" God, as that is further demonstrated in "right living" of a kind that reflects his character.

Paul's primary concern in this sentence, however, is with "righteousness" as reflecting one's (right) relationship with God. Such a relationship is "through[42] faith in Christ," a phrase that is shorthand for "by grace through faith,"[43] where Christ's death is the way God has graciously expressed his love in our behalf, which is realized by those who fully trust him to have so loved and accepted them — warts and all. Or at least that seems most likely Paul's point, despite a growing number of interpreters who think this phrase means "through Christ's [own] faith[fulness]," thus

---

the righteousness that comes from God and sought to establish their own, they did not submit to God's righteousness"); these emphases can be seen already in the OT (Ps 71:16, emphasizing God's righteousness alone; Isa 64:6 [LXX 64:5], indicating human "righteousness" as "filthy rags").

40. Gk. ἐμήν, not τὴν ἐμήν, which as Lightfoot rightly pointed out would imply that such a righteousness actually existed.

41. So also Müller; cf. RSV and REB ("based on the law"; but changed in the NRSV to "that comes from the law"); GNB ("gained by obeying the law"). For this kind of twofold sense to the same preposition in a single sentence, see M. J. Harris, *NIDNTT,* 3.1177-78. Most scholars are more impressed with the repetition of ἐκ and thus argue for "source" in both cases.

42. Gk. διά, which carries the nuance of secondary agency. Thus, the "source" (ἐκ) of new covenant righteousness is God; it has been mediated through (διά) Christ (cf. 1 Cor 8:6 for the same use of these prepositions). In the present case, of course, it is not mediated through Paul's faith, but through Christ in whom Paul has put his trust.

43. See, e.g., Eph 2:8-10 ("for by grace you have been saved through faith"); cf. Rom 4:16 ("the promise comes by faith, so that it might be by grace"). This is always what "through faith" means in Paul; it is never something believers do in exchange for God's acceptance; rather it reflects their utter trust in God's gracious love and acceptance.

referring to what Christ has done for us on the cross in faithful obedience to God.[44]

While there is a certain theological attractiveness to this option — particularly since it would then refer back to the narrative in 2:6-8 — it seems unlikely that Paul intended such here, for a number of contextual reasons, quite beyond those of usage already noted (n. 44): (a) It is altogether unlikely that in the second occurrence of "faith" in this sentence,[45] Paul intends "based

---

44. The phrase διὰ (or ἐκ) πίστεως Χριστοῦ occurs first in the Pauline corpus in Gal 2:16 (2x, cf. 2:20) and again in 3:22 and Rom 3:22, 26. At issue is whether the genitive is "objective" (Christ as the object of faith) or "subjective" (Christ as the one who lives "faithfully"). For a bibliography to 1980 of those who take it as subjective, see Longenecker, *Galatians,* 87; for a more recent — and influential — advocacy, see R. B. Hays, *Faith;* cf. M. D. Hooker, "ΠΙΣΤΙΣ ΧΡΙΣΤΟΥ," and esp. the debate between Hays and Dunn in *SBL 1991 Seminar Papers,* 714-44 (see Hultgren, *"Pistis Christou,"* and Koperski, "Meaning," for advocacy of an objective genitive); for commentaries that take it as subjective see Martin and O'Brien. Although there are places where it could well refer to "the faithfulness of Christ" (e.g., Rom 3:22, on the pattern of "God's faithfulness" in 3:3, and Abraham's in 4:12, 16 — although it is clear that πίστις carries a considerably different nuance in these two passages, *pace* Hays and O'Brien), it is unlikely to do so here. Most damaging to the subjective genitive view is its first occurrence (Gal 2:16), where it is immediately explained in terms of "even we *believed* in Christ Jesus" (the common appeal to tautology does not wash here, since the power of Paul's rhetoric lies in the threefold repetition of "works of law" and "belief in Christ"). Not only so, but the analogies of Rom 3:3 and 4:16 are not precise; in all six instances of πίστεως Χριστοῦ both words occur without the definite article, thus implying "through faith in Christ" (as in 2 Thess 2:13 [the real analogy in Paul to Phil 3:9, overlooked by O'Brien]; cf. Mark 11:22; the usage in Rom 4:16 may seem to be "an exact parallel" [O'Brien], but in fact it is dependent on 4:12, where the article makes Paul's sense clear, which is then picked up in v. 16), whereas in Rom 3:3 the definite article points to *"the* faithfulness of the [one and only] God." Most likely the phrase was coined in its first instance (Gal 2:16) in antithesis to ἐξ ἔργων νόμου, where "works" can only refer to what we do. By analogy, and in total antithesis, ἐκ πίστεως Χριστοῦ is also what we "do"; we put our trust in Christ. Although Silva's objection needs some modification, it is noteworthy that Paul regularly refers to believers as putting their trust in Christ, both with the verb "to believe" and with this noun where its usage is unambiguous; whereas Christ is never the subject of a verb that carries the connotation of "faithfulness" found in this noun when so interpreted. What needs to be emphasized is that nowhere does Paul unambiguously refer to our salvation as "through Christ's faithfulness," whereas he repeatedly and unambiguously so speaks of our faith. To make this genitive subjective, therefore, would seem to require stronger evidence than has been thus far presented.

45. Gk. ἐπὶ τῇ πίστει; the article is anaphoric, referring back to Paul's faith in the preceding clause, *contra* Martin and O'Brien, who would have it refer now to our human response to Christ's faith[fulness] in the preceding phrase. One wonders how the Philippians could possibly have caught on to such a radical shift of subject and object in a clause that seems so clearly designed to repeat the first for emphasis.

on Christ's faithfulness."[46] As noted, this second clause basically repeats the first, in slightly different language, so as to reinforce its point; and there is simply no analogy for "based on faith" to refer to Christ's activity, rather than ours. (b) In the present sentence Paul's emphasis is between "my own righteousness" and that which is "through faith," which makes more sense as referring to Paul's faith rather than to Christ's faithful obedience. (c) In the letter to this point, Paul has expressed concern about the Philippians' "faith" in the context of suffering. They have "not only believed in Christ, but have been graced with suffering" (1:29), and their suffering, expressed in the sacrificial metaphor of sacrifice, is the result of their "faith" (2:17). Since the present passage reflects a similar context (vv. 10-11), it seems likely that the "faith" that leads to righteousness also leads to "the participation in Christ's sufferings" in the next clause.

Thus, as usual in Paul, the contrast is between "works" and "faith," not so much referring to forensic "justification"[47] — there is no hint here (including vv. 3-6) of a juridical setting, and therefore of God's "justification" of those who have "broken the law" — but referring to the means to and expression of one's relationship with God. Such righteousness comes "from God," he insists, in contrast to being "my own" predicated on the law. And it has been made available through Christ, in whom Paul is now "found" and in whom he "boasts," hence it is "through faith in Christ."

**10-11** Returning to the theme of "knowing Christ Jesus my Lord," Paul concludes this long sentence (from v. 8) with a final purpose clause, now offering the primary reason for the rehearsal of his story. In keeping with Paul's OT roots, "knowing Christ" is the ultimate goal of being in right relationship with God; and "knowing Christ" is both "already" and "not yet."[48] Because of the righteousness Christ has effected for his people, we know him now, both the power of his resurrection and participation in his sufferings; but the ultimate "prize," to have present knowledge of him fully realized, awaits resurrection. This, then, is the decisive word over against those who would bring the Philippians under the old covenant. Obedience under that covenant could issue

---

46. That is, Paul can speak of "faith" without a qualifier when he prefers (cf. Rom 3:30-31); but it seems highly unlikely that he would use this word to speak of Christ's activity without the genitive qualifier.

47. *Contra* most interpreters; but it is doubtful in the extreme whether this noun can ever be extended to mean "justification." Paul uses δικαίωσις for this idea; it would require solid proof to demonstrate that δικαιοσύνη and δικαίωσις are indiscriminate synonyms in Paul.

48. *Contra* Beare, who on the basis of the aorist γνῶναι suggests that this also points to Paul's future resurrection. The context, including v. 11, speaks strongly against such a view. Indeed, this suggestion serves as an excellent (negative) illustration of the wrong use of the "punctiliar" view of the aorist.

in blameless Torah observance, but it lacked the necessary power — the gift of the eschatological Spirit (v. 3) who alone brings life (2 Cor 3:6) — to enable God's people truly to know him and thus bear his likeness (being "conformed to Christ's death," that is, living a cruciform existence — which is true "righteousness" in the "right living" sense).

Before looking at the parts, some grammatical and structural matters need resolution. First, the precise relationship of this clause to vv. 8-9 is not certain. It is possibly coordinate with the preceding clause ("that I may gain Christ and be found in him"),[49] in which case Paul is offering a twofold reason for "suffering the loss of all things and considering them street garbage": first, that he might gain Christ and be found in him, having the new righteousness provided by Christ; second, that he might know him, including the power of his resurrection and participation in his sufferings. Far more likely, however, in light of the grammar, the first clause presents the penultimate purpose and thus the ground for the ultimate purpose of "knowing Christ."[50] The latter, of course, cannot exist without the former; but in terms of the goal of life in Christ, everything points toward our present and future knowing of Christ. Thus:

> *in order that*
>   I  might gain Christ
>       and
>     be found in him
>           having the righteousness that is from God based on
>                 faith in Christ
>     *so that*
>           I may know him etc.

Second, one cannot be certain how "the power of his resurrection and participation in his sufferings" are related to the verb "know" and its object

---

49. So Barth, Gnilka, Hawthorne, Silva, O'Brien; but Pauline usage does not seem favorable (see next n.). Some (e.g., Calvin, Bengel, Hendriksen, Collange, Martin) take it to qualify "faith," but that puts the emphasis in a different place from Paul's, who is now picking up the motif of "knowing Christ" from earlier in the sentence.

50. So Meyer, Vincent, Loh-Nida. Two things make one think so: (1) Elsewhere where Paul intends coordinate purpose clauses (e.g., 1 Cor 7:5; Gal 3:14; 4:5) both clauses are introduced by ἵνα; whereas he alters the conjunctions when the second clause is dependent on, or elaborates, the first (e.g., ἵνα . . . ὅπως, 2 Thess 1:11-12; 1 Cor 1:28-29; 2 Cor 8:14; εἰς τὸ . . . ἵνα, Rom 7:4; 15:16); this seems clearly to be the pattern here; (2) there is no analogy to this use of an articular infinitive of purpose (τοῦ γνῶναι), which rarely (if ever) functions as a purpose *clause,* rather than as a simple complementary infinitive of purpose modifying what has immediately preceded (e.g., 1 Cor 10:13; 16:4). *Contra* Hawthorne, whose analysis of these clauses is suspect.

"him." It is possible, as the NIV, to see a threefold object — him, the power of his resurrection, participation in his sufferings — the latter two coordinated with the first by the double *kai* ("and").[51] But more likely Paul intends the first *kai* to be epexegetic, so that the phrases explain, or give content to, what "knowing Christ" means.[52] Thus:

> either: *so that* I may know him,
> both the power of his resurrection
> and participation in his sufferings
> or: *so that* I may know him,
> that is, the power of his resurrection
> and
> participation in his sufferings[53]

This option is preferable since it coordinates the elements that are truly coordinate and makes better sense of how these two items from elsewhere in the letter function in the present narrative. Indeed, these are the surprising matters in this final clause, since we are so poorly prepared for them here; but in light of the whole letter, they are scarcely surprising, since concern for the Philippians' remaining steadfast (with a keen eye to the future) in the midst of present suffering is a primary reason for the letter.[54] Moreover, the emphasis on the future is what gets the larger billing in what follows.

51. So KJV, NRSV, REB; Hendriksen, Caird; Forestell, "Perfection," 124.

52. So most interpreters; cf. the translations by Williams ("that is, the power of His resurrection") and Moffatt ("I would know him in the power of his resurrection").

53. On the basis of the absence of the article with κοινωνία (see n. 2 above), this is the more likely of the two options. Paul intends the closest kind of link between the two phrases; thus "the power of his resurrection and participation in his sufferings" form a single, two-sided reality in his thinking.

54. Missing this point has caused many interpreters to "spiritualize" this passage, so that "the power of his resurrection" has to do with living "above sin," etc., and "participation in his sufferings" is understood in light of Rom 6:1-6 and thus refers to "sanctification." So, *inter alia* and in a variety of forms, Calvin, Meyer, Kennedy, Jones, Müller, Hendriksen, Caird, Loh-Nida, Hawthorne, Silva. But only by the most strained interpretation can "participation in his sufferings" yield something like "our spiritual transformation into the image of Christ" (Silva). That might work for the next clause ("being conformed to his death"), but not very well for this one. Paul's language is nearly a repeat of 2 Cor 1:7, where "being participants in the sufferings" cannot possibly refer to something "spiritual." One would seem to need the strongest kind of linguistic and contextual evidence to overthrow the clear context of this letter, which has his and their sufferings regularly in view.

Even more difficult to find here is the emphasis on Paul's apostolic authority, as Pfitzner maintains (his being conformed to Christ's death is "the enactment of his apostolic commission," *Agon,* 145; cf. nn. 1 and 18 on vv. 4-6).

Third, as pointed out in the structural analysis (p. 313), the four modifiers of the verb are expressed in perfect chiasm, emphasizing in turn Christ's resurrection and sufferings and how Paul participates in both of them. Thus:

<pre>
        so that I may know him
    A            both the power of his resurrection
      B              and participation in his sufferings
      B′             being conformed to his death
    A′           if somehow I might attain the resurrection from the dead
</pre>

The forcefulness of this structure lies in lines A-A′, as they surround the B lines. In turn they point (1) to Christ's resurrection (line A) — as the means whereby Paul is enabled to endure suffering (line B); and (2) to Paul's resurrection as the eschatological issue of such suffering (A′) — as the latter is a portrayal of the Crucified One (B′).

On the meaning and significance of "knowing Christ" see on v. 8. We repeat here only that it implies intimate relationship. However, "knowing intimately" is not a form of mysticism, as the concrete appositional phrases that follow make clear.[55] The "intimacy" comes in the B lines, where Paul sees present suffering as a participation in Christ's suffering, as Paul's way of being conformed into Christ's likeness, whose "obedience unto death, even death on a cross" (2:8) is the ultimate paradigm of all Christian life.

As to the four lines:

(A) To know Christ now means first of all to know "the power of his resurrection," that is, the power that comes to believers on the basis of Christ's resurrection. Along with the gift of the eschatological Spirit, it was the resurrection of Christ that radically altered Paul's (and the early church's) understanding of present existence — as both "already" and "not yet." In Jewish eschatological expectations these two events, above all, would mark the beginning of God's final wrapup. Very early on the church recognized that *the* Resurrection (Christ's) had already set the future in motion. Paul in particular saw the implications of this reality, which are spelled out in some detail in 1 Corinthians 15. The resurrection of Jesus, he argues there, makes our future resurrection both necessary and inevitable: necessary, because even though death has been defanged as it were, it still remains as God's and our final enemy, but it will cease to be with our resurrection; and inevitable, because Christ's resurrection set something in motion as "first-fruits" that guarantees the final harvest. Precisely

---

55. This, of course, assumes the correctness to the view that the καί is epexegetic, i.e., that these clauses give "concreteness" to "knowing Christ"; cf. Forestell ("Perfection," 124): "the [participation in his sufferings] is necessarily the object of some experience, as is made clear from what follows: *Symmorphizomenos tō thanatō autou.*"

because of the latter (Christ's resurrection as guaranteeing ours), Paul understands the life of the future to be already at work in the present.

The reason for starting his explanation of "knowing Christ" with this word is twofold, and related to the ultimate concerns of the rest of the present appeal. First, the primary focus in what follows lies on the future, hence the connection between the two A lines: the power inherent in Christ's resurrection guarantees our own resurrection.[56] Second, and more apropos to Paul's immediate concern, present suffering, and especially Paul's urging the Philippians to "rejoice in the Lord" in the context of suffering (2:17-18), makes sense only in light of the resurrection of Christ.[57] Without the power inherent in Christ's resurrection, present suffering (even for Christ's sake) is meaningless.

That alone explains the unusual language of this phrase, "the *power* of his resurrection." Nowhere else does Paul speak of Christ's resurrection in quite this way, of its inherent power, which by implication is made available to those who are his.[58] Indeed, when speaking elsewhere of the "power" available to believers in the present age, he associates power with either God or the Spirit.[59] But here "knowing Christ" first of all means knowing "the *power* of *his* resurrection" because the present subject matter is "knowing *Christ*," and the empowering dimension of knowing him is reflected in his resurrection. Thus Paul has come to know, and continues to desire to know, the *power* of Christ's resurrection at work in his present mortal body. As he puts it in the similar passage in 2 Cor 4:7-17, in these present "jars of clay" we "are always being given over to death for Jesus' sake so that his life might be revealed in our mortal body" (2 Cor 4:11).

On the other hand, we know enough about Pauline theology from what he says elsewhere to add that his experience of the Spirit is the way the power of the resurrection is available to him — and them. After all, this personal

56. On the apparent hesitation Paul expresses in the final clause ("if somehow"), see the discussion of line A'.

57. Cf. Barth (103): "To know Easter means, for the person knowing it, as stringently as may be: to be implicated in the events of Good Friday"; see esp. the discussion in O'Brien, 405-6. Martin, based on his view of the "polemical" nature of this passage, has all of this in reverse by suggesting, "that intimacy of union with the living Lord in the power of his resurrection is only possible as the apostle first comes to share his sufferings."

58. The closest analogies are 1 Cor 6:14 (God raised Christ and will raise us by his power) and Eph 1:19-20 (God's present power toward us is that by which he raised Christ); cf. Rom 8:10-11, which speaks of the "body" as presently "dead" because of sin but alive to God by the Spirit, whose presence in our lives guarantees that the God who raised Christ from the dead will give life to our mortal bodies as well (see Fee, *Presence*, 542-54).

59. But see v. 21 below, where a similar transfer occurs in terms of Christ as the one who transforms our present bodies into the likeness of his present glory "in keeping with the power that enables him to bring everything into subjection to himself."

narrative begins with the assertion that must be understood to be presuppositional throughout: that in contrast to the backward-looking Judaizers, Paul and the Philippians presently live the life of the future by the power of the (eschatological) Spirit of God (v. 3).

A final theological word is needed regarding the inherent tension created by this line in light of the second one, and the frequent ambivalence one finds in the church toward these two clauses, so that it often becomes a matter of *either/or* rather than of Paul's *both/and*. The power of Christ's resurrection is neither the only way of knowing Christ in the present nor a way of knowing him independently from participation in his sufferings. In Paul's sentence the two go together hand-in-glove. Thus, there is not a moment of triumphalism in this first phrase; but neither does Paul emphasize suffering in such a way as to diminish the power of Christ's resurrection as genuinely present for us. Paul knows nothing of the rather gloomy stoicism that is so often exhibited in historic Christianity, where the lot of the believer is basically that of "slugging it out in the trenches," with little or no sense of Christ's presence and power. On the contrary, the power of Christ's resurrection was the greater reality for him. So certain was Paul that it had happened — after all, he had been accosted and claimed by the Risen Lord on the Damascus Road — and that Christ's resurrection guaranteed his own, that he could throw himself into the present with a kind of holy abandon, full of rejoicing and thanksgiving; and that not because he enjoyed suffering, but because Christ's resurrection had given him a unique perspective on present suffering (spelled out in the next two lines) as well as an empowering presence whereby the suffering was transformed into intimate fellowship with Christ himself.

(B) With the phrase, "and participation in his sufferings,"[60] Paul gives perspective both to the present warning (v. 2) and to his, and therefore especially to the Philippians', present circumstances. What began as yet another warning against the Judaizers (v. 2) evolved into his own personal story in which he has made clear to them that there is no future in going backward. He has been that route and has gladly suffered the loss of it all — and everything else — for the surpassing worth of knowing Christ, because, as he

---

60. Gk. κοινωνία παθημάτων; cf. κοινωνοί ἐστε τῶν παθημάτων in 2 Cor 1:7 ("you are participants in the sufferings"). This latter usage seems to render impossible the suggestion by Lohmeyer that "sufferings" is a subjective genitive here. For the meaning of κοινωνία in Paul see on 1:5. For the absence of the article with both κοινωνία and παθημάτων, see nn. 2 and 53 above. Both the usage in 2 Cor 1:7 and Paul's use of παθήματα would seem to render nearly impossible the "spiritualized" view of this line noted in n. 54 above. Despite the appeals to Rom 6:1-11 on the part of many, there is scarcely a linguistic tie to that passage, while there are both linguistic and conceptual ties with several passages in Paul where "present suffering" preceding final glory are juxtaposed (including Rom 8:17-30).

has said repeatedly and will say again, this alone has future to it. But the way forward lies with the "road less traveled," through the present with its suffering for the sake of Christ, not through the past with its safe, religious conformity. Although more speculative, all of this makes a great deal of sense if the possible attraction to Torah observance for the Philippians might lie in its being a way of avoiding suffering, while maintaining faith in Christ.[61] But Paul will have none of that, precisely because from his perspective any genuine knowing of Christ means participation in his sufferings, since only in such sufferings does one truly know Christ — as 2:6-8 has made plain.

Here, then, we come to the heart of Paul's understanding both of his relationship with Christ and of the nature of existence in the "already/not yet." He frequently refers to suffering on behalf of Christ as the ordinary lot of believers.[62] With the present phrase we get some theological insight into such an understanding. First, as was made plain in the Christ narrative (2:6-11), Christ's resurrection and present exaltation is the direct result of his having suffered for us to the point of death on a cross; by analogy, therefore, the only way for his followers to experience resurrection is through the same path of suffering. Second, and more importantly, the language "participation in *his* sufferings" gives the theological clue to everything. While believers' sufferings do not have the expiatory significance of Christ's, they are nonetheless seen as intimately related to his. Through our suffering the significance of Christ's suffering is manifested to the world,[63] which is why in 1:29-30 Paul describes such suffering as "on behalf of Christ."[64] This also further explains

61. Martin, following P. Siber *(Mit Christus)* and Collange, sees the context as polemical, against a kind of "over-realized eschatology" (on the basis of "perfect" in v. 12); but this founders on the way Martin treats the two phrases, as though the second were the condition of the first (see n. 57).

62. See, e.g., 1 Thess 1:6; 3:2-3; 2 Cor 1:5; 4:7-18; Rom 8:17; Col 1:24; and Phil 1:29 (!).

63. Cf. 1:13 above, where Paul's imprisonment is "manifested to be 'in Christ'." Both the language (κοινωνία = participation in) and the context render nearly impossible the "spiritualized" understanding of this line noted above (nn. 54 and 60), as though "participation in" = "a mystical sharing in all Christ's experiences" (Jones, 54) or the "spiritual process which is carried on in him who is united to Christ," which through baptism marks their "definitive breach with sin" (Silva, 191).

64. It is doubtful, therefore, whether Paul has any kind of "mystical union" with Christ in view (as, e.g., Vincent, Kennedy, Jones, Michael, Silva), including the kind of "Christ-mysticism" advocated by Deissmann and Schweitzer, or that which is read into this passage from Rom 6:1-6 (as Michael, Silva, *et al.*) or from the concept of the "body of Christ" (Proudfoot, "Imitation"). The "participation" inherent in κοινωνία, as in 1:5 above, means that Paul participates in the same reality as exemplified in Christ's sufferings; the "connection" between the two is that Paul's sufferings reflect Christ's inasmuch as they have the same goal. Christ's sufferings, which culminated in his death, were "for our

the reason for the sacrificial metaphor in 2:17-18 that follows hard on the heels of their "holding firm the message of life in the world," including "the world" that stands in opposition to them: Paul's suffering is the drink offering poured out in conjunction with their "sacrifice" and service resulting from their faith. As noted above on v. 8, it is difficult to imagine that Paul is not here reflecting the teaching of his Lord, that those who follow Christ will likewise have to "bear the cross" on behalf of others.

Hence, "knowing Christ" for Paul involves "participation in his sufferings" — and is a cause for constant joy, not because suffering is enjoyable, but because it is certain evidence of his intimate relationship with his Lord. Now at last the opening imperative, "rejoice in the Lord," which reiterates the same imperative in 2:18 in the context of suffering, begins to fall into place. The grounds for joy in the Lord come from "knowing him," as one participates in his sufferings, while awaiting our glorious future.

(B′) With this participial phrase ("becoming like him in his death") and its companion clause that follows (v. 11), Paul now responds to the twofold way he desires to know Christ. Although grammatically dependent on the verb "to know," the participle first of all amplifies "participation in his sufferings," indicating the character of that participation,[65] while at the same time it probably reaches beyond that to the whole of present life in Christ, which is to be marked by the death of Christ above all else. Several matters of significance converge here:

First, the combination "being conformed" *(summorphizomenos)* and "death" recall the Christ narrative in 2:6-11, offering the strongest kind of linguistic ties between Paul's story and the story of Christ. In pouring himself out by taking on human likeness, Christ, who is in the "form" *(morphē)* of God, also took on the *morphē* of a slave; and "being found" in human likeness, he humbled himself to *death* on a cross. Now Paul — and by implication the

---

sakes"; Paul's — and by implication the Philippians' as well — are for "the sake of the gospel," both in the sense of "because of" and "in behalf of."

65. Very likely, therefore, the participle is "modal," modifying the verb by way of the preceding clause. Thus: "that I may know him, including participation in his sufferings, by being conformed to his death." O'Brien, who argues against the "spiritualizing" of the preceding line, also argues against chiasm here, so that he can "spiritualize" this participle, thus making it refer to both "the power of his resurrection and participation in his sufferings," so as to be "incorporated into Christ" on the basis of his death. This view seems to have been taken against those who see "being conformed to his death" as referring to martyrdom (Meyer, Lohmeyer). But martyrdom is not a necessary inference — indeed, it is altogether unlikely. Being "conformed to his death" means the same as in 2 Cor 4:10-12, where Paul views present suffering as "carrying about in his body the death of Christ," not meaning that he will suffer martyrdom, but that his sufferings are to be understood in light of Christ's death.

Philippians should as well — sees his and their sufferings in Christ's behalf as God's way of "conforming" them into the likeness of Christ, which was quite the point of the prior narrative in the first place. Thus Christ's sufferings do not refer to "sufferings in general," but to those sufferings that culminated in his death, all of which was for the sake of others. Likewise, it is not just any kind of present suffering to which Paul refers in the preceding phrase, but to those which in particular express participation in *Christ's* sufferings; and the aim, as well as the character, of such suffering is to "become like him in his death," which almost certainly means suffering that is in some way on behalf of the gospel, thus for the sake of others, since no other suffering is in conformity to his.[66]

Second, and at the same time, this expression, which focuses simultaneously on Christ's *death* and Paul's being "conformed" to it, probably includes more than the suffering in line B. That is, since "participation in his sufferings" (B) is not an end in itself, but embraces Paul's life as lived in behalf of the gospel, so also "being conformed to his death" (B') very likely includes the whole of his life, including suffering, as that which marks, or characterizes, life in Christ. Thus it reaches back at least to 2:5-11, where "obedience unto death" is what ultimately marks the life of him who thereby manifests what "being equal with God" was all about. Since that passage was primarily paradigmatic, so here "being conformed to his death" means for those who "know" Christ to live in such a way that their lives bear that same likeness. Thus they are continually in process of "being conformed to his death."[67]

Third, since "resurrection" and "sufferings" are not naturally antithetical, this phrase thus serves as the transition between Paul's knowing the power of Christ's resurrection (A) in the context of participating in his sufferings (B) and his own future resurrection (A') noted in v. 11. Resurrection applies only to those who have first experienced "death." Christian life is cruciform in charac-

---

66. The idea that Paul is referring to his actual anticipated death is to read into this phrase what is simply not there (as, e.g., Meyer, Lohmeyer; G. Braumann, *NIDNTT,* 1.707). Paul is not talking about dying, but about suffering — of a kind that is in keeping with Christ's death.

67. It is common to see in this language an allusion to baptism, which is found in the text through the circuitous route of reading v. 10 in light of Rom 6:1-11. But that is to find what one is looking for, not what Paul himself hints at. The present tense of the participle seems to spell death to such an idea. One's death with Christ may well have been enacted at baptism, but "being continually conformed to that death," as this text has it, is far removed from the imagery of baptism. Paul's concern is first of all with his and the Philippians' ongoing sufferings as God's way of bringing them into conformity to Christ in his death, and thus with the whole of life as reflecting a cruciform existence. Baptism lay at the beginning of that process; the ongoing "conformation" in Paul's understanding is the work of the Spirit (cf. Rom 12:1-2).

ter; God's people, even as they live presently through the power made available through Christ's resurrection, are as their Lord forever marked by the cross. The heavenly Lion, one must never forget, is a slain Lamb (Rev 5:5-6).

Fourth, this participle is picked up again in its adjectival form in v. 21, indicating once more the closest possible ties between death and resurrection and especially the close relationship between our present suffering (by which we are being "conformed" into the likeness of his death) and our future resurrection (in which our present bodies "of humiliation" will be "conformed" into the likeness of his present resurrected, and therefore "glorified," body).

Together these phenomena demonstrate not only that chapter 3 is an integral part of this letter in its present form, but also that with this clause (vv. 10-11) Paul has now brought the narrative to the point it has been heading all along. The rest of our chapter 3 is a spelling out and application of what is said here.

(A') Finally, Paul moves from "knowing Christ" in the present to its full realization in the future. The point of this final clause is easy enough: Conformity to Christ's *death* in the present, which is possible for Paul because he also "knows the power of Christ's *resurrection*" in the present, will be followed by his own "resurrection from among the dead"[68] at the end. But how he says it is especially puzzling, particularly since the next paragraph (vv. 12-14), which concludes his story, and which has some equally puzzling moments, is an elaboration of this clause. The puzzles are two, but belong together: why he should begin the sentence with "if somehow," which might seem to imply doubt;[69] and why he should refer to his own resurrection as "attaining unto"[70] the "resurrection from among the dead."

The answer seems to be twofold and interrelated. First, this hesitation is not to be understood as lack of confidence about his own — or their — future; rather, it emphasizes that the resurrection of believers is intimately tied

---

68. Gk. τὴν ἐξανάστασιν τὴν ἐκ νεκρῶν. This unusual expression (ἐξανάστασιν is a NT hapax legomenon; the doubling of the article, thus intensifying "from among the dead"; the repeated ἐκ) is probably best explained as putting emphasis in two directions at once: first, it is a way of making clear that in contrast to the preceding mention of Christ's resurrection, whose power is *now* available to believers, this clause unmistakably refers to the future resurrection of believers; second, in its own way it emphasizes that resurrection follows "death" — in this case for those whose lives in the present are marked by "conformation to his death." This language, while it does not deny a general resurrection, emphasizes singularly the resurrection of believers from among the dead.

69. Gk. εἴ πως; cf. Rom 1:10; 11:14. But see esp. J. Gundry Volf (*Perseverance*, 257-58), who argues on the basis of the uses in Romans that "doubt" is not implied at all.

70. Gk. καταντήσω εἰς; the combination literally means "to arrive" at a given place, hence the NAB ("I hope that I may arrive at resurrection from the dead"). The GNB has probably captured Paul's sense: "in the hope that I myself will be raised from death to life."

335

to their first "being conformed to his death."[71] Without "death" of this kind, there is no resurrection.[72] Thus, in keeping with the soaring certainties of Rom 8:1-17a, where Paul qualifies our being heirs to future glory with the proviso "that we also suffer with him," so here, Paul's certain future resurrection (when viewed "from above") has the similar proviso (when viewed "from below"), expressed in this case by the "if somehow." As Luke has reported Paul and Barnabas to have "encouraged" (!) the believers in Asia Minor, here is Paul's way of saying, "we must go through many hardships to enter the kingdom of God" (Acts 14:22). But his future itself is not in doubt — everything in Paul, including vv. 12-21 that follow, refutes such a notion; what is uncertain for him is whether his certain future is to be realized by resurrection or by transformation (as implied in vv. 20-21). This matter is in God's hands, to which Paul gladly submits by his use of this language.[73]

Second, this is his way of moving toward the concern that they "stand firm" in the present (4:1; cf. 1:27), and, above all, not lose their clear focus on, and keen anticipation of, their certain future in Christ. Hence this last clause exists primarily as the direct lead-in to the final section of the narrative (vv. 12-14) and its final application (3:15–4:1). In whatever way the future is realized — through resurrection or transformation at the Parousia (as in vv. 20-21) — the present involves knowing the power of his resurrection as key to participating in Christ's sufferings. But the final, complete knowing of Christ is "not yet"; neither he nor they have attained to it. Nonetheless, such a future prize is the one certain reality of present existence and is thus worth bending every effort in order to realize. Thus, the "perhaps" is partly for their sakes, to encourage them to join with him in pursuing the prize that has not yet been attained.

As suggested earlier, this text in particular — because it is so popular and thus so easy to read apart from its context — needs careful detailed analysis; but when the analysis is over, one should return to the text and read it again and again. Here is quintessential Paul, and a quintessential expression of the NT view of Christian life. Such life means to be finished with one's religious past as having value before God or as a means of right relationship with God; it

71. Cf. Barth, 105; Collange, 132. All kinds of other suggestions have been made: an expression of humility (Meyer, Vincent, Hendriksen, Hawthorne); distrust in himself (Kennedy); as referring to the manner rather than the whether (Lenski, Martin, Motyer, O'Brien).

72. In light of his reconstruction (see n. 60 on v. 3) Koester argues that it emphasizes death as a presupposition to resurrection vis-à-vis the "over-spiritualized eschatology" of the alleged "opponents," who consider "resurrection as already achieved" ("Purpose," 323; cf. Schmithals). But that assumes the presence of "opponents," who in fact are not mentioned throughout this narrative.

73. Cf. Gundry Volf (n. 69).

means to trust wholly in Christ as God's means to righteousness. But such "righteousness" has as its ultimate aim "the surpassing worth of knowing Christ Jesus our Lord"; and "knowing Christ" means to experience the power of his resurrection now through the Spirit, as God's empowering presence for present "participation in his sufferings," as those sufferings are in "conformity with his death." The final two clauses put it all in perspective: to "know Christ" in the present means to be "conformed to his death," so that all of Christian life is stamped with the divine imprint of the cross as we live out the gospel in the present age, while we await the hope of resurrection.

As with 1:21 and 2:5-11, this selective personal history once again demonstrates how totally Christ-focused Paul is. For him Christian life is not simply a matter of "salvation" and "ethics"; it is ultimately a matter of knowing Christ. So too with resurrection; Paul's focus is not on "everlasting life" or anything else such. The goal of the resurrection, the "prize" for which Paul strains every effort in the present, is Christ himself.

If suffering and the temptation to become religious were causing the dimming of such vision for some in Philippi, in contemporary Western (and much of the rest of the world) culture the dimming is for different reasons, more often connected with values related to material gain. Paul's "vision" seems to have the better of it in every imaginable way; and a common return to "the surpassing worth of knowing Christ Jesus our Lord" could go a long way toward renewing the church for its task in the post-modern world. Our lives must be cruciform if they are to count for anything at all; but that word is preceded by the equally important one — the power of his resurrection, which both enables us to live as those marked by the cross and guarantees our final glory.

## 3. The Future Lies with the Future — Attaining Christ (3:12-14)

12*Not that I have already obtained all this, or*[1] *have already been made perfect, but I press on to*[2] *take hold of that for which Christ*

---

1. P[46] and several Western witnesses (D* [F G] a [b] Irenaeus[lat] Ambrosiaster) read a text with ἢ ἤδη δεδικαίωμαι ("or am already completely justified") added between "have already obtained" and "have already been made perfect." Although a case can be made for the others to have omitted this clause on the grounds that it seems so contradictory to Pauline theology or because of homoeoteleuton (so E. López, "En torno"; J. D. Price, "Textual Commentary," 281; Silva, 203-4; Hawthorne is open), such a view has enormous difficulties to overcome in terms of finding any scribal analogies (especially so early) for such "theologically astute" *omissions,* especially when it fits so nicely with vv. 8-11. On the other hand, such additions are the well-known proclivities of the Western text, who by adding such a clause quite missed the fact that they give a meaning to this verb not otherwise known to Paul. See further, Metzger, *Textual Commentary,* 614-15.

2. The Gk. behind the NIV reads: διώκω δὲ εἰ καὶ καταλάβω (lit., "but I press

*Jesus[3] took hold of me. 13Brothers [and sisters],[4] I do not consider myself yet[5] to have taken hold of it. But one thing I do: Forgetting what is behind and straining toward what is ahead, 14I press on toward the goal to win the prize for which God[6] has called me heavenward[7] in Christ Jesus.[8]*

With a considerable change of metaphors Paul's story takes a final turn, which simultaneously looks back to vv. 4-8 (forgetting the past), embraces the present (he is neither fully conformed to Christ's death nor has he arrived at the goal; vv. 10-11), and emphasizes his present pursuit of the final goal. But in light of how the story began (vv. 4-6) and where it got to in vv. 10-11, this turn in

---

on if also I might take hold of"). The καί has been omitted in several witnesses (P[16vid] ℵ* D* F G 326 2495 pc lat sy[p]) either because of homoeoteleuton or under the influence of the versions, which have great difficulty turning this combination into a receptor language (as the English translations bear witness).

3. As often with the Lord's name in Paul's letters, variation occurs between "Christ Jesus" (P[46] P[61] ℵ A Ψ Maj vg sy) and "Christ" (B D[2] F G 33 pc b Tertullian Clement Ambrosiaster). This is nearly impossible to call. On the one hand, omission could easily have occurred by homoeoteleuton (esp. since by the time of our earliest MSS, the divine names are abbreviated XY IY); on the other hand, an "addition" like this does not require intentionality on the part of scribes, since they would often write the name in full without even thinking about it. Very likely the shorter reading is original, but one has no guarantee here.

4. See n. 9 on 1:12.

5. Several significant witnesses (P[16vid] p[61vid] ℵ A D* P 33 81 104 365 614 1175 1241[s] al a sy[h**] bo Tertullian) read οὐπώ ("not yet") for οὐ ("not," P[46] B D[2] F G Ψ Maj lat sy[p] sa), apparently followed by the NIV. But this is a clearly secondary reading, which in light of the context is easy to account for. We may want Paul to have said "not yet" because of our understanding of how this sentence relates to vv. 9-11, but had Paul originally written οὐπώ, there is no conceivable reason for the "yet" to have been omitted (so often and so early); Müller's argument (123 n. 6) that it better fits the context is precisely why the variant occurred at all. Paul said "not" because he is speaking eschatologically, not theologically or ethically — which should also be noted by those who think either reading makes basically the same point (e.g., Hawthorne, Silva, O'Brien). Cf. Metzger, *Textual Commentary,* 615.

6. Paul's sentence concludes τοῦ θεοῦ ἐν Χριστῷ Ἰησοῦ ("of God in Christ Jesus"). This is altered in a variety of ways by several early witnesses: P[46] omits the final phrase (almost certainly due to homoeoteleuton); F G omit "of God" for the same reasons; while D* F G add "Lord" to the final phrase. None of these commends itself as original.

7. Instead of ἄνω κλήσεως ("upward calling") Tertullian and a marginal gloss in 1739 read ἀνεγκλησίας ("blamelessness"). This has purely historical interest: Tertullian is keen on "blamelessness"; that this reading is known — or conjectured — by the scribe of 1739 says something about the complex history of the early transmission of the NT text (even though 1739 is a tenth c. MS, its exemplar for the Pauline Epistles dated from the third or fourth century and contained a text very close to that of B).

8. See n. 6.

the argument is so unexpected (by us) that it is hard to hold it in context. Indeed, at the popular level, the contextual question is scarcely raised; thus these sentences, like their predecessor, are read in a very personal way and understood to mean pretty much whatever the reader intends. Unfortunately, this kind of reading has been abetted by scholarship — which tends to view this passage as beginning something altogether new, as though Paul were intending to use his story to fight on two fronts — and by translations like the NIV and GNB, which not only make a major paragraph break here, but (in the case of the GNB) offer a new title as well.[9]

But such a reading of the text is unwarranted, especially since the "not that" with which Paul's new sentence begins requires one to read what follows as standing in some form of contrast to what has just been said.[10] To be sure, in contrast *with what* may not be immediately apparent, since two of the key verbs in v. 12 (obtained, take hold of) have no object(s). And even if we could be sure of the "what," there still remains the question of "why."

As usual in such moments, the way forward lies first with a careful look at the structure of the whole and at how the narrative proceeds. First, the structure (in this case in a "literal" presentation of the Greek text that tries to capture the various linguistic connections):

[12]Not that
    already  I have taken *(elabon)*
  or already  I have been completed/perfected
*but*
    <u>I press on</u>
      if    I also may      take hold of *(kata-labo)*
            that for which
            I also have been taken hold of
                     by Christ Jesus
[13]Brothers and sisters,
  I do *not* consider myself to have taken hold
    *but* one thing:
        on the one hand,
            the things behind   disregarding

---

9. This is a nearly universal point of view, most scholars denoting the new "paragraph" as vv. 12-16, a view that has caused no end of grief in terms of understanding the point of vv. 15-16. But what they never speak to is how either the οὐχ ὅτι that begins v. 12 or the inferential οὖν in v. 15 supports this paragraphing.

10. Indeed, the idea that Paul is addressing new subject matter is read into the text primarily on the basis of the verb τετελείωμαι, usually translated as the NIV, "been made perfect," although probably incorrectly so in this case; see the discussion below.

on the other hand,
>    the things before    straining toward,
[14]I press on
>    toward the goal
>    for the prize
>        of the upward calling of God
>            in Christ Jesus.

Some observations:

(1) The passage comes in two similar, fairly balanced sentences (vv. 12 and 13-14). In both cases (a) the main verb is "I press on," which is (b) preceded by a disclaimer about "not having arrived" and (c) followed by a word about what he is pressing toward, which in each case (d) is qualified by a "divine passive" (he presses toward something Christ has already "taken hold" of him for). The only additional point made in the second sentence not found in the first is the notation about "disregarding what lies behind."

(2) Our difficulties with interpretation lie for the most part with the first sentence, resulting from two factors: (a) some unusual language, which stems from two word plays (on the verb *lambanō* and its compound *katalambanō;* and on the verb *teleiō* and its cognate adjective *teleioi* in v. 15 and noun *telos* in v. 19);[11] and (b) the fact that the *lambanō* verbs have no expressed object.

(3) Under the ordinary "rules" of rhetoric, such repetition leads one to expect the second sentence to reinforce the first, often by clarification as well — which seems to be exactly what has happened in this case. Fortunately for us, the second sentence is much easier to grasp, because by taking up the main verb from the first sentence, Paul transforms the whole into a metaphor from the races at the games.[12] At each point, therefore, we can first of all isolate what is pictured about the "runner" and then find the analogy in Paul's life in terms of his reasons for this rehearsal of his personal story; and it is precisely at this point (vv. 13-14) that the present paragraph wraps up the narrative that has preceded.

(4) Finally, in both sentences there is nearly as strong an emphasis on the disclaimer not to have "arrived *already*" as there is on his present eager pursuit of the goal. We should thus take seriously that, even though pursuit

11. The root word is the noun τελός (v. 19), which appears as the verb τετελείωμαι in v. 12 and the adjective τέλειοι in v. 15. Paul has not been "completed" yet, by which he now means "reached the 'goal' "; and those who have achieved "maturity" should have the same mindset, while the "destiny" of others, who resist a cruciform existence, is not glory but destruction.

12. Cf. Pfitzner (*Agon,* 139-41), O'Brien, et al., *contra* Meyer, Collange, Caird, Loh-Nida (cf. GNB), who see the metaphor as already beginning in v. 12.

of the goal is his primary — and last — word in each case,[13] he intends them to hear the disclaimers with equal stress.[14]

But *what,* then, is the goal, and *why* this conclusion to his story, and this emphatic way of putting it? On the first matter we can be fairly certain: in light of what has just been said in vv. 10-11, the "goal" is not "perfection" but the eschatological conclusion of present life, while the "prize" is none other than the final realization of his lifelong passion — the full "knowing" of Christ. To this end all else is not only "loss" and "street garbage" (v. 8) but is to be "forgotten" altogether.

The *why* remains speculative, especially in light of the double emphasis on his "not being there yet" and on his straining every nerve "to get there." Many see the primary emphasis to lie on the disclaimers and are prepared to see that emphasis in light of alleged "opponents." The difficulty with doing so, however, is that it requires one to "mirror read" the text with remarkable clairvoyance, since nothing else explicit in the letter comes forward to offer help; the nature of the "opposition," therefore, lies strictly in the eyes of the beholder, not in the text of Paul.[14] What we can point to from the letter, as we have noted throughout, are the twin emphases on (a) their "rejoicing in the Lord even in the midst of suffering" as (b) they "stand firm in the Lord" in the face of opposition with a keen eye toward future realities. That much at least belongs to the letter as a whole, and it is precisely the double note on which the present passage concludes (3:20-21 and 4:1). A careful look at the parts seems likewise to point in this direction.

13. Except for the final qualifier about Christ's prior activity — of "having appre-hended" him (v. 12), and as the sphere of God's upward calling (v. 14).

14. But to read the disclaimers as indicating "a decidedly polemical tone" (Pfitzner, *Agon,* 139) moves considerably beyond what Paul actually says. This appears to assume that Paul's "not/but" contrasts are always a polemical mode of argumentation, which is simply not the case. As the interpretation of vv. 15-16 below demonstrates, one can make good sense of the whole passage if one assumes only what is necessary in context, that Paul is concerned for the Philippians themselves, and that exhortation does not equal opposition, but warning and encouragement.

15. The suggestions are as varied as one should expect when explicit statements are lacking to guide reconstructions: some see "perfectionism" within the Philippian congregation ("obvious," Michael; Beare [129] is certain that this "is *their* language; [Paul] takes it over from them" [emphasis his]); others see "perfectionism" from outside "op-ponents," often seen as "enthusiasts" with an "over-spiritualized eschatology" (Koester, "Purpose"; Gunther, *Opponents,* 76, 84; Pfitzner, *Agon,* 152; Lincoln, *Paradise,* 93-95; O'Brien); while Plummer sees exactly the opposite, a "clear" attack on antinomianism (= "freedom from Judaism, which relies so much on external conformity to law, implies no encouragement to laxity of life"). The fundamental premise of all such views is that this material is polemical, which then must be "mirror read" to determine the view of the "opposition." See the Introduction, pp. 7-10.

The reason for the disclaimers is more difficult to assess. Perhaps a temptation toward the Judaizers also carried with it the idea that Torah observance makes one "more complete" in Christ,[16] not in the sense of "moral perfection" but of having achieved ultimate status in the people of God. One simply cannot know Paul's mind here, although historically it can be noted that the tendency to settle into a religious mode, especially by becoming "observant," is often accompanied by a dulling of one's eagerness for Christ himself, either conformity to his death or keen anticipation for his coming.

**12** The "not that"[17] which begins this sentence is a Greek idiom that qualifies something previously said, so that the readers will not draw the wrong inference from it.[18] Along with the repeated adverb "[not] already" Paul thus offers a twofold disclaimer — what not to infer about the already present future — plus a contrast presenting the "not yet" dimension of that same future. The elaboration in vv. 13-14 indicates that the disclaimer has to do with realities that will be realized only at the eschatological consummation. The context, therefore, suggests that what is being disclaimed as "already brought to full completion" is the knowing of Christ which can only be Paul's when the eschatological goal,[19] referred to in terms of the resurrection from the dead in v. 11, is realized at the coming of Christ (cf. vv. 20-21).

To this point Paul has asserted that he has left his religious past behind

---

16. This is my way of stating what Koester ("Purpose"; followed by O'Brien) argues to be the position of the "opponents," that they preach "a doctrine of obtainable perfection based on Judaizing practices." The view of Forestell ("Perfection") that Paul is basically teaching about "Christian perfection" seems to read the passage apart from its full literary context.

17. Gk. οὐχ ὅτι; cf. 4:11 and 17; 2 Thess 3:9; 2 Cor 1:24; 3:5; John 6:46; 7:22. The combination is an ellipse (BAGD suggest οὐ λέγω ὅτι) which in idiomatic English means something like, "this is not to say that. . . ." It should also be noted that in no other instance in the NT does this combination mark a paragraph break; it is especially doubtful that it does so here. See n. 9 above.

18. In Romans Paul employs the idiom τί οὖν ἐροῦμεν for this identical purpose. The difference between what Paul says here and what he does in Romans is that between "argumentation," which Romans is but Philippians is not, and personal narrative, which this passage is.

19. Cf. Kent, Bruce, O'Brien; others come close to putting it this way by simply referring to the object as "Christ" (so Pfitzner, *Agon,* 144-45; Hawthorne). There have been many other suggestions: the "prize" itself (Meyer, Bonnard, Beare, Collange; A. Ringwald, *NIDNTT,* 1.648-49), Meyer interpreting that to mean "the bliss of the Messiah's kingdom"; "the purified life in heaven" (Kennedy, 458); "life eternal" (Beare); "righteousness" (Barth; A. F. J. Klijn, "Opponents," 281-82). What is surprising in the literature is the lack of references to Paul's eschatology, which seems to dominate this passage, and without which one would seem to be able to make very little sense of it at all. This is the "not yet," set up by v. 11, which corresponds to the "already" of vv. 8-10. Pfitzner (*Agon,* 141-42) notes the eschatological "tension" but dismisses it much too casually.

him so that he might "gain Christ and be found in him" — already but not yet — having now the new righteousness effected by Christ. The goal of everything is *to know Christ*, which in the present means to experience the power of Christ's resurrection as Paul participates in Christ's sufferings, thereby being conformed to Christ's death — marked by the cross — so that he might also thereby attain the resurrection from the dead. Now he qualifies, "not that I already obtained."[20] Since this verb seems to cry out for an object, the question is, "obtained what?" The NIV suggests "all this," but that probably reaches too far back into the preceding sentence. Despite an early scribe who thought otherwise and added, "or am already fully justified,"[21] it is unlikely that Paul considers his present "righteousness" as something yet to be realized.[22] Righteousness is the given, which has made possible his "knowing Christ" in the present at all. What he has not yet "obtained," therefore, is the eschatological realization of the goal expressed in vv. 10-11, the kind of knowing of Christ that will be his only when he has "attained unto the resurrection from the dead" — or its equivalent, as vv. 20-21 clarify.

In that case, and both the preceding and ensuing contexts clamor for such a meaning, then the next verb probably carries a nuance other than "have already been made perfect,"[23] as though it dealt with "righteousness"

---

20. Gk. ἔλαβον, the common verb for "take" or "receive," which BAGD understand here to mean "make one's own." Hawthorne argues for "mental comprehension"; but that seems to miss the eschatological thrust of the passage by too much. Lightfoot argued that we should take seriously the change in tenses between this aorist and the perfect the follows, the aorist referring to his not having "obtained" at some point in the past (perhaps at his conversion), the perfect referring to something begun in the past that holds good in the present. But as O'Brien points out, the "already" seems to rule that out. More likely this is an example of the "constative aorist," which, in the words of J. H. Moulton, is "a line reduced to a point by perspective" (MHT, 1.109).

21. See n. 1 above for those who think this is the original reading.

22. *Pace* Barth, 106-7, whose reading of the text at this point is characteristically theological.

23. Gk. τετελείωμαι, only here in the Pauline corpus, although it appears as a textual variant for τελεῖται in 2 Cor 12:10. The adjective τέλειος ("complete, perfect, mature"), which occurs in v. 15, appears 8 times in all (1 Cor 2:6; 13:10; 14:20; Rom 12:2; Col 1:28; 4:12; Eph 4:13); and the noun τελειότης once (Col 3:14). Cf. the discussion by G. Delling in *TDNT*, 8.79-84; and H. Hübner, *EDNT*, 3.344-45. Most earlier commentators considered it to refer to "moral and spiritual perfection" (e.g., Vincent, 107). More recently this has been nuanced to denote "spiritual," eschatological perfection, with less emphasis on the moral-ethical side, and has been "mirror read" to be the language of his "opponents" (e.g., Jones, Koester, Jewett, Polhill, Lincoln, O'Brien; see following nn.). Some (e.g., Beare, Houlden) see Paul as using the language of the Mystery cults here, but that seems especially far-fetched in this context, since nothing in the surrounding matter would seem to give him reason to do so. For a rejection of "mirror reading" this word as reflecting the opposition in Philippi, see Lüdemann, *Opposition*, 106-7.

or some form of "perfectionism."[24] Although this verb and its cognates can sometimes mean "perfect," its origins lie with the noun *telos,* whose primary sense has to do with the "goal" or "aim" toward which something is pointing, often in the sense of "completing" or "fulfilling" it. Since there is nothing elsewhere in this letter, nor anywhere else in the Pauline churches for that matter, that smacks of "perfectionism,"[25] it is doubtful whether Paul is here intentionally countering such a point of view. More likely, since this verb seems intended to further clarify the first one,[26] it carries the sense of having "been brought to completion," by having arrived at the final goal

24. It has been common to read this double disclaimer ("not already obtained, not already made perfect") as parallel, so that the "object" of the first is supplied by the concept "perfect" in the second verb (e.g., Schmithals; Jewett, "Conflicting Movements," 373; Polhill, "Twin Obstacles," 167). Such an understanding is the direct result of seeing v. 12 (despite the οὐχ ὅτι) as starting a new paragraph, basically unrelated to what has preceded (see n. 9 above). Neither the grammar (there are no analogies in Paul where the "verb" of a second clause supplies the "object" of a former one) nor the context supports such a view.

That this verb reflects Paul's opposition to some form of perfectionism is asserted with a great deal more confidence in the literature than the full context of this personal history and its application would seem to allow. Thus O'Brien (423): "Most commentators agree that by using [this verb] here (note also τέλειος at v. 15) the apostle is taking over the terminology of his opponents for the purpose of correcting their false views" (cf. Jones, 56, "The Apostle at this point . . . fixes his attention upon a section of the Philippian Church which was in its tendencies identical with the party in the Church of Corinth which arrogated to itself the title of 'spiritual,' was filled with overweening pride, and claimed spiritual perfection"). While possible, that seems to place an enormous amount of weight on a verb which is capable of a different sense altogether. And it goes quite beyond the evidence to assert that Paul, vis-à-vis alleged opponents, "asserts or claims his imperfection" (Pfitzner, *Agon,* 142). Indeed, it seems impossible to verify this view on the basis of what is written in this letter alone; and since one can make perfectly good sense of Paul's usage without resorting to "opponents," this seems to be the better approach. On the problems with this kind of "mirror reading" of texts, which make too much of the use of certain vocabulary when there are not accompanying explicit statements, see J. Barclay, "Mirror Reading," 81-84; cf. the Introduction, pp. 7-8.

25. Some would argue that 1 Cor 4:8 suggests that Paul had a similar problem in Corinth (see n. 60 on v. 3). But there is nothing in 1 Corinthians to suggest "perfectionism" as the issue; rather, the point of conflict between him and the Corinthians had to do with what it meant to be "spiritual," in the sense of "people of the Spirit." They apparently took the presence of the Spirit as evidence that they had already arrived at the ultimate state of spiritual existence; but moral perfection does not seem to be part of their claim. It was certainly not a part of their reality! See Fee, *First Corinthians,* 4-15.

26. So also O'Brien (correctly), 423: "The expression is parallel with the preceding ἤδη ἔλαβον and is a further explanation in more literal terms of what was described figuratively of obtaining the goal. The ἤ ('or') connects two similar processes, not distinct or alternative ones."

with regard to his knowing Christ.[27] Together, therefore, these two disclaimers emphasize that the future, even though Paul considers it certain, has not yet been fully realized. But *what* future, and how are the two clauses related? Most likely Paul is affirming two things: that he has not yet come to know Christ in the way that only the eschaton will bring, and therefore that even though he knows Christ now, including the power of his resurrection, such knowledge does not mean either that his is now "completed" or that he has arrived at the final goal.

The future, however, belongs only to those who persevere (to use the language of theology). Paul thus immediately sets them right regarding the future that is "not yet": "but I press on,"[28] he says. In this first case the object of his present "pursuit" is expressed with a set of clauses that play on a compound of the verb "take" in the first disclaimer: "whether I also may take hold of[29] that for which I was also taken hold of by Christ Jesus." If that comes out a bit awkwardly, both in Greek and English,[30] it is because Paul is simultaneously playing on the word "take hold of" while "putting it straight" theologically. His meaning is plain enough, since it is clarified by the elaboration in vv. 13-14. Precisely because he has not yet arrived at the goal specified in vv. 10-11, he is "pursuing" it with all his might, which in

---

27. Cf. Kennedy, 457, "It means literally 'to bring to an end' determined by God"; and Hübner (*EDNT*, 3.344): "not as if I already *had reached my goal.*" Pfitzner (*Agon*, 139) seems to turn all of this on its head when he speaks of "the τελειότης which is the goal of the Apostle's striving." To turn the verb into a noun and make it the goal mentioned in v. 14 is methodologically suspect at best; at worst it represents a distortion of what Paul actually said.

28. Gk. διώκω, whose primary sense was "push, drive, set in motion," which then came to be the most common verb for "persecute" (pursue with a malevolent aim), but which is also used figuratively for "striving hard after" a good aim (as in 1 Thess 5:15; 1 Cor 14:1; Rom 9:30, 31; 12:13; 14:19; 1 Tim 6:11; 2 Tim 2:22; cf. Heb 12:14; 1 Pet 3:11); cf. O. Knoch, *EDNT*, 1.338-39.

29. Gk. καταλάβω, a compound which means "to take aggressively," hence "grasp" or "seize," occurring three times in these three consecutive clauses. The combination διώκω . . . καταλαμβάνειν is common (see, e.g., Sir 11:10; Lam 1:3; Herodotus 9.58).

30. The clause reads:   εἰ      καὶ καταλάβω,

                       ἐφ' ᾧ   καὶ κατελήμφθην

                             ὑπὸ Χριστοῦ 'Ιησοῦ.

The εἰ followed by a subjunctive introduces an indirect question (= [to see] whether I might take hold of). The double καί is best understood as going with the verb in each case (= "both/and" or "also/also"); hence in the first clause it is not an example of εἰ καί ("if indeed"; *contra* Collange [= concession, hence doubt] and O'Brien; cf. nn. 58 and 59 on 2:17). J. Gundry Volf (*Perseverance*, 255-56), although basically skipping the καί, nonetheless correctly recognizes that Paul's point is not to express doubt but precisely the opposite, to communicate "expectancy."

this first instance is expressed in terms of "taking hold of" the very thing[31] for which Christ first "took hold of" him. While Paul is indeed pursuing the eschatological goal with all his might, that is only because Christ was there first, pursuing him as it were, and "apprehending" him so as to make Paul one of his own.[32] Paul's point, as always, is that Christ's work is the prior one, and that all his own effort is simply in response to, and for the sake of, that prior "apprehension" of him by "Christ Jesus my Lord."

It is hard to imagine that this could refer to anything other than his final apprehension of Christ. Granted the mention of the resurrection in v. 11; but vv. 20-21 indicate that for Paul it is not resurrection per se that interests him but the final glory. The one whose motto is "to live is Christ, to die is [to] gain [Christ]" is not focusing now on the means to that end, but on the eschatological culmination itself — the ultimate apprehension of Christ.

**13-14** With an introductory vocative, "brothers and sisters," Paul elaborates the point of v. 12 with an athletic metaphor,[33] picturing himself as a runner whose every muscle and nerve is singularly focused on the goal, in hopes of winning the prize. Although he begins by emphatically repeating the disclaimer,[34] that is now secondary to the emphasis on the pursuit of the prize itself — Paul's primary concern regarding the Philippians, and his reason for concluding his story in this way.[35] That all of this is being narrated for their sakes is equally evidenced by the sudden — and surprising — appearance of

---

31. This is to read the ἐφ' ᾧ which introduces the second clause as the object of the verb (= τοῦτο ἐφ' ᾧ, "that with a view to which"); most regard it as causal (= ἐπὶ τούτῳ ὅτι, "for the reason that"), on the basis of its usage in Rom 5:12 and 2 Cor 5:4, and because the earlier verb does not have an object (as though that were significant here). But it is not at all certain that Paul intends "cause" in the sense of "cause and effect" in the Romans and 2 Corinthians passages. He certainly does not in Phil 4:10 below. Cf. the thorough discussion of this idiom by J. Fitzmyer ("Consecutive Meaning," 330), who likewise questions the causal sense here.

32. This surely points to his conversion (so most interpreters), thus indirectly verifying the basic accuracy of the narrative in Acts 9. See Barth (108) for a typically energetic exposition of the theological dimension of this text.

33. Cf. 1 Cor 9:24-27, where Paul uses similar imagery for a quite different point, namely that "receiving the prize" requires self-discipline.

34. Gk. ἐγὼ ἐμαυτόν οὐ λογίζομαι κατειληφέναι; the ἐμαυτόν ("myself") is best understood as the subject of the infinitive. Bringing it forward in the sentence is what creates the emphasis. Some see the emphasis as over against the Philippians; but it is equally possible (more probable, in terms of context) that the emphasis is his own, setting up what follows in the strongest possible way.

35. Thus it does not seem to be quite precise to suggest (as Pfitzner, *Agon,* 141) that Paul's *stress* is on the disclaimer "that he has *not yet* reached the goal of his endeavour" (emphasis his). Granted the emphasis in this disclaimer, but it goes beyond Pauline analogy to argue that the main stress in a "not/but" contrast lies on the "not" side of the contrast.

the vocative (the first explicit reference to the Philippians since vv. 2-3) in the middle of his own personal story.[36]

The disclaimer in this case repeats the verb from the immediately preceding clauses: "I do not consider myself to have taken hold." The reference seems to be so clearly to the eschatological wrapup, with the final gaining of Christ as its focus,[37] that to add an object (even the "it" of the NIV) seems pedestrian. This is what he longs for with regard to his Philippian brothers and sisters as well, that they not lose their "eager expectation" of Christ's coming (v. 20) in the midst of present difficulty and opposition. Perfectionism is hardly an issue; but perseverance with regard to Christ and the gospel is.

Thus he presents himself to them as a runner, whose reason for running is "one thing"[38] — winning the prize. As most analogies do, this one breaks down at one crucial point; in this case, all who run to the finish receive the prize. But Paul's point is not winning as such; rather his focus is on the *runner,* who runs so as to win.[39] The analogy is in three parts.

First, he pictures the runner as one who is not distracted by other things, presumably by others in the race. The imagery is probably that of the runner who is in the lead and does not look back to see where the competitors are; rather he focuses all his energy on the goal. Thus: "paying no attention to[40] what is behind and straining toward what is ahead."[41] Paul's interest in this

36. Lightfoot (152) sees it as "arresting attention"; Michael (160) thinks rather that it attempts to "mitigate any seeming severity in his words." But what is "severe" about this imagery, one wonders.

37. Cf. Martin, who, however, would see this double focus as "either/or" rather than "both/and."

38. Gk. ἓν δέ, an ellipse to which most would append an "I do," while some (e.g., Meyer) would argue for "I think." But the strength of Paul's rhetoric lies in the ellipse itself; the rest of the sentence indicates what "the one thing" is. Cf. his appeal to them to "think one thing" (2:2), that is, to be toward one another the way Christ himself exhibited "God likeness" (2:5-11).

39. On the danger, and exegetical perversity, of making Paul's analogies "walk on all fours" so as to miss Paul's own point, see Fee, *First Corinthians,* 434 n. 5, 608-9; and Fee, *1 and 2 Timothy,* 260-62; cf. Kennedy (458), "but pressing metaphors is always hazardous."

40. Gk. ἐπιλανθανόμενος, only here in Paul (although it occurs 7 times elsewhere in the NT). Although the word can sometimes mean "forget" in the sense of "not remembering," in figurative usage such as this one it more likely means "to pay no attention to, be unconcerned about" (cf. Heb 13:2).

41. These participles are especially poetic:

τὰ μὲν ὀπίσω ἐπιλανθανόμενος,
τοῖς δὲ ἔμπροσθεν ἐπεκτεινόμενος,

which probably accounts for both the choice of the first verb and the fact that "what lies before" is plural. The two participles express "manner." The second brings special vividness to the imagery, picturing the runner who is extending himself or herself by leaning toward the goal (Vincent notes that our idiom "home-stretch" picks up this same imagery).

part of the imagery is not with others in the race. Indeed, it is quite possible that this is simply part of the imagery to emphasize his eager pursuit of the goal and therefore that he does not "mean" anything by it at all, in the sense that the analogy has a real life counterpart of some kind. If he does "mean" something, which seems likely, it is probably to be understood in light of vv. 4-8: Paul as a runner who "pays no attention to the things that are behind" is probably a parting shot at what some of the Philippians might now be finding attractive. By "pursuing" Torah observance as "advancement," they would in fact be after the very things Paul has gladly put behind him as refuse.[42] In any case, as the rest of the analogy makes clear, the present accent is on "straining toward what is ahead."

The second point in the analogy is contained in the clause, "straining toward those things that lie before, I press on toward the goal."[43] The "goal" in the imagery, of course, is the finish line. For Paul the "goal" is the eschatological consummation of what is "already" his in Christ. Thus, it is not the resurrection as such, but the conclusion itself that is the goal; and despite what the imagery on its own might yield in terms of meaning, Paul is concerned only that the Philippians follow him in keeping a firm grip on their certain future, that they not be distracted along the way with lesser things (either Torah observance or opposition). Hence the concern expressed in 1:25, that he has "their progress and joy in the faith" uppermost in his concern for them. Progress in the faith means to hold steady to their future orientation, that they are a people headed for final glory with Christ himself.

Third, Paul images himself as a runner whose pursuit of the goal has "the prize"[44] as his — and by implication their — ultimate reason for running.[45] No

---

42. In light of v. 16, and the appeal for them to live up to where they currently are in Christ, it seems altogether unlikely that "the things behind him" denotes the measure of "knowing Christ" that he has already attained (as, e.g., Meyer, Vincent, Jones, Michael, Beare, Caird). This is a clear case of letting the imagery rather than the context dictate meaning (Michael, blatantly so), which is always a hazardous procedure. Such a view not only focuses on the wrong things in Paul's story, but it fails to take seriously enough the basic "already/not yet" framework of Paul's thinking that dominates this passage. What is "already" is not what is to be "disregarded," but rather what does not count for a thing at all in light of Christ — even though at one time in Paul's life he thought of it in terms of "gain."

43. Gk. κατὰ σκοπόν; only here in the NT. The word occurs in the sense of "target" in Job 16:12; Lam 3:12. On this use of κατά (= "in the direction of"), see Acts 8:26.

44. Gk. τὸ βραβεῖον; used of the "prize" in a contest. For an identical use of the noun see 1 Cor 9:24.

45. The εἰς is best understood as telic, indicating the purpose or goal of his "pursuit" (cf. GNB, NIV, O'Brien), rather than simply directional (as Lightfoot, Kennedy). Having missed this point, and thus seeing it as directional, later scribes changed it to the more proper ἐπί (D F G Maj).

mere celery wreath for Paul;[46] his prize is of "surpassing worth by far" — to gain Christ fully and completely. Not one to leave such imagery alone without mentioning the God whose love for him has made it possible, Paul adds a series of (mostly genitive) qualifiers — "of the upward (= heavenward) calling of God in Christ Jesus" — whose sense is easier to sort out than its grammar.[47] Whatever names we may give to his genitives, Paul intends the following relationships: First, God has "called" Paul to himself, which will culminate in glory; second, that call, which began at his conversion, is "heavenward" in terms of its final goal; third, God's call found its historical and experiential locus "in Christ Jesus"; and fourth, at the end of the race Paul will gain the prize, the tangible evidence that the goal of God's call has been reached.[48]

Paul tends to see all of Christian life in terms of "God's calling."[49] It begins as a call, call into fellowship with his Son (1 Cor 1:9), thus a call to "be saints," and thereby joined to his people who are destined for glory. The present usage is unusual in that it looks at the believer's calling from the perspective of its completion rather than its beginnings, as in most instances.

46. On the withered celery wreath as the "crown" for the victor in a race, see Broneer, "Crown"; cf. the discussion in Fee, *First Corinthians,* 436-37.

47. In this case, "of God" is clearly "subjective" (= God called me/us); Silva and O'Brien would make "calling" subjective as well, which sees the direction of relationship correctly but presses that nomenclature by too much (the calling does not offer the prize). This is probably an example of what Beekman-Callow (*Translating,* 265), call "result-means" (the call is the means that has brought about the promised result, the prize). In any case, it can scarcely be "appositional," as many suggest (e.g., Lohmeyer, Dibelius, Barth, Gnilka, Collange, Caird, Loh-Nida [GNB]), since that not only presents the singular difficulty of introducing a new idea altogether into the metaphor as to the meaning of the prize, but makes "calling" and "prize" mean the same thing, which seems scarcely possible, in that the calling has happened previously, while the prize is totally eschatological.

48. Gunther (*Opponents,* 182) sees this language as reflecting the alleged "opponents' " point of view, and, read in conjunction with vv. 19-21, he suggests that they consider themselves thus to be in "contact with angels." This seems to be an expression of "mirror reading" without controls.

49. Gk. κλῆσις; cf. 2 Thess 1:11; 1 Cor 1:26; 7:20; Rom 11:29; Eph 1:18; 4:1, 4; 2 Tim 1:9. Although the verb occurs far more frequently, and moves in several directions (e.g., Paul's calling to apostleship), this noun, which accents the event of calling rather than status or condition, is a nearly technical term for God's call of the believer to himself. Cf. the discussions in *EDNT,* 2.242-43 (J. Eckert); *NIDNTT,* 1.275-76 (L. Coenen); *TDNT,* 3.487-536; cf. the useful outline in *DPL,* 84-85 (C. G. Kruse). In an attempt to keep the metaphor alive, many interpreters see here an allusion to the announcement of the victor, his father's name, and his country, at the Olympic games (so Collange, followed *inter alia* by Bruce, Martin, Hawthorne). But that seems more fanciful than real, since there is no evidence that such an announcement was ever termed a κλῆσις, and this word is an especially Pauline one, full of theological grist that this suggestion would neutralize (cf. O'Brien).

This has been the aim of God's call right along, to lift them "heavenward"[50] to share in his eternal Presence. Here, then, is the first note of what will be emphasized at the end of the appeal in vv. 19-21: some, who are no longer "walking" in the way set forth by Paul, have their "minds set on earthly things"; whereas Paul and the Philippians are among those whose "citizenship is [already] in heaven," from whence they await the coming of the Savior.

But as in the preceding sentence (v. 12), the final word is "Christ Jesus"; in this case God's call has been effected for him and them "in Christ Jesus." As throughout the letter, this preposition is probably locative, not instrumental,[51] pointing to the sphere in which God's calling took place; it happened "in Christ Jesus," meaning in his death and resurrection, and it has been effected for Paul as one who trusts in and therefore lives "in Christ Jesus." Thus Christ is both the means and the end of God's call; and "knowing him" finally and fully is the "prize" toward which Paul stretches every nerve. As he will now go on to urge (vv. 15-16), by way of application, they should do the same.

This singular and passionate focus on the future consummation, which Paul clearly intends as paradigmatic, often gets lost in the church — for a whole variety of reasons: in a scientific age, it is something of an embarrassment to many; in a world "come of age," only the oppressed think eschatologically, for reasons of weakness we are told; in an affluent age, who needs it? But Paul's voice should not be muffled so quickly and easily. For a race who by their very nature are oriented to the future but who have no real future to look forward to, here is a strikingly and powerfully Christian moment. The tragedy that attends the rather thoroughgoing loss of hope in contemporary Western culture is that we are now trying to make the present eternal. Hence North Americans in particular are the most death-denying culture in the history of the race. How else, pray tell, can one explain cosmetic surgery having become a multi-million dollar industry?

In the midst of such banal hopelessness the believer in Christ, who recognizes Christ as the beginning and end of all things meaningful, needs to be reminded again — and to think in terms of sharing it with the world — that God's purposes for his creation are not finished until he has brought our salvation to its consummation. Indeed, to deny the consummation is to deny what is essential to any meaningful Christian faith. Paul finds life meaningful

---

50. Gk. ἄνω, the adverb for "above, upward"; cf. Col 3:1, 2; Gal 4:26. See esp. Acts 2:19 for the combination, "the heaven (= sky) above." Paul's usage here reflects the common cosmology, still used in popular parlance, which pictures heaven as "above" the earth; cf. GNB "to the life above." Given the context, "heaven" is the direction toward which Paul is heading, not the source of God's call; nor should one understand it by the totally bland "high vocation" suggested by Beare.

51. As GNB has it (cf. Loh-Nida).

precisely because he sees the future with great clarity, and the future has to do with beginnings — the (now redeemed) realization of God's creative purposes through Christ the Lord. There is no other prize; hence nothing else counts for much except "knowing Christ," both now and with clear and certain hope for the future.

## C. APPLICATION AND FINAL APPEAL (3:15–4:3)

Having used himself as an example of one who not only rejected his Jewish privileges for the gospel but also lives in the present totally oriented to the future, Paul now explicitly turns to apply this remarkable testimony to the situation in Philippi. But it is an application singularly difficult for the average reader to follow, and full of pitfalls for the scholar. Some things are clear enough: (1) Paul intends his story to be exemplary for them, since he makes that point two times running (vv. 15-16 and 17);[1] (2) after this twofold application, the second of which is accompanied by a contrasting indictment (vv. 18-19), he returns in turn (a) to his and their certain future in Christ (vv. 20-21), specifically picking up the latter part of the narrative (vv. 12-14, by way of vv. 10-11), (b) to the imperative to "stand firm in the Lord" (4:1), thus repeating the primary appeal from 1:27, and (c) to the appeal "have one mindset" (4:2-3) from 2:2-5, this time specifically applying it to two leaders of the community. Thus, Paul's application of his story recalls the two major concerns addressed in the two sections of the letter given to their "circumstances": steadfastness (including their keeping a steady gaze on Christ and their sure future) and unity.

But there are difficulties as well: to determine (a) what in his story Paul wants them to emulate in the appeals in vv. 15-16 and 17, and thus to determine precisely what he is after in these appeals; (b) how the various parts described above are related to one another in terms of the "argument" of the letter;[2] and (c) how the indictment of vv. 18-19 in particular is related to these materials. These in turn are related (in a typical exegetical circle) to our difficulties in determining with precision the meaning of a considerable number of details along the way.

As a way of approaching these matters, we should note that between the story itself and this application the three-way bond that holds the letter

---

1. And will do so again in 4:9, as the final wrapup to the larger section (3:1–4:9).

2. Or indeed whether they are related at all, or whether this is simply a form of first-century "stream of consciousness." But most likely Paul knows very well where he is going; and in any case, the first assumption of exegesis should be that authors are intentional, whether we can discover that intent or not.

together[3] is in full evidence; and this may help us to resolve some of the larger contextual questions. The narrative (vv. 4-14) was devoted altogether to the relationship of Paul to Christ; these appeals now link that with the other two "sides of the triangle" (see p. 13): First, his secure relationship with them allows him to tell his story for purposes of "imitation," as he now explicitly tells them; moreover, he begins (vv. 15-16) and ends (20-21) with verbs in the first plural, rather than second, thus reinforcing that he and they are in this together. Second, the clear aim of all this is with the Philippians' relationship with Christ, which is specifically picked up in the three final appeals (vv. 20-21; 4:1, and 2-3). Thus, there is no evidence, including in vv. 18-19, of "opposition" between him and them; some of them apparently need correction and exhortation, but that is not the same thing as "opposition."[4] This suggests further that vv. 18-19, rather than pointing to opponents, function exactly as Paul indicates — as a negative example of some who have stopped "running" and who are thus no longer either friends of the cross or eagerly pursuing the heavenly prize; rather, "their minds are set on present earthly existence," whose only future is "destruction." Even if we cannot identify these people with certainty, and we cannot, their *function* in the appeal is clearly expressed.

## 1. Application — Having a "Mature" Mindset (3:15-16)

> 15*All of us who are mature should*[5] *take such a view of things. And if on some point you think differently, that too God will make clear to you.* 16*Only let us live up to what*[6] *we*[7] *have already attained.*

---

3. See the Introduction, pp. 13-14.

4. And to speak of the "heresy at Philippi," as some do (e.g., Gnilka, Collange) is to move far beyond the evidence, especially in terms of what Paul explicitly says.

5. This reflects Paul's φρονῶμεν, which is almost certainly original; a few witnesses (א L 326 1241ˢ pc Clement) read the indicative. Collange (followed by Martin) leans toward this reading, which he turns into an interrogative, but for strictly presuppositional, not textual, reasons. The indicative could have been an error of hearing; more likely it represents an attempt to smooth out the text (= "As many as are mature, we think this way").

6. This reflects the τῷ αὐτῷ στοιχεῖν of Paul's original text (read by P16 P46 א* A B Ivid 6 33 1739 pc b co Hilary Augustine). Under the influence of the similar appeal in Gal 6:16 and Phil 2:2, the Western and Byzantine traditions added, in different configurations, κανόνι, τὸ αὐτὸ φρονεῖν (= "let us conform to the same *rule, thinking the same thing*"). This is an obviously secondary attempt to make sense of Paul's otherwise laconic clause. Very likely it captures the larger concern.

7. P16 (apparently) and a few MSS of the Sahidic version have turned this first plural into a second plural; while that reflects Paul's primary concern, it misses the rhetoric of this appeal.

Paul just concluded his personal story with a passionate declaration of his pursuit of the prize, knowing Christ fully and completely. He now turns to apply his story to the situation in Philippi. Exactly how — and how much — he expects them to apply it is not at all certain;[8] nonetheless, some items seem obvious and are therefore worth noting.

First, in contrast to v. 17, Paul makes this first application in the first person plural.[9] Whatever else, this is not the language or mode of polemics.[10] In clearly polemical contexts, Paul explicitly indicates the presence of outsiders and dissociates himself from his readers by addressing them with second plural imperatives. But here he does not say, "All of you who are mature, have this mindset." On the contrary, this is application and appeal, pure and simple; the first plural is Paul's way of including himself with his readers when the exhortation applies equally to him as to them,[11] and it is his story, after all, that he is urging them to join with him in following. That not all of them would necessarily see things his way is implied, but that much has been implied throughout the letter.

---

8. Jones (58) calls these two verses "one of the few passages in the Epistle that are difficult to interpret." That may be a bit sanguine as to the rest of the epistle, but it does reflect a reality about this passage. Here is a place where the scholarly pitfalls noted above (p. 351) are especially in evidence; but many of these are of our own making, partly resulting from a number of (sometimes unquestioned) presuppositions, which deeply affect how these verses are read: (a) The unwarranted paragraph break at v. 12 (which the grammar disallows; see on vv. 12 and 15), and the inclusion of vv. 15-16 in this new "paragraph" (thus vv. 12-16); (b) that vv. 12-14 in particular are directed against "opponents," whose language Paul is using against them; (c) and related to (b), that there is some kind of "theological" tension between "parties" in Philippi, and that Paul is addressing now one and then the other; and (d) that the word play in v. 15 determines the meaning of the text, rather than the grammar and context (this is blatant in Jones; it is unquestioned by many). To read the epistle as a letter of friendship and exhortation, as suggested in this commentary, brings about a quite different reading of the same data.

9. On this use of the first person plural in paraenetic sections of his letters, see above on v. 3.

10. Cf. Meyer (173): "A tone of *irony* . . . is utterly alien to the heartfelt character of the whole discourse, which is, moreover, in this application . . . so expressed as to include the apostle in common with his readers." So also Kennedy, Caird, Kent, Loh-Nida, O'Brien; *contra* Lightfoot, Jones, Schmithals, Beare, Gnilka, Collange, Martin, Bruce, Hawthorne, Silva. The difficulties with this latter point of view, besides the fact that a straight reading of the text is so much against it, is highlighted when one reads the secondary literature through in chronological order. Those who see the text as polemical in some way either avoid the grammar altogether (for good reason, one might add), or indicate the difficulties with the grammar — which exist primarily because of the presuppositions — and then try to settle them by the method of exegetical "divide and conquer" (where a series of unusual [and unlikely] meanings is proposed for individual words or phrases, which are then adopted en masse as Paul's overall intent; see esp. Hawthorne on v. 15b; cf. n. 23).

11. Cf., e.g., Rom 14:19; 1 Cor 15:49.

Second, the most striking thing about this application is that it *concludes* his narrative on the same note with which he *begins* the Christ narrative in 2:5, thus returning to the crucial verb which dominated the appeal in 2:1-5 (and will occur again in v. 19 and 4:2). Just as he told the Christ story so that they would have a "mindset" *(phroneite)* in keeping with Christ's, so now he has told his story so that they will "take a view" *(phronōmen)* of things in keeping with his own. Given that he specifically applies both stories by means of this verb, it seems hardly coincidental that Paul's story corresponds at several crucial points with Christ's. But as always for Paul, correct "thinking" leads to right living, so he concludes this application (v. 16) by urging them to conform their lives to their knowledge of Christ, as it has now been put on display through his own story.

That, at least, is the *how* of things; our difficulties lie with the *what* and *why*. Although very compressed and some of its grammar ambiguous,[12] *what* Paul says is in three parts:[13]

(1) A direct application: Therefore,
> as many of us as are *teleioi, this* let us "think" *(phronōmen)*.
(2) A qualification: And if you "think" *(phroneite)* anything differently,
> *this* also God will reveal to you.
(3) A rejoinder (to the qualification):
> In any case, unto whatever we have attained [already, is implied],
> [let us] conform to the same.

He thus begins by urging that they have *this* mindset, the one revealed in his

---

12. So that it is capable of different readings, both as a whole and in some of its parts. For example, to rework Caird's paraphrase (143-44), Paul might mean either:

> The point of view I have been expressing is the mark of a mature believer. If at any point you think otherwise, I can rely on God to reveal to you the correctness of my point of view. In any case, the one thing that matters is we should all act in accordance with the level of understanding already attained.

or:

> The point of view I have been expressing is the mark of mature believers like you and me. Granted this fundamental mindset, you may be sure that if there is anything on which you hold unsound opinions, God will lead you to the truth about that as well. The main thing is that we must conduct our life together by that one standard we all share.

On the former option, see Meyer (and most interpreters); for the latter see Lightfoot, Kennedy, Caird.

13. Cf. Lohmeyer (148): "drei rhetorischen Zweizeilen" (three rhetorical two-clause sentences).

story; then, as a kind of aside, he indicates that God will reveal to them where their "mindset" might need further help on unnamed matters; but he concludes by returning to the application, now in terms of behavior — of their living up to what God has already revealed, which they know well (rejoicing in the Lord even in present suffering, which conforms them to Christ's death, and to live in the present as those in eager pursuit of the eschatological prize). The basic *assumption* of the application, in any case, is *mutuality between him and them,* not fundamental differences of opinion on things that really matter. The passage overall is much too placid regarding central issues of Paul's understanding of the gospel to be construed as polemical.

**15** The inferential "therefore" with which this sentence begins[14] tells the story as to Paul's intent in rehearsing his pilgrimage: "In consequence of what I have been narrating," he says, "let us now hear the application." Which begins: "As many of us as are *teleioi.*"[15] This is a clear play on "I have not yet been brought to completion" in v. 12, and appears to be a bit tongue in cheek. After all, he includes himself in the present designation. So he who is "not yet" *teleios* ("completed") in the sense of *eschatological* hope, is "already" *teleios* ("mature"), along with them, in terms of how they live in the present as they await the final glory.[16] Thus *teleioi* probably means "mature" in the sense outlined in v. 16; those who live in keeping with what they have already attained are thus "complete" to that degree, even though the final completion, when all are fully conformed into the likeness of the Christ whom they desire to know above all else, still remains.

But who are intended by "as many as"? At the least he intends to include himself,[17] and apparently all others who share his point of view. Very

---

14. Gk. οὖν; unfortunately, as in 2:1, again left untranslated by the NIV; and scarcely noted even in the technical commentaries. Lohmeyer (147) and O'Brien (433) are notable exceptions. Hawthorne also notes it, but makes no effort to show how it functions. This clearly inferential conjunction, plus the total lack of any kind of paragraphing signal in v. 12, where the grammar demands a continuation of vv. 10-11, is what makes the common paragraphing (vv. 12-16) so suspect. In fact, just as in 2:1 and 2:28, this conjunction marks a turning point in the argument, in this case toward the application of what has been narrated from v. 4 — not just from v. 12!

15. On the basic meaning of this word, see nn. 11 and 23 on v. 12; cf. the discussion on 1 Cor 2:6 in Fee, *First Corinthians,* 102-3 (cf. on 14:20), where it refers to being "adults" as over against acting like children (cf. Eph 4:13).

16. As much as anything, missing the clearly eschatological thrust of vv. 10-11 and 12-14 with its "already but not yet" prespective has caused no end of generally irrelevant comments on this word play that seem quite foreign to Paul's concerns. Only O'Brien, among English commentaries over the past century, uses the language of eschatology to explain this text.

17. Although Schmithals (*Paul,* 74) thinks otherwise, that with this sentence "Paul . . . addresses his opponents, the τέλειοι, and sets himself at a distance from them." It is

often, therefore, this is understood to be partitive (= some do, and some don't).[18] But that would be a highly unusual use of this pronoun[19] for Paul. Technically, it is a correlative (= as many as . . . these), which seldom intends to say anything about those who do/are not, but only about those who do/are. Thus Rom 8:14, "as many as (= all who) are led by the Spirit, these are the children of God." This does not mean that God has some other children who are not led by the Spirit, but that being led of the Spirit characterizes all who are truly God's children.

Likewise here, in expanded form Paul probably intends, "As many as (= all who) are 'mature,' let us be those who have set our minds in keeping with mine described above." The awkwardness of the sentence comes from Paul's condensing the second clause into an imperative, and by including himself. Most likely, then, Paul intends to include all of them with himself in this imperative.[20] His concern lies in both parts of the sentence: that they "set their minds" in the same way as his own just described; and that this is precisely the frame of mind that characterizes "the mature" in Christ. On the verb itself see the discussion on 2:2. That he should use this verb here indicates that what is at stake for Paul is first of all a basic frame of mind, a way of looking at everything, which in turn leads to a way of behaving.

By "this"[21] (NIV, "such a view of things") Paul probably intends the whole narrative, including the rejection of his Jewish past. But it especially

---

difficult to see how the grammar of this sentence, especially the first person plural verbs (φρονῶμεν/ἐφθάσαμεν), allows for such an interpretation. On the inclusive "we" see the discussion on 3:3.

18. So Michael (164): "at the same time hinting that they have not all reached maturity"; cf. Kent (143), whose stance is the boldest ("exhorts those who are mature; . . . promises those who think differently"; cf. Silva [205], "the group of readers whose error Paul is addressing"). That is especially difficult to wrest from Paul's grammar, where the ὅσοι and first plural would ordinarily include them all and the second plural in the next clause can be read as "dividing the house" only by a severe wrenching of the text. Under any circumstances, Paul himself uses *no explicit language* indicating that he thinks of them as a divided community over this "issue."

19. Gk. ὅσοι, the correlative conjunction (= "as many as") used absolutely, but picked up as the subject of the next clause. Thus, e.g., Rom 2:12 ("as many as sinned apart from the Law shall perish apart from the Law; and as many as sinned having the Law will be judged by the Law"); in both halves of this sentence the "as many as" refers to all the people who fit the category. All others fit another category. What is not implied is that this fits a large number within the category, but not all.

20. Or at least in the sense suggested by Meyer (endorsed by O'Brien), that with this word "Paul leaves it to the conscientious judgment of every reader whether he [or she] . . . belongs to the number of the τέλειοι."

21. Gk. τοῦτο φρονῶμεν. On the pronoun with φρονεῖτε, see n. 25 on 2:5. Here it unquestionably points backward; the differences of opinion lie with what in vv. 4-14 the τοῦτο refers to. See next n.

includes his "participation in Christ's sufferings, by being conformed to his death" and his "eager pursuit of the eschatological prize," since that is the focus of vv. 18-19 and 20-21: those who are "enemies of the cross" and who have "set their minds on present earthly things" are set in sharp contrast to *us,* whose "citizenship is in heaven, from whence we eagerly await the Savior."[22]

But then Paul makes a surprising qualification:[23] "and if[24] you think *(phroneite)* anything differently,[25] this also God will reveal[26] to you." Our difficulties are several, some of them related to *what* is said: (a) what Paul intends by "anything differently" (NIV, "on some point") in the first clause, which is picked up by the "this" in the second clause; (b) the force of the

---

22. In context, both the immediate context of vv. 10-14 and 20-21 and the larger context of the letter that includes the Christ narrative in 2:6-11, one seems esp. hard pressed to limit the "this" to vv. 12-14, despite the large number of scholars who do so (mostly because they have already started a new "paragraph" at v. 12). Thus only a few see it as suggested here (e.g., Vincent, Barth; Fowl, *DPL,* 429). Otherwise Lightfoot ("the rule to forget the past and press ever forward"), and *inter alia* Meyer, Müller, Beare, Hendriksen, Loh-Nida, Bruce, Hawthorne, Silva, O'Brien. Many of these see the "mindset" to be limited to the language of "perfection"; thus, the only true "perfection" in the present is that which humbly acknowledges lack of perfection. But that is not only unnecessarily limiting (as vv. 17 and 4:9 indicate), but contextually unjustifiable; it misses the eschatological perspective of this passage by too much.

23. At least it seems "surprising" to us. Here our inability to fill their shoes as the letter was being read for the first time among them makes understanding especially difficult. Thus for us this is a "strangely prolix sentence" (Barth, 111).

24. Gk. χαὶ εἰ; although this could conceivably be an expression of intensive concession (= "even though"), that is unlikely, since in the only two certain instances of this idiom (χαί preceding a form of εἰ) in Paul (1 Cor 8:5; Gal 1:8) there are other indicators that make the concessive meaning certain; whereas the combination occurs in several instances where it is conjunctive (= "and if"), as here (cf. Rom 11:16; 13:9; 1 Cor 6:2; et al.). Hawthorne suggests that the χαί is adversative, that the εἰ = "since in fact," and that the τι is adverbial = "somewhat different," thus turning the whole sentence into a word over against the whole community ("But since you have a somewhat different attitude"); cf. n. 10 above.

25. Gk. τι ἑτέρως; the adverb occurs only here in the NT. Although it is correctly observed (e.g., Meyer) that the context implies an unfavorable sense, it is perhaps too much so to make it read "amiss" (as Lightfoot; cf. Caird). For Hawthorne's reading of the τι, see preceding n.

26. Gk. ἀποκαλύψει, Paul's regular verb for divine revelation, either the revelation of God's ways and the like, including prophetic utterances (e.g., 1 Cor 2:10; 14:30; Gal 1:16; 3:23; Eph 3:5) or of God's actions (e.g., Rom 1:18; 8:18). When Paul intends something lesser, he uses other verbs (as in 1:13, "manifest"). In Pauline theology such "revelation" as here intended would be the work of the Holy Spirit. Lincoln (*Paradise,* 94) sees this sentence as "ironical," reflecting on the "opponents' " boasting in "revelations." But that is a dubious reading of 2 Cor 11–12 into the present text (see n. 60 on v. 3).

"also" in the second clause; (c) and the nature of God's revealing "this" to them. These in turn impact the larger, and in some ways more difficult, contextual questions: how this sentence relates to what immediately precedes (v. 15a) and follows (v. 16) and how — or whether — it relates to the narrative of vv. 4-14. All of which is complicated for us by the tenor of the sentence, which does not carry even a whiff of the odor of controversy; indeed, it is almost nonchalant — a kind of "throw away" sentence — which makes one think that no great issue can be in view.[27]

It is common to read this as though there were some in the community in opposition to Paul. But this view has nearly insuperable difficulties. First, there is no hint elsewhere in the letter — nor in this sentence for that matter — that there is friction between him and them on some matter(s). Moreover, if this had been written in response to opposition, one would have expected something much more specific, like: "if *any* [*tines*] of you think differently *on these matters.*"[28] Instead he addresses the whole community,[29] and does so by repeating the verb *phroneite* from the first clause (*phronōmen*). Finally, the sentence that follows, which serves as a rejoinder to this momentary qualification, shows signs neither of anxiety on Paul's part nor of disagreeableness on theirs.

But if not addressing opposition, what then? Most likely, in light of the present context as well as the whole letter, it is best understood within the setting of friendship. In context Paul is especially concerned that they follow his

27. The best way to see this is to read it in contrast to another sentence (1 Cor 14:37-38) where Paul also anticipates that some might not share his view of things. In a clearly polemical context — as throughout the letter the Corinthians (at least many of them) are at odds with Paul on the matter at hand — Paul says, "If anyone thinks he or she is a prophet or a Spirit person, let them acknowledge what I am writing to you is the Lord's command; if they ignore this, they themselves will be ignored [by God, is implied]." The present sentence is a far cry from that one. While comparable in the sense that both sentences anticipate some differences of opinion with him, there is no resemblance between them in terms of tone and style. Thus, despite much that is written to the contrary, the casual nature of this sentence undermines the view that Paul is being *polemical,* either here or in the larger section (3:1–4:3). All the more so, when one considers that what he has just narrated about himself — righteousness from God based on faith, knowing Christ by participating in his sufferings so as to be conformed to the likeness of his death, eager pursuit of the eschatological goal of knowing Christ fully — are absolutely central matters to his theology. If they were at odds with him on any of these things, or if outsiders were among them leading them down forbidden paths, then this most casual of responses demonstrates that a leopard can change its spots after all!

28. Although that is exactly how some read the text, despite what Paul actually says (e.g., Kent, Loh-Nida).

29. Thus, whatever else, Paul is not here allowing for individual judgments on his teachings, as Caird points out.

example, which happens also to be part and parcel of a "patron/client" friendship. But throughout the letter he studiously avoids any hint of this kind of "superior to inferior" expression of friendship between him and them; in fact he goes out of his way to make sure that their friendship is understood in terms of mutuality.[30] That seems to be what is also going on here. On the one hand, he really is exhorting them to follow his example (as v. 17 will make even more clear); on the other hand, "exhortation" in this case is not "command," nor does it assume that all will see eye to eye with him on all matters. The emphasis in this sentence, after all, is not on any anticipated "disagreement" they might have with him, but on God's continuing to work among them through divine revelation. The sentence is thus predicated on their mutual friendship and mutual trust, which is so secure that Paul can simply leave it in God's hands to "reveal" to them what further understanding they may need on matters wherein they might not be ready fully to agree with him.

That would suggest, finally, in terms of the details, that the "something differently" and "this also" of his sentence do not so much reflect specifics that Paul has in mind, but generalities. Here is the offer of friendship; they may freely disagree with him at points — on many matters — and if any matter counts for something, Paul trusts God to bring them up to speed here as well. What both the immediate and larger contexts of this letter — not to mention what we know of Paul elsewhere — disallows is that "something differently" can refer either to their living a cruciform lifestyle or to the vigorous pursuit of the heavenly prize.[31] Paul goes on in vv. 18-19 to describe people who have abandoned these; and there the vigor and pathos return in such a way that forecloses on such eternally significant matters as belonging to this more "optional" approach to "thinking anything differently."

**16** Having allowed that they might see something differently from himself, but stipulating that God will redirect their collective "frame of mind" in any case, he returns to his first point, expressed now in terms of behavior. "In any case," he rejoins, "on the matter at hand you need not wait for divine revelation." At the same time he returns also to the first plural, "unto that which we have attained, to behave in conformity to 'the same.'" Some matters in this sentence are easier than others. First, the conjunctive adverb[32] is used

---

30. On this matter see both the Introduction, pp. 4-7, and (esp.) the discussion of 4:15-17 below. See also the discussion of 1:3-8, 12, 27; 2:1-2, 12, 17-18, 19-24; 3:1; 4:10, 14, 18-20.

31. Cf. n. 25; so also Meyer (176): "Certainly, therefore, the variations [= τι ἑτέρως], which Paul so forbearingly and confidently and without polemical handling commits to revealing correction on the part of God, were not on matters of principle or of an anti-Pauline character" (cf. Vincent, 113).

32. Gk. πλήν; used by Paul for "breaking off a discussion and emphasizing what is important" (BAGD); cf. 4:14; 1 Cor 11:11; Eph 5:33.

in this case to bring closure to the two preceding clauses. It therefore means, "under any circumstances," whether you see *all* things fully my way or not, "all of us, you and me together, must behave in conformity to the same standard." Second, the verb "behave in conformity to,"[33] which originally meant "to be drawn up in a line" (esp. as a military term), is used by Paul only figuratively, meaning to "bring one's life or behavior into conformity to" something (the Spirit; the "rule" that neither circumcision or uncircumcision counts for a thing, but only the new creation).

The difficulties have to do with (a) what Paul is referring to in saying "unto that which we have attained,"[34] (b) what "the same" refers to, to which he is urging[35] conformity, and (c) how these two relate to one another. Most likely:

(a) With the clause "unto that which we have attained," which can only mean "already," Paul seems to be calling them to live in keeping with how they have already followed Christ,[36] before they have received this letter.[37] Given Paul's longtime — and loving — relationship with this church,

---

33. Gk. τῷ αὐτῷ στοιχεῖν; in Paul see Gal 5:25 and 6:16 (cf. Rom 4:12), both of which throw light on this usage. In 5:25 he urges them, "since we have been brought to life by the Spirit, let us behave in conformity to the Spirit" (= in keeping with the "fruit of the Spirit"); 6:16 is very much like the present passage, καὶ ὅσοι τῷ κανόνι τούτῳ στοιχήσουσιν ("as many as conform to this 'rule' ").

34. Gk. ἐφθάσαμεν; used by Paul to mean to "reach a certain point (geographically)" (2 Cor 10:14) or, as here, to "attain" to a certain level of Christian conduct (cf. Rom 9:31). As Meyer correctly observes, this verb implies that "progress" has already been made (see on 1:25).

35. The verb is actually an infinitive. Burton (*Moods,* 146) considers it the one certain instance in the NT of an imperatival infinitive; but that would seem to need a degree of qualification, since the first person plural in the preceding clause (εἰς ὃ ἐφθάσαμεν) makes a straight imperative cumbersome at best — and without analogy in Paul. If imperatival, it is better to see it as hortatory ("let us behave").

36. Meyer (179) has rightly pointed out that this sentence in its entirety has to do with "living the gospel," not with "knowledge." Thus Paul is not here pointing to a certain level of "understanding," but of Christian behavior. Plummer (80) thinks "what we have attained" is equivalent to "the principle that we must never cease striving to make advance"; but that accords poorly with the verb στοιχεῖν.

37. Reading this passage as though in a polemical context presents no end of difficulties for its advocates, who must invariably read between the lines what Paul does not so much as hint at. Thus, e.g., V. Hasler (*EDNT,* 3.422, on the entry for φθάνω) considers this verb to indicate that they are to be "content with [!] what they have already *attained,*" vis-à-vis "striving enthusiastically after a higher level of faith not limited to a fellowship in suffering with the crucified Lord." Whereas the entry by E. Plümacher (under στοιχέω, 3.278) sees Paul as counteracting those "sure of their own spiritual maturity" that they "should *hold true to, stay in agreement with* what has been (spiritually) attained." To make these kinds of claims, the "we" must be treated as nonexistent (e.g., Jones), or as a rhetorical

and his frequent stops there, it is hard to imagine that he is telling them anything new in this letter. Indeed, in v. 1 he has said quite the opposite, that it is not burdensome for him to write the same things again as a safeguard. Thus, both the Christ narrative, which is foundational for his, and his own story do not present something new; rather they tell the "old, old story" all over again. This is that to which he and they have already attained, even if some are now slackening off in some way and for some reason.

(b) It is possible that "the same" means something like "to the same as mine as outlined in my story above," or "to one and the same 'rule' that we have always lived by."[38] More likely, however, it does not here refer to some external "rule" that he and they have in common,[39] but refers specifically to "that which we have already attained" in the preceding clause,[40] exemplified in the gospel.

(c) If so, then the clause functions as we have suggested, as a rejoinder following his momentary qualification in v. 15b. What he is therefore calling them to is to live in conformity to the gospel as that has been spelled out repeatedly in their hearing, and as it has now been repeated in the Christ narrative in 2:6-11 and in his own that has just preceded (vv. 4-14). What he and they have already "attained" is an understanding of the gospel in which the life of the Crucified One is the paradigm for those who would be his followers; and they may do so with joy because they are "already but not yet"; the power of the resurrection by which they now participate in his sufferings, thus being conformed to his death, is also the guarantee of their own sure future, toward which he has just urged them to follow him in eager pursuit.

The best explanation of the "why" of all this, therefore, is the one we have suggested right along, that in the face of opposition and some internal

---

ploy that does not really include Paul ("hypothetical," Plummer). But that runs roughshod over what can be clearly demonstrated about this feature of Pauline paraenesis (see the disc. on v. 3 above).

38. Which seems to be the understanding that lies behind the textual corruption found in the MajT (see n. 6 above; cf. KJV, "let us walk by the same rule, let us mind the same thing").

39. As, e.g., Lightfoot (154): "the rule of faith as opposed to works" (based on the parallel in Gal 6:16): cf. Hendriksen (177): "The rule has been established . . . : 'We are still far from perfect, but in Christ we should strive to become perfect" and GNB (endorsed by Loh-Nida), "let us go forward according to the same rules."

40. So also, *inter alia,* Vincent, Müller, Beare. Despite the fact that so many are prepared to add an understood noun or "rule" to "the same" (see preceding n.), Paul's syntax in particular seems to point in the direction here suggested. Both clauses begin with their respective modifiers; the symmetry in Paul's sentence, as well as the lack of a noun following τῷ αὐτῷ, suggests that it refers to the immediately preceding pronoun. Thus:

εἰς ὃ ἐφθάσαμεν,     Unto that which we have attained,
τῷ αὐτῷ στοιχεῖν.     to the same let us conform our conduct.

dissension, some of them have lost their vision for and focus on their crucified and risen Lord, including his coming again. Even in a Roman prison Paul has not lost his vision; here he urges them to follow his example and to see their participation in Christ's sufferings as Christ's way of "conforming them to his death," so that they, with Paul, may joyously gain the prize of his eternal presence.

## 2. Appeal and Indictment (3:17-19)

17*Join with others in following my example, brothers and sisters, and take note of those who live according to the pattern we gave you. 18For, as I have often told you before and now say again even with tears, many[1] live as enemies of the cross of Christ. 19Their destiny is destruction, their god is their stomach, and their glory is in their shame. Their mind is on earthly things.*

In the preceding sub-paragraph (vv. 15-16) Paul approached the concept of *imitatio,* as he specifically applied the "mindset" illustrated in his personal story to the Philippian situation, concluding with the exhortation that they conform their behavior to the pattern of Christ thus far attained. Paul now repeats his concern, this time in the express language of *imitatio.* At the same time he (apparently) amplifies so as to include not only the immediate concerns expressed in his personal history, but also some more general concerns that cover a larger scope of behavior.

He begins this sub-paragraph[2] with the basic imperative, that they "imitate" him in their behavior, and that they have a discerning eye for all who also walk according to his pattern (v. 17).[3] This is followed by an explanatory sentence (vv. 18-19), which gives the reasons for their "taking [careful] note of [others]" in this way — because there are many whose "walk" does not conform to the pattern. Although this last sentence is full of

---

1. In what appears to be the earliest attempt to tie vv. 18-19 to v. 2, P[46] adds a βλέπετε before τοὺς ἐχθρούς, thus creating a (nongrammatical) sentence that reads: "For many live, about whom I have told you often before and now say again with tears; watch out for the enemies of the cross, etc."

2. I use this language cautiously, since there are good reasons, as noted in the introduction to 3:15–4:3 (pp. 351-52), to see this larger section as a single flow of thought, which not only concludes the immediate exhortation (from 3:1) but the former exhortation (1:27–2:18) as well.

3. Since most of us read or study this letter in small pieces, it is easy to forget that just a few minutes earlier — in the actual reading of the letter — both Timothy (who looks out for the interests of Christ Jesus) and Epaphroditus (who risked his life for the sake of the gospel) are set before them as among those who "imitate" Christ in this way.

difficulties for the interpreter in terms of identifying both the persons alluded to and the nature of their "walk," their *function* in Paul's appeal seems clear. They not only stand in stark contrast to his example, as to the kind of behavior he is urging on the Philippians, but the final word about them ("their minds are set on earthly things") also serves as the foil for the final word about "us whose citizenship is in heaven" (vv. 20-21) and whose minds are thus set on winning the eschatological prize.

We will reserve our best guess as to who these people are — or represent — until we have looked at the sentence in detail. Here we simply note that in many ways this passage helps to tie together several items in the letter, especially the theme of joy in suffering and Paul's reasons for the narratives about Christ (2:6-11) and himself (3:4-14). At issue throughout is living a cruciform existence, discipleship marked by the cross and evidenced by suffering on behalf of Christ. This clearly lies behind the first hint of the *imitatio* motif (1:30; they are experiencing in Christ's behalf the same struggle they have known and seen in Paul); this is the central focus in both paradigmatic narratives (Christ as God humbled himself in becoming human, being *obedient* to death on a cross; Paul suffered the loss of all former things because of the surpassing worth of knowing Christ his Lord, so as finally to be conformed to his death). But in both cases there is "eschatological" glory — Christ's now and Paul's (and theirs) to come.[4] Hence, whatever we make of the two more difficult items that describe these "many" over whom Paul weeps (their god is their belly, and their glory is in their shame), the first and final items stand in stark contrast to both Christ and Paul at these crucial points: they are enemies of the cross and their minds are set on present, earthly things; that is, they have abandoned a lifestyle marked by the cross and have given up altogether on the sure future that belongs to those who are thus marked.

**17**   With the second vocative in this passage[5] Paul appeals to his Philippian "brothers and sisters" to "become imitators of me."[6] The idea of "imitating" a teacher had precedent in Paul's Jewish heritage,[7] where a pupil

---

4. For this basic point of view, see also Motyer, 183-84; O'Brien, 444-45; Bauder (*NIDNTT*, 1.491); and Fowl (*DPL*, 429).

5. See on v. 13 (also v. 1); cf. 4:1. See also n. 12 on 1:12.

6. Gk. συμμιμηταί μου; the compound appears only here in the NT (see the discussion) — indeed, only here in all of Greek literature. The non-compounded form appears in Paul's earliest letter (1 Thess 1:6; 2:14) and several times thereafter (the verb in 2 Thess 3:7, 9; the noun in 1 Cor 4:16; 11:1; Eph 5:1). Elsewhere in the NT, see Heb 6:12; 13:7; and 3 John 11.

7. As well as in the Greco-Roman world, sometimes of a worshiper and his/her deity, which may well serve as the background for it usage in Judaism, since it appears there in the later intertestamental period. On the role of exemplary paradigms in letters of moral exhortation, see the Introduction, pp. 11-12. For the Jewish background see Wis 4:2

learned not simply by receiving instruction but by "putting into practice" the example of the teacher; the one who "imitates" thus internalizes and lives out the model presented by the teacher. This language occurs in two kinds of contexts in Paul: suffering for the sake of Christ and the gospel, and behavior that conforms to the gospel.[8] In every case "imitation" of Paul means "as I imitate Christ" (expressly so in 1 Cor 11:1; cf. 1 Thess 1:6).

The key to our passage lies in its first occurrence in Paul (1 Thess 1:6), where the Thessalonians (fellow Macedonians, one should note) are reminded that in becoming believers they became followers of both Paul and Christ at the crucial point of having received the message in the context "of great affliction accompanied by the joy of the Holy Spirit."[9] That is very much like the present context. The two earlier hints of *imitatio* (of Paul) in Philippians (1:30; 2:18) occur in a context of suffering for Christ; the second concludes on the note of Paul's rejoicing — his own and together with them — and urges them to do "the same." This present section begins and ends with the imperative "rejoice *in the Lord*"; that they should do so in the context of suffering is the main point of his personal narrative (v. 10: "participation in Christ's sufferings" as his way of being "conformed to Christ's death").

Only here does Paul use the compound "fellow-imitators." Although this could go in one of three directions,[10] most likely Paul is calling on them

---

(imitating wisdom); *Ep. Ar.* 188, 210, 281 (imitating God); 2 Macc 9:23 (imitating a holy martyr); Jos. *Ant.* 1.68 (descendants of Seth who imitated his ways); 8.315 (Asa, who imitated David); Philo, *Virt.* 66 (Joshua imitating Moses); *Congr. Qu. Er.* 70. Philo's understanding is found in this latter reference: "for the practiser must be the imitator of a life, not the hearer of words, since the latter is the characteristic mark of the recipient of teaching, and the former of the strenuous self-exerciser" (LCL, 4.493). See Michaelis, *TDNT,* 4.659-74; Bauder, *NIDNTT,* 1.490-92; Larsson, *EDNT,* 2.428-30; Fowl, *DPL,* 428-31; De Boer, *Imitation;* H. D. Betz, *Nachfolge;* Brant, "Place" (see Larsson for a larger bibliography on this idea in the NT).

8. See esp. 1 Cor 4:16, where the Corinthians are to be reminded of Paul's "ways in the Lord." The early believers in Christ did not live by "principles" or by "the Book," but by the living example of those who taught by doing as well as by instruction. Thus the nature of Paul's argument with the Thessalonians in 2 Thess 3:7-10. See the discussion in Fee, *First Corinthians,* 187-88.

9. On this text and its significance for Pauline theology, see Fee *Presence,* 45-47.

10. Besides the view adopted here, it could mean either (a) that they are to be fellow-imitators with him of Christ, or (b) that they are to be fellow-imitators of others who are already imitating Paul. In support of (a), Paul has previously used "*syn*-compounds" to emphasize his and their mutuality (συγκοινωνούς μου in 1:7 [cf. 4:14]; συγχαίρω/συγχαίρετε in 2:18; συνεργῶν μου καὶ συστρατιώτην μου in 2:25; cf. συνήθλησάν μοι in 4:3); though frequently noted in the literature as an option, it has seldom been adopted (W. F. McMichael, "Followers Together"; and Pollard, "Integrity," are exceptions). The basic difficulty with this view is grammatical. Had Paul intended "together with me," the pronoun would have been dative and thus go with the συν. The genitive (μου) means the pronoun goes with μίμηται as

to join together in imitating him.[11] If so, Paul is once again picking up the theme of their being united on this matter, a theme that began as early as the repeated "all of you" in the salutation and thanksgiving (1:1-11),[12] and is brought to its concluding moment just a few sentences later (4:2-3).

Thus, they are urged to join together in following Paul's example (as he follows Christ is always implied), while at the same time they also "take note of those who live according to the pattern we gave you." For the sake of comment we need to put that more "literally": "and take note of those who walk[13] thus, just as you have us[14] as an example."[15] To "walk" has to do with behavior, living uprightly in all that one does. Although this may well include some among the Philippians "who walk thus" (Epaphroditus, for

---

the *object* of imitation, as always with the occurrences of the non-compounded noun (1 Thess 1:6; 2:14; 1 Cor 4:16; 11:1; Eph 5:1).

The second view supposes that Paul is here pointing to the second part of the sentence. Although adopted more often (e.g., Weiss, Ellicott, Meyer, Kent, Silva, Melick; Earle [*Word Meanings,* 56]; cf. NIV), this view is the least likely of all, since it runs roughshod over Paul's καί (*pace* Silva) and offers a forced sense to the correlative οὕτω . . . καθώς (as in Meyer, 180). It should perhaps be noted also that Michaelis (*TDNT,* 4.667 n. 13) allows that the compound noun might not have significance at all; but that seems highly doubtful, since the word seems to have been coined (from its cognate verb, to be sure) for the occasion.

11. So the majority of interpreters (*inter alia,* Lightfoot, Meyer, Vincent, Kennedy, Jones, Plummer, Beare, Collange, Martin, Kent, Bruce, Hawthorne, O'Brien; De Boer, *Imitation;* Betz, *Nachfolge*).

12. See on 1:1 (and n. 41 for further references).

13. Gk. περιπατοῦντας; only here and in v. 18 in this letter, but the primary verb in Paul for paraenesis (at least 20 of its 30 NT occurrences in his letters). The usage derives from his Jewish heritage, where God's people are to "walk in the ways of the Lord" (although the verb πορεύεσθαι is used most often in the LXX for this idiom). The point, of course, is that of the NIV, that these people "live" in this way; but the figure is a pregnant one and should not be easily laid aside. After all, the primary imperative in Paul is not, as many would have it, "love one another," but "walk in/by the Spirit" (Gal 5:16). Everything else follows from this one.

14. This a rare "editorial we" in this letter (see the disc. in Hawthorne, 160-61); in light of 2:20-22, it very likely includes Timothy as well (so many interpreters), since he has joined Paul in the writing of this letter and Paul says of him that he is like a son with his father with regard to his relationship to Paul and the gospel. Some (e.g., Lincoln, *Paradise,* 95) see the ἡμᾶς as including all of Paul's associates, thus suggesting they are also "those who walk thus."

15. Gk. τύπον, here denoting "pattern" or "model"; for this usage in Paul see 2 Thess 3:9; cf. 1 Thess 1:7; 1 Cor 10:6; 1 Tim 4:12; Tit 2:7. The later meaning of "prefigurement," in which one thing prefigures a later reality, is argued for as the sense here by Schunack (*EDNT,* 3.373); but this is such a forced meaning for the present context that one must judge it as an attempt to force a single sense on all Pauline uses, which does not work well either here or in several of the other texts.

example), the grammar and language of this clause imply a more comprehensive group of people, reaching beyond the Philippians themselves.[16] They are either to "take note of" or "be on the lookout for"[17] such people, who also walk in keeping with the example they find in Paul — especially as that has been expressed in the preceding narrative.[18] The final clause, "just as you have us as an example," then brings the two preceding clauses together. They are to walk, and to watch for others who so walk, in keeping with the example of Paul just given in vv. 4-14.

Who these people might be is more speculative; but in light of those who are singled out by way of contrast in vv. 18-19, very likely Paul is referring to various itinerants. Since Philippi was a small city on the main highway East and West, and a full day's walk from Neapolis on the coast, the Christian community in Philippi was undoubtedly frequented by all sorts of itinerants, who would be given the normal Christian hospitality. Paul himself was one of these, as both his letters and Acts bear witness.[19] Fully aware that not all who would come through were of the same mind as Paul regarding walking in the ways of Christ, he has frequently warned them of such itinerants (as vv. 1 and 18 indicate). This imperative, therefore, besides specifying the reason for vv. 4-14, moves toward warning, that when others come among them, they mark well those who "walk" in the way of the cross and who are living in eager anticipation of the future. For, he will now go on to explain, there are many who do not so "walk." The significance of such warning lies internal to Philippi; it could well be that this is where the friction between Euodia and Syntyche fits in — over the way one lives and "does" the gospel, especially in the face of current opposition and suffering.

**18** In a surprising turn of argument, Paul now goes on to give the

16. Not all think so (e.g. Jones, Plummer, Martin, O'Brien; De Boer, *Imitation*, 182-83). Plummer, O'Brien, and De Boer see Paul here pointing to leaders (Plummer, "pastors"!) within the congregation. But this seems to go against the plain sense of the language: He addresses the whole community in the first clause ("you [all] join together in imitating me"); it seem unlikely that the next clause then means, "you [all] take note of those [among you] who do in fact walk thus, just as you [all] have us for a pattern."

17. Gk. σκοπεῖτε; see on 2:4. Here it probably means to "mark, take note of" so as to follow (as Lightfoot); but in light of the very similar passage in Rom 16:17, where it means "mark so as to avoid," it may even here come closer to the sense of "watch for, be on the lookout for" (so *EDNT*, 3.255). Some (e.g., Martin) see a word play here between this verb and the σκοπόν in v. 14; but that is unlikely, since the point of the two words has no real "play" between them, even though they come from the same root.

18. Martin (142; following Michaelis, *TDNT*, 4.667-68) asserts: "The passage is really a call to obedience to apostolic authority more than a summons to imitate the apostle's way of life." That is to read foreign matter into this text on the basis of one's (questionable) presupposition that the *Sitz im Leben* of the text is primarily polemical; and it does special disservice to the plain sense of the present clause.

19. On this matter see the Introduction, p. 27.

reason, by way of contrast, for the second clause in v. 17. They must "take note of" those who walk in keeping with Paul's own imitation of Christ precisely because there are many whose "walk" is the exact opposite. The surprise comes not in the contrast as such, but in the way he describes these people, which has been the source of much difficulty — and speculation. The difficulty is with identification (who are they?), which is related to the fivefold description found here (vv. 18-19), two or three of which create problems for every proposed identification.

The difficulties of identification have to do with context, both the immediate and larger context of the letter, since nothing to this point in the letter has quite prepared us for some of this. Several matters are at issue: (1) how, or whether, they are related to those described as "dogs" in v. 2; (2) how, or whether, they are related to Paul's disclaimers in vv. 12-13; (3) how, or whether, they are related to any of the previous mention of alleged "opponents" in the letter (1:15-16, 28; 2:21); (4) whether they are internal or external to the Philippian community; and (5) whether Paul considers them to be believers at all, or former "believers" who are now headed for perdition. We will say a few further words about "identification" at the end; first, a look at the description itself.

First, Paul says that "many walk," a combination that suggests people associated with the Christian community but outside of Philippi.[20] On the one hand, the verb "walk," repeated from v. 17, is used primarily by Paul in this figurative way — to describe both positively and negatively how believers are to live as Christians.[21] Although it is common to regard these "many" as "false *teachers*,"[22] Paul does not in fact refer to their teaching as such,[23] but

20. Cf. Kennedy (461): "Plainly they were persons inside the Christian Church, although probably not at Philippi" (cf. Beare, Hendriksen, Kent, Bruce, Hawthorne). The majority agree in seeing them as believers (of a sort). On the other hand, most scholars assume them to be in Philippi (as, e.g., Martin), but the plain sense of these opening words of v. 18 is otherwise. Jewett ("Conflicting Movements," 376-77) argues otherwise on both counts, that they are not "valid Christians" from Paul's perspective, who were one-time members of the Christian community there but had "left the church."

21. The exceptions are Col 3:7; Eph 2:2, 4:17 (second occurrence), in each case referring to the "walk" of pagans (or former pagans) that is in contrast to that of believers — which could also be the case here, of course.

22. So esp. Gnilka (211, "Irrlehrer") and Martin (143): "These *teachers* [emphasis mine] were setting up themselves as 'models' of Christian leadership." This is the presupposition of most who use the language "opponents" to describe these people, which ordinarily means they are opponents of Paul who are teaching that which is contrary to what Paul teaches.

23. Except in the more circuitous language of "enemies of the cross." But as many point out (e.g., O'Brien, 453), this almost certainly does not refer to their *teaching* a doctrine of salvation that differs from Paul's, but to their way of life that spurns the cross. Cf. GNB, "there are many whose lives make them enemies of Christ's death on the cross."

to their "walk," to the way they live — although a poor understanding of the gospel for Paul obviously lies behind such behavior. On the other hand, it is unlikely that Paul would have spoken in the third person and used "many,"[24] if he had some of their own in mind. His way of referring to those within a given community who are out of step with the rest is with the (usually plural) indefinite pronoun, "some [of you]."[25]

But before describing them, he interrupts himself with an especially poignant word about his own feelings toward them.[26] Two things are said:

24. Gk. πολλοί; although a general term, it implies that a goodly number were like this (although Schenk and Silva think it more rhetorical and therefore not attempting to say anything about their number). In any case, it seems to exclude nonbelievers since, besides the reasons given in the discussion, that would require οἱ πλείονες ("the majority"; cf. 1:14). For a convenient listing of the reasons for this conclusion see either Caird, 146, or O'Brien, 452. All of this runs counter to the suggestion of some that Paul is here referring to non-Christian Jews (see n. 28 below).

25. As noted below, the next clause, οὓς πολλάκις ἔλεγον ὑμῖν ("whom I spoke to you about many times before"), with its combination of first, second, and third person pronouns, strongly implies that those mentioned to the Philippians in the third person ("about whom") are not a part of those to whom Paul is now speaking. For them to be currently within the Philippians community would seem to require the following presuppositions, some of which are highly dubious: (a) a community of considerable size (for "many" to make sense), which may or may not be so; (b) considerable "division" within this large community that would cause Paul to speak of some of them in this way, which is most doubtful; and (c) that the letter has excluded these people all along, since he has been writing to the whole community on the predicate of friendship, which is also doubtful.

26. It is often suggested that the grammar breaks down here, especially with the final clause (οἱ τὰ ἐπίγεια φρονοῦντες) appearing in the nominative, following the preceding accusatives (οὕς, τοὺς ἐχθροὺς); so Reumann, "Hymnic Fragment," 598. But even though the grammar gets admittedly stretched, very likely the final clause is intentionally nominative and should be understood to modify the subject πολλοί (cf. Kent). In that case, one should perhaps not be so hasty to see the two genitive relative clauses ("whose end is destruction; whose God is their belly and glory is in their shame") to be in apposition to "the enemies of the cross," but already to be grammatically pointing back to the subject πολλοί. If so, and this seems to be the best way to understand the whole grammatically, then the emphasis seems to lie on the first and final members. Thus:

πολλοὶ περιπατοῦσιν
οὓς πολλάκις ἔλεγον ὑμῖν
(νῦν δὲ καὶ κλαίων λέγω),
τοὺς ἐχθροὺς τοῦ σταυροῦ τοῦ Χριστοῦ,
ὧν τὸ τέλος ἀπώλεια,
ὧν ὁ θεὸς ἡ κοιλία
καὶ
ἡ δόξα ἐν τῇ αἰσχύνῃ αὐτῶν,
οἱ τὰ ἐπίγεια φρονοῦντες.

(a) Paul has told them about such people on frequent occasions.[27] This is both the language of warning and further indication that they are not members of the community in Philippi. The normal sense of "*whom* I told *you* about" is a reference to people other than those being addressed.

(b) But "outside" (the believing community) in what sense, is made difficult by the "now" side of this clause: "and indeed I now tell you with weeping." Although there is no reason to believe Paul would not "weep" over those who have never known Christ,[28] he otherwise reserves "weeping"[29] and tears for those within the Christian community. Thus, he now weeps over them not because they are pagans living like pagans who have never known Christ[30] — why make such a point at all, one wonders — but because as professed believers in Christ they should know better. Indeed, it is very much like the apostle to "weep o'er the erring one," even as he warns fellow believers not to walk in their ways (cf. Acts 20:31).

Thus the opening clauses seem to point to some outside the Philippian community who are not (or no longer) walking in the ways of the Lord — or who think of themselves as doing so despite the way they live. Although Paul undoubtedly has some specific people in mind, the language is ultimately generic and would include any and all who are like this.[31] The difficulties lie in squaring this with the fivefold description that follows:

(1) "The enemies of the cross of Christ." This first clause puts the

27. This is the clear sense of the combination of the adverb πολλάκις (= many times, frequently; cf. Rom 1:13; 2 Tim 1:16) and the iterative imperfect ἔλεγον (= "I used to tell you"). This is the language of parents to children. For this kind of reminder of former "warnings" see Gal 5:21.

28. Indeed, he comes very close to this in Rom 9:2, where he says about fellow Jews who have not believed in Christ that for the sake of Christ he has "great sorrow and unceasing anguish in my heart" over them. Hawthorne (164) rightly points out that Paul does not speak of weeping "for" anyone, and thus conjectures, in keeping with his viewpoint that the "opponents" are non-Christian Jews, that the weeping may be out of frustration.

29. Gk. κλαίων, a verb used elsewhere in Paul only of the mutual "weeping" that believers have for those who are "weeping" (1 Cor 7:30; Rom 12:15); he expresses the present sentiment twice elsewhere with the noun "tears" (2 Cor 2:4, over his "sorrowful letter"; 2 Tim 1:4, of Timothy's tears at their former parting); cf. Acts 20:19 and 31.

30. So Weiss. For those who think Paul is here speaking about non-Christian Jews, see n. 38 on v. 2. There are no analogies in Paul or the rest of the NT for describing non-Christian Jews with the content of these five phrases ("enemies of the cross" might be the one exception). In Paul, see, e.g., 1 Thess 2:14-16, which is especially harsh but has nothing in it that even borders on the present description.

31. Cf. Motyer (185): "In the long run it makes no odds whom he is decrying, and it is better not to attach the verses too firmly to any situation in the past . . . and the description is perfectly clear even if the names are absent." I am less convinced as to anything being "perfectly clear" in this passage; but this is a proper caution.

whole in perspective, and ties the present concern directly to the narrative about Christ in 2:6-11 and to his own that has just preceded (especially vv. 8, 10-11). For Paul the cross is simultaneously God's means of redemption (the "foolishness" by which God is "pleased to save those who believe," 1 Cor 1:21) and his way of "turning the tables" on all merely human schemes (1 Cor 1:17-25). Thus the cross stands as God's utter contradiction to human wisdom and power. Therefore, it inevitably creates enemies of those who refuse to go that route. Paul's concern is for the Philippians to "walk" in a way that conforms to the death of Christ, even death on the cross. Those who are to be "marked" as walking *contrary to the pattern Paul set* for them are first of all described as "enemies of the cross of Christ."[32]

But in what way? since this could be a fitting description of at least three kinds of people: (a) pagan compatriots in Philippi who "stand in opposition" to them and are the probable cause of their present suffering (1:28); (b) the Judaizers in v. 2, who would try to come among them and urge circumcision, since Paul describes such "Judaizers" in precisely this way in Galatians (6:11-14; cf. 3:1; 5:11); or (c) the kind of triumphalist antinomians Paul speaks against throughout 1 Corinthians, especially chapters 1–4, whose "spirituality" has put them beyond present suffering as they glory only in the Spirit and the present power of the resurrection.[33] It is not surprising, therefore, that each of these has had its advocates. But the very diversity of options demonstrates that this clause helps little toward their identification, except that it could fit in a variety of scenarios. My own attempt to put a face on these people appears at the end of v. 19 (p. 375).

**19** (2) "Their destiny is destruction." With something of a play on "completed" (v. 12) and "mature" (v. 15), Paul speaks about the eschatological outcome[34] of such "enemies of the cross"; it is "destruction."[35] This stands in

32. One can never divorce "walking (by the Spirit) in the ways of God" from a "theology of the cross" in Paul; nor does the present context allow for an interpretation of "enemies of the cross" that is purely theological (as, e.g., Koester, "Purpose," 325). It is ultimately that, of course, given the next clause ("whose τέλος is destruction"), but Paul's concern at this point is with their "walk," and in Paul that is never a simply theological matter.

33. On the alleged "Gnosticism" behind this language, see n. 21 on v. 8.

34. Gk. τέλος, the adjective from which the verb in v. 12 and noun in v. 15 have been formed. It means "the end" in the sense of "the goal" toward which something has been pointing; thus, "destiny." But it is hard to escape the conclusion that Paul is here offering a word play. His own destiny is to be "completed" (τετελείωμαι) by his full knowing of Christ at the eschaton; but he — and the Philippians — already have arrived at a measure of that destiny, hence they are "mature" (τέλειοι) in Christ, even if not yet fully completed. But these people have a different eschatological "end" (τέλος) altogether. Cf. Schenk, Silva, O'Brien. For this usage, cf. Rom 6:21, referring to the pagan past of his Gentile readers, τὸ τέλος ἐκείνων θάνατος ("the end of those things is death"); and

the starkest contrast, both by its wordplay and by its content ("utter loss"), to Paul's "goal" described in v. 14 ("the heavenward call of God in Christ"), which he reiterates in the final contrast in vv. 20-21. Our present bodies may exist in "humiliation"; but they are destined for a "glorious" transformation. But those who have abandoned the cross, both for themselves and as the paradigm for Christian life, are destined for "destruction." The contextual reason for its appearing second in this listing, as over against its logical place at the end, is probably for rhetorical effect. Since the way of the cross is central to Paul's concern, the "end" for those who are enemies of the cross is brought forward to a place immediately following, while the final position, though still climactic, expresses their present "mindset" that differs altogether from his which focuses on the glorious future; and thus it launches the final contrast.

But this phrase also creates difficulty for identification. This language ordinarily refers to those outside Christ altogether — and very well may do so here, even though that seems to stand in conflict with much else that is said. More likely, Paul is referring to some who have appeared as believers, but whose "end" demonstrates that something was wrong with their "faith." They probably consider themselves to be within the household of faith, and most likely are, or were, but whom Paul now assigns to a place outside Christ, precisely because they have abandoned Christ by adopting a lifestyle that is totally opposed to the redemptive work of the cross.

(3) "Whose god is their stomach."[36] Here is the clause, along with its companion, "and their glory is in their shame," that presents most of our

esp. 2 Cor 11:15, of the "false apostles" who preach "another gospel," ὧν τὸ τέλος ἔσται κατὰ τὰ ἔργα αὐτῶν ("whose end shall be in keeping with their works"). Koester ("Purpose," 326) takes the unlikely position that Paul is using the language of his "opponents" here, thus negating Pauline usage as offering any help.

35. Gk. ἀπώλεια; cf. 1:28 (n. 56) of those in Philippi who stand in opposition to the believers there. This is the language of eternal loss; it is generally reserved by Paul to describe the eternal destiny of those outside of Christ.

36. Gk. κοιλία; cf. 1 Cor 6:13 and esp. Rom 16:18. These two passages make it clear that Paul is referring to the "stomach" as such, not using it as a circuitous way of referring to the "flesh," as some would have it (Gnilka, Caird, Schenk, O'Brien; Klijn, "Opponents," 283; Lincoln, *Paradise,* 96). This seems to be theological wishfulness on the part of its proponents, since it lacks linguistic and contextual support.

In what appears to be a massive misreading of the evidence, Mearns ("Identity," 198-99) takes up the mistaken notion of Behm (*TDNT,* 3.186) that κοιλία in the LXX sometimes denotes "the male sexual organ." But the primary passages listed in support do not refer to the penis, but to "the fruit of the *loins,*" to use older terminology. In Mearns' "most blunt" passage (Sir 23:6) the RSV does not translate κοιλίας ὄρεξις as "lust," as Mearns asserts, but (correctly) "gluttony" (= "the longing of the belly"). It is συνουσιασμός that is translated "lust." Thus the idea that "κοιλία and αἰσχύνη are euphemisms for the circumcised male organ" (198) is a creation out of thin air.

difficulties.[37] Only one thing seems certain: that these two phrases belong with the final one, giving concrete expression to what that one generalizes, namely that they live only for the present; they have set their minds on earthly, not on heavenly, things. The present phrase, which from our distance is especially cryptic, is very close to what Paul says of some "divisive people" in Rom 16:17-18 ("they do not serve Christ but their own stomachs"); in both instances the imagery probably refers to some specific behavior. But to what? "Stomach" may be a metonymy for the craving after sumptuous fare, or perhaps for surfeiting.[38] One cannot be sure. Perhaps it is intended to be more representative — of those who are so given over to present bodily desires of all kinds, represented by the "appetites," that such has become a "god" to them.

In any case, this phrase is the basis for some to find "libertines" here. Which may well be the case for this phrase and the next one; but the phrases are otherwise so completely on their own in this letter that one can hardly argue on this basis for a libertine "threat" in Philippi. A greater difficulty rests with those who think Paul is here further describing the "dogs" of v. 2, as sarcasm for their being into "food laws" as well.[39] But that seems much too circuitous; and Paul is forthright about this issue elsewhere. All in all, we must again beg a degree of ignorance on this matter, except to repeat that it is almost certainly a specific illustration of the way in which these people have set their minds on earthly things.[40]

37. Grammatically, the two clauses are held together by a single relative pronoun, indicating that in Paul's mind they go together, probably as often with this kind of usage, as two sides of one reality. Both clauses are elliptical, requiring a copulative verb, which most likely should appear as in the NIV.

38. In 1 Cor 15:32 Paul cites Isa 22:13 to the effect that those without hope in the resurrection may just as well "eat and drink, for tomorrow we die." But that is hardly the same thing as making the stomach one's god. The closest analogy is found in Euripides (*Cyclops,* 334, 335), where Cyclops, with the words δαιμών and γαστήρ, says, "I offer sacrifice to no god but myself, and to this belly of mine." The "stomach" (usually γαστήρ) is used variously by Greco-Roman writers as a metonymy for gluttony and the like: Seneca refers to people who are "slaves of their bellies" (*Ben.* 7.26; cf. Xenophon *Mem.* 1.6.8; 2.1.2), and in another place of seeking "the good of man, not that of his belly" (*Vit. Beat.* 9.4); whereas Lucian (*Patr. Laud.* 10) uses "stomach" in a context of "people measuring happiness by their appetites."

39. An ancient view (held by Ambrosiaster, Hilary, Pelagius, Augustine, Theodoret, Bengel) and revived in modern times by Barth, Müller, Klijn, Hawthorne; Gunther, *Opponents,* 98. But there is no analogy for such usage anywhere in Paul or the NT. It is striking that Hawthorne, e.g., rejects the "libertine" view on the basis that there is no analogy in Paul, but then presents his own case as though there were, which in fact there is not. Besides the fact that nothing in the present language nor from any outside sources supports a metonymy for food laws, this seems to be much too strong a denunciation for what Paul elsewhere allows for Jewish Christians, as long as they do not thereby judge others (Rom 14:1-17); in fact by his own testimony he eats "kosher" when with Jews (1 Cor 9:20).

40. So also most interpreters.

(4) "Whose glory is in their shame." From our distance this clause is even more cryptic than its predecessor.[41] It is connected to "their god is their belly" by a single relative pronoun, suggesting that this is the flip side of whatever that one means.[42] "Glory" is what they delight in; "shame" is how they should perceive their behavior.[43] The word "glory" is undoubtedly another word play, setting up the contrast to our being transformed into the likeness of Christ's present body "of glory" in v. 21. Hence it is an especially striking bit of irony, where not only are they not destined for "glory" at all, because of their present enmity to the cross, but what "glory" they have in the present lies precisely in what should be for them a matter of shame.[44] But beyond that, in terms of specifics, we are largely in the dark.[45]

Again this clause creates all kinds of difficulties for some and opportunities for others in terms of speculations about identity. As with its predecessor, difficulties with this language are greatest for those who identify these people with the "dogs" of v. 2,[46] or with some form of enthusiasm. But such

41. It is common to find an allusion to sexual immorality here (Plummer, Collange; Bultmann, *TDNT,* 1.190; Schmithals, *Paul,* 110-11; Jewett, "Conflicting Movements," 381); this is sometimes objected to as not reflecting NT usage (so Koester, "Purpose," 326), but in light of Rom 1:27 that seems to be an assertion over against the evidence itself.

42. Hawthorne, 166, suggests that ἡ κοιλία and ἡ δόξα serve as compound predicate nouns to the subject "God." But see the critique in Silva, 212.

43. Silva (210), following Gnilka, suggests that αἰσχύνη here refers neither to immoral behavior nor to circumcision, but should be read in light of 1:20 as referring to "the objective disgrace that falls on those who come under divine judgment." But the context is that of moral/immoral behavior (as both the *imitatio* motif and the verb "walk" make certain). It is the Pauline view that life in sin is a life of "shame" (Rom 6:21, "the things of which you are now ashamed"; cf. 2 Cor 4:2). More unlikely still is Mearns's view (see n. 36 above) that "shame" refers to the circumcised male organ. Athough he suggests he will support this view with detailed exegesis, he offers no (valid) linguistic grounds nor parallels.

44. Two passages may serve as background to Paul's use of this language. In Hos 4:7, God says, "I will make your glory (δόξα) into dishonor (ἀτιμίαν)"; in Sir 4:21, in a context of not being ashamed to be oneself, the proverb goes, "For there is a shame that leads to sin, and there is a shame (αἰσχύνη) that is glory (δόξα) and grace" (cf. Prov 26:11a LXX). Paul's clause reads ἡ δόξα ἐν τῇ αἰσχύνῃ αὐτῶν. His point seems very close to that of Hos 4:7, even if his language is not.

45. It takes considerable confidence in one's ability to read between the lines, not to mention the need to make several exegetical "jumps" (e.g., to see "glory" here as related to "boasting" in v. 3!) to see this clause (as does Martin et al.) in terms of the opponents' "glorying" in "their powerful presence as charismatic figures in the church, claiming to be a special breed of Christian who had 'arrived' " (145).

46. Those who take this view (the majority) see the shame as referring either to the genitals or the nakedness exposed during circumcision. This is even more circuitous than its predecessor. And in any case Paul never considers circumcision shameful. Rather, it is irrelevant. Therefore, even though Jews may continue to practice it, they may not impose it on Gentile converts.

readings of the text cause the presuppositions to put more weight on the language than it seems able to bear, since there is nothing elsewhere in Paul or in other sources that hint of such things.

(5) "Their mind is on earthly things." Here is where the whole has been heading right along. Two things are significant for understanding. First, Paul once more uses the crucial verb from 2:2-5 and 3:15. They do not simply "think about" earthly things; their "minds are set on" such things, which stands in pointed antithesis to Paul's own mindset as portrayed in his personal story. His mind is set altogether on Christ, who for Paul is life and for whom to die is gain. Second, what their minds are set on is "earthly things,"[47] which not only sums up the preceding two clauses but at the same time sets up the contrast that follows. Here is the second crucial matter. These people over whom Paul weeps are first of all "enemies of the cross"; they are now characterized as those who have abandoned the pursuit of the heavenly prize, in favor of what belongs *only* to the present scheme of things.[48] Their focus is altogether earthward, even if we cannot be sure of how that specifically works out in their case.

Thus this final clause sums up the former two; this is what it means finally to be given over to the "stomach" as one's deity and to "glory" in what should be shameful. By their fruit, Paul says, you will know them; by their focus you will also recognize that they are not walking according to the pattern of Christ and his apostle.

Who, then, are these people? Some things seem more certain than others: first, they are almost certainly to be understood as "insiders" in the sense defined above (as professing Christians from their own point of view, despite how Paul views them); second, they are unlikely to be the same as those mentioned in v. 2; third, they also seem unrelated to anything Paul says about "not having arrived" in vv. 12 and 15;[49] fourth, since they are "believers" after a fashion, they can scarcely be the same as those mentioned in 1:28; fifth, it is highly unlikely that they are members of the Philippian community. Moreover, the language "opponents" seems ill-suited to describe them. They

---

47. Gk. τὰ ἐπίγεια; used by Paul primarily in contrast to "heavenly" things (cf. 1 Cor 15:40; 2 Cor 5:1), but only here in a pejorative sense (cf. Jas 3:15). Koester ("Purpose," 328; followed by Jewett, "Conflicting Movements," 378-89) sees Paul's use of the phrase as an "ironic" twist of the view of his "opponents" (they were into "heavenly things," but Paul sees them as merely "earthly"); but that is to turn Paul's own usage on its head for the sake of a hypothesis which exists only by reading between the lines.

48. Cf. Col 3:2: "Set your minds (φρονεῖτε) on things above (τὰ ἄνω), not on earthly things (τὰ ἐπὶ τῆς γῆς)."

49. Those who think otherwise are dependent on two exegetical "jumps" to make it work: that Paul is speaking about "perfectionism" and that the specific brand of "perfectionism" is "spiritual" not ethical. Neither of these accords well with the data in the respective texts.

are enemies of the cross, to be sure, but that is because of the way they live, rejecting a cruciform existence and a sure future for present self-indulgence. Paul weeps over them, and warns the Philippians against them; but he does not set them up as personal "opponents."

Most likely, therefore, Paul is here picking up on the major concerns of his personal narrative in vv. 4-14, by reminding the Philippians again of some about whom he has often warned them in the past, who have left the way of the cross and have "set their minds" on present, earthly concerns. He is probably describing some itinerants, whose view of the faith is such that it allows them a great deal of undisciplined self-indulgence. Whether they have taken Paul's view of "justification by faith" to a libertine conclusion,[50] as many think, is plausible, but probably too specific in terms of what Paul actually says in the text. In any case, they have not appeared heretofore in the letter, and do not appear again. They have served their immediate purpose of standing in sharp relief to Paul's own "walk" and to his heavenly pursuit, so crucial to this letter, and toward which Paul now turns once more as he begins to draw this appeal to an end.

## 3. Basis of the Appeal — Heaven, Now and to Come (3:20-21)

20*But*[1] *our citizenship is in heaven. And we eagerly await a Savior from there, the Lord Jesus Christ,* 21*who, by the power that enables him to bring everything under his*[2] *control, will transform our lowly bodies so that they will be*[3] *like his glorious body.*

---

50. As the wag in the Middle Ages is reported to have put it: "The world is remarkably well arranged; I like to sin and God likes to forgive sin."

1. The difficulty with Paul's γάρ, reflected in the NIV's "but," is found in early versions as well (d e f g m goth arm eth syr) and in a few isolated citations in the Fathers (Clement, Origen, Eusebius, Chrysostom), who read "but" for γάρ. The "evidence" from the Fathers is nearly worthless in this case, since they seldom attempt to carry over into their citations the precision of the Greek particles (on this matter see Fee, "Use," 355 [guideline 5.4]). That no *Greek* manuscript evidence lies behind these expressions of "but" is made clear by the bilingual MSS Dd Ff Gg, where the Greek side reads γάρ, while the Latin has *autem*. Martin (147) is so focused on the contrastive note in these verses that he actually says Paul uses *de* to introduce his "counter-position."

2. For the sake of clarity (that Christ is the "him" throughout the sentence), a large number of later MSS (including L Ψ 6 104 326 630 1175) changed Paul's αὐτῷ (or αὑτῷ) to the reflexive ἑαυτῷ ("his own"). See the discussion in Metzger, *Textual Commentary,* 615-16.

3. The later MS tradition (MajT syr; Ambrosiaster) clarified Paul's compressed grammar (= "who will transform the body of our humiliation similar in form [σύμμορφον] to the body of his glory") by adding (εἰς τὸ γένεσθαι αὐτὸ = so that it will be) before σύμμορφον. The difficulty is reflected in the NIV, which translates by adding these very words to the English text, although they were wanting in the Greek text being translated.

This sentence serves as Paul's immediate response to those "many" who "walk" contrary to the Pauline pattern, who are ultimately judged because "their minds are set on earthly things."[4] It also concludes the long exhortation that began in 3:1,[5] returning to the theme of the eschatological prize (vv. 11-14) by underscoring its certainty.[6] Whatever the current threat was, and whatever its source, Paul has apparently sensed an ebb in their eschatological anticipation, a matter he has spoken to throughout the letter.[7] At the same time, by picking up the play on their "dual" citizenship (cf. 1:27), plus the final affirmation that "our Savior" (a common title for the emperor) is the one who will also bring "all things under his control," Paul puts their present situation — opposition in Philippi resulting in suffering — into divine perspective. All of this is said in a sentence that rises to extraordinary christological heights; not only is Christ the focus and center of everything, but his activities here are those ordinarily attributed to God the Father in Pauline soteriological texts.[8]

Here is a classic expression of the eschatological framework of Pauline theology, that present life is "already/not yet," predicated on Christ and his coming(s). Although the passage begins with the "already," the accent falls on the "not yet," thus giving perspective to the Philippians' present situation — and to much else in the letter. Christ has gained his present glory through humiliation (2:7-11); he is now "in heaven" where we "eagerly await" his coming as "Savior"; when he comes he will "transform" us into his "likeness," so that our present bodies that know weakness and "humiliation" are

4. This is recognized by most interpreters. Some (Koester, Collange, Martin, Lincoln) see it as a response to "a false enthusiasm"; but it is difficult to derive that from anything said explicitly by Paul himself (cf. n. 45 on v. 19 above).

5. The passage in fact has several significant linguistic ties to what has preceded: to 1:20 (that Christ will be magnified in Paul's "body" whether through life or death); to 1:27 ("citizenship"); to 2:4-11 ("humiliation, transform [μετασχηματίσει], conform [σύμμορφον], the Lord Jesus Christ"); and to 3:10 ("conform").

6. Given the role and emphasis of vv. 12-14 in Paul's personal narrative (vv. 4-14), Hawthorne's judgment (168) about these verses seems a bit strong ("Nothing that has immediately preceded . . . has prepared the reader for this kind of happy outburst"). Silva (213) rightly judges the alleged contextual difficulties lying behind such statements to "have been greatly exaggerated."

7. See on 1:6 and 10; cf. 1:20, 21-24, 26; 2:9-11, 16; 3:11, 12-14, 15-16, 17-19.

8. Which some see as "condemning it" as Pauline (e.g., Güttgemanns, Strecker, Becker; see next n.). This is a remarkable judgment, since Paul himself dictated what is said here; and as noted on 2:6-11 (n. 3), methodologically we must assume as self-evident that what the apostle dictates for the hearing of the Philippians he also affirms — all the more so, one would think, when the passage brings this hortatory section that began in v. 1 (or at least v. 2) to its resounding conclusion. It is little wonder that the idea of a pre-Pauline, and therefore non-Pauline, hymn fragment has found such a small hearing in this case.

conformed into the likeness of his present "glory"; and he will accomplish that in keeping with the same divine "energy" (cf. 2:13) whereby he will also subject "all things" to himself (= "every knee shall bow").

Because of the exalted nature of this passage and its linguistic connections to 2:6-11, some see here another possible piece of pre-Pauline material (n. 8);[9] but as with the former passage, and even more so in this case, here is vintage Paul, whose thoroughly eschatological outlook and christological focus repeatedly merge in climactic moments like this.[10] For him to live is Christ; to die is to gain Christ; better yet is to be among those who participate in the Parousia of Christ.[11] If this were an Apocalypse, here would be the place to say, "even so, come Lord Jesus," and close the book. But this is a "hortatory letter of friendship,"[12] so Paul concludes as we should well expect, by drawing out the twofold consequences of this concluding word to their situation: first, that in light of such "glory," the Philippians (his "eschatological joy and crown") remain "steadfast *in the Lord*" (4:1); and second, that those who are primarily responsible for friction in the community "have the same mindset *in the Lord*" (4:2).

**20**   The relationship of this sentence to what has preceded is brought out by the second explanatory "for" in as many sentences.[13] The emphasis

---

9. For this point of view see Lohmeyer (150), Flanagan ("Note"), Güttgemanns (*Der leidende Apostel,* 240-47), G. Strecker ("Redaktion," 75-78), Becker ("Erwägungen"), Müller (*Prophetie,* 190-96), Hawthorne (168-70), Reumann ("Hymnic Fragment"); see Reumann (594-97) for a helpful survey of this development in (mostly German) NT scholarship. Cf. the critiques in Gundry, *SŌMA,* 177-83; Lincoln, *Paradise,* 87-89; and O'Brien, 467-72.

10. See, e.g., 1 Thess 1:9-10; 5:9-10; 2 Thess 2:13-14; 2 Cor 1:21-22; Gal 4:4-7; Rom 5:1-5. It is not surprising that most of these have been called into question, even though they are available only through Pauline dictation and none can be found in any other source. It is of some interest that this judgment is made at every lyrical or liturgical moment in Paul; apparently Paul is prejudged as incapable of such creativity, which may say more about the pedestrian nature of most Western theology than it does about the apostle! This does not mean that he was not drawing on available creedal or liturgical material (as, e.g., Lincoln, *Paradise,* 89), but that the sentence in its present form is a Pauline composition, which did not have prior existence in this form.

11. *Contra* many who assert otherwise about Paul's hopes in this letter, mostly by those who are convinced that Paul expects to die (e.g., Bruce, 134), despite what he plainly says to the contrary; see the discussion on 1:23-24.

12. See the Introduction, pp. 2-7; cf. on 1:12.

13. Gk. γάρ; see on v. 18. For this double γάρ, where a second clause further explains or elaborates the primary clause by way of the preceding clause ("Watch for those who walk thus, as you have us for an example; *for* many walk otherwise, . . . whose minds are set on earthly things; *for* our citizenship is in heaven"), see 1 Thess 3:3-4; 1 Cor 2:10-11; 9:15-16; Gal 1:11-12; et al. As in 1 Cor 2:10, to translate this as "but," as though it were related only in a contrastive way to what has immediately preceded, rather than in

is twofold; first, over against those who walk contrary to Paul and whose "minds are set on earthly things," Paul says, "*our*[14] citizenship is in heaven." He says "for" rather than "but," because, secondly, he is offering the ultimate reason for their following his example and for looking out for others who do so as well (v. 17). "For," he now explains, "our citizenship (hence our focus) is *in heaven*"[15] and our future is "glory" — in contrast to those whose "end" is destruction since they live only for the present.[16]

The linkage between this concluding word and v. 17 is also brought out by his returning to the inclusive "we" (see vv. 3 and 15-16), common to Pauline soteriological moments where the truth of the gospel *embraces him as well.* Perhaps we should say, in light of vv. 12-14, that Paul is now making sure that the Philippians recognize themselves as *included with him* as participants in the eschatological prize.

This is the second play on their Roman citizenship[17] in this letter; and

---

an explanatory way, is to miss Paul's grammar for our own inclinations (cf. n. 1 above). Loh-Nida are bold: " 'For' is not a natural connective with the previous verse. It is therefore best rendered as *however*" — and that despite the total lack of lexical evidence supporting an adversarial understanding of γάρ.

14. Gk. ἡμῶν γάρ, where the "our" stands in the emphatic first position, intending the strongest kind of contrast to "them." Cf. 1:28 and 3:3, where the identical thing happens. On the rare "vernacular possessive" in Paul, see on 2:2.

15. Gk. ἐν οὐρανοῖς; the plural reflects Jewish usage (which reflects the Hebrew plural found most often in liturgical texts). That the concept is singular for Paul is evidenced by the singular relative pronoun that follows. For a discussion of the "heavenly dimension" in Pauline thought, see Lincoln, *Paradise,* esp. the concluding chapter (169-95); see also U. Schoenborn, *EDNT,* 3.543-47.

16. Michael (177-78), who adopts a partition theory for chap. 3, sees the interpolation to end with v. 19 (mostly because he recognizes that the linguistic ties of vv. 20-21 to 2:6-11 are too significant to exclude those verses from the letter containing the latter — a point that goes begging with most who adopt a partition theory). Hence he is unimpressed by any of the links noted between vv. 20-21 and 17-19, and finds no explanation of the γάρ satisfactory. His presentation has the net effect of illustrating the extreme difficulties for all theories of interpolation.

17. Gk. πολίτευμα; cf. 1:27, where Paul used the cognate verb as his primary imperative in that appeal (for the interchange of that verb for this noun see the sentence in *Ep. Diog.* cited in n. 20 below). The word itself can refer either to the "constitution" by which a state is governed or for the "state" or "commonwealth" itself. The meaning "colony" can be found, the concept of "citizenship" itself is poorly attested, while "homeland" (as Lohmeyer, Beare, Hendriksen) is without support. In the present instance "colony" will not do as a translation (although the effects of that imagery are not far from what Paul is getting at), since the believers' πολίτευμα is in heaven, not on earth. Most likely Paul is using the term in its most common hellenistic sense of "commonwealth." But both the former word play in 1:27 and the present context of "walking" in righteousness imply that if their present "commonwealth" is in heaven, their "already/not yet" existence on earth is that of "citizens" of that heavenly commonwealth. Hence in terms of their

378

here it is a bold stroke indeed. Paul is not herewith renouncing their common citizenship in the earthly "commonwealth" of Rome; on the contrary, that citizenship is what will make the present sentence ring the changes for the Philippians. Citizens of the Roman "commonwealth" they may well be, and proudly so; but the greater reality is that they are subjects of the heavenly "Lord" and "Savior," Jesus Christ, and therefore their true "commonwealth" exists[18] in heaven.[19]

And they are citizens of the heavenly commonwealth "already," even as they await the consummation that is "not yet."[20] Although Paul's language will not quite allow the translation, "we are a colony of heaven" (Moffatt), the point of the imagery comes very close to that. Just as Philippi was a colony of Rome, whose citizens thereby exemplified the life of Rome in the province of Macedonia, so the citizens of the "heavenly commonwealth" were to function as a colony of heaven in that outpost of Rome. That this is Paul's concern lies in the context. They are to imitate Paul in their "walk," because ("for") their true "commonwealth" is in heaven; as such they live God's righteousness as an outpost of heaven in Philippi. And that life is cruciform in expression, which knows Christ in the power of his resurrection and participation in his sufferings, by being "conformed" to his death on the cross. Thus this passage serves as the basis for the preceding appeals, as well as for those that follow (calling for "steadfastness" and "unity").

This is the "already," and the emphasis in the preceding appeals rests

---

being constituted as the people of God who have a heavenly "commonwealth" that is both "already" and "not yet," Paul emphasizes their *commonwealth* that is in heaven; but in terms of their own participation in that heavenly commonwealth, both now and to come, it is their being *citizens* of that commonwealth that is in view here (similarly, Silva, 214). The primary discussion of the word is by W. Ruppel, "Politeuma." For a helpful overview see esp. Lincoln, *Paradise,* 97-100 (although the usage in 1:27 calls into question whether Paul is here taking over the language of "opponents," as Gnilka, Lincoln, et al. contend; cf. the critique by Reumann, "Hymnic Fragment," 605). The use of this word, which (a) corresponds to the usage in 1:27, (b) fits the Philippian situation specifically, and (c) is not found elsewhere in the NT, not to mention Paul, is especially damaging to the theory of a pre-Pauline hymn fragment (n. 8 above; cf. Gundry, *SŌMA,* 178).

18. Gk. ὑπάρχει; for this verb see on 2:6 above. As several point out, this usage, rather than a form of "to be," is probably significant, in that it emphasizes the actual existence of our heavenly commonwealth.

19. As Barth points out regarding this imagery, it reflects "a judicial order which at once both obliges and protects [people]."

20. Cf. the anonymous *Ep. Diog.* 5.9 (ἐπὶ γῆς διατρίβουσιν, ἀλλ' ἐν οὐρανῷ πολιτεύονται, "[Christians] go about their business on earth, but they live as citizens of heaven"), which is almost certainly dependent on a combination of this text and 1:27 (which also serves as evidence that the verb in 1:27 and this noun were understood to reflect the same reality).

here. But the ultimate concern is with the "not yet," with their living in the present as those in pursuit of the heavenly prize. Thus the rest of the sentence focuses on his and their sure future, which focuses altogether on their heavenly "Lord and Savior." The fact that their "commonwealth" already exists in heaven, and that they await their Savior from there, points to their divine vindication, to the full realization of what is "not yet," even though living out their heavenly citizenship "already" has led to persecution. Three points are made: (1) Our present citizenship is already "in heaven" from whence we "eagerly await [the coming of] our Savior," who is none other than "the Lord, Jesus Christ," the one who had the name "Lord" bestowed on him at his exaltation (2:9); thus Paul focuses first of all on the coming of Christ as the eschatological Lord and Savior. (2) At his coming Christ will "transform" the bodies of our present "humiliation," by "conforming" them into the likeness of his present "body of glory"; thus Paul also emphasizes the great "eschatological reversal" that they (and we) shall experience at his coming, that Christ himself experienced at his resurrection and exaltation. (3) He will do this "in keeping with the power" by which he is able to (and will) also subject all things to himself, thus emphasizing his absolute sovereignty over all things, including those in Philippi — and their "lord and savior," the emperor.

(1) While the language of this clause does not specify Christ's Parousia (coming), what Paul says does in fact presuppose it. First, we eagerly await him "from heaven,"[21] which can only mean, his Parousia from heaven; and second, we "eagerly await" him, a verb used exclusively by Paul in connection with the coming of Christ at the eschatological "wrap up."[22] By this verb Paul harks back to his own "eager pursuit" of the heavenly prize (vv. 12-14), likewise emphasizing how he lives in the present with his focus constantly on the goal.

Significantly, both for his readers' context and for our understanding of Paul's christology, the one whom we "eagerly await" is called "Savior."[23]

---

21. Gk. ἐξ οὗ καί. The "from whence" modifies "in heaven" (*contra* Jones, Lohmeyer, et al., who are troubled by the singular pronoun and suggest that its antecedent is πολίτευμα); the "also" (καί) functions to get the "not yet" part of the sentence under way.

22. Gk. ἀπεκδεχόμεθα; cf. 1 Cor 1:7; Gal 5:5; Rom 8:19, 23, 25 (elsewhere in the NT in Heb 9:28, also an eschatological context, and 1 Pet 3:20). This rare compound (intensifying ἐκδέχομαι [await] with ἀπό) appears for the first time in Greek literature in 1 Cor 1:7; it was probably coined by someone in the early church (perhaps Paul himself) to emphasize either the certainty of their expectation or, more likely, to express the eagerness with which they awaited Christ's coming.

23. Gk. σωτῆρα, which stands in the emphatic first position (the object before the verb) and without the definite article. But it is doubtful that Paul intended merely "*a*

The significance is highlighted by its rarity in Paul; only once heretofore (Eph 5:23) has he used this title to describe Christ.[24] That he does so here is almost certainly for the Philippians' sakes, since this is a common title for Caesar.[25] That he does so at all is especially significant christologically, since the title occurs frequently in the OT to refer to God our (my) Savior. As with the title "Lord," therefore (cf. 2:9-10), Paul has co-opted yet another OT term for God and unflinchingly attributed it to Christ. None of this would be missed by the Philippians, who know the term well in both of its contexts.

The clincher to all of this — as far as Paul's word of reassurance to the Philippians is concerned — is the final, otherwise unnecessary, appositive, "the Lord Jesus Christ," in which he picks up the precise language (including word order) from 2:11, the only two absolute uses of this combination in the letter. The Savior, they are thus reminded, is none other than "the Lord, Jesus Christ" himself, whose lordship every tongue will confess at the eschatological denouement. Here is the ultimate reason for their rejoicing *in the Lord.* The Lord is the Savior, by whose grace they have been redeemed and whose coming they eagerly anticipate, even as in their present suffering they are being "conformed into his likeness."

**21** (2) This second clause, "who will transform our lowly bodies so that they shall be like his glorious body," focuses on the way in which Christ will function as eschatological Savior. Although Paul's language is quite different here, the concept itself is to be understood in light of what Paul had written earlier to the Corinthians (1 Cor 15:42-57), in a context where some

---

Savior," as some contend. Rather the anarthrous usage is emphatic, as with the anarthrous κύριον Ἰησοῦν Χριστόν that follows. This is probably a variation on "Colwell's rule," that a definite predicate noun that precedes the verb is usually anarthrous (in this case a definite direct object, followed by an apposition, seems to function analogously).

24. Although it becomes more common in the letters that follow this one; see Tit 1:4; 3:6 (some would add 2:13); 2 Tim 1:10 (a context very much like this one). Many (e.g., Beare, Koester, Collange, O'Brien) emphasize the usage as reflecting Paul's use of the verb "save," which, it is alleged, is used exclusively to refer to the future of eschatological salvation. But that is simply not so, as 1 Cor 1:21; 15:2; Rom 8:25; and Eph 2:5 and 8 bear clear witness.

25. Cf. Foerster, *TDNT,* 7.1010-12. In its hellenistic derivation the term refers to anyone who "saves" or delivers, thus it has nothing to do with being "saved from sin" but with being delivered and protected, either by the gods (thus it is variously applied to Zeus, Apollo, Poseidon, Heracles, Asclepius, and Sarapis) or significant human figures (e.g., Pompey, the emperors). Caesar is thus called "the Savior of the World," Augustus himself being "the Savior of Humankind." K. H. Schelkle (*EDNT,* 3.326-27) denies that the usage here has any reference to the emperor, but the fact that it occurs in a sentence that deliberately places their "commonwealth" in heaven, from whence they await their true "Savior," seems to weigh more heavily in favor of the view espoused here; cf. Perkins, "Philippians," 93-94.

were denying a future, bodily resurrection of believers. The contrasts there were between our present bodies as perishable and "natural" (and when dead "sown in dishonor and weakness") and the transformed heavenly body as imperishable and "supernatural"[26] (and raised in "glory" and "power"); the present bodies are thus to be transformed into the "likeness" of the "man of heaven," who already bears such a body through his resurrection. And although the emphasis in that passage is on the resurrection per se, Paul concludes by emphasizing that the same transformation will occur for those living until the Parousia.

Apart from the words "body" and "glory," however, none of that language carries over into the present passage, which is here adapted to reflect the present emphases. The verb for "transformation" *(meta-schēma-tizō)*[27] and the adjective "conformed" *(sum-morphon)* pick up the language of 2:6-8, where Christ, who was in the "form" *(morphē)* of God, assumed the "form" of a slave in coming in the "likeness" *(schēma)* of human beings. Not only so, but the adjective "conformed" is the cognate of the verb that appeared in 3:10; those who are currently being "conformed" to Christ's death are someday to be "conformed" to his present glory. Moreover, the genitive describing our present bodies ("of humiliation") further echoes the "humiliation" of Christ in 2:8,[28] which expressed itself through "death on a cross." Finally, the body of the future is described as "the body of Christ's glory," the word which concludes the Christ narrative in 2:11, that Christ's present exaltation

---

26. For this as the proper contrast between ψυχικὸν σῶμα and πνευματικὸν σῶμα, as bodies "adapted to the present, natural, life and to the final eschatological life of the Spirit," see Fee, *Presence,* 262-64.

27. The verb means basically, "change the form of," hence "transform" or "change." For Pauline usage see 2 Cor 11:13, 14, 15; the usage in 1 Cor 4:6 is especially difficult. See the discussion by J. M. Nützel in *EDNT,* 2.419.

28. The genitive (ταπεινώσεως) is not descriptive (as the NIV, "lowly"), but expresses "belonging." The "our" and "his" in both cases go with "humiliation" and "glory" respectively, not with "body." Thus it is not "our lowly bodies," but "the body that belongs to our humiliation," or that "belongs to his glory." Thus, the body itself is not "lowly" but is the locus of present suffering and weakness, hence "the body of our present humiliation" in contrast to the body that shall be ours "in glory." Paul is not expressing contempt for the body, neither in the form found in the KJV ("our vile bodies"), which sounds far more dualistic than Paul could ever be, nor that suggested by Kennedy (463), that it refers to "the unfitness of the present bodily nature to fulfill the claims of the spiritual life" (it is not *sinful,* but full of weakness). After all, this is something Paul could well have said of Christ in his incarnation! It is also unlikely that this expression is "anti-Gnostic" (as Schmithals) or "anti-enthusiastic" (as Gnilka, Martin); the "Gnostics" have denied the body altogether, Paul is alleged here to be affirming it by way of polemical contrast. None of these suggestions takes seriously enough the linguistic ties with 2:6-11, while the latter must read a great deal more into the passage than Paul actually expresses (see n. 45 on v. 19).

as Lord of all will all redound to God's "glory," which is the word that also reminds the reader of the immediate context (of the "shameful glory" of those who are destined for destruction).[29] If those who have made a god of their bellies thus "glory" in their shame, we too have glory, but it is a coming glory, in which our present earthly existence is transformed into the likeness of Christ's own glory.

As to the future itself, two points are made: First, Christ's present existence is "bodily" in the sense of 1 Corinthians 15, that the "body" is the point of continuity between the present and the future; but the "form" that body has taken is the point of discontinuity — a "mystery" for Paul, but adapted to the final life of the Spirit, hence a "supernatural body," or as here, "the body of his [present] glory."[30] Second, the same future awaits those who are his, which is Paul's present concern. Our present lot, he has argued in 1:29-30, and alluded to in 2:17, is to "suffer for Christ's sake." But we can "rejoice in the Lord" in the midst of such suffering (2:18; 3:1; 4:4) because that suffering itself is enabled by "the power of his resurrection" (3:10), which resurrection at the same time guarantees our certain future. Hence in our present "humiliation" we await the coming of the Savior, and with that coming the transformation of our humiliation into the likeness of his glory. That is worth the eager pursuit of vv. 12-14.

(3) Finally, the power by which Christ will bring about this transformation is "in keeping with[31] the working that enables him also to bring everything under his control." In some ways this is the most remarkable "transformation" of all, in that Paul here uses language about Christ that he

---

29. As Michael recognized (see n. 16 above), these linguistic ties are such that it makes theories of interpolation which include these verses in the interpolated matter very difficult to sustain. On the other hand, while one is intrigued by the suggestion that this sentence is the next phase of the "Christ-hymn" of 2:6-11 (vv. 6-8, Christ becoming as us; vv. 9-11, what he now is; 3:20-21, his making us like him; as Hooker, "Interchange," 356-57), it is not finally demonstrable.

30. Even more than with the preceding genitive (see n. 28), it is especially doubtful whether Paul intended "glorious body," as though he were describing the nature of the new body itself. Paul's point is not the *nature* of this body, but that it is the body that is Christ's by virtue of his present glorified state. Vincent (121; followed by Plummer, 85) rightly says that this translation "dilutes and weakens the conception," not to mention causes the reader to miss the contrast with v. 19.

31. Gk. κατά; see Fee, *Presence*, 481 n. 24, for a discussion and rejection of the view that this preposition ever functions in a purely instrumental way. This is especially so here; not only does the preposition *not* denote instrumentality (*pace* NIV, NASB, NRSV, NAB, REB, NJB), but what it *does* convey is the "norm" or "standard" in keeping with which something is done. Hence Paul intends not "by the working" but "in keeping with that working" that is already recognized to have been at work in his own resurrection/transformation.

elsewhere uses only of God the Father. First, it is "in keeping with the working,"[32] which is then defined, "that enables him also to subject all things to himself." Second, the phrase "able to subject all things to himself" is Paul's eschatological interpretation of Ps 8:7, where God will "subject all things" to his Messiah, who in turn, according to 1 Cor 15:28, will turn over all things to God the Father so that "God might be all and in all." Remarkably, in the present passage the "subjecting" of all things to himself is said to be by Christ's own power.

The little word "also" is much too important to be omitted, as in many English translations.[33] Here is the final word of assurance to the Philippians. In keeping with the same power by which he will transform their present bodies that are suffering at the hand of opposition in Philippi, Christ will *likewise* subject "all things"[34] to himself, including the emperor himself and all those who in his name are causing the Philippians to suffer. As Paul has already said in 1:28 and implied in 3:19, their own salvation "from God" will at the same time result in the "destruction" of the opposition.

It simply cannot be said any better than that — for them or for us. This passage reminds us that, despite appearances often to the contrary, God is in control, that our salvation is not just for today but forever, that Christ is coming again, and that at his coming we inherit the final glory that belongs to Christ alone — and to those who are his. It means the final subjugation of all the "powers" to him as well, especially those responsible for the present affliction of God's people.[35] With Paul we would do well not merely to "await" the end, but eagerly to press on toward the goal, since the final prize is but the consummation of what God has already accomplished through the death and resurrection of our Savior, Jesus Christ the Lord.

---

32. Gk. κατὰ τὴν ἐνέργειαν; cf. Eph 3:7, κατὰ τὴν ἐνέργειαν τῆς δυνάμεως αὐτοῦ ("in keeping with the working of his power"; also Eph 1:19, "in keeping with the working of his might," and 3:20, "in keeping with the power that is at work in us"), texts referring to the way God's power is (or will be) tangibly at work in the world. The verb occurred in Phil 2:13 of God's working all things in/among them for his good pleasure.

33. Cf. NIV, GNB, NAB, REB; translated "also" in NRSV, or "even" in RSV, NASB, NJB.

34. Gk. τὰ πάντα, used by Paul when he wants to refer to the whole of the created universe or the whole of a given subject; for present usage cf. 1 Cor 8:6 (2x); 15:27-28 (4x); and Rom 11:36. The present passage is a direct reflection of the argument of 1 Cor 15:25-28.

35. This was "penned" in late April, 1994, when thousands of believers in Rwanda were suffering in the midst of a terrible civil war. Such realities are a constant reminder that Philippians is not "ivory tower" stuff, but was written to realities unlike those of most of us who write commentaries on such passages. It is hard not to believe that Rwandan Christians hear texts like this better than do many of us whose lives have currently fallen in more pleasant places.

## 4. Final Appeals — To Steadfastness and Unity (4:1-3)

1*Therefore, my brothers [and sisters,]*[1] *you whom I love and long for, my joy and crown, that is how you should stand firm in the Lord, dear friends*[2]*!*

2*I plead with Euodia and I plead with Syntyche to agree with each other in the Lord.* 3*Yes, and I ask you, [true companion*[3]*],*[a] *help these women who have contended at my side in the cause of the gospel, along with Clement and the rest of my co-workers,*[4] *whose names are in the book of life.*

[a]Or *loyal Syzygus*

With these two appeals Paul brings 3:1-21 to its proper conclusion. At the same time he reaches further back into the letter to bring closure to the twin issues raised in 1:27–2:18 — that they "remain steadfast" in the gospel and do so "as one person in the one Spirit." The appeals belong together;[5] they are expressed with great skill, full of indicators that Philippians is a "hortatory letter of friendship."[6]

The first appeal (v. 1)[7] is directed toward the whole community; simultaneously it (a) applies the immediately preceding word of eschatological

---

1. See n. 9 on 1:12.

2. This final word, ἀγαπητοί, is a repetition of the vocative the NIV translates "whom I love." It has been omitted by D* pc a b (as a translational phenomenon as well?); B 33 syᵖ add a μου ("my").

3. NIV, "loyal yokefellow"; Gk. γνήσιε σύζυγε. Since it is possible, though unlikely, that Paul is addressing Lydia here, the English rendering needs to be more open-ended. For further discussion, and the semantic unlikelihood of the NIV's "loyal," see n. 40 below (cf. n. 44).

4. NIV, "fellow workers." In place of Paul's τῶν λοιπῶν συνεργῶν μου, P16vid and ℵ* read τῶν συνεργῶν μου καὶ τῶν λοιπῶν ("my co-workers and the rest"), evidently concerned to include the whole community in the final eschatological affirmation (rather than simply "scribal inadvertence," as Metzger, *Textual Commentary,* 617). Silva (223) is willing to give this patently secondary reading more consideration than it deserves. P16 and ℵ* bear common witness to the same alteration of the text. Since that (more inclusive) reading makes perfectly good sense, how, if it were original, does one explain its being changed so early and often (across all textual traditions) to the more exclusive reading?

5. Noted also by Hawthorne, 178.

6. On this matter, see the Introduction, pp. 2-7.

7. One of the more bizarre results of partition theories is to be found in Beare's commentary. In the Introduction (p. 24) he includes 4:1 in his letter 1 (3:2–4:1); but in the commentary itself he omits this verse altogether, apparently resulting from the way he reconstructs his letter 3 (1:1–3:1; 4:2-9, 21-23).

hope[8] to the Philippian situation,[9] (b) recalls the primary exhortation of 1:27 with which the hortatory sections of the letter began,[10] and (c) leads into the specific appeal of vv. 2-3.[11] The second appeal (vv. 2-3) is directed specifically toward two named women; closely linked to the first by its grammar, word order, and repetition of "in the Lord,"[12] the sentence recalls the exhortation to unity in 2:2, while it also echoes "contending alongside [me, in this case] in the cause of the gospel" (1:27).

Here, then, is the case-specific wrapup both of the earlier exhortation in 1:27 and of both hortatory sections of the letter (1:27–2:18; 3:1-21). The concerns have been threefold, "steadfastness" and "unity," as they contend for the gospel in Philippi in the face of opposition. All three of these found expression in the initial exhortation in 1:27:

(1) that you stand firm
(2) in the one Spirit, as one person
(3) contending for the faith of the gospel

The third item is the backdrop — indeed, the urgency — of the whole, while the two hortatory sections of the letter take up items (1) and (2), but in reverse order (2:1-16 is primarily concerned with their unity, 3:1-21 with their standing firm). The present appeals bring closure to all of this by repeating the primary verbs

8. Meyer thinks v. 1 concludes vv. 17-21 only; whereas Jones skips the latter verses altogether in the interest of making it go back to 1:27–2:18. Both views are too constrictive.

9. By means of the inferential conjunction ὥστε ("so then"; cf. 2:12) and the eschatological vocatives, "my joy and crown." Some striking similarities between this appeal and that of 2:12-13 should also be noted: Both apply what has immediately preceded directly to the situation in Philippi (2:6-11 in the first instance, 3:20-21 here); and both presuppose their surrounding exhortations (1:27–2:5 and 3:15-19, "*thus* stand fast") and therefore themselves take the form of appeal (by way of imperative). Cf. Becker, "Erwägungen," 16-18 (endorsed by Reumann, "Hymnic Fragment," 598), who also notes these parallels.

10. The verb στήκετε occurs only here and in 1:27 in this letter; on the other hand, the concern expressed in this verb lies behind the whole of 3:1-21.

11. Partly by the lavish expressions of affection, which ease him into the appeal in v. 2; and partly by relationship of vv. 1-3 to the earlier appeals in 1:27–2:5. Just as the initial appeal to "stand firm" (1:27) was expressed in conjunction with an appeal for unity, so here the imperative "stand firm" is immediately followed by the concluding appeal in the letter, that Euodia and Syntyche "have the same mindset" (2:2).

12. Thus Paul's sentences read (literally): "In this way *stand firm in the Lord,* beloved. Euodia I entreat and Syntyche I entreat to *have the same mindset in the Lord.*" The grammar has to do with the asyndeton of v. 2 (lack of a nuancing connective; see on 3:1-2). The word order is marked by the name Euodia appearing immediately following the final vocative, the repeated ἀγαπητοί ("beloved"), which suggests that the proper name is not so much in the emphatic first position in its own sentence as that it was purposely brought forward to be heard immediately following the repetition of "beloved."

from the former exhortations ("stand firm" [1:27] and "have the same mindset" [2:2, 5; 3:15, 19]), concluding finally with a very case-specific application, toward which everything has apparently been heading from the beginning.[13]

The most striking features of the two appeals are related directly to matters of friendship. In v. 1 this takes the form of the remarkable elaboration of the vocative, where the ordinary "brothers and sisters" becomes *"my* brothers and sisters, *beloved and longed for, my joy and crown,"* the appeal itself being followed by the repetition of *"beloved."* This profusion of modifiers reminds them once again of his deep feelings for them, as well as of his deep concern for their present and future. In v. 2 friendship takes the form of Paul's actually naming two women and appealing to another member of the community to come to their aid, while repeating the appeal "to have the same mindset."

**1** For the "so then"[14] with which this appeal begins, see on 2:12 above. As there and elsewhere in his letters, Paul uses this conjunction specifically to apply the preceding "argument" to the local situation. But in this case the application nearly gets lost in the profusion of vocatives, which are emphatic and move in two directions. First, Paul modifies the standard "brothers and sisters"[15] with terms of friendship from earlier in the letter. They are his "beloved[16] and longed for[17] brothers and sisters." If the preceding exhortation has at times sounded strong, here he assuages any of that by reminding them of their first relationship, of his love for them that carries with it a deep longing for them, both to be with them and to know that even in his absence they are remaining steadfast in the Lord. So much does this relational concern matter to him that he repeats — awkwardly from the perspective of grammar, but effectively from the perspective of relationship — the vocative "beloved" at the end of the imperative. In any other letter, one might think he was trying too hard; but here, in returning to think about them more specifically, he

---

13. Cf. Garland, "Composition," 172-73; but I doubt whether to this point "Paul has *covertly* addressed the *dissension that had sundered the unity* of the church," so that all the rest of the letter has led to this "pastoral *confrontation* of these two women" (172, emphases mine to indicate points of disagreement). For a different reason for naming names, see the discussion below (and nn. 24 and 25).

14. Gk. ὥστε; see n. 7 on 2:12. As noted there, this conjunction is used by Paul when he intends to apply a preceding argument to their specific situation.

15. See on 1:12 above; cf. 3:1, 13, 17 in the immediately preceding exhortation. The present passage is the clear evidence that even though expressed in the generic masculine plural, Paul intends "brothers and sisters" with his vocative, since in this case he immediately, without a break and with asyndeton, speaks directly to two of the sisters.

16. Gk. ἀγαπητοί; for this word see on 2:12 above (n. 9).

17. Gk. ἐπιπόθητοί, a NT hapax legomenon and (understandably, given its strangeness as a noun) otherwise relatively rare word in Greek literature. The adjective is formed from the verb ἐπιποθέω, for which see on 1:8 and 2:26 above. This is one of the standard motifs in letters of friendship in antiquity; see Stowers, "Friends," 109.

simply cannot stop the flood of affectionate terms that characterizes his feelings toward them.[18]

The second set of vocatives is eschatological, which are as prospective as the former are retrospective.[19] As in a similar context in 1 Thess 2:19, where these same appellations occur, the Philippians are also "my [eschatological] joy and crown [of boasting]." Although the bracketed words do not appear in the text, on the basis of what Paul has said in the other passages this is certainly his intent.[20] Of course they are his present "joy" as well; but in this context he is pointing to the time when, along with the Thessalonians and others of his converts and friends, they will stand together with him in the presence of Christ. The joy is first of all over their being there at all; but they are also *"my* joy" in the sense of deep personal fulfillment at their being there with him. And therefore they will serve as his victor's "crown."[21] With this second set of modifiers, therefore, Paul adds a further reason for their standing fast (in the present) so as to achieve the eschatological prize (3:12-21); as his own converts and dear friends, they will function as his eschatological crown, and thus his joy at Christ's appearing (cf. 2:16).

Following this piling up of endearing vocatives, the application itself takes the form of appeal, repeating the imperative from 1:27, but with the modifiers "thus" and "in the Lord."[22] During their present distress they are to "stand fast *in the Lord,*" firmly planted in relationship with the same Lord whose coming they eagerly await and who will then subject all things to himself (3:20-21). And they are to *"thus* stand firm" (NIV, "that is how"), referring probably to the whole of 3:1-21, but especially to their "imitation" of Paul by their upright "walk" even as they bend every effort to attain the eschatological prize.[23] With these words, then, Paul renews the appeal to

---

18. It would be unfortunate indeed if, in recognizing that Paul is here using language common to friendship in the Greco-Roman world, one were to see this as a merely formal phenomenon and not the outpouring of his heart for his friends.

19. O'Brien thinks otherwise, that all of these modifiers refer to the present. But this usage is so singularly that of 1 Thess 2:19 and so closely follows 3:20-21 that it is hard not to see them as eschatological (as most interpreters).

20. This is especially in keeping with what he has already said in 2:16, that they are his "grounds for boasting for the day of Christ."

21. Gk. στέφανος, used by Paul literally in 1 Cor 9:25 to refer to the "crown" (usually made of dried celery leaves) worn by the victor in an athletic contest, deliberately contrasted, as "perishing," with the "imperishable crown" that believers will wear on the day of coronation. Thus he uses it figuratively here and in 1 Thess 2:19 to refer to his own "crown," in both cases denoting the presence of his converts with him at the coming of the Lord.

22. On the appearance of this phrase in Philippians see on 1:13 (nn. 28, 29). Here it can only be locative, indicating the sphere in which they are to stand fast, namely in their relationship to the Lord.

23. Lohmeyer, followed by Hawthorne, sees this οὕτως as pointing forward to vv.

steadfastness with which the exhortations in this letter began (1:27), but does so by way of the more recent exhortation (3:15-21).

**2** Having addressed the congregation with words of endearment and eschatological hope in v. 1, Paul now proceeds (in vv. 2-3) to make his final appeal, which is where much of the letter has been heading right along. But because the situation here addressed is so case-specific, we are left in the dark about much: who Euodia and Syntyche are, the nature of their disagreement, and who the "true companion" is. Nonetheless, the reason for this final appeal and its function in the letter are reasonably clear; and some good guesses can be made about the specifics.

For the Pauline letters, this is a remarkable moment indeed, since Paul does here what he seldom does elsewhere in "conflict" settings — he names names. In a media-saturated culture like ours, where naming the guilty or the grand is a way of life, it is hard for us to sense how extraordinary this moment is. Apart from greetings and the occasional mention of his co-workers or envoys, Paul rarely ever mentions anyone by name.[24] But here he does, and not because Euodia and Syntyche are the "bad ones" who need to be singled out; precisely the opposite, here are long-time friends and co-workers, leaders in the believing community in Philippi,[25] who have fallen on some bad times in terms of their "doing the gospel."[26] That he names them at all is evidence of friendship, since one of the marks of "enmity" in

---

2-9; but that seems to miss the force of the ὥστε and the link with 1:27. Pauline usage seems decisive (cf. 2 Thess 3:17; 1 Cor 7:17; 9:24; 11:28; 15:11; Gal 6:2). Without the extended vocative Paul's sentence reads, ὥστε οὕτως στήκετε ἐν κυρίῳ. Paul uses ὥστε like this only to apply a preceding argument. The οὕτως, therefore, must point backward, just as the ὥστε does. Silva and O'Brien would have it both ways, i.e., pointing backward primarily, but also forward; but that, too, seems doubtful. How would the hearer/reader know?

24. Indeed, one can think of a good number of exegetical puzzles that might never have arisen had he done so! The exceptions: Hymenaeus and Alexander (1 Tim 1:20; cf. 2 Tim 2:18); and perhaps Crispus, Gaius, and Stephanas (1 Cor 1:14-15), although one is not at all sure in the latter case that they are part of the controversy itself. Cf. Garland ("Composition," 172-73) and O'Brien, who have also noted this unusual feature, although O'Brien makes nothing further of it and Garland takes it in a quite different direction (see n. 13). As noted below, it is best explained as a feature of friendship.

25. Evidenced not only by the language of v. 3, but by the fact that he names them at all; *contra* Garland ("Composition," 172), who sees it as "pastoral confrontation."

26. I put it this way, rather than in terms of personal conflict, since this seems to be Paul's own concern whenever he speaks to this issue in the letter. See the discussion below (and n. 35). L. M. White ("Morality," 214 n. 59) "suspects" that "one or another of Paul's house church patrons (perhaps Euodia or Syntyche) had decided no longer to support Paul, thus creating the sense of crisis and distress." But that assumes more than we can know (would a town the size of Philippi have had that many house churches? and "crisis and distress" seem a bit strong for this letter).

polemical letters is that the enemies are left unnamed, thus denigrated by anonymity.[27]

We do not know who Euodia and Syntyche were.[28] Their names, which (roughly) mean "Success"[29] and "Lucky," tell us very little except that the latter, named after the goddess of fortune,[30] indicates pagan origins, and that both were given names indicative of parental desire for their making good in the world. What we do know is that in v. 3 Paul refers to them as his co-workers, having "contended at his side in the gospel." That he had women as co-workers in Philippi should surprise us none, since the church there had its origins among some Gentile women who, as "God-fearers," met by the river on the Jewish Sabbath for prayer (Acts 16:13-15). The evidence from Acts indicates that at her conversion, Lydia became patron both of the small apostolic band and of the nascent Christian community. By the very nature of things, that meant she was also a leader in the church, since heads of households automatically assumed the same role in the church that was centered in that household. Moreover, Macedonian women in general had a much larger role in public life than one finds elsewhere in the

27. See 1 Cor 4:18; 5:1-13; 6:1-11; 14:37; cf. Gal 5:10; 6:12; Rom 16:17. For this phenomenon, see P. Marshall, *Enmity,* 341-48.

28. Both names are common in inscriptions. Either one or the other has sometimes been treated as a man's name (so KJV, "Euodias"), but no evidence for such has ever turned up (cf. on Junia in Rom 16:7), and the αὐταῖς in v. 3 requires them to be women.

Because the name Lydia (Acts 16:14) literally means "the Lydian woman" (cf. Achaicus in 1 Cor 16:17), W. Ramsay (*Bearing,* 309) suggests that she might also have a more formal name and thus be identified with either of these women, preferably Syntyche, since that name was known in Lydia. He notes that Paul frequently uses a person's more proper name rather than the familiar form (e.g., Silvanus instead of Silas, Prisca instead of Priscilla). Although intriguing (Hawthorne is attracted to it), "there is nothing to lift the suggestion out of the region of conjecture" (Michael, 188).

29. Gk. Εὐοδία, which more literally means "prosperous journey"; Martin suggests "pleasant," as though it were a form of εὐωδία (4:18); but there is no evidence for this derivation, and it assumes the o/ω interchange to have been much more common in Greek antiquity than it actually was.

30. For males named in honor of "Dame Fortune" *(Tyche* is the Greek equivalent of the Latin, *Fortuna),* see Eutyches (Acts 20:9), Fortunatus (1 Cor 16:17), and one of Paul's erstwhile traveling companions, Tychicus. On the significance of this goddess to the everyday life of the Greco-Roman world, see the scathing rebuke in the elder Pliny, *Natural History* ("Everywhere in the whole world at every hour by all men's voices Fortune alone is invoked and named, alone accused, alone impeached, alone pondered, alone applauded, alone rebuked and visited with reproaches; deemed volatile and indeed by most men blind as well, wayward, inconstant, uncertain, fickle in her favours and favouring the unworthy. To her is debited all that is spent and credited all that is received, she alone fills both pages in the whole of mortals' account; and we are so much at the mercy of chance that Chance herself, by whom God is proved uncertain, takes the place of God." LCL).

empire;[31] in Philippi in particular they were also well known for their religious devotion.[32]

Paul now entreats[33] these two leaders "to have the same mindset in the Lord." The first part of this appeal, "to have the same mindset," is precisely the language of 2:2, where he had already urged the community on the basis of his and their common relationship in Christ and the Spirit, to "'complete' my joy" by *setting your minds on the same thing.*" Moreover, this is also the verb he uses to urge their collective following of his example in 3:15, in contrast to others whose "minds are set" on earthly things (v. 19).

---

31. See esp. the description in Tarn, *Hellenistic Civilization,* 98-99: "The great Macedonian princesses of the two generations after Alexander exercised much influence on the position of Greek women. If Macedonia produced perhaps the most competent group of men the world had yet seen, the women were in all respects the men's counterparts; they played a large part in affairs, received envoys and obtained concessions for them from their husbands, built temples, founded cities, engaged mercenaries. . . . From the Macedonian courts, (relative) freedom broadened down to the Greek home; and those women who desired emancipation — probably a minority — were able to obtain it in considerable measure." Cf. Acts 17:4, 12, where Luke refers to some early converts in Thessalonica (a Macedonian city) in terms of "not a few of the leading women." For the role of women in the church in Philippi see W. D. Thomas, "Place"; F. X. Malinowski, "Brave Women"; V. Abrahamsen, "Women"; E. Barnes, "Women"; F. M. Gillman, "Christian Women"; K. Torjesen, *When Women,* 53-109.

32. Which seems to be the best explanation for the many rock reliefs that mark the way up to the acropolis. On this matter, see esp. V. Abrahamsen, "Rock Reliefs."

33. Gk. παρακαλῶ, the common verb in Paul for exhortation, although "exhortation" at times borders on "comfort" and "encouragement" (cf. the noun on 2:1 above). See, e.g., in 1 Thessalonians, where Paul uses this verb to refer to his earlier time among them (2:12), of Timothy's intermediate visit to them (3:2), and of the exhortations in that letter (4:1, 10; 5:14); meanwhile this is what they are to do for one another (5:11). Cf. J. Thomas (*EDNT,* 3.26-27), and esp. S. R. Llewelyn (*New Docs,* 6.145-46), who offers an overview and schematic of verbs of petition in Paul (based on an unpub. diss. by D. Hartman, "Social Relationships"). He offers that in general παρακαλῶ is used predominantly in private letters, and is "less courteous" than ἐρωτῶ (see v. 3), which tends to be "more courteous and humble." For this usage of παρακαλῶ in Paul, Llewelyn lists 1 Thess 4:1, 10; 5:10; 2 Thess 3:12; 1 Cor 1:10; 4:16; 16:15; 2 Cor 2:8; 6:1; 10:1; Rom 12:1; Phlm 9, 10; Eph 4:1; Phil 4:2; 1 Tim 2:1. This distinction between using παρακαλῶ here and ἐρωτῶ in v. 3 is very likely an indication of "status" as well; that is, even though Euodia and Syntyche had "contended by Paul's side in the gospel," they were his subordinates, thus he "entreats" them; whereas his "loyal yokefellow" in v. 3 is probably to be recognized as Paul's equal (cf. O'Brien, 479), hence "I ask."

On the basis of a somewhat outdated study by C. J. Bjerkelund (*Parakalô*), many (e.g., L. M. White, "Morality," 206) see this verb as belonging to a "formal Parakalo (exhortation)" section at the end of the letter. But that is to press for something formal that in this case does not exist. Such "parakalo-periods," when they do occur in Paul, are never asyndetic as this one is; and the existence of the same verb in 2:12 makes this alleged "formal" matter quite irrelevant in this letter.

Given (a) the brevity of this letter, (b) that the letter would have been read aloud in the gathered community in a single sitting, and (c) that appeals to "have the same mindset" are part of the "stuff" of letters of friendship, one can be sure that the present appeal is to be understood as the specific application of the earlier ones.[34] How much this might also be related to the foregoing warning and appeal (3:1-21) is moot, but it seems probable.

Paul refuses to take sides, thus maintaining friendship with all. He appeals to both women — indeed the identical repetition of their names followed by the verb has rhetorical effect — to bury their differences by adopting the "same mindset," which in this case, as in the immediately preceding imperative, is qualified *"in the Lord."* Here is the evidence that we are not dealing with a personal matter, but with "doing the gospel" in Philippi.[35] Having "the same mindset *in the Lord*" has been specifically spelled out in the preceding paradigmatic narratives, where Christ (2:6-11) has humbled himself by taking the "form of a slave" and thus becoming obedient unto death on a cross, and Paul (3:4-14) has expressed his longing to know Christ, especially through participation in his sufferings so as to be conformed into the same cruciform lifestyle. The way such a "mindset" takes feet[36] is by humbly "looking out for the interests of others" within the believing community (2:3-4).

**3** In one of the more intriguing moments in his letters, Paul turns momentarily from Euodia and Syntyche to address another co-worker, asking him to help them respond to the appeal in v. 2: "Yes,[37] I ask[38] you (sing.) also,[39] true companion,[40] to assist[41] them." In so doing he further describes

34. As noted on 1:1 (p. 69 above), this passage is very likely the reason Paul also includes "along with the overseers and deacons" in the salutation, since he will eventually single out two of them in this way.

35. Otherwise Meyer, Jones, Kent, who see it as personal conflict ("a clash of personalities," Kent); cf. n. 26 above.

36. That is, "walks" in the ways of the Lord; see on 3:17 above.

37. Gk. ναί (the TR has καί, which is clearly an error in reading its own textual tradition [see Metzger, *Textual Commentary,* 616]). This is the Greek affirmative particle, which functions very much like "yes" in English. Here it indicates an "emphatic repetition of one's own statement," consisting in this case "in the fact that one request preceded and a similar one follows." The usage is rare in Paul, but see Phlm 20.

38. Gk. ἐρωτῶ, the "more courteous" verb of petition; see the disc. in n. 33 above.

39. Gk. ἐρωτῶ καί σε, which the NIV takes as conjunctive, "*and* I ask," but which is almost certainly ascensive, "I ask you *also,* loyal yoke-fellow" (= in addition to entreating them, I ask you as well to come to their aid).

40. Gk. γνήσιε σύζυγε. For γνήσιε see on 2:20 above. The NIV's "loyal" and GNB's "faithful" are hard to justify; the word has to do with "legitimacy," hence "genuine" or "true." The noun is the first of four συν-compounds in this sentence (see συλλαμβάνου, συνήθλησαν, συνεργῶν). The compound in this case means "yoked together with," and was chosen in this case, one would think, because of his/her role as a

Euodia and Syntyche, noting their relationship to Paul as co-workers from a long time back (along with Clement and some others), and concluding on yet another eschatological note[42] — that their names are recorded "in the book of life."

What intrigues is twofold: that in a letter addressed to the whole church he should single out one person in this way, which is unique to this moment in all his community-directed letters; and that Paul does not address him by name, leaving us to try to identify him on the basis of the appellation "true companion." These two matters are inter-related; we begin with the former.

Both its uniqueness and the nature of this address imply that Paul's "true companion," although well known in Philippi, is probably not a native Philippian, but one of Paul's itinerant co-workers who is presently on the scene there. This cannot be proven, of course, but it seems to make the best sense of the data.[43] It is altogether unlikely that Paul is speaking to a person named Syzygus,[44] since (a) there is no such name known in the Greco-Roman world and (b) the use of *syn*-compounds is an especially Pauline feature (there are no less than four in this immediate sentence; see n. 40). The appellation itself, therefore, indicates the closest kind of relationship — indeed partnership — between him and Paul; and the qualifier "genuine" is used elsewhere in

---

conciliator. The word occurs with frequency in Greek literature, but never as a proper name. Since it is sometimes used to refer to one's wife (e.g., Test. Reub. 4:1), a very early view (found in Clement of Alexandria and Origen) is that Paul is addressing his wife (thought to be Lydia). On the unlikelihood of Paul's being married at the time of his writing 1 Corinthians, see Fee, *First Corinthians,* 288 and 403.

Houlden (followed by Motyer, Hawthorne, and Silva) offers the unlikely suggestion that Paul is addressing the congregation collectively (Hawthorne in fact translates it as a plural). The problem lies not with the metaphor but with the vocative in the second person singular (Silva's "analogies" are not really so).

41. Gk. συλλαμβάνου (present middle imperative), found only here in the NT in this sense (in Acts 26:21, the middle carries the sense of "seize, arrest"). For this usage see esp. the letter of Dionysios to Nikanor published in *New Docs* 4.56 (παρακαλῶ σε, ἄδελφε, τῷ ἀδελφῷ μου Δημητρίῳ συλλαβέσθαι ("I request, brother, that you assist my brother Demetrius"); it also offers a good comparison between the aorist (in Dionysios's case it is a one-time affair, to help him "measure the grain") and the present, as in our passage, where Paul envisions an ongoing process.

42. In this regard see on 1:6, 10, 21-23; 2:11, 16; 3:12-14, 20-21; 4:1; cf. 4:5b that follows.

43. A view that goes back at least as far as Theodoret and Pelagius.

44. As in the NIV margin, a view suggested as an alternative by several (e.g., Jones, Plummer) and favored, *inter alia,* by Meyer, Vincent, Kennedy, Michael, Barth, Müller, Gnilka, Kent; see n. 40 above. Not only is such a "name" unknown, but it is difficult to imagine the circumstances (*pace* Meyer) in which a parent would give a child such an unusual moniker; finally, the qualifier "genuine" almost totally disqualifies it as a proper noun.

the Pauline corpus to refer to his intimate co-workers.[45] It surely cannot refer to Epaphroditus,[46] who is present at the dictation of the letter. It is unlikely that Paul would otherwise single out one person among equals to offer this help,[47] since he concludes the sentence by noting still other long-time co-workers who also "contended at his side" in Philippi.

If we are correct in identifying "true yokefellow" as one of Paul's intimate companions in itinerant ministry, then it cannot refer to Timothy,[48] who is coming at a time later than this letter. Of the others who are available, the most likely candidate is Luke.[49] Two things make this plausible, if one also considers Luke as the most likely person to be identified with the "we-passages" in Acts.[50] First, the "we" narrative takes Luke to Philippi in Acts 16, where it leaves off *until Paul's return to Philippi* some four to six years later in 20:1-5. The author of Acts, whether Luke or not, surely intends his readers to infer that he had spent these intervening years in Philippi. If so, then as one of Paul's most trusted companions, he had given oversight to that work for some years in the past.[51]

Second, if our view of the date and place of this letter is correct,[52] then Luke had recently been with Paul during the earlier period of this same

45. See on 2:20 above; cf. 1 Tim 1:2; Tit 1:4. The only exception is found in 2 Cor 8:8, where he refers to the "genuineness" of their love.

46. *Pace* Lightfoot (and allowed as an alternative by Jones). It makes very little sense that Paul should speak directly to someone at his side who would then be bearing the letter to Philippi (why would he need to do so at all, and why in this oblique way?); nor are there any analogies for it.

47. Unless in fact he is here addressing Lydia (so Renan, *St. Paul*), not because she is his wife (see n. 40), but because the church meets in her house, and these two women may have been among the first converts noted in Acts 16:13-15, who may also have been members of her household. Lightfoot objects that had a woman been intended Paul would more likely have written the adjective γνησία; but that is not certain.

48. *Pace* Jones (65; cf. Collange), who makes the unlikely suggestion that this is addressed to Timothy as he is writing the letter, for him to carry out when he gets there.

49. Adopted, *inter alia,* by Ramsay (*St Paul,* 358); M. Hájek ("Comments," 261-62); Bruce (130). G. Delling (*TDNT,* 7.748-50) opts for Silas.

50. Despite the strong historical and literary evidence in favor of this traditional view, it is not currently popular among NT scholars. But the evidence against Luke is based almost altogether on *theological* grounds, which is the flimsiest kind of evidence to use in the reconstruction of history, since the "theology" tends to be of our own making, not of the texts themselves. The historical case in favor of the tradition has recently been given a thorough hearing by C. Hemer, *Book of Acts,* 308-64, who concludes, "I am content to accept the identification of the author with Luke the physician but not to build on it" (362-63). Since the actual historical data favor the tradition so strongly, I am willing to build on them in a case like this where the data fit together so well.

51. Under this view, he is also then the most likely candidate for the glowing commendation in 2 Cor 8:16-24.

52. See the Introduction, pp. 37, 34-36.

imprisonment when Paul wrote the letters to Colossae and Philemon (Col 4:14; Phlm 23). The letter to Philippi, however, which appears to have been written toward the end of that imprisonment (see on 2:24 above), is especially noticeable for its lack of mention of the names of any of Paul's companions. All of this makes perfectly good sense if Luke had at some earlier point left for Philippi — and was perhaps the catalyst of their recent revival of material support (4:10). None of this can be proved, of course. Nonetheless, it fits all the available historical data, and the epithet "true yokefellow" would be especially fitting of Luke, especially in light of the affectionate language in Col 4:14. At the same time the reason for addressing one person among them in the second singular is also resolved.

Paul's erstwhile companion is thus asked "to assist" Euodia and Syntyche, obviously to "have the same mindset in the Lord." But Paul's focus is still on them, not on his "yokefellow." Hence, having mentioned them again (as the object of his assistance) he goes on, surely now for their own sakes, further to describe them (literally), "inasmuch as[53] in the gospel they have contended at my side." Paul's word order tells the story. His concern throughout is with the gospel in Philippi. Thus in this indirect way he reminds them that they were in partnership with him "in the gospel" from the very beginning, which is reason enough for them to get on with it still. On the athletic metaphor "contended at my side" see on 1:27 (cf. 2:13-14). Although it does not on its own necessarily imply leadership of some kind, it does so when used in this way in conjunction with Paul's own ministry, followed by a further notation about "the rest of my co-workers."

About "Clement and the rest of my co-workers" we know nothing. The context demands that they are fellow-Philippians. But why he should single out Clement is a singular mystery,[54] made all the more so by the unusual way it is attached to the former clause, "along with Clement and the rest." What this means seems clear enough, that "Clement and the rest of my co-workers"[55] also "contended at my side along with Euodia and Syntyche"

---

53. Gk. αἵτινες; the NIV (cf. NASB, REB; Hawthorne) is probably wrong to translate this as a simple relative pronoun (αἵ "who"), since Paul could have used that form so naturally and easily. Here it is almost certainly "qualitative" (BAGD, 2), to indicate that they "belong to a certain class" or "to emphasize a certain characteristic." Hence, "assist them, inasmuch as they belong among those who. . . ." Cf. O'Brien (481) who argues for a straight causal clause (= "because they").

54. Very early on (Origen, Eusebius) he was identified with Clement of Rome, on the grounds that 1 Clement was written to Corinth; which then became the standard Roman Catholic interpretation. But the dates of these two documents (probably separated by 35 years) makes that extremely doubtful, not to mention that the name Clement was so common among Roman citizens. Cf. the discussion in Lightfoot, 168-71.

55. For this word see the discussion on 2:25.

in the cause of the gospel in Philippi.[56] But why they should be attached to that clause in this way can only be conjectured. Most likely it is as close to an "aside" as one gets in Paul's letters; having just mentioned two in particular who "have contended at his side" for the sake of the gospel in Philippi, he includes the others who were with him in that ministry from the beginning, for some good reason mentioning Clement in particular, perhaps not wanting to mention the rest by name lest he exclude any. In its own way, therefore, the clause probably functions as a gentle reminder to all who lead the believing community in Philippi to "have the same mindset in the Lord," even though that is not specifically said of or to them.

The eschatological note on which this concludes is equally unique to the Pauline corpus. Elsewhere when he offers a moment of eschatological assurance to those to whom he writes, it takes a variety of forms, and usually, as in 2:16 and 4:1, includes some note of his being there with them. But here the focus is altogether on Euodia and Syntyche, and now by elaboration includes Clement and the rest as well. The ultimate reason for their getting it together in Philippi as they await from heaven the coming of their Savior, the Lord Jesus Christ (3:20), is that their "names [all of their names[57]] are in the book[58] of life." This unusual (for Paul) language is common stock from his Jewish heritage,[59] where

56. At least that would seem to be the "clear" sense. Lightfoot, however, thinks it goes with συλλαμβάνου (= "assist them . . . along with . . ."). Although grammatically possible, it seems unlikely in context. Paul has deliberately asked one person to "assist" the women. "Clement and the rest" are mentioned because he is recalling the "early history" of the church in Philippi, as it were.

57. *Contra* Meyer, Vincent, Hendriksen, Martin, et al., who would restrict it to "and the rest of my co-workers," as though Paul had forgotten their names, but that they are known to God and hence written down in his book. Grammatically, it should include at least Clement; contextually it must surely embrace all of Paul's "co-workers," hence include all who are mentioned in this sentence. So also Lohmeyer, Gnilka, Loh-Nida, Bruce, Hawthorne, Silva, O'Brien, Melick. Some (e.g., Bengel, Vincent, Barth, Beare, Müller) take the phrase to imply that Clement and the others have died; but the implication is unnecessary since elsewhere in the NT the phrase is used of the living (e.g., Luke 10:20; Rev. 3:5).

58. Gk. βίβλῳ. For this word in contrast to other words for "writings," see M-M (110): "As distinguished from χάρτης, the single sheet of papyrus for writing purposes, βίβλος was the roll, made up of χάρται glued together . . . , while in contrast to βιβλίον and βιβλίδιον it implies a literary work." It is the word that regularly occurs in conjunction with sacred writings, although in the LXX and NT it is nearly synonymous with βιβλίον; cf. H. Balz, *EDNT,* 1.218.

59. The idea of names inscribed by God in a heavenly book is found as early as Exod 32:32-33 ("blot out my name in the book you have written"); it is actually called "the book of life" in Ps 69:28 (LXX 68:29, "book of the living"). The term was especially congenial to apocalyptic (cf. Dan 12:1; 1 Enoch 47:3; Herm. *Sim.* 2.9), as evidenced by its sevenfold occurrence in the Revelation (3:5; 13:8; 17:8; 20:12, 15; 21:27; 22:19). This is the same tradition to which Jesus refers in Luke 10:20 ("your names are written in

the faithful were understood to have their names recorded in the heavenly "book of the living," meaning "the book that has recorded in it those who have received divine life [thus 'the book of the living,' Ps 68:29] and are thus destined for glory."

Hence with these words Paul brings the specific hortatory sections of the letter to conclusion. In both cases (vv. 1 and 2-3) he has picked up the eschatological note from 3:20-21 that has immediately preceded; and in both cases the note is affirmation and reassurance. If his concern in these exhortations is with the present — their "steadfastness" and "unity" for the sake of the gospel in Philippi — his focus has regularly been on their certain future. He and they together have their names recorded "in the book of life," and for that reason, as a colony of heaven in the Roman colony of Philippi, they need to live the life of the future now as they await its consummation.

It is not possible from this distance for us to know the specific nature of Euodia's and Syntyche's lack of agreement. We have speculated at various points along the way[60] that they may have been involved in whatever may have lain behind the exhortation in 3:1-21; but we admit to the speculative nature of such suggestions. In light of the total letter, however, and the nature of Paul's exhortations, it seems most likely that their disagreements were not substantial, and had more to do with "how to do the gospel" in Philippi in the context of their present suffering, rather than over substantive matters as such. One of them may have found the "Jewish" option attractive, as a way of getting the opposition to ease off. But we simply cannot know. It is male chauvinism pure and simple that thinks the issue is more purely personal, and related to their being women. At issue in this letter is not some petty quarrel between two people, but the gospel in Philippi. Everything in the letter points in that direction; there is no reason at this point to think otherwise. And almost certainly the significance of singling these two out in this way is related to the significance of their roles in leadership. But details elude us, precisely because they knew exactly what the issue was, which is why we do not; Paul did not have to reiterate in their hearing what they already knew in this regard.

When the dust clears, and one gets beyond the specifics about names and "women in leadership," it is hard to imagine NT exhortations that are more contemporary — for every age and clime — than these. To "stand firm in the Lord" is not just a word for the individual believer, as such words are so often taken, but for any local body of believers. The gospel is ever and always at

---

heaven"); cf. Heb 12:23. Caird reminds us that a civic register with the names of all citizens undoubtedly existed in Philippi; this is the register of citizens of the heavenly commonwealth (3:20).

60. See the introductions to 3:1-4a (p. 289); and on 3:17 (p. 366).

stake in our world, and the call to God's people, whose "names are written in the book of life," is to live that life now in whatever "Philippi" and in the face of whatever opposition it is found. But to do so effectively, its people, especially those in leadership, must learn to subordinate personal agendas to the larger agenda of the gospel, "to have the same mindset in the Lord." This means humbling, sacrificial giving of oneself for the sake of others; but then that is what the gospel is all about in any case. So in effect these exhortations merely call us to genuine Christian life in the face of every form of pagan and religious opposition.

At the same time, here is one of those pieces of "mute" evidence for women in leadership in the NT, significant in this case for its off-handed, presuppositional way of speaking about them. To deny their role in the church in Philippi is to fly full in the face of the text. Here is the evidence that the Holy Spirit is "gender-blind," that he gifts as he wills; our task is to recognize his gifting and to "assist" all such people, male and female, to "have the same mindset in the Lord," so that together they will be effective in doing the gospel.

# VI. CONCLUDING MATTERS (4:4-23)

The "concluding matters" of Philippians have long puzzled scholars, mostly because of the presence of 4:10-20, where Paul acknowledges their gift. The problem is twofold. Some scholars are particularly disturbed by the presence of this acknowledgment at the end of the letter; they cannot believe that Paul would have waited so long before he thanks them for their gift (although in fact he has already done so in an oblique way in 1:5 and 2:25 and 30). Their solution is to dismember the letter into three letters, viewing vv. 10-20 as one of these letters, inserted at this point by a rather "unthinking" collator. Others, equally disturbed by the presence of vv. 10-20, find themselves at something of a loss to know how to handle vv. 4-9, since these verses include the very items — and only such items — that belong to the "conclusions" of Paul's letters.[1]

The resolution of these matters is to be found at three points, which

---

1. The evidence for this is to be found in the commentaries, which are more divided over how to understand vv. 4-9 in the overall scheme of the letter than over any other section. Besides those who divide the letter into three parts (Michael, Beare, Gnilka, Collange), some make it a section of its own (Vincent); others as belonging with 4:1-3 (Lohmeyer, Müller, Hendriksen, Martin, Loh-Nida, Kent, Hawthorne, O'Brien) or 4:2-3 (Barth, Houlden, Caird) as a section on its own; others as belonging to 3:1–4:3 (Plummer, Melick). Of those commentaries consulted, only Silva recognizes vv. 4-9 as belonging to "final matters," but he includes vv. 2-3 as well.

together suggest that all of 4:4-23 function in this letter as "concluding matters," and that only the length of vv. 10-20 has kept us from seeing it this way right along. First, we need to take seriously the nature of the Pauline "conclusions," which not only lack "form" but are a study in variety. Nonetheless, when all of them are put side by side certain elements emerge in common — although not all of them in each letter — and these elements tend also to follow a common pattern, but again not consistently in each case. The elements that are common to five or more of the letters occur in the "purest" form in 2 Cor 13:11-13(14); they include:[2]

1. A series of (usually "staccato") imperatives
2. The wish of peace
3. The holy kiss
4. Greetings from Paul and others
5. A grace-benediction

The only one of these missing in this letter is the holy kiss. Indeed, if one were to remove vv. 10-20 for the moment, what is left (vv. 4-9 and 21-23) also constitutes a relatively "pure" form of these "concluding matters." The resolution to the present "form" of Philippians, however, does not lie in excising vv. 10-20, as some suggest, but with the next two observations.

Second, in 1 Corinthians Paul also has these same elements (minus the wish of peace), plus a couple of items unique to that letter. They begin with the "staccato" imperatives at 16:13-14. But just as in Philippians, the next "common" elements (the holy kiss and greetings) do not appear until v. 19, having been "interrupted" by a "letter of commendation" for the bearers of the letter (Stephanas, Fortunatus, and Achaicus), of whom Paul says, "I *am rejoicing* over their coming." At the very same point in our letter, Paul also "interrupts" the "concluding matters" with his acknowledgment of their gift. Only we should now change our language, for vv. 10-20 are not an "interruption" of a "form," since the "form" exists only as our discovery and for our convenience in figuring out what Paul is doing. Rather than a so-called interruption, in this case what is presented lies at the heart of these "concluding matters."

Third, the key to all of this lies with Paul's reasons for leaving the acknowledgment of their gift until the very end, which, as we will note below (at vv. 10-20), have to do with friendship and rhetorical emphasis. For now I

---

2. The only element that otherwise occurs at least three times is the autographic greeting ("this greeting is in my own hand"), which occurs in 2 Thess 3:17, 1 Cor 16:21, and Col 4:18 (although some would also include Gal 6:11, where it serves a considerably different function). Otherwise there are elements that are unique to a given letter (e.g., the "anathema" in 1 Cor 16:22).

simply point out that one can make a great deal of sense of these various final parts to the letter, including the "finally" in v. 8, when looked at in this way.

## A. CONCLUDING EXHORTATIONS (4:4-9)

It was suggested above that the appeals to "steadfastness" and "unity" in 4:1-3 function to bring closure to the main body of the letter (from 1:27). That a break occurs at the end of 4:3 is further demonstrated by the present series of exhortations. Paraenesis[3] of this kind occurs regularly in the Pauline letters, in a couple of different ways. On the one hand, there is the kind found in Gal 6:1-10;[4] Rom 12:1–13:14; Col 3:5–4:6, and Eph 4:1–6:9, which by and large spell out the ethical implications of the arguments of those letters. On the other hand, there are those found in 1 Thess 5:12-22, and much more briefly in 1 Cor 16:13 and 2 Cor 13:11, which function as part of the formal conclusions to these letters.[5] In the latter cases, the imperatives are often "staccato" and have some similarities from letter to letter.

The present passage belongs to this latter "genre." In form (and somewhat in content) these imperatives are similar to those of 1 Thess 5:12-22, which were apparently adapted to the urgencies of 1 Thessalonians,[6] while in content (esp. vv. 4-7) they also correspond to 2 Cor 13:11.[7] In this sense, then, they belong to the more "formal" matters that conclude the Pauline letters. But they also have some unusual features that mark them off from the others, and which also have given interpreters some difficulty in terms of their "placement" in this letter. A word about each of these.

As to the content, four matters are noteworthy. (1) These imperatives are in two sets (vv. 4-7 and 8-9), formally marked by the "finally" that begins the second set. The first set deals primarily with Christian piety (corporate and individual devotion), the second primarily with ethics (how

---

3. This is the technical term for moral exhortation and is frequently applied to a series of brief exhortations of this kind.

4. Some would include parts of Galatians 5 as paraenesis, but that material seems rather to be part of the argument of the letter (see Fee, *Presence,* 420-25; cf. *idem.* "Freedom"; J. M. G. Barclay, *Obeying,* 106-45, 216-20).

5. For a fuller discussion of these matters, see Gamble, *Textual History,* 56-83; *contra* the "pattern" observed by F. Filson, *Yesterday,* 22-23. For their adaptation in 1 Corinthians, see Fee, *First Corinthians,* 825-26.

6. On this matter see Fee, "Pneuma and Eschatology," 211-13.

7. The following items from 2 Cor 13:11 correspond to Philippians: "rejoice" (v. 4), "have the same mindset" (v. 2), "keep the peace" (cf. v. 7)," plus the conclusion "the God of love and peace will be with you" (cf. v. 9b). Our passage also has in common with 1 Thess 5:13b and 16-18: "rejoice, pray, give thanks, and peace."

Christians "think" and "behave"). Each concludes with a variant form of the "wish of peace" ("the peace of God will keep you"/"the God of peace will be with you"). (2) The actual number of "staccato" imperatives (vv. 4-7) is small, just three in fact, although one takes the form of a "not/but" contrast, which is considerably elaborated. (3) Not everything is imperative. Besides the affirmations of "peace" which conclude each set, the first set is "interrupted" by the striking indicative, "the Lord is near." (4) The final set is unique to this letter in the Pauline corpus, being full of "friendship" motifs and striking correspondences to the moral world of Hellenism.[8] At the same time it picks up the twin concerns of "thinking" and "doing" that run throughout the letter, concluding on the note of "imitating" Paul. The whole may be set out thus:

SET ONE (vv. 4-7):
    (1) Rejoice in the Lord always, and again I say it, rejoice.
    (2) Let your gentleness be evident to all.
        (a) The Lord is near.
    (3a) About nothing        be anxious;
    (3b) but in every situation   make your requests known to God
                              by prayer and petition
                              with thanksgiving
        ($b^1$) And the peace of God       will guard your hearts and minds
            which transcends all understanding

SET TWO (vv. 8-9) [introduced by, "finally, brothers and sisters"]:
    (1) Whatever things are . . . virtuous and praiseworthy,
                  these things consider.
    (2) What you have learned, received, heard, seen in me,
                  these things practice.
        ($b^2$) And the God of peace will be with you

Given these various "formal" features and their adaptations to the Philippian context, what are they doing at *this* point in the letter? And why another "finally" (v. 8) which does not seem to be "finally" in terms of the letter as a whole (cf. 3:1)? The answers lie both with the purpose of the present paraenesis and the (apparently deliberate) placement of vv. 10-20 at the end of the letter. First, these exhortations really do function as the "concluding

8. The differences between the two sets are perhaps best illustrated by their language. Except for "gentleness," the language of vv. 4-7 is that of the Psalter, while the language of v. 8 is common to Jewish wisdom and hellenistic moral philosophy. The one is the language of worship; the other of morality. And Paul will urge both.

paraenesis" of the letter; hence, the "finally" in this case means just that, "finally, with regard to the matters of the letter that have to do with my concerns over you." But they also appear to be transitional, from the letter body and its concerns to the final (in some ways, first) concern of the letter, to express his profound gratitude for their gift. On the other hand, the placement of vv. 10-20, which seems deliberate and carefully crafted to be the "last word" of the letter, appears at the end, even after the "concluding exhortations," for reasons of friendship. Occurring in the emphatic final position, these will be the final words left ringing in their ears as the letter is concluded, words that have had to do with "their concerns for the apostle."[9]

## 1. A Call to Christian Piety — and Peace (4:4-7)

> 4*Rejoice in the Lord always. I will say it again: Rejoice!* 5*Let your gentleness be evident to all. The Lord is near.* 6*Do not be anxious about anything, but in everything, by prayer and petition, with thanksgiving, present your requests to God.* 7*And the peace of God,*[10] *which transcends all understanding, will guard your hearts and your minds*[11] *in Christ*[12] *Jesus.*

In contrast to the second set of imperatives (vv. 8-9), which reflect the language of Greco-Roman moralism, this set is distinctively Christian — and Pauline. Indeed, it is so well known that one hesitates to comment on it. But a few observations are in order.

First, these initial imperatives have to do basically with piety. Piety is expressed in this imperatival way because, in keeping with his OT roots, devotion and ethics for Paul are inseparable responses to grace. The truly godly person both *longs* for God's presence, where one pours out his or her heart to God in joy, prayer, and thanksgiving, and *lives* in God's presence by "doing" the righteousness of God. Otherwise piety is merely religion, not devotion.[13]

Second, the heart of these exhortations reflects the threefold expression of Jewish piety — rejoicing in the Lord, prayer, and thanksgiving — which

9. *Contra* Beare (148); see the discussion on 4:10-20 below.
10. A few MSS (A t vg^mss sy^hmg) substitute "Christ" for "God," probably reflecting a liturgical alteration.
11. Probably on the analogy of 1 Thess 5:23, several Western witnesses (F G a d; Marius Victorinus, Pelagius) substitute σώματα ("bodies") for "minds." The very early P16 apparently reads "your minds and your bodies."
12. P46 has the singular substitution of "Lord" for "Christ."
13. This is especially evident in the Psalter, where being in God's presence requires blamelessness (Psalm 15; 101; cf. 51).

are basic to the Psalter: "the righteous rejoice in the Lord" (Ps 64:10; 97:12) as they "come before him with thanksgiving" (Ps 95:2; 100:4) to "pray" in his "sanctuary" (Ps 61:1-4; 84:1-8). Paul already expressed them in this way, and in this order, in his earliest extant letter as God's will for his people in Christ Jesus;[14] they found expression together in the present letter in the formal thanksgiving (1:3-4). For him they are the work of the Holy Spirit in the life of the believer and especially of the believing congregation.

Third, in Paul's understanding of the life of the Spirit, "joy" and "peace" also go together. "The Kingdom of God" has nothing to do with Torah observance ("food and drink") but everything to do with "righteousness and *peace and joy* in the Holy Spirit" (Rom 14:17; cf. 15:13; Gal 5:22). In 1 Thess 5:13, 16 and 2 Cor 13:11, both joy and peace are commanded; in this case, "joy" is commanded, while "peace" is promised.

Fourth, also in keeping with the Psalter, these imperatives, all expressed in the second person plural, exemplify the conjunction between individual and corporate piety. As always in Paul, "joy, prayer, and thanksgiving," evidenced outwardly by their "gentleness" and inwardly by God's "peace" in their midst, first of all have to do with the (gathered) people of God; but the fact that "the peace of God shall guard *your hearts and minds*" reminds us that what is to be reflected in the gathered community must first of all be the experience of each believer.[15]

The series has its own brand of "logic."[16] It begins on the note of joy (v. 4), which not only marks this letter as a whole, but also, with 3:1, frames the final hortatory section (3:1–4:3) in particular. But in contrast to 3:1, which was followed by an inward focus (warning and appeal), this one is followed by an outward focus (5a, that their "gentle forbearance be known by all people"), which in turn is followed by an (apparently) eschatological affirmation regarding the Lord's "nearness" (5b). The reality of that "nearness" also calls for "no anxiety," but rather for prayer and thanksgiving (v. 6),

---

14. See 1 Thess 5:16-18; cf. the discussion in Fee, *Presence,* 53-55, for their role in Pauline spirituality. For the same combination elsewhere see 1 Thess 3:9-10 and Col 1:9, 11-12.

15. Cf. Motyer, 205; Melick, 148. Many interpreters think otherwise, rejecting altogether a corporate dimension to this passage (e.g., Meyer, Vincent).

16. I put it this way because these kinds of imperatives are almost always asyndetic (without connecting or nuancing particles), as here. Hence in that sense, as O'Brien emphasizes (484-85), they are "independent" of one another. But that does not mean they lack "logic," in the sense that there is no conceptual connection between them, or that they are independent of the overall context of the letter. On the other hand, O'Brien rightly rejects the attempt to make the whole a "history of joy," to use Moffatt's language (*ExpT* 9 [1897-98] 334-36), seconded by Morrice, *DPL,* 512. So also with those (e.g., Melick, 148) who would subsume them all under the rubric "peace." What holds the whole together is Christian piety, which includes joy, prayer, and thanksgiving, and issues in peace.

concluding with the promise of God's "peace" to "guard their hearts and minds" (v. 7).[17]

Thus, even though only the first imperative ("rejoice") is distinctively "Philippian," and many of these items are common to other letters, beneath the surface lie hints of adaptation to the Philippian situation: (a) The earlier appeal to steadfastness in the face of opposition (1:27-30) is undergirded here by the repeated call to rejoice, the concern that their gentleness be evident to all, and the word against anxiety with its inverse call to prayer and thanksgiving;[18] (b) the concern for "unity" is reflected both in the exhortation to "gentleness" and the affirmation of "God's peace" guarding their hearts and minds; and (c) all of this is punctuated with "the Lord is near," the final reference to the eschatological theme found throughout the letter.

**4** In the final set of imperatives in v. 8 Paul will sanctify as equally Christian the best of Greco-Roman virtues. He begins, however, with what is distinctively Christian. Combining the "framing" exhortation of 3:1 ("rejoice *in the Lord*") with the "staccato" imperative that began the Thessalonian triad ("rejoice *always*"), he says it one more time, this time with verve:[19] "Rejoice in the Lord always; again I will say it, Rejoice!"[20]

"Joy," unmitigated, untrammeled joy, is — or at least should be — the distinctive mark of the believer in Christ Jesus.[21] The wearing of black and the long face, which so often came to typify some later expressions of Christian piety, are totally foreign to the Pauline version; Paul the theologian of grace is equally the theologian of joy. Christian joy is not the temporal kind, which comes and goes with one's circumstances; rather, it is predicated altogether on one's relationship *with the Lord,* and is thus an abiding, deeply spiritual quality of life.[22] It finds expression in "rejoicing," which is not a Christian option, but an imperative. With its concentration "in the Lord," rejoicing is

17. The affirmation that God's peace will guard their "minds" in turn prepares the way for the final set (vv. 8-9), that they "think on" whatever is praiseworthy.

18. Michael (194) sees it as reflecting only the concern for steadfastness; cf. Martin, Beare, O'Brien.

19. Both the assonance and chiasm effect striking — and memorable — rhetoric:

χαίρετε ἐν κυρίῳ πάντοτε;
πάλιν ἐρῶ χαίρετε.

20. On the impossibility of the translation suggested by Goodspeed, "Good-bye, and the Lord be always with you," see n. 25 on 3:1, *pace* Lightfoot and Beare.

21. For a discussion of this motif in Paul and the rest of the NT, see esp. *NIDNTT,* 2.356-61 (E. Beyreuther; G. Finkenrath); cf. also Morrice, *DPL,* 511-12. This imperative has nothing to do with martyrdom (Lohmeyer); and Collange's curious comment (144) that it has to do with believers for whom "the future stands open . . . and its realization . . . on the way," sounds far more like Bultmann than Paul.

22. In many ways Charles Wesley caught the essence of this imperative in his

"always" to mark their individual and corporate life in Philippi. The presence of the Holy Spirit in their lives and in their midst meant the experience of joy, whatever else may be their lot. In this letter the "whatever else" includes opposition and suffering at the hands of the local citizens of the empire, where Caesar was honored as "lord." In the face of such, they are to "rejoice in *the* Lord *always.*"

Although a recurring motif in this letter, joy is not a random motif. The word group appears 16 times, equally divided between Paul's joy and theirs. He begins by reminding them of *his own joy* as he prays for them (1:4), which he also experienced over their recent gift to him (4:10). Indeed, they will be his "joy" and "crown" when Christ comes (4:1). Meanwhile, his own "rejoicing in the Lord always" in his imprisonment (1:18 [2x]) serves as paradigm for their rejoicing in suffering (2:17-18),[23] a joy which he longs for them to bring to full measure by having one mindset (2:2).

Likewise, references to *their joy* are integral to the concerns of the letter. Two occurrences are case-specific (2:28, 29, renewed joy over the return of Epaphroditus). The others frame the two main hortatory sections that make up the heart of the letter (1:27–2:18; 3:1–4:3). The motif begins in 1:25, where Paul expects to be with them again "for their progress *and joy*" in the gospel. This is followed immediately, given his current absence, by the exhortation to steadfastness and unity, which concludes (2:18) with the double imperative, (a) to "rejoice" since their own suffering is a "sacrificial offering" to God, and (b) to "rejoice with me" inasmuch as his suffering is the accompanying drink offering. Thus joy in suffering is part of the friendship motif, of their mutuality in Christ. Likewise the second exhortation (3:1–4:3), which began with warning and appeal and concluded with the twin appeals to steadfastness

---

hymn, "Rejoice, the Lord is King." The first lines of each stanza wonderfully capture both Ps 97:1 and the eschatological context of the present imperative:

| [1]Rejoice, the Lord is king; | [3]His kingdom cannot fail, |
|---|---|
| Your Lord and king adore; | Our Lord the Judge shall come; |
| [2]The Lord the Savior reigns, | [4]Rejoice in glorious hope! |
| the God of truth and love; | he rules o'er earth and heaven. |

While the refrain joins this text with the heart of Ps 100:1 (and perhaps 28:7b):

Lift up your heart, lift up your voice!
    Rejoice, again I say, rejoice.

23. This is one of those aspects of the gospel that they have more than once "heard and seen in him" (4:9). Besides 1:12-26 in this letter, they have their memory of his first visit to Philippi. According to the narrative in Acts 16:25-34, it was while Paul and Silas were rejoicing in the Lord in the jail in Philippi, many years earlier, that God came to their aid and thus added to the number of those who became believers in the Lord.

and unity, is framed by the exhortation to "rejoice *in the Lord,*" and now to do so "always," even in the midst of their presently untoward circumstances.[24]

**5a**   This second imperative, "let your gentleness be evident to all," follows from the first. As they continually rejoice in the Lord even in the face of opposition and suffering, what others are to see is "gentleness." In what may be something of a word play with "let your requests *be made known* to God" that follows,[25] Paul here urges (literally) "let your 'gentleness' *be known*[26] to all people," that is, to those on the outside,[27] including those who oppose them. "Gentleness,"[28] however, is one of those terms that is difficult to pin down with precision. It is used by hellenistic writers and in the LXX primarily to refer to God (or the gods) or to the "noble," who are characterized by their "gentle forbearance" with others.[29] That is

24. Barth (120) says of these passages as a whole, " 'joy' in Philippians is a defiant 'Nevertheless!' which Paul sets as a full stop against the Philippians' *anxiety.*"

25. *Contra* Lohmeyer, 170, who suggests that both should be understood as prayer.

26. Gk. γνωσθήτω, which here probably = "be recognized by" (cf. Phillips, "have a reputation for gentleness," and Montgomery, "let your reasonableness be recognized by every one"); on the second verb, γνωριζέσθω, see n. 44.

27. While one would not deny in light of vv. 2-3 that he also intends them to have this disposition toward one another, in Paul the combination πᾶσιν ἀνθρώποις regularly points outward, to the whole of humankind; cf. 1 Thess 2:15; 2 Cor 3:2; Rom 5:18 (2x); 12:17, 18; 1 Tim 2:1, 4; 4:10; Tit 2:11; 3:2 (cf. Martin, 154; O'Brien, 488). To translate it simply "all" may leave the impression in context that it is inward looking.

28. Gk. ἐπιεικές; elsewhere in Paul only in the Pastoral Epistles (1 Tim 3:3; Tit 3:2); the noun occurs in 2 Cor 10:1, in conjunction with πραΰτης, to denote the characteristic attitude of Christ during his earthly life, an attitude espoused by Paul but apparently rejected by the Corinthians. As Lightfoot notes (160), it is "the opposite to a spirit of contention and self-seeking." For more complete discussions of this word, cf. J. Preisker, *TDNT,* 2.588-90; W. Bauder, *NIDNTT,* 2.256-59; H. Giesen, *EDNT,* 2.26 (which also contains a useful bibliography); and H. Leivestad, "Meekness," who offers a much-needed corrective to Preisker (see next n.).

29. See, e.g., (of God); Ps 86:5 (LXX 85:5), "You, Lord, are kind (χρηστός) and gently forbearing (ἐπιεικής); and plenteous in mercy (πολυέλεος) toward all who call upon you"; Bar 2:27, "You have dealt with us, O Lord our God, according to all your gentle forbearance and according to all your great mercy" (cf. Prayer of Azariah 19; Wis 12:18; 2 Macc 2:22; 10:4). So also of earthly rulers who show "clemency" (3 Macc 3:15; 7:6). It is the collocation of ἐπιείκεια with "mercy" in these texts that suggests the meaning "gentle forbearance," where the emphasis is on the "gentle" or "kind" disposition of God which lies behind his "clemency." Similarly when applied to the righteous man whom the wicked persecute (Wis 2:19): "Let us test him with insult and torture, so that we may find out his gentleness (ἐπιείκεια), and make trial of his forbearance" (NRSV, slightly revised). This latter text indicates that Preisker's emphasis on the believer's "sovereignty in Christ" is probably incorrect (cf. Leivestad's critique), and that all such translations suggesting "clemency" on the part of believers (e.g., "moderation" [Collange]; "magnanimity" [NEB, Hawthorne]; "consideration of others" [REB]) probably move in the wrong direction; cf. O'Brien, 487.

most likely its sense here, only now as the disposition of *all* of God's people.[30]

In the midst of their present adversity, the Lord, to whom they belong, has graciously set them free for joy — always. At the same time others should know them for their "gentle forbearance" toward one another and toward all, including those who are currently making life miserable. This is the Pauline version of 1 Pet 2:23, spoken of Christ but urged of Christian slaves, "when they hurled their insults at him, he did not retaliate; when he suffered, he made no threats. Instead, he entrusted himself to him who judges justly." It is this "gentle forbearance" and "meekness" of Christ, to which Paul appealed in 2 Cor 10:1, which he here calls the believers to exhibit in Philippi.

**5b** The sudden appearance of an indicative ("the Lord is near") is as surprising as its intent is obscure. The asyndeton typical of this kind of paraenesis[31] also holds true for this indicative, so that one cannot tell whether Paul intends it to conclude what precedes or introduce what follows, and therefore whether it expresses future or realized eschatology.[32] Does he intend, "Rejoice in the Lord always; *and* let your gentle forbearance be known by all, *for* the [coming of] the Lord is near"?[33] or "*Because* the Lord is [always] near, do not be anxious about anything, but let your requests be made known to God"?[34] Or does he intend a bit of both,[35] perhaps something as close to intentional double entendre as one finds in the apostle?[36]

On the one hand, this looks very much like another instance of intertextuality,[37] purposely echoing Ps 145:18, "the Lord is near all who call upon him."[38] In which case it introduces vv. 6-7 as an expression of "real-

30. Cf. TCNT, "let your forbearing spirit be plain to everyone."

31. Cf. the asyndeton in 3:1 and esp. 3:2.

32. The difficulty lies with the adverb ἐγγύς, which, as with the English "near," has either "spatial" or "temporal" connotations, depending on the context. On its own in a sentence like this it is totally ambiguous; unfortunately, in context it can go either way as well.

33. So Lightfoot, who notes the similarity with Jas 5:8, where μακροθυμία ("forbearance") is called for in light of the Parousia; cf. Meyer, Kennedy, Jones, Plummer, Michael, Lohmeyer, Barth, Müller, Beare, Hendriksen, Gnilka, Houlden, Martin, Loh-Nida, Kent, Silva, Melick.

34. So Calvin, Michaelis, Caird; Bugg, "Philippians 4:4-13"; cf. NEB, which starts a new paragraph with this indicative ("The Lord is near; have no anxiety, etc.").

35. So Alford, Ellicott, Vincent, Collange, Bruce, Craddock, Hawthorne, O'Brien.

36. As I tend to think; cf. Hawthorne, 182.

37. Cf. Lohmeyer, 169; Stanley, "Boasting," 106; J. Baumgarten, *Paulus,* 205-8; O'Brien, 489. For this phenomenon in Philippians see 1:19; 2:10, and 15-16.

38. LXX 144:18, ἐγγὺς κύριος πᾶσιν τοῖς ἐπικαλουμένοις αὐτόν; cf. 34:18 (LXX 33:19), ἐγγὺς κύριος τοῖς συντετριμμένοις τὴν καρδίαν ("the Lord is near the contrite in heart"); cf. 119:151 (118:151), where it appears in the second singular. Paul has ὁ κύριος

ized" eschatology: "Because the Lord is ever present, do not be anxious but pray." On the other hand (or perhaps at the same time), it also echoes the apocalyptic language of Zeph 1:7 and 14 ("the Day of the Lord is near"), picked up by Paul in Rom 13:12, and found in Jas 5:8 regarding the coming of the Lord.

On the whole it seems likely that this is primarily intended as the last in the series of eschatological words to this suffering congregation, again reminding them of their sure future, despite present difficulties. Thus, it is a word of encouragement and affirmation.[39] Since their present suffering is at the hands of those who proclaim Caesar as Lord, they are reminded that the true "Lord" is "near." Their eschatological vindication is close at hand. At the same time, by using the language of the Psalter, Paul is encouraging them to prayer in the midst of their present distress, because the "Lord is near" in a very real way to those who call on him now.

**6** Paul now turns to the second consequence of the Lord's being "near." They are to live without anxiety, instead entrusting their lives to God with prayer and thanksgiving. In so doing, he borrows from the Jesus tradition,[40] that the children of the Kingdom are to live without care — but not "uncaring" or "careless." Jesus invites his followers to live "without anxiety" because their heavenly Father knows and cares for them; in Paul's case it is because their "Lord is near." Apprehension and fear mark the life of the unbelieving, the untrusting, for whom the present is all there is, and for whom the present is so uncertain — or for many so filled with distress and suffering, as in the case of the Philippians.

On the contrary, Paul urges, "in everything, by prayer and petition, with thanksgiving, let your requests be made known to God." "In every-thing"[41] stands in contrast to "not about anything," and means "in all the

---

ἐγγύς, whose word order, in contrast to the Psalm, puts emphasis on "the Lord" more than "near." Baumgarten (preceding n.) correctly emphasizes the implicitly high Christology in such language; cf. on 2:10 above.

39. It is possible, but less likely, that Paul intended a word of motivation (= "be gently forbearing, because the Lord is near").

40. See the "Q" material included in Matthew's Gospel in the Sermon on the Mount (6:25-34) and in Luke 12:22-32. The language of the Gospels is μὴ μεριμνᾶτε τῇ ψυχῇ ("Do not be anxious about your life"); Paul has it μηδὲν μεριμνᾶτε ("Be anxious about nothing"). That Paul is reflecting the Jesus tradition best explains why the verb is pejorative here, the only such instance in the corpus (although see the adjective in 1 Cor 7:32); elsewhere it is positive (as in 2:20 above; cf. 1 Cor 7:32-34 [4x]; 12:25; and the use of the noun in 2 Cor 11:28). As Müller nicely put it, "to care is a virtue, but to foster cares is sin."

41. Gk. ἐν παντί, which is neuter singular and therefore cannot (*pace* Loh-Nida) modify "with prayer and petition," as in GNB ("in all your prayers") and NAB ("in every form of prayer").

details and circumstances of life."[42] In situations where others fret and worry, believers in "the Lord" submit their case to God in prayer, accompanied by thanksgiving. For this combination see on 1:4. The three words for prayer are not significantly distinguishable; "requests"[43] are "made known"[44] before[45] God "by prayer[46] and petition."[47] In so doing one acknowledges utter dependence on God, while at the same time expressing complete trust in him.

Especially striking in the context of petition is the addition, "with thanksgiving" — although it is scarcely surprising of Paul. His own life was accentuated by thanksgiving; and he could not imagine Christian life that was not a constant outpouring of gratitude to God.[48] Lack of gratitude is the first step to idolatry (Rom 1:21). Thanksgiving is an explicit acknowledgment of creatureliness and dependence, a recognition that everything comes as gift, the verbalization before God of his goodness and generosity. If prayer as petition indicates their utter dependence on and trust in God, petition "accompanied by thanksgiving" puts both their prayer and their lives into proper theological perspective. Thanksgiving does not mean to say "thank you" in advance for gifts to be received; rather, it is the absolutely basic posture of the believer, and the

42. So most interpreters, although some (e.g., Calvin, Meyer) would see it as limited to "circumstances." Some (Moffatt, Beare) see it as temporal, "always," but the context is quite against it.

43. Gk. τὰ αἰτήματα, only here in Paul (cf. 1 Jo 5:15, "we have the *requests* which we have *requested* from him"). The verb, which means to "request" or "ask for," also occurs rarely in Paul as a verb for prayer (only Col 1:9 and Eph 3:20). The noun denotes what is asked for as such, over against the act of praying. For the word group, see G. Stählin, *TDNT,* 1.191-95.

44. Gk. γνωριζέσθω. That one "lets God know" is probably a word play on letting their "gentle forbearance" be known to all people. Although this is something of a colloquialism — after all, God hardly needs to be informed by us of our requests — our doing so nonetheless carries theological import. For the believer it is an expression of humility and dependence; so also O'Brien, 493. The NIV's "present to God" is perhaps a dynamic equivalent, but it also misses something.

45. Gk. πρὸς τὸν θεόν, indicating "in the presence of" as much, or more than, "to," as though Paul had written τῷ θεῷ. Cf. Vincent, 135; Kennedy, 467; O'Brien, 493.

46. Gk. τῇ προσευχῇ, the standard biblical word for "prayer" — of any and all kinds.

47. Gk. τῇ δεήσει, which basically means "supplication" (see n. 41 on 1:4). Its fourfold occurrence in this letter (1:4 [2x], 19; here) probably reflects his and their situation.

48. In this regard see esp. the comments on 1 Cor 4:7 in Fee, *First Corinthians,* 170-71. One of the more intriguing realities of the Pauline letters is how seldom one finds the language of "praise" (in a significant way only in the thrice repeated "to the praise of his glory" in Eph 1:6, 12, 14). Very likely we should understand the language of "joy" and "thanksgiving," and in some instances "boasting/glorying," as also embracing "praise." On this matter see O'Brien, *DPL,* 68-71, and "Thanksgiving within Pauline Theology."

proper context for "petitioning" God.[49] Gratitude acknowledges — and begets — generosity. It is also the key to the final affirmation that follows.

**7** With a rare expression of parataxis[50] Paul deliberately conjoins the "peace of God" with the exhortation to pray in trusting submission with thanksgiving, and thus offers God's alternative to anxiety. This is a slight variation on what he had written not long before to the Colossians, that they should let "the peace of Christ serve as the arbiter in their hearts (individually)," since "they were called into one body."[51] But here it is affirmation and promise. As they submit their situation to God in prayer, with thanksgiving, what they may expect from God is that his "peace" will "guard" their hearts and minds as they remain "in Christ Jesus."

That Paul expresses "peace" in such terms is probably an indication that one can make too much of the differences within the community, implied in 2:1-4 and made explicit in 4:2. He is indeed concerned about all of them "having the same mindset" as they "do" the gospel in Philippi; but in this letter "friendship" prevails, and their need for encouragement in the midst of difficulty exceeds the need to be admonished.[52] Thus in contrast to other letters, he does not express "peace" as an imperative but as an indicative, closely related to their trusting God in prayer.

As with joy, peace for Paul is a fruit of the Spirit (Gal 5:22). It is especially associated with God and his relationship to his people. Here it is called "the peace of God"[53] because God is "the God of peace" (v. 9), the God who dwells in total *shalom* (wholeness, well-being) and who gives such *shalom* to his people. And it is the "peace of God" that "transcends[54] all understanding."[55] This could mean "beyond all human comprehension," which in one sense is certainly true. More likely Paul intends that God's peace "totally transcends the merely human, unbelieving mind," which is full of anxiety because it cannot think higher than itself.[56] Because the God to whom

---

49. As Kennedy (467) put it: "To pray in any other spirit is to clip the wings of prayer."

50. Beginning a Greek sentence with the conjunction "and." On this phenomenon in Paul, see n. 3 on 2:8; cf. the discussion in O'Brien, 495.

51. In Col 3:15 both "thanksgiving" and "peace" occur as imperatives ("let the peace of Christ rule in your hearts; . . . and be thankful").

52. For a similar view, see Kennedy and Caird.

53. Only here in Paul; but peace is regularly noted as coming from God (most Pauline salutations), which is what this genitive intends. Cf. "peace of Christ" in Col 3:15.

54. Gk. ὑπερέχουσα; for this word see on 3:8 above (n. 19).

55. Gk. πάντα νοῦν, the word for "mind," which here takes on the associated sense of "understanding."

56. Cf. Lightfoot, Meyer, Vincent, Jones, Plummer, Müller, Collange, Martin, Hawthorne, Silva; *contra* Calvin, Alford, Kennedy, Hendriksen, Kent, O'Brien, many of

we pray and offer thanksgiving, whose ways are higher than ours, is also totally trustworthy, our prayer is accompanied by his peace. And that, not because he answers according to our wishes,[57] but because his peace totally transcends our merely human way of perceiving the world. Peace comes because prayer is an expression of trust, and God's people do not need to have it all figured out in order to trust him!

Such peace will therefore "guard"[58] their "hearts and thoughts." In the Hebrew view the heart is the center of one's being, out of which flows all of life (e.g., Mark 7:21). God's peace will do what instruction in "wisdom" urged the young to do: "above all else, guard your heart, for it is the wellspring of life" (Prov 4:23). In the present context "God's peace" will be his "garrison" around their "hearts" so that they do not fall into "anxiety." It will also guard their "thoughts."[59] Since God's peace surpasses merely human understanding in any case, it will protect the mind from those very thoughts that lead to fear and distress and that keep one from trusting prayer.

As with so much else in this letter, the location of such "protection" is "in Christ Jesus." It is their relationship to God through Christ, in whom they trust and in whom they rejoice, that is the key to all of these imperatives and this affirming indicative. And this is what distinguishes Pauline paraenesis from that of both hellenistic moralists and Jewish wisdom.[60] Thus this is (literally and theologically) the final word in this series of exhortations. Everything that makes for life in the present and the future has to do with their being "in Christ Jesus."

Even though the experience of God's "peace" happens first of all at the individual level, it is doubtful that "peace" in this context refers only to

---

whom base their view on the alleged parallel with Eph 3:19 (the parallel seems to exist far more in our minds than in the actual language of Paul; cf. Schenk). Michael and Beare are ambivalent.

57. Cf. several (Meyer, Plummer, O'Brien) who note that God's peace is not contingent on "answered prayer," but on his character.

58. Gk. φρουρήσει, used literally by Paul of the ethnarch Aretas in 2 Cor 11:32, who set a guard at the city gates, and figuratively of the Law in Gal 3:23, in the sense of "keep in custody" until "faith" should come. This is a military metaphor, where a garrison, such as the one always stationed in Philippi, "guards the Roman *pax*."

59. Gk. τὰ νοήματα, found only in Paul in the NT and elsewhere only in pejorative contexts (2 Cor 2:11; 3:14; 4:4; 10:5; 11:3). As over against the "mind" (νοῦς, found in the preceding phrase, "which exceeds every mind"), this word, as with most nouns ending in -μα, denotes the concrete expression or activity of the mind, hence "your thoughts." Cf. J. Behm, *TDNT,* 4.960-61.

60. Cf., e.g., Dio Chrysostom, on covetousness, "It is not our ignorance of the difference between good and evil that hurts us, so much as it is our failure to heed the dictates of reason on these matters and to be true to our personal opinions" (*Or.* 17.1; LCL 2.189). For Paul the secret to peace lies not in reason but "in Christ Jesus."

"the well-arranged heart."[61] For Paul peace is primarily a community matter. As noted below (v. 9), the ascription "God of peace" occurs in Paul in contexts where community unrest is lurking nearby. Not only so, but the mention of peace in his letters (apart from the standard salutation) occurs most often in community or relational settings.[62] Thus Christ is "our peace" who has made Jew and Gentile one people, one body (Eph 2:14-17), who are thus urged to "keep the unity of the Spirit through the bond of peace" (4:3); similarly in the argument of Rom 14:1–15:13, Jew and Gentile together are urged to "make every effort to do what leads to peace" (14:19); or in the community paraenesis of Col 3:12–4:6, they are urged to "let the peace of Christ rule in your hearts, *since as members of one body you were called to peace*" (v. 15).

Given the context of this letter, in particular the simultaneous appeals to "steadfastness" and "unity" in the face of opposition, this is a most appropriate penultimate affirmation. They need not have anxiety in the face of opposition, because they together will experience the "protection" of God's "peace" in the midst of that conflict; and they who have been urged over and again to "have the same mindset" are here assured that the peace of God which surpasses merely human understanding will also protect their thoughts as they live out the gospel together in Philippi. Nor is it surprising, therefore, that the final, immediately following imperative (v. 8) is for them "give their minds only to higher and better things."

Joy, prayer, thanksgiving, peace — these identify Pauline spirituality. Such lives are further marked by gentle forbearance and no anxiety. The key lies with the indicative, "the Lord is near" — now and to come. The Lord is now present by his Spirit, who prompts prayer and thanksgiving, among whose "fruit" in the life of the believer and the believing community are joy and peace. Here is God's ultimate gift to those who trust in Christ, *shalom* and joy.

In a post-Christian, post-modern world, which has generally lost its bearings because it has generally abandoned its God, such spirituality is very often the key to effective evangelism. In a world where fear is a much greater reality than joy, our privilege is to live out the gospel of true *shalom,* wholeness in every sense of that word, and to point others to its source. We can do that because "the Lord is near" in this first sense, by the Spirit who turns our present circumstances into joy and peace, and who prompts our prayer and

---

61. Esp. so in light of the similar passage, probably recently dictated, in Col 3:15, where the imperative calls for them "to let the peace of Christ rule in your hearts, to which [peace] you were called in the one body." So also Kennedy, 467; *contra* Meyer (cf. Silva et al.), who sees the community expression only in v. 9.

62. Cf. Hasler, *EDNT,* 1.396.

thanksgiving. And we should be at that task with greater concern than many of us are, because "the Lord is near" in the eschatological sense as well.

## 2. A Call to "Wisdom" — and the Imitation of Paul (4:8-9)

> 8Finally, [brothers and sisters],[1] whatever is true, whatever is noble, whatever is right, whatever is pure, whatever is lovely, whatever is admirable — if anything is excellent or praiseworthy[2] — think about such things. 9Whatever you have learned or received or heard from me, or seen in me — put it into practice. And the God of peace will be with you.

In most of Paul's letters the preceding set of imperatives would have functioned as the "concluding exhortations," to be followed only by the wish of peace and the closing greetings. But this is a letter of friendship, so Paul adds a final set of exhortations, both sides of which are the "stuff" of friendship.[3] Here is material with which the Philippians would have felt very much at home before they had ever become followers of Christ and friends of Paul.[4]

The imperatives are twofold, expressed with striking rhetoric.[5] The

---

1. See n. 9 on 1:12.
2. Some key "Western" witnesses (D* F G a vg^cl; Ambrosiaster) add ἐπιστήμης following ἔπαινος (= "if anything is in praise of understanding"); this reflects either a failure on the part of scribes to recognize the passive sense of ἔπαινος (as Silva suggests) or an attempt to put the whole totally within the framework of the "mind."
3. The "friendship" dimension of the first part (v. 8) lies in Paul's adopting the language of their culture as a way of encompassing them; in v. 9 it rests with the repeated "imitatio" motif.
4. Some have suggested that these two verses are the insertion of the "final redactor" of the Philippian correspondence (e.g., Gnilka, 219; P. Fielder, *EDNT*, 3.238), which looks very much like an attempt to square what the text says with one's prior reconstruction of the "genuine" Paul.
5. Both sentences have a three-part structure. They begin (a) with a series of "whatever things," emphasized rhetorically by the repeated ὅσα in v. 8 and repeated καί in v. 9; (b) both lists are then "qualified," in the first instance by compounded "if" clauses, in the second by the prepositional phrase "in me"; and (c) both conclude with an appositional ταῦτα, followed by the imperative. Thus:

| (a) | ὅσα ἐστιν ἀληθῆ | ἃ | καὶ ἐμάθετε |
|     | ὅσα σέμνα |    | καὶ παρελάβετε |
|     | ὅσα δίκαια |    | καὶ ἠκούσατε |
|     | ὅσα ἀγνά |    | καὶ εἴδετε |
|     | ὅσα προσφιλῆ |    |    |
|     | ὅσα εὔφημα, |    |    |
| (b) | εἴ τις ἀρετὴ |    | ἐν ἐμοί |

first seems designed to place them back into their own world, even as they remain "over against" that world in so many ways. Expressed in the language of hellenistic moralism,[6] in effect it tells them to take into account the best of their Greco-Roman heritage, as long as it has moral excellence and is praiseworthy. The second *puts that into perspective,* by repeating the motif of "imitation."[6] They obey the first set of exhortations by putting into practice what they have learned from him as teacher and have seen modeled in his life. The whole concludes with the promise of God's abiding presence, as none other than "the God of peace."

Paul was a man of two worlds, which had become uniquely blended through his encounter with the Risen Christ. Christ's death and resurrection, marking the end of the old era and the beginning of the new, radically transformed Paul's (Jewish) theology, which he in turn radically applied to the Greco-Roman world with which as a Diaspora Jew he was so familiar. Thus people whom Christ had rescued from being without God and hope in the world are now encouraged in the language of that world to consider what is noble and praiseworthy, as long as it conforms to what they have learned and seen in Paul about Christ.

That Paul is not embracing Stoicism or pagan moralism as such[8] is made clear not only by his own theology everywhere but in particular by what he does with the Stoic concept of "contentment" in vv. 11-13 that follow. There he uses their language and intends the same general perspective toward circumstances as the Stoics. But he breaks the back of the Stoic concept by transforming their

---

$$\varkappa\alpha\grave{\iota}$$
$$\varepsilon\check{\iota}\ \tau\iota\varsigma\ \check{\varepsilon}\pi\alpha\iota\nu\circ\varsigma,$$
(c) ταῦτα λογίζεσθε          ταῦτα πράσσετε.

The first is as strikingly asyndetic (without connectives) as the second is polysyndetic (the same connective in each case). Each is thus a sentence unto itself (*pace* O'Brien, 508, who strangely argues that the ἅ in v. 9 has the preceding ταῦτα as its antecedent, whereas the structure of both sentences together makes it certain that the ταῦτα in both cases is in apposition to the preceding relative pronoun in their respective sentences). The difference between ὅσα and ἅ is that of "indefinite" and "definite" (i.e., "whatever things in general" and "what things in particular").

6. But in Paul's own case almost certainly mediated by way of Jewish wisdom as well. See the discussion below.

7. Expressed explicitly in 3:17, but hinted at in the various moments of reciprocity and mutuality that recur throughout the letter (e.g., 1:29-30; 2:17-18; 3:15).

8. *Pace,* e.g., Beare, who says that "Paul sanctifies, as it were, the generally accepted virtues of pagan morality. . . . These are nothing else than the virtues of the copybook maxims" (148). The language, yes; but their morality, no — even if outwardly they may correspond at various points. The "in Christ" formula which has just preceded (v. 7) and which dominates this letter disallows such a view.

"*self*-sufficiency" into "*Christ*-sufficiency." So here, using language the Philippians would have known from their youth, he singles out values held in common with the best of Hellenism. But as v. 9 implies, these must now be understood in light of the cruciform existence that Paul has urged throughout the letter.

**8** With this "finally," and its accompanying (final) vocative,[9] "brothers and sisters," Paul concludes the "hortatory" dimension of this "hortatory letter of friendship." There is one further item to add, his grateful recognition of their renewed material support (vv. 10-20); but that belongs to the dimension of friendship altogether (without being "hortatory"), and has basically to do with *their relationship with him*. This "finally" concludes *his concerns about them* (and is thus also "hortatory").

What is striking about this sentence is its uniqueness in the Pauline corpus. Take away the "finally, brothers and sisters," and this sentence would fit more readily in Epictetus's *Discourses* or Seneca's *Moral Essays* than it would into any of the Pauline letters — except this one. The six adjectives and two nouns that make up the sentence are as uncommon in Paul as most of them are common stock to the world of Greco-Roman moralism. However, they are also the language of Jewish wisdom;[10] indeed, the closest parallel to this sentence in the NT is not in the Pauline letters but in Jas 3:13-18,[11] where some of this same language (as well as that of vv. 4-7) occurs in speaking of "the *wisdom* that is from above."

But what Paul says here is much less clear than the English translations would lead one to believe. The impression given is that he is calling on them one final time to "give their minds" to nobler things. That may be true in one sense, but the language and grammar suggest something slightly different. The verb[12] ordinarily means to "reckon" in the sense of "take into account," rather than simply to "think about." This suggests that Paul is telling them not so much to "think high thoughts" as to "take into account" the good they have long known

---

9. For this vocative in the letter see on 1:12 (nn. 9 and 12).

10. Lohmeyer (173-76) and Michaelis (68-69) make too much of this correspondence, as though Paul were dependent on the LXX for the language itself. O'Brien (502-3) and others have rightly critiqued them at this point. But the critique has been stated too "either-or," as though the usage in Jewish wisdom had no bearing on how Paul would have understood these words. That this is unlikely is evidenced by O'Brien's own discussions of the individual words, where he regularly appeals to LXX usage.

11. Of all places (!), given that James is the one of the least hellenized documents in the NT.

12. Gk. λογίζεσθε, used also in 3:13. This is the verb that is well known to English Bible readers through its frequent use in Romans (18x), where it has been traditionally translated "reckon," where much of that usage is the result of his citing Gen 15:6 from the LXX (cf. Gal 3:6). It appears frequently also in 2 Cor 10–12 (6x), carrying basically the sense that it does here (= focused consideration of something).

from their own past, as long as it is conformable to Christ. This seems confirmed by the double proviso, "if anything," that interrupts the sentence.[13] The six words themselves, at least the first four, already point to what is virtuous and praiseworthy; so why add the proviso unless he intends them to *select out* what is morally excellent and praiseworthy from these "whatever things" that belong to the world around them, and to do so on the basis of Christ himself? Thus, he appears to be dipping into the language of hellenistic moralism, in his case tempered by Jewish wisdom, to encourage the Philippians that even though they are presently "citizens of heaven," living out the life of the future as they await its consummation, they do not altogether abandon the world in which they used to, and still do, live. As believers in Christ they will embrace the best of that world as well, as long as it is understood in light of the cross.

Despite its several correspondences to hellenistic moralism and Jewish wisdom, however, this is Paul's own enumeration.[14] It neither reflects the four cardinal virtues of Hellenism,[15] nor is there anything else quite like it as a *list* in the ancient world, either in form or content. As with all such "virtue" lists in Paul, it is intended to be representative, not definitive. The six adjectives

---

13. *Contra* the majority of interpreters, who repeatedly speak of these clauses as "summarizing" the former six words. Paul's actual language and grammar seem quite opposed to such an idea. The indefinite τις (whether subject = "if anything has"; or adjective = "if there is any") rules out the meaning "since" for the εἰ, as many would have it (e.g., Hawthorne, O'Brien, whose grammatical explanations and translations quite ignore the τις; to say "if, as is the case, there is *any* excellence" [O'Brien, 506, but without the "any"] as a way of *summarizing* the preceding clauses makes very little sense). The twin clauses are thus the protases of simple first class conditions (see Burton, *Moods,* 102-3), which in this sentence (in simplified form) say, "If there is anything morally excellent [to them], consider whatever things are. . . ." Finally, had Paul intended these two words to be of a kind with the former six, the shift from ὅσα to εἴ τις is inexplicable, even on rhetorical grounds. In Paul's grammar, the two words "moral excellence" and "praiseworthy" do not "summarize" the preceding virtues, they *qualify* them. Otherwise grammar would seem to be for naught (the appeal to BDF §372.1 counts for little because of the τις).

14. The closest thing to it is found in Cicero, *Tusculan Disputations,* 5.23.67: "But what is there in man better than a mind *(mente)* that is sagacious and good *(bona)?* . . . The good of the mind is virtue *(virtus);* therefore happy life is necessarily bound up with virtue. Consequently all that is lovely *(pulchra),* honourable *(honesta),* of good report *(praeclara)* . . . is full of joys" (LCL, 493). But Paul is obviously not "dependent" on this or any other such "list." For a succinct summary of the contrast between Paul and Hellenism on the matter of "virtue," see Link and Ringwald, *NIDNTT,* 3.927-28.

15. That is, "self-control" (σωφροσύνη); "prudence" (φρόνησις); "justice" (δικαιοσύνη); and "courage" (ἀνδρεία), which together are classified as "virtues" (ἀρεταί), first articulated by Plato, but generally taken over by the Greek and Roman philosophical tradition. They are baldly taken over by the author of Wisdom and made the virtues of the Jewish wisdom tradition (8:7)! It should also be pointed out here that the words προσφιλῆ and εὔφημα (nos. 5 and 6) do not appear in *any* of the pagan virtue lists.

416

cover a broad range — truth, honor, uprightness, purity, what is pleasing or admirable.[16] Since they also reflect what the teachers of Wisdom considered to be the best path for the young to adopt, very likely this language in part came to Paul by way of this tradition. In any case, in Paul they must be understood in light of the cross, since that is surely the point of the final proviso in v. 9 that whatever else they do, they are to follow Paul's teaching and thus imitate his cruciform lifestyle.[17] Thus:

(1) *Whatever is true.*[18] For Paul truth is narrowly circumscribed, finding its measure in God (Rom 1:18, 25) and the gospel (Gal 2:5; 5:7). As a virtue, especially in Jewish wisdom, it has to do with true speech (Prov 22:21) over against the lie and deceit (cf. 1:18 above) or is associated with righteousness and equity.[19] Just as suppression of the truth about God, which leads to believing the lie about him, is the first mark of idolatry (the worship of false deities), so the first word in this virtue list calls them to give consideration to whatever conforms to the gospel.

(2) *Whatever is noble.*[20] Although this word most often has a "sacred" sense ("revered" or "majestic"), here it probably denotes "honorable," "noble," or "worthy of respect." It occurs in Prov 8:6 also in conjunction with "truth" and "righteousness," as characteristic of what Wisdom has to say. Thus, whatever is "worthy of respect," wherever it may come from, is also worth giving consideration to.

(3) *Whatever is right.*[21] As with "truth," what is "right" is always

---

16. Lightfoot (161) sees the words as "roughly . . . arranged in a descending scale," the first two being "absolute," the next two "relative," and the final two "point to the moral approbation which they conciliate." This may be "neater" than Paul intended.

17. This sentence offers clear evidence that the distinctions between "secular" and "sacred" are most often of our making, based on our embracing an OT point of view regarding "holy things," even though it was brought to an end with the coming of Christ and the Spirit. Paul takes a different view, that being "in Christ" sanctifies whatever else one is and does, so that what is honorable, lovely, and pleasing, as long as it also worthy of praise, is also embraced by life in Christ. Although the articulation of a later time, this passage seems to embrace the notion of "common grace." Here is where Mozart and Beethoven (not only Bach!) come under Christian embrace.

18. Gk. ἀληθῆ, for which the English translations consistently render "true." For a useful discussion of "truth" in Paul, see L. Morris, *DPL,* 954-55.

19. In fact Bultmann (*TDNT,* 1.248) considers it to mean "upright" here.

20. Gk. σεμνά, found elsewhere in the NT only in the Pastoral Epistles, where it is used to describe the character of leaders (and others): 1 Tim 3:8, 11; Tit 2:2 (cf. the noun σεμνότητος in 1 Tim 2:2; 3:4; Tit 2:7). See the discussion by Foerster, *TDNT,* 7.191-96. The English translations offer "honest" (KJV), "honorable" (ASV, NASB, NRSV), "all that deserves respect" (NAB), as well as "noble" (NIV, GNB, REB).

21. Gk. δίκαιος, the adj. of the significant theological words δικαιοσύνη ("righteousness") and δικαιόω ("justify"). When used substantivally it often carries the sense

defined by God and his character. Thus, even though this is one of the cardinal virtues of Greek antiquity, in Paul it carries the further sense of "righteousness," so that it is not defined by merely human understanding of what is "right" or "just," but by God and his relationship with his people.[22]

(4) *Whatever is pure*.[23] This word originated in the cultus, where what had been sanctified for the temple was considered "pure"; along with the related word "holy," it soon took on moral implications. In Proverbs it stands over against "the thoughts of the wicked" (15:26) or "the way of the guilty" (21:8, in conjunction with being "upright"). Thus, "whatever things are pure" has to do with whatever is not "besmirched" or "tainted" in some way by evil. As with "truth" it occurs earlier in this letter (1:17) to contrast those whose motives are "impure" in preaching the gospel so as to "afflict" Paul.

(5) *Whatever is lovely*.[24] With this word and the next we step off NT turf altogether onto the more unfamiliar ground of Hellenism — but not hellenistic moralism (see n. 15). This word has to do primarily with what people consider "lovable," in the sense of having a friendly disposition toward. The NJB catches the sense well by translating, "everything that we love." Here is the word that throws the net broadly, so as to include conduct that has little to do with morality in itself, but is recognized as admirable by the world at large. In common parlance, this word could refer to a Beethoven symphony, as well as to the work of Mother Teresa among the poor of Calcutta; the former is lovely and enjoyable, the latter is admirable as well as moral.

(6) *Whatever is admirable*.[25] Although not quite a synonym of the preceding word, it belongs to the same general category of "virtues." Not a virtue in the moral sense, it represents the kind of conduct that is worth considering because it is well spoken of by people in general.

---

of its cognate noun (ὁ δίκαιος = "the righteous person"); otherwise it means "the right" or "just" thing (cf. on 1:7 above).

22. For this usage in Jewish wisdom see especially Sir 10:23 ("It is not right to despise one who is intelligent but poor," NRSV) and 27:8 ("If you pursue justice, you will attain it, and wear it like a glorious robe," NRSV).

23. Gk. ἅγνα; cf. 2 Cor 7:11; 11:2; 1 Tim 5:22; Tit 2:5; and Jas 3:17. The English translations consistently render it "pure."

24. Gk. προσφιλῆ, only here in the NT, and only in Sir 4:7; 20:13; and Esth 5:1[b] in the LXX. Translated variously as "lovely" (KJV, NIV, NASB, RSV, GNB), "lovable" (REB, TCNT), "pleasing" (NRSV), "admirable" (NAB, NEB).

25. Gk. εὔφημα, as with the preceding word, a NT hapax legomenon (although Paul uses the cognate noun in 2 Cor 6:8). It is also the only word in the list that is not found in the LXX, and the word for which there is the greatest variety among the English translations: "good report" (KJV), "gracious" (RSV, NEB), "admirable" (NIV; cf. NJB "everything we admire"), "high-toned" (Moffatt), "commendable" (NRSV), "honorable" (GNB), "decent" (NAB), "of good repute" (NASB, NEB[mg]), "attractive" (REB).

It is probably the lack of inherent morality in the last two words that called forth the interrupting double proviso[26] that follows, "if anything is excellent, if anything is praiseworthy." The word "excellent"[27] is the primary Greek word for "virtue" or "moral excellence." It is generally avoided, at least in this sense, by the LXX translators.[28] Although not found elsewhere in Paul, the present usage, along with "contentment" in v. 11, is clear evidence that he felt no need to shy away from the language of the Greek moralists. What he intends, of course, is that "virtue" be filled with Christian content, exemplified by his own life and teaching (v. 9). Likewise with "praiseworthy."[29] Although this word probably refers to the approval of others, the basis has been changed from "general ethical judgment"[30] to conduct that is in keeping with God's own righteousness. While not inherent in v. 8 itself, such an understanding of these words comes from the immediately following exhortation to "imitate" Paul, which in turn must be understood in light of what has been said to this point.

**9** With this sentence Paul brings the exhortations to conclusion.[31] It is not surprising that they end on the note of "imitation." Not only is such imitation urged on them explicitly in 3:17, but this motif belongs to "friendship" and is probably in view from the beginning of the letter (1:12).[32] In effect this sentence summarizes, as well as concludes, the letter. Paul's concern throughout has been the gospel, not its content ("doctrinal error" is not at issue), but its lived out expression in the world. To get there he has informed them of his response to his own present suffering (1:12-26), reminded them of the "way of Christ" (2:6-11), and told his own story (3:4-14), all of which were intended to appeal, warn, and encourage them to steadfastness and unity in the face of opposition. Now he puts it to them plainly, as the final proviso

---

26. For the grammar of these qualifying protases, see n. 13 above.

27. Gk. ἀρετή; elsewhere in the NT only in 1 Pet 2:9 and 2 Pet 1:3, 5 (2x), in the latter passage under the influence of Hellenism. For background and a discussion of NT usage see Bauernfeind, *TDNT,* 1.457-61; and Link and Ringwald, *NIDNTT,* 3.925-28.

28. Although it appears in the later, Greek works of the Septuagint (Wisdom and the Maccabees) as "virtue."

29. Gk. ἔπαινος; cf. 1:11 and n. 3 on 1:9-11. Apart from the three occurrences in Ephesians (1:6, 12, 14), where, as in Phil 1:11, it is God-directed, the word occurs twice to refer to "praise from God" (1 Cor 4:5; Rom 2:29), which in both cases is made clear by the qualifier "from God," and twice to refer to human praise (2 Cor 8:18; Rom 13:3).

30. So Hofius, *EDNT,* 2.16.

31. As with v. 1, Beare omits comment on this verse altogether (see n. 7 on 4:1-3). That he does so can scarcely be due to oversight, but is probably related to his view of Philippians as a collection of letters. This verse does not fit well with his having placed it in his "letter 1," since 3:17 (the earlier express mention of "imitating" Paul) belongs to his "letter 2."

32. See the introduction to 1:12-26 (p. 106) and n. 37 on 1:18.

to the preceding list of "virtues" that they should take into account. Read that list, he now tells them,[33] in light of what "you have learned and received and heard and seen in me," and above all else "put these things (you have learned, etc.) into practice."[34]

What he calls them to "practice" is "what things"[35] they have "learned" and "received" from him by way of instruction and what they have heard about him (from this letter? Epaphroditus? Timothy?) and seen in him by way of example. The first two verbs reflect his Jewish tradition, where what is "learned" is thus "received" by students.[36] For the combination "heard and seen in me" see on 1:30. In that context in particular it had to do with their common struggle of suffering for Christ's sake. Given the overall context of this letter, one may rightly assume that, whatever the specifics, Paul is once again calling them to the kind of cruciform existence he has been commending and urging on them throughout. Only as they are "conformed to Christ's death," as Paul himself seeks continually to be, even as they eagerly await the final consummation at his coming, will they truly live what is "virtuous" and "praiseworthy" from Paul's distinctively "in Christ" perspective.

The exhortations are thus finished; so Paul rightly concludes with a "wish of peace," which here takes the form of ultimate benediction, that "the God of peace will be with you." They will get "peace" because the God of peace, by his Spirit, is in their midst. The ascription "God of peace," derived from the OT, is frequent in Paul.[37] What is striking is that in every instance it occurs in contexts where there is strife or unrest close at hand. Thus the antidote to unruly *charismata* in the community is the theological note that God himself is a "God of peace" (1 Cor 14:33); or in a community where the unruly/idle live off the largess of others, Paul prays that the God of peace

33. O'Brien (508) rightly rejects the view of Sevenster *(Paul)* that would drive a wedge between vv. 8 and 9. But neither should one think of reading v. 8 without understanding it as finally qualified by v. 9. After all, v. 9 summarizes much of the letter; thus the indefinite "whatsoever things" mentioned in v. 8 are to be understood within the framework of the specific "what things," having to do with the gospel, they have learned from him. Cf. n. 5 above.

34. Gk. πράσσετε, a synonym for the word "do," and used interchangeably by Paul (see 1 Thess 4:11; 2 Cor 5:10; Eph 6:21; but more often negatively of "wrong practices": 1 Cor 5:2; 2 Cor 12:21; Gal 5:21; Rom 1:32; 7:15, 19, etc.).

35. On this relative, see n. 5

36. Gk. καὶ ἐμάθετε καὶ παρελάβετε; the combination only here in Paul. More often he uses the technical vocabulary of his rabbinic training ("received and handed down"; cf. 2 Thess 3:6; 1 Cor 11:23; 15:1-3). For the use of "learned" in Paul see Col 1:7; Eph 4:20; for "received" in the sense of "what has been taught" see 1 Thess 2:13; 4:1; Gal 1:9, 12; Col 2:6.

37. See 1 Thes 5:23; 2 Thes 3:16; 1 Cor 14:33; 2 Cor 13:11; Rom 15:33; 16:20; and here.

will give them peace at all times (2 Thes 3:16); or in a context where believers are warned against those who "cause divisions and put obstacles in your way," he assures them that the God of peace will bruise Satan under their feet shortly (Rom 16:20). Although "strife" is hardly the word to describe the Philippian scene, he nonetheless signs off with this affirmation, perhaps significantly so in light of the repeated exhortation to "have the same mindset."

The desire for "God's presence" determines much in Jewish piety and theology, both in the OT and in the intertestamental period. For Paul, and the rest of the NT, the way God is now present is by his Spirit, who is the fulfillment of the eschatological promises that God will put his Spirit into his people's hearts, so that "they will obey me." Thus, even though the Spirit is not mentioned, in Paul's understanding this is how the "God of peace will be — and already is — with you."[38] After all, the fruit of the Spirit is . . . peace.

If our interpretation is correct, three things happen simultaneously in these concluding and summarizing exhortations: (a) that they embrace what is good wherever they find it, including the culture with which they are most intimately familiar; (b) but that they do so in a discriminating way, (c) the key to which is the gospel Paul had long ago shared with them and lived before them — about a crucified Messiah, whose death on a cross served both to redeem them and to reveal the character of God into which they are continually being transformed. It is hard to imagine a more relevant word in our post-modern, media-saturated world, where "truth" is relative and morality is up for grabs.

The most common response to such a culture is not discrimination, but rejection. This text suggests a better way, that one approach the market-place, the arts, the media, the university, looking for what is "true" and "uplifting" and "admirable"; but that one do so with a discriminating eye and heart, for which the Crucified One serves as the template. Indeed, if one does not "consider carefully," and then discriminate on the basis of the gospel, what is rejected very often are the mere trappings, the more visible expressions, of the "world," while its anti-gospel values (relativism, materialism, hedonism, nationalism, individualism, to name but a few) are absorbed into the believer through cultural osmosis. This text reminds us that the head counts for something, after all; but it must be a sanctified head, ready to "practice" the gospel it knows through what has "been learned and received."

38. So also Meyer, 209, who sees the predicate "of peace" as unmistakably pointing to the special agency of the Spirit.

# B. ACKNOWLEDGING THEIR GIFT: FRIENDSHIP AND THE GOSPEL (4:10-20)

With his major concerns about "their circumstances" now addressed, and the "concluding exhortations" given, Paul turns at last to the first reason for the letter — to acknowledge their recent gift and thus to rejoice over this evidence of friendship. To this point he has not thanked them directly, although his gratitude is clearly implied in 1:3-7 and 2:25, 30 (perhaps 2:17). Some, to be sure, see this delay in saying "thank you" as evidence that Paul could not have written our Philippians in its present form: How could he wait to the very end, it is argued, before finally offering thanks for the gift?[1] And others look on its content as evidence of a strained relationship between him and (some of) them: How could a genuine "thank you" be expressed so reluctantly, and why does he twice tell them he really did not need their help (vv. 11-13, 17) before he actually thanks them for it (v. 18)?[2] These objections, however, overlook the primarily oral (and thus aural) culture within which this letter would be read and ignore the sociological framework of "friendship" in which it was written.[3]

As to the matter of placement: The first reason for the letter (acknowl-

---

1. See e.g., Beare (150), who finds it "inconceivable that Paul should wait all that time to express his thanks for the gifts." Cf. Michael (209), "Had the present letter been the first to go to Philippi with his thanks, he would surely not have deferred his reference to their gift until he had said everything else that he had to say." For a critique see n. 3.

2. What some have pejoratively called "thankless thanks," a phrase noted by Vincent (146) and thus traceable to the nineteenth c., regaining currency through Dibelius, Lohmeyer, and Gnilka (cf. Capper, "Dispute," 207-8). See also Michael (209-11), followed by Caird, who thinks he finds evidence here that Paul had written an earlier note of thanks, to which the Philippians had taken some exception, "complaining of what appeared to them to be a lack of adequate appreciation for their kindness" (209). Michael thus finds "the presence of . . . rebuke . . . unmistakable" in vv. 15 and 18, which also accounts for Paul's "extraordinary emphasis on his independence."

3. Indeed, much that has been written on this passage (e.g., about the alleged "long delay," Paul's not using the verb εὐχαριστεῖν, his placing this passage at the end of the letter, its form and content) reflects modern (basically Western) conventions, which tends to render them speculative and irrelevant (cf. Peterman, "Giving," 19-24). See, e.g., (1) Dodd's psychologizing of the apostle and his "bourgeois" attitude toward money (n. 18 on v. 15); (2) Collange's (149) mirror reading v. 17 as evidence of Paul's having actually solicited material help from them, because the situation in (Rome) had deteriorated (per 1:15-18); (3) Buchanan's view ("Epaphroditus' Sickness," 162, followed by Hawthorne) that what Paul is really about is a "delicate" combination of "gratitude" with a stern reminder that he does not want such gifts since it goes against his avowed policy (e.g., 2 Thess 3:7-10; 1 Cor 9:15-18); (4) Capper's view ("Dispute") that the lack of overflowing gratitude is due to a prior rift between Paul and the Philippians that has just been barely healed (see n. 4 on vv. 14-17).

edgment of their gift), it turns out, is almost certainly not its primary reason for having been written, which is to speak directly into their present circumstances before either Timothy or he comes on the scene (2:19-24). The latter, at least, is what gets the major attention; so much so, that even Paul's first report about "his affairs" (1:12-26) already has their situation in view. But having now dealt with his and their circumstances, and knowing full well what he was about, he concludes the letter on the same note with which it began (1:3-7) — their mutual partnership/participation in the gospel[4] — thus placing this matter in the emphatic, climactic position at the end. When read aloud in the gathered community, these will be the final words that are left ringing in their ears: that their gift to him has been a sweet-smelling sacrifice, pleasing to God; that God in turn, in keeping with his rich supply in Christ Jesus, will "fill them to the full" regarding all their needs; and that all of this redounds to God's eternal glory. At the same time, they will scarcely be able to overlook the exhortations and appeals that have preceded, given the predominance of these concerns in the large middle section of the letter. This is rhetoric at its best;[5] and the theory (predicated on our own sociology) that sees a later, rather mindless redactor "pasting" things together in this way turns out in the end to make him more clever than Paul.

As to the matter of "friendship": Although dealing primarily with "his affairs," in reality this section links his and their affairs together at the most significant point of "friendship," that of mutual giving and receiving (v. 15).[6] Indeed, much that puzzles us in this section is related to this phenomenon. Three matters intertwine: First is his genuine gratitude for their recent gift, expressed three times in three variations (vv. 10a, 14, 18). This is set, secondly, within the framework of Greco-Roman "friendship," based on mutuality and reciprocity, evidenced by "giving and receiving" — a theme that gets "strained" in this case because of (a) his being on the receiving end of that for which he has nothing to give in return and (b) their "mutuality" also carries some of the baggage of a "patron/ client" relationship,[7] due to his role as apostle of Jesus Christ.[8] Third, and most significantly (and typically!), this

---

4. For the difficulty in gaining precision on this important language, see on 1:5.

5. *Contra* Lightfoot (163), and many who have followed him, that "it is as if the Apostle said. I must not forget to thank you for your gift.'"

6. On this matter see the Introduction, pp. 4-7, which in many ways is essential reading for the discussion that follows (and esp. for vv. 14-17). The most significant primary source dealing with this matter is Seneca's *De Beneficiis;* cf. the somewhat condensed version in his *Ep. Mor.* 9. For helpful overviews see Saller, *Personal Patronage,* 1-39, and P. Marshall, *Enmity,* 1-33; cf. the more thorough discussion in Peterman, "Giving," 31-104.

7. See the Introduction, pp. 5-6; see also on 3:15.

8. Indeed, much of the discussion on this passage has been carried on as though Paul had never spoken to this issue previously (or by a misreading of the earlier evi-

sociological reality is rather totally subsumed under the greater reality of the gospel; thus the whole climaxes in doxology.[9]

All of this is fashioned with consummate artistry, some might say "tactful diplomacy," so that their "giving," his "receiving," and their long-term friendship ("partnership" in the gospel), which their gift reaffirms, climax in vv. 18-20 with gratitude (from Paul), accolade and promise (from God to them), and doxology (from both to God). To get there Paul repeats a pattern in vv. 10-13 and 14-17, in which: (a) he begins by acknowledging their recent gift (vv. 10a, 14); (b) he then qualifies what he says about them (10b, 15-16); and (c), with two clauses that begin "not that," he (more sharply) qualifies his "receiving" in relationship to his "need" (vv. 11-13, 17). The climax in vv. 18-20, it should be noted, begins with this same pattern (acknowledgment of their gift [v. 18] and the "qualifier" that God will thus meet their needs [v. 19]), but in place of the third element (Paul's "not that") he bursts into praise (v. 20). At the same time there is an interweaving of words and ideas, by repetition and wordplays, plus the "christianizing" of matters that are common stock in the culture, which makes the whole a marvelous tapestry.[10] All of which says "thank you" — to them for their long-term friendship and to God to whom all glory is due. Thus:

---

dence). But he had, in 1 Cor 9:1-18, where he defends his "right" (ἐξουσία) as an apostle to material support from his churches (vv. 3-12a, 13-14), in a context where he "explains" (in the form of a defense) why he has given it up in their case (vv. 12b, 15-18). The principle on which both "reciprocity" and "rights" are predicated is articulated in v. 11 ("If we have sown 'spiritual' seed among you, is it too much if we reap 'material' harvest from you?"). See further n. 5 on 4:14-17.

9. Some of those who have seen the sociological dimension of this passage have also tended to interpret it almost altogether along sociological lines (e.g., L. W. White, "Morality,"; Stowers, "Friends"; Capper, "Dispute"). The problem with doing so is that it slights the essential Paul, for whom everything, including the rhetorical and literary conventions to which he is a cultural heir, have been "transmuted" into the "shape" of the gospel. Thus, although one misses too much in this passage if one is not aware of the sociological realities that give it a cultural frame, one also misses too much if the "frame" gives meaning to the content, rather than the other way about. In Paul's hands the gospel gives new meaning even to the sociological reality of "friendship."

10. The linguistic ties between this passage and much that has preceded are so significant that any dismembering of this letter destroys the very "magic" that makes it work so marvelously as a letter of friendship. These include: the opening "I rejoiced in the Lord" (cf. 3:1; 4:4); the (now word play) on the verb φρονεῖν in v. 10 (cf. 1:7: 2:2-5; 3:15, 19; 4:2); the "christianizing" of Stoic terminology in v. 11 (cf. 4:8-9); the use of the ὑστερέω word group ("be lacking") in vv. 11-12 to refer to his "needs" (cf. 2:30); similarly, the use of "my needs" to refer to the same reality in v. 16 and 2:25; the use of the verb συγκοινωνέω in v. 14 (cf. 1:7) to refer to their "partnership with" Paul "in his affliction"; the language ἐν ἀρχῇ τοῦ εὐαγγελίου (lit., "in the beginning of the gospel") in v. 15, which echoes the identical idea in 1:5; and the use of the sacrificial

424

(a) 10a  Acknowledgment of their "renewed concern" for Paul in his need;

 (b) 10b  The qualifier: the intermediate hiatus in their "giving" was due to lack of opportunity, not lack of concern

  (c) 11-13 Pauline qualifier: "Not that" he speaks according to "need"; thus he "christianizes" the Stoic doctrine of "contentment": Neither want nor weal determined his life; in Christ he can handle either.

(a) 14  Second acknowledgement, now as "partnership in his affliction";

 (b) 15-16 The qualifier: reminder of their laudable history in this matter

  (c) 17  Pauline qualifier: "Not that" he desires the gift per se, but what the gift represents (an "ever-increasing balance in your account")

(a) 18  Third acknowledgment: Paul "abounds"; he has been "filled up"; at the same time, their "fragrant, sacrificial offering" pleases God

 (b) 19  The qualifier: Paul's reciprocity will come from God, who will "fill them up," supplying their "needs" in keeping with his own rich supply in Christ

  (c) 20  Doxology: To our God and Father be glory through endless ages.

The disturbing element for many are the two "not that" qualifiers, which in contemporary sociology would effect the opposite of what Paul intends. We instinctively have questions about one who begins an expression of gratitude as though the Philippians had finally gotten around to "showing concern for him again," then in effect tells them that he really did not need their gift in any case, and finally expresses his personal gratitude in terms of their making a sacrificial offering to God. What gives with such a fellow? But the key to the passage lies with these very elements that disturb us, which in fact make this a Christian expression of a first-century convention. Besides denying that their friendship is based on "usefulness" (the lowest form of "friendship"), Paul's point is that his joy lies not in the gifts per se — these he really could do with or without — but in the greater reality that the gifts represent:[11] the tangible evidence, now renewed, of his and their long-term

---

metaphor in v. 18 to refer to their "ministering" to his need (cf. 2:25 and 30). One must dance with unlimited sidesteps to remove this passage from the rest of the letter. Cf. Dalton ("Integrity," 99-101).

 11. So, e.g., Hawthorne and O'Brien, without however noting the significance of the convention of friendship.

friendship, which for Paul has the still greater significance of renewing their long-term "partnership/participation" with him in the gospel. This is why the climax is expressed in terms of their gift being a "fragrant and pleasing offering *to God,*" who in turn promises to pick up Paul's end of the reciprocity, all of which outbursts in praise of God's glory, the very glory that God has already abundantly lavished upon them both in Christ Jesus.[12]

A passage like this, one needs finally to note, should be read in light of Paul's unsolicited, lavish praise of this church in 2 Cor 8:1-5, with its thoroughly Christian equation of "affliction + poverty = abounding in generosity." It is unlikely that the Philippians have changed radically in the intervening few years. To the contrary, it is precisely this quality of their Christian life, expressed in his case within the cultural context of friendship, that causes Paul to give thanks in this way — as "rejoicing in the Lord" and as an outburst of praise to God's glory. Here is a community where the gospel had done its certain work.

## 1. Their Gift and Paul's "Need" (4:10-13)

> 10*I rejoice greatly in the Lord that at last you have renewed your concern for me. Indeed, you have been concerned, but you had no opportunity to show it.* 11*I am not saying this because I am in need, for I have learned to be content whatever the circumstances.* 12*I know what it is to be in need, and I know what it is to have plenty. I have learned the secret of being content in any and every situation, whether well fed or hungry, whether living in plenty or in want.* 13*I can do everything through him*[13] *who gives me strength.*

Despite the long history of the English translations' making this a separate paragraph, in reality it is simply the first step in acknowledging their gift. As noted, Paul's greater joy is in what the gift represents — tangible evidence of the rejuvenation of "friendship," and that as a demonstration of their "partner-

---

12. For convenience, the ensuing analysis will proceed according to the three "parts" noted above (cf. Bruce), recognizing that the "parts" are of our making, not Paul's — as are the two traditional paragraphings (10-13, 14-20 [NA[26], NIV, GNB, NAB, Jones, Müller, Hendriksen]; and 10-14, 15-20 [UBS[4], NRSV, REB, Lohmeyer, Kent]), both of which wrongly break up what is in fact a single piece in Paul's letter (so correctly, NASB, NJB).

13. According to the earliest and best evidence (ℵ* A B D* I 33 629 1739 pc lat co, Clement), Paul's sentence ends, ἐν τῷ ἐνδυναμοῦντί με ("in the one who strengthens me"). Given the preponderance of the "in Christ" language in this letter, and that he certainly intends "Christ" in this clause, the later scribes (F G Ψ Maj syr, Jerome) made explicit what Paul left implicit, by adding Χριστῷ at the end. And so it was transmitted to generations of English-speaking Christians, so that this well-known text will probably be "cited" in the same explicit way for some generations to come.

ship" with him in the gospel. Thus two matters are taken up in these opening sentences. First (v. 10a), Paul rejoices over their renewing the first feature of friendship, "giving and receiving." But having expressed that in terms of "now at last," he is quick to demur that they must not hear him wrongly (v. 10b). He knows, as they do, that the long hiatus in this tangible evidence of friendship (= partnership in the gospel) was due to their lack of opportunity.

Second (vv. 11-13), because his first concern is to express joy over friendship renewed, Paul feels compelled also to make sure that they do not understand what he has just said in terms of "need." This demurrer probably arises out of "friendship" as well. Very likely this is his way of reminding the Philippians that theirs is not based on "usefulness," but belonged to the highest level of friendship.[14] Thus Paul digresses momentarily to reject any notion that their friendship is based on "need," and thus has utilitarian origins. But in so doing, he has left us with one of his more remarkable moments, in which he uses the language — and outwardly assumes the stance — of Stoic "*self*-sufficiency," but radically transforms it into *Christ*-sufficiency. The net result is that Paul and Seneca, while appearing to be close, are a thousand leagues apart. The Stoic's (and Cynic's) "sufficiency/contentment" comes from within oneself; Paul's comes from without, from his being "a man in Christ," on whom he is totally "dependent" and thus not "independent" at all in the Stoic sense. Because Paul and the Philippians are both "in Christ," neither is dependent on the other for life in the world; but also because they are both "in Christ," Paul received their gift with joy, because this is how Christ helped him to "abound" in this case.

Finally, coming directly after v. 9 as it does, the language and the length of the passage suggest that it also serves as a final moment of *imitatio* in this letter. He has just urged them not to be anxious about anything, but to leave their situation in God's care, who as "the God of peace" will keep their hearts and minds in Christ. Paul now models what that means, that in Christ one can truly know "contentment" in any and all circumstances.[15]

---

14. Note the three kinds of friendship isolated by Aristotle (*Eth. Nic.* 8.3.1), and followed by others (Plutarch, *De Util.*; Seneca, *Ben.* 1.11.1; *Ep. Mor.* 9.8-9; cf. Cicero, *Inv.* 2.50), the "good," the "pleasant," and the "useful." Two things emerge in the discussions: that (1) the good" is the best of friendships, and somewhat idealistic, while "useful" is the commonest form, and can be entered into even by evil people for their mutual advantage; and (2) that the kind of "giving and receiving" that marked the latter also marked the former, so that pains are taken to distinguish the "good" from the merely "useful." Furthermore, Epicurus and his followers believed that even though friendship should be sought for its own sake, "it has its origins in the need for help" (*Gn* 5.23), a view that is rebuked by Cicero (*Fin.* 2.26.82-85). See the discussion in Marshall, *Enmity,* 25-30, although he does not connect these distinctions with what Paul is doing here.

15. Cf. Silva (234), who also notes this connection.

**10** The (correctly) untranslated *de* with which this sentence begins marks the transition to something new, but hardly an afterthought.[16] Paul is as good as his word, in this case his word of exhortation. Using the precise language of v. 4, but now in the past tense,[17] and with the addition of the adverb "greatly,"[18] he tells them that he burst into joy[19] at the arrival of Epaphroditus. They, his eschatological "joy" and "crown" (v. 1), are also cause for much past and present joy. Whatever else, they are his friends — his partners — in Christ.

His imprisonment had already resulted in rejoicing, since it became a catalyst for the advance of the gospel in Rome (1:18); now he tells them that their tangible reviving of friendship has likewise caused him to rejoice yet again while in detainment. As he twice exhorted them (3:1; 4:4), his rejoicing was "in the Lord," another subtle indication of the three-way bond (between him, them, and Christ) that holds the letter together. Paul rejoiced "in the Lord," the author of their common salvation, over the tangible evidence that they together belong to the Lord and thus to one another.[20]

But his stated reason for joy catches us by surprise: "that[21] at last you

16. As Lightfoot suggests (see n. 5); he is followed by Hawthorne (196), who makes altogether too much of this particle, which functions here as it did in 1:12 and 2:19 (cf. O'Brien, 516). Although δέ, the most common of the Greek particles, almost always carries a contrastive sense, the contrast is not always adversative. It is used by writers in all periods to mark the transition to a new section, and is thus contrastive in that sense.

17. Gk. ἐχάρην. Interpreters are divided as to whether this is a genuine aorist (Michael [but for some wrong reasons], Bruce, Silva, O'Brien; cf. Moffatt, Goodspeed, NEB) or an epistolary aorist (most interpreters and translations), which in the latter case may be translated as an English present (as the NIV, "I rejoice greatly"). But since Paul's first point of reference is to something in his own past, not just in the past from the perspective of their reading the letter, there seems to be no good reason to make it epistolary here (all the more so, since his "rejoicing" in 1:18 is expressed in the present tense). This is further supported by the addition of "greatly," which makes sense as referring to his joy at seeing Epaphroditus, but little sense as an epistolary aorist. In this regard, cf. Apion (Antonius Maximus) to Sabina (2nd c. CE): "When I learned that you were well, I rejoiced exceedingly (λίαν ἐχάρην)" (J. L. White, *Light,* 160). This does not exclude Paul's joy "running over" into the present as he writes. But his rejoicing in this case began with the arrival of Epaphroditus.

18. Gk. μεγάλως, one of the several NT hapax legomena in this passage.

19. On the phrase "rejoice in the Lord," its OT background and verbalizing implications, see the discussion on 3:1. It is of some interest that Paul's language here (4:10) is very close to what he says in 1 Cor 16:17 in response to the coming of Stephanas, Fortunatus, and Achaicus, although in that case it had nothing to do with a gift.

20. Barth (127), following Bengel, notes how "un-Stoic" these opening words are. A Stoic would have received the gift, but would scarcely have taken pleasure in it! Paul lives in a different world.

21. Gk. ὅτι, which in this instance is ambiguous. It introduces either a noun clause, giving the content of Paul's rejoicing, or an adverb clause, indicating its cause or basis. While either comes out at pretty much the same point, given the past tense of the verb

have renewed your concern for me." Paul's own qualifier that follows makes it clear that even though not intending these words pejoratively, he recognized that they could be taken so.[22] Three things lie behind the sentence: that "giving and receiving" is the first mark of friendship in the Greco-Roman world; that they had had a long history of "giving" to him (as vv. 15-16 make clear); that, as the various elements of this sentence indicate, some (probably considerable) time has elapsed since they had last ministered to his needs in this way.[23] How much time is impossible to say, but very likely several years. It is this lapse of time that accounts for how the sentence is expressed.

The verb "you have renewed" is a botanical metaphor, meaning to "blossom again"[24] — like perennials or the Spring shoots of deciduous trees and bushes. After a period of some dormancy in the matter of "giving and receiving," they have thus "revived" this dimension of their friendship with Paul. The adverb "at last"[25] likewise implies a hiatus in their giving. However, it probably does not mean "finally, at last," as though he had been expecting something in the meantime — which the qualifier that follows denies — but points rather to the conclusion of the hiatus. Thus, "now, finally, you were able to do what for a long time you could not."

What they were finally able to do again is expressed in language special to this letter: "to 'think' about me." Here begins the first in a series of word repetitions and word plays that dominate this final section of the letter. The verb "to think"[26] appeared first in the thanksgiving (1:7) to refer to Paul's

---

(n. 17), this ὅτι most likely expresses cause, "I rejoiced greatly because . . ." (cf. Loh-Nida, Hawthorne, O'Brien).

22. As some do; see, e.g., Capper ("Dispute," 207): "Paul's tone is virtually condescending, where his gratitude should overflow," because the Philippians have "reneged" on their "contract" (see n. 3 above and n. 4 on 4:14-17).

23. On this matter see further vv. 15-16.

24. Gk. ἀνεθάλετε, which in this case may be either transitive (= "you caused to grow") or intransitive (= "you bloomed again"), meaning either that they "revived their care for him" or that "they blossomed again, as far as their care for him is concerned." Cf. the metaphorical use in Sir 1:18 ("The fear of the Lord is a crown of wisdom, causing peace and health to bloom again") and 11:22 ("The blessing of the Lord is the reward of the godly, and the Lord shall cause his blessing to bloom again quickly"). Meyer (211-12) takes the improbable view that what has "blossomed again" is their prosperity, which now made it possible for them to give again. But 2 Cor 8:1-5 makes clear that "affliction and poverty" have long been their lot and had scarcely hindered their generosity!

25. Gk. ἤδη ποτέ; the combination occurs elsewhere in the NT only in Rom 1:10, where it is anticipatory and means something like "finally at last." It can scarcely mean that here, since in Romans it refers to something that had not yet happened, while here it refers to a renewal of something that has (apparently) lain dormant. Cf. 2 Clem 13:1 ("let us now at last repent"; which Lightfoot [AF²] translates, "let us repent immediately").

26. Gk. φρονεῖν; see on 1:7; 2:2, 5; 3:15-16, 19; 4:2.

"feeling this way" about them. Elsewhere in the letter it means "have a (certain) mindset." Some of the earlier uses occur in relational contexts, and therefore may lean toward "have the same mindset toward one another" (2:2; 4:2), in the sense of "show mutual care for each other."[27] That is certainly the sense here; hence the English translations have either "care for" or "be concerned about." In any case, this usage is hardly accidental. What has brought him joy is the renewal of their "thinking about/caring for" him in this way.

That this is Paul's intent is made certain by the qualifier, "indeed, you have been concerned, but you had no opportunity to show it." Two points of grammar in this clause indicate he is trying to deflect possible misunderstanding of the first clause. He begins, first, "with reference to which[28] indeed," a combination that picks up the infinitive "to be concerned" and intensifies it (= "with reference to which you were indeed[29] continually concerned"). Second, both verbs in this clause are imperfects, implying a continual concern for Paul with a likewise ongoing lack of opportunity[30] to do anything about it. Thus he is quick to acknowledge that he well understands the hiatus had nothing to do with their lack of concern but of opportunity.

**11** Having qualified his opening expression of joy against possible misunderstanding, Paul proceeds to qualify the event itself still further. But this time he is not so much qualifying something specifically said as he is putting the whole matter into perspective. His "not that"[31] is thus intended

27. On this matter see Stowers, "Friends," 111-12, although he tends to see the "one another" in terms of his and theirs together, rather than within the community itself, which seems to be a misreading of the text. A very similar thing happens in the occurrences in Romans, where the verb most often means to "have a certain disposition toward something or someone," but in 12:16 means "show mutual concern for one another."

28. Gk. ἐφ' ᾧ, a combination that is extraordinarily difficult in Paul; see on 3:12 above (cf. Rom 5:12, which is one of the classical exegetical cruxes in the Pauline corpus). As Fitzmyer notes ("Consecutive," 331), "the causal sense . . . does not impose itself." Rather, it either means (most likely) something like, "to which end," referring to the "concern about him" just mentioned, or (less likely) the ᾧ refers to Paul (as Calvin, Kennedy, Fitzmyer). For a complete discussion of the options and defense of the meaning suggested here, see Meyer, 212-14; see Fitzmyer for a thorough airing of the idiom in Greek antiquity.

29. Gk. ἐφ' ᾧ καὶ ἐφρονεῖτε, which Vincent (142) and others (e.g., O'Brien; Thrall, Greek Particles, 90) would translate "also," meaning that besides their recent gift they had *also* been thinking about him right along. That correctly recognizes the sense of "addition" inherent to the καί, but does not seem adequately to represent in English its intensive force.

30. Gk. ἠκαιρεῖσθε, lit. "have no time," here meaning "without time" in the sense of "lacking opportunity"; another NT hapax.

31. Gk. οὐχ ὅτι, cf. v. 17; for this usage in Paul see esp. on 3:12, where we suggested it represents our idiom, "this is not to say that."

to guard against anyone's drawing wrong inferences from what he has just said. The wrong inference would be that his joy is over their gift as such, as though joy had to do with finally being able to eat again.[32] On the contrary, he says, I have not said any of this because "I speak according to need."[33] His joy is over their friendship; and their friendship, he is quick to point out, is not utilitarian, related to what he can secure from it.[34]

Here is also the second in the series of word repetitions and wordplays in this passage. He had told them in 2:30 that he *did* have "lack" — of their presence! — which was made up in part by Epaphroditus's coming. Now he says that his joy is *not* over their filling his "lack" in the material sense (although he gladly acknowledges in v. 18 that he was "filled to the full" by their gift). But that also calls for further explanation; so rather than take up the matter of what his joy *is* all about (which comes next in vv. 14-17), he instead goes on to elaborate why their ministering to his "need" was not the reason for his joy.

On the surface, his explanation[35] looks like a meteor fallen from the Stoic sky into his epistle: "For I have learned to be content whatever the circumstances."[36] The word translated "content"[37] expresses the ultimate

---

32. On the fact that prisoners in the Roman world had to be provided for by friends, see on 2:25; cf. Rapske, *Acts,* 209-16.

33. Gk. καθ' ὑστέρησιν. The noun, which means "want, need, lack, poverty," occurs only here in Paul (and elsewhere in the NT only in Mark 12:44, of the widow casting in her "mite" out of "penury"). But see ὑστέρημα in 2:30 (cf. 1 Thes 3:10; 1 Cor 16:17; 2 Cor 8:14; 9:12; 11:9). These usages illustrate the differences between -ησις and -ημα nouns, the former emphasizing the verbal idea, the latter denoting a concrete expression of the idea. Thus Paul is not here referring to a specific expression of need, but to "being in need." The preposition in this case may be an instance of κατά = cause, reason (so Hawthorne, O'Brien); but it makes just as good sense to keep its basic sense of "the standard by which something is measured." Thus, "in speaking this way, it is not my personal 'need' which sets the standard for what I say."

34. On this matter see n. 14 above.

35. Thus we meet one of the relatively few explanatory γάρ's in this letter; see above on 1:19, 21; 2:13, 20, 21, 27; 3:3, 18, 20. Which indicates how little this letter is "argumentation."

36. Gk. ἐν οἷς εἰμι, meaning "in the situations in which I find myself." Curiously, many object to translating this "whatever the circumstances," since Paul uses a form of ὅς rather than ὅσος. They prefer to translate "in the state in which I am" (Vincent), meaning in his present circumstances (cf. Kent, Hawthorne). But both the plural and the elaborating phrase "in every and in all circumstances" in the next verse suggest that Paul is referring not simply to his present imprisonment, but to all the circumstances of his life.

37. Gk. αὐτάρκης; the adj. occurs only here in the NT, the noun (αὐταρκεία) only in 2 Cor 9:8 and 1 Tim 6:6. The usage in 2 Cor 9:8 is certain evidence that the word is part of Paul's regular vocabulary and that it can come close to "sufficiency," without the sense of "self-sufficiency." Too much can be made of its usage by Stoic and Cynic moral philosophers, since by the first Christian century it had become common parlance for "contentment," in

431

goal of Stoicism: to live above need and abundance in such a way as to be "self-sufficient," not meaning that one is oblivious to circumstances, but that the truly *autarkēs* person is not determined by such. One is "independent" of others and of circumstances in the sense of being free from their either causing distress or effecting serenity. Serenity comes from being sufficient unto oneself. Although one cannot be sure that Paul is deliberately echoing Stoic language, it is difficult to imagine the Philippians' not having recognized it as such. The potency of what Paul does — which they undoubtedly would have picked up on — is to use language similar to that of Stoicism to describe an attitude toward life that outwardly looks like theirs, but whose source, and therefore significance, is radically different. But before that (v. 13), Paul elaborates in terms of material needs (v. 12) what he has here avowed.

**12** The explanatory sentences in this verse are typically balanced, and somewhat rhythmical.[38] He begins with the broader vocabulary of want and plenty, "I know both how to be humbled;[39] I know also how to abound."[40] Although these will lead to the more specific matters of material needs, there is every good reason to think that by starting with these verbs, he intended, "to be humbled and to abound in every which way," including in the specific ways he will pick up next, but not limited to these.[41] After all, to be "humbled"

---

very much the sense that word carries in English. Thus Polybius speaks of Lycurgus, who, while having made the private lives of Spartan citizen "contented" (αὐτάρκεις), did not "make the spirit of the city as a whole likewise contented (αὔταρκες) and moderate" (LCL, p. 379); cf. the many occurrences in Josephus and Philo as well. What makes the word "Stoic-sounding" here is its usage in context. This sentence sounds exactly like something Seneca or Epictetus could have written. Cf., e.g., Seneca (*Vit. Beat.* 6.2): "The happy man is content with his present lot, no matter what it is, and is reconciled to his circumstances" (LCL, p. 115); thus he can say, "The wise man is sufficient unto himself for a happy existence" (*Ep. Mor.* 9.13; LCL, p. 51), although he qualifies the latter so as not to exclude "friendship" for the one who is at the same time "self-sufficient." Cf. Epictetus 4.7.14, "Wherever I go it will be well with me, for here where I am it was well with me, not because of my location, but because of my judgments [δόγματα = reasoned principles], and these I shall carry with me; . . . and with possession of them I am content [ἀρκεῖ], wherever I be and whatever I do" (LCL, p. 365). See also Sevenster, *Paul and Seneca,* 113-14.

38. Cf. Lohmeyer, Gnilka, and Martin, who, however, make far too much of this, as though something "poetic" were involved. One may as well argue for "poetry" in 1 Cor 7, where over and again this kind of balanced, rhythmic sentence occurs (cf. also 1 Cor 6:12-14, 16-17). This is simply the way Paul speaks and writes about every kind of matter.

39. Gk. ταπεινοῦσθαι, used of Jesus in 2:8; elsewhere in Paul only in 2 Cor 11:7, referring to his "humbling himself" by working with his own hands, and 12:21, referring to God's humbling him again before the Corinthians.

40. Gk. περισσεύειν; used again at the end of the sentence, and in 4:18 to refer to their gift. Most often in Paul it is used for "abounding" in spiritual qualities.

41. *Contra* O'Brien (523), who because of the context would limit it to "economic deprivation." The word seems too rich in content for such specific limitation.

is not the ordinary verb for "being in want"; moreover, it is a thoroughly non-Stoic word. Some Stoics may have reveled in "want"; none of them could tolerate "humiliation," which often headed their lists of attitudes to be avoided. Whether deliberately chosen over against them or not, and that is moot, for Paul this verb not only indicates "poverty," but embraces a way of life similar to that of his Lord (2:8; cf. Matt 11:28), a way of life that finds expression elsewhere in his various "hardship lists."[42]

Thus, "in every and in all circumstances,"[43] and now in reverse order, Paul specifies: "I have learned the secret"[44] of what it means "both to be well fed or go hungry,[45] both to abound and to be in need." Although the verb "learn the secret" is primarily a technical term for initiation into the mysteries, Paul is obviously using it metaphorically. While others have been "initiated into the mysteries," he says, "I have been initiated into both having a full stomach and going hungry." This passage joins others to make clear that, although Paul often ate well, he also knew very little of the cultural equivalent of our "three square meals a day." But the addition "to abound and to suffer need" probably point — on the "down" side, as do his hardship lists — to other material deprivations or supply, such as clothing (being in "rags"), shelter (homelessness), and less material ones such as toil and lack of rest.[46]

What is striking, of course, is his insistence that he knows the secret of *both* plenty and want.[47] His various "hardship lists" make it clear that he has experienced "plenty" of "want." But in contrast to some of the Cynics, he did not choose "want" as a way of life, so as to demonstrate himself *autarkēs;* rather he had learned to accept whatever came his way, knowing that his life was not conditioned by either, and that his relationship to Christ made one or the other essentially irrelevant in any case. Where we otherwise lack direct evidence from him are situations in which he "abounded" in "plenty" — at least on the material side of things, although in this letter he

42. See, e.g., 1 Cor 4:11-13; 2 Cor 6:4-5; 11:23-29; cf. 2 Cor 4:8-9.

43. Gk. ἐν παντὶ καὶ ἐν πᾶσιν, lit. "in everything and in all things"; cf. 2 Cor 11:6.

44. Gk. μεμύημαι, only here in the NT. The word is a technical term for initiation into the Mystery cults. Some (e.g., Lightfoot, Beare, Hawthorne) probably make too much of its origins, especially since it is so clearly metaphorical here.

45. Gk. καὶ χορτάζεσθαι καὶ πεινᾶν, the same combination occurs in Matt 5:6.

46. Not to mention "a day and night in the deep" (2 Cor 11:25), which has always struck me as too casually read by most of us. As one who has lived most of his life by the sea, I can only imagine the nightmare that must have been. That may not have been as "humiliating" in one way as the five times he received the thirty-nine stripes; but the desperation and loneliness of such "humbling" must have been intense — and this before the shipwreck at Malta.

47. With insight Calvin (292) notes that learning how to "abound" is "an excellent and rare virtue, and much greater than the endurance of poverty."

may very well be alluding to the generous patronage of the Philippians, both when he and his co-workers lived in Lydia's household and when they repeatedly supplied his material needs in Thessalonica and Corinth, and perhaps elsewhere.

**13** With the well-known words of this verse, Paul brings closure to this brief digression (vv. 11-13), in which he explains that his *joy* in receiving their gift was not predicated on their meeting his *need*. How has he learned to live in either want or plenty? His response: "I can do everything through[48] him who gives me strength." With that he transforms the very Stoic-sounding sentences that have preceded from appearing to promote any sense of sufficiency within himself to a sufficiency quite beyond himself, to Christ,[49] the basis and source of everything for Paul. Thus he turns "self-sufficiency" into "contentment" because of his "Christ-sufficiency." In effect this sentence spells out at the practical level the slogan of his life, expressed in 1:21: "for me to live is Christ."

"Everything" in this case, of course, refers first of all to his living in "want or plenty."[50] Paul finds Christ sufficient in times of bounty as well as in times of need. Although he appears to have had less of the former than the latter, here is his way of handling the warning to Israel given in Deuteronomy 8 that they not forget the Lord once they have experienced plenty. Thus, this passage is not an expression of Stoicism, not even a christianized version of the Stoic ideal; rather, it is but another of scores of such passages that indicate

48. Gk. ἐν τῷ ἐνδυναμοῦντι (cf. n. 13), which, given the frequency of the "in Christ" kind of phrase in Philippians, almost certainly does not primarily express agency here — although such an idea does not lag very far behind. Paul is referring to his being "in him, that is, in the one who enables." The problem with translating it "through him" is that it often leads to a kind of triumphalism that "when . . . empowered by Christ, nothing was beyond [Paul's] capabilities" (O'Brien, 526). O'Brien rightly contends against such a reading of the text (but see further n. 50).

49. That Paul intends Christ can scarcely be doubted; see on n. 13. For a similar use of the verb, but in the aorist, see 1 Tim 1:12.

50. This is made certain by the emphatic position of the πάντα, which in this case picks up the ἐν παντὶ καὶ πᾶσιν in v. 12. Missing this grammatical and contextual point has allowed some to quote this sentence out of context as a kind of eternal "gnomic" promise of Christ's help for any and everything, sometimes in a triumphalistic way that stands in total contradiction to its intent. On the other hand, to limit it merely to "want" or "plenty" (as, e.g., O'Brien, 526) is too constricting, since for Paul it does in fact express the reality of his entire life. Just as with "being humbled" in v. 12, so "everything" in this sentence should be understood more broadly as well, as long as it is understood within Paul's theological frame of reference. That is, his singular focus on Christ (1:21), whom he longs to know and to whose death he wants his entire life to be conformed, already dictates what "all things" means for him. To take this sentence out of that singular Christ-focused context of his life is to doom it to serve for lesser, more often selfish, things.

the absolute Christ-centeredness of Paul's whole life. He is a "man in Christ." As such he takes what Christ brings. If it means "plenty," he is a man in Christ, and that alone; if it means "want," he is still a man in Christ, and he accepts deprivation as part of his understanding of discipleship.

Therefore, although this passage belongs in part to the conventions of "friendship," as with all such cultural conventions, in Paul's hand they are transformed into gospel. Moreover, given the context, one should recognize this brief autobiographical moment also to serve in a paradigmatic way. He has just urged them to "practice" what he both taught and modeled (v. 9). In the midst of their own present difficulties, here is what they too should learn of life in Christ, that being "in him who enables" means to be "content" whatever their circumstances.

And all of this (vv. 11-13), one must remember, has been said in order to inform the Philippians that his joy is not simply over their gift — although he will finally express his deep gratitude for that as well. Thus, with the issue of "need" spoken to, he returns in v. 14 to the acknowledgment of their gift and their friendship.

This marvelous passage has also had its own unfortunate history of interpretation, in the hands both of its friends and of Paul's detractors. His detractors look on the text as unbearable ingratitude, that he should begin the thanksgiving for their gift by brushing it aside in an apparently peremptory fashion. Better not to give such people gifts who treat the gift so unfeelingly, so "stoically" as it were! But such detractors understand neither the nature of first-century friendship nor the apostle's own aim, which is to focus on their friendship and partnership *in the gospel,* which their gift represents and which is greater by far than the "mere gift" itself. Only in a culture like ours, where "things" tend to be more significant than people, would one remonstrate at what the apostle has done here.

On the other hand, Paul's friends have sometimes mangled the text by quoting it apart from its present context. The worst expression of this abuse occurs with v. 13, which is sometimes made to say that "I can do *all things* (especially extraordinary things) through Christ who strengthens me." Very often the application takes a form exactly the opposite of Paul's — with a bit of v. 19 thrown into the mix, "when in want I shall receive plenty" because of my relationship with Christ. Paul's point is that he has learned to live in either want or plenty through the enabling of Christ. Being in Christ, not being self-sufficient, has rendered both want and weal of little or no significance. Experience in the church should teach one what the Stoics themselves recognized, that either "want" or "wealth" can have deleterious affect on one's life, those in "want" because their "want" consumes them, those in "wealth" because their "wealth" does the same. The net result is a tragically small person. On the other hand, the Pauline perspective — life as cruciform, being "conformed to his death so as to attain the resurrection" — raises God's people above the dictates of either. Those in "want" learn patience and trust in suffering; those in "wealth" learn humility and dependence in prospering, not to mention the joy of giving without strings attached!

## 2. Their Gift as Partnership in the Gospel (4:14-17)[1]

> 14*Yet it was good of you to share in my troubles.* 15*Moreover,*[2] *as you Philippians know, in the early days of your acquaintance with the gospel, when I set out from Macedonia, not one church shared with me in the matter of giving and receiving, except you only;* 16*for even when I was in Thessalonica, you sent me aid*[3] *again and again when I was in need.* 17*Not that I am looking for a gift, but I am looking for what may be credited to your account.*

Returning to the language of the thanksgiving in 1:3-8, Paul resumes what he began in v. 10, moving it a step forward. In v. 10 he joyfully received their gift as tangible evidence that *their care for him* had "blossomed afresh." Since their gift met his material needs while imprisoned, it is also evidence of their being *partners with him in his affliction* (v. 14), and thus of their partnership with him *in the work of the gospel* (v. 15). As in 1:5-7, their love for Paul and serving the cause of the gospel blend. After all, to love Paul is to love the gospel.

In vv. 15-16 this "partnership" is expressed in the language of Greco-Roman friendship, language that untangles much in this letter.[4] He

---

1. As noted above (n. 12 on vv. 10-13) this is not a paragraph in its own right, but it follows the "pattern" of vv. 10-13 and makes its own distinct contribution to the overall expression of gratitude. Hence the reason for isolating it in the present discussion.

2. Lying behind this "moreover" is a δὲ καί. The δέ is omitted by P⁴⁶ D* pc, probably due to homoeoteleuton (οἴδατε δέ).

3. Paul's Greek reads εἰς τὴν χρείαν μοι ἐπέμψατε (= you sent to me for my need), which is just awkward enough for it to have been considerably tampered with in the process of transmission. One strand of "correction" (P⁴⁶ A D* 81 104 326 1175 1241ˢ 2464 pc) omitted the εἰς (= "you sent what I needed"), although this is most likely purely accidental (resulting from homoeoteleuton, δὶς εἰς). Another strand (D L P 323 614 629 630 pc) changed the μοι to μου, an understandable, "logical" variation.

4. *Contra* many who see it as some form of "thankless thanks," in a pejorative sense; see nn. 2 and 3 on 4:10-20. Sampley (*Partnership,* 51-77), on the basis of the commercial language (see on vv. 15-16, 17) suggests that the passage represents a version of "consensual *societas,*" in which Paul and the Philippians have entered into a form of contractual "partnership" in the gospel. Simply put, Paul preaches, they pay — although in Sampley's version the gospel modifies the relationship somewhat. This suggestion has

recounts their history of material support in terms of their having entered into a "giving and receiving" relationship with him, which is the first mark of friendship. "Giving" is what has been renewed. But friendship also presupposes reciprocation. In terms of the principle established in 1 Cor 9:11,[5] their gift is already to be understood as reciprocation; but having now "received" their gift, it is Paul's turn to reciprocate, which he does beginning in v. 17. The gift itself, he reminds them (cf. v. 11), is incidental; what he desires is for them to experience "an ever-increasing balance in their [divine] account" (= divine reciprocation), which in this first instance has to do with *eschatological* reward. *Present* "reciprocation" is promised in v. 19, now in terms of God supplying their various needs (including material ones).

As with the preceding sub-paragraph, where Paul transformed the language, and thus the significance, of the Stoic idea of "contentment" into something radically Christian, so here. The language is that of Greco-Roman friendship, which in this case is not so much "transformed" as it is totally subsumed under the greater reality of the gospel, thus giving friendship new meaning.

**14** The "yet" with which this sentence begins is the certain evidence that vv. 10-13 do not constitute a paragraph on their own. This particular adversative is Paul's way of "breaking off a discussion and emphasizing what is important" (BAGD).[6] Thus, even though Paul's life is not determined by "need" — he has learned "contentment" whether full or hungry — "none-

---

been picked up and applied vigorously by Capper ("Dispute"), who reads the whole letter in light of an alleged "dispute" between Paul and the Philippians over (a) Paul's ending up in prison, thus not fulfilling his end of the "contract"; (b) the Philippians' not sending him money as a result; and (c) our letter as his follow-up after their "pay" has been re-instated, explaining that they have read his imprisonment incorrectly and thus barely giving thanks for what he saw as his due. Besides missing the fact that the commercial language had already been co-opted by writers on friendship, this view strains Paul's language considerably (see nn. 30, 34, 35 below), and must reinterpret the friendship motifs in purely "utilitarian" terms (see n. 14 on 4:10-13). Capper's version in particular reflects a trend to mirror read "opposition" between Paul and his churches behind every sentence in his letters where moderns feel uncomfortable with the way Paul expresses himself (see further the Introduction, p. 7 n. 24).

5. That is, "material" support from his churches is his due because he has minis-tered the life of the Spirit to them (see n. 8 on vv. 10-13). Meyer, Hawthorne, *et al.,* object to the use of the 1 Corinthians reference with regard to the present passage because it "mixes" two kinds of giving and receiving, which stands over against their "literal" understanding of the commercial language. But the objection misses the friendship (and therefore metaphorical) dimension of the language here, which has to do with reciprocity, not an actual business transaction.

6. Gk. πλήν, see above on 3:16 and the discussion on 1 Cor 11:11 in Fee, *First Corinthians,* 522; cf. Zerwick-Grosvenor (602), "but still."

theless," he now comes back, picking up the thread of v. 10, "what you did in my behalf was a good thing."[7]

Paul's emphasis lies on the "good" they did. But not yet is the "good" the gift itself; that is reserved for the end (v. 18). This sentence resumes the acknowledgment begun in v. 10, where Paul referred to the gift as "a renaissance of your caring for me." Here that is elaborated in terms of their "partnership/participation with him[8] in his affliction." This returns to the language of 1:7, where Paul gives reason for his thanksgiving in terms of their being "partners/participants" together with him in his chains and in the defense of the gospel. In the present instance he refers to his imprisonment with the broader word "affliction,"[9] used most often to refer to afflictions suffered by

---

7. Gk. καλῶς ἐποιήσατε (cf. Acts 10:33), for which the American slang, "you did good," offers a literal, if ungrammatical, "translation." Καλῶς is the adverb of the adj. καλός, which variously means "good, beautiful, pleasant, noble, splendid." The English equivalent "well" would lose too much of the sense of the Greek. The NIV chose to keep the sense of the adverb, but did so at the expense of the verb; "it was good of you" seems a bit bland for the Greek idiom. It should also be pointed out that the combination καλῶς ἐποιήσατε also plays havoc with those views which see Paul in 4:10-20 as "virtually condescending" (Capper) or as involving "some measure of rebuke" (Michael). See n. 4 above and nn. 2 and 3 on 4:10-20.

8. Gk. συγκοινωνήσαντες (cf. the adj. in 1:7), a modal participle (= in this way); thus they "did good" *by sharing* his affliction with him. This anticipates the noncompounded form of the verb that recurs in v. 15, for whose meaning see the discussion on 1:5. My infelicitous "translation" is an attempt to capture both nuances in the verb, the primary one of "participating" in something, which in 1:5-7 and here means also to "participate" as "partners" with Paul in both his suffering and the gospel. The redundant συν prefix in particular emphasizes their participating together with him *in his affliction.* Cf. Lightfoot (164), "It was not the actual pecuniary relief, so much as the sympathy and companionship in his sorrow, that the apostle valued." See further n. 87 on 1:7.

The attempt by Sampley (see n. 4 above) to make κοινωνία the equivalent of the Roman *societas* (= contractual "partnership") has special difficulty with this compound, since the dative μου τῇ θλίψει indicates that the *koinonia* is in Paul's affliction, not "partnership" in a financial pact. Thus Sampley sees this usage as "incidental" (p. 60). It is not surprising that Capper avoids discussion of this verb and its corresponding adjective (1:7) altogether (cf. Beare [153], whose fault is even greater, since he wrote a commentary and did not so much as mention this verb and its prepositional phrase in commenting on this verse). This passage joins 1:7 and 3:10 (in light of 1:29-30) to indicate that the *first* meaning of the word group in Philippians has to do with "participation" in the sufferings of Christ, which Paul, by way of paradigm, declares to be his highest value and to which he desires his whole life to be conformed.

9. Gk. μου τῇ θλίψει; for θλῖψις cf. 1:17 above. See the helpful overview by J. Kremer, *EDNT,* 2.151-52; cf. *NIDNTT,* 2.807-9 (R. Schippers). Although it is true that this word often inherently carries eschatological overtones (so Schlier, *TDNT,* 3.144-47, followed by Kremer; cf. Martin [164, followed by Melick], who rejects any reference here to Paul's imprisonment — despite 1:7 and 17), such overtones are only minimally present

believers because of their relationship to Christ. It is an especially appropriate word in this case because not only did they "participate" with him in *his* affliction by sending their gift, but they did so in the context of *their own* affliction, noted in 1:29-30 and 2:17 and hinted at elsewhere.

**15-16** Reintroduction of the language "participation" launches Paul into a brief rehearsal of the Philippians' considerable — and exemplary — history in this regard. He begins with an emphatic reminder, "now you know, even you Philippians yourselves."[10] The content, which elaborates the theme of their "participation/partnership" with him, is in some ways quite remarkable, since it tells *their* story, and is thus well known to them.[11] Our interest in the passage is with both the *what* and *how* and the *why*. The *why* we will note briefly at the end; first a look at *what* Paul says, including *how* he says it, which is of interest in two ways.

First, he reminds them of their past "partnership with him in the gospel"; but, second, that reminder is couched in the language of friendship, indeed of the primary expression of friendship in Greco-Roman antiquity,

---

in this case, where there is no *eschatological significance* attached to Paul's present "affliction" *by imprisonment.*

The grammar is difficult. Ordinarily one would have expected μοι τῆς θλίψεως, had Paul intended "sharers together with me in the affliction," in which case the μοι would pick up the "together" in the συν, and τῆς θλίψεως would be a genitive with κοινωνέω. Nonetheless, this is probably what Paul in fact intended with the present combination. By bringing the "my" forward for emphasis (a rare "vernacular possessive" [see on 2:2], which occurs with the pronoun μου only in Rom 11:14; 1 Cor 9:27; Phil 2:2; and Phlm 20 among scores of occurrences), Paul puts θλῖψις in the dative as his way of emphasizing the "togetherness" inherent in the συν. The result is even greater emphasis on their being sharers in the affliction itself, while the "vernacular possessive" emphasizes that they share it with Paul.

10. Gk. οἴδατε δὲ καὶ ὑμεῖς, Φιλιππήσιοι. The δέ marks a transition in the narrative; the combination καὶ ὑμεῖς ("even you yourselves") and the vocative, "Philippians," together create the impression of strong emphasis on what he is about to narrate — a way of saying, "sit up and take note of what I am about to say." As noted on 1:2, the rare use of the designation "Philippians" also calls attention to their present earthly situation. Here it is used as an expression of affection (so most interpreters), *contra* Michael (218; cf. Hawthorne, 203), who sees it as intended "to soften or tone down a rebuke, lest perchance it might seem too severe."

11. One might compare this passage with sentences in Cicero and Seneca, which appear in their discussions of friendship: "Services . . . ought to be kept in mind by him for whom they were performed and should not be mentioned by him who performed them" (Cic. *Amic.* 71; LCL 20.181); "In the case of a benefit . . . the one should straightway forget that it was given, the other should never forget that it was received" (Sen. *Ben.* 2.10; LCL 3.67). Paul's sentence is evidence that he does "not forget it"; at the same time, he "mentions it" for the Philippians — hence the emphasis on their "knowing it" — since it would be impolitic for them to do so.

"partnership in the matter of giving and receiving." The narrative itself forms an "inclusio" around the theme of friendship:

A      15At the beginning of the gospel,
             when I set out from Macedonia,
   B          not one church shared with me
                  in the matter of giving and receiving,
             except you only;
A′      16for even in Thessalonica,
                  once and again,
             you sent (aid) for my need.

Part A takes them back to the beginning of their association with Paul, from the time he first departed from Philippi, carrying through beyond his departure from Philippi to his departure from the province (Macedonia). Part B takes up the theme of friendship, their "partnership with him in the matter of giving and receiving," emphasizing in particular their singular history in this matter. Part A′ reemphasizes both of these realities by reminding them that "even in Thessalonica," at his first stopover after leaving Philippi and even before leaving Macedonia, they had already ministered to his physical needs on several occasions. The result is a threefold emphasis: (a) on their friendship (= "partnership in giving and receiving"); (b) that it goes back to the beginning of his association with them; and (c) that they were the only church with whom he had entered into this kind of "contractual friendship."

(A) What Paul reminds them of first is that their "partnership" with him in "giving and receiving" has to do with the gospel, that it goes back to "the beginning of the gospel," which, given that the narrative is for their benefit and thus from their point of view, refers back to the time of their origins as believers in Christ.[12] His emphasis in this initial phrase is twofold:

12. Thus the NIV's expanded translation, "in the early days of *your acquaintance with* the gospel." For this understanding, cf. the discussion of the similar phrase in 1:5 (so most interpreters, e.g., Meyer, Vincent, Kennedy, Jones, Plummer, Dibelius, Lohmeyer, Müller, Hendriksen, Gnilka, Collange, Martin, Bruce, O'Brien). There has been an unusual amount of speculation over this phrase (cf. the articles by Glombitza, "Dank"; Suggs, "Concerning" [see the overviews and critique by O'Brien, 531-32]; Beare, who finds no solution satisfactory; and Capper, "Dispute," 204-6). For its meaning here, see the identical usage in *1 Clem* 47:1 ("what did he [Paul] first write to you in the beginning of the gospel?"). Writing to Corinth some forty-five years after the founding of the church and some forty years after 1 Corinthians, to which he is referring, Clement uses this phrase from the Corinthians' point of view to refer to their origins as Christians, even though 1 Corinthians was written several years after their "beginnings." The present context calls for the same sense.

440

(1) that the "friendship" into which he and they had entered, of which he will speak next, has its focus not just on his and their own personal relationship, but is a three-way bond that includes Christ and the gospel — the "glue" that has cemented their relationship and that gives it significance (see on 1:5); and (2) that this partnership goes back to their beginnings as Christians.

Second, he reminds them that the outworking of this "partnership in the gospel" stems from the time[13] he "set out from Macedonia." This phrase is somewhat ambiguous, since on the one hand Paul frequently uses the provincial name when referring to Philippi in particular,[14] while on the other hand it technically refers to the province and should refer to the time when (or after) he left Berea (Acts 17:10-15). Given the preceding vocative, "you Philippians," which particularizes them within Macedonia, and the way he further qualifies their role even in Thessalonica, a Macedonian city, he almost certainly intended them to hear this clause in the sense of his departing the province.[15] Why he should mention this aspect first, before that of Thessalonica (v. 16) which chronologically came first, is something of a puzzle.[16] Most

---

13. Gk. ὅτε ἐξῆλθον, which can mean either, "at the moment I set out" (Meyer, *et al.*), or (more likely) "after I had set out," where the Greek aorist has a pluperfect sense, as it often does in narrative (Burton, *Moods,* 23-24; so, e.g., Lightfoot, O'Brien). Which view one takes depends in part on how one understands this initial clause in relation to the final clause in v. 16. Since the "pluperfect aorist" is such a common practice, there is no good reason to suppose that the Philippians were tracking Paul's moves from the moment he left Berea (his last stop in Macedonia) so as to offer him financial support; and in any case we have firm evidence of such ministry in Corinth (2 Cor 11:9). Moreover, the evidence in 1 Thess 2:9 and 2 Thess 3:8 demonstrates that their "ministry to his needs" did not begin to cover all the living expenses for him and his companions.

The very awkwardness of the sentence when taken literally (that he entered into partnership with them *after* he had left Macedonia, hence well after he had left *them*) suggests that Paul's sentence is expressed "carelessly," which I take to mean "casually," precisely because it is *not* calculated but is the stuff of personal narrative. After dictating v. 16, Paul saw no need to "clean up" the sentence because he knew the Philippians would understand him well enough, even if we are less sure. This rather "casual" way of expressing himself throws considerable doubt on Capper's reconstruction that it refers to a *prior arrangement* they had made with Paul that their "consensual partnership" with him should begin after he left Macedonia. That is conjecture, pure and simple, and does not accord well with what Paul actually says.

14. This could have been guessed at in several instances (2 Cor 1:16; 2:13; 7:5); it is made certain by 2 Cor 11:9, quoted below, which in combination with this verse narrows "Macedonia" down to Philippi alone.

15. Which, along with the ascensive καί in v. 16 (*"even* in Thessalonica"), makes it extremely unlikely that he intended at this point to include the instances mentioned in v. 16 as well (as Michael contends [which he says is the "natural" reading of the text!]; cf. Loh-Nida).

16. Not to mention the cause for all kinds of conjectures and "solutions" to the rather imprecise way in which all of this is said. See n. 13.

likely the "narrative" is typically imprecise, as such personal recountings of "history" often are. He begins, as the emphasis in the context dictates, by focusing on their long-term relationship, hence "after he left Macedonia"; but since Thessalonica is also in Macedonia and the Philippians had already been serving him in this way even while he was in Macedonia, he (apparently) adds the qualifier in v. 16.

The concrete evidence for such "partnership" beyond Macedonia is to be found in 2 Cor 11:8-9, where in defense of his not having entered into such a contractual friendship with the Corinthians Paul argues: "I 'robbed' other churches by receiving support from them so as to serve you. And when I was with you and needed something, . . . the brothers who came from Macedonia supplied what I needed."[17] Whether, and if so how extensive, this ministry carried on beyond the time in Corinth cannot be known. Lacking other such fortuitous moments of verification like the one in 2 Corinthians, we can only guess that it extended beyond Corinth, but we cannot be certain.

(B) This material functions as the main clause in Paul's sentence. Its primary concern is to point out that they are the only church with whom Paul had entered into "contractual friendship." That is expressed twice, at the beginning and end of the clause: "no other church . . . except you only." It is further emphasized by the addition of the final clause (v. 16) which not only points to their repeated expression of this dimension of friendship, but also joins v. 15 to exclude Thessalonica from such an arrangement with Paul.

The nature of this "arrangement" is to be found in the language "in the matter of giving and receiving," which is the key to much, not only in the present passage but also to the letter as a whole. This has long been recognized as a metaphorical use of "commercial" language, traditionally

---

17. This bracketed emphasis on "you only among the churches," with the obvious exclusion of Thessalonica, creates some tension with the plural in 2 Cor 11:8-9 ("I robbed other *churches,*" in a context of mentioning the brothers *from Macedonia*), which has been variously handled (if at all). B. Holmberg (*Power,* 91-92) reads the present sentence (on the basis of "at the beginning") to imply that by the time Philippians was written, other churches by now had joined in such "giving and receiving"; he then finds the plural in 2 Cor 11:8 to confirm this view. While this is attractive, it seems to run counter to the evidence from the Thessalonian and Corinthian correspondence noted below (p. 445; cf. n. 24), and especially to that of the 2 Corinthians passage, which refers to an event very soon after he left Macedonia for the first time! Reumann ("Contributions," 441-42) adopts Holmberg's reconstruction, adding that the bracketed emphasis in the present passage is an "exaggerated *captatio benevolentiae*" (a polite way of "buttering people up"). A *captatio* may praise someone (or group) highly, but to *emphasize* (as Paul does here) what amounts to be a flatout lie (on the view that 2 Cor 11:8-9 has it right, and this is a polite "gesture" toward the Philippians) is hardly the stuff on which friendship is built. The best solution to the plural in 2 Cor 11:8 has to do with Paul's emphasis there; most likely "other churches" means "other believers."

interpreted as indicating Paul's stance toward their gift(s).[18] Thus the phrase "in the matter"[19] means that they have "opened an account" with Paul (Goodspeed), in which there is mutual "credit" (giving) and "debit" (receiving).[20] This understanding is corroborated by the extension of the metaphor in v. 17, where their giving is understood by Paul in terms of "interest that accumulates in this way to your divine credit" (Moffatt), and further in v. 18 with the expression, "you have paid me in full" (Goodspeed). This usage is so well established both in the papyri and in literary works that it is quite impossible for the Philippians to have understood it differently.

What was not recognized traditionally is that this commercial metaphor had already been co-opted within the context of Greco-Roman "friendship," especially to refer to "consensual" friendship, which would be evidenced by a mutual "debt and credit" (giving and receiving), that is, gifts and services understood as "benefits" mutually given and received.[21] This is almost cer-

---

18. Which ranges from "embarrassment" to an actual business transaction. Cf., e.g., C. H. Dodd, "Mind (I)," 71-72, who sees Paul as having "a well-to-do *bourgeois*" attitude toward money, needing it, on the one hand, but embarrassed by such a need, on the other. Thus he "covers up his embarrassment by piling up technical terms of trade, as if to give the transaction a severely 'business' aspect"; he is followed by Beare (155). Earlier Kennedy (472; cf. Beare, Martin) saw the usage as intentionally offering "a genial strain of humour" to the word of acknowledgment. J. Fleury ("Société"), on the other hand, considers Paul to have actually entered into a business partnership with Lydia, to which he is here referring, which has rightly been described as "fanciful" (Capper, "Dispute," 201). Cf. the summary of such views in Peterman, "Giving," 19-24.

19. Gk. εἰς λόγον, which as a commercial idiom means literally to "settle an account" (see the references in BAGD, 2 b). See esp. Sir 42:3, among a list of things for which one should not feel ashamed (v. 1): "of keeping accounts with a partner [περὶ λόγου κοινωνοῦ]" (NRSV). Thus, NEB, "my partners in payments and receipts."

20. Gk. δόσις καὶ λῆμψις; for this usage in commercial transactions, see Sir 42:7 (in the same list of items from the preceding n.): "and when you give or receive, put it in writing [καὶ δόσις καὶ λῆμψις, πάντα ἐν γραφῇ]" (NRSV). That the same language refers to "social reciprocity," see Sir 41:21; cf. the discussion in Peterman, "Giving," 53-54.

21. In this regard see the discussion by P. Marshall, *Enmity,* 160-64; and Peterman, "Giving," 59-60, 63-104. See, e.g., Plutarch, *De Lib. Educ..* 14 (11B), regarding Antigonus, king of the Macedonians, who sent to Theocritus that he should come to him καὶ λόγον δοῦναι καὶ λαβεῖν, which Babbitt translates (LCL, 1.53) "engage him in discussion." The usage in Herm. *Man.* 5.2.2 (περὶ δόσεως ἢ λήμψεως) also seems to be a case in point. Lightfoot (165) understands it literally, as referring to the passing of money between the two, but the context suggests otherwise. The "mandate" is discussing how "an angry temper works," in that it leads astray those who are "empty-headed and double-minded" (5.2.1). "For," Hermas picks up in 5.2.2, when it insinuates itself into the head of such people they become "embittered over worldly concerns, either about food or something trivial, or some *friend, or about giving or receiving,* or some such foolish matters" (Lightfoot, *AF²*, 220-21). The collocation of "giving and receiving" with "friend" is probably not accidental, and belongs to the context of reciprocity in friendship, rather than to financial transactions as such.

tainly how we should understand Paul's usage. The combination "shared with me in"[22] also reflects the metaphorical use of this technical language, thus meaning something like, "you alone entered into partnership with me in this matter." The language is intended to express both the mutuality and the reciprocity of such "giving and receiving." What is unique to Paul's relationship with the Philippians is that their "partnership" with him was not so much "one on one," as it were, but a *three-way bond* — between him, them, and Christ (and the gospel).[23]

This third factor results in a considerable "skewing" of the convention. Left intact is reciprocity and mutuality; "skewed" is the form these take in Paul. The discussions in Greco-Roman literature of "giving and receiving" in relation to friendship indicate that they often ended up in (sometimes destructive) one-up-manship. If reciprocity did not exceed the former gift, the original recipient came under long-term "obligation"; thus mutuality degenerated into a kind of "patron-client" relationship where one party "held the upper hand." But in Christ, Paul's relationship with the Philippians has been "leveled out" in its own divine way. On the one hand, a "patron-client" relationship already existed between him and his churches, in his role as apostle. This is why even in a letter of friendship like this one Paul can take such a strong hortatory stance. What is remarkable is how little he plays that note in this letter at all; rather, he and Timothy are "slaves of Christ Jesus" in their behalf, and rather than simply exhort by way of imperative, he appeals to his own example as the model for them to follow. Whatever else, they are in this (that is, in Christ) together.

On the other hand, another form of "patron-client" relationship had also long ago been established between him and them with regard to his personal, material needs. As far as we have records to guide us, in Philippi alone among his churches did he accept patronage while present with them, in this case in the household of Lydia. When he went on to Thessalonica, he chose a different course, deliberately "working with his own hands" so as to set such a model before the Thessalonians (2 Thess 3:7-10), a practice he continued when he went to Corinth (1 Cor 4:12).[24] As a result, the Philippians

---

22. Gk. μοι . . . ἐκοινώσησεν εἰς. This idiom explains both the specialized use of the verb in this case as well as the unusual usage of εἰς with it. For the usage see Plato, *Rep.* 5.453A (τῇ τοῦ ἄρρενος γένους κοινωνῆσαι εἰς ἅπαντα τὰ ἔργα; [whether the female human nature can] share with the male in all tasks."

23. See the phrase "at the beginning of the gospel" (v. 15). Cf. O'Brien (535), who suggests, "Marshall's point may be taken further by noting that both the Philippians' gifts and their friendship with the apostle derive from and are an expression of their 'partnership in the gospel from the first day until now'."

24. See also the testimony recorded in Acts 20:33-34 for the same practice in Ephesus. See n. 17 for some who take a different view. On the larger question of how

also alone among his churches had entered into "partnership with him" regarding his material needs, apparently assisting him as they were able and had opportunity. Thus, he became "client" to their "patronage," in this sense.

But precisely because their "friendship" was predicated on their mutual belonging to Christ, these two expressions of "patron-client" relationship were leveled by total mutuality and reciprocity. How he deals with his end of the "reciprocity" is what vv. 17 and 19 are all about. In any case, this is the relationship to which Paul is here calling their attention by way of reminder; his concern is to remind them that he has this unique relationship with them alone among all "his" churches.

(A′) As a further reminder of the uniqueness of their "friendship," Paul adds a final explanatory clause, "for[25] even[26] (when I was) in Thessalonica, once and again, you sent unto my need." This clause does three things. First, it joins v. 15 to exclude Thessalonica from the same kind of contractual friendship that he has with them; "Macedonia" means the province, and when he set out from the province, Thessalonica did not join with them in sending him aid,[27] even though it was the much larger and more influential city in Macedonia. Second, it reminds them of how they had repeatedly upheld their end of the "giving and receiving" from the time he first left Philippi. "Once and again"[28] believers from Philippi traveled the 145 kilometers (95 miles) down the Egnatian Way to Thessalonica to assist with Paul's material needs. In comparison with getting to Corinth or Rome (and especially to Caesarea),[29]

---

"itinerants" (philosophers/religious propagandists) were supported (fees, begging, patronage, working) see Hock, *Social Context,* 52-59.

25. Gk. ὅτι, which some (e.g., Kennedy, Michael, Gnilka, Collange, Hawthorne) see as a second object clause dependent on οἶδα. But that seems unlikely, since it makes the sentence more "calculated" than it probably was (see n. 13).

26. Not all are persuaded that this καί is ascensive. Some (Morris, "ἅπαξ," 208; Martin; Reumann, "Contributions," 439-40 [Bruce and O'Brien are favorably inclined]) see this καί and the καί preceding ἅπαξ as coordinate, meaning "both . . . and" (= "both in Thessalonica and once and again [beyond Thessalonica]"). But that is an altogether unnatural reading of the Greek. There is nothing grammatically coordinate (or in keeping with Paul's own "balancing" style) between "in Thessalonica" and "once and again"; and the usage in 1 Thess 2:18 includes the καί with the idiom καὶ ἅπαξ καὶ δίς (see next n.).

27. *Contra* Reumann ("Contributions," 440), who on the basis of the plural in 2 Cor 11:8 (see n. 17) asserts, "Thessalonica must have contributed." This passage stands squarely against that.

28. Gk. καὶ ἅπαξ καὶ δίς, lit. "both once and twice," which is equal to our idiom "once and again," or "more than once" (so Morris, "ἅπαξ"); cf. 1 Thess 2:18. Morris also points out that the idiom does not intend many such occasions (as the NIV, following BAGD, "again and again"), but two or three at the most.

29. The fact that Caesarea and Philippi are not on a "beaten path" best explains the hiatus in their giving.

this was "a piece of cake." Third, as in 2:25, he now mentions their gift to him as "for the sake of supplying *my need.*"[30] If he felt compelled to establish in vv. 11-13 that his joy over their gift was not grounded at this level, which could be viewed as utilitarian, neither did he intend to deny that they had in fact ministered to his "need." At the same time, he sets up the reciprocal language of v. 19, where God picks up Paul's end of the mutuality by supplying "all their needs" in Christ Jesus.

Finally, the question of "*why* this sentence at all" needs to be addressed, even if our answer is more speculative. That is, why this reminder of what, by his own admission, they well know? And why this emphasis on their being the only church to have entered into this kind of "partnership" with him? A couple of reasons may be suggested. First, such a reminder is itself an indication of the happy relationship he has with this church. The mention of "being paid in full" in v. 18 makes clear that no hidden motive, such as "putting them under obligation," lies behind it. Rather, as often happens in an interchange between friends, one partner in the friendship takes delight in reminding the other how that one has expressed friendship in the past. Paul's point, then, is that their present gift, even though after a hiatus of some years, represents yet another in their long and laudatory history in this regard. Second, in ways far more profound than the use of the verb "to thank," this is Paul's way of saying thank you for this long history of their "giving" and his "receiving." There is good evidence from the Greco-Roman world that the actual expression of "thank you" was not a part of friendship as such. As strange as it may seem to us, true friends did not need to express thanksgiving directly in order for it to be received.[31]

---

30. Gk. τὴν χρείαν, again in v. 19. This is the common word for "need"; the word ὑστέρησις in v. 11 indicated "lack," which often could mean "need" as well, but not necessarily so. The definite article probably indicates "*the* need at that time." Sampley (*Partnership,* 55), in the interest of his view of this relationship as "consensual *societas*" (n. 4), suggests on the basis of an entry in LSJ that the word should be broadened to include "requests." But his discussion has moments of questionable methodology, in which he rejects what he calls "corpus harmonization" (= finding meaning here from usage elsewhere in Paul), but accepts a classical usage for which he offers no hellenistic data in support. The word clearly means "need" in Paul; to make it mean "request" here would require not only firm contemporary evidence, but evidence within the context of "contractual partnership." Not only so, but Paul has just used the appropriate language for "request" in v. 6.

31. In this regard see esp. Peterman, " 'Thankless Thanks'," who cites P. Merton 12 (CE 58), "I may dispense with writing to you with a great show of thanks (μεγάλας εὐχαριστίας); for it is for those who are not friends that we must give thanks in words." Peterman points out that at issue in the citation is *verbal* gratitude, with which he may dispense because of friendship, but that such a disclaimer followed by an expression of indebtedness nonetheless functions as "thankless thanks" — of a positive sort.

What Paul is most likely doing here in keeping with social convention is thus expressing his "thank you" indirectly, but even more tellingly, by rehearsing their history in this way.[32]

The final "why" question, why he should have entered such a relationship with only one church, lies in the area of pure speculation and will not detain us. That he did so, is what we learn from this passage, and nothing more.

**17** With another "not that" (cf. v. 11), Paul interrupts his expression of gratitude with yet another qualifier against possible misunderstanding.[33] His short recital of their exemplary history of friendship with him in the matter of "giving and receiving" is not to be taken as an indirect request for more help.[34] Exactly the opposite, and now picking up on the commercial metaphor itself, what he "seeks,"[35] he tells them, is "the fruit that increases into your account," by which he means metaphorically, "an accrual of 'interest' against your divine 'account'." When unpacked, the metaphor expresses Paul's real concern for them, found as early as 1:25 in terms of "your progress in the faith." Their giving to him is an expression of love, of the gospel at work in their midst. For Paul every time they do so, it is also evidence of "fruitfulness," of the kind for which he prayed in 1:11. Such "fruitfulness" has the effect of being entered on the divine ledger as "interest," as the certain indication of the increase of their "fruitfulness," which will find its full expression at the coming of Christ. They themselves will be Paul's eschatological "reward" (2:16; 4:1); their gift to him has the effect of accumulating "interest" toward *their* eschatological "reward."

The metaphor, however, does not need to "walk on all fours" to be

32. Lightfoot (164) thinks otherwise, that he is reminding them of his willingness to receive such gifts from them, in light of his refusal to do so from other churches.

33. On the "pattern" involved with this demurrer, see p. 425 above; for a detailed examination of the similarities between vv. 11 and 17 see Schenk (44-46; O'Brien [536-37] gives a convenient overview in English).

34. Gk. τὸ δόμα, elsewhere in Paul only in Eph 4:8, in a citation of the LXX. It is used especially in the contexts of friendship to describe the "gifts" of reciprocity; thus it here refers to their most recent gift, picked up in v. 18, as τὰ παρ' ὑμῶν ("the things from you"). *Contra* Sampley and Capper (n. 4), who on the basis of some scattered papyrological evidence, suggest "payment" here; but such a sense in not found anywhere in biblical Greek, and runs counter to the context of friendship that pervades this discussion.

35. Gk. ἐπιζητῶ, only here (twice) and Rom 11:7 in Paul. It is an intensified form of ζητέω, meaning here something close to "strive for." On Collange's mirror reading this verb to suggest that Paul had actually asked them for help, see n. 3 on 4:10-20 (cf. Capper, "Dispute," 199 n. 10 = "a legal 'demand'"). The repetition of this verb in the second clause seems to render this view impossible. Does Paul intend to say, "but I request/demand that you receive interest etc."?

understood, or even to carry punch. Paul's interest is not in their "reward" as such, but in their gift as evidence that their relationship with Christ is in good order and is continuing to grow. He does not thereby negate the gift; indeed, he finally speaks directly to that in the next sentence. But here is the certain evidence that his ultimate concern is for them — far more than for his own material needs. Their gift, which serves his "physical health," serves more significantly as evidence of their "spiritual health." What else would one "seek," one wonders, in a relationship such as theirs, which is predicated altogether on their mutual belonging to Christ?

Many years ago a wise preacher counseled some younger ministers that Satan has three hounds with which he pursues those in ministry: pride, money, and sex. Money is surely not the least of these. It is therefore of some interest for us to note how sensitive Paul is on this matter. He can scarcely speak about it, and especially his relationship to receiving it, without offering a demurrer such as one finds in v. 17. This may well account for his (apparent) change of policy when he got to Thessalonica. There were enough itinerant religious and philo-sophical hucksters about, who, according to Dio Chrysostom, "used flattery as a cloak for greed" (cf. 1 Thess 2:4), for Paul to set out on a different course of maintenance upon leaving Philippi. Thus he can appeal to both Thessalonica and Corinth that his motives were totally free of pecuniary interests (1 Thess 2:1-10; 2 Cor 12:14-15). Paul did not "seek what is yours, but you" (2 Cor 12:14). A lesson in paradigm for all who are in Christian ministry of any kind.

The uniqueness of this passage in the corpus comes into focus here. For in Philippi he did accept their material support once and again. This says something significant about his relationship with this church, and here it is hard not to see the hand of Luke (and Lydia?) at work. Thus he gladly acknowledges their gift, but even here one finds the demurrer. These verses put much into perspective. They know him well; they also know that from them alone among his churches has he accepted gifts on an ongoing basis. The key to all of this is v. 14, read in light of 1:29-30; 2:6-8; and 3:8-10. Their relationship is not a kind of business transaction, despite the use of commercial metaphors throughout; rather, their gift is evidence of their being in partnership with him "in affliction" and for the sake of the gospel.

Thus he concludes that money — material support of his own needs — is ultimately irrelevant; what counts is what God is doing in their lives. Their gift serves as evidence of "fruitfulness" that will only gain interest toward their eschatological "reward." In an oppressively materialistic culture, these words are written off as saccharine spirituality — or "sour grapes" — so as to justify ongoing greed. My sense is that Paul has the better of it, and that truly Christian life lies closer to where he and they were than where many of us are.

## 3. Their Gift as a Fragrant Offering to God (4:18-20)

18*I have received full payment and even more; I[1] am amply supplied, now that I have received from Epaphroditus the gifts you sent. They are a fragrant offering, an acceptable sacrifice, pleasing to God.* 19*And my God will meet[2] all your needs according to his glorious riches in Christ Jesus.*
20*To our God and Father be glory for ever and ever. Amen.*

These sentences belong intimately with vv. 14-17,[3] continuing the commercial metaphor while offering reciprocity to their meeting his "need" in v. 16, thus concluding the narrative begun in v. 10. The reason for isolating them is to highlight their relationship with what has preceded and to demonstrate that the passage as a whole is anything but reticent thanks. With a considerable change of metaphors, Paul suggests that the ultimate recipient of their service to Paul is none other than the living God. Their material gift to Paul functioned as a sacrificial offering to God.

Although still using metaphors, this is about as straightforward as one gets in Paul. In v. 18, keeping to the commercial/friendship metaphors from vv. 15 and 17, he specifically acknowledges their gift, sent by way of Epaphroditus (cf. 2:25-30), which he further describes with a sacrificial metaphor. In v. 19, referring back to their meeting his "need" from v. 16, he indicates that God himself will pick up Paul's end of the reciprocity by meeting *all* their needs. All of which, especially v. 19, leads to a final outburst of praise in the form of a typical Pauline doxology (v. 20).

1. Apparently uncomfortable with the asyndeton on this sentence, P[46] and 2495 have added a δέ. As with the other expressions of asyndeton in this letter (3:1, 2; 4:4-9), it is part of the letter's rhetorical power, in this case of the cumulative effect of the piling up of verbs expressing lavish generosity.

2. A significant group of early MSS (including D* F G Ψ 6 33 81 104 326 365 1175 1241[s] 1739 1881 and the entire Latin tradition, plus the Sahidic) read an optative (πληρώσαι) for Paul's future indicative (πληρώσει). While the change is understandable and fits what Paul well might have done (praying that God will supply their needs in light of their supply of Paul's), the (almost surely original) indicative, besides having the better support (P[46] ℵ A B D[2] P Maj bo) also better fits the overall sense of the passage, especially the reciprocation of friendship. *Contra* Wiles (*Intercessory Prayers*, 101-7, followed by Martin, Hawthorne, and O'Brien), who argues that even though it is declarative, it nonetheless functions as a summarizing wish-prayer. That is to divest it of its contextual roots for the sake of "pan-liturgism." This is not prayer, nor does it function as such. It is theology in the interest of friendship (i.e., reciprocity). Worship comes next (v. 20), as a direct response to the *theology* expressed in this promise.

3. Indeed, one can no more justify a paragraph break here than at v. 14 or 2:8. See n. 12 on 4:10-20.

At the same time, word plays and repetitions abound, some of which are difficult to express in translation, but all of which tie these final sentences to what has immediately preceded (vv. 10-17) as well as to the earlier mention of their gift to him in 2:25-30.[4] He begins in v. 18 by capping off the commercial metaphor from vv. 15 and 17 (= "you have paid me in full," Goodspeed), to which he immediately appends the twice repeated verb from vv. 11-12, "I am in plenty"! He starts the next sentence with the verb "I have been filled to the full," which he repeats in v. 19 of God's reciprocation, "God will fill you to the full." His description of their gift as an "acceptable sacrifice" echoes the same metaphor used to refer to their suffering in 2:17 while the metaphor as a whole echoes the language of Epaphroditus's "priestly ministry" on their behalf in 2:25 and 30. That God will "fill to the full" their "need," picks up their ministering to his "need" in v. 16 (and 2:25); while the mention of God in the first position in v. 19, designated as "*my* God," is picked up again, also in the first position but as "*our* God and Father," in the doxology in v. 20. And God's supplying their needs in keeping with his riches "in glory" leads to the doxology, where Paul ascribes "glory" to God through eternal ages. All together it is an altogether exquisite passage.

**18** With a slightly contrastive "but"[5] Paul finally ("at long last" for Western tastes) mentions their gift directly. And he says it expansively, piling up verbs at the beginning[6] by which he indicates how richly his own needs have been met by their lavish generosity, and concluding with a change of metaphors expressing God's pleasure over their gift. Apparently concluding the commercial/friendship metaphor, he thus begins, "I have received (payment) in full."[7] In this context that probably refers first of all to the

---

4. Not to mention some interesting parallels to the prayer in 1:9-11, pointed out by Wiles (*Intercessory Prayer,* 104-6); cf. O'Brien, 543-44.

5. Gk. δέ, used in this case to set what follows in contrast to the final demurrer of v. 17, that he is not seeking their gift as such. "But in fact," he now goes on, I have received it as "full payment."

6. Paul's sentence reads, ἀπέχω δὲ πάντα καὶ περισσεύω. πεπλήρωμαι . . . (lit., "I have received in full all things and I abound; I have been filled to the full . . ."). That may be "thankless thanks," in the sense of not using the verb, but it is not "thankless." To the contrary, these words abound with gratitude without using the unnecessary (for friends) verb εὐχαριστεῖν (see n. 31 on 4:16).

7. In commercial papyri, the verb, which generally means "I have received," means something close to "paid" (= "to receive a sum and give a receipt for it"); see the sources cited in BAGD; cf. Deissmann (*Light,* 111-12, 331). The combination ἀπέχειν πάντα would thus mean something like "paid in full." On the other hand, Lightfoot (166) points out the frequency of this combination among Stoic writers, as a near equivalent of αὐταρκεία. Just as the "wise man" is "self-sufficient (contented)," so he also "has all things" in this philosophical sense (see, e.g., Epictetus 3.2.13, 3.24.17; Diogenes L. 7.100). Although the

matter of their "giving" and his "receiving," hence "full payment." If so, the language is metaphorical, pure and simple, indicating that his "receipt" of what they have "given" puts the "obligation" of friendship back on his side.

But his use of "all things" as the object of the verb, plus his immediately adding "and I abound," seems equally intended to recall vv. 11-13. Paul, who knows both how to be "abased" and how to "abound," has experienced both in his present imprisonment — "humiliation" from the imprisonment itself, the "abounding" at least in part from their gift, as he now acknowledges. Thus, he who has learned to be "content" in all situations "in Christ who empowers him," can say, in acknowledgment of their generosity, "I have all things; indeed, I have more than enough."

As clear indication that this passage is not "thankless," Paul starts all over again, this time with the verb for "being filled to the full."[8] As the NIV puts it, and in keeping with the context, "I am amply supplied." The rest of the verse modifies this verb, in two ways: first, by directly mentioning their gift(s) (lit., "the things from you") and their agency ("having received [them] from Epaphroditus"); second, by describing the gift(s) with a metaphor from the OT sacrifices ("a fragrant offering, an acceptable sacrifice"[9]), so as also to indicate divine approval with what they have done ("pleasing to God"[10]).

On Epaphroditus and his role in bringing their gift to Paul, see on 2:25-30. Paul has already referred to Epaphroditus's "ministry" as a "priestly service" to Paul on their behalf. Here he spells out what that means with language borrowed directly from the LXX, used to indicate the interplay between the human and the divine in the sacrifices. The imagery is that of the burnt offering, which was understood as a "fragrant offering" to God. The picture is that of the "aroma" of the sacrificial fire wafting heavenward — into God's "nostrils," as it were. Properly offered, it becomes "an acceptable sacrifice, pleasing to him." This, Paul says, is what their gift has amounted to from the divine perspective.

In its own way this sentence thus responds directly to v. 17. Although he does not "seek the gift" as such, in fact he has received their gift and it has resulted in his now "having plenty." What he does seek, he told them, is

---

present usage may thus conclude the commercial metaphor, the combination ἀπέχω πάντα καὶ περισσεύω (= "I have all things and more than enough") also clearly harks back to vv. 11-13, and thus at the same time brings closure to that theme by way of their gift.

8. Gk. πεπλήρωμαι, which can also mean to "fulfill" or "complete" (as in 2:2), but here and in v. 19, as in 1:11, it carries its basic denotation of "filling up."

9. For this imagery see n. 51 on 2:17.

10. Gk. εὐάρεστον τῷ θεῷ; for this imagery in Paul see on Rom 12:1-2; 14:18.

"an accrual of interest against your divine account." That, he now tells them with this splendid shift of metaphors, is exactly what has happened. Their gift, which has met Paul's material needs, has by that very fact pleased God, who from this point on becomes the focus of the rest of the passage.

**19** The mention of God at the end of the preceding sentence leads directly to this final wrapup of his "rejoicing in the Lord" over their gift, which serves as evidence both of their care for him (v. 10) and their long-standing friendship with him (vv. 15-16). Friendship presupposes reciprocity, mutual giving and receiving. This sentence is a master stroke.[11] Although he cannot reciprocate in kind, since their gift had the effect of being a sweet-smelling sacrifice, pleasing to God, Paul assures them that God, whom he deliberately designates as "*my* God," will assume responsibility for reciprocity. Thus, picking up the language "my need" from v. 16 and "fill to the full" from v. 18, he promises them that "my God will fill up every need of yours."

They obviously have the better of it! First, he promises that God's reciprocation will cover "*every* need of yours," especially their material needs, as the context demands — but also every other kind of need, as the language demands.[12] One cannot imagine a more fitting way for this letter to conclude, in terms of Paul's final word to them personally. In the midst of their "poverty" (2 Cor 8:2), God will richly supply their material needs. In their present suffering in the face of opposition (1:27-30), God will richly supply what is needed (steadfastness, joy, encouragement). In their "need" to advance in the

---

11. Because of its content (simultaneously concluding the friendship motif with the most exalted of theological language), not its "form." The attempts to divide the sentence into two halves (by Lohmeyer, followed by Wiles, into a 123/123 scheme; by Schenk, followed by O'Brien, into a 123/321 scheme) are less than persuasive, and each cancels the other out as evidence that Paul's sentence is not self-evidently poetic.

12. Gk. πᾶσαν χρείαν ὑμῶν; it is the addition of the otherwise unnecessary πᾶσαν, plus the expansive conclusion, "in keeping with his wealth in glory in Christ Jesus," that makes one think Paul is embracing both their material needs and all others as well. *Contra* Meyer, Kennedy, Jones, Plummer, Wiles, Martin, *et al.,* who see the combination of the future tense of the verb with the prepositional phrase ἐν δόξῃ ("in glory"), in some cases combined with an eschatological reading of v. 17, to refer to eschatological fulfillment exclusively. That an eschatological dimension is inherent in the promise I would not deny (after all, Paul's basic theological framework is his "already/not yet" understanding of present existence); but this object ("every need of yours") makes very little sense as an exclusively — indeed, even as a primarily — eschatological referent. On the other hand, to limit the phrase to material needs in the present, as Hawthorne does, is likewise to miss the force of its sweeping grandeur. Paul could easily have said "your needs"; rather, reflecting on "God's riches in glory in Christ Jesus," he says on an equally grand scale, "every need of yours." It is precisely the expansive quality of this sentence that makes Sampley's suggestion that χρεία also implies "request" come aground (see n. 30 on v. 16, a view that is linguistically suspect at best).

faith with one mindset (1:25; 2:1-4; 4:2-3), God will richly supply the grace and humility necessary for it. In the place of both "grumbling" (2:14) and "anxiety" (4:6), God will be present with them as the "God of peace" (4:7, 9). "*My* God," Paul says, will act for me in your behalf by "filling to the full *all* your needs."[13]

And God will do so, Paul says, "in keeping with his riches in glory in Christ Jesus." The Philippians' generosity toward Paul, expressed lavishly at the beginning of v. 18, is exceeded beyond all imagination by the lavish "wealth" of the eternal God, who dwells "in glory" full of "riches"[14] made available to his own "in Christ Jesus."[15] God's "riches" are those inherent to his being God, Creator and Lord of all; nothing lies outside his rightful ownership and domain. They are his "in glory" in the sense that his "riches" exist in the sphere of God's glory, where God "dwells" in infinite splendor and majesty, the "glory" that is his as God alone.[16] It is "in keeping with"

13. This kind of theology, promissory as it is in expression, has inherent in it that "God's riches in glory" and "every need of theirs" are "filled to the full" in God's way and in keeping with his (only good) purposes, not at the Philippians' (or our) beck and call, as it were.

14. Gk. κατὰ τὸ πλοῦτος αὐτοῦ. The noun is the common one for "wealth," but occurs with that sense only in 1 Tim 6:17 in the Pauline corpus. Beginning in Romans, and extensively so in the Prison Letters, Paul uses it primarily to refer to some specific aspect of God's "wealth" (Rom 2:4; 9:23; 11:33; Col 1:27; Eph 1:7, 18; 2:7; 3:8, 16). See the useful overview by H. Merklein in *EDNT,* 3.115-17.

15. These kinds of exquisite moments call for worship (v. 20) because all of our analogies and metaphors are too impoverished to try to catch the sense. One thinks of Annie Johnson Flint's

His love has no limit,
His grace has no measure,
His power has no boundary known unto men,
    For out of his infinite riches in Jesus,
    He giveth and giveth and giveth again.

Wrap up all the personal moments of "riches" into one (the small boy given full rein in the ice cream shoppe; landing on a patch of wild blackberries so full that one could not pick them all in a day; finding pool upon pool of eighteen to twenty-four inch trout in an unfished stream in the Sierra Nevada; and many such experiences) and one can only catch a faint glimmer of what Paul is here recognizing of God's wealth and lavish love for his people — expressed to the full "in Christ Jesus."

16. Gk. ἐν δόξῃ, which I take to be locative here (as with the following ἐν Χριστῷ Ἰησοῦ), not meaning "in heaven" as such (which is rightly objected to by most scholars), but referring to the ineffable and eternal "glory" in which God dwells, as the context within which God lavishes his riches on his own in Christ Jesus. This is not the common view — indeed the locative is very often dismissed out of hand — but it seems to make the best sense of the sentence as a whole, in which (a) this phrase follows the phrase κατὰ τὸ πλοῦτος αὐτοῦ, and therefore more naturally qualifies it than the verb, (b) most

all of this — not "out of" his riches, but in accordance with this norm,[17] the infinite "riches" of grace that belong to God's own glory — that God's full supply will come their way to meet their every need. The language is deliberately expansive; after all, Paul is trying to say something concrete about the eternal God and God's relationship to his people. That is why the final word is not the heavenly one, "in glory," but the combined earthly and heavenly one, "in Christ Jesus." Because Paul has beheld the "glory of God in the face of Christ Jesus" (2 Cor 4:6), expressed in this letter in the majestic Christ narrative in 2:6-11, Paul sees clearly that Christ Jesus is the way God has made his love known and available to his human creatures. This is what the letter has ultimately been all about. It began "in Christ Jesus"; it now concludes "in Christ Jesus." Indeed, even the customary closing greetings focus on Christ Jesus. For Paul, "to live is Christ, to die is gain." Thus the final word in the body of the letter proper is this one, "every need of yours in keeping with the wealth that is his in glory made available to you in Christ Jesus."

---

immediately follows the pronoun αὐτοῦ, which refers to God (= the riches of *him,* in glory), and thus (c) naturally leads to the final qualifier, "in Christ Jesus," as indicating both where and how the riches that belong to God's own ineffable glory are made available to his people.

This view thus solves the inherent difficulties that most interpreters have with the phrase, which they acknowledge, yet reluctantly adopt one option over the others. See n. 12 for a rejection of the totally eschatological view. The other two options are equally difficult to sustain contextually and/or grammatically. Some (e.g., Vincent, Rienecker-Rogers) would take it as adverbially modifying the verb "will fill to the full" (= will gloriously fill to the full), thus indicating the mode or manner of fulfillment. This is possible, but would seem more likely had it immediately followed the verb or otherwise preceded, not followed, "in keeping with his riches." One wonders how the hearer of the letter in Philippi could ever had heard it this way. Others take it, as I do, to modify the preceding phrase; but with an indefensible jump in grammar they turn the adverbial idea of "gloriously" into an adjective "glorious," so as to produce the translation represented by the NIV ("his glorious riches," cf. GNB, NAB, Confraternity, Phillips; the REB's "out of the magnificence of his riches," where an adverbial prepositional phrase now becomes a noun, seems to be based on grammatical wishfulness altogether). This is conceptually congenial, and in the case of Eph 1:18 is grammatically justifiable since "glory" appears in the genitive (= a "descriptive genitive") and may be translated "the riches of his glorious inheritance" (NIV). Even there an adjectival interpretation is unnecessary and seems to miss the sense of the noun "glory" — but how does one justify that grammatically in this instance where there is no genitive? One wonders whether the concept of "dynamic equivalent" should ever allow one to dismiss grammar so casually.

17. While the context of the sentence may also imply "out of," the preposition κατά in fact refers to a standard or norm in accordance with which something is done. Thus Michael's oft-quoted words, "in a manner that befits His wealth — on a scale worthy of His wealth" (226).

This says it all; nothing more can be added.[18] So Paul simply bursts into doxology before concluding with his customary greetings.

**20** It is no wonder that Paul now concludes the preceding sentence with doxology. The indicative yields to the imperative of worship. When one thinks on the "riches of God" lavished on us in Christ Jesus, what else is there to do but to praise and worship? Christ is indeed the focus of everything that God has and is doing in this world and the next, but God the Father is always the first and last word in Paul's theology. "*My* God" is now "*our* God *and Father*"; and the living God, the everlasting one, who belongs to the "ages of ages,"[19] and who dwells "in glory," is now ascribed the "glory" that is due his name.[20] All of this, because the Philippians have sent him material assistance to help him through his imprisonment! True theology is doxology, and doxology is always the proper response to God, even — especially? — in response to God's prompting friends to minister to friends.

This passage thus belongs to several such doxologies in the Pauline corpus, which come at varied moments and reflect Paul's true theological orientation. The "amen" with which they conclude, taken over by Christians from the Jewish synagogue, is the last word, our "so be it," not only to the doxology itself but especially to the ultimate eschatological words, "forever and ever." This is our way of acknowledging that "glory to God forever and ever" is the way it is and will be, no matter what we do. So let us, God's people in all times and climes, join the chorus.

---

18. We need to add a final theological word, however, since this sentence offers the theological basis for everything else in the letter. It is because Paul has caught a glimpse of "God's riches in glory, made available in Christ Jesus," that he speaks as he did in vv. 11-13; in the light of such "wealth," lavishly given in Christ, present "want" or "plenty" has very little bearing. This is also the reason for his counting all things but loss for the surpassing value of knowing Christ Jesus my Lord (3:8-10) and for his straining every effort in order to secure the eschatological prize, "the upward call of God in Christ Jesus" (3:13-14). Paul has caught a glimpse of God's "riches in glory," put on full display "in Christ Jesus." For Paul that determines everything. And this is the glory that he longs for his Philippian friends to see and experience. Thus the whole letter finds its theological focus in this final word.

19. Gk. εἰς τοὺς αἰῶνας τῶν αἰώνων; lit. "unto the ages of the ages," most often translated "for ever and ever." A semitism (although usually in the singular), it occurs in Paul in Gal 1:5; 1 Tim 1:17; 2 Tim 4:18; cf. 1 Pet 4:11 and throughout the Revelation.

20. For this use in doxologies in Paul, see Gal 1:5; Rom 16:27; Eph 3:21; 1 Tim 1:17; 2 Tim 4:18. The word "glory" is one of those biblical words that has entered the casual vocabulary of the church, which in fact is extremely difficult to pin down with precision. See the useful discussions in *EDNT,* 1.344-48 (H. Hagermann); *NIDNTT,* 2.44-48 (S. Aalen); *TDNT,* 2.233-53 (G. Kittel); *DPL* 348-50 (R. Gaffin).

## C. CLOSING GREETINGS (4:21-23)

> 21*Greet all the saints in Christ Jesus. The brothers who are with me send greetings.* 22*All the saints send you greetings, especially those who belong to Caesar's household.*
> 23*The grace of the Lord Jesus Christ be with your spirits.*[1]

As with most of his letters, and in keeping with the conventions of letter-writing in the Greco-Roman world, Paul concludes with the standard greetings (vv. 21-22) and a grace-benediction (v. 23).[2] In this letter these are notably brief, most likely because of the nature of the preceding promise (v. 19) and doxology (v. 20) — after which anything longer would be intrusive.

Although the closing greetings take a variety of forms in Paul's letters, frequently including the mention of people by name, cumulatively there are three basic components, all three of which occur here in their tersest expression:

1. The imperative to greet "all the saints" (which is his greeting to each of them).[3]
2. Greetings from his immediate companions.[4]
3. Where appropriate, greetings from other "saints" in his present location.[5]

The only elaboration, and only surprise, is the inclusion of "those who belong to Caesar's household" in the final greeting. These kinds of greetings are one

---

1. Apparently uncomfortable with this distributive singular, and perhaps with the language itself, later scribes (ℵ[2] Ψ Maj sy) changed Paul's τοῦ πνεύματος to πάντων (= with you all).

2. Galatians, Ephesians, and 1 Timothy, each for its own reason, are the exceptions with regard to the closing greetings. All the letters have the concluding grace-benediction.

3. This component takes two basic forms: either Paul calls on his readers to "greet *one another* with a holy kiss" (1 Cor 16:20; 2 Cor 13:12), or as here he calls on them to "greet *the saints* (or its equivalent)" (Col 4:15 [the brothers and sisters in Laodicea!]; Tit 3:15; 2 Tim 4:19); both appear in Rom 16:16 and 3-15. In three instances his personal greeting takes the form of personal note ("my greeting in my own hand"; 2 Thess 3:17; 1 Cor 16:21; Col 4:18). In all of these cases, including those where the imperative is to "greet one another," one may assume that this is Paul's way of greeting the whole community (except, of course, Rom 16:3-15 and 2 Tim 4:19, where individuals are singled out).

4. This occurs in 1 Cor 16:20 and Tit 3:15, as here, without mentioning names; elsewhere, where this dimension of greeting occurs, he includes names (Rom 16:21-23; Col 4:10-14; Phlm 23-24; 2 Tim 4:21).

5. See 1 Cor 16:19; 2 Cor 13:12.

of the ways (the collection for the poor in Jerusalem was another) that Paul used to keep the various churches aware of and in touch with one another. In its own small way, therefore, it functions as a part of his concern for the "unity of the body of Christ."

**21a**  The imperative to "greet[6] all the saints in Christ Jesus" is notable both for its uniqueness and brevity. For a community with whom he is on such friendly terms, one might have expected more. But the brevity is explicable both in terms of friendship — such letters in the Greco-Roman world are notable for their laconic closing greetings — and the preceding theological-doxological conclusion. Just as friends do not need to express thanks, neither do friends need elaborate greetings. And further greetings would detract from the words he most wants to leave with them — God's glory out of which he lavishes riches on them in Christ Jesus, to whom all glory is now due.

On the meaning of "saint(s)" see on 1:1. Although it is arguable that at the end they come out at the same place, Paul does not in fact say, as the NIV has it, "greet *all the* saints"; rather, he has, "greet *every saint*."[7] Since he regularly uses the plural when he intends to refer to a congregation or group as a whole, his use of the singular here is deliberate, functioning in a kind of "distributive" way. The greeting is not to the community lumped together as a whole, but to each member of the community individually. He does not single anyone out, but he does greet each of them in this fashion. Thus, "greetings to each one of God's people" (GNB).

---

6. Gk. ἀσπάσασθε. The question is sometimes raised (e.g., Müller, Beare, Hawthorne, O'Brien) as to whom this is addressed, since it is assumed that the church cannot greet itself, as it were. Thus many see it as addressed to the "overseers and deacons" of 1:1. But as we pointed out on that verse, the letter is addressed in the first instance to the whole community collectively, among whom the leaders are also mentioned. It is our own sociology (sense of logic?) and need for precision that both raises and answers the question in this way. In fact the greeting is from Paul to the whole church, not from Paul through others to the rest. If that is not precise to our thinking, it is surely what Paul intends, and keeps one from the eccentricity of having this singular instance of the second plural imperative addressed to others than those to whom the whole letter is addressed. Incidental evidence for this understanding is to be found in Rom 16:3, where Paul singles out Prisca and Aquila as first to be greeted (ἀσπάσασθε), in a letter that was very likely to be read first in their own house church by one of them (on the grounds that the letter was being carried by Phoebe, one of their [assumed] friends from nearby Cenchrea, who would almost certainly go to their house first, as Paul's order of greeting implies).

7. Gk. πάντα ἅγιον; for a discussion of this usage of πᾶς, see Moule, *Idiom Book,* 94-95. Grammatically, the alternative is not between "all the" and "every," but between "the whole" (apparently a semitism) and "every." There does not seem to be any grammatical justification for the plural of the NIV. Nor does "every" mean "of every kind," as Plummer (107) supposes.

What is less clear is the meaning of "in Christ Jesus," which is similar to the ambiguous "in the Lord" in 1:14. Does Paul intend, "greet each of God's people who belong to Christ Jesus" (GNB), or "give my greetings in Christ Jesus to every member" (NAB, cf. REB)? As in 1:14 the word order would seem to favor the former; but as there, that also creates an unusual — and unnecessary — redundancy. To be a "saint" is to be "in fellowship with Christ Jesus." On the other hand, this phrase, which is especially frequent in this letter, usually modifies the verb in its sentence (although 4:19 is a notable exception). Most likely, therefore, Paul intends the greeting to find its locus "in Christ Jesus,"[8] just as he has twice urged them to "rejoice in the Lord" (3:1; 4:4). In sum: Paul is sending his own greetings to each member of the believing community; they are to pass it on to one another for him, and the greeting is to be "in Christ Jesus," who is both the source and focus of their common life together.

**21b** The next greeting comes from his immediate circle of associates, "the brothers who are with me." His failure to mention names in this case has led to considerable speculation, especially since he mentions several by name in two other letters (presumably) from this captivity.[9] We have already suggested on 2:20-21 and 4:3 that Luke had probably returned to Philippi. As to the others, we know nothing; indeed, we cannot be sure even about Luke. And speculation is not terribly helpful here, since we cannot be sure why he mentions names in other instances. In some cases it is almost certainly because they were known to the recipients; but that is not likely in every case.[10] All we know is that just as he does not mention anyone in Philippi by name, neither does he mention any of his companions, even though this greeting makes it clear that some of them are still with him.[11] In any case, it is in keeping with the terseness of these greetings.

---

8. Esp. so in light of 1 Cor 16:19, where "in the Lord" functions in the same way (*pace* Müller, Collange). So Lightfoot, Meyer, Kennedy, Jones, Plummer, Lohmeyer, Bonnard, Beare, Martin, Silva. Those who think otherwise (Vincent, Müller, Collange, Loh-Nida, Kent, Bruce, Hawthorne, O'Brien) point to the usage in 1:1.

9. This assumes the traditional view also to be correct regarding Colossians and Philemon.

10. E.g., in Phlm 23 he sends greetings from Epaphras, who has recently come from Colossae; but in v. 24 he isolates apart from Epaphras four others: Mark, Aristarchus, Demas, and Luke. Does he do so because even though not known to Philemon, the five of them are the only companions currently with him? Likewise, it is unlikely that the church in Rome knew Tertius (Rom 16:22; but this is more complicated because the letter is being written from Corinth and the first house church to receive it [apparently] will be that of Prisca and Aquila [16:3-5], who are well known in Corinth and thus would presumably have known Tertius).

11. And very likely some of these are known to them. For example, Aristarchus, mentioned in Col 4:10 and Phlm 24, is noted in Acts 20:4 as from Thessalonica.

**22**   The third in the series of greetings reaches out to the broader circle of believers in Rome. Here he does indeed say, "all the saints," and he surely intends that, even if many of them would not so much as know they were being included — and in light of 1:15 and 17 some of those might not wish to be included! But they are all included simply because they all belong to one another, those in Rome to each other and those in Rome to those in Philippi as well.

But in this case Paul adds the intriguing, "especially[12] those who belong to Caesar's household." Two matters are noteworthy. First, despite objections from those who hold a different view, this little phrase joins with the mention of "Praetorian Guard" in 1:13 as the strongest kind of evidence for the Roman origins of this letter. All objections to this must take the form of trying to gainsay a simple historical reality, namely, that both of these groups are especially "at home" in Rome; whereas one must look under all kinds of "stones" to turn up evidence for their existence in Ephesus or Caesarea.[13] And to argue, as some do, that this does not necessarily mean the presence of Caesar's household as such, but of people who were at one time members of that household, is both an unnatural reading of the text and fails to grasp the significance of this notation, which is the next point.

Second, and related to the first, the significance of this greeting could hardly be lost on the Philippian believers, opposition to whom in part at least stems from the fact that Philippi is a Roman colony, where devotion to Caesar had a long history.[14] Besides having the gospel in common, and now suffering for Christ in common, Paul and the Philippians also have a common source of opposition. While the Philippians suffer at the hands of Roman citizens loyal to Caesar, Paul is an actual prisoner of Caesar. But in making him a prisoner at the heart of the empire, Rome has brought in a member of the "opposition" who is in the process of creating a "fifth column" within the

---

12. Gk. μάλιστα, the superlative of the adv. μάλα, which means "most of all"; in a context like this it has the effect of singling out a few from among a larger group (cf. Phlm 16, of Onesimus, "most of all to me, but even more so to you"; 1 Tim 4:10; 5:17; Tit 1:10; 2 Tim 4:13). This is another usage, incidentally, which this letter has in common with the Captivity and/or Pastoral letters, but not with others in the corpus.

13. Such evidence can be found for Ephesus (see Duncan, *Ephesian Ministry,* 110; although it is not at all clear that the inscriptions he notes refer to *residents of Ephesus* who would be ordinarily included under the rubric "household of"); it must be hypothesized for Caesarea. Intent on maintaining an Ephesian origin for the letter, Collange incautiously asserts (155), "so the reference here to 'those of Caesar's household' in no way supports the thesis of a Roman imprisonment." That is to put it exactly backwards! Whatever else, it does in fact support a Roman provenance for our letter; what others must do is to "discover" evidence that such language was used of people living outside Rome.

14. On this matter see the Introduction, pp. 30-32; cf. the discussion at various points in the commentary, esp. on 1:12-18, 22, 27-28; 2:9-11.

very walls of the emperor's domicile. Paul either has found[15] or has made disciples of the "Lord" Jesus among members of the imperial household,[16] who are thus on the Philippians' side in the struggle against those who proclaim Caesar as Lord!

Paul is an indomitable apostle of Christ Jesus. Let him loose and he will be among those "who turn the world upside down" (Acts 17:6; a charge of sedition!) for his Christ; incarcerate him too close to home and he will "turn Caesar's household upside down" as well. Thus, here is a word of encouragement to the Philippians in the midst of their present struggle. The "word of life" to which they hold firm in the midst of their "crooked and perverse generation" (2:15-16) has already penetrated the heart of the empire. They have brothers and sisters in Caesar's own household, who are on their side and now send them greetings; and therefore the Savior whom they await (3:20) in the midst of their present struggle will gather some from Caesar's household as well as from Caesar's Philippi when he comes.

**23**   In all of the extant letters that bear Paul's name, he signs off with this, or a similar, grace-benediction. The standard "good-bye" in Greek letters was *errōso* (lit., "be strong"), found in the NT in the letter of James (Acts 15:29). As with his salutations, Paul's closing greetings are thus "christianized." It is "grace," the favor of God that is theirs through "the Lord Jesus," that he wishes for them.[17] What is common to all his letters is that the "grace," when qualified,[18] is from "our Lord Jesus Christ." Although "grace" is primarily from God in Paul's letters,[19] on a few occasions he attributes grace directly as from Christ.[20] But in the grace-benedictions, it is invariably "the grace of our Lord Jesus Christ" that he "prays" will be with

---

15. As Lightfoot (173) believes (cf. Vincent, Plummer), perhaps rightly so.

16. Gk. οἱ ἐκ τῆς Καίσαρος οἰκίας; noting that this refers to Nero's household, Calvin (295) writes, "for it is no common evidence of divine mercy that the Gospel had penetrated that sink of all crimes and iniquities." What it meant for the gospel to have penetrated that "sink" has been the subject of all kinds of (often wild) speculation. Although it could include relatives and people of note, most likely it refers to slaves and freedmen attached to the palace. For the extent of the imperial household and the number and kinds of functionaries it included, based on funerary inscriptions, see the excursus in Lightfoot (171-78), who also notes the large number of correspondences between these names and those listed in Rom 16:6-16.

17. Some would wish to make the supplied verb indicative (G. Delling, *Worship*, 75); but since it takes the place of the standard ἔρωσσο, most likely an optative is intended. After all, this final word functions as a benediction or blessing.

18. In Colossians and the Pastoral Letters it is shortened simply to "grace be with you."

19. See, e.g., 1 Cor 1:4; 3:10; 15:10; 2 Cor 1:12; 6:1; 8:1; 9:14; Gal 2:21; Rom 5:15; Col 1:6; Eph 3:2, 7; Tit 2:11.

20. See 2 Cor 8:9; Gal 1:6; Rom 5:15; 1 Tim 1:14.

them. Thus the final grace serves to "book end" his letters, which begin with "grace (and peace)" as part of the greeting (see on 1:2). It is of some interest that where he also includes the wish of "peace" at the end, Paul always connects that with God the Father, as in 4:7 and 9.[21] In effect, therefore, the "grace and peace" that appear as the opening greeting as "from God the Father and the Lord Jesus Christ" are distinguished at the end as "the peace of God" and the "grace of our Lord Jesus Christ."

This is one of four letters[22] in which the ordinary "be with you" appears in the form "be with your spirits."[23] Reasons for this substitution are difficult to find. Three of the letters (Philemon, 2 Timothy, and this one) have in common that they are the most overtly affectionate of his letters. But that hardly accounts for its usage in Galatians(!), unless it is there as a kind of final offer of affection in a letter that otherwise bristles with distress. In the final analysis we must admit to not knowing why. What we do know is that the distributive singular, "with your (pl.) spirit (sing.)," in effect, as with the first of the greetings in v. 21, individualizes the grace-benediction, so that each of them (in the "spirit" of each) will experience the desired grace that is here prayed for.

On this note the letter comes to an end. One would hesitate to draw out too much theology from these more conventional closing formulas. But as noted

21. See 2 Thess 3:16; Rom 15:33; cf. 1 Thess 5:23; 2 Cor 13:11. In Gal 6:16 the peace benediction appears without a qualifier.

22. Cf. Gal 6:18; Phlm 25; 2 Tim 4:22. On this matter see the discussion of Gal 6:18 in Fee, *Presence,* 468-69.

23. R. Jewett (*Anthropological Terms,* 184) has made a considerable point out of the singular of πνεῦμα occurring with the plural pronoun, asserting that "since the word 'spirit' is in the singular, reference is clearly being made to the single divine spirit rather than to the various human spirits with which the members of the congregation could have been thought to have been born." He adds: "But one thing is certain: the tradition which shaped this formula did not distinguish between the divine spirit and the spirit which a man could possess." But this is not nearly as "clear" and "certain" as Jewett would have it. In fact, this use of the plural pronoun with a singular noun is but another reflection of Paul's (semitic) preference for a distributive singular, wherein "something belonging to each person in a group of people is placed in the singular" (N. Turner, *MHT,* 3.23; for this usage in Paul see [with σῶμα] 1 Cor 6:19, 20; 2 Cor 4:10; Rom 6:12; 8:23; [with καρδία] 2 Cor 3:15; Rom 1:21; Eph 1:18; 4:18; 5:19; 6:5). Therefore, Paul almost certainly does *not* intend by this usage to refer to "the single divine spirit," nor is he thinking of the Spirit as apportioned to each of them and in effect taking the place of the human spirit, as Jewett maintains. Paul simply means "be with your spirits," which he here substitutes for the more common "with you" that appears elsewhere.

Even more improbable, in that it ignores Pauline usage, is the suggestion by Jones (78) that it might go back to the "one spirit" in 1:27 (a text on which he misses Paul's usage as well).

at the beginning and elsewhere (e.g., 4:8, 11-13, 15-16) in Paul's hand conventions are never merely conventional. Eventually everything, including these conventions, is brought under the influence of Christ and the gospel. Thus the final greetings, which by their threefold elaboration presuppose the church as the body of Christ, are to be given and received as "in Christ Jesus." And the final grace is also "from the Lord Jesus Christ," so that everything in this letter, from beginning to end and everywhere in between, focuses on Christ, who as Paul's life (1:21) is magnified both in his language and in the two narratives that point specifically to him (Christ's in 2:6-11 and Paul's in 3:4-14). To miss this central focus on Christ is to miss the letter altogether, and to miss the heart of Pauline theology in particular.

To live is Christ; to die is to gain Christ; and for the sake of such "gain," namely the surpassing value of knowing Christ Jesus as one's own Lord, all else is merely refuse. Thus, may the grace of our Lord Jesus Christ be with all the readers of this letter, and with those who use this commentary to help better understand it as the Word of Christ.

# INDEX OF SUBJECTS

Adam, 209
adoption, 110
affection, 90-91, 93-95, 99
affliction, 118-19, 438-39
    *see also* Paul, imprisonment; suffering
already/not yet, 47, 50-51, 86, 97, 103, 145-46, 147n37, 219, 242, 244, 287, 320-21, 326, 329, 332, 376, 379-80
antinomians, 370
Antony, Mark, 25-26
anxiety, 408-11, 453
argumentation. *See* polemics
athletic metaphor, 250, 340, 346-49, 352, 395

baptism, 334n67
behavior, 97, 99, 201, 355, 359-60, 400-401
blamelessness, 102-3, 244-46
boasting, 154-55, 241, 249, 301-2
body, 137-38, 382-83
brothers and sisters, 110, 114-16, 291
burnt offering, 451

Caesarea, 35-36, 445, 459
Caesar's household, 36, 456, 459-60
calling, 349-50
chains, 59, 92, 118, 120
    *see also* Paul, imprisonment; suffering
character, 268
Christ-sufficiency, 415, 427, 434
Christian life, 52-53, 81, 87-88, 97, 101, 135, 227, 238-39, 270, 336-37, 409

church:
    hierarchy in, 67
    leadership, 67-69, 71
    persecution of, 308
circumcision, 101, 122-23, 289-90, 294-303, 306-7, 316, 322-23
citizenship, 19
    dual, 31, 93, 141, 161-62, 376
    heavenly, 162-63, 241, 287, 350, 378-79
    Roman, 66, 161-62, 222-23, 378-79
Clement, 26, 395-96
comfort, 178-80
commercial metaphor, 442-44, 447-48, 449-50
community, 190, 200, 232, 234-35, 403, 412
concern for others, 266-67, 270
confession, 225
confidence, 116, 138
conforming to Christ, 333-34, 360-62
consciousness, 148-49
Constantianism, 310
consummation, 50-51, 86
contentment, 414, 419, 427, 431-34, 437, 451
Corinth, 28, 445
crucifixion, 31
cruciform life, 104, 287, 337, 415, 420, 436
Cynics, 433

day of Christ, 86, 97, 244, 248, 257, 320-21
day of the Lord, 85, 408
deacons, 66, 69

death, 107, 126-27, 138, 140-50, 146, 172, 274, 334-35
destruction, 370-71, 384
Diaspora, 307, 414
different gospel, 303
discernment. *See* moral insight
discipleship, 113, 125, 147n37, 197, 208, 435
doctrine, 21
dogs, 295-97, 319, 367, 372, 373
doxology, 17, 424, 449, 450, 455
dread, 236
drink offering, 30, 124, 251-55, 280

earthly mindedness, 371-75, 391
election, 77
emotion, 95
encouragement, 180
enemies of the cross, 10, 33-34, 369-70, 374
envy, 118n5, 119, 122
Epaphroditus, 12, 20, 29, 37-39, 93, 259-61, 271-84, 286, 394, 405, 428, 431, 449-51
Ephesus, 35, 459
eschatology, 30, 47, 50-52, 86-88, 126, 145-46, 153, 168-69, 197, 223, 228, 248, 341-42, 348, 388, 404
    *see also* already/not yet
eternity, 149
ethics, 10-11, 337, 400
Euodia, 26, 33, 69, 81, 389-93, 395-97
evangelicalism, 231
evangelism, 111, 116, 118, 123-24, 229, 244, 247-48, 258, 283, 412
evil doers, 295-96
exhortation, 10-11, 12, 20, 29, 37, 156, 180, 359

faith, 101, 324-26
faithfulness, 318n21
false teachers, 367
fellow-imitators, 364
fellowship, 59, 82
flesh, 142-45, 300-303, 306, 310, 322
form, 204-5, 208, 211, 213, 333, 382-83
friendship, 2-7, 10-11, 16, 19-20, 27, 38, 73, 76, 358-59, 387, 389, 402, 410, 415, 419, 422-31, 435, 439-47, 449-51
fruit of righteousness, 101, 103-5
fruit of the Spirit, 104, 410

fruitfulness, 143-44, 447-48
future, 30, 126-27, 223, 345, 350, 407-8
    *see also* eschatology

gain/loss metaphor, 312-20
gaining Christ, 141-42, 144
garbage. *See* refuse
generosity, 28
Gentiles, 122-23, 294-302, 306-7, 412
gentleness, 404, 406-7
gift, 83, 92, 398-99, 422-26, 429-31, 436, 442-43, 448, 450-51
glorification, 249, 346, 363, 371
glory, 187, 228, 373-74, 382-83
gluttony, 372n38
Gnosticism, 318n21, 382n28
goal, 338-40, 344, 384
God:
    character, 191, 214, 418
    the Father, 48, 71, 461
    as first and last, 170
    glory, 226, 227, 231, 238, 453-55
    love, 98-99, 180-82, 185, 208, 217, 240
    mercy, 279-81
    pleasure, 239-40
    presence, 421
good work, 85-86, 87, 95, 96, 105
goodwill, 5, 120, 239
gospel, 13-14, 20, 38, 47, 81-84, 92-93, 125-26, 136, 158
    advancement of, 107, 108-11, 117, 120, 124, 138, 150, 261
grace, 70-71, 91, 92, 171, 320, 402, 460-61
gratitude, 5
Greco-Roman culture, 4, 63, 187-88, 252, 295, 414, 429
    friendship in, 436-37, 439, 443
    moralism of, 401, 402, 404, 414-19
grumbling, 243-44, 453

hardship lists, 433
healing, 279
heart, 90, 411-12
heaven, 349-50
hedonism, 421
Holy Spirit, 48-49, 80-81, 132-35, 163-66, 173, 181-82, 225, 227, 238-39, 299-302, 330, 403, 405, 421
hope, 20, 135, 138, 151
humiliation, 371, 432-33, 451

humility, 33, 50, 63, 153, 187-89, 191,
196, 200, 208, 227, 271, 436
hymn, hymnody, 40-43, 192-94, 217, 219

idolatry, 409, 417
image of God, 209
imitation, 229, 362-65, 367, 388, 401,
414, 419, 427
imperative(s), 156, 159-62, 227, 231-37,
240-41, 256, 281-82, 287, 399, 400-
401, 413-14
indicative, 227, 407
individual, 190, 234-35, 403, 411, 421
intertextuality, 17-18, 130, 136, 220,
222, 242, 246n26, 257, 407
intimacy, 318, 329, 333
Israel, 64, 242-43, 245, 258, 434

jealousy. *See* envy
Jesus Christ:
    centrality, 13-14, 49-50, 228, 376, 462
    coming, 86, 380-82
    death, 99, 125, 216-18, 228, 274, 334-
    36
    deity, 198, 207-8, 213
    emptying himself, 203
    equality with the Father, 220
    exaltation, 196, 218-22, 226, 228
    example, 227-28
    glorification, 105, 134, 136-39, 168
    humiliation, 64, 157, 196-97, 211-17,
    315, 333, 382-83
    humility, 187-89, 208
    incarnation, 198, 203n41, 211-14, 223
    "in Christ Jesus," 65, 71, 112-13, 178,
    180, 181-82, 200, 321, 411, 453-54,
    462
    Lordship, 31-32, 157, 197, 222-25,
    381
    love, 95, 226, 318-19
    meekness, 407
    nearness, 407-8, 412-13
    obedience, 216
    person and work, 82
    pre-existence, 198, 202-3
    resurrection, 125, 225, 227, 327-28,
    329-30, 331, 334-37, 414
    sufferings, 327-28, 332-37
Jewish piety, 402
Jewish wisdom, 411, 415-17
Job, 130-31
joy, 20, 28, 52-53, 75, 81-82, 95, 118,

124, 126-27, 130, 150, 153-54, 183-
85, 280, 255-58, 388, 403-6, 412, 427-
31, 434-36
    *see also* rejoicing
Judaizers, 9, 17, 33, 122-23, 286-99,
302, 306-10, 319, 324, 331, 342, 356,
370
justification, 322n35, 326

Kingdom of God, 403
knowing Christ, 304-5, 306, 310-14, 317-
18, 326-37, 341-45, 350-51
knowledge, 97, 99-101

labor, 250
law, 309-10, 313
leadership, 189, 397-98
letters, 2-4
    of commendation, 259-61, 262-63,
    272, 281
    of friendship, 10, 12-14, 23, 37, 106,
    108, 110, 257, 286, 377, 385, 413,
    415
liberalism, 173
libertines, 372, 375
like-mindedness, 266-69
likeness of Christ, 227
Lord's Prayer, 105
love, 96, 98-101, 104, 120, 153, 180-81,
185-86, 191, 227, 447
Luke, 27, 394-95
Lydia, 26, 444

Macedonia, 28, 440-42, 445
martyrdom, 29, 252, 254
materialism, 173, 421, 448
maturity, 355-56
mercy, 279
military imagery, 275-76
mindset, 89-90, 156, 168, 175-76, 185-
89, 191-96, 214, 228-29, 315, 353-55,
362, 371, 391-92, 430, 453
mirror-reading, 7n, 8, 10, 341
money, 448
moral excellence, 419
moral insight, 97, 99-101
morality, 419, 421
mutilation, 296-300, 302
mutuality, 5-6, 11, 12, 90, 405, 423, 444-46
mysticism, 65, 329, 332n64

nationalism, 421

need(s), 427, 431, 433, 434, 446, 450, 452-54
Nero, 31-32, 36, 116, 157, 197
new covenant, 298-99, 318n21, 322n35

oath, 93-94
obedience, 197, 216, 226, 227, 229, 231-37, 363
obligation, 5
Octavian, 25-26, 161
offering. *See* gift
old covenant, 326-27
    *see also* torah observance; Judaizers; circumcision
Old Testament:
    sacrificial system, 251
    use by Paul, 17-18, 103, 130, 188, 235, 236, 241-43, 251, 318, 381, 402-3
opponents, 7-10, 121, 122, 295, 341, 367, 374
opposition, 29-30, 241, 341, 352, 358, 404, 452
oral culture, 16-17, 18, 79n35, 178
overseers, 66-69

paganism, 245-46, 370, 414
partnership in the gospel, 10, 23, 73, 76, 80, 84-87, 90-92, 423-28, 435, 436, 438-41
patience, 436
Paul:
    apostleship, 62, 147n37
    Christology, 49-50, 125, 127, 150, 170-71, 197, 199, 435
    death, 252-53
    eschatology, 149, 150
    ethics, 191, 218, 227, 402
    imprisonment, 28, 30, 32, 34-37, 92-93, 108-17, 120-21, 152, 173, 428, 438, 451
    Jewish status, 305-8
    rhetorical style, 42
    spirituality, 80, 81, 95, 412
    theology, 20, 46-47, 217, 228, 284, 462
    use of OT, 17-18, 103, 130, 188, 235, 236, 241-43, 251, 318, 381, 402-3
peace, 70-71, 403-4, 410-12, 420-21, 461
perfection, 341-42, 344, 347
perseverance, 183-84, 345
persuasion, 11

petition, 77, 81
Pharisees, 308-9
Philippi (church), 26-34, 445
Philippi (city), 24-26, 31-32, 36-37, 244-46, 459
Philippians (letter):
    authenticity, 45-46
    *hapax legomena*, 18-19
    integrity, 21-23
    provenance, 34, 36, 277-78, 459
    redactor, 23, 423
    text, 23-24
piety, 400, 403
pluralism, religious, 111, 125
poetry, 40-42, 193-94, 196
polemics, 17-18, 20, 353-55
post-modern world, 150, 173, 412, 421
posturing, 32-33, 52, 81, 158, 273
    *see also* selfish ambition
poverty, 28, 433, 452
power, 330-31
powers, 384
Praetorian Guard, 34-36, 112-14, 275, 459
prayer, 72-73, 75, 80-81, 96-105, 132-35, 402-3, 412
preaching, 116-17, 124
prize, 326, 346-49, 362
progress, 107, 150, 153-54, 161, 233, 405
prose, 41-42
Psalter, 403

race. *See* athletic metaphor
realized eschatology, 407-8
reciprocity, 12, 19, 27, 452
refuse, 319-23, 341
rejoicing, 286-87, 289-94, 333, 364, 402-6, 426, 452, 458
relativism, 421
religiousness, 310
remembrance, 75-79
resurrection, 149, 304, 314-15, 334-36, 346, 382-83
reward, 447-48
rhetoric, 14-17, 42, 178
riches, of God, 453-55
righteousness, 52, 96-97, 101, 105, 296, 300, 302, 313-16, 321-27, 337, 343, 417-19
    in the law, 309-10
Rome, Roman Empire, 25-26, 30-36,

113-17, 121-24, 161, 167, 172, 222-23, 277-78, 405, 445, 459-60

sacrifice, 254
saints, 64-65, 457-59
salvation, 71, 87, 128-32, 134, 138, 169-71, 229-31, 234-37, 337
sanctification, 328n54
sarcasm, 293
scandal of the cross, 197
sectarianism, 173
self-gratification, 150, 375
self-interest, 190-91
self-sufficiency, 415, 427, 432, 434, 435
selfish ambition, 157, 186-191, 198, 202
    see also posturing
selflessness, 202, 227
serenity, 432
Servant of the Lord, 212
servanthood, 197
shame, 136, 373-74
Silas, 27-28
slaves, 6, 211-14, 333
    of Jesus Christ, 62-64, 71, 444
sociology, 423-25
sorrow, 279-81
steadfastness, 385-86, 388-89, 397, 400, 405, 412
stoicism, 331, 414, 427, 431-34, 435, 437
stomach, 371-72, 374
story, 47
strife, 118n5, 421
struggle, 172-73
suffering, 21, 29-30, 33, 51, 52, 59, 125, 170-74, 228, 229-30, 254-55, 273, 304, 314-15, 331-36, 408, 436

Syntyche, 26, 33, 69, 81, 389-93, 395-97
Syzygus, 393

thanksgiving, 13, 17, 22-23, 30, 72-81, 88, 93, 95, 402-3, 409-11, 412
Thessalonica, 441-42, 444-45, 448
time, 149
Timothy, 8, 12, 20, 27-28, 29n, 33, 38-39, 60-64, 163, 259-261, 262-71, 394
Titus, 28
Torah observance, 122, 290-1, 300-304, 306, 308-10, 323-24, 327, 342, 348
transformation, 382-84
Trinity, 48, 179, 180, 182, 302
triumphalism, 197, 331
trust, 5
truth, 417, 421

unity, 157, 166, 185, 189, 385-86, 397, 400, 404, 405-6, 412
usefulness, 425, 427

vain conceit, 157, 186, 188-89
vindication, 130-32, 134, 138, 170, 197, 219-20, 228, 315, 408
virtue(s), 5, 415-20
vocabulary, 18-20

weakness, 236
wisdom, 100, 411, 415-17
"wish of peace," 401, 420, 461
women, 26, 390-91, 397-98
world, 421
worship, 455

# INDEX OF AUTHORS

Aalen, S., 455
Abbott, E., 184
Abrahamsen, V., 391
Achtemeier, P. J., 16, 17
Alexander, L., 3, 4, 291
Alford, H., 115, 183, 221, 292, 407, 410
Arzt, P., 72
Augustine, 372
Aune, D. E., 15

Babbitt, C. J., 443
Bahr, G. J., 60
Bakken, N. K., 203
Balch, D. L., 63
Balz, H., 135, 137, 299, 396
Bandstra, A. J., 209
Barclay, J. M. G., 7, 299, 344, 400
Barclay, W., 177, 179, 181
Barnes, E., 391
Barrett, C. K., 181
Bartchy, S. S., 63
Barth, K., 69, 74, 78, 123, 135, 140,
    141, 161, 164, 167, 178, 186, 187,
    189, 191, 216, 219, 222, 233, 236,
    243, 244, 245, 246, 250, 267, 277,
    288, 295, 311, 327, 330, 336, 342,
    343, 346, 349, 357, 372, 379, 393,
    396, 398, 406, 407, 428
Barth, M., 132
Basevi, C., 15
Bauder, W., 363, 364, 406
Bauer, W., Arndt, W. F., Gingrich, F. W.,
    and Danker, F., 78, 88, 89, 102, 109,
    110, 115, 120, 121, 130, 133, 147,
    148, 169, 180, 186, 187, 190, 202,
    239, 250, 252, 254, 263, 281, 282,

315, 317, 318, 342, 343, 359, 395,
    437, 443, 445, 450
Bauernfeind, O., 419
Baumgarten, J., 407, 408
Beare, F. W., 43, 69, 78, 90, 103, 113,
    115, 123, 128, 132, 136, 140, 169,
    178, 179, 180, 183, 192, 201, 207,
    211, 212, 217, 220, 221, 222, 224,
    229, 233, 235, 243, 246, 252, 255,
    261, 270, 273, 280, 291, 300, 317,
    318, 320, 326, 341, 342, 343, 348,
    350, 353, 357, 361, 365, 367, 378,
    381, 385, 396, 398, 402, 404, 407,
    409, 411, 414, 419, 422, 433, 438,
    440, 443, 457, 458
Beck, H., 70
Becker, J., 376, 377, 386
Beekman, J., 143, 153, 317, 349
Behm, J., 204, 371, 411
Bengel, J. A., 274, 327, 372, 396, 428
Benoit, P., 69
Bertram, G., 135, 138
Best, E., 66
Betz, H. D., 14, 364, 365
Beutler, J., 110
Beyer, H. W., 68
Beyreuther, E., 404
Bjerkelund, C. J., 391
Black, C. C., 14
Black, D. E. 176, 177, 178, 183, 193
Blass, F., Debrunner, A., and Funk, R.
    W., 207, 239, 250, 252, 253
Blevins, J. L., 29
Bloomquist, L. G., 15, 16, 29, 73, 106,
    135, 261
Broneer, O., 349

Bonhöffer, 99

Bonnard, P., 91, 143, 148, 152, 163, 175, 266, 273, 293, 314, 342, 458

Bornkamm, G., 212

Bousset, W., 65, 301

Boyer, J. L., 177

Brant, J. A., 364

Brauch, M., 231

Braumann, G., 334

Brewer, R. R., 162

Brown, C., 70, 163

Bruce, F. F., ix, 35, 36, 61, 63, 78, 90, 91, 113, 114, 115, 121, 131, 134, 143, 148, 161, 164, 170, 208, 211, 213, 222, 238, 243, 244, 265, 266, 278, 288, 290, 291, 292, 296, 307, 320, 322, 342, 349, 353, 357, 365, 367, 377, 394, 396, 407, 426, 428, 440, 445, 458

Buchanan, C. O., 275, 276, 278, 422

Bugg, C., 407

Bühner, J.-A., 276

Bultmann, R., 137, 154, 181, 318, 373, 404, 417

Burton, E. D. W., 252, 253, 277, 360, 416, 441

Caird, G. B., 87, 103, 192, 201, 209, 212, 217, 220, 233, 235, 243, 246, 255, 268, 270, 278, 283, 288, 291, 292, 293, 294, 295, 317, 328, 340, 348, 349, 353, 354, 357, 358, 368, 371, 397, 398, 407, 410, 422

Callow, J., 143, 153, 317, 349

Calvin, J., 114, 143, 203, 230, 246, 254, 265, 266, 290, 292, 300, 321, 327, 328, 407, 409, 410, 430, 433, 460

Capper, B. J., 111, 422, 424, 429, 437, 438, 440, 441, 443, 447

Carr, W. A., 224

Carson, D. A., 1, 34

Cerfaux, L., 212

Chapa, J., 15

Christou, P., 266

Coenen, L., 68, 349

Collange, J.-F., 64, 65, 66, 69, 74, 78, 81, 87, 90, 91, 94, 103, 110, 111, 120, 130, 131, 134, 135, 141, 143, 146, 147, 148, 163, 167, 169, 176, 179, 180, 181, 183, 186, 187, 192, 193, 201, 205, 207, 209, 210, 214, 222, 223, 233, 234, 236, 237, 239, 246,
252, 254, 261, 263, 266, 267, 276, 277, 278, 280, 292, 298, 303, 316, 320, 321, 327, 332, 336, 340, 342, 345, 349, 352, 353, 365, 373, 376, 381, 394, 398, 404, 406, 407, 410, 422, 440, 445, 447, 458, 459

Colwell, E. C., 230

Conybeare, W. J., 278

Conzelmann, H., 246

Coppens, J., 43

Craddock, F., 136, 407

Cullmann, O., 148, 209, 224

Culpepper, R. A., 261

Dailey, T. E., 145, 147

Dalton, W. J., 425

Dana, H. E., 153

Dassmann, E., 68

Dautzenberg, G., 172

Davies, W. D., 302

Dean, H., 206, 210

De Boer, W. P., 364, 365, 366

Deissmann, A., 35, 65, 93, 201, 282, 301, 322, 450

Delling, G., 100, 343, 394, 460

Denis, A. M., 252, 254

Denton, D. R., 135

de Silva, D. A., 290

de Vogel, C. J., 148, 149

Dibelius, M., 123, 141, 163, 201, 224, 233, 266, 292, 349, 422, 440

Dodd, C. H., 422, 443

Droge, A. J., 141, 147

Duncan, G. S., 34, 35, 459

Dunn, J. D. G., 44, 181, 203, 209, 297, 325

Dupont, J., 146

Eadie, J., 134, 164, 178, 221

Earle, R., 365

Eckert, J., 349

Edgar, C. C., 59, 72, 106

Ellicott, C. J., 112, 118, 183, 365, 407

Ellis, E. E., 115, 27

Erasmus, 163

Ernesti, 209

Esser, H.-H., 187, 188

Evans, O. E., 65

Ewald, P., 78, 163

Exler, F. X. J., 59, 291

Fairweather, E. R., 210

Fee, G. D., ix, 28, 40, 41, 42, 47, 48,
    64, 65, 67, 68, 80, 82, 87, 89, 95,
    97, 98, 100, 102, 110, 119, 122,
    130, 132, 134, 137, 142, 150, 151,
    161, 164, 181, 183, 187, 190, 192,
    194, 202, 208, 211, 223, 224, 235,
    238, 239, 253, 254, 279, 283, 292,
    297, 299, 300, 302, 318, 319, 320,
    330, 344, 347, 349, 355, 364, 375,
    382, 383, 393, 400, 403, 409, 437,
    461
Feinberg, P. D., 193, 203, 206, 209, 212
Ferguson, E., 63
Fielder, P., 413
Filson, F., 400
Finkenrath, G., 404
Finlayson, S. K., 246
Fitzgerald, J. T., 35, 45
Fitzmyer, J., 171, 346, 430
Flanagan, N., 377
Fleury, J., 443
Flint, A. J., 453
Foerster, W., 381, 417
Forestell, J. T., 328, 329, 342
Fortna, R. T., 38, 183
Fowl, S. E., 67, 192, 193, 196, 205, 206,
    357, 363, 364
Fridrichsen, A., 185, 265
Funk, R. W., 258, 259
Furness, J. M., 193, 206
Furnish, V. P., 72, 181, 286, 290, 292

Gaffin, R., 455
Gamble, H., 400
Garland, D. E., 20, 69, 78, 107, 131,
    140, 286, 290, 292, 293, 387, 389
Georgi, D., 44, 296, 307
Gibbs, J. G., 212
Giblin, C. H., 71
Giesen, H., 236, 406
Gillman, F. M., 391
Glasson, T. F., 209, 210
Gloer, W. H., 40
Glombitza, O., 236, 440
Gnilka, J., 66, 75, 78, 83, 87, 99, 109,
    123, 130, 131, 135, 136, 143, 163,
    175, 177, 178, 180, 201, 212, 224,
    233, 243, 247, 266, 273, 280, 292,
    299, 306, 320, 327, 349, 352, 353,
    367, 371, 373, 379, 382, 393, 396,
    398, 407, 413, 422, 432, 440, 445
Goldstein, H., 102

Goodspeed, E. J., 161, 252, 291, 317,
    404, 428, 443, 450
Grayston, K., 295
Green, J. B., 218
Grundmann, W., 146, 187, 190
Guhrt, J., 225
Gundry, R. H., 137, 148, 323, 377, 379
Gundry Volf, J., 250, 320, 335, 336, 345
Gunther, J., 7, 36, 307, 309, 341, 349
Günther, W., 98, 372
Gutbrod, W., 307
Guthrie, D., 1, 34
Güttgemanns, E., 376, 377

Hagermann, H., 455
Hagner, D. A., 297
Hahn, H.-C., 137, 154
Hainz, J., 82
Hájek, M., 394
Hamilton, N. Q., 135
Hanhart, K., 141, 148
Harnack, A., 78
Harris, J. R., 274
Harris, M. J., 315, 324
Harrison, P. N., 22
Hartman, D., 391
Harvey, J., 203
Hasler, V., 70, 360
Hauck, F., 292
Haupt, E., 141
Hawthorne, G. F., xii, 34, 36, 62, 64, 66,
    67, 69, 71, 75, 78, 82, 84, 85, 87, 90,
    91, 93, 94, 96, 98, 99, 109, 127, 129,
    130, 131, 133, 135, 140, 141, 144,
    146, 153, 162, 164, 165, 167, 168,
    169, 171, 177, 178, 179, 180, 181,
    182, 183, 189, 198, 200, 202, 204,
    205, 206, 207, 208, 210, 213, 214,
    216, 222, 232, 234, 235, 236, 239,
    243, 244, 246, 252, 254, 255, 259,
    261, 266, 269, 273, 274, 275, 277,
    280, 288, 290, 293, 294, 295, 300,
    302, 307, 311, 315, 317, 319, 320,
    327, 328, 336, 337, 338, 342, 343,
    349, 353, 355, 357, 365, 367, 369,
    372, 373, 376, 377, 385, 388, 390,
    393, 395, 396, 398, 406, 407, 410,
    416, 422, 425, 428, 429, 431, 433,
    437, 439, 445, 449, 457
Hays, R. B., 17, 130, 319, 325
Headlam, A. C., 63
Hemer, C., 394

Hendriksen, W., 78, 87, 90, 103, 132, 133, 141, 143, 145, 152, 162, 167, 178, 180, 183, 200, 201, 202, 207, 210, 212, 222, 231, 233, 234, 238, 243, 255, 263, 265, 266, 279, 280, 290, 293, 307, 316, 327, 328, 336, 357, 361, 367, 378, 396, 398, 407, 410, 426, 440

Hendrix, H. L., 25

Hengel, M., 217, 218

Heriban, J., 212

Hock, R. F., 445

Hofius, O., 224, 419

Hoffmann, P., 141

Holmberg, B., 267, 442

Holmes, M. W., 22

Hooke, S. H., 206

Hooker, M., 46, 192, 193, 209, 211, 314, 325, 383

Hoover, R. W., 205, 206, 207

Houlden, J. L., 67, 78, 109, 114, 115, 138, 170, 209, 213, 220, 233, 243, 266, 320, 343, 393, 398, 407

Howard, G., 203, 220

Howson, J. S., 278

Hübner, H., 343, 345

Hultgren, A. J., 325

Hunt, A. S., 59, 72, 106

Hurst, L. D., 203

Hurtado, L. W., 196, 203, 213, 225, 226

Jaeger, W. W., 206

Jeremias, J., 212, 214

Jewett, R., 73, 78, 88, 119, 237, 265, 268, 289, 290, 292, 343, 344, 367, 373, 374, 461

Johnson, L. T., 1, 2, 12, 163, 185

Jones, M., 61, 128, 131, 143, 145, 163, 170, 178, 180, 187, 189, 201, 205, 208, 210, 212, 243, 244, 246, 254, 255, 266, 288, 293, 314, 328, 332, 343, 344, 348, 353, 360, 365, 366, 380, 386, 392, 393, 394, 407, 410, 426, 440, 452, 458, 461

Käsemann, E., 43, 45, 192, 196, 199, 201, 204, 206, 207, 208, 209, 212, 216, 220, 224, 235, 314

Kee, H. C., 254, 288

Kendrick, G., 218, 226

Kennedy, G., 14, 16

Kennedy, H. A. A., 65, 74, 75, 78, 87, 98, 101, 102, 110, 111, 115, 118, 122, 127, 131, 140, 143, 145, 145, 153, 169, 170, 174, 177, 180, 182, 187, 198, 199, 200, 201, 204, 208, 213, 222, 223, 234, 238, 243, 244, 246, 249, 252, 255, 271, 277, 281, 288, 293, 316, 319, 328, 332, 336, 342, 345, 348, 353, 365, 367, 382, 393, 407, 409, 410, 412, 430, 440, 443, 445, 452, 458

Kent, H. A., 128, 134, 164, 165, 172, 183, 209, 210, 243, 246, 255, 265, 266, 273, 280, 288, 293, 310, 342, 347, 353, 354, 356, 358, 365, 367, 368, 392, 393, 398, 407, 410, 426, 431, 458

Kertelge, K., 322

Kidd, R., 67

Kilpatrick, G. D., 293

Kim, C.-H., 259

Kittel, G., 455

Klijn, A. F. J., 294, 342, 371, 372

Knoch, O., 345

Koester, H., 290, 294, 296, 298, 299, 318, 336, 341, 342, 343, 370, 371, 373, 374, 376, 381

Koperski, V., 325

Koskenniemi, H., 4

Kreitzer, L. J., 149, 193, 222, 226

Kremer, J., 438

Kruse, C. G., 349

Kümmel, W. G., 1, 22, 34, 36

Kurz, W. S., 23

Lang, F., 319

Larsson, E., 364

Leivestad, H., 406

Lemaire, A., 66

Lenski, R. C. H., 161, 336

Lietzmann, H., 181

Lightfoot, J. B., xii, 22, 65, 66, 68, 75, 78, 84, 90, 111, 113, 123, 131, 132, 134, 139, 141, 143, 144, 145, 147, 152, 164, 166, 170, 171, 174, 176, 178, 180, 182, 184, 187, 189, 200, 202, 204, 206, 207, 210, 221, 224, 233, 239, 243, 244, 246, 250, 252, 255, 265, 266, 271, 275, 279, 280, 288, 291, 292, 293, 300, 303, 317, 320, 324, 343, 347, 348, 353, 354, 357, 361, 365, 366, 394, 395, 396, 404, 406, 407, 410, 417, 423, 428,

429, 433, 438, 441, 443, 447, 450, 458, 460

Lincoln, A. T., 148, 149, 294, 296, 299, 318, 341, 343, 357, 365, 371, 376, 377, 378, 379

Link, H. G., 62, 98, 416, 419

Linton, O., 119

Llewelyn, S. R., 306, 391

Lohmeyer, E., 36, 40, 43, 75, 78, 83, 90, 98, 109, 115, 128, 134, 140, 141, 142, 145, 152, 155, 159, 164, 177, 179, 201, 220, 223, 250, 266, 292, 294, 312, 331, 333, 334, 349, 354, 355, 377, 378, 380, 388, 396, 398, 404, 406, 407, 415, 422, 426, 432, 440, 458

Loh, I.-J., 91, 136, 141, 143, 163, 180, 182, 183, 192, 196, 199, 207-8, 214, 217, 222, 223, 229, 233, 235, 236, 243, 244, 248, 252, 254, 266, 277, 280, 293, 294, 301, 302, 317, 321, 327, 328, 340, 349, 350, 353, 357, 358, 361, 378, 396, 398, 407, 408, 429, 441, 452, 458

Lohse, E., 68

Longenecker, R. N., 325

López, E., 337

Losie, L. A., 196, 199, 201

Lüdemann, G., 343

Lütgert, W., 88

Luther, M., 168

Lyons, G., 107, 303

Mackay, B. S., 278, 283, 293, 294

Malherbe, A., 2, 4, 10, 11

Malinowski, F. X., 391

Manson, T. W., 254

Mantey, J. R., 153

Marshall, I. H., xii

Marshall, J. W., 15

Marshall, P., 4, 5, 201, 390, 423, 427, 443, 444

Martin, R. P., 12, 40, 43, 45, 69, 75, 78, 83, 85, 87, 90, 91, 106, 115, 141, 147, 152, 155, 162, 163, 175, 179, 180, 181, 184, 189, 192, 196, 199, 201, 204, 205, 206, 210, 212, 214, 220, 223, 224, 227, 233, 235, 236, 243, 244, 246, 255, 266, 273, 274, 277, 287, 292, 294, 295, 298, 299, 303, 306, 307, 309, 318, 320, 325, 327, 330, 332, 336, 347, 349, 352, 353, 365, 366, 367, 373, 375, 376, 382,

390, 396, 398, 404, 406, 407, 410, 432, 438, 439, 440, 443, 445, 449, 452, 458

Mayer, B., 261, 272

McMichael, W. F., 364

Mearns, C., 371, 373

Meeks, W. A., 63

Melick, R. R., 75, 78, 87, 90, 91, 123, 131, 143, 144, 163, 180, 206, 208, 210, 233, 243, 266, 365, 396, 398, 403, 407, 438

Metzger, B. M., 60, 96, 109, 271, 288, 337, 338, 375, 385, 392

Meyer, H. A. W., xii, 61, 69, 78, 83, 85, 90, 91, 92, 94, 118, 123, 128, 129, 131, 132, 134, 139, 143, 144, 151, 164, 168, 177, 178, 179, 180, 181, 183, 186, 187, 200, 202, 203, 204, 205, 207, 209, 211, 213, 214, 220, 221, 222, 226, 230, 231, 234, 238, 243, 244, 245, 246, 252, 254, 255, 263, 265, 266, 280, 288, 290, 292, 293, 295, 327, 328, 333, 334, 336, 340, 342, 347, 348, 353, 354, 356, 357, 359, 360, 365, 386, 392, 393, 396, 403, 407, 409, 410, 411, 412, 420, 429, 430, 437, 440, 441, 452, 458

Michael, J. H., 62, 69, 74, 75, 78, 87, 90, 112, 115, 118, 128, 130, 132, 134, 139, 143, 144, 152, 153, 163, 164, 165, 170, 171, 178, 180, 187, 192, 201, 202, 208, 210, 212, 219, 222, 223, 229, 233, 235, 239, 243, 244, 247, 252, 254, 255, 260, 261, 263, 265, 266, 270, 272, 274, 277, 280, 288, 307, 316, 317, 319, 320, 332, 341, 347, 348, 356, 378, 383, 390, 393, 398, 404, 407, 411, 422, 428, 438, 441, 445, 454

Michaelis, W., 159, 311, 364, 365, 366, 407, 415

Michel, O., 211

Miller, E. C., 162

Moehring, H. R., 302

Moffatt, J., 78, 93, 98, 114, 133, 136, 139, 143, 153, 162, 180, 182, 192, 201, 213, 252, 288, 317, 320, 328, 379, 403, 409, 418, 428, 442

Mommsen, 113

Montgomery, E., 205, 406

Moo, D. J., 1, 34, 193, 238

Morrice, W. G., 403, 404

Morris, L., ix, 1, 34, 417, 445
Motyer, J. A., 67, 91, 132, 134, 142, 177, 179, 182, 183, 298, 336, 363, 393, 403
Moule, C. F. D., 43, 115, 134, 148, 163, 178, 201, 202, 206, 207, 211, 213, 221, 304, 307, 369, 457
Moulton, J. H., and Milligan, G., 111, 133, 145, 180, 202, 204, 206, 268, 290, 316, 319, 396
Moulton, J. H., Howard, W. F., and Turner, N., 221, 288, 343, 461
Müller, J. J., ix, 61, 78, 91, 133, 153, 180, 183, 192, 200, 207, 210, 222, 234, 243, 246, 266, 280, 293, 324, 328, 338, 357, 361, 372, 377, 393, 396, 398, 407, 408, 410, 426, 440, 457, 458
Mullins, T. Y., 106, 258
Mundle, W., 237
Murphy-O'Connor, J., 43, 44, 203

Neugebauer, F., 112
Nida, E. A. *See* Loh, I.-J.
Nützel, J. M., 224, 382
Nygren, A., 98

O'Brien, P. T., xii, 7, 12, 14, 34, 40, 67, 72, 75, 78, 85, 87, 90, 91, 94, 98, 100, 103, 105, 111, 113, 115, 116, 120, 121, 122, 127, 130, 131, 132, 134, 135, 136, 137, 140, 141, 143, 145, 146, 147, 153, 161, 164, 167, 169, 170, 175, 177, 178, 179, 180, 183, 185, 187, 192, 193, 196, 203, 204, 206, 208, 209, 210, 212, 213, 216, 219, 223, 230, 234, 235, 238, 243, 244, 246, 247, 248, 250, 253, 254, 255, 263, 264, 266, 272, 275, 280, 288, 290, 291, 293, 294, 296, 298, 299, 307, 308, 311, 315, 317, 319, 320, 321, 322, 325, 327, 330, 333, 336, 338, 340, 341, 342, 343, 344, 345, 348, 349, 353, 355, 356, 357, 363, 365, 366, 367, 368, 370, 371, 377, 381, 388, 389, 391, 395, 396, 398, 403, 404, 406, 407, 409, 410, 411, 414, 415, 416, 420, 425, 428, 429, 430, 431, 432, 434, 440, 441, 444, 445, 447, 449, 450, 452, 457, 458
Omanson, R. L., 75, 111
O'Neill, J. C., 205, 206, 207

Oswalt, J., 136

Palmer, D. W., 140, 142, 147
Panikulam, G., 83
Patitsas, C., 210
Pedersen, S., 236
Perkins, P., 290, 381
Peterlin, D., 29, 66
Peterman, G., 5, 12, 78, 83, 84, 107, 185, 422, 423, 443, 446
Pfitzner, V. C., 172, 249, 287, 290, 303, 309, 328, 340, 341, 342, 344, 345, 346
Plümacher, E., 360
Plummer, A., 78, 83, 85, 90, 92, 111, 112, 131, 136, 166, 170, 179, 180, 192, 202, 209, 210, 211, 212, 216, 222, 223, 224, 244, 246, 252, 253, 255, 271, 275, 277, 279, 280, 281, 317, 320, 321, 341, 360, 361, 365, 366, 373, 383, 393, 398, 407, 410, 411, 440, 452, 457, 460
Pohlmann, W., 204
Polhill, J. B., 294, 299, 319, 343, 344
Pollard, T. E., 294, 314, 364
Porter, S. E., 68, 90
Preisker, J., 406
Price, J. D., 337
Proudfoot, C. M., 332

Quell, G., 98

Rahtjen, B. D., 121, 273, 274, 293, 294, 296
Ramsay, W. M., 113, 390, 394
Rapske, B., 27, 92, 431
Reed, J. T., 90, 147
Reeves, R. R., 148
Reicke, B., 34, 113, 278
Renan, E., 394
Rengstorf, K. H., 62
Reumann, J., 18, 68, 78, 368, 377, 379, 386, 442, 445
Ridderbos, H., 209
Rienecker, F., and Rogers, C., 280, 454
Ringwald, A., 342, 416, 419
Robbins, J., 195
Roberts, R., 161, 162
Robertson, A. T., 78, 83
Robinson, D. W. B., 31, 298
Robinson, H. W., 212
Robinson, J. A. T., 137
Rohde, J., 68

Ross, J., 96, 206
Ruppel, W., 379
Russell, R., 70

Saller, R. P., 4, 5, 6, 423
Sampley, P., 83, 91, 185, 436, 438, 446, 447
Sanday, W., 63
Sanders, E. P., 297, 323
Sanders, J. A., 43, 214
Sass, G., 62
Schelkle, K. H., 381
Schenk, W., 66, 67, 321, 322, 368, 370, 371, 411, 447, 452
Schippers, R., 438
Schlier, H., 316, 438
Schmithals, W., 115, 121, 123, 294, 309, 318, 336, 344, 353, 355, 373, 382
Schmitz, O., 141, 318
Schneider, G., 98
Schnider, F., 59
Schoenborn, U., 378
Schöllgen, G., 68
Schönweiss, H., 224
Schubert, P., 59, 72, 78
Schunack, G., 365
Schütz, J. H., 119, 162
Schweitzer, A., 65, 332
Schweizer, E., 66, 137, 212
Scott, E. F., 162, 192
Seesemann, H., 83, 181
Seifrid, M. A., 112, 201
Sevenster, J. N., 420, 432
Siber, P., 332
Silva, M., xii, 69, 75, 76, 78, 79, 81, 82, 83, 87, 90, 91, 97, 98, 107, 113, 115, 119, 122, 128, 131, 134, 138, 140, 141, 143, 162, 164, 167, 170, 171, 177, 178, 180, 181, 183, 193, 200, 201, 202, 204, 206, 208, 209, 210, 211, 212, 215, 219, 220, 221, 224, 230, 234, 235, 238, 243, 244, 246, 252, 253, 255, 261, 263, 264, 266, 269, 272, 273, 278, 280, 288, 290, 292, 293, 295, 302, 314, 315, 316, 319, 320, 321, 325, 327, 328, 332, 337, 338, 349, 353, 356, 357, 365, 368, 370, 373, 376, 379, 385, 389, 393, 396, 398, 407, 410, 412, 413, 427, 428, 458
Simpson, E. K., ix
Snyman, A. H., 15

Spicq, C., 98
Stählin, G., 111, 409
Stalder, K., 68
Stambaugh, J. E., 63
Stanley, D. M., 407
Stauffer, E., 98, 172
Steenberg, D., 209
Stein, R. H., 231, 234
Stenger, W., 59
Stowers, S. K., 1, 2, 4, 5, 11, 12, 59, 89, 185, 286, 293, 387, 424, 430
Strecker, G., 376, 377
Strimple, R. B., 43, 45, 193, 201, 205, 206, 208, 209, 212
Stumpff, A., 316
Suggs, M. J., 27, 440
Sullivan, K., 100
Swift, R. C., 235, 290
Synge, F. C., 192

Talbert, C. H., 203
Tarn, W. W., 26, 391
Tellbe, B. M., 30, 289
Thekkekara, M., 196
Thomas, J., 391
Thomas, T. A., 210, 211
Thomas, W. D., 290, 391
Thornton, L. S., 148
Thräde, K., 4
Thrall, M., 130, 250, 290, 317, 430
Torjesen, K. J., 27, 391
Towner, P. H., 67
Traub, H., 224
Tucker, F. B., 226
Tuente, R., 62
Turner, N., 78, 288, 461

Vincent, M. R., xii, 62, 66, 85, 90, 91, 101, 111, 116, 118, 122, 128, 131, 132, 136, 137, 138, 143, 144, 145, 153, 165, 170, 177, 178, 179, 180, 183, 200, 202, 204, 209, 210, 213, 221, 231, 237, 238, 243, 246, 255, 263, 266, 280, 288, 290, 292, 293, 320, 327, 332, 336, 343, 347, 348, 357, 359, 361, 365, 383, 393, 396, 398, 403, 407, 409, 410, 422, 430, 431, 440, 454, 458, 460
Vokes, F. E., 206
Volf, J. See J. Gundry Volf
Von Campenhausen, H., 66
Vos, G., 148

Wagner, G., 192, 212
Wallace, D. H., 209
Wanamaker, C. A., 203
Wanke, J., 308
Warnach, V., 99
Warren, W., 210
Watson, D. F., 15, 16, 261
Wedderburn, A. J. M., 136
Weiser, A., 62
Weiss, B., 183
Weiss, J., 139, 163, 192, 292, 365, 369
Wesley, C., 404
White, J. L., 2, 59, 72, 78, 106, 258, 261, 273, 277, 428
White, L. M., 2, 12, 18, 389, 391, 424
Wikgren, A., 25

Wilder, A. N., 16
Wiles, G. P., 134, 449, 450, 452
Williams, S. K., 322, 328
Windisch, H., 181
Wong, T. Y.-C., 203
Wright, N. T., 193, 202, 205, 206, 207, 208, 209, 211, 304, 314

Yorke, G. L. O. R., 201

Zahn, T., 74, 78
Zerwick, M., 132, 134, 201, 315
Zerwick, M., and Grosvenor, M., 145, 199, 200, 252, 437
Ziesler, J. A., 103, 322, 323
Zmijewski, J., 154

# INDEX OF SCRIPTURE REFERENCES

## OLD TESTAMENT

### GENESIS
| | |
|---|---|
| 1:14-19 | 246 |
| 1:26-27 | 209 |
| 2–3 | 209 |
| 2:2 | 87 |
| 3:5 | 209 |
| 3:22 | 209 |
| 5:23 | 427 |
| 15:6 | 415 |
| 17:1 | 242, 244 |
| 17:3-14 | 306 |
| 35:14 | 254 |

### EXODUS
| | |
|---|---|
| 10:2 | 318 |
| 15:16 | 236 |
| 15:29 | 254 |
| 16:7-12 | 243 |
| 16:12 | 242 |
| 17:3 | 243 |
| 19:6 | 64 |
| 32:32-33 | 396 |

### LEVITICUS
| | |
|---|---|
| 19:5 | 251 |
| 19:18 | 98 |
| 21:5 | 296 |

### NUMBERS
| | |
|---|---|
| 4:16 | 68 |
| 14:1-38 | 243 |
| 14:27-29 | 243 |
| 15:3-4 | 251 |
| 15:5 | 254 |
| 16:41 | 243 |
| 17:5 | 243 |
| 17:10 | 243 |
| 28:7 | 251 |
| 31:14 | 68 |

### DEUTERONOMY
| | |
|---|---|
| 2:25 | 236 |
| 6:5 | 98 |
| 7:7 | 98 |
| 8 | 434 |
| 11:25 | 236 |
| 21:23 | 308 |
| 30:6 | 299 |
| 32:5 | 229, 242, 243, 244, 245 |
| 33:12 | 307 |

### JOSHUA
| | |
|---|---|
| 22:27 | 94 |
| 24:29 | 63 |

### JUDGES
| | |
|---|---|
| 9:28 | 68 |

### 1 SAMUEL
| | |
|---|---|
| 12:5 | 94 |
| 17:43 | 295 |
| 20:23 | 94 |
| 24:14 | 295 |

### 2 SAMUEL
| | |
|---|---|
| 9:8 | 295 |
| 16:9 | 295 |

### 1 KINGS
| | |
|---|---|
| 18:28 | 296 |

### 2 KINGS
| | |
|---|---|
| 8:13 | 295 |
| 9:36 | 295 |
| 18:12 | 63 |

### ESTHER
| | |
|---|---|
| 5:1 | 418 |

### NEHEMIAH
| | |
|---|---|
| 1:6 | 63 |

### JOB
| | |
|---|---|
| 11:12 | 207 |
| 13 | 130 |
| 13:16 | 130, 131 |
| 13:18 | 131 |
| 14:13 | 79 |
| 16:12 | 348 |

### PSALMS
| | |
|---|---|
| 5:5 | 296 |
| 6:8 | 296 |
| 8:7 | 384 |
| 13:4 | 296 |
| 15 | 402 |
| 15:2 | 103 |
| 16:3 | 65 |
| 16:4 | 252 |
| 21:13 | 105 |
| 28:7b | 405 |
| 32:11 | 291 |
| 33:21 | 291 |

| | | | | | |
|---|---|---|---|---|---|
| 34:3-5 | 136 | 11:30 | 103 | **EZEKIEL** | |
| 34:3-6 | 131 | 13:2 | 96 | 21:32 | 79 |
| 34:9 | 65 | 15:26 | 418 | 25:10 | 79 |
| 34:18 | 407 | 21:8 | 418 | 34:23 | 63 |
| 35 | 136 | 22:21 | 417 | 38:17 | 63 |
| 35:9 | 291 | 26:11a | 373 | | |
| 35:12 | 296 | | | **DANIEL** | |
| 35:24-28 | 131 | **ISAIAH** | | 7:8 | 65 |
| 35:26-27 | 136 | 19:16 | 236 | 7:18 | 65 |
| 35:28 | 105 | 22:13 | 372 | 7:21 | 65 |
| 40:16 | 291 | 23:16 | 79 | 7:22 | 65 |
| 51 | 402 | 28:10 | 279 | 9:6 | 63 |
| 52:4 | 296 | 41–55 | 222 | 9:10 | 63 |
| 54:6 | 236 | 41:17 | 222 | 12:1-4 | 246 |
| 54:14 | 265 | 41:21 | 222 | 12:1 | 396 |
| 55:5 | 236 | 42–53 | 212 | 12:3 | 242, 246, 247, 248 |
| 58:2 | 296 | 42:5 | 222 | | |
| 58:5 | 296 | 42:6 | 222 | **HOSEA** | |
| 61:1-4 | 403 | 42:8 | 222 | 4:1 | 318 |
| 64:10 | 403 | 42:13 | 222 | 4:7 | 373 |
| 68:29 | 397 | 42:21 | 222 | 6:6 | 318 |
| 69:28 | 396 | 43:3 | 222 | | |
| 71:16 | 324 | 43:10 | 222 | **AMOS** | |
| 74:3 | 65 | 43:12 | 222 | 3:7 | 63 |
| 84:1-8 | 403 | 45:18 | 224 | 6:12 | 103 |
| 86:5 | 406 | 45:18-24a | 224 | | |
| 91:7 | 296 | 45:18-24 | 220 | **JONAH** | |
| 91:9 | 296 | 45:22-24a | 224 | 1:9 | 63 |
| 93:4 | 296 | 45:23 | 220, 222, 223, 224, 225 | 4:5 | 269 |
| 93:16 | 296 | | | | |
| 95:2 | 403 | 49:18 | 222 | **ZECHARIAH** | |
| 95:6 | 224 | 52:13 | 212 | 10:7 | 291 |
| 97:1 | 405 | 53 | 212, 216 | 13:2 | 79 |
| 97:12 | 403 | 53:8 | 212 | | |
| 100:1 | 405 | 53:12 | 212 | **ZEPHANIAH** | |
| 100:4 | 79, 403 | 53:13 | 212 | 1:7 | 408 |
| 101 | 402 | 64:6 | 324 | 1:14 | 408 |
| 104:26 | 63 | 65:23 | 242, 249 | | |
| 110:4 | | | | **NEW TESTAMENT** | |
| 118:3 | 296 | **JEREMIAH** | | | |
| 119:151 | 407 | 9:23-24 | 154, 301 | **MATTHEW** | |
| 124:5 | 296 | 9:23-25 | 299 | 5:6 | 433 |
| 136:1 | 48 | 9:25 | 299 | 5:29 | 252 |
| 144:4 | 296 | 25:4 | 63 | 6:25-34 | 408 |
| 144:9 | 296 | 31:34 | 318 | 7:6 | 295 |
| 145:18 | 407 | 38:20 | 79 | 9:37-38 | 296 |
| | | 42:5 | 94 | 10:10 | 296 |
| **PROVERBS** | | | | 10:16 | 245 |
| 3:9 | 96, 103 | **LAMENTATIONS** | | 11:25 | 188 |
| 4:23 | 411 | 1:3 | 345 | 11:28 | 433 |
| 8:6 | 417 | 3:12 | 348 | | |

| | | | | | |
|---|---|---|---|---|---|
| 11:29 | 188 | 6:1 | 243 | 26:21 | 393 |
| 16:24-26 | 316 | 7:60 | 224 | 27:23 | 77 |
| 23:15 | 308 | 8:26 | 348 | | |
| 26:37 | 277 | 9 | 346 | **ROMANS** | |
| | | 9:1-2 | 308 | 1:1 | 63 |
| **MARK** | | 9:40 | 224 | 1:2-4 | 216 |
| 7:21 | 411 | 10:33 | 438 | 1:3-4 | 193 |
| 8:34-36 | 316 | 13:26 | 282 | 1:4 | 66 |
| 11:22 | 325 | 14:22 | 336 | 1:5 | 233 |
| 12:18-27 | 149 | 15:5 | 305 | 1:8 | 73, 77, 233 |
| 12:44 | 431 | 15:23 | 70 | 1:9 | 73, 78, 79, 94, 288, 299 |
| 14:33 | 277 | 15:23-29 | 59 | 1:10 | 335, 429 |
| 15:16 | 35, 113 | 15:29 | 460 | 1:11 | 94, 271 |
| 15:19 | 224 | 16 | 394 | 1:11-14 | 124 |
| | | 16:1 | 61 | 1:13 | 110, 121, 143, 369 |
| **LUKE** | | 16:10-16 | 27 | 1:18 | 357, 417, 428 |
| 1 | 194 | 16:11 | 25 | 1:19 | 112 |
| 1:46-55 | 41 | 16:11-15 | 26 | 1:20 | 299 |
| 1:68-79 | 41 | 16:11-40 | 27 | 1:21 | 244, 409, 461 |
| 2 | 194 | 16:13 | 61 | 1:25 | 299, 417 |
| 2:34 | 120 | 16:13-15 | 390, 394 | 1:27 | 373 |
| 5:8 | 224 | 16:14 | 390 | 1:28-30 | 245 |
| 9:23-25 | 316 | 16:15 | 84 | 1:29 | 119 130 |
| 10:20 | 396 | 16:25-34 | 405 | 1:32 | 420 |
| 12:22-32 | 408 | 17:4 | 61, 391 | 2:2 | 252 |
| 14:7 | 247 | 17:6 | 460 | 2:4 | 453 |
| 14:8 | 282 | 17:10-15 | 441 | 2:5 | 86, 102 |
| 22:41 | 224 | 17:12 | 391 | 2:7 | 87 |
| 23:2 | 217 | 17:14 | 61 | 2:10 | 87 |
| | | 19–20 | 35 | 2:12 | 356 |
| **JOHN** | | 19:22 | 61, 247 | 2:16 | 86, 102 |
| 1:1 | 230 | 20:1-5 | 394 | 2:18 | 101 |
| 4:24 | 300 | 20:3 | 28 | 2:28-29 | 299 |
| 4:34 | 216 | 20:3-4 | 61 | 2:29 | 419 |
| 5:18 | 207 | 20:4 | 278, 458 | 3–15 | 456 |
| 5:30 | 216 | 20:9 | 390 | 3:3 | 325 |
| 6:38-40 | 216 | 20:19 | 369 | 3:9 | 124 |
| 6:46 | 342 | 20:28 | 68 | 3:20 | 100 |
| 7:12 | 243 | 20:31 | 369 | 3:22 | 325 |
| 7:17 | 216 | 20:33-34 | 444 | 3:25 | 169 |
| 7:22 | 342 | 21–26 | 278 | 3:26 | 169, 325 |
| 7:53–8:12 | 45 | 21:29 | 278 | 3:30-31 | 326 |
| 10:15 | 216 | 21:34 | 292 | 4:12 | 325, 360 |
| 10:17 | 216 | 22:4-5 | 308 | 4:14 | 211 |
| 19:12 | 5 | 22:30 | 292 | 4:16 | 324, 325 |
| 20:30-31 | 95 | 23–24 | 35 | 4:22 | 220 |
| | | 23:6-9 | 308 | 5:1-5 | 179, 298, 377 |
| **ACTS** | | 23:35 | 35, 113 | 5:3 | 140 |
| 2:19 | 350 | 24:17 | 278 | 5:3-4 | 170 |
| 2:36 | 225 | 25:26 | 196, 292 | 5:4 | 268 |
| 3:5 | 247 | 26:5 | 308 | 5:5 | 180, 181, 268 |
| 4:32 | 164 | 26:9-11 | 308 | | |

| | | | | | |
|---|---|---|---|---|---|
| 5:5-8 | 179 | 9:23 | 145, 453 | 15:5-8 | 201 |
| 5:6-8 | 99 | 9:30 | 345 | 15:8 | 69 |
| 5:12 | 346, 430 | 9:31 | 345, 360 | 15:13 | 99, 403 |
| 5:12-21 | 209 | 10:3 | 323 | 15:16 | 65, 251, 252, |
| 5:15 | 99, 460 | 10:9 | 225 | | 276, 327 |
| 5:18 | 506 | 10:16 | 233 | 15:16-17 | 254 |
| 5:19 | 216 | 11:1 | 305, 307 | 15:18 | 233, 249 |
| 6:1-6 | 328, 332 | 11:1-2 | 307, 316 | 15:22 | 220 |
| 6:1-11 | 146, 331, 334 | 11:7 | 447 | 15:23 | 121, 124 |
| 6:12 | 461 | 11:14 | 335, 439 | 15:23-24 | 36 |
| 6:15 | 124 | 11:16 | 357 | 15:24 | 264 |
| 6:21 | 370, 373 | 11:25 | 110 | 15:26 | 82, 83 |
| 7:4 | 231, 327 | 11:29 | 349 | 15:29 | 251 |
| 7:5-6 | 238, 299 | 11:33 | 453 | 15:31 | 128 |
| 7:7-12 | 310 | 11:33-36 | 46, 194, 219 | 15:33 | 420, 461 |
| 7:7-25 | 239, 309 | 11:36 | 384 | 16 | 250 |
| 7:12 | 231 | 12–15 | 89 | 16:1 | 69, 275 |
| 7:13 | 246 | 12:1 | 137, 182, 251, | 16:1-2 | 259, 272, 281 |
| 7:15 | 420 | | 252, 299, 391 | 16:2 | 274 |
| 7:18 | 234, 238 | 12:1-2 | 238, 334, 451 | 16:3 | 275, 457 |
| 7:19 | 520 | 12:1–13:14 | 400 | 16:3-5 | 458 |
| 8:1-17a | 336 | 12:2 | 343 | 16:3-15 | 121, 456 |
| 8:3 | 213, 298 | 12:3 | 184 | 16:3-16 | 120 |
| 8:5 | 185 | 12:5 | 189 | 16:6-16 | 460 |
| 8:6-7 | 89, 185 | 12:8 | 279 | 16:7 | 390 |
| 8:9 | 134, 301 | 12:9 | 87 | 16:9 | 275 |
| 8:9-10 | 134 | 12:10 | 174, 189 | 16:16 | 456 |
| 8:10-11 | 330 | 12:11 | 292 | 16:17 | 366, 390 |
| 8:14 | 356 | 12:13 | 345 | 16:17-18 | 372 |
| 8:15 | 298 | 12:15 | 369 | 16:18 | 371 |
| 8:16 | 245 | 12:16 | 184, 189, 430 | 16:19 | 87, 233, 245 |
| 8:17 | 332 | 12:17 | 406 | 16:20 | 420, 421 |
| 8:17-18 | 170 | 12:18 | 406 | 16:21 | 275 |
| 8:17-30 | 171, 331 | 12:19 | 232 | 16:21-23 | 456 |
| 8:18 | 357 | 13:3 | 87, 419 | 16:22 | 61, 458 |
| 8:19 | 135, 380 | 13:4 | 69 | 16:25-26 | 216 |
| 8:21 | 245 | 13:8 | 189 | 16:26 | 145 |
| 8:23 | 380, 461 | 13:9 | 357 | 16:27 | 455 |
| 8:24 | 264 | 13:12 | 86, 408 | | |
| 8:25 | 380, 381 | 14:1 | 244 | **1 CORINTHIANS** | |
| 8:28-30 | 137 | 14:1-17 | 372 | 1–4 | 370 |
| 8:29 | 110 | 14:1–15:13 | 122, 309, | 1:1 | 62 |
| 8:32 | 171 | | 412 | 1:4 | 77, 78, 460 |
| 8:37 | 221 | 14:11 | 220, 222, 223 | 1:4-9 | 86 |
| 9–11 | 279 | 14:14 | 116 | 1:6 | 89 |
| 9:1 | 94 | 14:17 | 81, 122, 292, | 1:7 | 380 |
| 9:1-5 | 316 | | 310, 403 | 1:7-8 | 87 |
| 9:2 | 369 | 14:18 | 451 | 1:8 | 86, 102 |
| 9:3 | 305 | 14:19 | 189, 345, 353, | 1:9 | 349 |
| 9:4 | 299 | | 412 | 1:10 | 154, 391 |
| 9:8 | 245 | 15:2 | 190 | 1:10-12 | 33 |
| 9:22 | 145 | 15:5 | 184 | 1:11 | 32 |

| | | | |
|---|---|---|---|
| 1:14-15 | 389 | 5:5 | 86, 102, 151 |
| 1:17 | 211 | 5:7 | 102, 237, 298 |
| 1:17-25 | 370 | 5:8 | 102 |
| 1:17-31 | 197 | 6:1-11 | 390 |
| 1:18 | 169, 224, 298 | 6:2 | 357 |
| 1:18-25 | 208 | 6:9-10 | 245 |
| 1:21 | 370, 381 | 6:11 | 65 |
| 1:22-25 | 42 | 6:12-13 | 42 |
| 1:26 | 349 | 6:12-14 | 432 |
| 1:26-28 | 42 | 6:13 | 371 |
| 1:28-29 | 327 | 6:13-14 | 137 |
| 1:30 | 298 | 6:14 | 330 |
| 1:31 | 249, 301 | 6:16-17 | 432 |
| 2:1 | 120 | 6:19 | 461 |
| 2:3 | 236 | 6:20 | 461 |
| 2:6 | 343, 355 | 7 | 432 |
| 2:6-8 | 224 | 7:2-4 | 42 |
| 2:7 | 216 | 7:5 | 327 |
| 2:8 | 216 | 7:11 | 253 |
| 2:10 | 357, 377 | 7:17 | 190, 389 |
| 2:10-11 | 377 | 7:18-19 | 289 |
| 2:10-16 | 165 | 7:19 | 101, 290, 297 |
| 2:12 | 171 | 7:20 | 190, 349 |
| 3:5 | 69 | 7:21 | 253 |
| 3:6-8 | 143 | 7:24 | 190 |
| 3:7 | 231 | 7:26 | 279 |
| 3:9 | 275 | 7:28 | 253 |
| 3:10 | 91, 460 | 7:30 | 369 |
| 3:13 | 86 | 7:31 | 215 |
| 3:15 | 316 | 7:32 | 408 |
| 3:17 | 168 | 7:32-34 | 408 |
| 3:18 | 306 | 7:38 | 231 |
| 3:20 | 244 | 8:2 | 306 |
| 3:21 | 231 | 8:5 | 357 |
| 3:21-23 | 142 | 8:6 | 226, 324, 384 |
| 4:4-5 | 137 | 9:1-18 | 424 |
| 4:5 | 231, 419 | 9:3-12a | 424 |
| 4:6 | 382 | 9:3-18 | 111 |
| 4:7 | 253, 409 | 9:11 | 437 |
| 4:8 | 344 | 9:12b | 424 |
| 4:8-13 | 317 | 9:12 | 111 |
| 4:11-13 | 433 | 9:13 | 251 |
| 4:12 | 250, 444 | 9:13-14 | 424 |
| 4:13 | 319 | 9:14 | 120 |
| 4:16 | 363, 364, 365, 391 | 9:15 | 211 |
| 4:16-20 | 259 | 9:15-16 | 377 |
| 4:17 | 264, 268, 269, 275 | 9:15-18 | 422, 424 |
| 4:18 | 390 | 9:16 | 111, 150 |
| 4:19 | 77, 264 | 9:18 | 111 |
| 4:21 | 165 | 9:19-22 | 42, 142 |
| 5:1-13 | 390 | 9:19-23 | 111 |
| 5:2 | 520 | 9:20 | 297, 372 |

| | |
|---|---|
| 9:22 | 267, 316 |
| 9:24 | 348, 389 |
| 9:24-25 | 249 |
| 9:24-27 | 346 |
| 9:25 | 172, 388 |
| 9:27 | 439 |
| 10:1 | 110 |
| 10:1-11 | 18 |
| 10:6 | 365 |
| 10:10 | 243 |
| 10:12 | 231 |
| 10:13 | 327 |
| 10:14 | 232 |
| 10:18 | 251 |
| 10:24 | 190, 268 |
| 10:26 | 44 |
| 10:32 | 102 |
| 10:33 | 190, 268 |
| 11:1 | 363, 364, 365 |
| 11:3 | 110 |
| 11:9 | 279 |
| 11:11 | 359, 437 |
| 11:22 | 221 |
| 11:23 | 420 |
| 11:26 | 120 |
| 11:27 | 231 |
| 11:28 | 389 |
| 11:33 | 231 |
| 12:3 | 145, 225 |
| 12:6 | 237 |
| 12:8-10 | 174 |
| 12:9 | 279 |
| 12:11 | 237 |
| 12:13 | 165, 166, 279 |
| 12:14 | 279 |
| 12:25 | 189, 266, 408 |
| 12:26 | 256 |
| 12:28 | 67, 279 |
| 12:30 | 279 |
| 13 | 41 |
| 13:4 | 99 |
| 13:5 | 190, 268 |
| 13:6 | 256 |
| 13:10 | 343 |
| 13:12 | 100 |
| 14:1 | 345 |
| 14:4 | 180 |
| 14:8 | 279 |
| 14:12 | 99 |
| 14:15 | 124 |
| 14:18 | 77 |
| 14:20 | 343 |

| | | | | | |
|---|---|---|---|---|---|
| 14:22 | 231 | 1:2 | 182 | 5:9 | 220 |
| 14:26 | 124 | 1:3 | 180, 182 | 5:10 | 420 |
| 14:30 | 357 | 1:5 | 180, 332 | 5:14 | 181 |
| 14:33 | 420 | 1:7 | 328, 331 | 5:16 | 231 |
| 14:34-35 | 45 | 1:8-11 | 35 | 5:17 | 231 |
| 14:36 | 116 | 1:10 | 128 | 5:21 | 322 |
| 14:37 | 306, 390 | 1:12 | 102, 460 | 6:1 | 391, 460 |
| 14:37-38 | 358 | 1:14 | 86, 102, 249 | 6:3 | 111 |
| 14:39 | 231 | 1:15-20 | 36 | 6:4-5 | 433 |
| 15 | 329, 383 | 1:16 | 28, 441 | 6:7 | 117 |
| 15:1 | 145 | 1:20 | 220 | 6:8 | 418 |
| 15:1-3 | 420 | 1:21-22 | 377 | 7:1 | 232 |
| 15:2 | 381 | 1:23 | 9 | 7:5 | 28, 441 |
| 15:3 | 298 | 1:24 | 275, 342 | 7:11 | 85, 408 |
| 15:9 | 305, 308 | 2:2 | 144, 291 | 7:15 | 232, 236 |
| 15:10 | 249, 460 | 2:3 | 85 | 8:1 | 145, 460 |
| 15:11 | 389 | 2:4 | 369 | 8:1-5 | 28, 426, 429 |
| 15:21-22 | 209 | 2:8 | 391 | 8:1-6 | 99 |
| 15:25-28 | 384 | 2:9 | 232, 268 | 8:2 | 268, 452 |
| 15:27-28 | 384 | 2:11 | 411 | 8:6 | 235 |
| 15:28 | 384 | 2:13 | 28, 441 | 8:7 | 99 |
| 15:31-32 | 35 | 2:14-15 | 252 | 8:8 | 266, 394 |
| 15:32 | 372 | 2:17 | 102, 116 | 8:9 | 202, 203, 211, 460 |
| 15:40 | 374 | 2:17–3:18 | 123 | 8:14 | 327, 431 |
| 15:42-57 | 381 | 2:17–4:6 | 289 | 8:16-24 | 259, 264, 272, |
| 15:45-49 | 209 | 3:2 | 406 | | 278, 394 |
| 15:49 | 353 | 3:5 | 342 | 8:17 | 280 |
| 15:51 | 149 | 3:6 | 69, 299, 327 | 8:18 | 22, 28, 419 |
| 15:52 | 149 | 3:9 | 234 | 8:23 | 275, 276 |
| 15:55 | 142 | 3:11 | 234 | 8:24 | 169, 281 |
| 15:58 | 99, 110, 231, | 3:12 | 264 | 9:3 | 211 |
| | 232, 249, 271 | 3:14 | 411 | 9:8 | 87, 99, 431 |
| 16:4 | 327 | 3:15 | 461 | 9:10 | 132 |
| 16:5 | 28 | 4:1 | 279 | 9:12 | 99, 251, 421 |
| 16:7 | 264 | 4:2 | 116, 373 | 9:13 | 82, 83, 268 |
| 16:10 | 266, 271 | 4:3 | 224, 253 | 9:14 | 460 |
| 16:12 | 264 | 4:4 | 204, 411 | 9:15 | 83 |
| 16:13 | 165, 278, 400 | 4:6 | 454 | 10–12 | 415 |
| 16:13-14 | 399 | 4:7-17 | 330 | 10–13 | 8, 9, 22, 118 |
| 16:15 | 281, 391 | 4:7-18 | 332 | 10:1 | 391, 406, 407 |
| 16:15-18 | 259, 272 | 4:8-9 | 433 | 10:5 | 232, 411 |
| 16:16 | 249 | 4:10 | 137, 461 | 10:5-6 | 232 |
| 16:17 | 283, 390, 428, | 4:10-12 | 333 | 10:6 | 232 |
| | 431 | 4:11 | 330 | 10:14 | 360 |
| 16:19 | 399, 456, 458 | 4:12 | 231 | 10:15 | 135, 136 |
| 16:20 | 456 | 4:13 | 220 | 10:17 | 249, 301 |
| 16:21 | 61, 399, 456 | 4:15 | 99 | 11–12 | 29, 357 |
| 16:22 | 225, 399 | 4:17-18 | 170 | 11:1-23 | 123, 294 |
| | | 5:1 | 148, 374 | 11:2 | 408 |
| **2 CORINTHIANS** | | 5:3 | 215 | 11:3 | 411 |
| 1–9 | 22 | 5:4 | 346 | 11:4-22 | 289 |
| 1:1 | 66 | 5:8 | 148 | 11:6 | 433 |

| | | | | | |
|---|---|---|---|---|---|
| 11:7 | 432 | 1:23 | 305, 308 | 6:2 | 189, 190, 283, 389 |
| 11:8 | 442, 445 | 1:24 | 137, 214 | 6:6 | 109, 116 |
| 11:8-9 | 442 | 2:2 | 211, 214, 249 | 6:10 | 87 |
| 11:9 | 278, 431, 441 | 2:5 | 111, 417 | 6:11 | 61, 399 |
| 11:13 | 295, 382 | 2:6-10 | 123 | 6:11-13 | 123 |
| 11:13-14 | 294 | 2:9 | 91 | 6:11-14 | 370 |
| 11:13-15 | 294 | 2:14 | 111 | 6:12 | 390 |
| 11:14 | 382 | 2:16 | 325 | 6:15 | 101, 123, 297 |
| 11:15 | 253, 294, 295, | 2:17 | 215 | 6:16 | 70, 352, 360, |
| | 371, 382 | 2:20 | 318, 325 | | 361, 461 |
| 11:21-23 | 306 | 2:21 | 460 | 6:18 | 132, 461 |
| 11:22 | 123, 305, 308 | 3:1 | 370 | | |
| 11:23 | 35, 295 | 3:2 | 133 | **EPHESIANS** | |
| 11:23-29 | 433 | 3:2-3 | 301 | 1:3-7 | 216 |
| 11:23–12:12 | 303 | 3:3 | 86, 87 | 1:3-14 | 72 |
| 11:25 | 433 | 3:5 | 133, 134 | 1:6 | 409, 419 |
| 11:28 | 408 | 3:6 | 415 | 1:7 | 453 |
| 11:31 | 94 | 3:10 | 85 | 1:8 | 99 |
| 11:32 | 411 | 3:13 | 308 | 1:9 | 145, 211 |
| 12:10 | 343 | 3:14 | 299, 327 | 1:12 | 409, 419 |
| 12:14 | 268, 448 | 3:18 | 171 | 1:13 | 117 |
| 12:14-15 | 448 | 3:22 | 325 | 1:14 | 409, 419 |
| 12:18 | 22, 278 | 3:23 | 357, 411 | 1:15 | 98 |
| 12:19 | 232 | 4:3 | 231 | 1:15-23 | 72 |
| 12:21 | 77, 420, 432 | 4:4-5 | 213 | 1:16 | 73, 78, 79 |
| 13:2 | 114 | 4:4-6 | 110 | 1:17-21 | 73 |
| 13:3 | 268 | 4:4-7 | 377 | 1:18 | 349, 453, 461 |
| 13:7 | 246 | 4:5 | 298, 327 | 1:19 | 384 |
| 13:11 | 290, 291, 400, | 4:6 | 134, 211 | 1:19-20 | 330 |
| | 403, 420, 461 | 4:9 | 237 | 1:20-21 | 224 |
| 13:11-13 | 399 | 4:11 | 249 | 2:1 | 98, 214 |
| 13:12 | 64, 456 | 4:26 | 350 | 2:2 | 224, 367 |
| 13:13 | 179, 181, 214 | 5 | 400 | 2:5 | 381 |
| 13:14 | 179, 181, 214, | 5:5 | 264, 380 | 2:7 | 453 |
| | 399 | 5:6 | 101, 297 | 2:8 | 381 |
| | | 5:7 | 249, 417 | 2:8-10 | 324 |
| **GALATIANS** | | 5:7-12 | 123 | 2:14-17 | 412 |
| 1:4 | 216, 220 | 5:10 | 116, 390 | 2:18 | 165 |
| 1:5 | 455 | 5:11 | 370 | 3:2 | 460 |
| 1:6 | 294, 460 | 5:12 | 294, 296 | 3:3 | 145 |
| 1:8 | 357 | 5:13 | 64, 161, 211 | 3:5 | 145, 347 |
| 1:9 | 420 | 5:16 | 161, 365 | 3:7 | 384, 460 |
| 1:10 | 63 | 5:17 | 148, 223 | 3:8 | 453 |
| 1:11 | 145 | 5:19 | 112 | 3:10 | 145, 224 |
| 1:11-12 | 377 | 5:19-21 | 187 | 3:14 | 224 |
| 1:12 | 420 | 5:20-21 | 119 | 3:14-19 | 73 |
| 1:13 | 305 | 5:21 | 369, 420 | 3:16 | 453 |
| 1:13-14 | 305, 306, 308 | 5:22 | 81, 292, 403, 410 | 3:18 | 172 |
| 1:13–2:14 | 303 | 5:22-23 | 104 | 3:19 | 411 |
| 1:14 | 214, 305, 308 | 5:25 | 360 | 3:20 | 384, 409 |
| 1:16 | 137, 357 | 5:26 | 186, 187 | 3:21 | 455 |
| 1:20 | 94, 141 | 6:1-10 | 400 | 4:1 | 161, 349, 391 |

4:1–6:9          400
4:2       172, 187, 189
4:4       165, 166, 349
4:8               447
4:13         343, 355
4:16              132
4:17              367
4:18              461
4:20              420
4:25              189
4:30       86, 102, 130
4:32         171, 189
5:1          363, 365
5:2          251, 252
5:19             461
5:21             189
5:23             381
5:33             359
6:5          236, 461
6:12             224
6:21   110, 145, 275, 420
6:21-22    20, 108, 272
6:22         85, 264

**PHILIPPIANS**
1–2         21, 285
1:1      6, 20, 50, 60, 74,
  80, 90, 146, 152, 211,
  265, 269, 277, 290, 365,
          392, 457, 458
1:1-2         3, 54, 60
1:1-11    38, 54, 59, 365
1:1–2:30          291
1:1–3:1a           21
1:1–3:1           385
1:2      48, 50, 60, 66, 70,
       86, 91, 439, 461
1:3      61, 74, 75, 76, 77,
       88, 90, 104, 266
1:3-4      13, 81, 89, 403
1:3-5         75, 76, 89
1:3-6         75, 88, 90
1:3-7         422, 423
1:3-8      12, 30, 54, 74,
  127, 287, 359, 436
1:3-11    3, 15, 23, 54, 72
1:3-26             15
1:4   6, 75, 80, 96, 97, 98,
  152, 154, 184, 255, 256,
          405, 409
1:4-5              23
1:5    13, 14, 20, 47, 75,

78, 80, 81, 85, 88, 89,
  90, 107, 111, 119, 156,
  162, 181, 231, 256, 269,
  276, 283, 331, 332, 398,
  423, 424, 438, 440, 441
1:5-7         436, 438
1:6     13, 23, 24, 30, 48,
  50, 51, 71, 73, 76, 84,
  85, 89, 97, 102, 103,
  105, 115, 127, 152, 200,
  228, 237, 238, 248, 285,
          320, 376, 393
1:6-8              75
1:7      6, 13, 19, 20, 23,
  30, 34, 38, 47, 66, 75,
  76, 82, 83, 88, 89, 90,
  91, 93, 107, 110, 112,
  120, 124, 135, 152, 162,
  171, 184, 199, 230, 232,
  364, 418, 424, 429, 438
1:7a               90
1:7b               90
1:7-8   13, 62, 74, 75, 79,
                   96
1:8     6, 66, 74, 76, 89,
  90, 91, 93, 98, 99, 182,
  231, 232, 233, 271, 277,
                  387
1:9      13, 18, 52, 95, 97,
  104, 107, 115, 154, 184,
          185, 323
1:9-11   12, 54, 76, 87, 95,
  162, 244, 419, 450
1:10     13, 19, 23, 30, 50,
  51, 65, 86, 95, 100, 104,
  127, 153, 241, 244, 248,
          320, 376, 393
1:10-11   13, 73, 228, 320
1:11     17, 18, 23, 48, 49,
  52, 65, 71, 84, 96, 101,
  103, 151, 241, 310, 419,
          447, 451
1:11a             104
1:12      3, 19, 22, 47, 83,
  106, 107, 109, 111, 112,
  114, 115, 119, 126, 142,
  151, 153, 156, 158, 162,
  230, 259, 260, 269, 270,
  287, 291, 338, 359, 363,
  377, 385, 387, 413, 415,
          419, 428
1:12-13           156

1:12-14   15, 54, 108, 109
1:12-18a      30, 54, 108,
          125, 126
1:12-18b       131, 138
1:12-18    23, 107, 132,
       136, 137, 459
1:12-26   3, 6, 11, 12, 30,
  31, 38, 54, 76, 84, 89,
  106, 128, 155, 156, 172,
  173, 184, 230, 244, 257,
  258, 260, 263, 405, 419,
                  423
1:13     19, 34, 35, 36, 92,
  107, 108, 109, 110, 112,
  114, 201, 264, 275, 321,
  332, 357, 388, 459
1:13-14        22, 112
1:13-18a          106
1:14     8, 24, 34, 92, 107,
  108, 109, 110, 114, 118,
  119, 121, 124, 152, 154,
  248, 264, 270, 321, 368,
                  458
1:15   107, 108, 111, 115,
  117, 118, 119, 120,
  162, 239, 268, 459
1:15-16       82, 117, 367
1:15-17       6, 8, 9, 37,
  107, 118, 124, 127, 154,
          157, 186
1:15-18a      15, 54, 108,
          115, 117
1:15-18        49, 84, 142
1:16     47, 93, 107, 117,
  118, 120, 135, 186,
                  230
1:16-17      24, 108, 117,
       118, 119, 120
1:17    18, 19, 24, 33, 34,
  92, 107, 110, 117, 118,
  119, 120, 122, 124, 127,
  186, 268, 418, 438, 459
1:18     12, 47, 106, 108,
  114, 117, 119, 120, 124,
  127, 131, 139, 152, 154,
  184, 230, 250, 256, 317,
  408, 419, 428, 454
1:18-24            47
1:18a       118, 130, 255
1:18b  106, 127, 128, 255
1:18b-19          130
1:18b-20   54, 127, 151

1:18b-26  16, 30, 54, 106,
126, 150, 156
1:18b–4:7  16
1:18c  118
1:19  6, 18, 19, 49, 111,
127, 130, 132, 153, 165,
170, 184, 199, 242, 260,
407, 409, 431
1:19-20  93, 107, 120,
126, 128, 130, 139, 141,
154, 172, 253, 259, 263
1:20  84, 128, 130, 131,
135, 139, 140, 147, 154,
220, 222, 260, 264, 268,
373, 376
1:20-23  65, 108, 111
1:21  16, 49, 113, 119,
139, 140, 142, 143, 144,
171, 200, 264, 266, 285,
312, 316, 317, 320, 337,
431, 434, 462
1:21b  144
1:21-22  207
1:21-23  156, 248, 270,
393
1:21-24  30, 54, 126,
127, 139, 169, 228, 376
1:22  137, 139, 142,
145, 146, 147, 150, 152,
199, 200, 266, 459
1:22-23  38, 140, 141
1:23  19, 24, 88, 139,
141, 144, 145, 234,
253, 259, 260
1:23-24  38, 144, 145,
152, 377
1:23b-24  146
1:24  49, 107, 137,
139, 145, 146, 147, 151,
152, 253, 270
1:24-25 94, 138, 143, 163
1:24-26  108, 109, 126,
138, 141, 147, 156, 233,
259, 263, 270
1:24b-26  140
1:25  39, 47, 66, 107,
111, 113, 115, 150, 151,
152, 156, 167, 191, 199,
233, 256, 280, 286,
291, 348, 360,
405, 447, 453
1:25-26  38, 54, 62,

126, 146, 147, 150, 151,
155, 163, 249, 253, 259
1:26  28, 36, 112, 151,
154, 173, 241, 248, 249,
263, 264, 301, 376
1:27  3, 12, 13, 19, 31,
32, 47, 49, 52, 62, 65,
66, 71, 82, 83, 84, 87,
100, 108, 110, 123, 141,
146, 151, 153, 155, 156,
158, 161, 166, 170, 175,
176, 177, 181, 183, 184,
185, 186, 191, 219, 227,
229, 230, 231, 233, 234,
240, 241, 258, 259, 260,
261, 263, 265, 285, 286,
336, 351, 359, 376, 378,
379, 386, 387, 388, 389,
395, 400, 461
1:27-28  8, 9, 29, 93,
121, 459
1:27-28a  177
1:27-30  15, 16, 29, 54,
155, 157, 158, 175, 176,
177, 230, 245-46, 254,
266, 404, 452
1:27–2:5  232, 386
1:27–2:16  124
1:27–2:18  3, 10, 11,
16, 23, 38, 54, 76, 97,
106, 107, 151, 154, 166,
245, 246, 256, 258, 260,
261, 264, 265, 286, 287,
292, 293, 295, 361, 385,
386, 405
1:27–4:3  286
1:28  6, 19, 24, 31, 48,
128, 129, 158, 159, 167,
168, 170, 172, 184, 224,
230, 231, 234, 246, 367,
370, 371, 374, 378, 384
1:28b  170
1:28-30  121
1:29  49, 51, 52, 91,
92, 159, 170, 180, 218,
221, 326, 332
1:29-30  6, 8, 9, 29, 30,
167, 173, 175, 178, 179,
180, 228, 255, 256, 285,
332, 383, 414, 438, 439,
448
1:30  92, 107, 157,

159, 166, 170, 172, 200,
254, 363, 364, 420
2  4, 51
2:1  6, 10, 11, 19, 49,
65, 82, 112, 156, 165,
166, 174, 176, 177, 227,
228, 264, 321, 355, 391
2:1-2  29, 62, 158, 161,
303, 359
2:1-4  32, 54, 157, 165,
166, 173, 174, 189, 192,
199, 230, 410, 453
2:1-5  354
2:1-11  15
2:1-16  386
2:1-18  157
2:1–3:21  15
2:2  19, 32, 33, 52,
84, 89, 91, 97, 98, 104,
107, 124, 132, 153, 156,
165, 174, 175, 176, 182,
186, 189, 191, 197, 200,
244, 255, 265, 285, 352,
356, 378, 386, 387, 391,
405, 429, 430, 439, 451
2:2a  177
2:2b  177
2:2-3  161
2:2-4  177, 182, 199,
200, 202, 216
2:2-5  6, 351, 374, 424
2:2-16  180
2:2c-4  177
2:3  11, 19, 33, 52, 99,
102, 107, 121, 123, 174,
176, 186, 189, 190, 191,
196, 199, 202, 208, 211,
216, 274, 312, 316, 317
2:3-4  12, 29, 97, 153,
176, 189, 191, 200, 213,
228, 234, 265, 267, 268,
270, 300, 323, 392
2:3-8  104
2:4  8, 12, 20, 24, 33,
64, 87, 175, 176, 188,
189, 190, 197, 198, 200,
208, 209, 239, 256, 260,
268, 366
2:4-5  236
2:4-11  376
2:5  24, 44, 64, 89,
112, 176, 184, 185, 189,

194, 197, 198, 199, 209, 219, 238, 347, 354, 356, 387, 429

2:5-7    55, 197, 300

2:5-8    323

2:5-11    40, 41, 42, 45, 54, 65, 97, 156, 157, 158, 172, 175, 191, 192, 194, 219, 227, 228, 263, 334, 337, 347

2:6    18, 19, 44, 45, 50, 186, 188, 194, 198, 202, 203, 212, 214, 215, 217, 220, 221, 239, 274, 316, 379

2:6a    40

2:6b    40, 211

2:6c    40, 42

2:6-7a    176

2:6-7    50, 209, 220

2:6-8    30, 32, 71, 193, 195, 196, 217, 219, 325, 332, 382, 383, 448

2:6-11    6, 11, 15, 19, 30, 32, 39, 40, 46, 47, 50, 104, 141, 185, 186, 187, 193, 199, 203, 209, 211, 215, 220, 226, 229, 231, 232, 235, 240, 259, 304, 314, 332, 333, 357, 361, 363, 370, 376, 377, 378, 382, 383, 386, 392, 419, 454, 462

2:7    19, 64, 186, 194, 198, 204, 205, 208, 210, 216, 269, 315

2:7a    40

2:7b    40, 215

2:7b-8    176, 188

2:7c    41

2:7d    41

2:7-8    6, 50, 194, 202

2:7-11    376

2:8    19, 31, 49, 55, 71, 176, 187, 189, 192, 195, 203, 208, 213, 214, 215, 226, 229, 233, 274, 282, 315, 321, 329, 370, 382, 410, 432, 433, 449

2:8a    41

2:8b    41

2:8c    41

2:8d    42

2:9    19, 24, 71, 195, 216, 219, 220, 223, 320, 380

2:9a    41

2:9b    41

2:9c    41, 42

2:9-10    381

2:9-11    30, 31, 42, 48, 50, 51, 55, 88, 192, 193, 195, 196, 212, 215, 219, 228, 233, 237, 248, 262, 264, 376, 383, 459

2:10    19, 192, 195, 219, 222, 223, 407, 408

2:10a    41, 42

2:10b    41

2:10c    41, 42

2:10-11    18, 220, 242, 370

2:11    48, 50, 71, 114, 187, 195, 219, 222, 225, 241, 334, 381, 382, 393

2:11a    41

2:11b    41, 42

2:11c    41, 42

2:12    3, 12, 18, 19, 34, 46, 62, 67, 88, 110, 128, 153, 156, 158, 197, 227, 229, 230, 231, 237, 238, 286, 359, 386, 387, 391

2:12-13    55, 87, 157, 216, 229, 230, 386

2:12-16    32

2:12-18    15, 55, 229

2:12-28

2:13    48, 49, 71, 87, 107, 120, 123, 182, 190, 197, 200, 230, 237, 240, 241, 377, 384, 431

2:13-14    395

2:14    19, 33, 52, 69, 114, 153, 161, 187, 189, 197, 239, 240, 241, 242, 243, 453

2:14-15    65

2:14-16    18, 157, 158, 162, 184, 220, 229, 230, 232, 258, 261, 299

2:14-18    55, 229, 240, 259

2:15    19, 31, 48, 52, 69, 102, 156, 172, 233, 235, 240, 248, 268, 309

2:15-16    84, 230, 407, 460

2:15-16a    244

2:15a    241

2:15b-16a    241

2:16    30, 47, 50, 51, 86, 102, 154, 156, 211, 219, 229, 240, 250, 255, 256, 257, 320, 376, 388, 393, 396, 447

2:16b    241, 244, 248

2:16c    241

2:16-18 64, 156, 158, 184

2:17    6, 18, 29, 38, 66, 71, 102, 125, 152, 153, 156, 158, 240, 250, 256, 257, 270, 276, 280, 285, 326, 345, 383, 422, 439, 450, 451

2:17a    241

2:17b-18    241

2:17-18    30, 62, 124, 156, 158, 229, 230, 250, 263, 323, 330, 333, 359, 405, 414

2:18    12, 53, 124, 125, 154, 161, 240, 256, 286, 289, 291, 333, 364, 383, 405

2:19    3, 19, 37, 38, 49, 61, 112, 163, 260, 261, 262, 263, 266, 269, 270, 282, 292, 321, 428

2:19b    259

2:19-20    33

2:19-22    61

2:19-23    61, 259

2:19-24    12, 29, 38, 55, 108, 233, 259, 260, 262, 359, 423

2:19-30    3, 15, 16, 55, 156, 230, 250, 258

2:20    12, 18, 19, 126, 261, 262, 263, 265, 267, 268, 270, 392, 394, 408, 431

2:20-21    20, 33, 190, 458

2:20-22    32, 262, 263, 365

2:21    6, 8, 9, 12, 121,

123, 260, 262, 265, 268, 270, 367, 431
2:22    64, 146, 262, 263, 266, 267, 268
2:23    3, 19, 201, 259, 261, 262, 264, 269, 280
2:23-24    33, 260, 263
2:24    28, 36, 37, 38, 49, 94, 112, 116, 126, 138, 141, 152, 163, 233, 253, 259, 261, 262, 264, 265, 270, 282, 292, 321, 395
2:25    19, 78, 184, 188, 251, 264, 271, 272, 274, 280, 284, 316, 364, 395, 398, 422, 424, 425, 431, 446, 450
2:25-26    64
2:25-27    272
2:25-30    12, 29, 39, 55, 259, 260, 271, 449, 450, 451
2:26    19, 36, 37, 94, 271, 272, 273, 274, 276, 283, 387
2:27    19, 48, 271, 272, 279, 281, 283, 431
2:28    18, 154, 256, 271, 272, 273, 274, 280, 286, 291, 355, 405
2:28-30    272
2:29    19, 112, 256, 264, 271, 272, 273, 274, 281, 282, 286, 405
2:29a    282
2:29b    282
2:30    12, 19, 20, 24, 37, 78, 251, 252, 271, 272, 274, 276, 278, 279, 280, 283, 398, 422, 424, 425, 431, 450
3    4, 17, 21, 33, 51, 286, 335
3:1    10, 17, 18, 19, 21, 22, 39, 49, 110, 112, 115, 154, 167, 256, 257, 264, 286, 287, 288, 290, 293, 321, 323, 359, 361, 362, 363, 366, 376, 383, 387, 401, 403, 404, 407, 424, 428, 449, 358

3:1a    285, 288
3:1b    285, 286, 288, 289, 306
3:1bff.    21
3:1-2    288, 386
3:1-4a    55, 285, 287, 314, 397
3:1-11    101
3:1-16    16
3:1-21    15, 97, 287, 385, 386, 388, 392, 397
3:1–4:3    3, 11, 39, 55, 151, 152, 257, 285, 358, 398, 403, 405
3:1–4:9    3, 351
3:2    6, 9, 19, 21, 101, 118, 121, 122, 123, 167, 246, 285, 286, 288, 289, 290, 293, 298, 300, 303, 304, 306, 308, 314, 319, 331, 362, 367, 369, 370, 372, 373, 374, 376, 407, 449
3:2-3    8, 33, 289, 303, 304, 305, 313, 347
3:2-8    323
3:2-9    123
3:2-11    97
3:2-21    22
3:2–4:1    385
3:3    7, 47, 49, 65, 112, 154, 252, 264, 288, 296, 298, 302, 306, 321, 327, 331, 336, 344, 353, 356, 357, 361, 373, 378, 431
3:3-4    293, 322
3:3-6    155, 295, 324, 326
3:3-9    294
3:3-14    20, 47, 286
3:4    19, 104, 288, 355
3:4a    302, 306
3:4b    305, 306
3:4-6    304, 313, 314, 328, 338
3:4-8    338, 348
3:4a-9    285
3:4b-6    55, 287, 288, 302, 303, 305
3:4b-14    55, 303
3:4-9    9, 286, 287, 304
3:4-14    6, 11, 23, 30, 32, 50, 88, 97, 142, 285,

287, 298, 352, 356, 358, 361, 363, 366, 375, 376, 392, 419, 462
3:4–4:1    30
3:5    19, 305
3:5-6    306, 315, 317
3:6    102, 104, 302, 305, 309, 312, 320, 321, 322, 323
3:6b    312, 313
3:7    24, 88, 199, 311, 312, 313, 315, 317, 320, 323
3:7b    313, 317
3:7-8    188, 274, 310, 313
3:7-9    303, 304, 314
3:7-11    16, 55, 65, 141, 311
3:8    19, 49, 104, 142, 189, 285, 289, 304, 311, 316, 323, 326, 329, 333, 341, 370, 410
3:8a-b    317
3:8a    312, 313, 314
3:8b    312, 313
3:8c    312, 313, 315, 316
3:8c-9    313, 319
3:8-9    291, 310, 327
3:8-10    342, 448, 455
3:8-11    52, 337
3:9    20, 47, 48, 71, 104, 153, 215, 264, 302, 310, 311, 312, 313, 314, 316, 325
3:9-11    71, 338
3:9-16    248
3:10    19, 49, 51, 82, 113, 140, 141, 228, 311, 313, 317, 318, 320, 334, 364, 376, 382, 383, 438
3:10b    323
3:10-11    30, 50, 104, 125, 285, 287, 304, 311, 312, 313, 314, 320, 321, 322, 323, 326, 335, 338, 341, 343, 345, 351, 355
3:10-14    9, 51, 357
3:10-21    10
3:11    19, 51, 52, 311, 313, 326, 333, 342, 346, 376

3:11-14   228, 285, 287, 320, 376
3:11-15   256
3:12   49, 71, 77, 323, 332, 337, 339, 340, 341, 342, 344, 346, 350, 353, 355, 357, 370, 374, 430
3:12-13   367
3:12-14   19, 30, 51, 55, 88, 97, 125, 126, 127, 141, 148, 285, 304, 314, 335, 336, 337, 351, 353, 355, 357, 376, 378, 380, 383, 393
3:12-15   309
3:12-16   339, 353, 355
3:12-21   146, 336, 388
3:13   19, 110, 115, 337, 339, 363, 387, 415
3:13-14   30, 47, 49, 88, 249, 340, 342, 345, 346, 455
3:14   19, 48, 112, 148, 250, 264, 321, 337, 340, 341, 345, 366, 371
3:14-21   153
3:15   11, 19, 30, 89, 168, 184, 199, 286, 339, 340, 343, 352, 353, 355, 370, 374, 387, 391, 414, 423, 424
3:15a   358
3:15b   353, 361
3:15-16   8, 55, 298, 339, 341, 350, 351, 352, 353, 362, 376, 378, 429
3:15-17   52, 88, 127, 287, 303
3:15-19   386
3:15-21   148, 287, 314, 389
3:15–4:1   304, 336
3:15–4:3   55, 351, 362
3:16   348, 352, 354, 355, 358, 359
3:17   19, 30, 110, 115, 125, 161, 190, 286, 351, 353, 357, 359, 362, 363, 367, 378, 387, 392, 397, 414, 419

3:17-19   6, 55, 65, 285, 362, 376, 378
3:17-20   162
3:17-21   286, 386
3:17–4:1   305
3:17–4:7   16
3:18   10, 49, 121, 161, 286, 292, 293, 362, 365, 366, 367, 377, 431
3:18-19   9, 34, 52, 88, 101, 121, 285, 287, 290, 294, 351, 352, 357, 359, 362, 366, 367
3:18-21   248
3:19   89, 184, 340, 354, 362, 370, 376, 378, 382, 384, 319, 424, 429
3:19-21   256, 349, 350
3:20   19, 31, 52, 66, 88, 141, 161, 162, 184, 347, 375, 377, 396, 397, 431, 460
3:20-21   30, 47, 51, 55, 71, 88, 149, 228, 285, 287, 298, 336, 341, 342, 343, 346, 351, 352, 356, 357, 363, 371, 375, 378, 383, 386, 388, 393, 397
3:21   19, 21, 51, 228, 304, 312, 314, 323, 330, 335, 373, 375
4:1   6, 13, 17, 19, 23, 30, 62, 94, 109, 110, 112, 115, 165, 184, 232, 249, 250, 264, 285, 304, 321, 336, 341, 351, 352, 363, 376, 377, 385, 387, 389, 393, 396, 397, 405, 428, 447
4:1-2   286
4:1-3   29, 55, 76, 184, 244, 285, 287, 385, 386, 398, 400, 419
4:1-9   21
4:1-20   16
4:2   19, 26, 33, 89, 109, 112, 165, 179, 183, 184, 185, 187, 285, 289, 354, 377, 385, 386, 387, 389, 391, 392, 400, 410, 424, 429, 430
4:2-3   6, 32, 69, 101,

124, 161, 166, 189, 351, 352, 365, 386, 389, 397, 398, 406, 453
4:2-9   385, 389
4:3   19, 27, 166, 266, 275, 364, 390, 391, 392, 400, 412, 458
4:4   21, 22, 39, 49, 53, 112, 124, 154, 256, 257, 264, 285, 291, 383, 400, 403, 404, 424, 428, 458
4:4-7   55, 81, 287, 400, 401, 402, 415
4:4-9   30, 39, 51, 55, 398, 399, 400, 449
4:4-13   407
4:4-23   55, 398, 399
4:5a   403, 406
4:5b   403
4:5   18, 30, 50, 393
4:6   19, 80, 403, 408, 446, 453
4:6-7   48, 407
4:7   48, 65, 189, 264, 321, 400, 404, 410, 414, 453, 461
4:8   19, 21, 22, 65, 70, 89, 99, 110, 199, 285, 290, 291, 400, 401, 404, 412, 413, 415, 419, 420, 462
4:8-9   16, 55, 97, 101, 287, 400, 401, 402, 404, 413, 424
4:8-20   16
4:9   17, 48, 125, 126, 199, 286, 317, 351, 357, 405, 410, 412, 413, 414, 415, 417, 419, 420, 427, 435, 453, 461
4:9b   400
4:10   18, 19, 62, 78, 89, 112, 184, 233, 256, 264, 284, 346, 359, 395, 405, 424, 426, 428, 436, 438, 449, 452
4:10a   423, 424, 425, 427
4:10b   424, 425, 427
4:10-13   55, 424, 426, 436, 437
4:10-14   426

4:10-17 450
4:10-20 3, 4, 6, 17, 21,
23, 39, 55, 69, 287, 398,
399, 401, 402, 415, 422,
438, 447, 449
4:11 18, 19, 283, 342,
419, 424, 426, 437, 446,
447
4:11-12 19, 99, 276, 424,
450
4:11-13 70, 414, 422,
424, 425, 427, 434, 435,
446, 451, 455, 462
4:12 19, 154, 426, 432,
434
4:13 24, 99, 426, 432,
434, 435
4:14 3, 6, 19, 82, 83,
91, 124, 184, 185, 359,
364, 423, 424, 425, 435,
436, 437, 448, 449
4:14-15 19
4:14-16 62
4:14-17 55, 83, 111,
422, 424, 429, 431, 436,
449
4:14-19 273
4:14-20 276
4:15 19, 27, 47, 66,
82, 412, 422, 423, 424,
436, 438, 440, 442, 445,
449, 450
4:15-16 6, 27, 83, 84,
424, 425, 429, 436, 439,
452, 462
4:15-17 359
4:15-20 426
4:16 276, 424, 436,
440, 441, 442, 449, 450,
452
4:17 112, 342, 422,
424, 425, 430, 436, 437,
443, 445, 447, 448, 449,
450, 451, 452
4:18 18, 48, 78, 154,
231, 251, 252, 255, 273,
274, 275, 276, 390, 422,
423, 424, 425, 431, 432,
438, 443, 446, 447, 449,
450, 452, 453
4:18-20 23, 55, 359,
424, 449

4:19 17, 47, 48, 112,
264, 276, 321, 424, 425,
435, 437, 445, 446, 449,
450, 451, 452, 456, 458
4:19-20 30, 47
4:20 48, 71, 105,
424, 425, 449, 450, 453,
455, 456
4:21 66, 110, 112,
146, 264, 267, 275, 321,
456, 461
4:21a 457
4:21b 458
4:21-22 3, 17, 456
4:21-23 21, 39, 55, 385,
399, 456
4:22 19, 34, 36, 64,
114, 456, 459
4:23 3, 24, 456

COLOSSIANS
1:1 62
1:2 116
1:3 73, 77
1:4 98
1:5 117
1:6 460
1:7 63, 69, 420
1:9 100, 403, 409
1:9-11 59
1:9-14 73
1:10 87, 161
1:11-12 403
1:12 87
1:14-15 41
1:15 40, 41, 193, 204
1:15-18 43
1:16b 41
1:18 40
1:18b 41
1:24 171, 332
1:25 116
1:27 145, 453
1:28 120, 343
1:29 172, 249
2:1 110, 187
2:6 420
2:7 99
2:11 289
2:13 171
2:16-23 289
2:18 187

2:19 132
2:23 187
3:1 350
3:2 350, 374
3:5–4:6 400
3:7 367
3:10-11 275
3:12 182, 187
3:12–4:6 412
3:13 189
3:14 343
3:15 410, 412
3:16 117, 172
4:3 109, 116
4:7 63, 110, 145, 275
4:7-8 108, 269
4:7-9 259, 272
4:8 20, 85, 264
4:9 145
4:10 458
4:10-14 456
4:12 172, 249, 343
4:14 395
4:15 456
4:18 399, 456

1 THESSALONIANS
1:2 77, 78, 79
1:2-3 73
1:3 87, 98, 249, 264
1:5 89
1:6 98, 109, 116, 214,
292, 332, 363, 364, 365
1:7 365
1:8 117
1:9 214
1:9-10 298, 377
2:1-10 448
2:1-12 303
2:2 27, 172, 173
2:4 235, 448
2:5 94, 124
2:8 232
2:9 441
2:10 94, 244
2:12 161, 180, 391
2:13 116, 420
2:14 363, 365
2:14-16 369
2:15 406
2:17 148
2:17–3:6 259

| | | | | | |
|---|---|---|---|---|---|
| 2:18 | 60, 445 | 2:2 | 86 | 6:3-5 | 119 |
| 2:19 | 249, 388 | 2:13 | 77, 325 | 6:4 | 119 |
| 3:2 | 61, 69, 275, 391 | 2:13-14 | 377 | 6:6 | 431 |
| 3:2-3 | 170, 259, 263, | 2:16 | 264 | 6:11 | 345 |
| | 264, 332 | 2:17 | 87, 153 | 6:12 | 172, 249 |
| 3:3 | 120, 125 | 3:1 | 117, 290, 291 | 6:17 | 453 |
| 3:3-4 | 377 | 3:2 | 128 | | |
| 3:4 | 235, 279 | 3:5 | 98 | **2 TIMOTHY** | |
| 3:5 | 249 | 3:6 | 420 | 1:3 | 73, 78, 80, 299 |
| 3:5-8 | 264 | 3:7 | 363 | 1:4 | 94, 271, 369 |
| 3:6 | 78, 79, 94, 271 | 3:7-10 | 303, 364, 422, 444 | 1:9 | 349 |
| 3:8 | 165 | 3:8 | 441 | 1:10 | 381 |
| 3:9-10 | 75, 403 | 3:9 | 342, 363, 365 | 1:12 | 86 |
| 3:10 | 431 | 3:12 | 391 | 1:15 | 119 |
| 3:12 | 98, 99, 189 | 3:14 | 232 | 1:16 | 369 |
| 3:12-13 | 102 | 3:15 | 232 | 1:17 | 280 |
| 3:13 | 244 | 3:16 | 420, 421, 461 | 1:18 | 86 |
| 4:1 | 290, 291, 391, 420 | 3:17 | 61, 389, 399, 456 | 2:3 | 275 |
| 4:4 | 190 | | | 2:5 | 253 |
| 4:8 | 65, 134 | **1 TIMOTHY** | | 2:9 | 92, 117 |
| 4:9 | 189 | 1:2 | 266, 268, 394 | 2:15 | 295 |
| 4:10 | 99, 279, 391 | 1:3 | 28 | 2:18 | 117, 389 |
| 4:11 | 420 | 1:12 | 434 | 2:21 | 87 |
| 4:13 | 110, 264 | 1:13 | 279, 305, 308 | 2:22 | 345 |
| 4:14 | 149 | 1:13-16 | 309 | 3:6 | 134 |
| 4:16 | 149 | 1:14 | 460 | 3:17 | 87 |
| 4:17 | 146 | 1:16 | 137, 279 | 4:2 | 116 |
| 4:18 | 231 | 1:17 | 455 | 4:3 | 109 |
| 5:2 | 86 | 1:18 | 275 | 4:6 | 252, 253 |
| 5:8 | 264 | 1:20 | 389 | 4:7 | 172 |
| 5:9 | 298 | 2:1 | 391, 406 | 4:8 | 86, 148, 290 |
| 5:9-10 | 377 | 2:2 | 417 | 4:9 | 264 |
| 5:10 | 391 | 2:4 | 406 | 4:13 | 28, 459 |
| 5:11 | 146, 189, 235, 391 | 2:7 | 94 | 4:17-18 | 128 |
| 5:12 | 249 | 2:8 | 244 | 4:18 | 455 |
| 5:12-13 | 67, 281 | 3 | 68 | 4:19 | 456 |
| 5:12-22 | 400 | 3:2 | 68 | 4:21 | 456 |
| 5:13 | 403 | 3:3 | 406 | 4:22 | 461 |
| 5:13b | 400 | 3:4 | 417 | | |
| 5:14 | 391 | 3:5 | 68 | **TITUS** | |
| 5:15 | 87, 189, 345 | 3:8 | 69, 417 | 1 | 68 |
| 5:16 | 403 | 3:11 | 417 | 1:4 | 266, 268, 381, 394 |
| 5:16-18 | 74, 400, 403 | 3:14 | 264 | 1:7 | 68 |
| 5:23 | 244, 402, 420, 461 | 3:14-15 | 259 | 1:10 | 459 |
| | | 3:15 | 247 | 1:14-16 | 289 |
| **2 THESSALONIANS** | | 3:16 | 40, 41, 43, 193 | 1:16 | 87 |
| 1:3 | 77, 98, 189 | 3:16b | 41 | 2:2 | 417 |
| 1:5 | 169 | 4:10 | 172, 249, 406, 459 | 2:5 | 117, 418 |
| 1:8 | 233 | 4:12 | 365 | 2:7 | 365, 417 |
| 1:10 | 86 | 5:17 | 459 | 2:11 | 406, 460 |
| 1:11 | 349 | 5:18 | 295 | 2:13 | 381 |
| 1:11-12 | 59, 73, 327 | 5:22 | 418 | 3:1 | 87 |

| | | | | | |
|---|---|---|---|---|---|
| 3:2 | 406 | 6:19 | 292 | 4:11 | 455 |
| 3:3 | 245 | 9:28 | 380 | | |
| 3:6 | 381 | 10:5-9 | 216 | **2 PETER** | |
| 3:12 | 28 | 12:2 | 217, 269 | 1:3 | 419 |
| 3:15 | 456 | 12:14 | 345 | 1:5 | 419 |
| | | 12:23 | 397 | 2:22 | 295 |
| **PHILEMON** | | 13:2 | 347 | 3:1 | 102 |
| 1 | 62, 275 | 13:7 | 363 | | |
| 2 | 275 | | | **1 JOHN** | |
| 4 | 73, 77, 78, 79 | **JAMES** | | 2:28 | 136 |
| 5 | 98 | 1:1 | 70 | 5:15 | 409 |
| 6 | 73, 100 | 3:13-18 | 415 | | |
| 9 | 391 | 3:15 | 374 | **3 JOHN** | |
| 10 | 268, 391 | 3:17 | 418 | 2 | 72 |
| 12 | 274, 275 | 3:18 | 103 | 11 | 363 |
| 16 | 232, 459 | 5:8 | 407, 408 | | |
| 20 | 392, 439 | | | **REVELATION** | |
| 21 | 232 | **1 PETER** | | 3:5 | 396 |
| 22 | 138, 171, 264 | 2:4 | 282 | 5:5-6 | 335 |
| 23 | 395, 458 | 2:6 | 282 | 13:8 | 396 |
| 23-24 | 456 | 2:9 | 419 | 17:8 | 396 |
| 24 | 275, 458 | 2:23 | 407 | 20:12 | 396 |
| 25 | 461 | 2:25 | 68 | 20:15 | 396 |
| | | 3:11 | 345 | 21:27 | 396 |
| **HEBREWS** | | 3:20 | 380 | 22:15 | 245 |
| 5:7-10 | 216 | 4:3-5 | 245 | 22:19 | 396 |
| 6:12 | 363 | 4:9 | 243 | | |

# INDEX OF EARLY
# EXTRABIBLICAL LITERATURE

Note: If necessary, see ABBREVIATIONS (pp. xv-xx).

## JEWISH LITERATURE

### APOCRYPHA

**BARUCH**

| | |
|---|---|
| 2:27 | 406 |
| 4:27 | 79 |
| 5:5 | 79 |

**1 MACCABEES**

| | |
|---|---|
| 3:6 | 296 |

**2 MACCABEES**

| | |
|---|---|
| 2:22 | 406 |
| 8:8 | 111 |
| 9:23 | 364 |
| 10:4 | 406 |

**3 MACCABEES**

| | |
|---|---|
| 3:15 | 406 |
| 7:6 | 406 |

**PRAYER OF AZARIAH**

| | |
|---|---|
| 19 | 406 |

**SIRACH**

| | |
|---|---|
| 1:18 | 429 |
| 4:7 | 418 |
| 4:21 | 373 |
| 10:23 | 418 |
| 11:10 | 345 |
| 11:22 | 429 |
| 20:13 | 418 |
| 23:6 | 371 |
| 27:4 | 319 |
| 27:8 | 418 |
| 39:10 | 105 |
| 41:21 | 443 |
| 42:3 | 443 |
| 42:7 | 443 |
| 51:17 | 111 |

**WISDOM**

| | |
|---|---|
| 2:19 | 406 |
| 3:1-3 | 142 |
| 4:2 | 363 |
| 5:14 | 79 |
| 8:7 | 416 |
| 12:18 | 406 |

### PSEUDEPIGRAPHA

**2 BARUCH**

| | |
|---|---|
| 78:2 | 70 |

**1 ENOCH**

| | |
|---|---|
| 47:3 | 396 |

**EPISTLE OF ARISTEAS**

| | |
|---|---|
| 188 | 364 |
| 210 | 364 |
| 281 | 364 |

**SIBYLLINE ORACLES**

| | |
|---|---|
| 7.58 | 319 |

**TESTAMENT OF REUBEN**

| | |
|---|---|
| 4:1 | 393 |

### DEAD SEA SCROLLS

*1QSb*

| | |
|---|---|
| 4:25 | 105 |

### RABBINIC LITERATURE

| | |
|---|---|
| *Tanch 107b* | 295 |

### JOSEPHUS 432

*Ant.*

| | |
|---|---|
| 1.68 | 364 |
| 4.59 | 111 |
| 8.315 | 364 |
| 11.241 | 265 |

**BJ**
5.571        319

## PHILO

*Congr. Qu. Er.*
70        364
*Virt.*
66        364

## EARLY CHRISTIAN

**AMBROSIASTER**   372

**1 CLEMENT**
38:2      133
47:1      440
59:3       68

**2 CLEMENT**
13:1      429

**CHRYSOSTOM**
   66, 114, 143, 271, 375

**CLEMENT OF ALEXANDRIA**
   375, 393, 395, 426

**THE DIDACHE**
13:2      296

**EPISTLE TO DIOGNETUS**
5.9      379

**EUSEBIUS**   375, 395

**HERMAS**
*Man.*
5.2.2      443
*Sim.*
2:9      396

**HILARY**   372

**IGNATIUS**
Rom 2:2      252

**JEROME**   426

**ORIGEN**   223, 375, 393, 395

**PELAGIUS**   372, 393

**POLYCARP**
*Ep. Phil.*      22

**TERTULLIAN**   338

**THEODORET**   370, 393

## GRAECO-ROMAN

**ARISTOTLE**
*Eth. Nic.*
8      4
8.3.1      427
1163b      164

**CICERO**
*Amicitia*      4
71      439
*Att.*
11.15.1      60
*Fam.*
2.4.1      4
*Fin.*
2.26.82-85      427
*Inv.*
2.50      427
*Rab. Post.*
5.16      218
*Tusc. Disp.*
5.23.67      416
*Verr.*
5.66      217

**DIO CHRYSOSTOM**
*Or.*
17.1      411

**DIOGENES**
7.100      450

**EPICTETUS**
3.2.13      450
3.24.17      450
4.7.14      432

**EPICURUS**
*Gn.*
5.23      427

**EURIPIDES**
*Cyclops*
334      372
335      372
*Orest.*
1046      164

**HERODOTUS**
9.58      345

**LUCIAN**
*Patr. Laud.*
10      372

**PLATO**
*Rep.*
5.453A      444

**PLINY**
*Natural History*      390

**PLUTARCH**
*De Amic. Mult.*      4
96AB      5
*De Lib. Educ.*
14      443
*De Util.*      427
87B      5

**POLYBIUS**   432

**PSEUDO-DEMETRIUS**
   2, 4, 11, 158

**PSEUDO-LIBANIUS**
   2, 11

**SENECA**
*Ben.*      423
1.11.1      427
2.10      439
7.26      372
*Ep. Mor.*
9      423
9.8-9      427
9.13      432
11      4
40.1      12

| | | | |
|---|---|---|---|
| 75.1 | 12 | **XENOPHON** | |
| *Vit. Beat.* | | *Mem.* | |
| 6.2 | 432 | 1.6.8 | 372 |
| 9.4 | 372 | 2.1.2 | 372 |

# INDEX OF GREEK WORDS

ἀγάπη, 98
ἀγαπητοί, 232, 387
ἅγιοι, 64-65
ἅγνος, 18, 418
ἀγών, 172
ἀδελφοί, 109, 115
ἀδημονέω, 19, 277
ἀθλέω, 166
αἴσθησις, 18, 99, 100
αἰσχύνη, 373
αἴτημα, 19, 409
αἵτινες, 395
αἰῶν, 455
ἀκαιρέομαι, 18, 430
ἀκέραιος, 245
ἀληθής, 417
ἀλλά, 130, 250
ἀλλήλους, 77-78
ἄλυπος, 18, 280, 281
ἄμεμπτος, 244, 309
ἄμωμα, 245
ἀναγκαῖον, 274
ἀναγκαιότερον, 150
ἀναθάλλω, 18, 429
ἀναλύω, 19, 148
ἀναπέμπω, 274-75
ἀναπληρόω, 282
ἄνθρωπος, 213
ἄνω, 350
ἅπαξ καὶ δίς, 445
ἀπεκδέχομαι, 380
ἀπέχω, 450
ἀποβαίνω, 19
ἀποκαλύπτω, 357
ἀποκαραδοκία, 135
ἀπόστολος, 276

ἀπουσία, 18, 234
ἀπωλεία, 169, 371
ἀρετή, 19, 419
ἁρπάγμα, 206-7
ἁρπαγμός, 18, 205-7
ἀσθενέω, 277
ἀσπάζομαι, 457
ἀσφαλής, 19, 292
ἅτινα, 315
αὐτάρκης, 18, 431-32
αὐτὸ τοῦτο, 85
ἀφίδω, 19, 269
ἄχρι, 86

βεβαίωσις, 19
βίβλος, 19, 396
βλέπετε, 293
βραβεῖον, 348

γάρ, 91, 124, 139, 237, 298, 377
γένος, 307
γινώσκω, 406
γλῶσσα, 225
γνήσιος, 392
γνησίως, 18, 266
γνωρίζω, 145, 406, 409
γνῶσις, 317-18
γογγυσμός, 19, 243
γράφειν, 292

δέ, 146, 263, 268
δεήσις, 80, 132, 409
διά, 138, 315, 317, 319, 324
διάκονος, 69
διαλογισμός, 244
διατρέφω, 19

INDEX OF GREEK WORDS

διαφέροντα, 101
δίκαιος, 89, 417
δικαιοσύνη, 322-23, 326
διό, 220
δίς. See ἅπαξ
διώκω, 345
δοκιμάζω, 101
δοκιμή, 268
δόμα, 447
δόξα, 204, 373, 452, 453
δόσις, 19, 443
δοῦλος, 62, 212
δοῦλος κυρίου, 63
δουλεύω, 62, 269

ἑαυτῶν, 234
ἐγγύς, 407
ἐγκοπή, 111
εἰ καί, 253, 345
εἴ τις, 416
εἴ πως, 335
εἰκών, 204-5, 209
εἰλικρινής, 19, 102
εἰρήνη, 70, 71
εἰς, 81, 102, 111
εἰς λόγον, 443
ἐκ, 120
ἐλπίζω, 264
ἐν, 112, 136, 223
ἐν κυρίῳ, 112
ἐν παντί, 408
ἐν Χριστῷ, 112, 200
ἐν ὑμῖν, 200
ἐνάρχομαι, 86
ἔνδειξις, 169
ἐνέργεια, 384
ἐνεργέω, 237
ἔντιμος, 19, 282
ἐξανάστασις, 18, 335
ἐξαυτῆς, 19, 269
Ἐπαφρόδιτος, 19, 274
ἔπαινος, 419
ἐπεκτείνομαι, 19, 347
ἐπέχω, 247
ἐπί, 79, 80, 81, 254. See also ἐφ' ᾧ
ἐπιγείος, 374
ἐπιγνῶσις, 100
ἐπιεικής, 406
ἐπιζητέω, 447
ἐπιθυμία, 148
ἐπιλανθάνομαι, 19, 347
ἐπιμένω, 150

ἐπιπόθητοι, 19, 387
ἐπιποθέω, 94, 277
ἐπίσκοπος, 68
ἐπιτέλω, 86
ἐπιχορηγία, 132-33
ἐργάτης, 295
ἐριθεία, 121, 186-87
ἔρις, 119
ἐρωτάω, 392
ἑτέρως, 19, 357
ἔτι, 99
εὐαγγέλιον, 82
εὐάρεστον, 451
εὐδοκία, 120, 239
Εὐοδία, 19, 390
εὑρίσκω, 215, 321
εὔφημος, 19, 418
εὐψυχῶ, 19, 265
ἐφ' ᾧ, 346, 430

ζῆν, 143
ζημία, 19, 316

ἡγέομαι, 188, 274, 316, 317
ἤδη ποτέ, 429
ἡμέρα, 102, 248

θλῖψις, 438
θυσία, 251, 252

ἴσα, 19, 207
ἵνα, 98, 223
ἰσόψυχον, 19, 265

κἀγώ, 265
καθώς, 232
καί, 98, 114, 119, 144, 214-15, 220, 320, 441
καὶ γάρ, 279
καὶ εἰ, 357
καίπερ, 19, 302
Καίσαρος, 19
καλῶς, 438
καρπός, 141-42, 143
κατά, 186, 383, 454. See also τὰ κατ' ἐμέ
καταγγέλλω, 120
καταλαμβάνω, 340, 345
καταντάω, 335
κατατομή, 19, 296
καταχθόνιος, 19
κατεργάζομαι, 234, 237

495

καυχάομαι, 301
καύχημα, 154, 248
κεῖμαι, 120
κενοδοξία, 19, 186
κενόω, 210
κέρδος, 140, 316
κλαίω, 369
Κλήμεντος, 19
κλῆσις, 349
κοιλία, 371
κοινόω, 444
κοινωνία, 82-83, 91, 181, 331, 332
κόσμος, 246
κύριος, 31
κύων, 19

λαμβάνω, 340, 343
λατρεύω, 299
λειτουργία, 251
λειτουργός, 176
λῆμψις, 19, 443
λογίζομαι, 415
λόγος, 248. See also εἰς λόγον
λοιπός, 114. See also τὸ λοιπόν

μάλιστα, 459
μᾶλλον, 110, 306
μεγαλύνω, 135, 136
μεγάλως, 19, 428
μὲν οὖν, 269
μενοῦνγε, 38, 317
μένω, 125, 152
μεριμνάω, 266
μέσον, 245
μέχρι, 216
μιμητής. See συμμιμητής
μνεία, 78-79
μόνον, 161
μορφή, 19, 195, 203-4, 211, 333
μυέω, 19, 433

ναί, 392
νόημα, 411
νοῦς, 410

δ καί, 200, 201
οἱ πάντες, 267
οἴομαι, 19, 120
οἶδα, 120
οἰκία, 460
οἰκτιρμός, 182
ὀκνηρός, 292

ὀκταήμερος, 19
ὁμοίωμα, 213, 214
ὄνομα, 221
ὅς, 202
ὅσος, 356
ὅστις. See αἵτινα; ἅτινα
ὅτι, 85, 225, 428, 445
οὐ. See οὐχ ὅτι
οὖν, 177, 355
οὐρανός, 378
οὗτος. See τοῦτο
οὕτως, 388-89
οὐχ ὅτι, 342, 430

πάντοτε, 77
παραβολεύομαι, 19, 282
παρακαλέω, 391
παράκλησις, 179-80
παραμένω, 152
παραμύθιον, 19, 180
παραπλήσιος, 19, 279
παρρησία, 137
πᾶς, 77, 136, 457. See also τὰ πάντα; ἐν πάντι
πείθω, 115, 152
πέμπω, 274
περιπατέω, 161, 365
περισσεύω, 99, 154, 432
περισσοτέρως, 115
περιτομή, 296
πιστεύω, 129
πίστις, 153, 324
πίστις Χριστοῦ, 324
πληρόω, 103, 183, 451
πλήν, 124, 359, 437
πλοῦτος, 453
πνεῦμα, 164, 165, 181, 300, 461
πολιτεύομαι, 19, 161-62
πολίτευμα, 19, 378
πολύς, 368
ποτέ. See ἤδη ποτέ
πραιτώριον, 19
πράσσω, 420
προκοπή, 111, 153
προσευχή, 80, 409
πρόφασις, 124
προσφιλής, 19, 418
πτύρω, 19, 168

σάρξ, 142
σεμνός, 417
σκολιός, 19

σκοπέω, 190, 366
σκοπός, 19, 348
σκύβαλα, 19, 319
σπλάγχνα, 94, 182
σπουδαιοτέρως, 280
στέφανος, 388
στήκω, 386
στοιχέω, 360
συγκοινωνέω, 19, 438
συγκοινωνός, 83, 91
συγχαίρω, 19, 255
σύζυγος, 19, 385, 392-93
συλλαμβάνω, 19, 393
συμμιμητής, 19, 363-64
συμμορφίζω, 19, 228, 314, 333
σύμμορφον, 314
σύμψυχος, 19, 183, 185
σύν, 67, 146
συναθλέω, 19, 166
συνδοῦλος, 63
συνεπίσκοπος, 60
συνεργός, 275
συνέχομαι, 147
σύνεσις, 100
Συντύχη, 19, 390
συστρατιώτης, 275
σχῆμα, 215
σῶμα, 137
σωτήρ, 31, 380-81
σωτηρία, 128, 131

τὰ κατ᾽ ἐμέ, 110
τὰ πάντα, 384
τὰ πρός σε, 3
τὰ περὶ ἐμέ, 269
τὰ περὶ ὑμῶν, 110, 158, 263
ταπεινόω, 216, 432
ταπεινοφροσύνη, 187, 216
ταπείνωσις, 19, 382
ταχέως, 264
τέκνον, 245, 268

τέλος, 340, 370
τέλειος, 340, 343, 355
τετελειόω, 340, 343-44
τί γάρ, 124
τις, 118
τὸ λοιπόν, 21, 290
τοῦτο, 89, 131, 144, 170, 199, 356
τρόμος, 236
τύπος, 365

ὑπακούω, 232
ὑπάρχω, 202, 379
ὑπέρ, 171, 239
ὑπερέχω, 189, 317, 410
ὑπερυψόω, 19, 221
ὑστέρημα, 283
ὑστέρησις, 19, 431

φαίνω, 246
Φαρισαῖος, 19
φθάνω, 360
φθόνος, 119
Φιλιππήσιοι, 19, 439
φόβος, 236
φρονέω, 89, 165, 187, 208-9, 429
φρόνημα, 89
φρουρέω, 411
φύσις, 204
φωστήρ, 19, 246

χαίρω, 19, 291, 404, 428
χαρά, 184
χαρίζομαι, 171, 221
χάρις, 91
χορτάζω, 19, 91
χρεία, 276, 446, 452

ψυχή, 158, 164, 282

ὡς, 94, 234
ὥστε, 231, 387